INSTITUTIONAL FRAMEWORKS OF COMMUNITY HEALTH AND SAFETY LEGISLATION

Committees, Agencies and Private Bodies

Institutional Frameworks of Community Health and Safety Legislation

Committees, Agencies and Private Bodies

ELLEN VOS

·HART·
PUBLISHING

OXFORD
1999

Hart Publishing
Oxford and Porland, Oregon

Published in North America (US and Canada) by
Hart Publishing c/o
International Specialized Book Services
5804 NE Hassalo Street
Portland, Oregon
97213-3644
USA

Distributed in Australia and New Zealand by
Federation Press Pty Ltd
PO Box 45, Annandale
NSW 2038, Australia

Distributed in the Netherlands, Belgium and Luxembourg by
Intersentia, Churchillaan 108
B2900 Schoten, Antwerpen
Belgium

Hart Publishing is a specialist legal publisher based in Oxford, England.
To order further copies of this book or to request a list of other
publications please write to:

Hart Publishing, 19 Whitehouse Road, Oxford, OX1 4PA
Telephone: +44 (0)1865 434459 or Fax: +44 (0)1865 794882
e-mail: hartpub@janep.demon.co.uk

British Library Cataloguing in Publication Data
Data Available
ISBN 1 901362–74–4

Typeset in 10pt Sabon
by Hope Services (Abingdon) Ltd.
Printed in Great Britain on acid-free paper
by Biddles Ltd, Guildford and King's Lynn.

Per Mimmo

To my mother and my sisters Yvonne and Marga
To the memory of my father

Foreword

The European Commission's White Paper of 1985 on the "Completion of the Internal Market" and the accompanying documents announced the largest legislative programme in the history of the European Community. In many respects, that programme was striking in its modesty. To many, its main ambition, the elimination of barriers to trade resulting from differences in national product regulation, appeared little more than a milder version of the older idea of establishing a common market. And its promoters repeatedly highlighted its limited implications: no major institutional reform was proposed, nor did the programme require the transfer of new powers or additional resources to the Community.

Less than a decade later, when Ellen Vos began the research that was to lead to this book, it had already become clear that this "soft" reading of the 1992 programme was fallacious: the European Community was struggling with new issues (health and safety, consumer and environmental protection, etc.) and it was contemplating new structures to handle these new tasks. At the same time, Member States had become more vocal, and the populace more concerned, in reaction to what appeared a seemingly endless transfer of powers to the European level.

The discrepancy between the emphasis on the material benefits of the Internal Market and the benign neglect of its manifold institutional implications was striking. Why then, one might wonder, did this important and so forcefully promoted initiative have so little to say about the series of issues this book deals with?

We should nevertheless not content ourselves with noting just another paradox in the legal life of the European Community and/or praising the author for her courage to embark upon an uncharted sea. We should rather reflect upon the wisdom of a legislative programme which *avoided* tackling all the follow-up problems it was bound to produce. At least in hindsight, one cannot but be struck by the way the 1992 programme was launched as an extraordinarily successful example of "legislative experimentalism". We know that nobody could foresee back in 1985 whether and under what conditions the internal market programme was to become a success. To be sure, the promoters of the programme could build upon strong political support in many quarters and point confidently to the modernising impact their initiative promised to exert throughout the Community; what they could by no means imagine were the dynamics of this programme. It would have been extremely difficult, if not impossible, to consider in any depth all the institutional issues and alternatives which the implementation process would bring to the fore.

Even within our relatively well consolidated constitutional states, important reasons militate in favour of an experimental design of legislative programmes. Since legislatures very often are unable to foresee the impact of their action, they should place greater emphasis upon scrutinising the actual development of their "products" and be ready to learn from successes and failures. At the European level, an incremental approach, exposing adopted legislation progressively to controlled experience and learning processes seems even more important. Europe's complicated legislative machinery cannot be controlled simply by regular elections. The accountability of this legislation has to be ensured by leaving national legislatures room for manoeuvre, by judicial controls and by a design which foresees adaptation and correction. Seen in this light, the apparent modesty of the single market programme should neither come as a surprise, nor be seen as a paradox, but rather be perceived as a fortunate legislative self-restraint, which paved the way for continuous institutional innovations, self-corrections and learning processes.

The merits of this book and the approach it adopts are to be evaluated in the same light. Of course one should expect institutional political actors themselves to reflect carefully upon their practices. But it takes the patience and independence of academic discussions to explore systematically and in depth the implications of ongoing developments. It is this mixture of an enormous patience and intellectual unrest which has guided Dr Vos and which makes her work so valuable.

This book blends together an in-depth discussion of major institutional issues and remarkably precise analyses of the development of secondary Community law in the field of product regulation. It presents and evaluates the pros and cons of all conceivable institutional alternatives – ranging from mutual recognition, standardisation by self-regulatory bodies, comitology and agencies. Most remarkable is the author's research on the infrastructures of the internal market. This research is not only based on a careful scrutiny of Community legislation, but also implementation studies, and as well as the author's own empirical investigations. The insights these analyses reveal not only relativise the practical importance of seemingly fundamental theoretical differences (such as those between "agencies" and "committees"); they also shed new light on very old and very basic questions (such as the dependence of functioning markets on functioning institutions).

Ellen Vos has not only delivered a narrative of past and present European efforts to establish and manage the internal market; her study also points to the future; it shows how the success of Europe's market building efforts and the achievements of the law in disciplining this development are overshadowed by internationalisation processes and new institutional problems. Fortunately enough, she contented herself with indicating what is about to concern us in the future, without trying to pre-empt future analyses of these developments. In that respect, too, this book is an exemplary study of European "law in context": the author, being well aware of the necessarily preliminary character of such a thorough analysis, has managed to place her (contextual) findings in a broader context.

This book is of invaluable help for anybody interested in understanding and evaluating the ongoing transformation of European governance structures. It will also prove to be a most useful guide to the study of future developments.

RENAUD DEHOUSSE
Paris/Florence

CHRISTIAN JOERGES
Bremen/Florence

Acknowledgements

The research for this book was carried out at the European University Institute in Florence and was generously funded by the Dutch Ministry of Education, the European University Institute, the Fundatie van de Vrijvrouwe van Renswoude the 's-Gravenhage, the Stichting Dr. Hendrik Muller's Vaderlandsch Fonds and the Stichting Admiraal van Kinsbergen Fonds.

A number of persons have been a source of support and inspiration during the writing of this book. They are too numerous to mention individually, but I would like to thank some persons in particular. I am most grateful to Christian Joerges and Renaud Dehousse, not only for their supervision and "scientific expertise", but also for their kindness and sympathy. I would also like warmly to thank Judge P.J.G. Kapteyn and René Barents for their constructive criticism and generous support. Special thanks are due to the persons interviewed in the course of this research, especially those active in "comitology", who kindly took the time to explain the practical functioning of committees. Many thanks go to the staff of the European University Institute, in particular to Marlies Becker, and the Centre of European Law and Politics at the University of Bremen (ZERP).

I would also like to thank Josef Falke, Mel Kenny, Jürgen Neyer, Andreas Furrer and Stephen Vousden for stimulating discussions; Michelle Everson for all her help, comments and sense of humour; and Wolf Sauter and Harm Schepel for their valuable criticism and the many conversations we had during the times of the Weser Troika. Chris Engert corrected the English of this book, for which I am most thankful. Particular thanks are also due to Richard Hart for his professional and friendly support.

Furthermore, I would like to express my gratitude to friends for all their understanding, patience and warmth. I am indebted to my family and the Monda family for the constant encouragement they have given me throughout. Last, but not least, I would like to thank my partner Cosimo Monda for all his help with this book and his loving support.

ELLEN VOS

Contents

Abbreviations   xxi
Table of Cases   xxiii
Treaty of Amsterdam   xxix
Table of Legislation   xxxiii

Introduction

1. REGULATING RISK   2
2. DEALING WITH RISK UNDER COMMUNITY LAW   5
3. REGULATORY MODELS: COMMITTEES, AGENCIES AND PRIVATE BODIES   9

CHAPTER 1
The Community's Involvement in Health and Safety Regulation

1. INTRODUCTION   11
2. THE EMERGENCE OF COMMUNITY HEALTH AND SAFETY REGULATION   13
   2.1. The Elimination of Obstacles to Trade and the Exceptions
        Thereto: "Negative Integration"   14
      2.1.1. Article 36, First Sentence, and the Rule of Reason   15
      2.1.2. Article 36, Second Sentence   17
   2.2. The Dual Basis of Community Involvement in Health
        and Safety Regulation: "Positive Integration"   18
3. COMMUNITY COMPETENCE AND ITS LEGAL BASIS   21
   3.1. The Functions of the Legal Basis Requirement   22
   3.2. The Treaty of Rome   24
   3.3. The Single European Act   27
      3.3.1. Article 100a in Relation to Article 100   27
      3.3.2. Article 100a as a Legal Basis for Health and Safety Regulation   28
      3.3.3. The Approximation Requirement   30
      3.3.4. Article 100a(4) and (5) (Derogation Clauses)   31
   3.4. The Treaty of Maastricht   33
      3.4.1. Articles 2 and 3   34
      3.4.2. Articles 129a and 129   34
      3.4.3. Subsidiarity   36
   3.5. The Treaty of Amsterdam   36
      3.5.1. Amendment to Article 100a(3)   37
      3.5.2. Amendment to Article 100a(4) and (5)   37
      3.5.3. Amendment to Article 129   38
      3.5.4. Amendment to Article 129a   38

3.6. The Problem of Demarcation 38
   3.6.1. The Theory of the "Centre of Gravity" 39
   3.6.2. Demarcation between the Various Treaty Provisions 41
   3.6.3. Alternatives to the Theory of the "Centre of Gravity"? 43
4. CONCURRENT POWERS BETWEEN THE COMMUNITY AND THE MEMBER
STATES 43
   4.1 The Methods of Harmonisation 44
   4.2 Supremacy and Pre-emption 45
   4.3 Towards Shared Competence on Health and Safety 46
      4.3.1. Residual Competence of Member States 46
      4.3.2. Shared Member State and Community Powers 48
5. CONCLUSION 50

CHAPTER 2
Deepening of Community Health and Safety Regulation

1. INTRODUCTION 52
2. DEEPENING OF COMMUNITY INVOLVEMENT IN HEALTH AND SAFETY
REGULATION: TOWARDS COMMUNITY IMPLEMENTATION 54
   2.1. The Difficulties Inherent in the "Traditional" Approach to
Harmonisation 54
   2.2. The New Approach to Harmonisation 56
   2.3. Deepening of Community Health and Safety Regulation 58
      2.3.1. The Limits of the Mutual Recognition Principle 60
         2.3.1.1. A "Race to the Bottom"? 60
         2.3.1.2. Compulsory Mutual Recognition? 64
      2.3.2. The Creation of Trade Barriers by Means of Procedural
Rules 65
      2.3.3. Wide Discretion of Member States and Vague
Terminology in Directives 66
      2.3.4. Dangerous Products and Accidents 67
      2.3.5. Innovation and New Technology 68
      2.3.6. Community Responsibility for Ensuring Health and
Safety Protection 68
3. THE RELATIONSHIP BETWEEN COMMUNITY LEGISLATION AND
IMPLEMENTATION 70
   3.1. The Blurring of the "Legislation–Execution" Distinction and
the Principle of the Separation of Powers 70
   3.2. Implementation of Community Law 71
      3.2.1. The Power to Adopt Measures under Primary
Community Law and the Power to Implement Rules
Developed by the Community Institutions 71
      3.2.2. The Concept of Implementation 72
      3.2.3. Do Member States Have a Right to Implement? 74

3.3. The Legal Basis of Community Implementation 75
    3.3.1. Harmonisation under Article 100a 75
    3.3.2. Other Relevant Provisions 77
4. THE IMPLICATIONS OF THE PRINCIPLES OF SUBSIDIARITY AND
PROPORTIONALITY FOR THE DEEPENING OF COMMUNITY ACTIVITIES IN
HEALTH AND SAFETY REGULATION 77
  4.1. The Subsidiarity Principle 78
    4.1.1. The Introduction of the Subsidiarity Principle by the
        Maastricht Treaty 78
    4.1.2. Criteria 79
    4.1.3. Justiciability of Subsidiarity? 81
  4.2. The Proportionality Principle 82
5. THE INSTITUTIONAL BALANCE OF POWERS 83
  5.1. The Principle of the Institutional Balance of Powers 83
  5.2. The Principle of the Institutional Balance—More than a
    Restatement of Article 4? 84
  5.3. Functions of the Principle of Institutional Balance 85
  5.4. The Principle of the Institutional Balance and the *Trias Politica* 86
  5.5. The Member States within the Institutional Balance of Powers 87
6. DIFFICULTIES FLOWING FROM THE INCREASING RELIANCE ON THE
COMMISSION IN HEALTH AND SAFETY REGULATION 88
  6.1. Delegation of Implementing Powers to the Commission 89
    6.1.1. The Concept of Delegation 89
    6.1.2. The Introduction of Article 145, Third Indent, by the
        Single European Act 90
    6.1.3. The Scope of Delegation 91
    6.1.4. Delegation of Implementing Powers to the Commission
        and the Institutional Balance of Powers 92
  6.2. The Concept of Legitimacy 93
    6.2.1. Legitimacy 94
    6.2.2. Legitimacy in the Community Context 95
  6.3. Participation of Member States in the Exercise by the
    Commission of Implementing Powers on Health and Safety 96
    6.3.1. Explaining the Participation of the Member States from
        the Institutional Balance of Powers 96
    6.3.2. The *Sui Generis* Character of the Community 97
    6.3.3. National Constitutions 97
    6.3.4. Community Law: Article 36 and Secondary Law 97
    6.3.5. The Specific Nature of Risk Regulation 98
    6.3.6. Addressing Subsidiarity 98
    6.3.7. Compliance 99
  6.4. Means to Enhance Legitimacy 100
    6.4.1. Scientific Expertise 100
    6.4.2. Public Interest and Interest Participation 102

6.4.3. Transparency and Access to Documents   103
6.4.4. Due Process Requirements   104
6.4.5. Judicial Control and Duty to State Reasons   105
6.4.6. Accountability of Community Health and Safety
        Regulation   106
7. CONCLUSION   106

CHAPTER 3

**Health and Safety Regulation through Committees—the Case of
Foodstuffs**

1. INTRODUCTION   110
2. THE RISE OF COMMITTEES WITHIN THE COMMUNITY'S INSTITUTIONAL
   STRUCTURE   113
   2.1. Origins of Committees   113
   2.2. Typology of Committees   114
   2.3. Committees in Figures   115
3. THE COMPETENCE OF THE COMMUNITY TO CREATE COMMITTEES   117
   3.1. The Power of the Council to Create Committees   119
   3.2. The Power of the Commission to Create Committees   119
4. COMMITTEES AND THE INSTITUTIONAL BALANCE OF POWERS   120
   4.1. The Search for More Efficient Decision-making   121
   4.2. The Comitology Decision   122
   4.3. Inter-Institutional Controversies   124
        4.3.1. Shortcomings of the Comitology Decision   124
        4.3.2. The Plumb–Delors Agreement   125
        4.3.3. The *Modus Vivendi*   126
   4.4. The Court's Approval of Committee Procedures   129
5. HEALTH AND SAFETY REGULATION THROUGH COMMITTEES: THE CASE
   OF FOODSTUFFS   131
   5.1. The Peculiarities of Foodstuffs   132
   5.2. The Community's Regulatory Approaches to Foodstuffs   133
        5.2.1. The "Traditional" Approach to Foodstuffs   133
        5.2.2. The New Approach to Foodstuffs of 1985   133
        5.2.3. Various Regulatory Patterns of Food Regulation   134
        5.2.4. Towards a Third Phase of Integration: the Deepening
                of Community Food Regulation   135
   5.3. Main Committees Set Up in the Food Sector: Description 140
        5.3.1. Scientific Committee: The Scientific Committee on Food   140
               5.3.1.1. The Scientific Committee for Food prior to
                        the BSE Crisis   141
               5.3.1.2. The Outbreak of the BSE Crisis and the
                        Findings of the Temporary Committee of
                        Inquiry into BSE   143

5.3.1.3. The Commission's New Approach to Food
Safety in the Aftermath of BSE 145
5.3.1.4. The New Scientific Committee on Food 147
5.3.2. Interest Committees: the Advisory Committee on
Foodstuffs and the Consumer Committee 148
5.3.2.1. The Advisory Committee on Foodstuffs 148
5.3.2.2. The Consumer Committee 150
5.3.3. Policy-making/implementation Committee: the
Standing Committee on Foodstuffs 152
5.4. The Interrelation between the Member States and the
Community Institutions through the Standing Committee on
Foodstuffs 154
5.4.1. Bridging between the Member States and the
Commission 156
5.4.2. The Paradox of Denationalisation and the Growing
Importance of National Interests 159
5.4.3. Safeguard clauses 161
5.4.4. The Use of the Regulatory Committee Procedure in
Food Regulation 162
5.4.5. Objections to the Use of the *Contre-filet* Variant of the
Regulatory Committee Procedure in Emergency Cases
and Administrative Procedures 163
5.5. Integrating Scientific Expertise in Community Food
Regulation through the Scientific Committee on Food 166
5.5.1. The Resort to the Scientific Committee on Food as a
Source of Scientific Advice 166
5.5.2. Principles of Excellence and Independence of Scientific
Expertise 169
5.5.3. Diversification of Expertise on the SCF 170
5.5.4. Towards the Building Up of European and
International Scientific Expertise through the SCF 170
5.5.5. The Scientific Co-operation Model (SCOOP) 171
5.6. Interest Participation by Means of Committees? 173
5.6.1. The Need for Plural Decision-making on Food Issues 173
5.6.2. The Role of the Economic and Social Committee 173
5.6.3. Participation of Various Interests through Committees 174
5.7. Transparency and Access to Documents 177
5.8. Accountability of Community Food Regulation 179
5.9. Towards Indirect Judicial Review of Committee Activities 179
5.10. Right of Hearing 181
5.11. Reform of the Comitology Decision 182
6. CONCLUSION 183

CHAPTER 4

Health and Safety Regulation through Agencies—the Case of Pharmaceuticals

1. INTRODUCTION   188
2. THE RISE OF AGENCIES WITHIN THE COMMUNITY'S INSTITUTIONAL STRUCTURE   189
   - 2.1. Origins of Agencies   189
   - 2.2. Classification of Agencies   191
3. THE COMPETENCE TO ESTABLISH AGENCIES UNDER THE TREATY PROVISIONS   193
   - 3.1. The Legal Basis for Agencies   194
     - 3.1.1. Article 235   194
     - 3.1.2. Article 130s   196
     - 3.1.3. Article 100a   196
   - 3.2. Delegation of Powers to Agencies   200
     - 3.2.1. The *Meroni* Principles   200
     - 3.2.2. The Influence of the *Meroni* Principles on Community Practice   201
     - 3.2.3. The Relevance of *Meroni* for the Creation of Agencies: the Institutional Balance of Powers   202
4. HEALTH AND SAFETY REGULATION THROUGH AGENCIES: THE CASE OF PHARMACEUTICALS   203
   - 4.1. The Peculiarities of Pharmaceuticals   204
   - 4.2. The Community's Regulatory Approach to Pharmaceuticals   206
     - 4.2.1. Partial Harmonisation Combined with Mutual Recognition: the Former Authorisation Procedures   206
       - 4.2.1.1. The Multi-state Procedure   207
       - 4.2.1.2. The Concertation Procedure   209
     - 4.2.2. The Deepening of Community Action on Medicinal Products   210
       - 4.2.2.1. The Limits of the Voluntary Application of the Mutual Recognition Principle   210
       - 4.2.2.2. The New System for the Free Movement of Medicinal Products   211
       - 4.2.2.3. The Centralised Market Authorisation Procedure   212
       - 4.2.2.4. The Decentralised Market Authorisation Procedure   214
       - 4.2.2.5. Supervision and Reinforced Pharmacovigilance   215
   - 4.3. The Agency for the Evaluation of Medicinal Products: Description   216
     - 4.3.1. The Structure of the EMEA   217

4.3.2. The Tasks of the EMEA   220

4.3.3. The Operation of the EMEA and the Community
Authorisation Procedures   221

4.4. The Interrelation between the Member States and the
Community Institutions through the EMEA and Committees   222

4.4.1. The EMEA   223

4.4.2. The Standing Committee on Medicinal Products for
Human Use, the CPMP and the Management Board   225

4.4.3. The Pharmaceutical Committee   227

4.4.4. The Mutual Recognition Facilitating Group   228

4.5 Integrating Scientific Expertise into Community Regulation
on Pharmaceuticals through the EMEA   228

4.5.1. Models for the Authorisation of
Medicinal Products   228

4.5.2. The Community's "Two-tiered" Model of Integrating
Scientific Expertise   229

4.5.3. Principles of Objectivity and Independence   230

4.5.4. Requirements concerning the Plurality of Scientific Expertise   232

4.5.5. The Scientific Committee on Medicinal Products and
Medical Devices in the BSE Aftermath   233

4.6. Participation of Interested Parties   234

4.7. Transparency and Access to Documents   238

4.8. Accountability of Community Pharmaceutical Regulation   238

4.9. The Right to a Hearing and Appeal Procedures   239

4.10. The EMEA as an "Independent" Regulatory Agency?   240

4.10.1. The Possibility of Delegating Decision-making
Powers to the EMEA under Current Law   241

4.10.1.1. The Commission's Powers: Supervision of
the Agency   242

4.10.1.2. Judicial Review   245

4.10.2. Capture   247

5. Conclusion   247

Chapter 5
Health and Safety Regulation through Private Bodies—the Case of Technical Product Standards

1. Introduction   251

2. Health and Safety Regulation through Private Bodies: the Case
of Technical Product Standards   253

2.1. The Peculiarities of Technical Consumer Products and
Standardisation   253

2.2. Standard-setting by the European Standardisation Bodies CEN
and CENELEC: Description   255

2.2.1. The Creation of CEN and CENELEC   255
2.2.2. The Organisational Structure of CEN and CENELEC   256
2.2.3. The Standard-setting Process   262
        2.2.3.1. European Standards   262
        2.2.3.2. The Drafting Process of European Standards   265
2.3. The Community's Regulatory Approach to Technical
Consumer Products and Standards   268
    2.3.1. The Information Directive of 1983   268
    2.3.2. The "General Orientations for Co-operation" of 1984   269
    2.3.3. The New Approach's Dichotomy between Law and
    Technical Specifications   270
        2.3.3.1. The New Approach to Technical
                 Harmonisation and Standards   270
        2.3.3.2. The Model Directive   271
    2.3.4. The Success and Shortcomings of the New Approach   272
    2.3.5. The Need to Deepen the New Approach   277
        2.3.5.1. The Global Approach to Certification and
                 Testing   277
        2.3.5.2. The Green Paper on the Development of
                 European Standardisation and its Follow-Up   278
        2.3.5.3. Increased Community Activities on Product Safety   280
3. DELEGATION OF POWERS TO THE EUROPEAN STANDARDISATION BODIES?   281
    3.1. The Reference to Standards Technique   281
        3.1.1. Methods of Referring to Standards   281
        3.1.2. Admissibility of the Reference to Standards Technique
               in the National Context   282
        3.1.3. The Reference to Standards Technique under the New
               Approach   283
    3.2. Delegation of Powers to CEN and CENELEC?   283
        3.2.1. Nature of the Standards and the Presumption of
               Conformity   285
        3.2.2. Delegation of Powers to the Commission   287
4. LEGITIMACY OF DECISION-MAKING AND STANDARD-SETTING   288
    4.1. The Commission's Attempts to Democratise the
    Standardisation Process   289
        4.1.1. A European Standardisation System   289
        4.1.2. A European Standardisation Forum   290
    4.2. The Interrelation between the Member States, the Community
    Institutions and the European Standardisation Bodies through
    Committees: Bridging the Public and Private Divide   291
    4.3. Integrating Technical Expertise into Community Regulation
    through CEN and CENELEC   296
        4.3.1. The Co-ordination of Technical Expertise at Community
               and International level   297

4.3.2. The Diversification of Expertise 297
4.3.3. Unbalanced National Expertise? 297
4.4. The Participation of Interested Parties 298
4.4.1. Consumer Participation in Standardisation 299
4.4.1.1. The Troubled History 299
4.4.1.2. The Creation of ANEC 300
4.4.2. The Remaining Difficulties 301
4.4.3. In Search of a Discussion and Policy Platform: a
European Standardisation Forum or Enlarging the
"Enlarged" 83/189 Committee 303
4.5. Transparency and Access to Documents 304
4.6. Accountability of Community Product Safety Regulation 305
4.6.1. Supervision of the Standard-setting Procedure 305
4.6.2. Post-market Control of Harmonised Standards 307
5. Conclusion 308

Conclusion

1. Community Health and Safety Regulation through Committees,
Agencies and Private Bodies 312
2. In Search of Legitimate Community Health and Safety Regulation 318
3. Towards a Theoretical Conceptualisation of Community Risk
Regulation 320

Bibliography 325

Index 353

Figure 1. Proliferation of committees set up by secondary Community
legislation since 1980 117
Figure 2. Appropriations and expenditure of committee meetings
1980–1998 118
Figure 3. Simplified scheme of consultation and decision-making
procedure in the food sector 155
Figure 4. The contre-filet variant of the regulatory committee
procedure used in the authorisation of medicinal products 167
Figure 5. Budget of the Community Agencies 1994–1998 192
Figure 6. The organisational structure of the EMEA 218
Figure 7. Budget of the EMEA 1995–1998 222
Figure 8. The organisational structure of CEN 263
Table 1. Scheduled expenditure of the relevant committees in the
food sector 154
Table 2. The inclusion of committee procedures in Community food
legislation involving health and safety issues 157

Table 3. Frequency of systematic objections raised by the Member
States against the first market authorisation of a medicinal
product as a percentage   209

Table 4. Overview of the progress made by CEN in the development
of standards in the framework of Commission mandates
relating to the relevant New Approach Directives (involving
safety standards) in June 1994 and in June 1997   275

Abbreviations

AFNOR	Association Française de Normalisation
AG	Advocate General
ANEC	European Association for the Co-ordination of Consumer Representation in Standardisation
BEUC	Bureau Européen des Unions des Consommateurs
BS	British Standard
BSE	Bovine Spongiform Encephalopathy
BSI	British Standards Institution
BT	Technical Board
Bull. EC	Bulletin of the EC
BVerfG	Bundesverfassungsgericht
BVerfGE	Entscheidungen des BVerfG
CC	Consumer Committee
CCC	Consumer Consultative Council
CDE	*Cahiers de Droit Européen*
CEN	Comité Européen de Normalisation
CENELEC	Comité Européen de Normalisation Electrotechnique
CML Rev.	*Common Market Law Review*
CMLR	Common Market Law Reports
COREPER	Committee of Permanent Representatives
DG	Directorate General
DIN	Deutsches Institut für Normung, Deutsche Industrienorm
DIN-Mitt.	DIN-Mitteilungen
DKE	Deutsche Elektrotechnische Kommission
EC	European Community
ECJ	European Court of Justice
ECR	European Court Reports
ECSC	European Coal and Steel Community
ECU	European Currency Unit
EEA	European Economic Area
EEC	European Economic Community
EFLR	*European Food Law Review*
EFTA	European Free Trade Association
ELJ	*European Law Journal*
ELR	*European Law Review*
EMEA	European Agency for the Evaluation of Medicinal Products
EN	European Standard
EOTC	European Organisation for Testing and Certification

ETSI	European Telecommunications Standardisation Institute
EU	European Union
EuR	*Europarecht*
Euratom	European Atomic Energy Community
EWG	Europäische Wirtschaftsgemeinschaft
ff.	and following pages
GATT	General Agreement on Tariffs and Trade
GRUR	*Gewerblicher Rechtsschutz und Urheberrecht*
HD	Harmonised Document
ICLQ	*International and Comparative Law Quarterly*
IEC	International Electrotechnical Commission
ISO	International Standardisation Organisation
JCMS	*Journal of Common Market Studies*
JCP	*Journal of Consumer Policy*
JEPP	*Journal of European Public Policy*
LIEI	*Legal Issues of European Integration*
MJ	*Maastricht Journal of European and Comparative Law*
MLR	*The Modern Law Review*
NF	Norme Française
NJB	Nederlands Juristenblad
NJW	*Neue Juristische Wochenschrift*
OJ	Official Journal of the European Communities
OECD	Organisation for Economic Co-operation and Development
Pol.Q.	*Political Quarterly*
R&D	Research and Development
RabelsZ	*Rabels Zeitschrift für ausländisches und internationales Privatrecht*
RMC	*Revue du Marché Commun*
RTD Eur	*Revue Trimestrielle de Droit Européen*
SCF	Scientific Committee on Food
SEA	Single European Act
SECO	European Secretariat for the co-ordination of standardisation
SEW	*Tijdschrift voor Europees en economisch recht*
TC	Technical Committee
TEU	Treaty on European Union
ULR	*Utilities Law Review*
VDE	Verband Deutscher Elektrotechniker
VuR	*Verbraucher und Recht*
WTO	World Trade Organisation
YEL	*Yearbook of European Law*
ZaöRV	*Zeitschrift für ausländisches öffentliches Recht und Völkerrecht*
ZHR	*Zeitschrift für das gesamte Handels- und Wirtschaftsrecht*
ZLR	*Zeitschrift für das gesamte Lebensmittelrecht*

Table of Cases

Air France *v* Commission Case T-3/93 [1994] ECR II-121............................166
AKZO Chemie BV et al *v* Commission Case 5/85 [1986] ECR 2585 243
Amsterdam Bulb Case 50/76 [1977] ECR 137 74
Angelopharm *v* Freie und Hansestadt Hamburg Case C-212/91 [1994]
    ECR I-171..9, 37, 104, 105, 114, 166, 168
Association de défence des brûlers d'huiles usagées (ADBHU) Case 240/83
    [1985] ECR 531 ....13, 16, 17, 26, 34, 40
Association des centres distributeurs Edouard Leclerc et al *v* Sarl "Au blé vert"
    et al Case 229/83 [1985] ECR 1...17
Azienda Agricola "Le Canne" Srl *v* Commission Case T-218/95 [1997]
    ECR II-2055 180
Bellon Case C-42/90 [1990] ECR I-4863 16
Biologische producten Case 272/80 [1981] ECR 3277................................57
Brandsma Case C-293/94 [1996] ECR I-3159 ....18, 47
Brunner et al *v* European Treaty Cases 2BvR 2134/92 & 2159/92,
    Bundesverfassungsgericht, judgment of 12 Oct 1993 [1994]
    CMLR 57..6, 13, 59
BSE cases *see* Queen (The) *v* Ministry of Agriculture, Fisheries and Food
    ex p National Farmers' Union et al and United Kingdom *v* Commission
Bundesanstalt für den Güterfernverkehr *v* Gebrüder Reiff Case C-185/91
    [1993] ECR I-5801..105, 170, 242, 288
Butter-Absatz *v* Germany Case C-345/88 [1990] ECR I-159 72
Carvel and Guardian Newspapers *v* Council Case T-194/94 [1995]
    ECR II-2767 178
Cassis de Dijon case *see* Rewe Zentrale AG *v* Bundesmonopolverwaltung
    für Branntwein
Clin-Midy Case 301/82 [1984] ECR 259 206
Comitology case *see* Parliament v Council
Commission *v* Belgium Case 263/96 [1997] ECR I-7453 276
Commission *v* Council (ERTA) Case 22/70 [1971]
    ECR 263 ....25, 45, 45, 166, 246
Commission *v* Council Case 45/86 [1987] ECR 1493 ....22, 23, 26, 39
Commission *v* Council Case C-155/91 [1993] ECR I-939 ....34, 39, 42, 131
Commission *v* Council (Commodity Coding) Case 165/87 [1988]
    ECR 5545 ....39, 40
Commission *v* Council (Erasmus) Case 242/87 [1989] ECR 1425 39
Commission *v* Council Case 131/87 [1989] ECR 3743................................40
Commission *v* Council Case 11/88 [1989] ECR 3799 41

Commission *v* Council (Fisheries) Case 16/88 [1989]
ECR 3457..73, 92, 93, 130, 203
Commission *v* Denmark (Danish bottles) Case 302/86 [1988] 4607 17
Commission *v* European Parliament (Titanium Dioxide)
Case C-300/89 [1991] ECR I-2867.......................................23, 29, 39, 40, 41
Commission *v* France (Woodworking machines) Case 188/84 [1986] ECR 419.....62
Commission *v* Germany (Reinheitsgebot) Case 178/84 [1987]
ECR 1227..16, 17, 18, 100, 140
Commission *v* Germany Case 205/84 [1986] ECR 3755 62
Commission *v* Germany Case C-51/94 [1995] ECR I-3599 18
Commission *v* Greece Case 176/84 [1987] ECR 1193 ....16, 17, 18
Commission *v* Greece (Alfonsina) Case 68/88 [1989] ECR 2965 ....73, 74
Commission *v* Greece Case C-205/89 [1991] ECR I-1361 16
Commission *v* Greece Case C-391/92 [1995] ECR I-1621 15
Commission *v* Ireland Case 113/80 [1981] ECR 1625 ....15, 17
Commission *v* Italy Case 7/68 [1968] ECR 423 17
Commission *v* Italy Case 123/76 [1977] ECR 1449 281
Commission *v* Italy Case 100/77 [1978] ECR 879...................................47
Commission *v* Italy Case 144/77 [1978] ECR 1307..................................24
Commission *v* Italy Case 91/79 [1980] ECR 1099 ....24, 29
Commission *v* Italy Case 92/79 [1980] ECR 1115 ....24, 29
Commission *v* Italy Case 44/80 [1981] ECR 343 47
Commission *v* Italy Case C-334/89 [1991] ECR 93...................................66
Commission *v* United Kingdom Case 124/81 [1983] ECR 203 17
Commission *v* United Kingdom (pasteurised milk) Case 261/85 [1988]
ECR 547..17
Construction Products case *see* Germany *v* Commission
Costa *v* ENEL Case 6/64 [1964] ECR 585 ....6, 45
Council *v* Parliament Case 34/86 [1986] ECR 2155 83
Cremonini and Vrankovich Case 815/79 [1980] ECR 3583....................281, 285
Dassonville case *see* Procureur du Roi *v* Dassonville
De Dapper *v* Parliament Case 54/75 [1976] ECR 1381...............................119
De Peijper Case 104/75 [1976] ECR 613 ....16, 62
Debus Joined Cases C-13/91 & C-113/91 [1992] ECR I-3617.....................16, 18
Denkavit Case 15/83 [1984] ECR 2171 82
Deutsche Grammophon *v* Metro Case 78/70 [1971] ECR 487 73
Deutsche Milchkontor GmbH *v* Germany Joined Cases 204-215/82
[1983] ECR 2633 ....73, 74
Dulciora *v* Amministrazione delle Finanze dello Stato Case 95/78 [1979]
ECR 1547 129
Einfuhr- und Vorratstelle für Getreide und Futtermittel *v* Köster Case 25/70
[1970] ECR 1161 ....72, 83, 92, 119, 129
Établissements Armand Mondiet SA *v* Armement Islais SARL (Mondiet)
Case C-405/92 [1993] ECR I-6133 ....83, 101

European Parliament *v* Council Case C-295/90 [1992] ECR I-4193 39

Fédération Charbonière de Belgique *v* High Authority Case 8/55 [1954-6]
ECR 292...120

France *v* Commission Case C-325/91 [1993] ECR I-3283 ....166, 246

France *v* Commission Case C-327/91 [1994] ECR I-3641 27

France *v* Commission (Pentachlorophenol) Case C-41/93 [1994]
ECR I-1829.....................................22, 23, 27, 28, 33, 37, 48, 106, 171

France, Italy and UK *v* Commission Joined Cases 188-190/80 [1982]
ECR 2545 ....23, 72, 73

Frans-Nederlandse Maatschappij voor Biologische Producten BV
Case 272/80 [1981] ECR 3277 ....18, 47

Freistaat Bayern *v* Eurim-Pharm GmbH Case C-347/89 [1991]
ECR I-1747 16

Galli Case 31/74 [1975] ECR 47 47

GB-INNO-BM *v* Confédération du Commerce Luxembourgeois
Case C-362/88 [1990] ECR I-667..15, 69

Geddo *v* Ente Nazionale Risi Case 2/73 [1973] ECR 865....................14

General Product Safety case *see* Germany *v* Council

Germany *v* Commission Case 278/84 [1987] ECR 1 159

Germany *v* Commission Case C-240/90 [1992] ECR I-5383.....................72, 92

Germany *v* Commission (Construction Products) Case C-263/95 [1998]
ECR I-441 ....180, 181, 295

Germany *v* Council (General Product Safety) Case C-359/92 [1994]
ECR I-3681..31, 49, 53, 75, 76, 77, 82, 139, 199

Germany *v* Council Case C-280/93 [1994] ECR I-4973 83

Germany *v* European Parliament and Council Case C-233/94 [1997]
ECR I-2405 ....34, 81

Germany *v* Parliament and Council Case C-233/94 [1997] ECR I-2405 23

Greece *v* Commission Case 30/88 [1989] ECR 3711 129

Greece *v* Council Case C-62/88 [1990] ECR I-1527......................................41

Haegeman *v* Belgian State Case 181/73 [1974] ECR 449.............................246

Hansen & Søn Case C-326/88 [1990] ECR I-2911..74

Hauptzollamt Bremerhaven *v* Massey Ferguson Case 8/73 [1973]
ECR 897 2

Hauptzollamt München-Mitte *v* Technische Universität München
Case C-269/90 [1991] ECR I-5469 ....105, 166, 170, 171, 181, 233, 240, 297

Heijn Case 94/83 [1984] ECR 3263..47

Hoche Case C-174/89 [1990] ECR I-2681 82

Hopermann *v* Bundestalt für Landwirtschaftliche Marktordnung
Case C-257/88 [1990] ECR I-1669 72

Hormones case *see* United Kingdom *v* Council

Hünermund et al *v* Landesapothekerkammer Baden-Württemberg
Case C-292/92 [1993] ECR I-6787 15

IBM *v* Commission Case 60/81 [1981] ECR 2639.......................................166

Interporc Im- und Export GmbH *v* Commission Case T-124/96 [1998]
  ECR II-313 104
Italy *v* Council Case 166/78 [1979] ECR 2575 29
Jongeneel Kaas BV Case 237/82 [1984] ECR 483....................................16, 46
Keck and Mithouard Cases C-267 & 268/91 [1993] ECR I-6126....................15
Köster case *see* Einfuhr- und Vorratstelle für Getreide und Futtermittel Köster
Kraus Case C-19/92 [1993] ECR I-1663 61
Liggett *v* Lee 288 US 517 (1933) 60
Lingenfelser Case C-118/89 [1990] ECR I-2637..82
Maizena GmbH *v* Council (Isoglucose) Case 139/79 [1980] ECR 3393.....84, 85
Meroni & Co, Industrie Metallurgiche SpA *v* High Authority
  Case 9/56 [1957-8] ECR 113......................83, 86, 88, 200-203, 240, 284, 285
Meroni & Co, Industrie Metallurgiche SpA *v* High Authority
  Case 10/56 [1957-8] ECR 157 ....83, 86, 88, 200-203, 240, 284, 285
Mirepoix Case 54/85 [1986] ECR 1067..47
Miro (Belgian genever) Case 182/84 [1985] ECR 3731 17
Moskof AE *v* Ethinikos Organismos Kapnou Case C-244/95 [1997]
  ECR I-6441...180
Motte Case 247/84 [1985] ECR 3887 ....16, 18, 44, 47, 136, 140
Muller Case 304/84 [1986] ECR 1511 ....16, 18, 44, 47, 136, 140
National Carboning Company *v* Commission Case 109/75R [1975]
  ECR 1193...84
Netherlands *v* Commission (Standing Veterinary Committee)
  Case C-147/96, pending, [1996] OJ C 197/9 180
Netherlands *v* Council Case C-58/94 [1996] ECR I-2169 104
Nicolet Instrument *v* Hauptzollamt am Main-Flughafen
  Case 205/85 [1986] ECR 2049..106
Nijman Case 125/88 [1989] ECR 3533 ....16, 47
Officier van Justitie *v* Koninklijke Kaasfabriek Eyssen BV
  Case 53/80 [1981] ECR 409...16, 18
Pall-Dahlhausen Case C-238/89 [1990] ECR I-4827 15
Parliament *v* Commission Case C-156/93 [1995] ECR I-2019...................85, 92
Parliament *v* Council (Comitology) Case 302/87 [1988]
  ECR 5615 ....85, 125, 128, 161, 162, 182–3
Parliament *v* Council (Chernobyl) Case C-70/88 [1990] ECR I-2041,
  [1991] ECR I-4529 ....39, 42, 83, 84, 85, 125
Parliament *v* Council Case C-316/91 [1994] ECR I-625 85
Parliament *v* Council Case C-65/93 [1995] ECR I-643..................................85
Parliament *v* Council Case C-156/93 [1995] ECR I-2019 126
Parliament *v* Council (TACIS) Case C-417/93 [1995] ECR I-1185...92, 130, 131
Parliament *v* Council Case C-303/94 [1996] ECR I-2943.........................85, 92
Parliament *v* Council Case C-259/95 [1997] ECR I-5303 ....35, 127
Parliament *v* Council and Commission (Bangladesh) Joined
  cases C-181/91 & C-248/91 [1993] ECR I-3685 ....166, 246

Parti écologiste "Les Verts" *v* European Parliament
Case 294/83 [1987] ECR 2...6, 83, 85, 86, 88, 246
Pentachlorophenol case *see* France *v* Commission
Philipp Brothers Case C-155/89 [1990] ECR I-330 82
Piagème and others *v* BVBA Peeters Case C-369/89 [1991] ECR I-2971 18
Polydor Case 270/80 [1982] ECR 329 28
Procureur du Roi *v* Dassonville Case 8/74 [1974] ECR 837......................14, 15
Pubblico Ministero *v* Ratti Case 148/78 [1979] ECR 1629...........................16
Queen (The) *v* Intervention Board for Agricultural Produce, *ex p* Accrington
Beef Co Ltd and Other Case C-241/95 [1996] ECR I-6699 180
Queen (The) *v* Minister for Agriculture, Fisheries and Food and the
Secretary of State for Health, *ex p* Fedesa and others Case C-311/88
[1990] ECR I-4023 ....29, 83, 101, 102
Queen (The) *v* Ministry of Agriculture, Fisheries and Food, *ex p* National
Farmers Union et al (BSE) Case C-157/96 [1998] ECR I-2211 ....102, 103, 143
Ratti Case 148/78 [1979] ECR 1629..16
Rau *v* Commission (Christmas butter) Joined Cases 279, 280 285 and 286/84
[1987] ECR 1096 ....72, 129
Reiff case *see* Bundesanstalt für den Güterfernverkehr *v* Gebrüder Reiff
REWE-Handelsgesellschaft Nord mbH *v* Hauptzollamt Kiel Case 158/80
[1981] ECR 1805 22
Rewe-Zentrale AG *v* Bundesmonopolverwaltung für Branntwein (Cassis de
Dijon) Case 120/78 [1979] ECR 649....................15, 17, 18, 56, 61, 134
Rewe Zentrale *v* Landwirtschaftskammer Rheinland Case 37/83 [1984]
ECR 1229...44
Rey Soda *v* Cassa Conguaglio Zucchero Case 23/75 [1975]
ECR 1279 ....72, 91, 129
Romano *v* Inami Case 98/80 [1981] ECR 1241....................202, 203
Roquette Frères *v* Council Case 138/79 [1980] ECR 3333....................29, 84, 85
Sandoz BV Case 174/82 [1983] ECR 2445 ....16, 18, 47
Scheer *v* Einfuhr- und Vorratsstelle für Getreide und Futtermittel
Case 30/70 [1970] ECR 1197 ....72, 73, 83, 129
Schul Case 15/81 [1982] ECR 1409..28
Schumacher *v* Hauptzollamt Frankfurt aM Case 215/87 [1989]
ECR 617...16
Schutzverband gegen Unwesen in der Wirtschaft *v* Yves Rocher
Case C-126/91 [1993] ECR I-2361 15
Sevince *v* Staatssecretaris van Justitie Case C-192/89 [1990]
ECR I-3461 ....246, 247
SGEEM *v* European Investment Bank Case C-370/89 [1992]
ECR I-6211 ....88, 247
Simmenthal Case 35/76 [1976] ECR 1871 16
Tedeschi *v* Denkavit Commerciale srl Case 5/77 [1977]
ECR 1555..16, 44, 46, 130, 163

Technische Universität München case *see* Hauptzollamt München-Mitte *v*
    Technische Universität München
Titanium Dioxide case *see* Commission *v* European Parliament
United Foods and Van den Abeele *v* Belgium Case 132/80 [1981]
    ECR 995 136
United Kingdom *v* Commission (BSE) Case C-180/96 [1998]
    ECR I-2265 ....67, 102, 143
United Kingdom *v* Council (Hormones) Case 68/86 [1988]
    ECR 855 ....11, 23, 39, 40, 41, 101
United Kingdom *v* Council (Petra) Case 56/88 [1989] ECR 1615 39
United Kingdom *v* Council Joined cases C-51/80, C-90/89 and C-94/90
    [1991] ECR I-2757 26
United Kingdom *v* Council Case C-84/94 [1996] ECR I-5755 ......23, 39, 42, 102
United Kingdom *v* Council (battery hens) Case 131/86 [1988]
    ECR 906 ....40, 41
Van Bennekom Case 227/82 [1983] ECR 3883.....................16, 18, 46, 47, 206
Van den Hulst's Zonen *v* Produktschap voor Siergewassen
    Case 51/74 [1975] ECR 79 47
Van der Wal *v* Commission Case T-83/96 [1998] ECR II-545 104
Van Gend en Loos Case 26/62 [1963] ECR 1...6, 86
Vreugdenhil Case 22/88 [1989] ECR 2049 72
Westzucker *v* Einfuhr- und Vorratstelle für Zucker Case 57/72 [1973]
    ECR 321...72
Wilhelm *v* Bundeskartellamt Case 164/68 [1969] ECR 1 29
Woodworking machines case *see* Commission *v* France
WWF (UK) *v* Commission Case T-105/95 [1997] ECR II-313 104
Wybot *v* Faure Case 149/85 [1986] ECR 2391..83
Zoni (Italian pasta) Case 90/86 [1988] ECR 4285..17

Opinions

Opinion 1/76 [1977] ECR 741..194, 196, 202, 203
Opinion 1/91 [1991] ECR I-6079 ....6, 86, 246
Opinion 2/91 [1993] ECR I-1061 45
Opinion 2/92 [1995] ECR I-521..26

Treaty of Amsterdam

Numbering of the Treaty on European Union and the EC Treaty *before* and *after* the entry into force of the Treaty of Amsterdam

A. Treaty on European Union (TEU)

Before	*After*	*Before*	*After*	*Before*	*After*
Title I	*Title I*	Art J.7	Art 17	Art K.9	Art 37
Art A	Art 1	Art J.8	Art 18	Art K.10	Art 38
Art B	Art 2	Art J.9	Art 19	Art K.11	Art 39
Art C	Art 3	Art J.10	Art 20	Art K.12	Art 40
Art D	Art 4	Art J.11	Art 21	Art K.13	Art 41
Art E	Art 5	Art J.12	Art 22	Art K.14	Art 42
Art F	Art 6	Art J.13	Art 23	*Title VIa*	*Title VII*
Art F.1	Art 7	Art J.14	Art 24	Art K.15	Art 43
Title II	*Title II*	Art J.15	Art 25	Art K.16	Art 44
Art G	Art 8	Art J.16	Art 26	Art K.17	Art 45
Title III	*Title III*	Art J.17	Art 27	*Title VII*	*Title VIII*
Art H	Art 9	Art J.18	Art 28	Art L	Art 46
Title IV	*Title IV*	*Title VI*	*Title VI*	Art M	Art 47
Art I	Art 10	Art K.1	Art 29	Art N	Art 48
Title V	*Title V*	Art K.2	Art 30	Art O	Art 49
Art J.1	Art 11	Art K.3	Art 31	Art P	Art 50
Art J.2	Art 12	Art K.4	Art 32	Art Q	Art 51
Art J.3	Art 13	Art K.5	Art 33	Art R	Art 52
Art J.4	Art 14	Art K.6	Art 34	Art S	Art 53
Art J.5	Art 15	Art K.7	Art 35		
Art J.6	Art 16	Art K.8	Art 36		

B. Treaty establishing the European Community (EC)

Before	*After*	*Before*	*After*	*Before*	*After*
Part One	*Part One*	Art 4	Art 7	Art 7	– (repealed)
Art 1	Art 1	Art 4a	Art 8	Art 7a	Art 14
Art 2	Art 2	Art 4b	Art 9	Art 7b	– (repealed)
Art 3	Art 3	Art 5	Art 10	Art 7c	Art 15
Art 3a	Art 4	Art 5a	Art 11	Art 7d	Art 16
Art 3b	Art 5	Art 6	Art 12	*Part Two*	*Part Two*
Art 3c	Art 6	Art 6a	Art 13	Art 8	Art 17

Before	After	Before	After	Before	After
Art 8	Art 17	Art 43	Art 37	Art 73j	Art 62
Art 8a	Art 18	Art 44	– (repealed)	Art 73k	Art 63
Art 8b	Art 19	Art 45	– (repealed)	Art 73l	Art 64
Art 8c	Art 20	Art 46	Art 38	Art 73m	Art 65
Art 8d	Art 21	Art 47	– (repealed)	Art 73n	Art 66
Art 8e	Art 22	*Title III*	*Title III*	Art 73o	Art 67
Part Three	*Part Three*	*Chapter 1*	*Chapter 1*	Art 73p	Art 68
Title I	*Title I*	Art 48	Art 39	Art 73q	Art 69
Art 9	Art 23	Art 49	Art 40	*Title IV*	*Title V*
Art 10	Art 24	Art 50	Art 41	Art 74	Art 70
Art 11	– (repealed)	Art 51	Art 42	Art 75	Art 71
Chapter 1	*Chapter 1*	*Chapter 2*	*Chapter 2*	Art 76	Art 72
Section 1	*(deleted)*	Art 52	Art 43	Art 77	Art 73
Art 12	Art 25	Art 53	– (repealed)	Art 78	Art 74
Art 13	– (repealed)	Art 54	Art 44	Art 79	Art 75
Art 14	– (repealed)	Art 55	Art 45	Art 80	Art 76
Art 15	– (repealed)	Art 56	Art 46	Art 81	Art 77
Art 16	– (repealed)	Art 57	Art 47	Art 82	Art 78
Art 17	– (repealed)	Art 58	Art 48	Art 83	Art 79
Art 18	– (repealed)	*Chapter 3*	*Chapter 3*	Art 84	Art 80
Art 19	– (repealed)	Art 59	Art 49	*Title V*	*Title VI*
Art 20	– (repealed)	Art 60	Art 50	*Chapter 1*	*Chapter 1*
Art 21	– (repealed)	Art 61	Art 51	*Section 1*	*Section 1*
Art 22	– (repealed)	Art 62	– (repealed)	Art 85	Art 81
Art 23	– (repealed)	Art 63	Art 52	Art 86	Art 82
Art 24	– (repealed)	Art 64	Art 53	Art 87	Art 83
Art 25	– (repealed)	Art 65	Art 54	Art 88	Art 84
Art 26	– (repealed)	Art 66	Art 55	Art 89	Art 85
Art 27	– (repealed)	*Chapter 4*	*Chapter 4*	Art 90	Art 86
Art 28	Art 26	Art 67	– (repealed)	*Section 2*	*(deleted)*
Art 29	Art 27	Art 68	– (repealed)	Art 91	– (repealed)
Chapter 2	*Chapter 2*	Art 69	– (repealed)	*Section 3*	*Section 2*
Art 30	Art 28	Art 70	– (repealed)	Art 92	Art 87
Art 31	– (repealed)	Art 71	– (repealed)	Art 93	Art 88
Art 32	– (repealed)	Art 72	– (repealed)	Art 94	Art 89
Art 33	– (repealed)	Art 73	– (repealed)	*Chapter 2*	*Chapter 2*
Art 34	Art 29	Art 73a	– (repealed)	Art 95	Art 90
Art 35	– (repealed)	Art 73b	Art 56	Art 96	Art 91
Art 36	Art 30	Art 73c	Art 57	Art 97	– (repealed)
Art 37	Art 31	Art 73d	Art 58	Art 98	Art 92
Title II	Title II	Art 73e	– (repealed)	Art 99	Art 93
Art 38	Art 32	Art 73f	Art 59	*Chapter 3*	*Chapter 3*
Art 39	Art 33	Art 73g	Art 60	Art 100	Art 94
Art 40	Art 34	Art 73h	– (repealed)	Art 100a	Art 95
Art 41	Art 35	*Title IIIa*	*Title IV*	Art 100b	– (repealed)
Art 42	Art 36	Art 73i	Art 61	Art 100c	– (repealed)

Before	After	Before	After	Before	After
Art 100d	– (repealed)	Art 113s	Art 133	Art 130h	Art 165
Art 101	Art 96	Art 114	– (repealed)	Art 130i	Art 166
Art 102	Art 97	Art 115	Art 134	Art 130j	Art 167
Title VI	*Title VII*	Art 116	– (repealed)	Art 130k	Art 168
Chapter 1	*Chapter 1*	*Title VIIa*	*Title X*	Art 130l	Art 169
Art 102a	Art 98	Art 116 (new)	Art 135	Art 130m	Art 170
Art 103	Art 99	*Title VIII*	*Title XI*	Art 130n	Art 171
Art 103a	Art 100	*Chapter 1*	*Chapter 1*	Art 130o	Art 172
Art 104	Art 101	Art 117	Art 136	Art 130p	Art 173
Art 104a	Art 102	Art 118	Art 137	Art 130q	– (repealed)
Art 104b	Art 103	Art 118a	Art 138	*Title XVI*	*Title XIX*
Art 104c	Art 104	Art 118b	Art 139	Art 130r	Art 174
Chapter 2	*Chapter 2*	Art 118c	Art 140	Art 130s	Art 175
Art 105	Art 105	Art 119	Art 141	Art 130t	Art 176
Art 105a	Art 106	Art 119a	Art 142	*Title XVII*	*Title XX*
Art 106	Art 107	Art 120	Art 143	Art 130u	Art 177
Art 107	Art 108	Art 121	Art 144	Art 130v	Art 178
Art 108	Art 109	Art 122	Art 145	Art 130w	Art 179
Art 108a	Art 110	*Chapter 2*	*Chapter 2*	Art 130x	Art 180
Art 109	Art 111	Art 123	Art 146	Art 130y	Art 181
Chapter 3	*Chapter 3*	Art 124	Art 147	*Part Four*	*Part Four*
Art 109a	Art 112	Art 125	Art 148	Art 131	Art 182
Art 109b	Art 113	*Chapter 3*	*Chapter 3*	Art 132	Art 183
Art 109c	Art 114	Art 126	Art 149	Art 133	Art 184
Art 109d	Art 115	Art 127	Art 150	Art 134	Art 185
Chapter 4	*Chapter 4*	*Title IX*	*Title XII*	Art 135	Art 186
Art 109e	Art 116	Art 128	Art 151	Art 136	Art 187
Art 109f	Art 117	*Title X*	*Title XIII*	Art 136a	Art 188
Art 109g	Art 118	Art 129	Art 152	*Part Five*	*Part Five*
Art 109h	Art 119	*Title XI*	*Title XIV*	*Title I*	*Title I*
Art 109i	Art 120	Art 129a	Art 153	*Chapter I*	*Chapter I*
Art 109j	Art 121	*Title XII*	*Title XV*	*Section 1*	*Section 1*
Art 109k	Art 122	Art 129b	Art 154	Art 137	Art 189
Art 109l	Art 123	Art 129c	Art 155	Art 138	Art 190
Art 109m	Art 124	Art 129d	Art 156	Art 138a	Art 191
Title VIa	*Title VIII*	*Title XIII*	*Title XVI*	Art 138b	Art 192
Art 109n	Art 125	Art 130	Art 157	Art 138c	Art 193
Art 109o	Art 126	*Title XIV*	*Title XVII*	Art 138d	Art 194
Art 109p	Art 127	Art 130a	Art 158	Art 138e	Art 195
Art 109q	Art 128	Art 130b	Art 159	Art 139	Art 196
Art 109r	Art 129	Art 130c	Art 160	Art 140	Art 197
Art 109s	Art 130	Art 130d	Art 161	Art 141	Art 198
Title VII	*Title IX*	Art 130e	Art 162	Art 142	Art 199
Art 110	Art 131	*Title XV*	*Title XVIII*	Art 143	Art 200
Art 111	– (repealed)	Art 130f	Art 163	Art 144	Art 201
Art 112	Art 132	Art 130g	Art 164		

Before	After	Before	After	Before	After
Section 2	*Section 2*	Art 186	Art 243	Art 209a	Art 280
Art 145	Art 202	Art 187	Art 244	*Part Six*	*Part Six*
Art 146	Art 203	Art 188	Art 245	Art 210	Art 281
Art 147	Art 204	*Section 5*	*Section 5*	Art 211	Art 282
Art 148	Art 205	Art 188a	Art 246	Art 212	Art 283
Art 149	− (repealed)	Art 188b	Art 247	Art 213	Art 284
Art 150	Art 206	Art 188c	Art 248	Art 213a	Art 285
Art 151	Art 207	*Chapter 2*	*Chapter 2*	Art 213b	Art 286
Art 152	Art 208	Art 189	Art 249	Art 214	Art 287
Art 153	Art 209	Art 189a	Art 250	Art 215	Art 288
Art 154	Art 210	Art 189b	Art 251	Art 216	Art 289
Section 3	*Section 3*	Art 189c	Art 252	Art 217	Art 290
Art 155	Art 211	Art 190	Art 253	Art 218	Art 291
Art 156	Art 212	Art 191	Art 254	Art 219	Art 292
Art 157	Art 213	Art 191a	Art 255	Art 220	Art 293
Art 158	Art 214	*Chapter 3*	*Chapter 3*	Art 221	Art 294
Art 159	Art 215	Art 192	Art 256	Art 222	Art 295
Art 160	Art 216	Art 193	Art 257	Art 223	Art 296
Art 161	Art 217	Art 194	Art 258	Art 224	Art 297
Art 162	Art 218	Art 195	Art 259	Art 225	Art 298
Art 163	Art 219	Art 195	Art 259	Art 226	− (repealed)
Section 4	*Section 4*	Art 197	Art 261	Art 227	Art 299
Art 164	Art 220	Art 198	Art 262	Art 228	Art 300
Art 165	Art 221	*Chapter 4*	*Chapter 4*	Art 228a	Art 301
Art 166	Art 222	Art 198a	Art 263	Art 229	Art 302
Art 167	Art 223	Art 198b	Art 264	Art 230	Art 303
Art 168	Art 224	Art 198c	Art 265	Art 231	Art 304
Art 168a	Art 225	*Chapter 5*	*Chapter 5*	Art 232	Art 305
Art 169	Art 226	Art 198d	Art 266	Art 233	Art 306
Art 170	Art 227	Art 198e	Art 267	Art 234	Art 307
Art 171	Art 228	*Title II*	*Title II*	Art 235	Art 308
Art 172	Art 229	Art 199	Art 268	Art 236	Art 309
Art 173	Art 230	Art 200	− (repealed)	Art 237	− (repealed)
Art 174	Art 231	Art 201	Art 269	Art 238	Art 310
Art 174	Art 231	Art 201a	Art 270	Art 239	Art 311
Art 176	Art 233	Art 202	Art 271	Art 240	Art 312
Art 177	Art 234	Art 203	Art 272	Art 241	− (repealed)
Art 178	Art 235	Art 204	Art 273	Art 242	− (repealed)
Art 179	Art 236	Art 205	Art 274	Art 243	− (repealed)
Art 180	Art 237	Art 205a	Art 275	Art 244	− (repealed)
Art 181	Art 238	Art 206	Art 276	Art 245	− (repealed)
Art 182	Art 239	Art 206a	− (repealed)	Art 246	− (repealed)
Art 183	Art 240	Art 207	Art 277	Art 247	Art 313
Art 184	Art 241	Art 208	Art 278	Art 248	Art 314
Art 185	Art 242	Art 209	Art 279		

Table of Legislation

EC Treaty (as amended by the Treaty of Maastricht) 86, 87, 202
  Art 2...23, 34, 194
  Art 3 ....34, 194
  Art 3b 36, 82
  Art 3b(1) 72
  Art 3(g) 29
  Art 3(o), (s) 12, 34, 35, 50–51, 68, 312
  Art 4 ....21, 71, 72, 79, 83, 84, 85, 102, 108, 129, 200
  Art 4a..88
  Art 4b 88
  Art 5 ....72, 73
  Art 7 46
  Art 8 46
  Art 8a..27
  Art 9 14
  Arts 12–16 14
  Art 30 ....14, 15, 17, 56, 61
  Art 36 ....15, 16, 17, 29, 31, 32, 37, 43, 44, 46, 47,
                                    51, 56, 97, 210, 312, 315
  Art 39...40
  Art 39(1)..145
  Art 43 ....38, 40, 101
  Arts 48–58 14
  Art 57(1)...57
  Arts 59-66..14
  Art 75...194, 197
  Art 83..113
  Art 90...14
  Art 90(3)..72
  Arts 92–94 14
  Arts 95–98 14
  Art 100 ....11, 16, 21, 24, 25, 26, 27–29, 38, 40, 42, 46,
                              50, 55, 56, 76, 101, 196, 198
  Art 100a 11, 12, 16, 21, 22, 27–29, 30, 31, 32, 33, 34, 36,
             38, 39, 40, 41, 42, 43, 46, 50, 51, 58, 63, 64, 66,
             72, 75, 76, 82, 107, 111, 121, 126, 182,
             194, 195, 196–200, 272, 297, 312, 313
  Art 100a(1)..32, 76

EC Treaty (as amended by the Treaty of Maastricht) (*cont.*):

Art 100a(3) 9, 17, 18, 34, 37, 41, 63, 68, 102, 151, 169, 297
Art 100a(4) 12, 31–33, 37, 44, 48, 51, 106, 312
Art 100a(5) 31–33, 37, 47, 48, 51, 313
Art 100b 64
Art 100b(2) 32
Art 105 88
Art 113 41
Art 118a 39, 42
Art 124 113
Art 129 ....12, 18, 34, 35, 36, 38, 68, 312
Art 129a 12, 34, 35, 36, 38, 39, 43, 68, 77, 107, 312
Art 129a(b) 18
Art 129a(1) 77
Art 129a(2) 77
Art 129a(3) 38
Art 130 173
Art 130n 118
Arts 130r-t 39
Art 130r 78
Art 130r(2) 41
Art 130r(4) 79
Art 130s 39, 40, 41, 41, 42, 43, 194, 195, 196, 197
Arts 130s(1), (2), (3) 39
Art 143 ....106, 121
Art 144 ....106, 121
Art 145 ....54, 72, 73, 75, 84, 89, 92, 119, 119, 121, 122, 127, 130
Art 145, third indent 89, 90–1
Art 148 267
Art 148(2) 123
Art 151(1) 113
Art 153 119
Art 155 ....54, 72, 75, 89, 90, 91, 92, 127, 130
Art 155(4) 119
Art 155, fourth indent 89, 90
Art 158(2) 121
Art 164 246
Art 169 62
Art 171(2) 72
Art 173 ....85, 166, 245, 245, 246, 247
Art 175 245
Art 175(3) 166
Art 177 62
Art 177(b) 245

Art 177(c) 118, 246
Art 184 245
Art 188c 118
Art 189 ....66, 68, 72
Art 189a(1) 165, 183
Art 189b 39, 126, 127
Art 189c 39
Art 190 ....22, 105, 106, 166
Art 191a 104
Art 191(1) 127
Art 193 113
Art 198a 113
Art 198d-e 88
Art 203 130
Art 205 130
Art 214 119
Art 235 ....11, 21, 24, 25, 26, 27, 34, 38, 50, 72, 77, 82,
                               107, 122, 194-196, 197, 198, 199, 200, 211
Art 236 26

ECSC Treaty 120, 201, 202
  Art 3 83
  Art 53 200

EEC Treaty
  Art 2 ....24, 26
  Art 4 129
  Art 75(1)(c) 194
  Art 100 133
  Art 149(1) 165
  Art 155 129

Euratom Treaty
  Art 53 244

GATT (General Agreement on Tariffs and Trade)
  Art XX 102

Single European Act 11, 21, 27–33, 39, 48, 50, 59, 63, 64,
                               78, 91, 106, 107, 119, 151, 162
Treaty of Amsterdam 21, 22, 36-38, 48, 75, 91, 100, 104, 169, 312
  Art 2 20
  Art 100a(3) 100
  Amsterdam Protocol on Subsidiarity and Proportionality 36, 79, 80

Treaty on European Union (Maastricht Treaty) 33–36, 39, 58, 67, 71, 77, 78, 79, 91, 103, 107, 111

Preamble 79
Art 3b 78, 79
Art A 79
Art A(2) 104
Art N 128
Art N1 ....26, 199
Art N(1) 195, 196

REGULATIONS (in chronological order)

Council Reg 1 [1952-8] OJ Spec Ed 59
  Art 3 181
Council Reg 802/68 [1968] OJ L165 114
  Council Reg 803/68 [1968] OJ L170 114
Council Reg (EEC) 970/73 European Monetary Cooperation Fund [1973]
  OJ L89/2 190
Council Reg (EEC) 337/75 European Centre for the Development of
  Vocational Training [1975] OJ L39/1 190
  Art 18 243
Council Reg (EEC) 1365/75 European Foundation for the Improvement of
  Living and Working Conditions OJ L139/1 190
  Art 22 243
Council Reg ((EEC) 2784/79 Duty free importation of scientific apparatus
  [1979] OJ L318/32 105
  Arts 7(3)-(5) 105
Council Reg (EEC) 3252/87 on research in fisheries
  [1987] OJ L314/17 130
Commission Reg (Euratom) 944/89 Permitted levels of radiation in
  foodstuffs [1989] OJ L101/17 ....67, 139
Council Reg (EEC) 2219/89 Food export following nuclear emergency
  [1989] OJ L101/17 ....67, 139
Council Reg (EEC) 1210/90 European Environment Agency
  [1990] OJ L120/1 190
Council Reg (EEC) 1360/90 European Training Foundation
  [1990] OJ L131/1, amended by Council Reg (EC) 2063/94
  [1994] OJ L216/9 190
Council Reg (EEC) 2081/92 Protection of indications/origins for
  agricultural and foodstuffs, as amended by Council Reg 535/97
  [1997] OJ L83/3 135
Council Reg (EEC) 2082/92 Certificates of a specific character for
  agricultural products and foodstuffs [1992] OJ L208/9 136

Commission Reg (EEC) 207/93 Organic Agricultural products
[1993] OJ L25/5 126
Council Reg (EEC) 302/93 European Monitoring Centre of Drugs and
Drug Addiction [1993] OJ L36/1 190
   Art 17 246
Council Reg (EEC) 315/93 Contaminants in food
[1993] OJ L37/1 ....28, 138, 157, 162
   Arts 4, 8 157
Commission Reg (EEC) 2037/93 Protection of geographical indications
[1993] OJ L185/5, amended by Commission Reg 1428/97 [1997]
OJ L196/39 [1997] OJ L196/39...135–6
Council Reg (EEC) 2309/93 European Agency for Evaluation of Medicinal
Products [1993] OJ L 214/1 ....164, 191, 211, 212, 230, 233
   Preamble, 3rd recital 231
   Preamble, 7th recital...165
   Art 6(4) 212
   Art 6(5) 235
   Art 7(b) 212
   Art 9 212
   Art 10 212
   Art 10(1) 230
   Art 10(3) 164
   Art 12 238
   Art 12(1) 223
   Arts 15-17 216
   Art 50(1) 219
   Art 50(2) 217
   Art 50(3) 230
   Art 51 ....220, 231
   Art 51(j) 235
   Art 52 217
   Art 52(1) 217, 232
   Art 52(2) 224, 231
   Art 52(3) 219, 229
   Art 53(2) 218, 232
   Art 54 ....217, 231
   Art 54(2) 231
   Art 55 219
   Art 57(1) 222
   Art 58 235
   Art 65 ....220, 223, 235
   Art 73 164
   Recitals 9-14 217

European Parliament and Council Reg 258/87 on novel foods and
  novel food ingredients [1997] OJ L43/1 ....139, 157
  Arts 12, 13..156
Council Reg (EC) 40/94 Office for Harmonisation in the Internal Market
  (Trade Marks, Designs and Models) [1994] OJ L11/1...............191, 195, 244
  Art 57 245
  Art 63...2456
  Art 140...243
  Art 141...166
Council Reg (EC) 2062/94 European Agency for Safety and Health at Work
  [1994] OJ L216/1 191
  Art 22 243
Council Reg (EC) 2100/94 Community Plant Variety Office
  [1994] OJ L227/1 191
  Art 73 246
Council Reg (EC) 2965/94 Translation Centre [1994] OJ L314/1,
  amended by Council Reg (EC) 2610/95 [1995] OJ L268/1........................191
Council Reg (EC) 297/95 Fees payable to European Agency for the
  Evaluation of Medicinal Products [1995] OJ L35/1 222
Commission Reg (EC) 1662/95 Marketing authorisations for medicinal
  products for human and veterinary use [1995] OJ L158/4
  Art 3 ....213, 226
  Art 4 213
  Art 5 213
  Art 12(1) 213
  Art 12(2) 213
  Art 13 213
  Art 18(4) 213
Commission Reg (EC) 2868/95 Implementation of Community Trademark
  [1995] OJ L303/1 243
European Parliament and Council Reg (EC) 2232/96 Community procedure
  for flavouring substances [1996] OJ L299/1 ....157, 162, 164
  Art 3(3) 157
  Arts 7, 8...157, 162
  Art 8 235
Council Reg (EC) 1035/97 European Monitoring Centre on Racism and
  Xenophobia [1997] OJ L151/1...191

DIRECTIVES (in alphabetical order)

Active implantable medical devices Council Directive 90/385/EEC
[1990] OJ L189/17, amended by Council Dir 93/68/EEC [1993]
OJ L220/1 ....273, 276
Art 3 286
Art 5 286
Art 6(2) 294
Art 7 287
Appliances burning gaseous fuels Council Dir 90/396/EEC [1990]
OJ L196/15, amended by Council Dir 93/68/EEC [1993]
OJ L220/1 ....273, 276
Caseins and caseinates Council Dir 83/417/EEC [1983] OJ L237/25 135
Cocoa and chocolate Council Dir 73/241/EEC [1973] OJ L228/23,
amended by Council Dir 89/344/EEC [1989] OJ L142/19 ....133, 135
Colours for use in foodstuffs Council Dir 94/36/EC [1994]
OJ L237/13 ....65, 134, 157
Art 5 157
Colours (purity criteria) for use in foodstuffs Commission Dir 95/45/EC
[1995] OJ L226/1 154
Colourings for use in medicinal products Council Dir 78/25/EEC
[1978] OJ L11/18 196
Construction products Council Dir 89/106/EEC [1989]
OJ L40/12, amended by Council Dir 93/68/EEC [1993]
OJ L220/1 ....264, 273, 276, 276
Art 4 ....286, 294
Art 5 286
Art 19 294
Art 21 287
Cosmetics 12th Commission Dir 90/121/EEC [1990] OJ L71/40 166
Art 2(1) 168
Dangerous substances Council Dir 91/173/EEC (amending Dir 76/769/EEC)
[1991] OJ L85/34 33
Dehydrated milk Council Dir 76/118/EEC [1976] OJ L24/49.......................135
Door-to-door selling Council Dir 85/577/EEC [1985] OJ L372/31 46
Electromagnetic compatibility Council Dir 89/336/EEC [1989]
OJ L139/19, amended by Council Dir 93/68/EEC [1993]
OJ L220/1   273, 276
Extraction solvents Council Dir 88/334/EEC [1988] OJ L157/28, amended by
Eur. Parliament and Council Dir 97/60/EC [1997] OJ L331/7 134
Arts 5, 6 157
Flavouring agents Council Dir 88/388/EEC [1988] OJ L184/61, amended by
Commission Dir 91/71/EEC [1991] OJ L42/25 134
Arts 8, 10 157

Food additives for food for human consumption Council Dir 89/107/EEC
  [1988] OJ L40/27, amended by Eur. Parliament and Council Dir 94/34/EC
  [1994] OJ L237/1 ....65, 134
    Art 4 157
    Art 6 115
    Art 11 157
Food additives other than colours and sweeteners European Parliament
  and Council Dir 95/2/EC [1995] OJ L61/1 ....65, 134, 157
    Art 6 157
Foodstuffs for particular nutritional use Council Dir 89/398/EEC [1989]
  OJ L186/27, amended by Eur. Parliament and Council Dir 96/84/EC
  [1997] OJ L48/20 ....135, 157, 161
    Arts 11, 12, 13 157
Fruit juices Council Dir 75/726/EEC [1975] OJ L311/40, consolidated by
  Council Dir 93/77/EEC [1993] OJ L244/23..135
General product safety Council Dir 92/59/EEC [1992]
  OJ L228/24 ....30, 49, 53, 69, 76, 139, 162, 280
    Art 2b 49
    Art 4(2) 252
    Art 6 49
    Art 7 139
    Art 7(2)..69
    Arts 8–12..69
    Art 9..49, 76, 80, 139
    Art 10 296
    Art 11 163
Genetically modified micro-organisms Council Dir 90/219 [1990]
  OJ L117/1 43
Genetically modified organisms Council Dir 90/220 [1990] OJ L117/15.........43
Hazardous waste Council Dir 91/698..42
Health and safety at work Council Dir 89/391/EEC [1989] OJ L183/1...........63
Honey Council Dir 74/409/EEC [1974] OJ L221/10 135
Hormones in farming Council Dir 85/649/EEC 40, 101
Human blood or plasma products Council Dir 89/381/EEC [1989]
  OJ L181/44..210
Hygiene in foodstuffs Council Dir 93/43/EEC [1993] OJ L175/1 ...138, 157, 162
    Art 10 161
    Arts 11, 14..157
Immunological medicinal products consisting of vaccines, toxins or
  serums and allergens Council Dir 89/342/EEC extending the scope
  of Dirs 65/65/EEC and 75/319/EEC..210
Infant and follow-on formulae Commission Dir 91/321/EEC [1991]
  OJ L175/35, amended by Commission Dirs 96/4/EC and 96/5/EC
  Processed cereal babyfoods [1996] OJ L49/17............................126, 135, 156

Information on technical standards and regulations Council Dir 83/189/EEC
[1983] OJ L109/8, amended by Council Dir 88/182/EEC [1988]
OJ L81/75, and Eur. Parliament and Council Dir 94/10/EC [1994]
OJ L100/30..55, 138, 158, 183, 264, 268, 294
 Arts 4, 8, 9 269
 Art 5...286, 292
 Art 6(1) 292
 Art 6(3) 293
 Art 6(4) 293
 Art 6(4)(e) 293
 Art 6(5) 293
Information on technical standards and regulations, consolidated text
 Eur. Parliament and Council Dir 98/34/EC [1998] OJ L204/37,
 amended by Eur. Parliament and Council Dir 98/48/EC [1998]
 OJ L217/18..269
Jams, jellies, marmalade and chestnut puree Council Dir 79/693/EEC
 [1979] OJ L205/5 ....133, 135
Labelling, presentation and advertising of foodstuffs Eur. Parliament and
 Council Dir 97/4/EC [1997] OJ L43/214 18
Lifts European Parliament and Council Dir 95/16/EC [1995] OJ L213/1......273
Low voltage Council Dir 73/23/EEC [1973] OJ L77/29.........268, 269, 276, 281,
 283, 284
Machinery Council Dir 89/392/EEC [1989] OJ L183/9, amended by
 Council Dir 91/368/EEC [1991] OJ L198/16 and Council
 Dir 93/44/EEC [1993] OJ L175/12, and Council Dir 93/68/EEC
 [1993] OJ L20/1...63,158, 273, 276, 307
 Art 3 307
 Art 6 286
 Art 6(2) 294
 Art 7 287
 Art 11 287
Machinery, consolidated text, Eur. Parliament and Council Dir 98/37/EC
 [1998] OJ L207/1 273
Materials and articles in contact with foodstuffs Council Dir 89/109/EEC
 [1989] OJ L40/38 ....134, 157
 Art 5 157
 Art 9 157
Medical devices Council Dir 93/42/EEC [1993] OJ L169/1............273, 276, 277
 Art 5 286
 Art 5(2) 286
 Art 7 294
 Art 8 287
Medicinal products Council Dir 83/570/EEC amending Dirs 65/65/EEC,
 75/318/EEC and 75/319/EEC [1983] OJ L332/1 ....208, 239

Medicinal products Council Dir 93/39/EEC, amending Dirs 65/65/EEC,
    75/318/EEC and 75/319/EEC [1993] OJ L214/22 ....164, 211
    Art 1 223
    Art 2 212
    Art 3..214, 215, 216, 222
Medicinal products (high-tech/biotechnological) Council Dir 87/22/EEC
    [1987] OJ L15/38 209
    Art 5 209
Mineral water Council Dir 80/778/EEC [1980] OJ L229/11 135
Misleading advertising Council Dir 84/570/EEC [1994] OJ L250/17 46
Official control of foodstuffs Council Dir 89/397/EEC [1989]
    OJ L186/23..134, 137, 157
    Art 13 137
Official control of foodstuffs (additional measures) Council Dir 93/99/EEC
    [1993] OJ L290/14 ....137, 157
    Art 8 157
    Art 5 137
Non-automatic weighing instruments Council Dir 90/384/EEC [1990] OJ
    L189/1, amended by Council Dir 93/68/EEC [1993] OJ L220/1 ....273, 276
Personal protective equipment Council Dir 89/686/EEC [1989] OJ L399/18,
    amended by Council Dir 93/68/EEC [1993] OJ L220/1 ....273, 276
    Art 5 286
    Art 6(2) 294
    Art 7 ....286, 287
Plastic materials/articles intended for contact with foodstuffs
    Commission Dir 90/128/EEC [1990] OJ L75/19.....................................156
Pricing of medicinal products for human use Council Dir 89/105/EEC
    [1989] OJ L40/8 196–7
Prohibition of certain substances Council Dir 81/602/EEC [1981]
    OJ L222/32..101
Proprietary medicinal products Council Dir 65/65/EEC [1965]
    OJ 22/369 ....25, 206, 207, 210, 227
    Art 3 ....207, 223
    Art 4 207
    Art 6 223
Proprietary medicinal products (harmonisation of documentation)
    Council Dir 75/318/EEC [1975] OJ L147/1 ....207, 225
Proprietary Medicinal Products Committee (CPMP) Council
    Dir 75/319/EEC [1975] OJ L147/13..196, 207
    Art 9(4) 214
    Art 10(1) 214
    Art 10(2) 214
    Art 11 215
    Art 12 ....215, 222

Art 13 215
Art 14 239
Art 14(2) 215
Art 15a 215
Arts 29a–29f 216
Arts 30–33 216
Proprietary medicinal products Council Dir 89/341/EEC amending Dirs
    65/65/EEC, 75/318/EEC, 75/319/EEC [1989] OJ L142/11 210
Proprietary medicinal products – testing Council Dir 87/19/EEC
    amending Dir 75/318/EEC [1987] OJ L15/31...................................212, 225
Quick-frozen food Council Dir 89/108/EEC [1989] OJ L40/34 ....135, 157
Quick-frozen food temperature monitoring Commission Dir 92/1/EEC
    [1992] OJ L34/28 154
Quick-frozen food, sampling for temperature control Commission
    Dir 92/2/EEC [1992] OJ L34/30 154
Radiopharmaceuticals Council Dir 89/343/EEC extending the scope of
    Dirs 65/65/EEC and 75/319/EEC [1989] OJ L142/16 210
Recreational crafts European Parliament and Council Dir 94/25/EC [1994] OJ
    L164/15 273
    Art 6(3) 294
Regenerated cellulose film materials intended to come into contact with
    foodstuffs Commission Dir 93/10/EEC [1993] OJ L93/27 156
Scientific co-operation relating to food Council Dir 93/5/EEC 157, 171
    Art 5 157
Simple pressure vessels Council Dir 87/404/EEC [1987] OJ L220/48,
    amended by Council Dir 93/68/EEC [1993] OJ L220/1 ....273, 276
Sugars (certain) Council Dir 73/437/EEC [1973] OJ L356/71 135
Sweeteners for use in foodstuffs Council Dir 94/35/EC [1994]
    OJ L237/3 ....65, 134, 157
Telecommunications terminal equipment Council Dir 91/263/EEC [1991]
    OJ L128/1, amended by Council Dir 93/68/EEC [1993] OJ L220/1 ...273, 276
    Art 13 294
Telecommunications terminal equipment, consolidated text Eur. Parliament
    and Council Dir 98/13/EC [1998] OJ L74/1..273
Titanium dioxide waste Council Dir 89/428/EEC [1989] OJ L201/56 41
Toy safety Council Dir 88/378/EEC [1988] OJ L187/1, amended by Council
    Dir 93/68/EEC [1993] OJ L220/1..............................64, 273, 276, 308
    Art 5 286
    Art 6 286
    Art 7 287
Veterinary medicinal products Council Dir 93/40/EEC amending Dirs
    81/851/EEC and 81/852/EEC [1983] OJ L214/31 211
Waste disposal Council Dir 91/156/EEC [1991] OJ L78/32 42
Working time Council Dir 93/104/EC [1993] OJ L307/18 42

DECISIONS (in chronological order)

Council Dec 69/414/EEC Standing Committee on Foodstuffs [1969]
   OJ L291/9   152
      Preamble, first recital...152
      Art 2 153
      Art 3 152
Commission Dec 73/306/EEC Consumer Committee [1973] OJ L283/18,
   amended by Dec 80/1087/EEC [1980] OJ L320/33 150
Commission Dec 74/234/EEC Scientific Committee for Food [1974]
   OJ L136/1...141
      Art 2 141
      Art 3 141
      Art 4 141
      Art 5 141
      Art 6 141
      Art 7 141
      Art 8 141
Council Dec 75/320/EEC Pharmaceutical Committee [1975]
   OJ L147/23...119, 207, 227
      Art 2 227
Commission Dec 75/420/EEC Advisory Committee on Foodstuffs [1975]
   OJ L182/35, amended by Commission Dec 78/758/EEC [1978]
   OJ L251/18..148, 174
Commission Dec 80/1073/EEC Advisory Committee on Foodstuffs, new
   statute [1980] OJ L318/28 149
Council Dec 84/133/EEC Rapid exchange of information on the dangers
   arising from the use of consumer products [1984] OJ L70/16 138
      Art 8(2) 138
Council Dec 86/138/EEC Community information system on home and
   leisure accidents (EHLASS) [1986] OJ L109/23 280
Council Dec 87/373/EEC Exercise of implementing powers
   (Comitology Decision) [1987] OJ L197/33 ....93, 122–4
      Art 3 161
      Art 4 125
Council Dec 87/600 Euratom Information exchange in a radiological
   emergency [1987] OJ L371/76 ....67, 139
Council Dec 89/45/EEC Rapid exchange of information on the dangers
   arising from the use of consumer products [1989] OJ L17/51, amended
   by Council Dec 90/352/EEC [1990] OJ L173/49.....................................138
Commission Dec 90/55/EEC Consumers' Consultative Council [1990]
   OJ L38/40, amended by Commission Dec 94/146/EC [1994] OJ L64/28
   and Commission Dec 95/13/EC [1995] OJ L21/17 ....151, 296

Council Dec 90/683/EEC Modules for conformity assessment procedures
[1990] OJ L380/13..277
    Annex 277
Council Dec 91/341/EEC Vocational Training of Customs Officials
(Matthaeus Programme) [1991] OJ L187/41 199
Council Dec 92/247/EEC Research into measurements and testing [1992]
OJ L126/12..296
Commission Dec 93/72/EEC Advisory Committee for the Co-ordination
in the Internal Market Field [1993] OJ L26/18 117
Council Dec 93/465/EEC Conformity assessment procedures/CE marking
[1993] OJ L220/23..278
Council Dec 93/580/EEC Exchange of information of certain products which
may jeopardise consumer health or safety [1993] OJ L278/64..................280
Council Dec 93/662/EC Council's Rules of Procedure [1993] OJ L304/1,
amended by Council Dec 95/24/EC Euratom, ECSC [1995]
OJ L31/14 22
Commission Dec 93/701/EC General consultative forum on the
environment [1993] OJ L238/53 174
Council Dec 93/731/EC, ECSC, Euratom Public access to Council
documents [1993] OJ L340/43, amended by Council Dec 96/705/EC,
ECSC, Euratom [1996] OJ L325/19 ....104, 178
Commission Dec 94/90/ECSC, EC, Euratom Access to documents
[1994] OJ L47/45, amended by Commission Dec 96/567/Euratom,
ECSC, EC [1996] OJ L47/45 ....104, 178, 305
Commission Dec 94/652/EC Co-operation on questions relating to food
[1994] OJ L253/29, amended by Commission Dec 95/142/EC [1995]
OJ L92/26..154
Commission Dec 94/783/EC Prohibition of PCP notified by Germany
[1994] OJ L316/43 48
Council Dec 3092/94/EC Information system on home and leisure
accidents [1994] OJ L331/1, amended by Council Dec 95/184/EC
[1995] OJ L120/36 ....35, 49, 69, 77
    Preamble...280
    Art 7 296
Commission Dec 95/28/EC Implementation of Community legislation
required to achieve the internal market (Karolus Programme) [1995]
OJ L37/39 65
Commission Dec 95/173/EC Scientific Committee for Food [1995]
OJ L167/22 142
    Art 2 142
    Art 4 142
    Art 9 142
    Art 11 142
Commission Dec 95/492/EC Scientific co-operation relating to food 172

Council Dec 3052/95/EC Information exchange on national measures
  derogating from free movement [1995] OJ L321 64
Council Dec 95/468/EC Telematic data exchange (IDA) [1995]
  OJ L269/23 65
Commission Dec 96/211/EC Prohibition of PCP notified by Denmark
  [1996] OJ L68/32 48
Council Dec 96/239/EC Emergency measures against BSE [1996]
  OJ L78/47 ....67, 139, 143
Council Dec 96/646/EC Action plan for cancer [1996] OJ L95/9 35
Council Dec 96/647/EC Prevention of AIDS etc [1996] OJ L95/16 35
Commission Dec 97/404/EC Scientific Steering Committee [1997]
  OJ L169/85 169
Commission Dec 97/579/EC scientific committees in the field of health
  and safety [1997] OJ L237/18 ....140, 170
      Art 2(1) 168
      Art 2(2) 148
      Art 2(3) 147
      Art 2(5) 147
      Art 4 148
      Art 3(3) 147
      Art 5(1) 148
      Art 5(3) 147
      Art 6(1) 169
      Art 7 148
      Art 8 148
      Art 10 148
      Annex 234
Council Dec 97/1400/EC Health monitoring [1997] OJ L193/1 35
Commission Dec 98/100/EC Publication of Standard EN 692 [1998]
  OJ L23/24 307
Commission Dec 98/235/EC CAP advisory committees [1998]
  OJ L88/59 176

Decision of the Committee of the Regions concerning public access to their
  documents [1997] OJ L351/70 104
Decision on Public Access to European Environment Agency documents
  [1997] OJ C282/5 104
Decision 9/97 concerning public access to administrative documents of the
  EMI [1998] OJ L90/43 104
Economic and Social Committee Dec on public access to ESC documents
  [1997] OJ L339/18 104
European Parliament Dec 97/632/EC, ECSC, Euratom Public access to
  EP documents [1997] OJ L263/27 104

Introduction

The aim of this book is to analyse the emergence of product safety regulation by the European Community.[1] It seeks to categorise and analyse the legal and "practical" problems of Community health and safety regulation, investigates the manner in which the Community addresses these regulatory problems and attempts to identify its guiding principles.

Although the Community was primarily conceived as an "Economic Community", this has not prevented it from gradually becoming involved in health and safety regulation. On the one hand, Community involvement in this area originates from its sustained effort to achieve the free movement of goods within the internal market. On the other hand, Community involvement with consumer health and safety and other consumer interests has evolved as a genuinely independent "Community" objective. A high level of consumer health and safety protection has become one of the widely recognised (and self-legitimising) aspects of Community activity in this area. On this dual basis, the Community has gradually entered the complex and technical process of health and safety regulation.[2] Subsequently, due to factors such as the mutual distrust between the Member States, the "post-Maastricht" Community has increasingly been required to play a direct role in health and safety regulation. As a result, the Community is presently one of the prime actors in European consumer health and safety regulation. The regulation of these issues, however, is an intricate matter and confronts the Community with legal and practical problems which stem from both the specific nature of health and safety regulation and the very characteristics of the Community's transnational structure. In order to understand these problems clearly, it is essential to examine the particularities of health and safety regulation first.

---

[1] Throughout this book, unless otherwise indicated, cited Arts. refer to the EC Treaty as amended by the Treaty of Maastricht. For the re-numbering of the provisions of the Treaty of the European Union and the European Community Treaty by the Treaty of Amsterdam, the Table of Arts. is generally referred to.

[2] See Ch. Joerges/J. Falke/H.W. Micklitz/G. Brüggemeier, *Die Sicherheit von Konsumgütern und die Entwicklung der Europäischen Gemeinschaft* (Baden-Baden, 1988) (English version: *European Product Safety, Internal Market Policy and the New Approach to Technical Harmonisation and Standards*, EUI Working Paper LAW 91/10–14 (European University Institute, Florence, 1991; http://www.iue.it/LAW/WP-Texts/Joerges91/).

1. REGULATING RISK

The regulatory problems the Community faces in governing the "republic of science"[3] can be traced back to the specific character of health and safety regulation. It entails *inter alia* the gathering of the relevant scientific data, the assessment and management of risks and the establishment of monitoring procedures. The question whether a product is safe or not is measured with regard to the probability of its causing severe harm. A product is generally considered safe when its attendant "risks" are judged to be "acceptable".[4]

Risk

The concept of "risk" is often characterised in terms of probability measures. It can be defined as the possibility that an undesirable state of reality (adverse effects) may occur as a result of natural events or human activities. This definition implies that humans make causal connections between actions and their effects, and that undesirable outcomes can thus be avoided or modified if such actions or effects are circumvented or moderated. Accordingly, risk in itself already entails both a descriptive and a normative concept. It includes three elements: undesirable outcome, probability of occurrence and the state of reality.[5] In this vein, risk refers to human decision and can be distinguished from "danger" which takes account of external causes that may be imputed to the "environment".[6]

Acceptable Risk

"Acceptable risk" is a difficult concept to define. The elusive character of the term "acceptable" risk underlines the difficulty with which regulators are faced. For instance, acceptance may result from a mere passive continuation of a historical situation (people continuing to live in an earthquake zone or near a volcano); acceptance may occur because of ignorance or misperception of the risk;[7] acceptance may also be simply acquiescence in majority decisions.[8]

---

³ S. Jasanoff, *Science at the Bar, Law, Science and Technology in America* (Cambridge (MA)/London, 1995), 93.

⁴ W.W. Lowrance, *Of Acceptable Risk. Science and the Determination of Safety* (Los Altos, 1976), 75. See also P. Asch, *Consumer Safety Regulation, Putting a Price on Life and Limb* (New York/Oxford, 1988).

⁵ O. Renn, "Concepts of Risk: A Classification", in S. Krimsky/D. Golding (eds.), Social Theories of Risk (Westport/London, 1992), 56–8. The author starts from the assumption that the distinction between reality and possibility is accepted; if the future were either predetermined or independent from human activity, the term risk would make no sense.

⁶ In this sense, N. Luhmann, *Risk: A Sociological Theory* (Berlin/New York, 1993), 21–2.

⁷ See Asch, above n. 4, 76 ff.

⁸ See Lowrance, above n. 4, at 78.

Acceptance may however also stem from the perception that no other alternatives exist. In this instance, costly and highly toxic ("risky") medicines may still be judged "acceptable" for serious diseases where no other alternatives exist (e.g. in cases of cancer or aids).

"Risk Society"

Health and safety (risk) regulation encompasses both scientific findings and social values which are subject to constant alteration.[9] The application of science and technology in today's increasingly "technologised" world needs to be constantly weighed against the risks involved.[10] Hence, modern society has been described as a "risk society" (*Risikogesellschaft*),[11] as it seeks to ensure health and safety by eliminating or reducing the exposure of its citizens to certain potentially risky substances.[12] The regulatory activities of the "risk society" thus involve the assessment of the risks associated with specific substances or products (risk assessment) and the regulatory decisions on what to do about these risks (risk management).[13] Risk assessment and risk management together aim to prevent the occurrence of certain catastrophes. The acceptability of risks as a regulatory issue refers to the "choice" of society to accept certain risks, which consequently makes risk regulation a matter of ranking norms or values. When considering risks, for instance, several—not only scientific—elements must be taken into account: the general characteristics of the product (its usefulness); its technical aspects (are there safer alternatives?); the danger posed by the design of the product or by its incorrect or faulty use; the danger of the product through possible defects; the potential user of the product, as well as costs and other factors.[14]

---

[9] See, for instance, Lowrance, above n. 4. See, for more recent studies on the relation between science and normative values, D.G. Mayo/R.D. Hollander (eds.), Acceptable Evidence. Science and Values in Risk Management (New York/Oxford, 1991). See also O.A. Brekke/E.O. Eriksen, *Technology Assessment and Democratic Governance*, typescript, Norwegian Research Centre in Organisation and Management (Bergen, 1998).

[10] S.K. Siddhanti, *Multiple Perspectives on Risk and Regulation. The Case of Deliberate Release of Genetically Engineered Organisms into the Environment* (New York/London, 1991), 27.

[11] See U. Beck, *Risikogesellschaft. Auf dem Weg in eine andere Moderne* (Frankfurt, 1986), translated by M. Ritter, *Risk Society: Towards a New Modernity* (London, 1991). See, e.g., also G. Bechmann (ed.), *Risiko und Gesellschaft. Grundlagen und Ergebnisse interdisziplinärer Risikoforschung* (Opladen, 1993).

[12] Or even persons (unqualified doctors). See S. Breyer, *Breaking the Vicious Circle. Toward Effective Risk Regulation* (Cambridge, Mass., 1993), 3.

[13] Breyer, above n. 12, 9 ff. See also L.B. Lave (ed.), *Risk Assessment and Management* (New York/London, 1987).

[14] OECD, *Product Safety. Risk Management and Cost-Benefit Analysis* (Paris, 1983), 45–51.

Value-laden Nature of Risk Regulation

Risk assessment is, however, inherently plagued by uncertainty or controversy, so that no absolute value may be attached to it. The notion that scientists can or do limit themselves to addressing purely scientific issues may even be fundamentally misconceived.[15] Today, it is generally accepted that no such thing as "objective science" exists; given the present state of our knowledge, scientists are not likely to limit themselves to addressing "purely scientific issues".[16] Scientific experts can and do disagree: they are not infallible by virtue of their specialist access to a scientific methodology that can guarantee their "objectivity", whilst their seemingly "disinterested" advice may be influenced by professional, economic or political considerations.[17] Depending on various elements (for whom they work, for example), scientists may inevitably need to engage in normative assessments.[18] Science therefore finds its limits in, for example, the lack of sufficient knowledge which means that scientists themselves must postulate several hypotheses.[19] Furthermore, the day-to-day management of society cannot always wait for scientists to complete their cautious determinations of risks which may take long periods of time, thus necessitating the settlement of risks within political deliberations.[20]

Hence, adequate solutions for problems attended by great scientific uncertainty or having strong political overtones cannot be furnished by science and scientists alone.[21] Such "trans-scientific" problems confront regulators with the "choice" of whether or not to accept certain risks, and require them to judge the risks inherent to social and technological industrial development by balancing calculable and calculated dangers against any possible desired benefits.[22] Under these conditions of scientific uncertainty and/or controversy,[23] decision-makers are faced with the problem of how to make proper use of the scientific data and

---

[15] See S. Jasanoff, *The Fifth Branch. Science Advisers as Policymakers* (Cambridge, Mass./London, 1990), 249.

[16] *Ibid.*

[17] B. Martin/E. Richards, "Scientific Knowledge, Controversy and Public Decision Making", in S. Jasanoff/G.E. Markle/J.C. Petersen/T. Pinch (eds.), *Handbook of Science and Technology Studies* (Thousand Oaks/London/New Delhi, 1995), 507.

[18] Di Trocchio even speaks of the intentional lying of scientists: F. Di Trocchio, *Le bugie della scienza. Perchè e come gli scienzati imbrogliano* (Milano, 1993).

[19] See, for instance, in relation to animal studies, C.F. Cranor, *Regulating Toxic Substances. A Philosophy of Science and the Law* (New York/Oxford, 1993), 17 ff.

[20] Lowrance, above n. 4, at 79.

[21] See A.M. Weinberg, "Science and Trans-Science" (1972) 10 *Minerva* 209–22.

[22] See R. Damm/D. Hart (eds.), *Rechtliche Regulierung von Gesundheitsrisiken* (Baden-Baden, 1993), at 9. See, in general, R. Wilson/E. Crouch, *Risk/Benefit Analysis* (Cambridge, Mass., 1982). See for a classification of different approaches to risk assessment, Renn, above n. 5, 56 ff.

[23] See O. Godard, "Social Decision-Making under Conditions of Scientific Controversy, Expertise and the Precautionary Principle", in Ch. Joerges/K.H. Ladeur/E. Vos (eds.), *Integrating Scientific Expertise into Regulatory Decision-Making. National Traditions and European Innovations* (Baden-Baden, 1997), 39–73.

risk assessments submitted to them. In this context, it is difficult to sever risk assessment from risk management.[24]

2. DEALING WITH RISK UNDER COMMUNITY LAW

It is into this complex world of risk regulation that the Community is now entering. The gradual shift of health and safety regulation to the Community level forces the Community institutions to deal with risk and carry out risk assessment and management. It poses considerable regulatory difficulties for the Community, which differ from those faced at the Member State level. These problems may be categorised with the help of the dichotomy between legality and legitimacy. In addition, Community health and safety regulation raises problems of a more "practical" nature.

Problems of Legality

The gradual evolution of Community health and safety regulation raises questions about its impact upon the relationship between the Member States and the Community which results from the continuous transfer of powers from the Member States to the Community (Chapter 1). In this context, questions arise regarding the Community's competence in this field in relation to the principle of attributed powers, which determines that every binding measure of the Community must be based on the provisions of the Treaty.[25] This principle is explicitly recognised by the Treaty of Maastricht. Clearly, the growing Community involvement in this area must take account of the principles of supremacy, pre-emption and safeguard procedures which have been developed precisely to address the relationship between national legal orders and the Community legal order. Hence, the scrutiny of Community competence in these fields ultimately concerns fundamental constitutional issues.

However, Community involvement in health and safety issues not only leads to a restructuring of the vertical distribution of power (transfer of Member State powers to the Community), but also has an impact on the horizontal distribution of powers (shift from Parliament and Council legislation to Commission implementation) (Chapter 2). First, the analysis must focus on the reasons for increased involvement of Community activity in this area; which factors, notwithstanding the Commission's plea for mutual recognition, push the "post-Maastricht" Community to increase its activities in this area

[24] See Cranor, above n. 19, at 132. See also W.D. Rowe, "Risk Analysis", in M. Waterstone (ed.), *Risk and Society: The Interaction of Science, Technocracy and Public Policy* (Dordrecht/Boston/London, 1992), 23.

[25] See, e.g., R. Barents, "The Internal Market Unlimited: Some Observations on the Legal Basis of Community Legislation" (1993) 30 *CMLRev*. 85.

further?[26] The "deepening" of Community action in this field raises further legal questions about the Community's competence to implement its own rules, the principle of subsidiarity and the principle of the institutional balance of powers. Has the Community paid sufficient regard to its own institutional structure? These questions are of particular relevance as the Community has resorted to various bodies such as committees, agencies or standard-setting organisations, both within and outside the Community's institutional structure.

Problems of Legitimacy

Furthermore, increasing decision-making by the Community on consumer health and safety issues, previously decided upon in the national context, has generally been viewed as a less democratic form of decision-making. This view is also a reflection of more general concerns about the legitimacy of the Community legal order[27] based on the Rule of Law[28] and its law-making powers, due to the pervasiveness of Community integration in many fields.[29] Discussion of the "democratic deficit" of the Community generally refers to the weak role of the European Parliament in comparison with the national parliaments, holding the Community to the yardstick of the system of representative parliamentary democracy.[30] The problematic ratification of the Maastricht Treaty and the *Maastricht* judgment of the German Constitutional Court[31] all give expression to these concerns.[32]

In the field of health and safety regulation, these concerns are first and foremost directed to the increasing activity of the Commission (Chapter 2). This can be explained by analogy with the national and American context where delegation of discretionary powers is argued to move away from what has been

---

[26] COM(85)310 final.

[27] See, as early as Case 26/62, *Van Gend en Loos* [1963] ECR 1 and Case 6/64, *Costa v. ENEL* [1964] ECR 585.

[28] See, *inter alia*, Case 294/83, *Parti écologiste "Les Verts"* v. *European Parliament* [1987] ECR 2, confirmed in *Opinion 1/91* [1991] ECR I–6079.

[29] See, e.g., J.H.H. Weiler, "Problems of Legitimacy in Post 1992 Europe" (1991) 46 *Aussenwirtschaft* 411–37; E.-J. Mestmäcker, "On the Legitimacy of European Law" (1994) 58 *RabelsZ* 615–35.

[30] See, e.g., S. Williams, "Sovereignty and Accountability in the European Community" (1990) 61 *Pol.Q.* 3, 299; C. Harlow, "A Community of Interests? Making the Most of European Law" (1992) 55 *MLR* 332; D. Curtin, "'Civil Society' and the European Union: Opening Spaces for Deliberative Democracy?", in *Collected Courses of the Academy of European Law* (Florence, 1996, forthcoming 1998). See, e.g., the European Parliament Resolution on the democratic deficit [1988] OJ C187/229.

[31] *Brunner et al.* v. *The European Union Treaty*, Cases 2BvR 2134/92 & 2159/92, *Bundesverfassungsgericht*, judgment of 12 Oct. 1993 [1994] CMLR, 57.

[32] See, in general, Ch. Joerges, "Legitimationsprobleme des Europäischen Wirtschaftsrechts und der Vertrag von Maastricht", in G. Brüggemeier (ed.), *Verfassungen für ein ziviles Europa* (Baden-Baden, 1994), 91–130.

termed the "transmission belt" model of administrative law.[33] In this model, the wide degree of discretion may be argued to have weakened the administration's claim to be acting solely on the basis of the legislature's duly enacted laws and thus to have undermined administrative legitimacy. This situation leads, at national level, to a search for additional measures aimed at enhancing legitimacy, such as greater democratic and judicial control, increased transparency, greater expertise and stronger participation of citizens in the decision-making process by means of representative interest groups, open hearings and public debate, although such mechanisms, nevertheless, raise other difficulties in turn.[34]

However, legitimacy in the Community context cannot merely reproduce "national models". When observing the dynamics of integration one can detect the *sui generis* character of the Community, which is more than a mere association of states but less than a true supranational constitutional order.[35] The Community is not (yet) a kind of a new European "state"; instead it can be portrayed as what political scientists have termed a "multi-level system of governance".[36] Multi-level governance sees to decision-making by different levels of government and shifting fields of competence[37] and thus appears compatible with both the conservation of national administrative powers and the assumption of national powers by the Community. In search of greater legitimacy for decision-making by the Commission in particular, the Community's multi-level governance structure is therefore troubled with additional problems relating to the need to include the Member States in the implementation phase, the differing linguistic and cultural habits and the "representativity" of interests. Hence, in this book, the analysis of the institutional frameworks of Community health and safety regulation concentrates on the manner in which scientific expertise, the participation of diffuse interests, the transparency of the decision-making procedures and the accountability of Community decision-making are relied upon.

The search for legitimate risk regulation by the Community/Commission is based on the main premise that the Member States are an essential basis of the Community and that consequently their participation in balancing of political interests at the Community level is desired. The Member States' concern to be involved in Community risk regulation is not to be seen as just a matter of promoting national, parochial, protectionist interests, but is much more the

---

[33] See R. Stewart, "The Reformation of American Administrative Law" (1975) 88 *Harvard Law Review* 1669–70. This applies also to the European Community.

[34] See, in this context, M. Everson, "Administering Europe?" (1998) 36 *JCMS* 2, 195–216.

[35] See also M. Jachtenfuchs, "Theoretical Perspectives on European Governance" (1995) 1 *ELJ* 2, 115–33.

[36] See, in particular, F.W. Scharpf, "Community and Autonomy: Multi-level Policy-making in the European Union" (1994) 1 *JEPP* 2, 219–42 and M. Jachtenfuchs/B. Kohler-Koch, "Regieren im dynamischen Mehrebenensystem" in *id.* (eds.), *Europäische Integration* (Opladen, 1996), 15–44.

[37] For a comprehensive recent analysis, see V. Eichener, *Entscheidungsprozesse in der regulativen Politik der Europäischen Union* (Habilitation, University of Bochum 1997).

inevitable result of the fact that risk assessment and management are so complex, uncertain and controversial that they cannot be conducted without reference to normative social values. Community structures of risk regulation must therefore address the tensions arising from the opening up of markets on the one hand and the need to respond to "legitimate" regulatory concerns on the other.[38] The interdependence of national and Community regulatory concerns has become especially apparent in the aftermath of the BSE crisis.[39]

In addition, alongside the Member States, interested parties should also participate in Community risk regulation, since decision-making increasingly takes place at the Community level. At the same time, interest participation at the Community level will enable the various interested parties to free themselves from imposed national traditions and values.[40] Negotiation and deliberation with "civil society" (that is, non-governmental) actors,[41] and therefore with the citizens of the Community, is of great importance.[42] A particular role in this should be reserved for those who are most vulnerable to risks: the users of products. The structures of health and safety regulation will therefore be examined to determine the extent to which interested parties may participate in Community decision-making.

"Practical" Problems

Regulating risk at the Community level means that the Community is now required to collect, produce and evaluate scientific data[43] or, alternatively, to harmonise such activities at the national level. The Community, however, lacks the necessary scientific expertise and administrative capacity to carry out these tasks. As risk regulation incorporates both scientific expertise and normative elements, a certain degree of flexibility is required. In addition, the internal market objective pushes the Community into an increased involvement in health and safety regulation, since national legislative provisions on these issues create justified trade barriers. This leads not only to the implementation of a greater number of rules at Community level, but also engages the Community

---

[38] Ch. Joerges, "Scientific Expertise in Social Regulation and the European Court of Justice: Legal Frameworks for Denationalised Governance Structures", in Ch. Joerges/K.-H. Ladeur/E. Vos (eds.), *Integrating Scientific Expertise into Regulatory Decision-Making. National Traditions and European Innovations* (Baden-Baden, 1997), 322.

[39] An overview of the main events of the BSE crisis will be given in Chap. 4.

[40] See, in general, Everson, above n. 34.

[41] Curtin, above n. 30.

[42] See on the concept of deliberative democracy, e.g., J. Bohman/W. Rehg (eds.), *Deliberative Democracy* (Cambridge Mass./London, 1997); J. Cohen, "Deliberation and Democratic Democracy", in *ibid.*, 67–91; J. Cohen, "Procedure and Substance in Deliberative Democracy", in S. Benhabib, *Democracy and Difference. Contesting the Boundaries of the Political* (Princeton, NJ, 1996), 95–119 and J. Cohen/Ch. Sabel, "Direct-Deliberative Polyarchy" (1997) 3 *ELJ* 4, 313–42.

[43] See, for an analysis of the problems caused by value interpretation in collecting, interpreting, communicating and evaluating evidence of risks, with particular reference to the American debate, Mayo/Hollander (eds.), above n. 9.

in monitoring activities and the creation of emergency procedures which may be applied to dangerous products brought onto the Community market (post-market control). This inevitably results in an increasing workload for the Community institutions, in particular, the Commission. In so far as Community involvement in health and safety regulation may be considered to be an accidental consequence of the market integration objective (spill-over), this may explain why the Community has not been well-equipped to face these difficulties. In response, it has sought to expand its institutional frameworks to achieve the regulatory objectives of both the internal market and consumer health and safety protection, and to design appropriate provisions and regulatory frameworks to incorporate scientific expertise into decision-making. Today, in the aftermath of the BSE crisis, the importance of such frameworks needs hardly be emphasised. Not surprisingly, the pivotal place of scientific expertise in Community product regulation is recognised by the Treaty of Amsterdam, which explicitly inserts the obligation of the Commission to base its internal market proposals on new scientific evidence (Article 100a (3)).[44]

3. REGULATORY MODELS: COMMITTEES, AGENCIES AND PRIVATE BODIES

Both political science and legal literature characterise this type of regulatory activity as social regulation, mainly concerned with regulatory protection against risks to human health and safety and the environment.[45] Regulatory modes of social regulation can generally be distinguished as: statutory regulation by independent agencies, deregulation (or regulatory competition or mutual recognition) and self-regulation.[46] The Community has operated these three modes of regulation, whilst, in addition, it has resorted to a mode typical of the Community: the committee system. However, deregulation or mutual recognition as the sole means of achieving market integration and health and safety protection has not worked. Although the Commission launched this method as one of the main instruments for achieving the internal market objective in its 1985 White Paper,[47] practice soon demonstrated that this New Approach boiled down to a re-regulatory operation for Community health and safety regulation.[48] Instead of a "race to the bottom", a process of re-regulation at the Community level takes place in which another kind of "regulatory

---

[44] This seems to confirm the importance the Court has attached to scientific expertise. See, e.g., Case C–212/91, *Angelopharm* v. *Freie und Hansestadt Hamburg* [1994] ECR I–171.

[45] This terminology originates, in particular, from the USA. See, e.g., C.R. Sunstein, *After the Rights Revolution. Reconceiving the Regulatory State* (Cambridge Mass., 1990) and M.D. Reagan, *Regulation. The Politics of Policy* (Boston, Mass./Toronto, 1987).

[46] G. Majone, *Regulating Europe* (London, 1996), in particular ch. 1: Regulation and its modes, 9–27. Regulation through public ownership is a main mode of economic regulation.

[47] Above n. 26.

[48] Ch. Joerges, "Paradoxes of Deregulatory Strategies at Community Level: The Example of Product Safety Policy", in G. Majone (ed.), *Deregulation or Re-regulation? A Regulatory Reform in Europe and the United States* (London, 1990), 176–97.

competition" has emerged by which Member States strive to impose their own regulatory approaches on the whole of the Community.[49]

Hence, the regulatory models which the Community operates in an attempt to overcome the various difficulties arising from science-based decision-making and to ensure adequate and efficient decision-making are based on committees, agencies and private bodies (self-regulation). These three institutional frameworks form the core of the analysis in this book which examines these models in three fields: foodstuffs, pharmaceuticals and technical product standards (Chapters 3–5). These fields are exemplary in that they all are concerned with the dual regulatory objectives of both internal market policy and consumer health[50] (foodstuffs and pharmaceuticals) and safety[51] (technical product safety), but nonetheless differ in the regulatory approach through which the Community attempts to overcome legal and practical problems. The analysis seeks to reveal the particularities of these structures and the manner in which the various bodies operate, which hitherto have remained largely obscure. It concentrates on investigation of the legality and legitimacy of these frameworks and will seek to identify the principles which currently guide the Community in regulating risk.

This book, therefore, first examines the gradual evolution of Community involvement in health and safety regulation and elaborates on the fundamental EU law concepts of competence, subsidiarity, institutional balance of powers, delegation of powers and legitimacy in relation to health and safety (Chapters 1 and 2). These concepts are then used to appraise the legality and the legitimacy of the three basic regulatory patterns: the resort to committees, to agencies and to private bodies (Chapters 3–5). In conclusion, some suggestions for improvement of Community risk regulation are advanced.

---

[49] See for the case of air quality regulation, A. Héritier/S. Mingers/C. Knill/M. Becka, *Die Veränderung von Staatlichkeit in Europa. Ein regulativer Wettbewerb: Deutschland, Großbritannien, Frankreich* (Opladen, 1994).

[50] Which relates to the intake of products or substances by persons.

[51] Which relates to the physical contact with products by persons.

1

The Community's Involvement in Health and Safety Regulation

1. INTRODUCTION

This chapter examines the origins of Community involvement in health and safety regulation and investigates the Community's legal competence to operate in this area. Although the original Treaty of Rome contained no explicit provision on a Community competence for health and safety regulation, this has not prevented the Community from gradually stepping into this field. Health and safety regulation by the Community has evolved on a dual basis, being part of both an internal market policy and a consumer protection policy. However, over the years, the incremental development of Community activities in health and safety regulation and other consumer interests has been much contested. In the 1970s, the Community competence in this and other areas, such as environmental protection, was hotly debated in the literature.[1] However, as long as the Member States possessed the right of veto—based on the unanimity requirement, particularly in Articles 100 and 235—growing Community activities in this field were not disputed in practice, since Member States were able to block any Community action with which they did not agree.[2]

This rapidly changed with the 1987 Single European Act,[3] which introduced qualified majority voting in Article 100a to accelerate harmonisation measures aimed at the creation of an internal market, in accordance with the Community's "New Approach on Technical Harmonisation and Standards".[4]

---

[1] See, *inter alia*, the debates discussed by G. Close, "Harmonisation of Laws: Use or Abuse of Powers under the EEC Treaty?" (1978) 3 *ELR* 461–81. See also J.H Kaiser, "Grenzen der EG-Zuständigkeit" (1980) 15 *EuR* 2, 97–118, discussing the competences of the Community, in particular with respect to what Kaiser defined as the border areas (*"Grenzzonen"*) such as health, consumer protection, environment protection, social security, education and culture.

[2] In recent years the Member States have demonstrated that they are prepared to go to court in order to defend their voting right, in particular their veto. In several cases, Member States have attempted to demonstrate that the correct legal basis of the adopted measure in question was the one which provided for a unanimity voting in the Council, instead of the one allowing for qualified majority. See, for instance, Case 68/86, *United Kingdom* v. *Council* (*"hormones"*) [1988] ECR 855.

[3] See, in general, on the history of the Single European Act, J. De Ruyt, *L'Acte unique européen: commentaire* (Brussels, 1989).

[4] Council Resolution on a new approach to technical harmonisation and standards [1985] OJ C136/1. See, in more detail, Chap. 2.

Yet the price to be paid for the introduction of qualified majority voting,[5] which put the Member States at the risk of being outvoted,[6] was the introduction of an "opting out" clause in paragraph (4) of Article 100a. This paragraph, which is said to be the most troublesome provision of the SEA,[7] was especially designed to meet the concerns of the various Member States, in particular those of Denmark, that measures adopted by qualified majority voting might lower their existing high levels of consumer and environmental protection.[8] As a result, paragraph (4) allows Member States, in certain circumstances, to take measures to protect *inter alia* consumer health and safety even after the adoption of a harmonisation measure.

The Community's "dynamic" assumption of Member States' powers on the basis of Article 100a nonetheless reignited the competence issue.[9] The overall debate on the Community's "creeping" competence was continued during the 1991 Inter-Governmental Conference on Political Union. Once again, Member States were afraid to transfer greater powers to the Community, but agreed upon the need to do so. Thus, paradoxically, the Maastricht Treaty introduced a widening of Community competences, together with certain institutional changes which added various new subject-matters to the Community's activities but tempered their effects by the denial of the decision-making powers of the Community in some of these areas and the introduction of subsidiarity. As regards health and safety regulation, Article 3(o) and (s) stipulates that the Community's activities include "a contribution to the attainment of a high level of health protection" and "a contribution to the strengthening of consumer protection", whilst contemporaneously separate titles have been introduced on public health (Article 129) and consumer protection (Article 129a). In view of their supplementary character, however, both Articles have been argued to have brought about little change.[10] Not surprisingly, even after the conclusion of the

[5] J. Mertens de Wilmars, "Het Hof van Justitie van de Europese Gemeenschappen na de Europese Akte" (1986) 34 *SEW* 9/10, 605. See also C.D. Ehlermann, "The Internal Market Following the Single European Act" (1987) 24 *CMLRev.*, 389 ff.

[6] See, in general, on this subject-matter, Ch. Engel/Ch. Borrmann, *Vom Konsensus zur Mehrheitsentscheidung. EG-Entscheidungsverfahren und nationale Interessenpolitik nach der Einheitlichen Europäischen Akte* (Bonn, 1991).

[7] Ehlermann, above n. 5, at 389.

[8] See the unilateral declaration by the Danish Government on Art. 100a (4), annexed to the SEA. See C. Gulmann, "The Single European Act—Some Remarks from a Danish Perspective" (1987) 24 *CMLRev.*, 31 ff. and L. Krämer, "The Single European Act and Environmental Protection: Reflections on Several New Provisions in Community Law" (1987) 24 *CMLRev.* 681. See, in general, on the legislative history of this provision, De Ruyt, above n. 3.

[9] See the debate in M. Fallon/F. Maniet (eds.), *Sécurité des produits et mécanismes de contrôle dans la Communauté européenne* (Louvain-la-Neuve, 1990) and in particular the contribution by P. VerLoren van Themaat, "Some comments of a former Advocate-General at the Court of Justice of the European Communities", 129 ff. See in general, E. Steindorff, *Grenzen der EG Kompetenzen* (Heidelberg, 1990) and, more recently, A. Dashwood, "The Limits of European Community Powers" (1996) 21 *ELR* 113–28.

[10] See R. Lane, "New Community Competences Under the Maastricht Treaty" (1993) 30 *CMLRev.* 958–60.

Maastricht Treaty, "creeping" Community competences[11] remained subject to debate. This controversy was primarily apparent in the tortuous ratification process,[12] and the German Constitutional Court's 1993 *"Maastricht"* judgment.[13] However, the recent amendments by the Treaty of Amsterdam, although not yet in force,[14] appear to reinforce Community competence on health and safety regulation.

Hence, the legal questions addressed in this chapter relate to the Community's general competence to issue health and safety acts and to the correct legal basis for this. Once the general competence of the Community to regulate health and safety matters has been examined, the question accordingly arises of the impact of Community health and safety regulation on the relationship between Member States and the Community. This issue will be addressed in the final section of this chapter. First, however, the need for Community involvement activities on health and safety will be examined.

2. THE EMERGENCE OF COMMUNITY HEALTH AND SAFETY REGULATION

The free movement of goods is one of the Community's main instruments for achieving its objective of the creation of an internal market. It is a general principle of Community law[15] and requires Member States to refrain from hindering the entry of goods from other Member States into their markets. The internal market may be achieved through "negative" integration (elimination of trade barriers) and "positive" integration (creation of new policies), although this distinction has been blurred to some extent.[16]

[11] See M. Pollack, "Creeping Competence: The Expanding Agenda of the European Community" (1994) 14 Journal of Public Policy, 95–145.

[12] See, *inter alia*, A. Duff, "Ratification", in A. Duff/J. Pinder/R. Pryce, *Maastricht and Beyond. Building the European Union* (London, 1994), 53–68; F. Laursen/S. Vanhoonacker (eds.), *The Ratification of the Maastricht Treaty. Issues, Debates and Future Implications* (Maastricht, 1994).

[13] *Brunner et al.* v. *The European Union Treaty*, Cases 2BvR 2134/92 & 2159/92, *Bundesverfassungsgericht*, judgment of 12 Oct. 1993, in particular point C (before I) [1994] CMLR 57. See, for comments on this judgment, *inter alia*, M. Herdegen, "Maastricht and the German Constitutional Court: Constitutional Restraints for an 'Ever Closer Union'" (1994) 31 *CMLRev*. 235–49; D. Hanf, "Le jugement de la Cour constitutionnelle fédérale allemande sur la constitutionnalité du Traité de Maastricht" (1994) 30 *RTDE* 3, 391–423; Th. Koopmans, "Rechter, D-mark en democratie: het Bundesverfassungsgericht en de Europese Unie" (1994) 8 *NJB* 245–51; Ch. Joerges, *States Without a Market? Comments on the German Constitutional Court's Maastricht Judgment and a Plea for Interdisciplinary Discourses*, NISER Working Paper (Utrecht, 1996).

[14] The action against the introduction of the Euro brought before the German Constitutional Court by four German professors was rejected by the Court as being clearly unfounded: Order of 31 Mar. 1998, Az 2 BvR 1877/97 and 50/98.

[15] Case 240/83, *Association de défense des brûleurs d'huiles usagées (ADBHU)* [1985] ECR 531, at 584.

[16] The terms negative and positive integration were formulated by Tinbergen in 1954. He defines negative integration as measures consisting of the abolition of a number of impediments to the proper operation of an integrated area, and positive integration as the creation of new institutions and their instruments or the modification of existing instruments: J. Tinbergen, *International Economic Integration* (2nd edn., Amsterdam, 1965), 76. Pinder uses the term negative integration

2.1. The Elimination of Obstacles to Trade and the Exceptions Thereto: "Negative Integration"

Focusing on "negative integration", Article 30 enjoins the Member States from imposing quantitative restrictions on imports or measures having an equivalent effect. This prohibition is a means of dismantling national barriers in order to allow for the free movement of goods throughout the Community market.[17] Quantitative import (or export) restrictions include all legislative or administrative rules restricting the importation (or exportation) of one or more products according to quantitative norms.[18] However, the interpretation of "measures having equivalent effect" has proved more difficult and has consequently led to copious case law.[19] In *Dassonville*, the Court defined the concept of measures having equivalent effect as:

> "[a]ll trading rules enacted by Member States which are capable of hindering, directly or indirectly, actually or potentially, intra-Community trade are to be considered as measures having an effect equivalent to quantitative restrictions".[20]

for that part of economic integration that consists of the removal of discrimination and positive integration as the formulation and application of co-ordinated and common policies in order to fulfil economic and welfare objectives other than the removal of discrimination: J. Pinder, "Problems of European Integration", in G.R. Denton (ed.), *Economic Integration in Europe* (London, 1969), 145. The main difference between the two definitions is that Tinbergen's distinction between negative and positive integration is founded on whether policy instruments are to be eliminated or whether new policies must be formed, whilst Pinder's definition is based on whether the purpose is to remove discrimination or to maximise welfare in other ways. See, more recently, F.W. Scharpf, *Negative and Positive Integration in the Political Economy of European Welfare States*, Jean Monnet Chair Papers, EUI Working Paper RSC (Florence, 1995). See sect. 2.2.

[17] See also other examples of negative integration, in relation to other specific measures capable of restricting intra-trade: Arts. 9, 12–16 (customs duties and charges having equivalent effect); Arts. 48–58 (free movement for legal and natural persons); Arts. 59–66 (freedom to provide services); Art. 90 (State activities or other public or privileged undertakings acting as market participants); Arts. 92–94 (state aids) and Art. 95–98 (discriminatory taxation).

[18] E.g. Case 2/73, *Geddo v. Ente Nazionale Risi* [1973] ECR 865.

[19] See for an overview of the case law, P. Oliver, *Free Movement of Goods in the European Community Under Articles 30 to 36 of the Rome Treaty* (London, 1996); P.J.G. Kapteyn/P. VerLoren van Themaat, edited by L. Gormley, *Introduction to the Law of the European Communities* (Deventer, 1990), 377–87; L. Gormley, *Prohibiting Restrictions on Trade within the EEC* (Amsterdam/New York/Oxford, 1985). Bourgoignie gives a detailed overview up to 1983 of the national trade rules which have been viewed as measures of equivalent effect by the Court: Th. Bourgoignie, "Consumer Law and the European Community: Issues and Prospects", in Th. Bourgoignie/D. Trubek, *Consumer Law, Common Market and Federalism in Europe and the United States* (Berlin/New York, 1987), 160–5.

[20] Case 8/74, *Procureur du Roi v. Dassonville* [1974] ECR 837. Capotorti AG was even clearer when he stated in Case 788/79, *Gilli and Andres*, that a breach of Art. 30 is: "no less a contravention by the fact that the restrictive national rule subjects imported and national products to the same treatment. . . . The character of a national rule falling within the scope of Art. 30 lies in the fact of its being a complete barrier to the importation from other Member States of a given product; that fact is enough for it to be regarded as offending the rule of free movement of goods even if the said rule prevents the marketing of the product in question irrespective of the country in which it has been manufactured": [1980] ECR 2082.

The principle of equivalence was further refined in the celebrated *Cassis de Dijon* case, where the Court held that, in principle, a Member State must allow a product lawfully produced and marketed in another Member State into its own market, unless a prohibition of this product is justified by mandatory requirements (see below).[21] Such an interpretation paved the way for a very broad interpretation of measures of equivalent effect.[22] However, the Court has recently adopted a more restrictive approach and delimited the scope of Article 30 by distinguishing between product-related regulations and selling arrangements (*"modalités de vente"*), establishing that the latter fall outside the application of Article 30.[23]

2.1.1. Article 36, First Sentence, and the Rule of Reason

The prohibition of Member States from creating trade barriers is nevertheless tempered by various exceptions. These exceptions are laid down in Article 36 and developed by the Court in its case law on Article 30. In its first sentence, Article 36 enumerates the grounds which justify trade barriers: public morality, public policy or public security; *the protection of health and life of humans*, animals or plants; the protection of national treasures possessing artistic, historic or archaeological value or the protection of industrial and commercial property. Member States are thus allowed to maintain national rules where they aim to protect the health and life of humans, a value which the Court has considered as

---

[21] Case 120/78, *Rewe-Zentrale AG* v. *Bundesmonopolverwaltung für Branntwein* [1979] ECR 649, although this principle was only explicitly developed in Case 113/80, *Commission* v. *Ireland* [1981] ECR 1625.

[22] The scope of Art. 30 has been debated since the 1960s; see for an overview of the different schools of thought in the doctrine: Oliver, above n. 19, 90 ff. In *Dassonville*, the Court chose a broad interpretation: above n. 20. See, more recently, for instance, Cases C–238/89, *Pall-Dahlhausen* [1990] ECR I–4827; C–362/88, *GB-INNO-BM* v. *Confédération du Commerce Luxembourgeois* [1990] ECR I–667; C–126/91, *Schutzverband gegen Unwesen in der Wirtschaft* v. *Yves Rocher* [1993] ECR I–2361. See, in general, J. Steiner, "Drawing the Line: Uses and Abuses of Article 30 EEC" (1992) 29 *CMLRev.* 749.

[23] Cases C–267 & 268/91, *Keck and Mithouard* [1993] ECR I–6126. See *inter alia* U. Becker, "Von 'Dassonville' über 'Cassis' zu 'Keck'—Der Begriff der Maßnahmen gleicher Wirkung in Artikel 30 EGV" (1994) 29 *EuR* 2, 162–74; S. Moore, "Revisiting the Limits of Article 30 EEC" (1994) 19 *ELR* 19, 195; K.J.M. Mortelmans, "De interne markt en het facettenbeleid na het Keck-arrest: nationaal beleid, vrij verkeer of harmonisatie" (1994) 42 *SEW* 4, 236–50. Reich speaks in this context even of a "November Revolution" of the Court: N. Reich, "The 'November Revolution' of the European Court of Justice: *Keck*, *Meng* and *Audi* Revisited" (1994) 31 *CMLRev.* 459–92. According to Chalmers, the Court has decided to cut the Gordian knot and to rationalise its case law on Art. 30: D. Chalmers, "Repackiging the Internal Market—The Ramifications of the *Keck* Judgment" (1994) 19 *ELR* 385–403. Palacio Gonzalez brings the *Keck* judgment in connection with the principle of subsidiarity: J. Palacio Gonzalez, "The Principle of Subsidiarity (A Guide for Lawyers with a Particular Community Orientation)" (1995) 20 *ELR* 361. The path followed in *Keck* by the Court has been confirmed in its subsequent case law: see, for instance, Case C–292/92, *Hünermund et al.* v. *Landesapothekerkammer Baden-Württemberg* [1993] ECR I–6787 and Case C–391/92, *Commission* v. *Greece* [1995] ECR I–1621. See, for a discussion of the situation post-*Keck*, L.W. Gormley, "Two Years after *Keck*" (1996) 19 *Fordham International Law Journal* 866–86 and S. Weatherill, "After *Keck*: Some Thoughts on How to Clarify the Clarification" (1996) 33 *CMLRev.* 885–906.

ranking foremost among the property interests and general interests protected by Article 36.[24] The exceptions are of an *interim* nature: once the necessary protection for human health has been provided for at Community level through harmonisation directives based on Article 100 or 100a, recourse to Article 36 ceases to be justified.[25] However, if the harmonisation is incomplete, the Member States may adopt measures in the non-harmonised field and resort to Article 36 for justification.[26] As the Court held in *Motte*:

> "it is only when Community directives make provision for the full harmonisation of all measures needed to ensure the protection of health and institute Community measures to monitor compliance therewith that recourse to Article 36 ceases to be justified".[27]

In the absence of harmonisation, the Court has often preferred (particularly in cases involving complex scientific findings) to confirm the validity of national rules under Article 36. Although in such cases Member States have the power to decide what degree of protection for the health and safety of the life of humans they intend to assure,[28] this does not mean that Member States retain "exclusive" competence in these matters. As the Court ruled in *Simmenthal*:

> "Article 36 is not designed to reserve certain matters to the exclusive jurisdiction of the Member States but permits national law to derogate from the principle of free movement of goods to the extent to which such derogation is and continues to be justified for the attainment of the objectives referred to in that Article".[29]

Being an exception to the prohibition of trade barriers and measures of equivalent effect, the grounds of justification in Article 36 have initially been inter-

---

[24] See, e.g., Case 215/87, *Schumacher* [1989] ECR 617 and Case C–347/89, *Freistaat Bayern* v. *Eurim-Pharm GmbH* [1991] ECR I–1747. See, as regards the environmental protection in particular, Case 240/83, above n. 15, at 549.

[25] For instance, Case 5/77, *Tedeschi* v. *Denkavit Commerciale s.r.l.* [1977] ECR 1555; Case 148/78, *Pubblico Ministero* v. *Ratti* [1979] ECR 1629; Case 227/82, *Van Bennekom* [1983] ECR 3883.

[26] See, for instance, Case 227/82, above n. 25; Case 237/82, *Jongeneel Kaas BV* [1984] ECR 483.

[27] Case 247/84, *Motte* [1985] ECR 3887, at 3903. See also Case 304/84, *Muller* [1986] ECR 1511, at 1526; Case 104/75, *De Peijper* [1976] ECR 613; and Case 215/87, *Schumacher* v. *Hauptzollamt Frankfurt a.M.* [1989] ECR 617, para. 15.

[28] E.g., Case 53/80, *Officier van Justitie* v. *Koninklijke Kaasfabriek Eyssen BV* [1981] ECR 409; Case 174/82, *Sandoz BV* [1983] ECR 2445; Case 227/82, above n. 25; Case 176/84, *Commission* v. *Greece* [1987] ECR 1193; Case 178/84, *Commission* v. *Germany (Reinheitsgebot)* [1987] ECR 1227; Case 247/84, above n. 27; Case 304/84, above n. 27; Case 125/88, *Nijman* [1989] ECR 3533; Case C–205/89, *Commission* v. *Greece* [1991] ECR I–1361; Case C–42/90, *Bellon* [1990] ECR I–4863; Joined Cases C–13/91 & C–113/91, *Debus* [1992] ECR I–3617.

[29] Case 35/76, *Simmenthal* [1976] ECR 1871, at 1886. See, e.g., also *Ratti* where the Court determined that "pursuant to Article 100 of the Treaty, Community directives provide for the harmonisation of measures necessary to ensure the protection of the health and safety of humans and animals and establish Community procedures to supervise compliance therewith, recourse to Article 36 ceases to be justified and the appropriate controls must henceforth be carried out and the protective measures taken in accordance with the scheme laid down by the harmonising directive": Case 148/78, *Ratti* [1979] ECR 1629, para. 36. See equally the Commission's response to the Written Question No. 1421/84 (Bonde) [1985] OJ C118/5–6.

preted exhaustively by the Court.[30] Yet the rigidity of this rule has been undermined to some extent by the Court in its case law on Article 30, in which it developed further exceptions. As already mentioned, the Court ruled in *Cassis de Dijon* that trade barriers flowing from disparities between national laws must be accepted, in so far as these provisions may be recognised as being necessary in order to satisfy mandatory requirements, relating in particular to the effectiveness of fiscal supervision, the protection of public health, the fairness of commercial transactions and the defence of the consumer.[31] The exception thus developed by the Court by virtue of the latter Article is generally referred to as the *rule of reason*.

2.1.2. *Article 36, Second Sentence*

The question whether a national measure protecting human health and safety is justified or not is examined by the Court in the light of the principle of proportionality underlying the second sentence of Article 36.[32] This provision stipulates that prohibitions or restrictions "based on the grounds mentioned in Article 36 may not constitute a means of arbitrary discrimination or a disguised restriction on trade between the Member States. Hence, Member States are not allowed to adopt measures which are disproportionate with their legitimate aim. The substantial body of the Court's case law reveals that Member States cannot successfully invoke the exceptions of Article 36 or the rule of reason developed under Article 30, if it is possible to achieve the objectives aimed at with less intrusive means than the prohibition or the restriction of a product lawfully manufactured and marketed in other Member States:[33] Member States may not use a sledge hammer to crack a nut.[34] For instance, where Member States have sought to justify measures with regard to consumer health

---

[30] As the Court determined in, for instance, Case 7/68, *Commission v. Italy* [1968] ECR 423; Case 124/81, *Commission v. United Kingdom* [1983] ECR 203; and Case 229/83, *Association des Centres distributeurs Edouard Leclerc et al. v. Sàrl "Au blé vert" et al.* [1985] ECR 1. Consumer protection, for instance, is not mentioned and cannot therefore be invoked as a ground for justification by virtue of this Art: see Case 113/80, *Commission v. Ireland* [1981] ECR 1625.

[31] *Cassis de Dijon,* above n. 21. Although certain measures concerning the protection of the environment could be covered by the "protection of health and life of humans, animals and plants", this was viewed as a rather unsatisfactory way of ensuring the protection of the environment. In its decision in Case 240/83, above n. 15, and later in Case 302/86, *Commission v. Denmark (Danish bottles)* [1988] ECR 4607, the Court mentioned explicitly the protection of the environment as a mandatory requirement. Subsequent to the SEA, the protection of the environment has obtained next to health and safety and consumer protection an autonomous place in Art. 100a(3). See, on the relation between the common market and the environment, in particular A.R. Ziegler, *The Common Market and the Environment: Striking a Balance,* Dissertation, Hochschule St. Gallen nr. 1764 (Bamberg, 1995).

[32] See, e.g., G. de Búrca, "The Principle of Proportionality and its Application in EC Law" (1993) 13 *YEL* 105–50.

[33] See, for instance, Case 178/84, above n. 28; Case 176/84, above n. 28; Case 182/84, *Miro (Belgian genever)* [1985] ECR 3731; Case 261/85, *Commission v. United Kingdom (pasteurised milk)* [1988] ECR 547; Case 90/86, *Zoni (Italian pasta)* [1988] ECR 4285.

[34] De Búrca, above n. 32, at 109.

protection, the Court has in various cases emphasised that instead of prohibiting the circulation of a product, the interests of consumers may be adequately protected by means of labelling.[35] In such cases, the Court has demonstrated that it is particularly alert to the danger of Member States advancing arguments with a hidden protectionist agenda.[36] On the other hand, the Court has been generally very cautious in matters of human health,[37] and has habitually approved (always within the limits of the proportionality principle[38]) national rules which prohibit the circulation of certain products and upheld approval systems for such products.[39]

2.2. The Dual Basis of Community Involvement in Health and Safety Regulation: "Positive Integration"

Where the Community seeks to achieve an internal market by facilitating the free movement of goods, purely "negative integration" measures will, however, not suffice. Since national provisions on health and safety issues are likely to constitute justified obstacles to trade under Article 36, the only way to remove such barriers is through "positive integration" by means of Community legislation.[40] As a result, the Community has become active in the regulation of consumer health and safety. Community harmonisation activities in this and other fields tend to

---

[35] This has led to the adoption of various measures on labelling requirements by the Community. See, e.g., European Parliament and Council Dir. 97/4/EC amending Dir. 79/112/EEC on the approximation of the laws of the Member States relating to the labelling, presentation and advertising of foodstuffs [1997] OJ L43/214. As regards language requirements of labelling, see Case C–369/89, *Piagème and others* v. *BVBA Peeters* [1991] ECR I–2971 and the Interpretative Commission Communication concerning the use of languages in the marketing of foodstuffs in the light of the judgment in the Peeters Case, COM(93)532 final. For a critical evaluation of the Court's emphasis on product labelling, see H.C. Von Heydebrand u.d. Lasa, "Free Movement of Foodstuffs, Consumer Protection and Food Standards in the European Community: Has the Court of Justice Got It Wrong?" (1991) 16 *ELR* 319–415. See, as regards the Commission approach on foodstuffs, O. Brouwer, "Free Movement of Foodstuffs and Quality Requirements: Has the Commission Got it Wrong?" (1988) 25 *CMLRev.* 237–62.

[36] See Case 178/84, above n. 28 and Case C–51/94, *Commission* v. *Germany* [1995] ECR I–3599.

[37] It is to be noted that the Court uses the terminology protection of human health and protection of public health interchangeably: see, for instance, Case 174/82, above n. 28 and Case 227/82, above n. 25, where the Court refers to public health in connection with Art. 36. I, however, would rather distinguish, as the Treaty seems to do, between the protection of human health and the public health, the latter notion being directed towards public health care and relating more to activities such as prevention of diseases, including drug dependence (see Arts. 36: "protection of health and life of humans"; Art. 100a(3): "health, safety, environmental protection and consumer protection" (the Dutch text of the Treaty which mentions *"volksgezondheid"* (public health) seems to be an exception); Art. 129: entitled "public health"; Art. 129a(b): "to protect the health, safety and economic interests of consumers").

[38] See, e.g., Case 174/82, above n. 28; Case 176/84, above n. 28; Case 178/84, above n. 28; Case 247/84, above n. 27; Case 304/84, above n. 27; Joined Cases C–13/91 & C–113/91, above n. 28.

[39] See *Cassis de Dijon*, above n. 21. See also, for instance, Case 53/80, above n. 28; Case 272/80, *Frans-Nederlandse Maatschappij voor Biologische Producten BV* [1981] ECR 3277 and Case C–293/94, *Brandsma* [1996] ECR I–3159.

[40] See, as regards mutual recognition, also Chap. 2.

blur the traditionally strict distinction between "negative" and "positive" integration:[41] by harmonising the health and safety aspects of products, the Community aims at the elimination of trade barriers ("negative" integration), whilst at the same time it positively contributes to the development of a policy to protect the health and safety of consumers ("positive" integration). It follows that the internal market cannot be achieved without a europeanisation of product safety law.[42] Thus Community involvement in health and safety regulation stems foremost from its aim to achieve a common market. Political scientists have interpreted the expansion of Community tasks in the area of consumer protection primarily in terms of a functional spill-over:[43] if Member States wish to secure the advantages of their original agreement of market integration, they will be forced to expand the scope of integration into new sectors.[44]

However, Community involvement in health and safety has other sources as well. In the early 1970s, various scandals concerning dangerous products in several Member States made plain the need for greater consumer protection, and were followed by a blossoming of consumer movements at the national level. The activities of enterprises on a Community market also raised voices arguing for greater Community involvement in the promotion of social values and the quality of life for citizens throughout Europe; a task to be undertaken complementary to the pursuit of economic integration.[45] At the Paris Summit in October 1972, the Heads of State and Government gave the political green light to the expansion of Community activities into areas of consumer and environmental protection and social policy.[46] They recognised that economic expansion was not an aim in itself, but should also enable a reduction in disparities in living conditions and should be pursued with the participation of all social

---

[41] See P.J.G Kapteyn/P. VerLoren van Themaat *et al.*, *Inleiding tot het recht van de Europese Gemeenschappen. Na Maastricht* (Deventer, 1995), 449. See also R. Pitschas, "Europäische Integration als Netzwerkkoordination komplexer Staatsaufgaben", in Th. Ellwein/D. Grimm/ J.J. Hesse/G.F. Schuppert (eds.), *Jahrbuch zur Staats- und Verwaltungswissenschaft* (Baden-Baden 1996), 379–416.

[42] Ch. Joerges/J. Falke/H.-W. Micklitz/G. Brüggemeier, *Die Sicherheit von Konsumgütern und die Entwicklung der Europäischen Gemeinschaften* (Baden-Baden, 1988) (English version: *European Product Safety, Internal Market Policy and the New Approach to Technical Harmonisation and Standards*, EUI Working Papers LAW 91/10–14 (Florence, 1991; http://www.iue.it/LAW/WP-Texts/ Joerges91/), EUI Working Paper LAW 91/13, 81.

[43] In accordance with the classic work of E. B. Haas, *The Uniting of Europe* (Stanford, 1958); *id.*, "International Integration: The European and Universal Process", in D.J. Hekius et al. (eds.), *International Security* (New York, 1964), 229–60; *id.*, "Technocracy, Pluralism and the New Europe", in S.R. Graubard (ed.), *A New Europe?* (Boston, 1964), 62–88.

[44] Pollack, above n. 11, 125–6. In this context, Pollack adjudges a secondary, much less important role for the so-called political spill-over as identified by George, which emphasises the role of specific supranational and subnational groups in the functional spill-over process. See, for the latter concept, S. George, *Politics and Policy in the European Community* (New York, 1991). The important role which, in particular, the Commission as supranational actor has played in the integration process is underlined by G. Majone/R. Dehousse, "The Institutional Dynamics of European Integration: From the Single Act to the Maastricht Treaty", in S. Martin (ed.), *The Construction of Europe. Essays in Honour of Emile Noël* (Dordrecht/Boston/London, 1994), 91–112.

[45] Bourgoignie, above n. 19, 115–16.

[46] Sixth General Report of the EC, 11–12.

partners and result in an improvement in the quality of life as well as in standards of living. The Heads of Government promised, therefore, to give particular attention to "intangible values and to protecting the environment, so that progress may really be put at the service of mankind".[47] As regards consumer protection, the Community institutions were expressly requested to submit an action programme before 1 January 1974, making the widest possible use of all Treaty provisions.[48] Accordingly, the first Community programme on consumer protection and information policy, drawn up by the Commission in 1973, was approved by the Council in April 1975 and recognised the protection of health and safety as a basic consumer right.[49] Despite the "soft law" character of this programme, from that moment onwards the Community developed an active policy on consumer protection,[50] the growing importance of which has led to the creation of a separate Commission Directorate-General on consumer affairs, DGXXIV, which has, in the aftermath of the BSE scandal, been extended to Consumer Policy and Consumer Health Protection.[51] Over the years, various Community acts, in particular directives, concerning both the safety and economic interests of consumers have been adopted.[52] Health and safety regulation is therefore incorporated, both in the internal market policy and the consumer protection policy of the Community,[53] and has gradually evolved on this dual basis.

[47]   The Amsterdam Treaty has now included the protection of the environment among its objectives in Art. 2.

[48]   Sixth General Report of the EC, 8.

[49]   The other four rights granted are: the right to protection of economic interests; the right of redress; the right to information and education and the right of representation. Council Resolution on a preliminary programme of the EEC for a consumer protection and information policy [1975] OJ C92/1.

[50]   See Council Resolution on a second programme of the EEC for a consumer protection and information policy [1981] OJ C133/1; Communication from the Commission to the Council on a New Impetus for Consumer Protection Policy, COM(85)314 final; Council Resolution concerning the future orientation of the policy of the EEC for the protection and promotion of consumer interests [1986] OJ C167/1; Council Resolution on future priorities for relaunching the consumer protection policy [1989] OJ C294/1; Three year action plan of consumer policy in the EEC (1990–92), COM(90)98 final; Council Resolution on future priorities for the development of consumer protection policy [1992] OJ C186/1; Second Commission three-year action plan 1993–5: placing the single market at the service of European consumers, COM(93)378 final; Communication from the European Commission to the Council on the priorities for consumer policy, 1996–8, COM(95)519 final; Draft proposal for a decision of the European Parliament and the Council establishing a general framework for Community activities in favour of consumers (1999–2001), COM(97)684 final.

[51]   In 1988, the handling of consumer affairs was already separated from DGXI (environment) and brought into a single service of the Commission, charged solely with consumer affairs: the Consumer Policy Service.

[52]   See, for an overview of the acts adopted, European Commission, DGXXIV on Consumer Policy and Consumer Health Protection, *Inventory of Community Acts Relating to Consumer Affairs* (documentation office) (Brussels, Apr. 1997). As regards the literature examining the Community activities in consumer affairs, see Th. Bourgoignie, *Eléments pour une théorie du droit de la consommation* (Louvain-la-Neuve, 1988); Bourgoignie/Trubek, above n. 19; Joerges *et al.*, above n. 42; L. Krämer, *EEC Consumer Law* (Louvain-la-Neuve, 1986); T. Askham/A. Stoneham, *EC Consumer Safety* (London, 1994); N. Reich/G. Woodroffe (eds.), *European Consumer Policy after Maastricht* (Deventer, 1994); G. Woodroffe (ed.), *Consumer Law in the EEC* (London, 1984).

[53]   See Joerges *et al.*, above n. 42.

3. COMMUNITY COMPETENCE AND ITS LEGAL BASIS

The increasing involvement of the Community in health and safety regulation has given rise to much debate on whether the Community has competence in this field, as no specific provision on this issue was laid down in the Treaty. The absence of a specific Treaty provision, however, does not mean that the Community lacks competence. This section will, therefore, scrutinise which Treaty provisions may validly serve as a basis for Community competence to regulate health and safety matters. The need to establish the correct legal basis for health and safety regulation is of great importance in view of the principle of attributed (or enumerated or specific) powers (*compétence d'attribution*), which is generally believed to underlie the Community and which is, subsequent to the Maastricht Treaty, set out in the first paragraph of Article 3b.[54] The principle of attributed powers indicates that the Community does not possess the competence to create a power which it lacks simply by means of an act of law.[55] It deals with the vertical division of powers between the Member States and the Community, and relates to the allocation of powers.[56] It determines that each institution must act within the limits of the powers conferred upon it by the Treaty and means that every binding measure of the Community must (directly or indirectly—depending on whether it concerns an attributed or a delegated power) be based on the provisions of the Treaty.[57]

The possible legal basis of health and safety regulation is discussed in the light of the original Rome Treaty and its three main Treaty amendments: the Single European Act (SEA), the Treaty of Maastricht and, finally, the Treaty of Amsterdam. In this manner, account is given of the evolution of the Community's commitment to health and safety issues, adding continuously to the already existing Treaty Articles. Under the original Treaty of Rome, the Community largely relied on two legal instruments for the adoption of product regulation: Articles 100 and 235, requiring unanimous decision-making by means of the consultation procedure. The SEA added an important instrument to these two Articles: Article 100a. In particular, the Commission demonstrated

---

[54] Prior to the Maastricht Treaty, this principle was derived from Art. 4 EEC. See Kapteyn/VerLoren van Themaat, above n. 19, at 113; R. Barents, "The Internal Market Unlimited: Some Observations on the Legal Basis of Community Legislation" (1993) 30 *CMLRev.* 85–6; H.P. Ipsen, *Europäisches Gemeinschaftsrecht* (Tübingen, 1972), 89; G. Isaac, *Droit communautaire général* (Paris, 1989), 34–8; J. Schwarze, *Die Befügnis zur Abstraktion im europäischen Gemeinschaftsrecht* (Baden-Baden, 1976), 55; Steindorff, above n. 10, at 18; M. Zuleeg, "Die Kompetenzen der Europäischen Gemeinschaften gegenüber den Mitgliedstaaten" (1970) 20 *Jahrbuch des öffentlichen Rechts der Gegenwart* 3; A. Tizzano, 'Lo sviluppo delle competenze materiali delle Comunità europee" [1981] *Rivista di diritto europeo* 140–1.

[55] In German literature this is referred to as *Kompetenz-Kompetenz*. See, *inter alia*, Kaiser, above n. 1, at 115.

[56] R. Barents, "De wijzigingen van het materiële EEG-recht" (1992) 40 *SEW* 8/9, 687–8; K. Lenaerts, "Subsidiarity and Community Competence in the Field of Education" (1994/5) 1 *Columbia Journal of European Law* 1, 2.

[57] See Barents, above n. 54, at 85. Lenaerts speaks, therefore, of the *legal basis* principle: Lenaerts, above n. 56, at 2.

a strong preference for Article 100a as a legal basis, since its qualified majority voting requirement allows for faster decision-making. Article 100a was additionally attractive to the Parliament as it furnished it with greater powers under the co-operation procedure.[58] The Treaty of Maastricht has finally introduced a specific title on consumer protection, providing the Community with further means for the adoption of health and safety issues. The Treaty of Amsterdam, in conclusion, confirms and refines the Community's commitment to health and safety regulation. Before analysing the individual Articles as possible legal bases for health and safety regulation, however, the general importance and functions of the legal basis is addressed.

3.1. The Functions of the Legal Basis Requirement

An important principle of the doctrine of attributed powers is that every binding Community act requires a direct or indirect legal basis in the provisions of the Treaty itself. Strictly speaking, it is the existence of a Treaty provision which determines the existence of a Community competence. The choice of legal basis is of the utmost importance as it determines the "nature" of the Community's competence.[59] By virtue of Article 190, Community measures must also stipulate the grounds for their introduction and substance.[60] This requirement determines that such measures must include a statement of the facts and the law which led the institution in question to adopt them.[61] Moreover, the duty to state reasons includes an obligation to state the legal basis upon which the act is based: in principle,[62] every act must expressly mention the relevant Treaty provisions.[63] Compliance with this procedural requirement is extremely important since any infringement thereof invalidates the act in question.[64]

[58] Currently, this Art. requires the co-decision procedure.

[59] See, for a discussion of the legal basis issue, Barents, above n. 54; K.St.C. Bradley, "The European Court and the Legal Basis of Community Legislation" (1989) 14 *ELR* 379–402; N. Emiliou, "Opening Pandora's Box: The Legal Basis of Community's Measures before the Court of Justice" (1994) 19 *ELR* 488–507; M. O'Neill, "The Choice of Legal Basis: More Than a Number" (1994) 1 *Irish Journal of European Law* 44–58 and S. Weatherill, "Regulating the Internal Market: Result Orientation in the House of Lords" (1992) 17 *ELR* 309–16.

[60] An application of this principle can be found in Arts. 13(b) and 16 of the Council's Rules of Procedure which provide that every reg., dir. and dec. it adopts (alone or together with the Parliament) shall contain a reference to the provisions under which the measure is based, preceded by the words "Having regard to": Council Dec. 93/662/EC adopting the Council's Rules of Procedure [1993] OJ L304/1, as amended by Council Dec. 95/24/EC, Euratom, ECSC [1995] OJ L31/14.

[61] Case 158/80, *REWE-Handelsgesellschaft Nord mbH* v. *Hauptzollamt Kiel* [1981] ECR 1805.

[62] In *General System of Preference*, the Court admitted, though, that "failure to refer to a precise provision of the Treaty need not necessarily constitute an infringement of essential procedural requirements when the legal basis for the measure may be determined from other parts of the measure". It continued, nevertheless, by considering that such explicit reference is indispensable where the parties concerned and the Court are left uncertain as to the precise legal basis. Case 45/86, *Commission* v. *Council* [1987] ECR 1493, para. 9.

[63] Case 45/86, above n. 62, at 1519.

[64] See, e.g., Case C–41/93, *France* v. *Commission* (*Pentachlorophenol*) [1994] ECR I–1829.

The specific legal basis requirement may be argued to have two functions: an instrumental and a guarantee function.[65] The instrumental function relates to the fact that the Community needs to refer to a legal basis to demonstrate that it is performing its tasks in accordance with the Community objectives set forth in Article 2. The guarantee function regards the importance of the legal basis in ensuring individuals, Member States as well as the institutions themselves, that no decisions are taken where the Community lacks competence,[66] thus securing the institutional balance of powers.[67] This requirement not only enables the Court to review the act in question, but also ensures that the Member States and the nationals concerned have knowledge of the conditions under which the Community institutions have applied Treaty provisions. In Case 45/86 on the *General System of Preference*, the Court expressly placed the issue in the context of the organisation of powers of the Community.[68] The legal basis requirement must therefore be considered against the background of the extent of the powers the institutions enjoy under the specific Treaty provisions.[69] The Court required that:

> "the choice of a legal basis may not depend simply on an institution's conviction as to the objective pursued but must be based on objective factors which are amenable to judicial review".[70]

Those factors include, in particular, the aim and content of the measure.[71] The limits of the powers conferred upon the Community institutions by a specific Treaty provision are determined through the interpretation of the particular wording of the specific provision which needs to be analysed in the light of its purpose and place in the scheme of the Treaty.[72] The Community institutions must therefore refrain from subjective considerations in their choice of a legal basis. In practice, this requirement appears difficult to meet, as even an institution such as the Commission, the guardian of the Treaty *par excellence*, may not be free from certain political imperatives and constraints.[73]

[65] Barents, above n. 54, 91–4.

[66] *Ibid.*, at 92.

[67] G. Guillermin, "Le principe de l'équilibre institutionnel dans la jurisprudence de la Cour de Justice des Communautés européennes" (1992) 119 *Journal du droit international* 337–8. See Chap. 2 for more details on the latter principle.

[68] Case 45/86, above n. 62, at 1520.

[69] See, Joined Cases 188–190/80, *France, Italy and UK* v. *Commission* [1982] ECR 2545. See also Lenz AG in his Opinion in Case 45/86 who considers that the question of the legal basis raises the issue of the powers of the Community institutions: above n. 62, at 1506. See also Bradley, above n. 59, at 394.

[70] Case 45/86, above n. 62, para. 11. See also, *inter alia*, Case 68/86, above n. 2, at 898; Case C–41/93, above n. 64, at 1829.

[71] See, in particular, Case C–300/89, *Commission* v. *European Parliament* (*"Titanium dioxide"*) [1991] ECR I–2867; Case C–84/94, *United Kingdom* v. *Council* [1996] ECR I–5755; and Case C–233/94, *Germany* v. *Parliament and Council* [1997] ECR I–2405.

[72] Joined Cases 188–190/80, above n. 69.

[73] Barents, above n. 54, 91–2. This is once more demonstrated in the BSE crisis. Recent empirical research on the behaviour of the Commission indeed confirms that the Commission is more than just a technocratic institution. See C. Landfried, "Beyond Technocratic Governance: The Case of Biotechnology" (1997) 3 *ELJ* 253–72.

3.2. The Treaty of Rome

In the 1950s, the founders of the Treaty of Rome did not foresee that the Community would become involved in health and safety regulation. Consequently, although an accelerated raising of the standard of living was listed among the Community's goals in Article 2 EEC, the Treaty did not provide for a specific power of the Community in this area. Therefore, the generally formulated Articles 100 and 235[74] were both frequently resorted to. Article 100 provides for the harmonisation of laws, regulations and administrative provisions of the Member States which directly affect the establishment or functioning of the common market. In the 1970s, the broad use of Article 100 by the Community institutions, particularly in relation to the fields of environmental and consumer protection, provoked severe criticism for being *ultra vires*.[75] This criticism, however, was repudiated by some authors who pointed out the fact that even in purely economic terms, environmental and consumer protection legislation affects production and marketing costs, and thus would directly affect the establishment or functioning of the common market.[76] In Case 91/79, *Commission* v. *Italy*, the Court opted for a broad application of Article 100, deciding that:

> "it is by no means ruled out that provisions on the environment may be based upon Article 100. The provisions which are made necessary by considerations relating to the environment and health may be a burden upon the undertakings to which they apply and if there is no harmonisation of national provisions, competition may be appreciably distorted".[77]

Consequently, under this Article the Community is competent to issue directives (the only measures allowed for by Article 100) to harmonise national

---

[74] Described by Usher as "twins, if not as 'terrible' twins": J.A. Usher, "The Gradual Widening of European Community Policy on the Basis of Articles 100 and 235 of the EEC Treaty", in J. Schwarze/H.G. Schermers (eds.), *Structures and Dimensions of the European Community Policy* (Baden-Baden, 1988), 26.

[75] See, for instance, the House of Lords Select Committee on the European Communities, *Approximation of legislation*, session 1977–8, 22nd Report and 35th Report, HL 131 and HL 199 (London, 1978). For a discussion of this report, see R.H. Lauwaars/J.M. Maarleveld, "Het Britse Hogerhuis en de harmonisatie van wetgeving" (1979) 27 *SEW* 1, 9–14. See also the Danish report to the FIDE congress at Dublin, discussed by G. Close, "The Legal Basis for the Consumer Protection Programme of the EEC and Priorities" (1983) 8 *ELR* 222–3; E. Grabitz/C. Sasse, *Beiträge zur Umweltgestaltung* (Berlin, 1977). Likewise, the European Parliament criticised, for instance, several proposals of the Commission on product liability and consumer information, based on Art. 100, as such measures would not directly affect the common market. See European Parliament, Doc. 246/78, EP 51 378/fin (product liability). 1977–8, Doc. 114/77 (information).

[76] See, in particular Close, above n. 1. He distinguishes between a restrictive, a liberal and an intermediate approach to the Community competence in consumer protection issues.

[77] Case 91/79, *Commission* v. *Italy* [1980] ECR 1099. See also Case 92/79, *Commission* v. *Italy* [1980] ECR 1115. Prior to this, the Court had already ruled that the elimination of barriers need not be the only purpose of a measure based on Art. 100. A dir. on the stunning of animals, aiming at both elimination of trade barriers and the reduction of the suffering of animals was, therefore, according to the Court, validly based on Art. 100: Case 144/77, *Commission* v. *Italy* [1978] ECR 1307.

provisions concerning health and safety issues which constitute justified trade barriers and distortions of competition, with no prejudice to their health and safety protection substance. Where the Community institutions aim at both the protection of health and the elimination of disparities between national provisions, Article 100 thus may be validly resorted to. This has, for example, been the case with various directives on the approximation of provisions relating to proprietary medicinal products.[78]

Article 235 (the elastic clause of the Treaty[79]) has offered generous possibilities as a legal basis for measures which could not prove a direct link to the establishment or functioning of the common market or for the adoption of regulations. It provides a legal basis for appropriate measures to be taken by unanimity, if action by the Community proves it necessary to attain—in the course of the operation of the common market[80]—one of the objectives of the Community for which the Treaty has not provided a necessary power.[81] Unlike Article 100, Article 235 allows for the adoption of all "appropriate measures", and does not demand that the common market be directly affected. Article 235 thus requires a much looser link with the common market than Article 100 does. Following the period 1958–73, during which only sporadic resort was made to Article 235,[82] the 1972 Paris Summit's explicit call for the Community pursuit of consumer and environment protection resulted in a far more frequent use of

[78] See, e.g., Council Dir. 65/65/EEC on the approximation of provisions laid down by law, regulation or administrative action relating to proprietary medicinal products [1965] OJ 22/369.

[79] See, e.g., J.H.H. Weiler, "The Transformation of Europe" (1991) 100 *The Yale Law Review* 2403–83.

[80] The equivalent phrases in the French and Italian texts *"dans le fonctionnement du marché commun"* and *"nel funzionamento del mercato comune"* (literally: "in the functioning of the common market") point to the functioning of the common market, whilst the Dutch and the German texts seem rightly to allow a broader interpretation by articulating *"in het kader van de gemeenschappelijke markt"* and *"im Rahmen des Gemeinsamen Marktes"* (literally: "within the framework of the common market").

[81] It has been argued that the existence of Art. 235 signifies that the application of the theory of implied powers, a theory well-known in the law of federal states and international organisations, would not be applicable to Community law. However, Art. 235 and the theory of implied powers have different scopes of application. Art. 235 applies to a situation in which it is necessary to act in order to attain one of the objectives of the Community, whilst the power to act is lacking. The theory of the implied powers, on the other hand, can only be applied in relation to existing powers of action. It cannot fill a gap in the totality of the specific powers conferred upon the Community institutions, for which Art. 235 has been framed, but it may solely supplement an existing power which shows a gap. See Kapteyn/VerLoren van Themaat, above n. 19, 117–18. See Case 22/70, *Commission v. Council (ERTA)* [1971] ECR 263. See, in general, C. Denys, *Impliciete bevoegdheden in de Europese Economische Gemeenschap* (Antwerp, 1990).

[82] Lachmann mentions that before 1973 the Council had adopted no more than 35 acts based on Art. 235, which were all merely related to agricultural or custom matters: P. Lachmann, "Some Danish Reflections on the Use of Article 235 of the Rome Treaty" (1981) 18 *CMLRev.* 448. See, for a quantitative analysis, also J.H.H. Weiler, *Il sistema comunitario europeo* (Bologna, 1985), 195. In the cases in which Art. 235 was used, it was interpreted in a narrow way. See, for instance, Usher, who takes the view that Art. 235 was obviously intended as an exceptional measure: above n. 65, at 30. See also the Council's answer to Written Question 204/67 (Vredeling) [1968] OJ C17/2, considering that Art. 235 would not be applicable whenever it aimed to give rise to new obligations which went beyond the ones laid down in the Treaty.

Article 235 as a legal basis. Yet, as was the case with Article 100, the widespread use of this Article raised objections.[83] Whereas the amendments by the Maastricht Treaty have now put this issue beyond any doubt,[84] it appears that prior to these amendments Article 235 already provided a legal basis for health and safety measures which aimed to improve living and working conditions, one of the Community's goals formulated in Article 2 EEC.[85] An analogy for such an interpretation of Article 235 was found in the Court's case law regarding Community environmental legislation in which the Court categorically stated that environmental protection was one of the Community's essential objectives.[86] Hence, prior to the Maastricht Treaty, the Council decisions setting up a Community system for the rapid exchange of information on dangers arising from the use of consumer products, and a Community system of information on accidents involving consumer products were validly adopted by virtue of Article 235.[87]

The broad scope of Article 235 nonetheless begs the question whether there are any limits to the use of this Article. One evident limit is that the measures adopted may be contrary to any prohibition expressly included in the Treaty. In addition, according to more recent Court jurisprudence, recourse to Article 235 is justified only where no other Treaty provision gives the Community institutions the necessary powers to adopt the measure in question.[88] Importantly, Article 235 should not be used to adopt measures which would constitute an amendment to the Treaty, as Treaty amendments are dealt with by Article 236, currently Article N1 TEU. In *Massey-Fergusson*, the Court ruled that by reason of the specific requirements of Article 235, the action in question[89] could not be criticised, since, under the circumstances, the rules of the Treaty on the decision-making procedure of the Council and on the division of powers between the institutions were not prejudiced.[90] It suggests from this case law that no deci-

---

[83] See House of Lords Select Committee on the European Communities, which suggested that recourse to Art. 235 should be limited to economic and financial purposes: 22nd Report, above n. 75. See also, next to its objections to a wide use of Art. 100, the concern of the Danish Government for an uncontrolled use of Art. 235, discussed by P. Lachmann, above n. 82, 447–61. Not surprisingly, the generous resort to Art. 235 was considered by the German *Bundesverfassungsgericht* in its *Maastricht* judgment a point of preoccupation: above n. 9.

[84] See sect. 3.4.

[85] This aim was included in the Community goal of an accelerated raising of the standard of living, stipulated in Art. 2 EEC. See, in general, F. Murphy, "Towards a More Fairly Balanced and Better Quality of Life", in EEC Commission, *Thirty Years of Community Law* (Brussels, 1983), 487–98.

[86] See, e.g., Case 240/83, above n. 15.

[87] See, e.g., Council Dec. 86/138/EEC concerning a demonstration project with a view to introducing a Community system of information on accidents involving consumer products (European Home and Leisure Accident Surveillance System (EHLASS)) [1986] OJ L109/23.

[88] See, for instance, Case 45/86, above n. 62 and Joined Cases C–51/80, C–90/89 and C–94/90, *United Kingdom* v. *Council* [1991] ECR I–2757, para. 6 and *Opinion 2/92* of the Court [1995] ECR I–521, at I–560. See, however, earlier, Case 8/73, *Hauptzollamt Bremerhaven* v. *Massey-Fergusson* [1973] ECR 897.

[89] Council Reg. 803/68 (1968) OJ L148/6, on the valuation of goods for customs purposes, which had been enacted under Art. 235.

[90] Case 8/73, above n. 88, at 908.

sions which distort the institutional balance of powers as laid down in the Treaty may be based on Article 235.[91] This appears to indicate that the Community does not possess a comprehensive *Kompetenz-Kompetenz*, as was strongly insisted upon by the German Constitutional Court in its *Maastricht* judgment.[92]

3.3. The Single European Act

3.3.1. *Article 100a in Relation to Article 100*

Article 100a was one of the most important of the SEA's provisions on the internal market, as the institutional counterpart of the Community's new harmonisation strategy which responded to its need for accelerated decision-making. Pursuant to this provision:

> "the Council shall, acting by qualified majority . . ., adopt the measures for the approximation of the provisions laid down by law, regulation or administrative action in Member States which have as their object the establishment and functioning of the internal market".

Article 100a applies "[b]y way of derogation from Article 100 and save where otherwise provided in this Treaty" for the achievement of the objectives set out in the former Article 8a. Article 100a constitutes a *lex specialis* to Article 100, which determines that it must be applied once its conditions are met and that no free choice may be made between Article 100a and 100.[93] In comparison with Article 100, Article 100a introduces qualified majority voting, allows for the adoption of "measures", introduces the notion of the "internal market" with which it does not demand a direct link. The attractiveness of the introduction of the qualified majority voting procedure is self-evident. In addition, Article 100a allows for the adoption of "measures" which also include the adoption of

---

[91] See also T.C. Hartley, *The Foundations of European Community Law* (3rd edn., Oxford, 1994), 118. In the same sense, Kapteyn/VerLoren van Themaat, above n. 19, at 116. This issue will be examined in greater detail in the following Chaps.

[92] *Brunner et al.* v. *The European Union Treaty*, above n. 13. See, for a denial of *Kompetenz-Kompetenz* of the Community, also U. Everling, "Reflections on the Structure of the European Union" (1992) 29 *CMLRev.* 1069. Recently, the Court invalidated a Commission agreement with the USA concerning competition because the Commission had operated outside the limits of the powers conferred upon it by the Treaty in accordance with Art. 4(1): see Case C–327/91, *France* v. *Commission* [1994] ECR I–3641.

[93] Ehlermann, above n. 5, at 382; R. Hayder, "Neue Wege der EG-Rechtsangleichung?" (1989) 53 *RabelsZ* 658–9; Krämer, above n. 8, at 678; B. Langeheine, "Rechtsangleichung unter Art 100a EWGV—Harmonisierung vs. nationale Schutzinteressen" (1988) 23 *EuR* 3, 241; P.Ch. Müller-Graff, "Die Rechtsangleichung zur Verwirklichung des Binnenmarktes" (1989) 24 *EuR* 2, 122–3; J. Pipkorn, "Artikel 100A, Angleichung von Vorschriften mit Bezug auf den Binnenmarkt", in H. Von der Groeben/J. Thiesing/C.-D. Ehlermann, *Kommentar zum EWG-Vertrag* (Baden-Baden, 1991), 2826. This view seems also to be endorsed by the Court in its recent case law: see, *inter alia*, Case C–41/93, above n. 64, para. 21.

regulations,[94] although the Inter-Governmental Conference on the Single European Act urged the Commission to give precedence to the use of directives where harmonisation involves the amendment of legislative provisions in one or more Member States.[95] Although initially the use of the notion of "internal market" instead of the "common market"[96] appeared to be of great importance,[97] the Court ruled in *Pentachlorophenol* that both notions were equivalent.[98] The internal market is thus a market of which free movement and undistorted competition are the main features. It follows that the powers conferred by Article 100a may even be considered broader than those conferred by Article 100, since Article 100a does not require that the provisions "directly affect" the internal market.[99]

3.3.2. *Article 100a as a Legal Basis for Health and Safety Regulation*

The Community's competence for health and safety matters may be based on Article 100a in two cases; first, where national laws concerning such matters constitute justified trade barriers to the free movement of goods, thus discriminating against imported products; and secondly, where obstacles result from

---

[94] See, for instance, Council Reg. (EEC) 315/93 laying down Community procedures for contaminants in food [1993] OJ L37/1, which is based on Art. 100a. In general, see, *inter alia*, Kapteyn/VerLoren van Themaat, above n. 19, at 473.

[95] Declaration of the Intergovernmental Conference on Art. 100a of the EEC Treaty, annexed to the SEA.

[96] The notion common market is equally not defined in the Treaty. The Court has interpreted this concept as "the elimination of all obstacles to the intra-Community trade in order to merge the national markets into one single market bringing about conditions as close as possible to those of a genuine internal market": Case 15/81, *Schul* [1982] ECR 1409. See also Case 270/80, *Polydor* [1982] ECR 329, in which the Court ruled that "the Treaty seeks to create a single market reproducing as closely as possible the conditions of a domestic market".

[97] In the legal debate following the SEA, in the main three different viewpoints existed: some viewed the notion of internal market as encompassing less than that of the common market (for instance, Kapteyn/VerLoren van Themaat, above n. 19, at 473; P. Pescatore, "Some Critical Remarks on the 'Single European Act'" (1987) 24 *CMLRev.* 11; P. VerLoren van Themaat, "De Europese Akte" (1986) 34 *SEW* 7/8, 475; and N. Forwood/M. Clough, "The Single European Act and Free Movement. Legal Implications of the Provisions for the Completion of the Internal Market" (1986) 11 *ELR* 385); others viewed both notions to be interchangeable (for instance, Barents, above n. 54, 102–5; Langeheine, above n. 93, at 239; and A. Mattera, *Le marché unique européen—ses règles, son fonctionnement* (Paris, 1988), 13), whilst others again viewed the concept of internal market to be broader than the common market (for instance, E. Steindorff, "Gemeinsamer Markt als Binnenmarkt" (1986) 150 *ZHR* 689 and G. Bosco, "Commentaire de l'acte unique européen des 17–18 fevrier 1987" (1987) 23 *CDE* at 371).

[98] Case C–41/93, above n. 64, at I–1847. Already earlier, in *Titanium Dioxide* (above n. 71), the Court decided in this direction. See Barents, above n. 54, 104–5. In view of the fact that the Court already used both terms interchangeably in its earlier case law (see the *Schul* case in which the Court operated in defining the concept of common market the term "genuine internal market": above n. 96), this decision hardly comes as a surprise.

[99] Barents, above n. 54, 105–6. In this sense, see also Ehlermann, above n. 5, at 370. Barents observes that in this way Art. 100a includes in part the competence conferred by Art. 235. Crosby, in contrast, is of the opinion that currently Art. 100a is being misused and that too little attention is paid to the rule of law: S. Crosby, "The Single Market and the Rule of Law" (1991) 16 *ELR* 465.

disparities between the legislative provisions of Member States on these issues, thus causing a distortion of competition.[100]

As explained above, Article 36 allows the Member States to maintain legislative provisions, which, whilst constituting obstacles to trade, may yet be justified on ground of human health and safety protection. The adoption of measures by the Community is consequently the only means by which free movement (market concerns) may be reconciled with health and safety protection (regulatory concerns).[101] The general manner in which Article 100a is formulated inevitably results in the attribution of discretionary powers.[102] In such cases, the Court is likely to examine in a limited way the suitability of (and need for) a particular measure.[103]

In addition, it may be argued that disparities between national measures based on health and safety protection considerations are likely to distort competitive conditions. Where manufacturers must comply with more (stringent) laws than their national ones, their position on the foreign market may be adversely affected—or even made untenable—in comparison with the position of their colleagues on that market. Besides, measures based on Article 100a need not exclusively aim at economic objectives. This is confirmed by paragraph (3) of this Article, which requires the Commission to take a high level of protection as its starting-point when proposing harmonisation measures concerning health, safety, environmental and consumer protection.[104] This provision expressly indicates that the objectives of health and safety and consumer protection may be effectively pursued by means of harmonisation measures under Article 100a.[105] That Article 100a may serve as the legal basis of measures aimed at both the protection of health and safety and the improvement of the conditions of competition can be deduced from the Court's case law.[106]

---

[100] See Art. 3(g). For more details on discrimination and distortion, see R. Barents, "The Community and the Unity of the Common Market. Some Reflections on the Economic Constitution of the Community" (1990) 33 *German Yearbook of International Law* 18 ff. The main difference between these concepts is that discrimination regards the legislation of one single Member State, whilst distortion results from disparities caused by unilateral measures of at least two Member States: see Case 164/68, *Wilhelm* v. *Bundenskartellamt* [1969] ECR 1.

[101] See Chap. 2 on the limits of the mutual recognition principle in this field.

[102] See also Barents, above n. 54, at 89.

[103] See, *inter alia*, Case 166/78, *Italy* v. *Council* [1979] ECR 2575; Case 138/79, *Roquette Frères* v. *Council* [1980] ECR 3333; Case C–311/88, *The Queen* v. *The Minister for Agriculture, Fisheries and Food and the Secretary of State for Health, ex parte Fedesa and others* [1990] ECR I–4023. See also Barents, above n. 54, at 30.

[104] See, e.g. Bourgoignie, above n. 52, 246–7. See also the soft law initiatives adopted by the Council: above n. 50.

[105] As the Court held in relation to the environmental protection in Case C–300/89, above n. 71, at I–2901.

[106] By analogy with Case C–300/89, above n. 71, in which the Court expressly referred to Cases 91/79 and 92/79, above n. 68.

3.3.3. The Approximation Requirement

The wide powers of the Community to issue health and safety acts under Article 100a find their limit in the requirement of approximation or harmonisation[107] of laws.[108] The concept of approximation or harmonisation is not defined by the Treaty. In this book, the following definition of approximation or harmonisation is adhered to:

> "the creation of rules by an act of a Community institution or by an international agreement accorded in the framework of the Community which have as a result, or aim at changing or supplementing national legislation as is necessary for the achievement of a common purpose".[109]

For harmonisation it is not necessary for all Member States already to have legislation on the subject-matter concerned, since the absence of such a provision in some Member States may have a negative effect on the achievement or the functioning of the internal market, and thus distort competition.[110] For example, some Member States had already adopted horizontal legislation on product safety, in particular imposing a general obligation on economic actors to market only safe products, whilst other Member States did not have such legislation. As disparities in the existing legislation and the absence of horizontal legislation in some Member States might create barriers to trade and distort competition, too, the Council was entitled to issue a harmonisation directive on general product safety by virtue of Article 100a.[111] Likewise, it can be argued that even in situations where no prior national legislation exists, Community measures aimed at the prevention of the creation of trade barriers may constitute harmonisation measures in the sense of Article 100a.[112] Thus, harmonisation also includes the replacement of national rules by Community rules. In addition, as the Court has recently determined, harmonisation measures encom-

---

[107] At present, these two terms are to be considered as synonyms. See, for an overview of the different opinions on the terminology harmonisation, co-ordination and approximation, R.H. Lauwaars/J.M. Maarleveld, *Harmonisatie van wetgeving in Europese organisaties* (Deventer, 1987), 45–51 and H.C. Taschner, "Artikel 100", in H. Von der Groeben/H. Thiesing/C.-D. Ehlermann (eds.), *Kommentar zum EWG-Vertrag* (Baden-Baden, 1991), 2792–4. See also D. Vaughan (ed.), *The Law of the European Communities* (London, 1986), 636.

[108] Barents, however sees no actual limitation in this harmonisation requirement. In his view, in almost all areas national legislation which must be approximated exists: R. Barents, "Milieu en interne markt" (1993) 41 *SEW* 1, 25, n. 73. This view, however, does not take into account the measures of a more institutional nature (at Community level), which the Community institutions may want to base on Art. 100a.

[109] Lauwaars/Maarleveld, above n. 107, at 50. See, for the different harmonisation methods, sect. 4.1.

[110] A. Bleckmann, *Europarecht* (Köln/Berlin/Bonn/München, 1990), 440; Ehlermann, above n. 5, 385; B. Langeheine, "Artikel 100A", in E. Grabitz, *Kommentar zum EWG-Vertrag* (Munich, 1990), point 43; Pipkorn, above n. 93, at 2848; Taschner, above n. 107, at 2807.

[111] See the 2nd recital of Council Dir. 92/59/EEC on general product safety [1992] OJ L228/24.

[112] Bleckmann, above n. 110, at 440; Ehlermann, above n. 5, at 385; Langeheine, above n. 110, point 43; Pipkorn, above n. 93, at 2848; Taschner, above n. 107, at 2807. See also Chap. 4.

pass not only measures relating to a specific product or class of products but also, if necessary, individual measures concerning those products.[113] This means that the Community is empowered not only to adopt measures which lay down general rules, but may also apply those rules to specific cases.[114]

3.3.4. Article 100a(4) and (5) (Derogation Clauses)

Although Article 100a accordingly provides a legal basis for the adoption of a wide range of health and safety measures, it provides at the same time some important exceptions. Both paragraphs (4) and (5) allow Member States to adopt measures to protect consumer health and safety.

In accordance with paragraph (5), harmonisation measures shall in appropriate cases include a safeguard clause which enables the Member States to take provisional measures for one or more of the non-economic reasons referred to in Article 36. In practice, the inclusion of such clauses in directives was already common prior to the SEA.[115] As a result, virtually all Community directives involving health and safety issues now contain a safeguard clause.[116] Hence, where a Member State has good grounds for believing that a product satisfying the requirements set in a specific directive nonetheless poses a hazard to safety or health, it may temporarily prohibit this product, or attach special conditions to its circulation. Article 100a(5) explicitly stipulates that these measures are of a provisional nature; national measures are subjected to a Community control procedure. Member States must, therefore, immediately inform the Commission of the measures they have introduced, specifying the reasons for their adoption. It is the Commission then which takes a decision, after having consulted a committee composed of national representatives.[117] The safeguard clauses aim to prevent dangerous products from circulating in the Community market. At the same time, the ability to include safeguard measures, reflects a recognition of the constitutional obligation of most Member States to ensure the health and safety of their citizens.[118]

The same is true for Article 100a(4), the so-called "opting-out" clause. This paragraph allows Member States to appeal to the interests listed by Article 36, or those relating to the protection of the environment or of the working environment, even after the adoption of a harmonisation measure. Under this

---

[113] Case C–359/92, *Germany v. Council (General Product Safety)* [1994] ECR I–3681, at I–3711/3712.

[114] See, in more detail, Chap. 2.

[115] See the survey carried out by Krämer, above n. 52, points 242–6.

[116] See Chaps. 3–5.

[117] These procedures will be discussed into more detail in Chap. 3.

[118] See H.W. Micklitz, "Consumer Rights", in A. Cassese/A. Clapham/J.H.H. Weiler (eds.), *Human Rights in the European Community: The Substantive Law* (Baden-Baden, 1991), 53–109 and also H.W. Micklitz/Th. Roethe/S. Weatherill (eds.), *Federalism and Responsibility. A Study on Product Safety Law and Practice in the European Community* (London/Dordrecht/Boston, 1994).

provision, Member States may unilaterally apply their own stricter national measures which may hinder free trade in the products addressed by the harmonisation measure in question[119] and disregard a majority decision of the Council. The circumstances under which derogation from a harmonisation measure is possible are as follows. Where a Member State deems it necessary to apply its national measure on the grounds mentioned above, it must notify the Commission. The Commission subsequently confirms the measure after having verified that it is not a means of arbitrary discrimination or a disguised restriction on trade. If the Commission or a Member State considers that another Member State is making improper use of this provision, it may bring the matter directly before the Court.

In view of its potentially detrimental effect upon the internal market, it is not surprising that the introduction of this right of "opting out" in Article 100a has been much debated.[120] Some have argued that this provision[121] gives Article 36 and national protection of the environment and the working environment a permanent character, even after full harmonisation has taken place under Article 100a(1).[122] Equally, the usefulness of harmonisation for achieving the internal market has been questioned, since it appears possible that a Member State might, even after harmonisation, nonetheless forbid the import of products meeting the criteria established by the particular harmonisation measure.[123] At the same time, the unclear wording of Article 100a(4) creates a degree of uncertainty about the exact interpretation of this provision. It is not clear, for example, which Member States can invoke paragraph 4 (all Member States or only the ones which voted against), exactly when the Member State must notify the Commission of its intention to derogate, when the national legislation may be applied (before or after confirmation by the Commission), which national measures may be applied (existing or also new ones), the extent to which the Commission may verify whether national provisions do not constitute a means of arbitrary discrimination or a disguised trade barrier, the nature of the confirmation by the Commission (is it a decision?) and the possibility of review by the Court.

---

[119] This derogation also applies in cases where a dir. contains a safeguard clause on the meaning of Art. 100a(5). See Joerges *et al.*, above n. 42, EUI Working Paper LAW 91/13, at 162. But see H.J. Glaesner, "Die Einheitliche Europäische Akte" (1986) 21 *EuR* 2, 134.

[120] See J. Flynn, "How Will Article 100A(4) Work? A Comparison With Article 93" (1987) 24 *CMLRev.* 689–707; Forwood/Clough, above n. 97, 383–408; Glaesner, above n. 119, 119–52; Gulmann, above n. 8, 31–40; K. Hailbronner, "Der 'nationale Alleingang' im Gemeinschaftsrecht am Beispiel der Abgasstandards für Pkw" (1989) 16 *EuGRZ* 101–22; J.-P. Jacqué, "L'Acte unique européen" (1986) 22 *RTDE* 575–612; Langeheine, above n. 93, 235–56; Mertens de Wilmars, above n. 5, 601–19; P. Pescatore, "Die 'Einheitliche Europäische Akte'. Eine ernste Gefahr für den Gemeinsamen Markt" (1986) 21 *EuR* 2, 153–69; Pescatore, above n. 97, 9–18.

[121] Together with Art. 100b(2).

[122] Pescatore, above n. 120, at 158. See also EP Written Question no. 193/86 [1987] OJ C112/39, asking the Council whether it agreed that para. 4 constituted a threat to the realisation of a genuine single Community market and could make the common market more compartmentalised than it was already.

[123] Kapteyn/VerLoren van Themaat, above n. 19, at 474.

In practice, however, Article 100a(4) has rarely been invoked. To date, the only case tested was a German derogation to Council Directive 91/173/EEC on dangerous substances[124] under Article 100a(4).[125] In this case, the Commission had explicitly approved German recourse to Article 100a(4) under which it had sought to apply its stricter national legislation. The legislation concerned imposed an almost comprehensive ban on pentachlorophenol (PCP), justifying its measures on the grounds of health and environmental protection, in derogation from the Directive that allowed for a 0.1 per cent concentration of PCP. France, however, challenged the Commission's approval before the Court. The Court clarified some of the ambiguities listed above. It established that Commission confirmation constitutes a "decision" in the sense of Article 189. As a derogation from a harmonisation measure, it needed to be interpreted strictly. The Court ruled, therefore, that no Member State may apply national rules derogating from harmonisation measures without obtaining prior confirmation from the Commission.[126] However, the Court carefully avoided any pronouncement on the technical substance and annulled the Commission's decision on procedural grounds, underlining its failure to state reasons under Article 190.[127]

3.4. The Treaty of Maastricht

The Maastricht Treaty both introduced some important institutional changes, which gave the Parliament co-decision powers in areas such as the internal market (Article 100a) and widened Community competences in several areas. Contemporaneously, however, it expressly denied the Community decision-making powers in some of these areas and introduced the principle of subsidiarity.[128] The following changes are of particular relevance for health and safety regulation.

---

[124] Council Dir. 91/173/EEC, amending for the ninth time Dir. 76/769/EEC on the approximation of the laws, regs. and administrative provisions of the Member States relating to restrictions on the marketing and use of certain dangerous substances [1991] OJ L85/34.

[125] Case C–41/93, above n. 64.

[126] *Ibid.*, at I–1849.

[127] As submitted by France in one of its pleas. In the Court's view, the Commission could not discharge its obligation requirement by merely restating the objectives of the German legislation, namely the protection of health and the environment, but needed instead to state its own reasons, both of fact and law, for reaching the decision (at I–1850).

[128] See, for a thorough examination of the Maastricht Treaty, R. Dehousse (ed.), *Europe After Maastricht. An Ever Closer Union?* (Munich, 1994); A. Duff, above n. 12; D. O'Keeffe/ P.M. Twomey (eds.), *Legal Issues of the Maastricht Treaty* (London, 1994); Lane, above n. 10; *SEW* special issue on the Maastricht Treaty, no. 8/9, 1992.

3.4.1. Articles 2 and 3

First, Article 2, setting the scheme of Community goals, expressly adds "quality of life" to the objective of the raising of the standard of living.[129] Moreover, and clarifying this new parameter, reference to an "acceleration" in the raising of the standard of living is deleted. As a consequence, the activities of the Community which are to achieve this objective include "a contribution to the attainment of a high level of health protection" (Article 3(o)) and "a contribution to the strengthening of consumer protection" (Article 3(s)). Although these Articles cannot themselves be cited as an independent legal basis for secondary Community acts, they nonetheless strengthen the interpretation of Articles 100a and 235 highlighted earlier, confirming the broader, social character of the Community.

3.4.2. Articles 129a and 129

The Maastricht Treaty introduces special Articles on consumer protection, Article 129a, and on public health, Article 129. Article 129a (a provision long campaigned-for by the consumer movement[130]) explicitly confirms the Community competence to contribute to the attainment of a high level of consumer protection. It allows for the adoption of measures pursuant to Article 100a in the internal market context (paragraph 1(a)) and specific action supporting and supplementing national policies aiming at the protection of the health and safety of consumers and of their economic interests (paragraph 1(b)).[131] Actions adopted pursuant to paragraph 1(b), however, do not prevent Member States from pursuing more stringent protection if such measures are compatible with the Treaty.[132] Hence, paragraph 3 lays down a minimum harmonisation formula. Although the Community must ensure a high level of protection, it is not obliged to adopt the *highest* level of protection which can be found in a particular Member State.[133] Furthermore, in contrast to Article 100a (3), Article 129a requires the *Community*, and not merely the Commission, to contribute to a high level of consumer protection.[134] As distinct from environ-

---

[129] This was a codification of the Court's case law. See, e.g., Case 240/83, above n. 15.

[130] See M. Goyens, "Where There's a Will, There's a Way! A Practitioner's View", in N. Reich/G. Woodroffe, *European Consumer Policy after Maastricht* (Deventer, 1994), 93–104.

[131] See, *inter alia*, H.W. Micklitz/S. Weatherill, "Consumer Policy in the European Community: Before and After Maastricht" (1993) 16 *JCP* 285–321.

[132] This was once more expressly reaffirmed by the European Council in Edinburgh, see the Conclusions of the Presidency, Part B, annex 2, at 7b.

[133] Case C–233/94, *Germany* v. *European Parliament and Council* [1997] ECR I– 2405, para. 48. In this case, the Court recognised consumer protection as an objective of the Community, albeit not the only one (para. 48).

[134] See, in this context, the arguments of the Spanish government intervening in Case C–155/91, *Commission* v. *Council*, that the high level of protection obligation under Art. 100a(3) need be respected only by the Commission and not by the Council, [1993] ECR I–939, at I–953. The Court, however, did not consider this argument.

ment and public health protection, however, the Treaty does not demand that the goal of consumer protection be integrated into all other Community policies. Such a requirement may nonetheless be deduced from Article 3(o) and (s).

The introduction of Article 129a into the Treaty in principle severs the pursuit of consumer protection from the internal market rationale. Yet, in practice, the consumer protection objective is not easily distinguished from the internal market objective, which gives rise to demarcation problems in the identification of the correct legal basis (see below). In practice, therefore, the concrete significance of Article 129a for health and safety regulation has remained relatively low. So far, the Community institutions have used this Article only for the adoption of one (important) act on the protection of consumer safety, namely, Council Decision 3092/94/EC setting up a Community system of information on home and leisure accidents, aimed at the prevention of accidents.[135]

In addition to Article 129a, the Maastricht Treaty has also introduced a provision on public health: Article 129. This Article requires the Community to contribute towards the ensuring of a high level of human health protection by encouraging co-operation between the Member States and, if necessary, support for their action. Community action, however, may consist solely of incentive measures, excluding harmonisation measures, and will be directed at public health in the sense of the prevention of diseases such as cancer, AIDS and drug abuse by means of research and information. It does not apply to health requirements to be met by products.[136] Hence, Article 129 does not directly provide for a legal basis for product regulation. By requiring that health protection requirements form a constituent part of the Community's overall policies, it nonetheless reinforces the Community's general competence to regulate the health and safety aspects of products.

---

[135] Earlier versions of this dec. had been adopted under Art. 235, see n. 78. European Parliament and Council Dec. 3092/94/EC introducing a Community system of information on home and leisure accidents [1994] OJ L331/1. Following to the accession of the new Member States, this Decision has been amended by Council Dec. 95/184/EC [1995] OJ L120/36. The action for annulment of this Dec. brought by the Parliament before the Court on the ground that Art. 169 of the Act of Accession did not provide for the correct legal basis was dismissed by the Court. See Case C–259/95, *Parliament* v. *Council* [1997] ECR I–5303.

[136] This Art. has provided a legal basis for, *inter alia*, European Parliament and Council Dec. 645/96/EC adopting a programme of Community action on health promotion, information, education and training within the framework for action in the field of public health (1996–2000) [1996] OJ L95/1, European Parliament and Council Dec. 646/96/EC adopting an action plan to combat cancer within the framework for action in the field of public health (1996–2000) [1996] OJ L95/9; European Parliament and Council Dec. 647/96/EC adopting a programme of Community action on the prevention of AIDS and certain other communicable diseases within the framework for action in the field of public health (1996–2000) [1996] OJ L95/16. See also Council Resolution on the framework for Community action in the field of public health [1994] OJ C165/1 and more recently, European Parliament and Council Dec. 1400/97/EC adopting a programme of Community action on health monitoring within the framework for action in the field of public health (1997–2000) [1997] OJ L193/1.

3.4.3. Subsidiarity

The subsidiarity principle, laid down in Article 3b, is often linked with the determination of Community competences. Yet, subsidiarity is not so much concerned with the *allocation* of competences between the Member States and the Community which, as was argued above, is determined more by the principle of attributed powers. Rather, it constitutes a criterion for the *exercise* of the Community's non-exclusive competences, already established by other Treaty provisions.[137] The introduction of the principle of subsidiarity therefore does not concern the establishment of a Community competence *per se*.[138] Instead, it is a limiting measure, designed to restrict the far-reaching centralisation of competences at Community level.[139]

The proportionality principle, laid down in the third paragraph, also constitutes a limitation on the *exercise* of Community powers. Proportionality determines that the Community may, under certain circumstances, not be able to exercise its powers fully.[140] In this vein, both paragraphs 2 and 3 of Article 3b act as limits to be taken into account *intra vires*,[141] which is explicitly confirmed by the Amsterdam Protocol on Subsidiarity and Proportionality. These paragraphs will be discussed more extensively in Chapter 2, which analyses the extent of Community activities in health and safety regulation.

3.5. The Treaty of Amsterdam

The amendments of the Treaty of Amsterdam[142] which concern health and safety protection, present principally the institutional repercussions of the BSE crisis.[143] The re-formulation of Articles 100a, 129 and 129a must all be interpreted as the strong desire of the Member States and the Community institutions not to repeat the errors made in the BSE affair, hereby taking particular account of the allegedly market-influenced policy followed by the Commission.[144] As a result, the amendments reinforce the Community's competence to protect the health and safety of persons in relation to products.

[137] See Barents, above n. 56, at 688; Lenaerts, above n. 56, 2–3; A.G. Toth, "The Principle of Subsidiarity in the Maastricht Treaty" (1992) 29 *CMLRev*. 1092. In this sense, see also the Commission in its Communication of the Commission to the Council and the European Parliament on the Principle of Subsidiarity, SEC(92)1990 final, 3 ff. To be sure, the determination of the extent to which powers may be exercised by the Community or the Member States also implies, in turn, a distribution of powers between the Community and the Member States.

[138] See also R. Dehousse, "Community Competences: Are there Limits to Growth?", in R. Dehousse (ed.), *Europe after Maastricht. An Ever Closer Union?* (Munich, 1994), 110.

[139] See Barents, above n. 56, at 688.

[140] *Ibid*. 687–8; Lenaerts, above n. 56, at 2.

[141] Lenaerts, above n. 56, at 3.

[142] It is recalled that this Treaty is not yet in force.

[143] See European Policy Centre, *Making Sense of the Amsterdam Treaty* (Brussels, 1997), 100–1 and A. Duff (ed.), *The Treaty of Amsterdam* (London, 1997).

[144] See, for more details, Chap. 3, sect. 5.3.1.2.

3.5.1. Amendment to Article 100a(3)

The Treaty of Amsterdam importantly adds to Article 100a(3) the obligation on the Commission to take particular account of "any new development based on scientific facts" in addition to the already existing obligation on the Commission to start from a high level of health and safety protection when proposing harmonisation measures. This amendment, which was not addressed by the single preparatory documents for the Inter-governmental Conference,[145] appears to appease the need for a greater degree of "objectivity"[146] and quality of Community legislation in the aftermath of the BSE crisis. It confirms the importance attached by the Court to scientific expertise as the basis for decision-making by the Commission, particularly in *Angelopharm*.[147]

3.5.2. Amendment to Article 100a(4) and (5)

The amendments by the Treaty of Amsterdam to the "opting out" procedure of Article 100a(4) must mainly be considered as a consolidation of the Court's case law in *Pentachlorophenol*[148] and a further clarification of the vague wording of this paragraph.[149] The amendments first make a distinction between national measures which exist at the moment of adoption of a harmonisation measure (new paragraph (4)) and national measures which are introduced after the adoption of a harmonisation measure (new paragraph (5)).

New paragraph (4) retains the criteria for the possibility of maintaining the already existing national measures unaltered: the protection of the interests laid down in Article 36 and the protection of the environment or working environment. Strict limitations are, however, posed on the introduction of national measures after harmonisation.

New paragraph (5) allows Member States only to introduce new national measures based on new scientific evidence relating to the protection of the environment or the working environment on the grounds of a problem specific to that Member State which has arisen after the adoption of a harmonisation measure. The notification procedure to the Commission is laid down in the new paragraphs (6)–(8). It is explicitly recognised that the Commission takes a "decision", instead of using the vague term "confirms". New paragraph (6) stipulates that the Commission "approves" or "rejects" the national provisions, whilst in

---

[145] See, *inter alia*, http://europa.eu.int/en/agenda/igc-home. The Commission's Communication on the impact and effectiveness of the single market, COM(96)520 final (para. 4.5), however, emphasised the importance of scientific expertise.

[146] See R. Barents, "Het Verdrag van Amsterdam en het Europees Gemeenschapsrecht. De materieelrechtelijke en institutionele veranderingen" (1997) 45 *SEW* 10, 353.

[147] Case C–212/91, *Angelopharm v. Freie und Hansestadt Hamburg* [1994] ECR I–171. See, in more detail, Chaps. 2 and 3.

[148] Case C–41/93, above n. 64.

[149] See Barents, above n. 146. See sect. 3.3.4.

the absence of a "decision" from the Commission within six months, the national provisions are deemed to have been improved.

3.5.3. Amendment to Article 129

As a direct consequence of the BSE crisis, the Amsterdam Treaty amends Article 129 so as to require all Community policies and actions to "ensure" (and no longer "contribute to") a high level of human health protection in general. Importantly, Community action is no longer directed solely towards the prevention of diseases but towards the improvement of public health in general and the prevention of sources of danger to human health.

Paragraph (4) adds two elements of competence to the Community. First, the Community may adopt, under the co-decision procedure, measures setting high standards of quality and safety or organs and substances of human origin, blood and blood derivatives (clearly intended to combat the diffusion of transmissible viruses through trade in blood transfusion, following recent scandals). Secondly, it may adopt, by way of derogation from Article 43, measures in the veterinary and phythosanitary fields which have as their direct objective the protection of public health. Although, on the basis of this Article, the adoption of harmonisation measures to improve human health (and thus product regulation) is still excluded, the amendments imply an important recognition of the Community's commitment to human health protection.

3.5.4. Amendment to Article 129a

The new Article 129a also adds to the current text of Article 129a that the Community must contribute to protecting the health and safety and economic interests of consumers as well as to promoting their right to information, education and to organise themselves in order to safeguard their interests. It finally explicitly recognises that consumer protection requirements must be taken into account in the definition and implementation of other Community policies and activities. Consumer protection policy, for many years the "Cinderella" of the Community policies,[150] has thus obtained a central place among the Community activities.

3.6. The Problem of Demarcation

Problems arise where a measure may possibly fall under two different legal bases. Which legal basis should be chosen if one measure serves several purposes? This problem results from the general formulation of many Treaty provisions such as Articles 100, 100a and 235, which use such terms as harmon-

---

[150] European Policy Centre, above n. 143, 101.

isation and internal market.[151] Health and safety measures often do pursue a dual objective, both market integration and health and safety protection. Hence, the introduction of Article 129a on consumer protection by the Maastricht Treaty gave rise to the question of which should have precedence when determining the correct legal basis of several measures adopted by the Community institutions; internal market aspects (Article 100a), or consumer protection (Article 129a), since most measures adopted under the umbrella of consumer protection policy derive from the simple fact that national laws may hinder intra-Community trade and distort competition.[152]

In other fields too, the Treaty Articles provide several such dilemmas. As regards measures on environmental protection, for example, the introduction of a separate title on the protection of the environment by the SEA (Articles 130r–130t), gave rise to dilemmas in determining the correct legal basis of several measures adopted by the Community institutions; were they intended to cover internal market aspects (Article 100a), or the protection of the environment (Article 130s)? Difficulties exist where these Articles, depending upon the type of measure to be adopted, lay down different voting requirements.[153] Similar problems arise with relation to the protection of the health and safety of workers (Article 100a or Article 118a).[154] Although it is true that some of these Articles provide for the same decision-making procedure (i.e. Article 189b), so that the choice between two Articles is of less practical significance, the differences between the derogations which the Member States might invoke[155] nonetheless indicate that the determination of the proper legal basis remains significant.

3.6.1. The Theory of the "Centre of Gravity"

Not surprisingly, the choice between two legal bases has caused much Court jurisprudence.[156] Where, according to the Court, an institution's power is based on two Treaty provisions, it is obliged to adopt the specific measures by virtue of the two relevant provisions.[157] If the decision-making procedures of specific provisions are identical, the choice of the legal basis is more of a

---

[151] Barents, above n. 54, 88 ff.

[152] See in this context *inter alia*, Close, above n. 1, 461–81; Close, above n. 75, 221–40.

[153] Following the Maastricht Treaty, Art. 130s concerning the environment introduces no fewer than 4 different legislative procedures: the procedure under Art. 189c (co-operation) (Art. 130s(1)), under Art. 189b (co-decision) (Art. 130s(3)); consultation with unanimity (Art. 130s(2)); and qualified majority (decided with unanimity, Art. 130s(2)).

[154] See recently Case C–84/94, above n. 71. See, for more details on the latter legal basis issue, for instance, E. Steyger, *Medezeggenschap bij veiligheid en gezondheid* (Deventer, 1990), 274–351.

[155] This situation is not changed by the Amsterdam Treaty.

[156] See, for instance, Case 45/86, above n. 62; Case 68/86, above n. 2; Case 165/87, *Commission v. Council (Commodity Coding)* [1988] ECR 5545; Case 242/87, *Commission v. Council (Erasmus)* [1989] ECR 1425; Case 56/88, *United Kingdom v. Council (Petra)* [1989] ECR 1615; Case C–70/88, *Parliament v. Council* [1991] ECR I–4529; Case C–300/89, above n. 71, Case C–155/91, above n. 133 and Case C–295/90, *European Parliament v. Council* [1992] ECR I–4193.

[157] Case 165/87, above n. 156.

formality.[158] However, this is different where the relevant provisions provide for a different decision-making procedure. In such situations, the Council has frequently had recourse to reasoning based on the "centre of gravity" or the "main purpose" theory.[159] According to this theory, the choice of the legal basis depends on what the institution in question considers to be the principal objective of the measure concerned.[160]

However, for horizontal harmonisation measures, serving both market and policy integration purposes, the choice of the exact legal basis seems to be left to the discretion of the Community legislature.[161] In the literature, the theory of the "centre of gravity" has thus been criticised on the basis that it merely amounts to a free choice for the Community institutions, depending on their subjective political convictions, and that it thus constitutes a repudiation of the guarantee function of the legal basis requirement. Should a Community institution consider the internal market element to be of greater importance than the policy element, it would opt for Article 100a; should it consider the policy element to be more significant, it would instead choose Articles such as Article 43 or 130s. The subjective reasoning which this theory entails is clearly demonstrated in the Court's case law. For instance, in the context of agricultural policy, the Council long held the view that the main objective of agricultural harmonisation measures was the protection of human, animal and plant health which justified the choice of Article 100. When, however, no unanimous consensus could be reached on the Hormones Directive, the Council rushed to the defence of Article 43 as the correct legal basis, with the argument that agriculture was the centre of gravity of this measure.[162] Another example of subjective reasoning is found in *Titanium Dioxide,* where both the Council and the Commission referred to the theory of the centre of gravity in order to defend different Articles (Article 130s and Article 100a respectively) as the correct legal basis.

[158]   Case 165/87, above n. 156.

[159]   See, for instance, as regards the choice between Art. 43 and Art. 100 as the proper legal basis of Council Dir. 85/649/EEC prohibiting the use of hormonal substances in livestock farming, in particular the reports for the hearing of Case 68/86, above n. 2. For more details on the latter case, see R. Barents, "Hormones and the Growth of Community Agricultural Law" [1988] 1 LIEI 1–19. As regards the choice between Arts. 100a and 130s, see Case C–300/89, above n. 71.

[160]   See Barents, above n. 54, at 101.

[161]   See, in this context, Case 240/83, above n. 15.

[162]   Case 68/86, above n. 2. In response to the argument brought by the UK that Council Dir. 85/649/EEC was *inter alia* aimed at the protection of the health of consumers, and thus needed to be based on Art. 100 in addition to Art. 43, the Court held: "Article 43 of the Treaty is the appropriate legal basis for any legislation concerning the production and the marketing of agricultural products listed in Annex II to the Treaty which contributes to the achievement of one or more of the objectives of the common agricultural policy set out in Article 39 of the Treaty". Case 68/86, above n. 2, at 896. See equally Case 131/86, *United Kingdom* v. *Council (battery hens)* [1988] ECR 906, at 930 and Case 131/87, *Commission* v. *Council* [1989] ECR 3743, at 3770. See Barents, above n. 54, at 102.

3.6.2. Demarcation between the Various Treaty Provisions

With its clear choice in *Titanium Dioxide* in favour of Article 100a, to the detriment of Article 130s,[163] the Court seemed to have placed this theory firmly in the past.[164] Admitting that the directive at issue, concerning waste from the titanium dioxide industry,[165] was indissolubly concerned both with the protection of the environment and with the elimination of disparities in competitive conditions, the Court arrived at its decision on the basis of three considerations. First, it referred to Article 130r(2) which stipulates that environmental protection requirements are a component of the Community's overall policies, and consequently deduced that a Community measure is not dependent on Article 130s, for the simple reason that it also pursues environmental protection objectives. Secondly, the Court considered that provisions including environmental and health issues may distort competition. Action intended to approximate national provisions and thereby eliminate competition distortions was, in the view of the Court, conducive to the achievement of the internal market and thus fell within the scope of Article 100a. Thirdly, this view was reinforced by reference to Article 100a(3), which obliges the Commission to take a high level of protection as a base in its proposals. Some authors have argued that the Court's preference for Article 100a in this case is to be traced to institutional considerations relating to the stronger role of Parliament in the decision-making process.[166] However, the Court was far more cautious, and merely made reference to the different procedures which were involved in this case. Thus, the Court's choice is mainly to be explained by its wide interpretation of the concept of internal market in this case.[167]

Whereas, subsequent to the *Titanium Dioxide* judgment, it could still be asserted that all legislative provisions which in some way are pertinent to the competitive position of undertakings fall within the scope of Article

---

[163] See, on the relation between Arts. 100a and 130s, *inter alia*, D. Freestone, "European Community Environmental Policy and Law" [1991] *Journal of Law and Society* 135–54; L. Krämer, *EC Treaty and Environmental Protection* (London, 1995); P. Kromareck, "Commentaire de l'Acte unique européen en matière d'environnement" [1988] *Revue juridique de l'environnement* 76; F. Roelants du Vivier/J.P. Hannequart, "Une nouvelle stratégie européenne pour l'environnement dans le cadre de l'Acte unique" (1988) 316 *RMC* 205; A. Saggio, "Le basi giuridiche della politica ambientale nell'ordinamento comunitario dopo l'entrata in vigore dell'Atto unico" [1990] *Rivista di diritto europeo* 39–50.

[164] Case C–300/89, above n. 71, at I–2867, annotated by H. Somsen, "Comments to Case C–300/89, *Commission* v. *Council* (*Titanium dioxide*)" (1992) 29 *CMLRev.* 140–51. In this sense, see also Case 68/86, above n. 2; Case 131/86, above n. 153; Case 11/88, *Commission* v. *Council* [1989] ECR 3799. However, in Case C–62/88, *Greece* v. *Council* [1990] ECR I–1527, the Court still decided Art. 113 to be the correct legal basis for the reg. in question (on the import of contaminated agricultural products) as it was mainly intended to regulate trade between the Community and non-member countries.

[165] Dir. 89/428/EEC [1989] OJ L201/56.

[166] See, *inter alia*, Crosby, above n. 99, 464–5; Somsen, above n. 164, at 150; Micklitz/Weatherill, above n. 131, at 300. See also Tesauro AG in this case, who underlined the importance of the participation of the Parliament under Art. 100a: above n. 71, at I–2892/2893.

[167] See Barents, above n. 54, at 95.

100a,[168] the Court's recent judgments seem to have placed this notion in some doubt. Probably anxious about the implications of this judgment, which had considerably enlarged the scope of Article 100a and determined that a major part of future (environmental) directives would need to be based upon it,[169] the Court rethought its earlier considerations. In Case C–155/91 on the waste disposal directive,[170] the Court added several nuances to the *Titanium Dioxide* judgment, and ruled that the sole fact that the achievement and functioning of the internal market are involved is not sufficient to justify the choice of Article 100a.[171]

More recently when asked to decide upon the correct legal basis of a directive on certain aspects of the organisation of working time,[172] the Court quite outspokenly referred to the theory, considering that:

> "the delimitation of the respective fields of application of Articles 100, 100a, on the one hand, and Article 118a, on the other, rests not upon a distinction between the possibility of adopting general measures in the former case and particular measures in the latter, but upon the principal aim of the measure envisaged."

thus concluding:

> "[i]t follows that, where the principal aim of the measure in question is the protection of the health and safety of workers, Article 118a must be used, albeit such a measure may have ancillary effects on the establishment and functioning of the internal market."[173]

This case law seems thus to have resuscitated the "centre of gravity" theory, once again raising the conundrum of choice in accordance with "objective" factors; an "objectivity" of which the Court aspires to be the adjudicator.[174]

---

[168] Barents, above n. 54, at 107. Except, clearly, for the subjects relating to fiscal matters, the free movement of persons and protection of workers, summed up by Art. 100a itself, and the specific Treaty provisions with respect to sectoral policies and those relating to specific issues.

[169] See the express warning of Tesauro AG on the erosion of Art. 130s in his Opinion in Case C–155/91, above n. 133, at I–961.

[170] Dir. 91/156/EEC [1991] OJ L78/32.

[171] Case C–155/91, above n. 133, at I–968. See also Case C–70/88, handed down by the Court shortly after the *Titanium dioxide* judgment (above n. 71). The Court held that recourse to Art. 100a was not justified if the act at issue only had an incidental effect of harmonising the conditions for the free movement of goods: Case C–70/88, above n. 156, at I–4566. An action brought by the Commission against the Council (Case C–86/92 [1992] OJ C 97/7) on the legal basis of Council Directive 91/698 on hazardous waste was removed from the Court's register on 6 Sept. 1993.

[172] Council Dir. 93/104/EC [1993] OJ L307/18.

[173] Case C–84/94, above n. 71, at I–5802.

[174] See, e.g., D. Geradin, "Trade and Environmental Protection: Community Harmonisation and National Environmental Standards" (1993) 13 *YEL* 170–1; Micklitz/Weatherill, above n. 131, at 301; Mortelmans, above n. 23, at 243; H.G. Sevenster, "Annotation to Case C–2/90, Commission v. Belgium" (1994) 42 *SEW* 2, 111. For measures concerning the environment, the introduction of the different voting requirements by the Maastricht Treaty in Art. 130s does not seem to make the choice of the legal basis any easier. Disputes about the legal basis may now even arise within Art. 130s itself: see Lane, above n. 10, at 973.

3.6.3. Alternatives to the Theory of the "Centre of Gravity"?

In view of its subjectivity, alternatives to the "centre of gravity" theory have been proposed. In the environmental context, for example, it has been suggested that environmental measures might distinguish between Article 100a aspects and Article 130s aspects.[175] However, such a distinction seems inevitably to renew the necessity of the identification of the main purpose of the measure. In addition, the division of such a measure into two acts may contribute to more confusion regarding the existing Community acts. Furthermore, it is difficult to apply this suggestion to health and safety regulation, since health and safety matters are often difficult to isolate from product requirements. The composition or manufacturing features of a foodstuff, for instance, cannot generally be separated from health requirement issues. The use of certain ingredients may thus lead to the need for the harmonisation of certain additives.[176]

At present, therefore, in the absence of a better alternative, the choice between the various Articles still requires the identification of the main purpose of a measure. In this vein, the free movement of goods objective in health and safety matters would seem to indicate that internal market policy prevail in all such measures. Thus, the Directive on General Product Safety aiming at the elimination of trade barriers and distortions of competition, whilst at the same time ensuring a high level of health and safety protection, may validly be based on Article 100a.[177] Besides, in contrast to the provisions on the environment, Article 129a on consumer protection expressly refers to Article 100a for measures adopted in the context of the internal market, which seems to reinforce the importance of Article 100a. This is also confirmed by the Treaty of Amsterdam.

4. CONCURRENT POWERS BETWEEN THE COMMUNITY AND THE MEMBER STATES

From the above it follows that the Community is generally competent to regulate health and safety issues. However, its competence is not exclusive: Member States retain powers in this matter. Several Treaty provisions confirm Member States' competence. For example, the wording of Article 129a suggests that the Community is not alone in regulating health and safety issues: it needs to support and supplement the policies of the Member States. Furthermore, as observed in section 2.1, an important reservation for Member States is found principally in Article 36, which allows Member States to adopt measures in

---

[175] Sevenster, above n. 219, at 111. This technique has, for instance, been applied in environmental law. See Dir. 90/219 [1990] OJ L117/1, based on Art. 130s and Dir. 90/220 [1990] OJ L117/15, based on Art. 100a.

[176] Brouwer, above n. 30, at 249.

[177] Above, n. 111. Whether the Community had the competence to adopt such a measure has been debated at length. See, in general, Fallon/Maniet, above n. 9.

order to protect the health and safety of persons. Such measures, however, are likely to create obstacles to trade and the Community will sooner or later harmonise such national rules. Depending on the degree of harmonisation achieved, Member States may nonetheless still be able to adopt national measures, even after harmonisation. It is therefore important to discuss the different harmonisation methods deployed by the various Community acts first. Furthermore, concurrent powers between the Community and the Member States in health and safety regulation raise problems of demarcation. The principles of supremacy and pre-emption have been developed to address problems of this kind and consequently need to be examined.

4.1. The Methods of Harmonisation[178]

The first method is *total* or *exhaustive* harmonisation. In this case, national provisions are replaced by Community norms detailed in the directive. The Community regime thus entirely covers the subject-matter regulated so that resort to Article 36 is no longer possible. However, it remains possible for Member States to invoke safeguard clauses where this is provided for by the directive,[179] or by Article 100a(4) if the conditions required are met. The latter possibility in practice implies the dilution of total harmonisation in favour of geographically differentiated harmonisation.[180] *Optional* harmonisation allows producers to choose whether to apply national norms or the Community norms established in a particular directive.[181] Depending on whether a company wishes to circulate its products on the Community or solely on the national market, it will decide whether or not to conform with Community rules. *Minimum* harmonisation refers to the situation in which a directive stipulates minimum standards, but leaves the Member States free to establish higher standards.[182] Finally, *partial* harmonisation refers to cases in which a specific directive solely regulates some aspects of the subject-matter.[183] Here, recourse to Article 36

---

[178] See Lauwaars/Maarleveld, above n. 107, 149 ff. See also, Kapteyn/VerLoren van Themaat *et al.*, above n. 41, 460–1 and P.J. Slot, "Harmonisation" (1996) 21 *ELR* 378–97. In an annex to its draft proposal for a "General Programme for the elimination of technical barriers to trade that result from disparities between the provisions laid down by law, regulation or administrative action in the Member States", the Commission had originally proposed a typology of harmonisation methods: see EP Doc. 15/68, sub. VI. This typology however was not included in its final proposal [1968] OJ C48/24. See for a discussion of the proposed methods, Joerges *et al.*, above n. 42, EUI Working Paper LAW 91/13, 21–5.

[179] See, e.g., Case 5/77, above n. 25, at 1576–7.

[180] Kapteyn/VerLoren van Themaat *et al.*, above n. 41, at 460.

[181] See J. Curall, "Some Aspects of the Relation Between Articles 30–36 and Article 100 of the EEC Treaty with a Closer Look to Optional Harmonisation" (1984) 4 *YEL* 179–80.

[182] This method is for instance laid down in Art. 118a. See, in particular, H.A.G. Temmink, "Minimumnormen in EG-richtlijnen" (1995) 43 *SEW* 2, 79–105.

[183] See Case 247/84, above n. 27; Case 304/84, above n. 27; and Case 37/83, *Rewe Zentrale* v. *Landwirtschaftskammer Rheinland* [1984] ECR 1229. See L. Hancher, "The European Pharmaceutical Market: Problems of Partial Harmonisation" (1990) 15 *ELR* 10.

remains a possibility in relation to the aspects falling outside the scope of the directive. Mutual recognition of national standards, controls in a Community act and reference to standard techniques[184] might be identified as further methods of harmonisation.

4.2. Supremacy and Pre-emption

The distribution of powers between the Member States and the Community and the consequential conflicts between national and Community legislation have given rise to general questions of legislative prevalence. Thus, concepts have been developed by the Court and literature in order to determine the relationship between these orders and between conflicting legislative provisions. The doctrines of supremacy and pre-emption are both designed to ensure the primacy of Community over Member State law. The doctrine of supremacy applies to situations in which both Community and national legislation affect a relevant subject-matter. It determines that, in the event of conflict, a directly effective provision of Community law prevails over a provision of national law.[185] The principle of pre-emption is distinct from this in that it is a question of determining competence. It is "more clean-cut and more dramatic in its exclusionary effect on national powers".[186] In its most rigid form, pre-emption means that once the Community legislates in a field, it occupies that field and thereby precludes Member State action.[187] Member State action is precluded even though there are no Community provisions with which national rules can come into conflict. Non-exclusive Community powers might thus become "exclusive" to the extent to which they have been exercised.[188]

The attractiveness of this "classic" pre-emption is its rigidity: the Community establishes the rule through its acts, whilst the Member States may no longer act

---

[184] See, for a discussion of the latter technique, Chap. 5.

[185] See, e.g., Hartley, above n. 91, Chap. 7; J. Shaw, *Law of the European Union* (2nd edn., Houndmills, 1996), 257 ff. See, e.g., Case 6/64, *Costa* v. *ENEL* [1964] ECR 585 and Case 106/77, *Simmenthal* [1978] ECR 629.

[186] S. Weatherill, *Law and Integration in the European Union* (Oxford, 1995), chap. 5, 137.

[187] See M. Waelbroeck, "The Emergent Doctrine of Community Pre-emption—Consent and Re-Delegation", in T. Sandalow/E. Stein (eds.), *Courts and Free Markets* (Oxford, 1982), ii, 551; J.H.H. Weiler, "The Community System. The Dual Character of Supranationalism" (1981) 1 YEL 277–9; J.H.H. Weiler, "Community, Member States and European Integration: Is the Law Relevant?" (1982–3) 21 JCMS 1, 43 ff. See, more recently, E.D. Cross, "Pre-Emption of Member State Law in the European Economic Community: A Framework for Analysis" (1992) 29 CMLRev. 447–72; A. Furrer, *Die Sperrwirkung des sekundären Gemeinschaftsrechts auf die nationalen Rechtsordnungen*, Dissertation Hochschule St. Gallen, no 1515 (Baden-Baden, 1994).

[188] In the *ERTA* case concerning international agreements in the field of transport, the Court strictly applied this doctrine, ruling that "each time the Community, with a view to implementing a common policy envisaged by the Treaty, adopts provisions laying down common rules, whatever form these may take, the Member States no longer have the right, acting individually or even collectively, to undertake obligations with third countries which affect those rules": Case 22/70, above n. 81. See, in this sense, also *Opinion 2/91* [1993] ECR I–1061, para. 9.

unilaterally.[189] In this vein, each Community legislative provision pervades an area previously within national competence and pre-empts national action in this area.[190] In its case law on the interpretation of directives based on Articles 100 and 100a the Court has used this principle to secure market integration.[191] For health and safety measures based on Article 100a, pre-emption would imply that where the Community has issued measures under Article 100a, Member States may no longer issue unilateral measures by virtue of Article 36. However, it is clear that a strict application of pre-emption, particularly in this field, would put human health and safety at risk; Member States would not be able to adopt protective measures where the Community had already adopted legislation. A strict interpretation of pre-emption should therefore be rejected.[192] In practice, the Court has actually been more cautious where human health and safety is at issue and has applied a pragmatic and less rigid pre-emption in this field. It has often ruled that where a certain field is not (yet) completely harmonised, Member States nonetheless retain a competence to issue legislative provisions.[193]

4.3. Towards Shared Competence on Health and Safety

4.3.1. Residual Competence of Member States

To what extent Member State powers on health and safety matters may or must be pre-empted is to be determined foremost in the light of the harmonisation method used and of the exemption clauses included in the harmonisation measures. Under the "traditional" harmonisation strategy pursued in the 1970s, the Community aimed at the total harmonisation of national provisions, thus leaving little room for the Member States to act.[194] Its new harmonisation strategy of 1985, however, strived primarily to achieve minimum harmonisation. Yet, in contrast to measures concerning the protection of the economic interests of consumers,[195] Community measures relating to the protection of consumer health and safety, such as foodstuffs, medicines and technical products, generally do not apply the minimum harmonisation technique. Rather, they embody mea-

---

[189] S. Weatherill, "Beyond Preemption? Shared Competence and Constitutional Change in the European Community", in D. O'Keeffe/P.M. Twomey, *Legal Issues of the Maastricht Treaty* (London, 1994), 13–33.

[190] Weatherill, above n. 186, at 137.

[191] See, for instance, Case 5/77, above n. 25. See further sect. 2.1.

[192] The inappropriateness of strict pre-emption has been underlined by various academics. See, *inter alia*, Cross, above n. 187; Furrer, above n. 187; Weatherill, above n. 189.

[193] See, for instance, Case 227/82, above n. 25; Case 237/82, above n. 26. See sect. 2.1.

[194] See, in detail, Chap. 2.

[195] For instance, Dir. 84/570 concerning misleading advertising stipulates that the Dir. does not preclude the application of provisions of more extensive protection (Art. 7) [1994] OJ L250/17 and Dir. 85/577 on door-to-door selling, which provides for a similar provision in Art. 8 [1985] OJ L372/31.

sures of total[196] or partial[197] harmonisation, generally including a safeguard clause in the sense of Article 100a(5).[198]

Whether a Community measure entails exhaustive harmonisation or not, is decided by the Court according to the nature and the scope of the act, thus exploring in detail the text of the Community measure concerned.[199] As observed above, in determining the degree of harmonisation of health and safety issues, the Court has been very cautious. From this case law, it can be concluded that in the absence of full harmonisation, Member States retain powers on health and safety protection measures. Moreover, the greater the scientific uncertainty about the products or the risk-assessment procedures, the more willing the Court has been to allow Member States to decide which degree of protection of health and safety they intend to ensure.[200] The reliance of the Member States on these exemptions and the Court's jurisprudential confirmation of Member State competence, however, have forced the Community to adopt more legislation. This appears to confirm that partial harmonisation is often only the beginning of a process which ultimately leads to total harmonisation.[201]

---

[196] With respect to technical products under the New Approach, see D. Hoffmann, "Product Safety in the Internal Market: The Proposed Community Emergency Procedure", in Fallon/Maniet (eds.), above n. 9, 67.

[197] With respect to pharmaceuticals, see Hancher, above n. 183.

[198] Virtually all Community acts on foodstuffs, for instance, provide for such a safeguard clause. See Chap. 3.

[199] See, for instance, Case 31/74, *Galli* [1975] ECR 47; Case 51/74, *Van den Hulst's Zonen* v. *Produktschap voor Siergewassen* [1975] ECR 79; Case 100/77, *Commission* v. *Italy* [1978] ECR 879; and Case 44/80, *Commission* v. *Italy* [1981] ECR 343.

[200] See, *inter alia*, Case 174/82, above n. 28; Case 227/82, above n. 25; Case 247/84, above n. 27; Case 304/84, above n. 27. In its case law, the Court seems to distinguish between cases of scientific uncertainty and cases where it is not disputed that certain substances constitute a risk to health. The latter is, e.g., the case with pesticides. In such cases, the Court allows Member States to regulate the presence of residues of pesticides on foodstuffs: see Case 94/83, *Heijn* [1984] ECR 3263 and Case 54/85, *Mirepoix* [1986] ECR 1067; with respect to the use of pesticides on plants see Case 272/80, above n. 39 and Case 125/88, above n. 28 and the use of pesticides in a cleaning product, Case C–293/94, above n. 39. See, for an analysis of the Court's case law with respect to the role of scientific expertise, Ch. Joerges, "Scientific Expertise in Social Regulation and the European Court of Justice: Legal Frameworks for Denationalised Governance Structures", in Ch. Joerges/K.H. Ladeur/E. Vos (eds.), *Integrating Scientific Expertise into Regulatory Decision-Making. National Traditions and European Innovations* (Baden-Baden, 1997), 295–323.

[201] See also Kapteyn/VerLoren van Themaat *et al.*, above n. 41, at 461. Nevertheless, with respect to medicinal products the Commission has argued that even after the adoption of the so-called decentralised procedure for the authorisation of medicinal products, Member States are allowed to invoke Art. 36; COM(90)283 final—SYN 309–312 concerning the future system for the free movement of medicinal products in the European Community, 17 (for more details on this procedure, see Chap. 4). A case could arise where a producer wishes to extend the marketing of his/her medicinal product to a Member State which was not involved in the initial decentralised authorisation procedure. Whether the Court will accept a Member State's recourse to this Art. in such cases depends on the Court's willingness to consider whether a sufficient level of harmonisation has been achieved to protect the health and safety of persons. See L. Hancher, "Creating the Internal Market for Pharmaceutical Medicines—an Echternach Jumping Procession?" (1991) 28 *CMLRev.* 831.

4.3.2. Shared Member State and Community Powers

Elements of a concept of shared competence between the Community and the Member States in matters of human health and safety may be found in Article 100a(4) and (5) and secondary Community legislation on health and safety issues.

Some authors have interpreted Article 100a(4) as signifying that ultimately it is the Member States which determine the level of protection.[202] The strict interpretation of this provision by the Court in *Pentachlorophenol*,[203] discussed above, however, makes it clear that national rules cannot be applied by the Member States without the prior authorisation of the Commission.[204] At first sight, the interpretation by the Court appears to reject the calls for a more generous interpretation of the principle of pre-emption, which favours a national competence to act under Article 100a(4).[205] The Commission's practice following this judgment nonetheless seems to give evidence of its willingness to take account of the heterogeneity of the Community. First the Commission once again confirmed the German derogation—this time properly accounting for its approval on the basis of the scientific evidence sought.[206] Initially, this approach seemed to result in a reconsideration of the relevant Community measures and thus to promote increased Community involvement in this area, since the Commission announced its intention to assess the possibility of proposing a total ban of PCP.[207] However, almost two years later, the Commission gave up the prospect of proposing such a ban and approved another derogation. Demonstrating its particular awareness of the special problems PCP posed to Danish public health and to the Danish environment, the Commission thus sanctioned the Danish prohibition of PCP.[208] This attitude seems to ease the safeguarding of stricter national legislation even after harmonisation. A similar reasoning might be followed in relation to health and safety protection measures based on Article 129a(3), which contains a comparable provision to Article 100a(4).

In addition to this, the Community institutions pay careful attention to the Member States' competence and responsibility in health and safety matters. Hence, the Community legislative practice in health and safety often not only recognises Member States' competence by introducing safeguard clauses in accordance with Article 100a(5) (although this, too, is under Community con-

---

[202] See as regards environmental protection, L. Krämer, "Environmental Protection and Article 30 EEC Treaty" (1993) 30 *CMLRev.* 124. See also the declaration of the Danish Government on the use of Art. 100a(4), published in annex to the SEA.

[203] Case C–41/93, above n. 64.

[204] This is expressly confirmed by the Amsterdam Treaty. See sect. 3.5.2.

[205] Weatherill, above n. 189, 18 ff. See also Krämer, above n. 202.

[206] Commission Dec. 94/783/EC concerning the prohibition of PCP notified by Germany [1994] OJ L316/43.

[207] *Ibid.*, point IV.

[208] Commission Dec. 96/211/EC [1996] OJ L68/32. The Netherlands has also invoked the procedure of Art. 100a(4) in order to prohibit the use of PCP.

trol), but also explicitly preserves Member States' powers. For example, with the adoption of the General Product Safety Directive,[209] product safety is now regulated at the Community level. This Directive sets a general product safety obligation within the Community, requiring that producers place only safe products on the market and gives a definition of the "safe product".[210] In addition, the Directive confers upon the Commission the contested power[211] to act in emergency situations, although specifying that the risk can be eliminated effectively only through the adoption of appropriate measures at Community level should one or more Member States differ with regard to the measures they plan to adopt.

However, within this Directive itself, the Council expressly confirms the competences of the Member States on product safety. For example, Article 5 of the Directive leaves the Member States with the power to adopt the necessary regulatory provisions to make producers and distributors comply with their obligations under the Directive so as to ensure that products placed on the market are safe, to monitor the safety of products brought on the market and to give the competent national authorities the necessary powers to take appropriate measures, such as imposing suitable penalties in cases of breaches of the safety obligation. Article 6 additionally recognises the power of the Member States to adopt appropriate measures to organise, immediately and efficiently, the withdrawal of dangerous products already placed on the market.[212] The European Parliament and Council Decision 3092/94/EC on a Community system of

---

[209] Above, n. 111.

[210] It defines "safe product" in Art. 2(b) as: "any product which, under normal or reasonably foreseeable conditions of use, including duration, does not present any risk or only the minimum risks compatible with the product's use, considered as acceptable and consistent with a high level of protection for the safety and health of persons taking into account various circumstances". These circumstances include, in particular: the characteristics of the product, including its composition, packaging, instructions for assembly and maintenance; the effect on other products, where it is reasonably foreseeable that it will be used with other products; the presentation of the product, the labelling, any instructions for its use and disposal and any other indication or information provided by the producer and the categories of consumers at serious risk when using the product, in particular, children: above n. 111.

[211] Art. 9 of the Dir., above n. 111. This power was attacked before the Court by Germany: Case C–359/92, *Germany* v. *Council*, above n. 113. See, in more detail, Chap. 2.

[212] With a view, *inter alia*, to: (a) organising appropriate checks on the safety properties of products, even after their being placed on the market as being safe, on an adequate scale, up to the final stage of use or consumption; (b) requiring all necessary information from the parties concerned; (c) taking samples of a product or a product line and subjecting them to safety checks; (d) subjecting product marketing to prior conditions designed to ensure product safety and requiring that suitable warnings be affixed regarding the risks which the product may present; (e) making arrangements to ensure that persons who might be exposed to a risk from a product are informed in good time and in a suitable manner of the risk by, *inter alia*, the publication of special warnings; (f) temporarily prohibiting, for the period required to carry out the various checks, anyone from supplying, offering to supply or exhibiting a product or product batch, whenever there are precise and consistent indications that they are dangerous; (g) prohibiting the placing on the market of a product or product batch which has proved dangerous and establishing the accompanying measures needed to ensure that the ban is complied with; (h) organising the effective and immediate withdrawal of a dangerous product or product batch already on the market and, if necessary, its destruction under appropriate conditions. See Art. 6 of the General Product Safety Dir., above n. 111.

information on home and leisure accidents explicitly recognises this dual character, stipulating that "although the management of consumer safety is primarily the responsibility of each Member State", a Community framework of information on home and leisure accidents "appears . . . to be necessary to supplement and complement the policy carried out by the Member States . . . to achieve a high level of consumer protection".[213]

Taken together, these elements reveal a close intertwining of both Member State and Community powers on health and safety matters in Community law. Accordingly, we may observe the development of a concept of shared national and Community competence on health and safety issues.

5. CONCLUSION

The Community has gradually become involved in the field of the regulation of the health and safety aspects of products. This involvement stems foremost from its commitment to achieving an internal market. However, the protection of human health and safety has also been pursued as an independent objective. The Community competence in health and safety regulation may be based on various Treaty provisions. Prior to the SEA, Community competence in this area was validly based on Articles 100 and 235. Following the introduction of qualified majority voting in Article 100a by the SEA, this Article has been generally resorted to by the Community institutions. In general, Article 100a offers a valid legal basis for product regulation since it usually involves the internal market. Measures concerning foodstuffs, pharmaceuticals or technical consumer products may generally be adopted by virtue of Article 100a, as the differences between national laws relating to such products hinder the free movement of those products. Where these national provisions aim to protect the health and safety of persons and thus form justified trade barriers, Community measures based on this Article reconcile both free movement and health and safety protection.

The general formulation of Article 100a encompasses the attribution of discretionary powers which, in accordance with consistent case law, will only marginally be reviewed by the Court. Notwithstanding its broad scope, recourse to Article 100a is limited to harmonisation measures. Although this notion must also be interpreted broadly, it nonetheless excludes the adoption of measures of a purely institutional character. For such measures, the general clause of Article 235 may be resorted to. Notwithstanding the supposedly limited nature of the Community system (based on the principle of attributed powers) a considerably wide competence may be derived from the general wording of Articles 100a and 235. The Maastricht Treaty, for the first time, explicitly recognises in Article 3 that the attainment of a high level of health protection (letter (o)) and the

---

[213] Fourth and eleventh recitals of the preamble to this Dec., above n. 135.

strengthening of consumer protection (letter (s)) fall within the activities of the Community. In addition, the insertion of Article 129a by this Treaty has not only confirmed the Community's general competence in health and safety regulation, but has also provided it with a specific legal basis for the protection of consumer interests. Drawing lessons from the BSE crisis, the Treaty of Amsterdam reinforces this competence by amending Articles 100a, 129 and 129a, thereby clearly recognising the Community's commitment to the protection of human health and safety.

The general wording of the relevant Articles at the same time raises difficulties with respect to the demarcation of the scope of these Articles. Despite its troublesome nature, the Court has recently confirmed that the choice of legal basis must be made according to the theory of the "centre of gravity". Inevitably, this theory entails some subjective reasoning concerning the legal basis of health and safety measures.

The Community's competence in health and safety regulation is, however, not exclusive: the Member States may still take measures in this field. This is explicitly provided for by Articles 36 and 100a(4) and (5) in particular. The ability of the Member States to adopt measures under these provisions depends greatly on the method of harmonisation used and the degree of harmonisation achieved; that is the extent to which the Community pre-empts national law. In the absence of the total harmonisation of health and safety matters, the Court has confirmed its pragmatic approach to pre-emption, stating that the Member States may validly adopt unilateral measures to ensure human health and safety. Consequently, even where the Community has chosen to pursue partial harmonisation, this is likely to lead towards a greater degree of harmonisation of health and safety regulation by the Community.

However, Article 100a(4) also gives evidence of elements of shared competence between the Community and the Member States on human health and safety. The Commission's attitude to this procedure demonstrates its willingness to take account of the heterogeneity of the Community, and allows for a more generous interpretation of the principle of pre-emption, which favours a national competence even after harmonisation. In addition, in its harmonisation measures on health and safety, the Community legislature often not only recognises the Member States' competence on this matter by introducing safeguard clauses in accordance with Article 100a(5), but also expressly affirms Member States' powers in this field. For example, analysis of the General Product Safety Directive discloses that Member State powers and Community powers on product safety are closely intertwined. These elements indicate a development towards a concept of shared competence between the Community and the Member States in matters of human health and safety protection.

2

Deepening of Community Health and Safety Regulation

1. INTRODUCTION

Whilst the previous chapter examined the roots of Community activities in health and safety regulation and the general competence of the Community to regulate health and safety issues, this chapter scrutinises the various factors which push the Community to deepen its activities in health and safety and identifies a third phase of integration. It analyses the legal implications of such an increased involvement or "deepening", completing herewith the legal setting of Community health and safety regulation, against which the specific institutional structures of Community health and safety regulation will be measured.

Although the Commission's new strategy, in combination with the Single European Act (in particular, the introduction of qualified majority voting) was intended to overcome many of the drawbacks of the initial "slow" harmonisation strategy, this model has not had the hoped-for success in the area of health and safety regulation. In this area, a third phase of integration may now be observed; yet another phase in which the Community is responding to the demand that it deepen its involvement with health and safety regulation, and move towards the implementation of health and safety regulation at the Community, rather than at the national level. This latter phase has gradually evolved out of a second phase of integration, during which the Community, and in particular the Commission, has sought to realise its "1992" programme. Although no strict division may be made, it might generally be argued that the late 1980s and the early 1990s were to bring with them the realisation that the mere implementation of the Commission's White Paper would not suffice to achieve the internal market, and that new initiatives were necessary. Indeed, the need for more Community action in various areas in order to achieve the internal market had already been recognised shortly after the adoption of the Commission's White Paper, which argued that:

> "[i]t would be a tragic illusion to believe that the adoption of the 300 legislative measures would complete the internal market. The 300 measures are only the top of an immense iceberg of Community action".[1]

---

[1] H. Schmitt von Sydow, "The Basic Strategies of the Commission's White Paper", in R. Bieber/R. Dehousse/J. Pinder/J.H.H. Weiler (eds.), *1992: One European Market? A Critical Analysis of the Commission's Internal Market Strategy* (Baden-Baden, 1988), 91.

This chapter begins by examining this "iceberg" in the field of Community health and safety regulation. Arguments will be advanced to demonstrate the need for a deepening of Community action in this area; a deepening which will gradually result in a third phase of integration. The deepening of Community activities in health and safety matters, however, touches upon several legal questions. First, the power of the Community to implement the rules established by the Community legislature has itself been the subject of debate. For example, building on the distinction between legislative and administrative powers, it has been argued that, in the absence of a specific provision on the execution of Community law, the application of Community law is, in principle, a matter for the Member States, in accordance with the principle of attributed powers.[2] More specifically, it has been asserted that Article 100a does not provide a legal basis for a provision empowering the Commission to adopt decisions relating to emergency actions, as this would necessarily disturb the distribution of powers between the Community and the Member States.[3] Closely connected with this is the assertion that the Community runs the risk of a "regulatory deficit", since the Community's lack of "genuine" administrative powers (except for the ones directly provided for in the Treaty, such as competition and anti-dumping), together with the huge bottlenecks at the implementation level, might lead to a decline in efficiency and a lack of flexibility, and thus become a serious obstacle to the achievement of Community objectives.[4]

This chapter, therefore, investigates the powers of the Community to implement its legislation. To this end, it analyses whether the various Treaty provisions provide a basis for differentiation between legislative and implementing powers, and whether they create a presumption that the implementation of Community rules is a matter for the Member States alone. Secondly, the extent to which the Community may exercise the powers conferred upon it by the Treaty depends upon the principles of subsidiarity and proportionality. These principles require that it be proven that Community action is really necessary, and that the objectives of any proposed action cannot adequately be achieved at Member State level, and do not go beyond what is strictly necessary to achieve the Community objectives. Therefore, the implications of these principles for a deepening of Community health and safety regulation are scrutinised. Thirdly, the deepening of health and safety regulation by the Community must respect the institutional balance of powers laid down in the Treaty. This principle, as

---

[2] See for an overview of the viewpoints, A. Klösters, *Kompetenzen der EG-Kommission im innerstaatlichen Vollzug von Gemeinschaftsrecht* (Köln/Berlin/Bonn/München, 1994), 12–13.

[3] This view was held by the German government in Case C–359/92, *Germany* v. *Council* [1994] ECR I–3681, as regards the legal basis of Dir. 92/59/EEC on general product safety [1992] OJ L228/24, which delegates a power to the Commission to adopt decisions in emergency situations (Art. 9).

[4] R. Dehousse, *Integration* v. *Regulation? Social Regulation in the European Community*, EUI Working Paper LAW 92/23 (Florence, 1992); R. Dehousse/Ch. Joerges/G. Majone/F. Snyder (with M. Everson), *Europe After 1992. New Regulatory Strategies*, EUI Working Paper LAW 92/31(Florence, 1992), 5–6.

developed by the Court, demands that implementation of health and safety regulation respects the Community institutions' prerogatives, in particular the ones laid down in Article 145, third indent, and 155, fourth indent. Consequently, the final section of this chapter examines the impact of this principle on the delegation of greater power to the Commission resulting from a need for fast, flexible and efficient decision-making and a reduction in the workload of the Council/ Parliament. The exercise of wide discretionary powers by the Commission raises, in turn, problems of legitimacy which require examination.

2. DEEPENING OF COMMUNITY INVOLVEMENT IN HEALTH AND SAFETY REGULATION: TOWARDS COMMUNITY IMPLEMENTATION

2.1. The Difficulties Inherent in the "Traditional" Approach to Harmonisation

As explained in the previous chapter, the removal of obstacles to trade has been a major concern of the Community. The first step in a systematic approach to the abolition of technical barriers to trade was taken by the Council in 1969 through its adoption of a "General Programme for the elimination of technical barriers to trade that result from disparities between the provisions laid down by law, regulation or administrative action in the Member States".[5] This Programme was directed at the harmonisation of national regulations concerning the marketing and the use of products of particular importance through directives under Article 100. The General Programme embodied four resolutions and one agreement.[6] The first two resolutions included a detailed timetable for the release of numerous directives designed to remove obstacles to trade on both industrial products, such as motor vehicles and machinery, and foodstuffs. A subsequent resolution was devoted to the mutual recognition of national inspections, which the Council could, according this resolution, include in the directives envisaged. The fourth resolution provided for procedures to be followed to adapt directives to technical progress. A final document was included in the form of an "Agreement of the Representatives of the Governments of the Member States meeting in the Council of 28 May 1969 providing for standstill and notification to the Commission". This agreement required the Member States to abstain from adopting measures for the products

[5] Adopted on 28 May 1969 [1969] OJ C76/1.

[6] See, in general, Ch. Joerges/J. Falke/H.-W. Micklitz/G. Brüggemeier, *Die Sicherheit von Konsumgütern und die Entwicklung der Europäischen Gemeinschaften* (Baden-Baden, 1988) (English version: *European Product Safety, Internal Market Policy and the New Approach to Technical Harmonisation and Standards*, EUI Working Papers LAW 91/10–14 (Florence, 1991; http://www.iue.it/LAW/WP-Texts/Joerges91/); and R.H. Lauwaars, "The 'Model Directive' on Technical Harmonisation", in R. Bieber/R. Dehousse/J. Pinder/J.H.H. Weiler (eds.), *1992: One European Market? A Critical Analysis of the Commission's Internal Market Strategy* (Baden-Baden, 1988), 152–3.

covered by the Programme and to inform the Commission about draft measures concerning products not covered by the Programme.[7] In 1973, the General Programme was supplemented by another Council resolution in which a new list of sectors was added,[8] whilst in that same year the Council adopted a programme on industrial policy in which new, revised timetables for the removal of the trade barriers were determined.[9]

In the following years, the results of the "traditional" approach, however, left much to be desired. The shortcomings in the decision-making process became rapidly apparent.[10] It was soon clear that the procedures for the adoption of a directive were cumbersome and time-consuming since agreement was sought on all the finer details. In one instance, for example, the delay between the preparation of a directive and its final adoption by the Council was almost 10 years.[11] Such delays have, in part, been attributed to the attempt to incorporate very detailed technical provisions, which did not differ from technical standards in substance.[12] Besides, by the time agreement was reached on such provisions, they were often already outdated as a consequence of rapid technical evolution.

Further factors contributing to the cumbersome decision-making procedure were, for example, the insufficient delegation of powers from the Council to the Commission, and the discrepancy between harmonisation and European standardisation, since Community institutions did not make sufficient use of existing or possible European standards,[13] and paid no attention to certification and testing problems.[14] Such problems were nonetheless also closely connected with the institutional voting requirements attached to the directives adopted under Article 100.[15] The unanimity required by this Article seemed extremely difficult to attain. Moreover, the frequently deployed optional harmonisation method often seemed inadequate to achieve the goals of the common market. This method allowed Member States to recognise other standards on their own

[7] This Agreement has been replaced by Dir. 83/189/EEC [1983] OJ L109/8 which will be discussed in Chap. 5.

[8] [1973] OJ C38/1.

[9] [1973] OJ C117/1.

[10] See Commission Communication on technical harmonisation and standards, a new approach COM(85)19 final, part 1, para. 2 and the Commission's White Paper on the Completion of the Internal Market of June 1985, COM(85)310 final, para. 61. See also Joerges *et al.*, above n. 6, 272–6; Schmitt von Sydow, above n. 1, 80–5; Lauwaars, above n. 6, 155–6.

[11] See Joerges *et al.*, above n. 6, at 260.

[12] Joerges *et al.* mention, as a striking example, the 80-page long Commission proposal for a Council Dir. on the approximation of the laws of the Member States on steering wheels placed in front of the driver's seat on narrow-gauge machinery with pneumatic tires [1985] OJ C222/1, whilst dirs. on motor vehicles adopted up to 1985 already contained in total 602 pages primarily comprising technical specification and instructions: above n. 6, at 260 (EUI Working Paper LAW 91/13, at 27).

[13] Lauwaars, above n. 6, 155–6; J. Pelkmans, *Opheffing van technische handelsbelemmeringen in de EG, Pilot Study in opdracht van het UNO* (The Hague, 1985), 46–52. See also White Paper, above n. 10, in particular, paras. 61, 68 and 70.

[14] J. Pelkmans, "The New Approach to Technical Harmonisation and Standardisation" (1987) 25 *JCMS* 3, 251–3.

[15] White Paper, above n. 10, para. 68.

markets so that two parallel markets existed. It was essentially designed for manufacturers' interests, which were not always in accordance with health and safety protection. Therefore, the exceptions of Article 36 could still be validly invoked.[16] These difficulties forced the Community and, in particular, the Commission, to rethink its traditional approach, moving away from a situation where, in the words of Lord Cockfield, the Commission followed a policy of: "if it moves, harmonise it".[17] In addition, they revealed the need for institutional changes, in particular with regard to the unanimity requirement under Article 100.

2.2. The New Approach to Harmonisation

It was the Court's case law in particular which offered the Commission a helping hand in developing a new strategy to harmonisation. In *Cassis de Dijon*, which made legal history, the Court was asked to give a preliminary ruling on an issue which had arisen between a German firm, Rewe-Zentral, and the German public authorities, touching upon the question whether a German law could prohibit the import of a French, low alcohol (15–20%) liqueur, named "Cassis de Dijon", on the ground that only alcoholic beverages having a minimum alcohol percentage of 25%, might be marketed under the name "liqueur".[18] The Court held that products lawfully produced and marketed in one Member State must be admitted by another Member State, save where refusal is justified by virtue of mandatory requirements.[19] In a Communication of 1980, the Commission concluded from the Court's judgment that many obstacles to trade could simply be eliminated by strictly applying the prohibition contained in Article 30.[20] Where an imported product "suitably and satisfactorily" satisfied the legitimate objective of a Member State's rules (such as human health and safety, and protection of the consumer or the environment),

---

[16]   See J. Curall, "Some Aspects of the Relation Between Articles 30–36 and Article 100 of the EEC Treaty with a Closer Look to Optional Harmonisation" (1984) 4 *YEL* 179–80.

[17]   Speech of 22 Feb. 1988, delivered in London to the Federation of British Electrotechnical and Allied Manufacturers, quoted in: A. McGee/S. Weatherill, "The Evolution of the Single Market—Harmonisation or Liberation" (1990) 53 *MLR* 583. In a Communication to the Parliament of 1980, the Commission, though, declared that it had never been the Commission's policy to harmonise for the sake of harmonisation: see, G. Majone, *Deregulation or Re-Regulation? Policymaking in the European Community since the Single Act*, EUI Working Paper SPS 93/2 (Florence, 1993), 2–3.

[18]   This figure is mentioned by the Court in its judgment. In the summary of facts of the report for the hearing, however, a minimum alcohol level of 32% is referred to.

[19]   Case 120/78, *Rewe-Zentrale AG v. Bundesmonopolverwaltung für Branntwein* [1979] ECR 649.

[20]   Communication of the Commission concerning the consequences of the judgment given by the Court on 20 Feb. 1979 in Case 120/78 (*Cassis de Dijon*) [1980] OJ C256/2. See R. Barents, "New Developments in Measures Having Equivalent Effect" (1981) 18 *CMLRev.* 296–9; L.W. Gormley, "Cassis de Dijon and the Communication from the Commission" (1981) 6 *ELR* 454–9; D. Welch, "From 'Euro Beer' to 'Newcastle Brown', A Review of European Community Action to Dismantle Divergent 'Food' Laws" (1983–4) 22 *JCMS* 1, 62 ff.

the importing country, in the Commission's view, could no longer justify prohibitions on its sale by claiming that it fulfilled the legitimate objective in a different manner from domestic products. Therefore, it proclaimed its intention to concentrate its harmonisation activities mainly in areas where trade barriers were justified according to the criteria determined by the Court.[21]

This new strategy was enshrined by the Commission in its White Paper on the Completion of the Internal Market of June 1985, later also promoted as the "1992 programme".[22] The White Paper's terminology distinguished between the "new strategy" on the one hand and the "new approach" on the other. The "new strategy" was concerned with the choice to be made between harmonisation and the principle of mutual recognition, whilst the "new approach" concerned the possible methods of how to achieve harmonisation.[23] In this White Paper, the Commission relied heavily upon the equivalence of national legislative objectives, which would require the mutual acceptance of goods (mutual recognition) by the Member States.[24] The Commission's focus on the mutual recognition principle or negative integration was primarily motivated by tactical and practical considerations, namely the reduction of the Council's workload and the need to obtain rapid results.[25] In the Commission's words:

> "the objectives of national legislation, such as the protection of human health and life and of the environment, are more often than not identical. It follows that the rules and controls developed to achieve those objectives, although they take different forms, essentially come down to the same thing, and so should normally be accorded recognition in all Member States, not forgetting the possibilities of co-operation between national authorities".[26]

Supported by the Council,[27] the Commission thus declared that mutual recognition would be an effective strategy for the achieving a common market.[28] Hence, this strategy[29] abandoned the "traditional" approach of detailed, vertical harmonisation and was welcomed by some authors since it seemed to herald

---

[21] Commission Communication, above n. 20.

[22] White Paper, above n. 10.

[23] Schmitt von Sydow, above n. 1, at 92.

[24] See for the terminology Case 272/80, *Biologische producten* [1981] ECR 3277. The expression "mutual recognition" already appears in the Treaty itself with respect to the free movement of persons. So, Art. 57(1) stipulates that "[i]n order to make it easier for persons to take up and pursue activities as self-employed persons, the Commission shall . . . issue directives for the mutual recognition of diplomas, certificates and other evidence of formal qualifications".

[25] Schmitt von Sydow, above n. 1, at 96.

[26] White Paper, above n. 10, para. 58.

[27] In its Conclusions on standardisation of 16 July 1984, the Council expressly recognised that "the objectives being pursued by the Member States to protect the safety and health of their people as well as the consumer are equally valid in principle, even if different techniques are used to achieve them". Published as Annex I to the Council Resolution on a New Approach to technical harmonisation and standards [1985] OJ C136/2.

[28] White Paper, above n. 10, para. 63.

[29] Which was explicitly declared applicable to foodstuffs, see the Communication from the Commission to the Council and the European Parliament on the completion of the internal market: Community legislation on foodstuffs, COM(85)603 final.

an end to the danger that "Euro-bread" and "Euro-beer" would be the sole out-come of the internal market.[30] Accordingly, the Commission concentrated on the harmonisation of justified trade barriers and planned the adoption of approximately 300 legislative acts in order to achieve the internal market before 31 December 1992. As regards the approach to be taken towards such harmon-isation activities, the Commission referred to the "New Approach to Technical Harmonisation and Standards", already approved by the Council in its Resolution of 7 May 1985[31] and developed by the Commission in its communi-cation of 31 January 1985.[32] The basic keystone of this New Approach was its distinction between essential safety requirements, which were to be laid down by the Council, and technical specifications to be undertaken by the European standardisation bodies CEN and CENELEC.[33] The SEA's introduction of qual-ified majority voting in Article 100a (the White Paper's institutional corollary) provided the necessary means to accelerate decision-making.

2.3. Deepening of Community Health and Safety Regulation

Although by means of this approach important progress was made towards the completion of the internal market, with hindsight, the White Paper was some-what Utopian.[34] To be sure, in contrast to the lacklustre 1970s, the 1980s were a time of important progress for the Community. In particular, success was due to the following factors: political will, a clear objective (achievement of the internal market), a binding time-table (1992)[35] and the introduction of qualified majority voting. However, the "euphoric" 1980s were followed by a renewed "euro-scepticism" in the 1990s. In the "post-1992" era, public awareness of Community activities grew, interest being fuelled by the growing significance of the Community and its very public achievements during the 1980s.[36] Thus, increasing attention was paid to the democratic deficit,[37] and the legitimacy of the Community decision-making process. At the same time, the Community met, for the first time, real opposition from the public in the form of the Danish "no" vote against the ratification of the Maastricht Treaty,[38] its "first democra-

---

[30] See Welch, above n. 20, at 66 and P. Oliver, *Free Movement of Goods in the European Community Under Articles 30 to 36 of the Rome Treaty* (London, 1996), 98.

[31] Council Resolution, above n. 27, 1 ff.

[32] Commission Communication, above n. 10.

[33] This innovative technique will be examined in greater detail in Chap. 5.

[34] See, e.g., Schmitt von Sydow, above n. 1, 79–80.

[35] *Ibid.*

[36] See, for an overview of the harmonisation activities of the Community, I.E. Schwartz, "30 Jahre EG-Rechtsangleichung", in E.J. Mestmäcker/H. Möller/H.P. Schwarz, *Eine Ordnungspolitik für Europa* (Baden-Baden, 1987), 333–68.

[37] See, for instance, J.H.H. Weiler, "The Transformation of Europe" (1991) 100 *The Yale Law Review* 2403–83.

[38] On 2 June 1991 the Danish electorate voted against the Act approving the Maastricht Treaty by a majority of 50.7%. See P.J.G. Kapteyn, "Denemarken en het Verdrag van Maastricht" (1992) 25 *NJB* 781–3.

tic hiccup".[39] The *Maastricht* judgment of the German Constitutional Court may likewise be seen in this light.[40]

On the eve of its entry into force, Weiler sketched the situation in relation to the Maastricht Treaty as follows: "it will be recalled as a low, anti-climactic moment in the history of contemporary European integration, not as its crowning achievement", and so concluded that "*fin-de-siècle* Europe may, thus, be not the reflection of emptiness, but a sign of healthy suspicion of ideals as idolatry".[41] In part, the slow-down in post-Maastricht may also be attributed to the spill-over effects and unforeseen consequences of the common market objective;[42] effects which have led to a revival of regulatory interventionists policies at Community level.[43] It thus results from the fragmented ("adhocery") internal market policy followed by the Community. Fluctuations (slowdown–progress–slowdown) in the Community pharmaceutical market have, for instance, been compared with the "Echternach jumping procession": the Moselle valley pilgrimage where participants are required to take three steps forward and two steps back[44]—a metaphor which holds true for the entire field of product regulation.

These three periods of: (1) slowdown combined with "euro-sclerosis" sentiments; (2) progress combined with "euro-confidence"; followed by (3) a slowdown combined with a renewed "euro-scepticism" correspond to the conclusion of the various Treaties by intergovernmental conferences and the harmonisation strategies which followed as a consequence.[45] The first phase encompasses the period starting with the conclusion of the Rome Treaty and ending with the conclusion of the 1987 Single European Act. During this phase, the Community operated in accordance with the maxim that each national act called for a Community act.[46] The second phase starts with the adoption of the 1985 White Paper, followed by the SEA, which gave impetus to a new harmonisation strategy. However, quite apart from the fact that the 1992 deadline was

---

[39] D. Curtin, "The Constitutional Structure of the Union: A Europe of Bits and Pieces" (1993) 30 *CMLRev.* 67.

[40] *Brunner et al.* v. *The European Union Treaty*, Cases 2BvR 2134/92 & 2159/92, *Bundesverfassungsgericht*, judgment of 12 Oct. 1993 [1994] CMLR 57. .

[41] J.H.H. Weiler, "Fin-de-Siècle Europe", in R. Dehousse (ed.), *Europe After Maastricht. An Ever Closer Union?* (Munich, 1994), 203 and 215.

[42] See Chap. 1 and E.B. Haas/P.C. Schmitter, "Economics and Differential Patterns of Political Integration: Projections about Unity in Latin America" (1964) 18 *International Organization* 705–37.

[43] See Ch. Joerges, "Market ohne Staat? Die Wirtschaftsverfassung der Gemeinschaft und die regulatieve Politik", in R. Wildemann (ed.), *Staatswerdung Europas? Optionen für eine politische Union* (Baden-Baden, 1991), 225–68.

[44] L. Hancher, "Creating the Internal Market for Pharmaceutical Medicines—an Echternach Jumping Procession?" (1991) 28 *CMLRev.* 821–53. Such processions are also held in other European cities (for instance in Taranto, Italy). See for a detailed examination of the pharmaceutical field Chap. 4.

[45] See Weiler, who distinguishes in the three periods: (1) 1958 to the mid-1970s: the foundational period—toward a theory of equilibrium; (2) 1973 to the mid-1980s: mutation of jurisdiction and competences; and (3) 1992 and beyond: Weiler, above n. 37.

[46] See Commission Communication, above n. 29, at 2.

clearly too ambitious,[47] practice was to demonstrate that the mere adoption of the approximately 300 directives listed in the White Paper was not an adequate means to realise one single Community market. Consequently, in the 1990s, the "post-Maastricht" era, we are witnessing a third phase of integration in which the Community is responding to the demand that it deepen its activities in health and safety regulation towards more Community implementation of health and safety issues. This development may be explained by various factors, some of which are dealt with below.[48]

2.3.1. The Limits of the Mutual Recognition Principle

2.3.1.1. A "Race to the Bottom"?

Mutual recognition was foremost viewed as "a method that for all practical purposes amounts to a subtle form of deregulation".[49] The blunt instrumentalisation of the principle of mutual recognition by the Commission in its White Paper thus fostered increased fears that a "regulatory gap" would be created: the Member States' Treaty obligations would make it difficult for them to exercise the regulatory competences they had retained, whilst in theory, at least, the Community would only dispose of limited competences and instruments with regard to alert decision-making.[50] It was feared that the strong emphasis on negative integration would result in a "race to the bottom",[51] a declining spiral of deregulation[52] and *laissez-faire* policy-making.[53] Confronted with the stark

[47]   See E. Steindorff, "Unvolkommener Binnenmarkt" (1994) 158 *ZHR* 149.

[48]   See E. Vos, "Market Building, Social Regulation and Scientific Expertise: An Introduction", in Ch. Joerges/K.-H Ladeur/E. Vos, *Integrating Scientific Expertise into Regulatory Decision-Making. National Traditions and European Innovations* (Baden-Baden, 1997), 127–39. See also Chaps. 3–5.

[49]   W. Streeck/P.C. Schmitter, "From National Corporatism to Transnational Pluralism: Organized Interests in the Single European Market" (1991) 19 *Politics and Society* 149.

[50]   Th. Bourgoignie/D. Trubek, *Consumer Law, Common Markets and Federalism in Europe and in the United States* (Berlin/New York, 1987), 171–2.

[51]   The metaphor "race to the bottom" originates from the American debate on corporate law. Apparently Brandeis J introduced the term "race of laxity" in *Liggett* v. *Lee* (concerning the New Jersey corporate rules of 1896), 288 US 517, 557–60 (1933) (Brandeis' dissenting opinion), whilst Cary coined the term "race to the bottom": W.L. Cary, "Federalism and Corporate Law: Reflections Upon Delaware" (1974) 83 *The Yale Law Journal* 666. Cary discusses the classical example of a "race to the bottom", the lax corporate laws of the US state of Delaware meant a haven for corporations. Some authors have expressed strong reservations about the desirability of the actual occurence of a "Delaware" into the EC context. According to other authors, however, Arts. 54 and 56 of the EC Treaty (the right of establishment), are drawn up by the Member States so as to prevent "the Delaware effect", see I. Cath, "Freedom of Establishment of Companies: A New Step Towards Completion of the Internal Market" (1986) 6 *YEL* 246 and 260 (pointing out to Art. 56) and C.-D. Ehlermann, "Ökonomische Aspekte des Subsidiaritätsprinzips: Harmonisierung versus Wettbewerb der Systeme" (1995) 18 *Integration* 1, 14 (with reference to Art. 54(3)).

[52]   See, in particular, D. Charny, "Competition among Jurisdictions in Formulating Corporate Law Rules: An American Perspective on the 'Race to the Bottom' in the European Communities" (1991) 32 *Harvard International Law Journal* 423–57. See also, more generally, J.P. Trachtman, "International Regulatory Competition, Externalisation and Jurisdiction" (1993) 34 *Harvard International Law Journal* 47–104.

[53]   C.R. Sunstein, "Protectionism, the American Supreme Court, and Integrated Markets", in R. Bieber/R. Dehousse/J. Pinder/J.H.H. Weiler (eds.), *1992: One European Market? A Critical Analysis of the Commission's Internal Market Strategy* (Baden-Baden, 1988), 143.

choice between keeping their stricter standards (resulting in a reverse discrimination of national producers[54]) or lowering them (endangering human health and safety), national governments would rather be induced to diminish their regulatory activities in order to allow their national manufacturers to compete with firms from countries with less stringent standards on the Community market.[55] This "competition between rules" would then finally lead to a withdrawal of state intervention in several fields,[56] and so to a general deterioration in health, safety and quality standards.[57]

Practice, however, has revealed that these fears are generally unfounded.[58] In particular, the principle of mutual recognition, as envisaged by the Commission, has shown itself to have its limits.[59] The principle of mutual recognition has by no means voluntarily been applied by the national authorities. Particularly in fields of health and safety, where consumers are unable to evaluate the cost-safety trade-offs in relation to certain products, and national authorities have consequently adopted legislative provisions to provide additional protection, Member States have often refused to accept the products from another Member State. For instance, with respect to medicinal products, a field where politically highly sensitive decisions on "risky" medicines are taken, Member States have often been very distrustful towards other administrative

[54] See, e.g., R. Streinz, "Das Problem der 'umgekehrten Diskriminierung' im Bereich des Lebensmittelrechts" [1990] *ZLR* 488 and M. Nentwich, *Das Lebensmittelrecht der Europäischen Union* (Vienna, 1994), 255 ff. (and the references mentioned in n. 1056) and, very recently, M. Poiares Maduro, *We the Court. The European Court of Justice and the European Economic Constitution* (Oxford, 1998), 70 ff. In the absence of Community legislation, the Court has held reverse discrimination to be in conformity with the Treaty provisions: see, for instance, Case C–19/92, *Kraus* [1993] ECR I–1663.

[55] This view had already been put forward by the German government in *Cassis de Dijon*; its lawyers arguing that the inevitable result of the strict application of Art. 30 would be a situation whereby minimum requirements would be reduced to the lowest level to be found in the legislation of any one of the Member States: Case 120/78, above n. 19, at 656. See also the Economic and Social Committee (ESC), which has pointed to the fact that this "negative" integration is likely to pose a large number of consumer protection problems and leads, for instance, in the area of insurance, to what it calls "control authority shopping": a situation in which, in its example of insurance, insurance undertakings will choose to register their business in whichever Member State offers them the greatest freedom from supervision and to market their services from that Member State. ESC Opinion on consumer protection and completion of the internal market [1991] OJ C339/16.

[56] See, in general, N. Reich, "Competition between Legal Orders: A New Paradigm of EC Law?" (1992) 29 *CMLRev.* 861–96 and S. Woolcock, *The Single European Market. Centralisation or Competition among National Rules?* Working Paper (The Royal Institute of International Affairs, London, 1994) and with regard to environmental protection: A. Weale, "Environmental Protection, the Four Freedoms and Competition among Rules", in M. Faure/J. Vervaele/A. Weale (eds.), *Environmental Standards in the European Union in an Interdisciplinary Framework* (Antwerp/Apeldoorn, 1994), 73–89.

[57] G. Majone, *Mutual Recognition In Federal Type Systems*, EUI Working Paper SPS 93/1 (Florence, 1993), 12.

[58] See Woolcock, above n. 56, 38–41; J. Stuyck, "Free Movement of Goods and Consumer Protection", in G. Woodroffe (ed.), *Consumer Law in the EEC* (London, 1984), 95–6; Dehousse, above n. 4, 16–17.

[59] See, in general, Majone, above n. 57, 12 ff. See also Ch. Joerges, "European Economic Law, the Nation-State and the Maastricht Treaty", in R. Dehousse (ed.), *Europe After Maastricht. An Ever Closer Union?* (Munich, 1994), 42–4.

authorities and insisted on compliance with their own regulations, thus refusing entry to imported goods. These practices have been supported by the Court in various cases.[60]

The lack of mutual trust especially, has often led the national authorities to prefer to undergo the full Article 169 procedure or to confront actions brought by interested parties in the national courts before being eventually forced to accept mutual recognition by the Court (in the latter case by virtue of Article 177). In view of the time and energy which such procedures entail, it seems hardly appropriate to rely upon the principle of mutual recognition as a regulatory instrument to overcome the differences in national legislative provisions, especially if each tiny difference should lead to national courts and/or Court proceedings.[61] Moreover, mutual recognition also fails where the objectives of national legislation diverge or where there is no agreement on the means of achieving regulatory equivalence.[62] This is clearly illustrated by a judgment of the Court handed down a year after the presentation of the White Paper.[63] In the *Woodworking Machines* case, the Court was called upon to decide whether the divergent approaches to ensuring the safety of woodworking machines in France and Germany were to be considered equivalent. Whereas the French safety norms for such machines were based on a strict user-protection concept with a minimum of intervention by the user, thus requiring additional protective devices on the machines, the German norms were based on a safety-through-education approach, requiring special training for the users. The Court, recognising the sensitivity of the case, did not agree with the Commission's argument that both safety norms were essentially equivalent. Instead, it ruled that, in the absence of harmonisation at the Community level, France could insist on its own, stricter, safety norms by virtue of Article 36, and thus restrict the import of such machines into its territory.[64]

From the preceding observations, it follows that mutual recognition has not had the success which the Commission had envisaged in its White Paper. Instead, it has faltered in the face of the Member States' unwillingness simply to accept each other's products, and has likewise been unable to address health and safety regulatory concerns. The limits to mutual recognition and the need for harmonisation in this area were, in fact, predicted by one of the drafters of the White Paper. It was openly admitted that:

---

[60] See, *inter alia*, Case 104/75, *De Peijper* [1976] ECR 613.

[61] D. Hoffmann, "Product Safety in the Internal Market: The Proposed Community Emergency Procedure", in M. Fallon/F. Maniet (eds.), *Sécurité des produits et mécanismes de contrôle dans la Communauté européenne* (Louvain-la-Neuve, 1990), 63–4; see also Majone, above n. 57, at 13.

[62] J. Sedemund, "'Cassis de Dijon' und das neue Harmonisierungs- konzept der Kommission", in J. Schwarze (ed.), *Der Gemeinsame Markt, Bestand und Zukunft in wirtschaftsrechtlicher Perspektive* (Baden-Baden, 1987), 43–4.

[63] Case 188/84, *Commission v. France* (*"Woodworking machines"*) [1986] ECR 419.

[64] *Ibid*. In the context of national insurance policies see also Case 205/84, *Commission v. Germany* [1986] ECR 3755. In this case the Court judged the basic concepts underlying insurance products to be too different to allow for the application of the principle of mutual recognition.

"[i]ndeed, harmonisation is not dead and may sooner or later start to flourish again. It has been relegated only in the specific context of the White Paper and its objective of abolishing all barriers to the free movement of goods, persons, services and capital. Mutual recognition achieves this objective, but it does not satisfy all aspirations of consumers and producers. It will be possible to buy an electrical appliance in any part of the Community and to take it across the border without restriction, but, once at home, it may still prove impossible to plug it into the wall socket. Standardisation and compatibility of interfaces are particular important to industry where international competition in the world depends on the economies of scale and the pressure of—undistorted—competition which only a home market of dimensions of a continent can provide. Similarly, only harmonisation can implement effective Community policies for e.g. the protection of the environment or can give the Community a leading role in the fields of public health, technical security and consumer protection".[65]

In addition, the Community institutions have been very much aware that a "race to the bottom" might seriously endanger human health and safety.[66] Various Community measures, influenced by Article 100a(3)'s requirement of a high protection level, have indeed aimed at the maintenance or improvement of the safety level achieved in the Member States.[67] It may even be argued that Community policies have played an important role in strengthening national legislative frameworks of environmental and consumer protection, particularly for those countries which had not evolved an effective regulatory mechanism to protect consumer and environmental interests (mostly southern Member States).[68] Moreover, it has become apparent that the Community's competence is flexible enough to sustain its activities in fields such as environmental and consumer protection. In fact, the SEA's introduction of qualified majority voting in Article 100a has proved particularly significant for the adoption of product regulation. The threat of being outvoted has made Member States more willing to

---

[65] Schmitt von Sydow, above n. 1, at 97.

[66] Council Dir. 89/391/EEC on health and safety at work [1989] OJ L183/1 (ninth recital of the preamble).

[67] See Council Dir. 89/392/EEC on machinery [1989] OJ L183/9 (third recital of the preamble). This Dir. establishes in fact a level of protection which is even higher than the existing levels in the Member States: see V. Eichener, *Social Dumping or Innovative Regulation? Process and Outcomes of European Decision-Making in the Sector of Health and Safety at Work Harmonization*, EUI Working Paper SPS 92/28 (Florence 1992), 6 ff. See also Joerges, above n. 59, 44–7.

[68] See, for instance, on the *de facto* impact of EC consumer programmes on the developments in the Member States, N. Reich/H.-W. Micklitz, *Consumer Legislation in the EC Countries—A Comparative Analysis* (London, 1980), as regards advertising (63 ff.), door-to-door selling (67–9) and product liability (93–106). More recently, see N. Reich/G. Woodroffe, *European Consumer Policy after Maastricht* (Deventer, 1994). As regards the positive influence of Community legislation in this field, see, in particular, the articles in Reich and Woodroffe by K. Tonner, "The European Influence on German Consumer Law" at 225–36 and S. Cotterli/P. Martinello/C.M. "Verardi, Implementation of EEC Consumer Protection Directives in Italy", at 249–68, more critical of the importance of Community legislation for the French situation: A. Chambraud/P. Foucher/A. Morin, The Importance of Community Law for French Consumer Protection Legislation, 209–24. See also Dehousse, above n. 4, at 16.

negotiate, which has resulted in compromise solutions in fields where, for many years, no decision had been possible.[69]

Hence, instead of a "race to the bottom", the new Commission strategy has rather resulted in re-regulatory policies at the Community level in areas such as consumer and environmental protection, policies largely based on Article 100a.[70] It has resulted in the re-organisation of traditional legislative techniques and the establishment of comprehensive mechanisms for health and safety regulation within the internal market.[71]

2.3.1.2. Compulsory Mutual Recognition?

Certainly, if faced with unwillingness by Member States to apply the mutual recognition principle voluntarily, the Community might decide to impose mutual recognition by a decision of the Community institutions, either under the normal decision-making procedure of Article 100a or under Article 100b. However, apart from the fact that, in practice, action under Article 100b has been deemed unnecessary,[72] imposing mutual recognition would be highly undesirable since such a move would once again raise the spectre of the regulatory "race to the bottom".[73] The regulation of health and safety matters by the Community might thus be argued to be the only way to reconcile these regulatory objectives with the free trade requirement.[74] Moreover, the political sensi-

---

[69] The Commission proposal for an "old style" Council Dir. on the safety of toys, for instance, dated from 1980 [1980] OJ C228/10 and was modified in 1983 [1983] OJ C203/12. As soon as the SEA was adopted, the Commission redrafted its proposal in terms of the New Approach requirements [(1986) OJ C282/4] and after the presentation of its amended proposal, COM(87)467 final, the Council adopted on 3 May 1988 the Dir. 88/378/EEC on the safety of toys [1988] OJ L187/1. See also Dehousse, above n. 4, 17.

[70] See in general G. Majone (ed.), *Deregulation or Re-regulation? A Regulatory Reform in Europe and the United States* (London, 1990), with, in particular, the contributions by Ch. Joerges, "Paradoxes of Deregulatory Strategies at Community level: The Example of Product Safety Policy", 176–97 and E. Kaufer, "The Regulation of New Product Development in the Drug Industry", 153–75. See also Ch. Joerges, "Market ohne Staat? Die Wirtschaftsverfassung der Gemeinschaft und die regulatieve Politik", in R. Wildemann (ed.), *Staatswerdung Europas? Optionen für eine politische Union* (Baden-Baden, 1991), 225–68.

[71] Joerges, above n. 59, at 45.

[72] Instead, emphasis has been laid on a greater transparency and strengthening of mutual confidence; see the Commission in its Communication on the Management of the mutual recognition of national rules after 1992. Operational conclusions reached in the light of the inventory drawn up pursuant to Art. 100b of the EC Treaty [1993] OJ C353/4. To this end, a procedure is created for the exchange of information on national measures derogating from the principle of the free movement of goods, within the Community, European Parliament and Council Dec. 3052/95/EC [1995] OJ L321/1. See S. Weatherill, "Compulsory Notification of Draft Technical Regulations: The Contribution of Directive 83/189 to the Management of the Internal Market" (1996) 16 YEL 183 ff.

[73] In response to the call by the Amsterdam European Council of June 1997, the Commission has recently proposed to create a mechanism whereby the Commission can intervene in order to remove certain obstacles to trade [1998] OJ C10/14. However, being applicable to "clear, unmistakable and unjustified" obstacles to the free movement of goods, measures on health and safety issues will not be affected by this rule.

[74] R. Dehousse, "Some Reflections on the Crisis of the Harmonisation Model", in F. Snyder (ed.), *A Regulatory Framework for Foodstuffs in the Internal Market*, EUI Working Paper LAW 94/4 (Florence, 1994), 47–8.

tivity underlying health and safety regulation is likely to make it difficult, if not impossible, to arrive at a decision imposing mutual recognition. Where, for instance, the mutual recognition of products including additives was imposed by the Court, the Community has nonetheless continued to engage in legislative activities concerning additives.[75] This phenomenon may be explained in that the Member States apparently feel dissatisfied when the Court forces them to allow the use of certain substances in products on their market (although the Court is very prudent in this and generally allows the Member States a wide degree of discretion) and prefer harmonisation instead; the latter option giving them a voice in the matter.

2.3.2. The Creation of Trade Barriers by Means of Procedural Rules

Where mutual recognition breaks down and given the manner in which national administrative authorities exercise their powers of control, the Community has attempted to initiate a higher degree of mutual confidence between national administrations,[76] hereby enforcing administrative co-operation between them.[77] In addition, the Community has set up a telematic exchange of data between national administrations (IDA).[78] However, for health and safety regulation which includes politically sensitive matters, this has appeared not to be

[75] See Council Dir. 89/107/EEC on the approximation of the laws of the Member States concerning food additives authorised for use in foodstuffs intended for human consumption [1988] OJ L40/27, amended by European Parliament and Council Dir. 94/34/EC [1994] OJ L237/1; European Parliament and Council Dir. 94/35/EC on sweeteners for use in foodstuffs [1994] OJ L237/3; European Parliament and Council Dir. 94/36/EC on colours for use in foodstuffs [1994] OJ L237/13; European Parliament and Council Dir. 95/2/EC on food additives other than colours and sweeteners [1995] OJ L61/1.

[76] For instance, Council Dec. on the adoption of an action plan for the exchange between Member State administrations of national officials who are engaged in the implementation of Community legislation required to achieve the internal market [1992] OJ L286/65; Commission Dec. 95/28/EC establishing priorities for the action plan for the exchange between Member State administrations of national officials who are engaged in the implementation of Community legislation required to achieve the internal market (Karolus Programme) [1995] OJ L37/39; Council Resolution on the development of administrative co-ordination in the implementation and enforcement of Community legislation in the internal market [1994] OJ C179/1; Council Resolution on co-ordination with regard to information exchange between administrations [1994] OJ C181/1. See also earlier Written Questions nos. 1557/84, 1713/84 (both [1985] OJ C135/24 and 28) and no. 1006/85 [1985] OJ C334/19. See also Council Resolution on the effective uniform application of Community law and on the penalties applicable for the breaches of Community law in the internal market [1995] OJ C188/1, in which the Council encourages the Commission to continue to develop administrative co-operation where necessary.

[77] The necessity for administrative co-operation was underlined by the Sutherland report: *The Internal Market after 1992. Meeting the Challenge*, Report to the EEC Commission by the High Level Group on the operation of the Internal Market of 26 Oct. 1992. See also the Commission's Communication to the Council and the European Parliament, Reinforcing the effectiveness of the internal market, COM(93)256 final, 26–30 and the Commission's Communication to the Council and the European Parliament, The operation of the Community's internal market after 1992. Follow up to the Sutherland report, SEC(92)2277 final.

[78] Council Dec. 95/468/EC [1995] OJ L269/23. See also the Commission Communication concerning the evaluation of the IDA programme and a second phase of the IDA programme, COM(97)661 final. See http://www.ispo.cec.be/ida (IDA homepage).

the sole solution. To a certain degree, the lack of mutual confidence has also caused the creation of new obstacles to trade in the form of new national control and inspection procedures. Hence, more detailed Community intervention has been necessary, since these new national measures may again be considered to be justified trade barriers.[79] Hence, authorisation procedures for medicinal products have been set up, both of which grant the Commission the final say in authorisation and provide for a monitoring procedure.[80] Moreover, the need to lay down general co-ordinating principles for the carrying out of official control and inspection is commonly accepted in the food sector, and such principles have accordingly been laid down by the Community.[81]

2.3.3. Wide Discretion of Member States and Vague Terminology in Directives

Although Article 100a allows the Community institutions to use measures other than directives, directives still dominate and are the main legislative instrument in matters of health and safety regulation.[82] Directives leave to the Member States the choice of which form and methods are to be used to achieve the goals laid down in the specific directive.[83] The often highly technical nature of health and safety regulation determines that the Member States are usually given a wide degree of discretion. Whilst this flexibility is considered to be a vital element in the Community scheme, allowing for the evaluation of the local situation and apposite decision-making by local and regional authorities,[84] it has also given the Member States ample leeway for divergent and probably self-interested implementation,[85] thus endangering the homogeneous realisation of Community objectives.[86] Furthermore, the inclusion of vague and open-ended terms in directives on health and safety,[87] reflecting political compromise, often

---

[79] See, also, Communication of the Commission to the Council, Making the most of the internal market: strategic programme, COM(93)632 final, 7.

[80] See, in detail, Chap. 4.

[81] See, for instance, the preamble of Council Dir. 89/397/EEC on the official control of foodstuffs [1989] OJ L186/23. See Chap. 3.

[82] See the declaration on Art. 100a adopted by the Inter-Governmental Conference as an annex to the SEA.

[83] In accordance with Art. 189.

[84] See, for instance, Case C–334/89, *Commission* v. *Italy* [1991] ECR 93, at 105.

[85] J.H.H. Weiler, "The White Paper and the Application of Community Law", in R. Bieber/ R. Dehousse/J. Pinder/J.H.H. Weiler (eds.), *1992: One European Market? A Critical Analysis of the Commission's Internal Market Strategy* (Baden-Baden, 1988), 352; G. Majone, *The Development of Social Regulation in the European Community: Policy Externalities, Transaction Costs, Motivational Factors*, EUI Working Paper SPS 95/2 (Florence, 1995), 17.

[86] For environment analogous arguments can be advanced. See A.R. Ziegler, *The Common Market and the Environment: Striking a Balance*, Dissertation, Hochschule St. Gallen nr. 1764 (Bamberg, 1995), 181–2.

[87] See generally Council Resolution on the quality of the drafting of Community legislation [1993] OJ C166/1. See A.E. Kellerman, "The Quality of Community Legislation Drafting", in D. Curtin/T. Heukels (eds.), *Institutional Dynamics of European Integration, Essays in Honour of H.G. Schermers* (Dordrecht/Boston/London, 1994), 251–62. See for these problems in the agricultural context, R. Barents, "The Quality of Community Legislation" (1994) 1 *MJ* 101–14.

also results in divergent interpretation, implementation and intentional non-compliance at national level.[88] The use of such vague and open-ended terms is similarly one of the factors which have caused enormous delays in the national implementation of Community legislation, and thus in the application of Community law. In view of the politically sensitive and technical nature of health and safety regulation, these problems are not to be resolved by simply "urging" the Member States to transpose and apply Community directives fully and accurately.[89] Rather, it is vital that the Community should intervene more thoroughly in national legislation and administration in order to come to grips with the implementation of its acts.[90]

2.3.4. *Dangerous Products and Accidents*

As argued in the introduction to this book, risk regulation includes a whole set of regulatory measures which are closely intertwined. Products cannot be allowed to enter onto the market without, at the same time, providing for mechanisms for monitoring their safety. Therefore, the creation of a single Community market in which products may freely circulate brings with it the corollary that dangerous products are no longer restricted to the national market, but may potentially circulate throughout the Community. This forces the Community to consider the setting up of information and monitoring systems, and to take upon itself the necessary powers to withdraw such products from the Community market. Here, I need only mention the BSE problem which, although related to agricultural policy, readily demonstrates the potential danger that Community-wide circulation of meat from diseased cows may adversely affect the health and safety of Community citizens.[91] The need for Community intervention in such cases is readily apparent.[92] Community intervention seems indisputable in relation to worldwide catastrophes, such as the *Chernobyl* accident.[93]

---

[88] See, in general, the Commission Communication on the impact and effectiveness of the single market, COM(96)520 final, para. 4.

[89] See the IGC on the Political Union which, in a Declaration on the implementation of Community Law to the TEU, recognising these problems, urged the Member States to transpose fully and accurately into national law the Community dirs. addressed to them within the deadlines laid down therein. In addition, the necessity of applying Community law with the same effectiveness and rigour as used in the application of national law was stressed. See also, in this context, recently Council Resolution, above n. 76.

[90] J.P.H. Donner, "De nationale wetgever en de Gemeenschap" (1992) 40 *SEW* 6, 473.

[91] See, in more detail, Chap. 3.

[92] Commission Dec. 96/239/EC on emergency matters to protect against bovine spongiform encephalopathy [1996] OJ L78/47. See, for the unsuccessful attempt to annul this Dec., Case C–180/96, *United Kingdom* v. *Commission* [1998] ECR I–2265.

[93] See, for instance, Council Dec. 87/600/Euratom on Community arrangements for the early exchange of information in the event of a radiological emergency [1987] OJ L371/76 and Council Reg. (EEC) 2219/89 on the special conditions for exporting foodstuffs and feedingstuffs following a nuclear accident or any other case of radiological emergency [1989] OJ L211/4; Commission Reg. (Euratom) 944/89 laying down maximum permitted levels of radioactive contamination in minor foodstuffs following a nuclear accident or any other case of radiological emergency [1989] OJ L101/17.

2.3.5. Innovation and New Technology

Product innovation and technology may have an impact on human health and safety. Biotechnology used in the production of medicines or foodstuffs, for example, raises concern about a decline in food safety. Consequently, most Member States react with regulatory action, causing, however, justified trade barriers. The Community has therefore also taken up activities in this field.[94]

2.3.6. Community Responsibility for Ensuring Health and Safety Protection

Elements of Community responsibility for human health and safety constitute another component which may explain the need for an intensification of Community activities in health and safety. In contrast to the situation in most Member States, where governments have a constitutional obligation to ensure the health and safety of their citizens,[95] the Treaty does not contain an explicit provision obliging the Community to protect the health and safety of its citizens, nor does it guarantee a Community right to safety. Yet, it is possible to identify certain elements which indicate that wherever the Community issues product regulation, it implicitly assumes a positive responsibility to protect the health and safety of persons.[96] These can be found both in the Treaty provisions and in secondary Community legislation.

In the Treaty itself, Article 3(o) and (s), for example, lists amongst Community activities a contribution to a high level of health and consumer protection. This apparent obligation is strengthened by Articles 100a(3) and 129a and will be reinforced by the amendments of the Amsterdam Treaty, which in Articles 129 and 129a no longer sets as a Community objective the attainment of a *"contribution"* to ensure a high level of human health and consumer protection but straightforwardly requires the Community to *"ensure"* a high level of human health and consumer protection.[97]

In relation to secondary law, mention should be made of the Community's consumer policy programmes,[98] which have recognised the right to protection of health and safety since 1975.[99] Notwithstanding their "soft law" status,[100] the

---

[94] See Chap. 3.

[95] H.-W. Micklitz, "Consumer Rights", in A. Cassese/A. Clapham/J.H.H. Weiler (eds.), *Human Rights in the European Community: The Substantive Law* (Baden-Baden, 1991), 53–109.

[96] See Ch. Joerges, "Product Safety Law, Internal Market Policy and the Proposal for a Directive on General Product Safety", in M. Fallon/F. Maniet (eds.), *Sécurité des produits et mécanismes de contrôle dans la Communauté européenne* (Louvain-la-Neuve, 1990), 184 and 190.

[97] See Chap. 1.

[98] See the Community's consumer protection programmes mentioned in n. 50 to Chap. 1.

[99] See Council Resolution on a preliminary programme of the EEC for a consumer protection and information policy [1975] OJ C92/1.

[100] The notion "soft law" refers to such techniques as codes of conduct, voluntary agreements, recommendations resolutions and declarations which in principle have no legally binding status, in the sense of Art. 189 EC: see G.L. Close, "The Legal Basis for the Consumer Protection Programme of the EEC and Priorities" (1983) 8 *ELR* 234. See, more generally, for instance, K.C. Wellens/

Court appears to attach some value to these programmes and to recognise them as being a part of Community law. In its judgment in Case C-362/88, *GB-INNO-BM* v. *Confédération du commerce luxembourgoise*,[101] the Court held that the provision of information to the consumer—one of the rights recognised by the consumer policy programmes—was one of the principal requirements of Community consumer law.[102] This judgment may apply by analogy to the case of the right to protection of health and safety. In addition, several acts adopted by the Community in fact display an awareness of such a responsibility, since they seek to establish a level of safety which is even higher than that found in certain Member States.[103]

Without doubt, an important act in this context is the General Product Safety Directive of 1992.[104] As already argued in Chapter 1, although this Directive does not deny the Member States' responsibility for product safety, it actually takes on the competence to impose a general safety requirement upon producers, conferring on the Commission the responsibility for overseeing national measures and for adopting health and safety measures in emergency situations.[105] A similar approach is laid down in the European Parliament and Council Decision 3092/94/EC which introduces a Community information system on home and leisure accidents.[106]

Taken together, these elements have provoked a gradual deepening of Community involvement in health and safety regulation, and have encouraged the Community to move towards the consideration of "genuine" product safety issues in addition to "pure" internal market objectives. In this manner, the Community has been forced to confront health and safety regulation in all its complexity. Hence, where the Community takes decisions on the manufacturing and/or marketing of products, it must also ensure their safety.[107] This includes, for example, the establishment of supervisory systems of pre- and post-market control, which also contain emergency procedures.

G.M. Borchardt, "Soft Law in the European Community Law" (1989) 14 *ELR* 267–321; F. Snyder, "Soft Law and Institutional Practice in the European Community", in S. Martin (ed.), *The Construction of Europe, Essays in Honour of Emile Noël* (Dordrecht/Boston/London, 1994), 197–225.

[101] [1990] ECR I–667.

[102] *Ibid.*, at I–689.

[103] See, for instance, the Machinery Dir. 89/392/EEC reported by Eichener, above n. 67, at 5 ff.

[104] Council Dir. 92/59/EEC, above n. 3. The need to impose a general safety obligation on manufacturers was already set forth in the Commission's communication on a new impetus for consumer protection policy, COM(85)314 final, which was endorsed by the Council in its Resolution [1986] OJ C167/1. This objective of a safety obligation was further pursued by the Commission in a Communication concerning the safety of consumer products, COM(87)209 final, recognised by the Council on 25 June 1987 [1987] OJ C176/3. See also the opinion of the ESC on the general safety requirements for products [1988] OJ C175/12.

[105] Art. 7(2) and Arts. 8–12 of Dir. 92/59/EEC, above n. 104.

[106] [1994] OJ L331/1. See Chap. 1.

[107] Ch. Joerges, "The New Approach to Technical Harmonisation and the Interests of Consumers: Reflections on the Requirements and Difficulties of a Europeanisation of Product Safety Policy", in R. Bieber/R. Dehousse/J. Pinder/J.H.H. Weiler (eds.), *1992: One European Market? A Critical Analysis of the Commission's Internal Market Strategy* (Baden-Baden, 1988), 179.

3. THE RELATIONSHIP BETWEEN COMMUNITY LEGISLATION AND IMPLEMENTATION

The ever-growing Community activities in health and safety and, in particular, the implementation of certain of its own rules, primarily raises questions about the relationship between legislation, implementation and execution, with legal literature doubting whether the Community is generally competent to execute Community law. Since there is no provision expressly empowering the Community to execute its own legislation, it has been argued that the Member States possess constitutional autonomy in this field; an autonomy underpinned by the principle of attributed competences.[108] In this view, where the Treaty provisions do not explicitly confer powers on the Community institutions, executive powers are the sole provenance of the Member States—in accordance with Article 5. Yet, the observation that the Community has not been expressly assigned a general power on the implementation of the legislation adopted by it, does not necessarily mean that the Community is not competent to do so. This issue forms the main point of the analysis in the following section.

3.1. The Blurring of the "Legislation–Execution" Distinction and the Principle of the Separation of Powers

Analysis must first focus on the distinction between legislation and execution, which is derived from the principle of the separation of powers. This principle, which has influenced constitutional development in democratic states since the eighteenth century, is the most common (organic) manifestation of the concept of the *trias politica*, originally developed by Montesquieu[109] in 1748.[110] It draws a sharp distinction between legislative, executive and judicial powers.[111] However, the practical tendency of the modern nation-state to blur the distinction between legislation and execution has been generally recognised, and has resulted in the development of a more responsive system of "checks and balances".[112] Doubts, therefore, arise whether it is desirable to apply the concept of

[108] See Klösters, above n. 2, 12–13.

[109] V. Goldschmidt (ed.), *Montesquieu, "De l'esprit des lois"* (Paris, 1979).

[110] Whereas the *trias politica* has authoritatively been laid down by Montesquieu, several predecessors of this theory already existed, which can even be traced back to the works of Aristotle. See also Locke's *Two Treaties of Government* of 1690.

[111] A very strict separation of powers theory was developed, in particular, by Immanuel Kant in his book entitled *Die Methaphysik der Sitten* of 1797.

[112] Here, the concept of administration which is recognised to include, in addition to the mere application of rules, the issue of norms has been developed. See, for an overview of the definitions of public administration in the 12 Member States, in a search for conceptual understanding of public administration, J. Schwarze, *European Administrative Law* (London, 1992), in particular 18–19, and L. Prakke/C.A.J.M. Kortmann, *Het bestuursrecht van de landen der Europese Gemeenschappen* (Deventer, 1986). Instead of the "legislation–execution" distinction, it would, according to some legal writers, be "policy" which is determinant for both the issuing of rules and

the separation of powers at the Community level, when its limits have already become apparent at national level.[113] Moreover, the transfer of the concepts developed within the context of the nation-state to the Community level is a process to be treated with the utmost caution.[114] Indeed, legal literature[115] now recognises that it is virtually impossible to apply an organic understanding of the principle of the separation of powers—based on a strict distinction between those holding legislative, executive and judicial office—to the Community's currently pentapartite[116] institutional structure.

3.2. Implementation of Community Law

3.2.1. *The Power to Adopt Measures under Primary Community Law and the Power to Implement Rules Developed by the Community Institutions*

The Treaty provisions themselves equally fail to make a distinction between legislation and execution or administration. The absence of this distinction in the Treaty may be due to the fact that the Community was set up as an international organisation,[117] and concepts of legislation, execution and administration are

their execution, while the choice for laying down this policy in legislative provisions, policy formulations or individual decisions would to a great extent be determined by coincidental circumstances: F.C.L.M. Crijns, *Het Europese perspectief van het Nederlandse staatsrecht* (Zwolle, 1989), 176. In modern (Dutch) administrative law legislation is therefore considered by some to be an instrument of administration: see L.A. Geelhoed, *De interveniërende staat, aanzet tot een instrumentenleer* (The Hague, 1983); P. De Haan/T.G. Drupsteen/R. Fernhout, *Bestuursrecht in de sociale rechtsstaat* (Deventer, 1986); B.J.M. Van der Meulen, *Rechterlijk toetsing van wetgeving in Europees perspectief, in: Bestuursrecht na 1992, preadviezen voor de Vereniging voor Administratief Recht* (Alphen an der Rijn, 1989), 56. Van Male speaks therefore of "administrative legislation" (*bestuurswetgeving*), indicating that the drawing up of a generally valid primary regulation is an act of administration and not an act of secondary legislation: R.M. Van Male, *Rechter en bestuurswetgeving* (Zwolle, 1988), 4.

[113] See, on the application of the principle of separation of powers to the Community, P. Pescatore, "L'exécutif communautaire: justification du quadripartisme institué par les traités de Paris et Rome" (1978) 14 *CDE* 387–406. More recently, see K. Lenaerts, "Some Reflections on the Separation of Powers in the European Community" (1991) 28 *CMLRev*. 1–35. See also M. Everson, "Independent Agencies: Hierarchy Beaters?" (1995) 1 *ELJ* 180–204.

[114] See, *inter alia*, H.P. Ipsen, *Europäisches Gemeinschaftsrecht* (Tübingen, 1972), 319, and R. Dehousse, "Comparing National Law and EC Law: The Problem of the Level of Analysis" (1994) 42 *The American Journal of Comparative Law*, 771 ff.

[115] See Pescatore, above n. 113, 406; Lenaerts, above n. 113, 12–13; B. De Witte, "Community Law and National Constitutional Values" (1991) 2 *LIEI* 7; E.-W. Fuss, *Die Europäischen Gemeinschaften und der Rechtsstaatgedanke* (Heule, 1963), 21; and more cautiously, Dehousse, above n. 114, 774.

[116] Following the Maastricht Treaty, Art. 4 mentions five institutions: the EP, the Council, the Commission, the Court of Justice and the Court of Auditors.

[117] Albeit today Community law can, certainly, be distinguished from traditional public international law according to its content, its instruments and its sources of law: see P.J.G. Kapteyn / P. VerLoren van Themaat *et al.*, *Inleiding tot het recht van de Europese Gemeenschappen. Na Maastricht* (Deventer, 1995), 36–8. See also *Opinion 1/91* in which the Court judged the EEC Treaty, albeit concluded in the form of an international agreement, to constitute the constitutional charter of the Community based on the rule of law [1991] ECR I–6079.

generally thought to be national concepts. The Treaty, for example, generally stipulates that the Community institutions must carry out their tasks in accordance with the requirements laid down in the Treaty; in other words, adopting regulations, directives, decisions, recommendations or opinions (see Articles 3b(1), 4 and 189). Furthermore, it makes use of general terms such as "measures" (for example, Articles 100a, 145, 155, 235); "measures to ensure the fulfilment of obligations arising out of this Treaty or resulting from action taken by the institutions of the Community" (Article 5) and "for the implementation of the rules" (Articles 145 and 155). Hence, instead of distinguishing between legislative and administrative powers, the Treaty distinguishes between the power of the Community institutions to adopt measures or rules by virtue of primary Community law, and the power to implement such rules.[118]

3.2.2. The Concept of Implementation

The concept of implementation[119] needs some further explanation. It is explicitly used in Articles 145, third indent, and 155, fourth indent. A systemic interpretation of Article 155's positioning within the Treaty (together with certain practical requirements) has led the Court consistently to hold that "implementation by the Commission" is to be interpreted widely.[120] This determines that whilst the legislative organs[121] must regulate all essential elements, the power to adopt all measures necessary for the implementation of the rules established may safely be left to the Commission.[122] These detailed implementation rules[123] also include the imposition of sanctions.[124] In *France, Italy and United Kingdom v. Commission*, which concerned the Commission's legislative powers under Article 90(3), the Court further established that neither Article 155 (now Article 145), nor Article 189 made any distinction between legislative powers (to be exercised by the Council) and powers of administration or control (to be exer-

---

[118] This is underlined by the Court in various cases. See, for instance, Case 25/70, *Einfuhr- und Vorratstelle für Getreide und Futtermittel Köster* [1970] ECR 1161, at 1170 and Case 30/70, *Scheer v. Einfuhr- und Vorratsstelle für Getreide und Futtermittel* [1970] ECR 1197, at 1208.

[119] See for the concept of implementation, in particular in relation to the agricultural policy, for instance, R. Barents, *The Agricultural Law of the EC* (Deventer, 1994), 58–63.

[120] See, *inter alia*, Case 23/75, *Rey Soda v. Cassa Conguaglio Zucchero* [1975] ECR 1279, at 1300; Joined Cases 279, 280, 285 and 286/84, *Rau v. Commission (Christmas butter)* [1987] ECR 1069, at 1120; Case 22/88, *Vreugdenhil* [1989] ECR 2049, at 2079–80.

[121] On the question whether, after the Maastricht Treaty, Art. 145 third indent also includes acts of both Parliament and Council adopted under co-decision, see Chap. 3, sect. 4.3.3.

[122] See, *inter alia*, Case 25/70, *Köster*, above n. 118; Case C–345/88, *Butter-Absatz v. Germany* [1990] ECR I–159; Case C–357/88, *Hopermann v. Bundesanstalt für Landwirtschaftliche Marktordnung* [1990] ECR I–1669.

[123] It follows from the case law that the notion of detailed rules must likewise be interpreted widely. See Case 57/72, *Westzucker v. Einfuhr- und Vorratstelle für Zucker* [1973] ECR 321, at 338.

[124] See Case C–240/90, *Germany v. Commission* [1992] ECR I–5383, paras. 38–40. With respect to the imposition of sanctions on Member States for not having complied with a judgment of the Court, see Art. 171(2). See on the concept of sanctions in the Community agricultural law, Barents, above n. 119, 277–91. More generally, see A. Ward, "Effective Sanctions in EC Law: A Moving Boundary in the Division of Competence" (1995) 1 *ELJ* 205–17.

cised by the Commission).[125] The broad interpretation of implementation was confirmed by the Court in Case 16/88, *Commission v. Council (Fisheries)*.[126] In this case, the Council sought to determine that the Commission's decision-making powers were subject to a committee procedure which allowed the Council ongoing control over the Commission's exercise of its powers.[127] In order to defend its own, independent decision-making powers to implement the budget under Article 205, the Commission argued that a distinction needed to be made between "legislative implementation" (i.e. powers to determine the procedures for the application of the rules laid down by the Council) and "administrative implementation" (i.e. the application to individual situations of the rules laid down by the Council[128]), powers which do not fall within Article 145, third indent. The Court, however, refused to accept the Commission's distinction. It held that the concept of implementation, in the sense of Article 145, third indent, encompasses both the drawing up of implementing rules and the application of rules to specific cases by means of acts of individual application.[129] This interpretation was justified by the Court with reference to the fact that the Treaty itself contained no such restriction, and did not indicate that acts of individual application were to be excluded.[130]

The notion of implementation also includes the control of the application of Community law and its enforcement.[131] This may be derived from the general tenor of Article 5. As the Court ruled, this Article places a general duty upon the Member States, the exact details of which depend in each case upon the Treaty provisions at issue or on rules derived from the overall scheme of the Treaty.[132] By virtue of this Article, Member States are required to take all appropriate measures necessary to ensure the application of Community law and its supervision and effectiveness.[133] This means that Member States must implement Community legislation with the same rigour as national legislation. Where Community legislation, for example, does not provide any specific penalty for

---

[125] Joined Cases 188–190/80, [1982] ECR 2545.

[126] [1989] ECR 3457.

[127] See on the committee procedures Chap. 3.

[128] As reported by Darmon AG in this case, above n. 126, at 3469. The terminology "administrative implementation" is also used by Schwarze, above n. 112, in particular at 25 ff. (discussing the areas of administrative implementation of Community law).

[129] Case 16/88, *Commission v. Council* [1989] ECR 3457, at 3485 (para. 11).

[130] *Ibid.*

[131] See e.g., R. Mayntz, "Politische Steuerung: Aufstieg, Niedergang und Transformation einer Theorie", in K. Von Beyme/C. Offe (Hrsg.), *Politische Theorien in der Ära der Transformation* (Opladen, 1996), 149.

[132] See Case 78/70, *Deutsche Grammophon v. Metro* [1971] ECR 487.

[133] See, for instance, Case 30/70, *Scheer*, above n. 118, at 1206; Joined Cases 205–215/82, *Deutsche Milchkontor GmbH* v. *Germany* [1983] ECR 2633, at 2665–6; and Case 68/88, *Commission v. Greece (Alfonsina)* [1989] ECR 2965, at 2984. For an in-depth study of Art. 5, see in particular M. Blanquet, *L'article 5 du Traité C.E.E.—Recerche sur les obligations de fidélité des États membres de la Communauté* (Paris, 1993). See also J. Temple Lang, "Article 5 of the EEC Treaty: The Emergence of Constitutional Principles in the Case Law of the Court of Justice" (1986–7) 10 *Fordham International Law Journal* 503–37; O. Due, "Artikel 5 van het EEG-Verdrag. Een bepaling met een federaal karakter?" (1992) 40 *SEW* 5, 355–66.

an infringement, or refers for that purpose to national provisions, Member States must guarantee that infringements of Community law are penalised in the same way as infringements of national law. The penalties which may be imposed (including criminal penalties[134]) must be "effective, proportionate and dissuasive".[135]

Hence, the concept of implementation must be interpreted broadly, and includes the drawing up of rules, the application of rules to individual situations, and the effective supervision of the correct application of Community law, enforcement and the imposition of sanctions.[136] In this manner, the concept of implementation as developed in the Community context seems to reflect the modern approach of administration developed at the level of the nation-state.

3.2.3. Do Member States Have a Right to Implement?

At present, the greater part of Community law is implemented by the Member States. The main fields of indirect implementation are the Common Agricultural Policy and the Common Customs Tariff Policy.[137] The implementation of the Community's internal market policy has also often been left to the Member States. Yet this does not mean that implementation of Community law is *reserved a priori* to the Member States: Article 5 does not furnish Member States with (executive) implementation competence.

In *Deutsche Milchkontor*, the Court held that where Community measures make no specific reference to the question of implementation, it is for the Member States to implement Community law in accordance with any relevant national provisions.[138] This case law, together with the broad concept of implementation, indicates that the Community may, in accordance with its discretionary powers, regulate the implementation of its measures, determining in each case whether and to what extent (in accordance with the proportionality principle) implementation should be left to the Member States or whether the necessary powers need to be delegated to the Commission or may be exercised by the Community legislature itself.[139] This is explicitly accepted by the Declaration relating to the Protocol on Subsidiarity and Proportionality to the Treaty of Amsterdam, which states that although, in principle, the administrative implementation of Community law is the responsibility of the Member States in accordance with their constitutional arrangements, this does not affect

---

[134] Case 50/76, *Amsterdam Bulb* [1977] ECR 137.

[135] Case 68/88, *Commission* v. *Greece*, above n. 133, at 2985; Case C–326/88, *Hansen & Søn* [1990] ECR I–2911.

[136] See Barents, above n. 119, 58–9.

[137] See, in general, Schwarze, above n. 112.

[138] Joined Cases 205–215/82, *Deutsche Milchkontor GmbH* v. *Germany*, above n. 133, at 2665–6. See also, *inter alia*, Case 68/88, *Commission* v. *Greece*, above n. 133, at 2984.

[139] See K. Lenaerts, "Regulating the Regulatory Process: 'delegation of powers' in the European Community" (1993) 18 *ELR* 25 and as regards the CAP, Barents, above n. 119, at 63.

the supervisory, monitoring and implementing powers of the Community as provided under Articles 145 and 155.[140]

3.3. The Legal Basis of Community Implementation

By virtue of their institutional character, Articles 145, third indent, and 155, fourth indent, however, may not be used as the sole legal basis for Community health and safety measures. The question, therefore, arises whether the Treaty provisions lay down an adequate legal basis which allows for the implementation of measures by the Community institutions. Examination must hereby focus upon the Treaty Articles tackled in the previous chapter. Above all, this raises the question whether these Articles distinguish between general (legislative) measures and individual measures in the application of these rules to individual cases (implementing measures).

3.3.1. *Harmonisation under Article 100a*

As argued in Chapter 1, Article 100a includes broad discretionary powers which allow for the valid adoption of many acts regulating health and safety issues. However, it is controversial whether the concept of harmonisation under Article 100a also includes the adoption of implementing measures which apply rules to a specific case. For example, some observers perceive a "crisis of the harmonisation model" and argue that this model is no longer an appropriate means of addressing the problems which the Community currently faces.[141] However, here it is viewed that harmonisation measures do not distinguish between general and individual measures, and thus between legislative and implementation powers, and that by virtue of their discretionary powers under Article 100a, the Community institutions may determine which types of harmonisation measures are needed to achieve the internal market.

Under the general definition given in Chapter 1, the notion of harmonisation entails the creation of rules through a Community act and does not differentiate between legislation or implementation. Such an interpretation is primarily to be derived from the wording of Article 100a which speaks of "measures" in general. Furthermore, Article 100a explicitly refers to the approximation of administrative provisions in addition to those laid down by law or regulation.[142]

The question whether Article 100a differentiates between general and individual acts, the latter falling outside the scope of harmonisation, was tackled in *Germany* v. *Council*.[143] In this case, the Court had to consider the inextricable link between the pursuit of the internal market goal and regulatory intervention

---

[140] Declaration no. 43 on the Amsterdam Treaty.
[141] See the doubts expressed by Dehousse, above n. 74, at 49.
[142] See Jacobs AG in Case C–359/92, *Germany* v. *Council*, above n. 3, at I–3692/3693.
[143] Case C–359/92, above n. 3.

to ensure health and safety protection, the two aspects being brought together in the General Product Safety Directive.[144] Where, during the drafting of this Directive, Germany had demonstrated strong reluctance about its adoption, it came as no surprise that shortly after its adoption Germany attacked its validity. In essence the German government argued that Article 100a provides no legal basis for a provision in Article 9 of the Directive which empowers the Commission to adopt, in emergency situations, decisions requiring Member States to take certain specific actions on products which present a serious and immediate risk to the health and safety of consumers. In its view, the sole aim of Article 100 ff. of the Treaty and, in particular, Article 100a(1), was the approximation of laws, which would not include the power to apply the law in individual cases. The latter measures should be left to the national authorities. Not surprisingly, the Court rejected this argument. It acknowledged that in certain areas and, in particular, that of product safety, the approximation of general rules might not suffice to ensure the unity of the market. Consequently, the notion of "measures for the approximation" was to be interpreted as:

> "encompassing the Council's power to lay down measures relating to a specific product or class of products and, if necessary, individual measures concerning those products".[145]

In answer to Germany's analogy to the division of powers under the German Constitution, the Court further replied that the rules regulating the relationship between the Member States and the Community were different in character from those governing relations between the *Bund* and the *Länder*.[146]

In this judgment, the Court confirmed that the harmonisation model does not distinguish between measures of a "legislative" nature and measures of a mere "individual" character. The harmonisation model might also be used for implementing measures which empower the Commission to adopt individual measures in specific cases, and thus definitively departs from more "classical" notions of harmonisation, which would only see to the approximation of national measures of a more general "legislative" nature and allow for the Member States to continue to apply their national, albeit harmonised, legisla-

---

[144]   Case C–359/92, above n. 3.

[145]   *Ibid.*, at I–3711, para. 37. Jacobs AG, however, agreed with the distinction between the harmonisation measures on the one hand and measures of application, and, on the other, as drawn by the German government. He took the view that Art. 100a is concerned exclusively with the harmonisation of national provisions. The application of uniform rules, adopted under Art. 100a, to individual cases would therefore be a matter for national authorities. Nevertheless, he arrived at the conclusion that decisions adopted under Art. 9 of the Directive are measures of harmonisation as they require *each* Member State to ensure that *all* instances of the product in question are withdrawn from the market. In his view, a decision under Art. 9 lays down a uniform rule which is to be applied by the authorities of the Member States. In addition, the fact that a decision might be of individual concern to a particular undertaking would not in itself prevent such a decision from being a harmonisation measure, as long as its function is to harmonise national provisions for the benefit of the internal market: Opinion, above n. 3, paras. 37–8.

[146]   Above, n. 3, para. 38.

tion. Harmonisation may thus still prove important and constitute a flexible tool suited to present needs.

3.3.2. *Other Relevant Provisions*

The other Articles which govern the adoption of acts implementing health and safety regulation, in particular Articles 129a and 235, do not make specific reference to the notion of harmonisation, and instead generally empower the Community institutions to adopt "measures" (Articles 129a(1) and 235) and "specific action" (Article 129a(2)).[147] If viewed in the light of the Court's judgment in the *General Product Safety* case, the wording of these Articles suggests that they likewise provide a dual legal basis which allows for both legislative and implementing measures of a more individual character, which, in the absence of a hierarchy of norms, take the form of the decisions referred to in Article 189.[148] For example, the introduction of a Community information system on home and leisure accidents which both forms a fundamental part of consumer protection policy and is necessary to support and complement the policy carried out by the Member States, may be based on Article 129a(2).[149]

4. THE IMPLICATIONS OF THE PRINCIPLES OF SUBSIDIARITY AND PROPORTIONALITY FOR THE DEEPENING OF COMMUNITY ACTIVITIES IN HEALTH AND SAFETY REGULATION

The preceding sections clearly established that there is a need for the Community to engage more deeply in health and safety regulation and determined that the Treaty offers various provisions as the correct legal basis for it. This leaves an important question to be answered: to what extent may the Community employ its powers in this field? This question must now be measured against the two principles laid down in the second and third paragraphs of Article 3b: the subsidiarity and proportionality principles which, to a certain degree, overlap.

---

[147] See Chap. 1.

[148] The Commission's proposal for a hierarchy of norms to be included in the Maastricht Treaty was not accepted. At the conclusion of the Maastricht Treaty the IGC agreed, however, that IGC to be convened in 1996 would examine this issue; Declaration of the IGC on the hierarchy of Community acts. See G. Winter (ed.), *Sources and Categories of Europan Union Law: A Comparative and Reform Perspective* (Baden-Baden, 1995).

[149] European Parliament and Council Dec. 3092/94/EC, above n. 106.

4.1. The Subsidiarity Principle

4.1.1. The Introduction of the Subsidiarity Principle by the Maastricht Treaty

Article 3b of the Maastricht Treaty makes a great concession, explicitly stating that Community competences are limited and must be exercised in accordance with the principle of subsidiarity, "the word that saved Maastricht".[150] This principle reflects the Member States' reluctance to accept the Community's assumption of greater powers.[151] It thus counterbalances the TEU's increase in the number of areas governed by majority voting, and the introduction of "new" Community competences, such as consumer protection and public health.

The principle of subsidiarity is by no means a novel concept and may be traced back to Roman Catholic origins.[152] In the Community context, subsidiarity was to become a guiding principle for the future development of the Community, following a 1988 meeting between Jacques Delors and the representatives of the German *Länder* in which Jacques Delors became a subsidiarity "convert" after hearing the *Länder*'s concerns about the preservation of their own powers.[153] Not surprisingly, the elevation of this principle to a general principle of Community law[154] by Article 3b of the Maastricht Treaty, has given rise to furious debate on its significance.[155] Article 3b reads as follows:

---

[150] D.Z. Cass, "The Word that Saves Maastricht? The Principle of Subsidiarity and the Division of Powers within the European Community" (1992) 29 *CMLRev.* 1107–36.

[151] See R. Dehousse, "Community Competences: Are there Limits to Growth?", in R. Dehousse (ed.), *Europe after Maastricht. An Ever Closer Union?* (Munich, 1994), 107.

[152] For more details on the Roman-Catholic origins of the principle of subsidiarity, see, for instance, L.S.M. Besselink/H.S.J. Albers/W.T. Eijsbouts, "Subsidiarity in Non-federal Contexts: The Netherlands and the European Union" (1994) 42 *SEW* 5, 275–320; N. Emiliou, "Subsidiarity: An Effective Barrier Against 'the Enterprises of Ambition?'" (1992) 17 *ELR* 383–407; P.J.G. Kapteyn, "Community Law and the Principle of Subsidiarity" [1991] *Revue des Affaires européennes* 35–43; M. Wilke/H. Wallace, *Subsidiarity: Approaches to Power-sharing in the European Community*, Discussion Paper 27 (London, 1990).

[153] Wilke/Wallace, above n. 152, 3–5; Kapteyn, above n. 152, 37–8.

[154] Before its inception as a general principle in the Community setting, the subsidiarity principle was already laid down in Art. 130r in relation to Community environmental policy, as amended by the SEA, which stipulated that "[t]he Community shall take action relating to the environment to the extent to which the objectives referred to in para. 1 can be attained better at Community level than at the level of the individual Member States". The draft TEU designed by the European Parliament had already referred to the principle of subsidiarity [1984] OJ C77/33.

[155] See R. Barents, "De wijzigingen van het materiïle EEG-recht" (1992) 40 *SEW* 8/9, 684–701; Besselink/Albers/Eijsbouts, above n. 152; Cass, above n. 150; Dehousse, above n. 151; Emiliou, above n. 152; L.A. Geelhoed, "Het subsidiariteitsbeginsel: een communautair principe?" (1991) 39 *SEW* 7/8, 422–35; P.J.G. Kapteyn, "De complexe rechtsorde van het Unieverdrag: subsidiariteitsbeginsel en nieuwe bevoegdheden", in K. Hellingman (ed.), *Europa in de steigers: van Gemeenschap tot Unie* (Deventer, 1993), 41–52; K. Lenaerts, "Subsidiarity and Community Competence in the Field of Education" (1994–5) 1 *Columbia Journal of European Law* 1, 1–28; K. Lenaerts/P. Van Ypersele, "Le principe de subsidiarité et son contexte: étude de l'article 3B du Traité CE" (1994) 30 *CDE* 3–85; J. Palacio Gonzalez, "The Principle of Subsidiarity (A Guide for Lawyers with a Particular Community Orientation)" (1995) 20 *ELR* 355–70; A.G. Toth, "A Legal Analysis of Subsidiarity", in D. O'Keeffe/P.M. Twomey (eds.), *Legal Issues of the Maastricht Treaty* (London, 1994), 37–48. Very critical on introduction of the subsidiarity principle in the Treaty is Kapteyn,

"The Community shall act within the limits of the powers conferred upon it by this Treaty and of the objectives assigned to it therein.

In areas which do not fall within its exclusive competence, the Community shall take action, in accordance with the principle of subsidiarity, only if and in so far as the objectives of the proposed action cannot be sufficiently achieved by the Member States and can therefore, by reason of the scale or effects of the proposed action, be better achieved by the Community.

Any action by the Community shall not go beyond what is necessary to achieve the objectives of this Treaty".

It is evident that all three paragraphs of Article 3b aim to regulate Community activities, although their exact meaning has given rise to uncertainty. Article 3b encompasses three elements: it reiterates the principle of attributed powers, formerly restricted to Article 4 EEC (first paragraph); it lays down the principle of subsidiarity (second paragraph); and it codifies the principle of proportionality, already developed by the Court (third paragraph).[156] As recently confirmed by the Amsterdam Protocol on Subsidiarity and Proportionality, the principle of subsidiarity does not call into question the powers conferred on the Community by the Treaty as interpreted by the Court.

4.1.2. Criteria

As stated in the preamble to the TEU, the European Union, in its attempt to create an ever closer Union among the peoples of Europe, will adopt decisions "as closely as possible to the citizen in accordance with the principle of subsidiarity".[157] In fields not falling under the exclusive jurisdiction of the Community, the principle of subsidiarity determines that Community action is only possible if the objectives of the proposed action cannot be sufficiently achieved by the Member States and, for reasons of scale or effects, can consequently be better achieved by the Community. The literature identifies two tests for the application of the principle of subsidiarity: (a) the "more effective attainment" test, which determines that Community institutions may take action only if and in so far as the objectives of the proposed action cannot be sufficiently achieved by the Member States; and (b) the "better attainment" test, based upon the analogous application of Article 130r(4) combined with a "cross boundary dimension",[158] which stipulates that Community action is appropriate if the proposed measure

who argues that: "[i]n a system of limited powers conferred on the Community for the realisation of a limited objective, namely the establishment and operation of a common market, the importation of the subsidiarity principle is redundant, confusing and dangerous because it calls in question the system laid down in the Treaty and deprives the logic of functional integration of its driving force": Kapteyn, above n. 152, at 39.

[156] See also, in this sense, the Council Conclusions of the Edinburgh Summit of 1992, Bull. EC 12–1992, Annex 1 to part A: *Overall Approach to the Application of the Subsidiarity Principle and Article 3B of the Treaty on European Union*, 13–14; Barents, above n. 155, at 687; Lenaerts, above n. 155, at 2.

[157] See the preamble to the TEU. See also Art. A of this Treaty.

[158] Referring to the size or the dimension of the tasks extending beyond the national borders.

can, for reasons of scale or effects, be better achieved at the Community level.[159] In a Communication of October 1992 on the principle of subsidiarity, the Commission[160] labels these two tests, the "comparative efficiency test"[161] and the "value added test".[162] The Amsterdam Protocol on Subsidiarity and Proportionality finally lays down a three step approach, already set out by the European Council in Birmingham, when applying the subsidiarity principle: (1) the issue has transnational aspects which cannot satisfactorily be regulated by Member States' action; (2) actions by Member States or lack of Community action would conflict with Treaty requirements or would otherwise significantly damage Member States' interests; (3) Community action would produce clear benefits by reason of its greater scale or effects compared with action by the Member States.

In the case of health and safety regulation, the indissoluble link between market integration and health and safety protection generally determines that it will not be difficult for the Community to demonstrate that Community action is required. Application of the three criteria of the Amsterdam Protocol will generally result in the confirmation that regulation of the health and safety aspects of products has transnational elements which, in combination with the free movement requirement, will not be satisfactorily regulated by Member State action, thus necessitating Community action. For example, the adoption by the Community institutions of measures in emergency situations where products present a serious and immediate risk to the health and safety of persons, may be justified by the fact that in view of the need both to protect health and safety and the internal market, this risk may only be effectively eliminated through Community measures.[163] Furthermore, where administrative co-operation and mutual confidence between administrations have not sufficed to ensure the effective implementation of internal market legislation in specific fields of health and safety regulation, a need for action at the Community level is easily demonstrated. This is true, for example, in the area of medicinal products, where the need for Community action on the authorisation of medicinal products has clearly been necessary both to achieve an internal market for pharmaceuticals and to protect human health effectively.[164] Seen in this light, the subsidiarity principle is not likely to hinder the deepening of Community health and safety regulation.[165]

[159] Emiliou, above n. 152, at 401. In this sense, see also Dehousse, above n. 151, at 111; Kapteyn, above n. 152, 40 ff.

[160] Communication of the Commission to the Council and the European Parliament on the principle of subsidiarity, SEC(92)1990 final, 10 ff.

[161] Checking whether the Member States have at their disposal the means to the end to be achieved.

[162] Assessing the effectiveness of the Community action.

[163] See Art. 9 of the General Product Safety Dir., above n. 3. See also Communication from the Commission to the Council, the European Parliament and the Economic and Social Committee on the handling of urgent situations in the context of implementation of Community rules: follow-up to the Sutherland report, COM(93)430 final.

[164] See further Chap. 4.

[165] See, in this context, Declaration no. 43 relating to the Protocol on Subsidiarity and Proportionality to the Treaty of Amsterdam.

4.1.3. *Justiciability of Subsidiarity?*

The fact that these tests are carried out by policy-makers leaves much room for political discretion, and it therefore appears likely that the choices made will be political ones.[166] The subsidiarity principle has therefore generally been held to be a political rather than a legal principle.[167] This political character raises the question whether subsidiarity is truly justiciable.[168] In view of this essentially subjective character, it is likely that the Court will have great difficulty in examining whether Community measures respect subsidiarity in substance. Just as in cases of broadly formulated discretionary powers attributed to the Community in various Treaty provisions, the Court will probably opt for a "marginal" review of measures.[169] This will lead to a greater emphasis upon the duty to state reasons[170] and the legal basis requirement. Indeed, a recent case, *Germany v. European Parliament and the Council*,[171] explicitly addressed the principle of subsidiarity in relation to the obligation to state reasons. In this case, Germany attacked the validity of the European Parliament and Council Directive on deposit-guarantee schemes. Among the grounds for annulment of the Directive in question, Germany brought up the failure to explain Community action as regards its conformity with subsidiarity. Examining (superficially) the recitals of this Directive, however, the Court concluded that the Council and Parliament had fulfilled their duty. Therefore, it may be argued that whenever the Court is called upon to judge subsidiarity, it will engage in scrutinising the compliance with the duty to state reasons and in examining the measure on the basis of manifest errors or misuse of powers (marginal review).[172]

This determines that in the context of health and safety regulation, where the broad discretionary powers of the Community institutions under Article 100a or 235 commonly provide the legal basis, the Court will restrict itself to a limited review of the Community measure in question. The Court is similarly likely to restrict itself to a marginal review of whether a measure is in conformity with

---

[166] Kapteyn, above n. 152, at 41.

[167] Barents, above n. 155, at 688; Dehousse, above n. 151. By the same author, see also: *Does subsidiarity really matter?* EUI Working Paper LAW 92/32 (Florence, 1993); Emiliou, above n. 152, at 406; Geelhoed, above n. 155; House of Lords Select Committee on the European Communities, *Report on Political Union. Law-Making Powers and Procedures*, Session 1990–1, 17th report (London, 1991), in particular at point 165; H.-W. Micklitz/Ch. Roethe/S. Weatherill, *Federalism and Responsibility. A Study on Product Safety Law and Practice in the European Community* (London/Dordrecht/Boston, 1994), 32.

[168] See, in this context, in particular, Emiliou, above n. 152, 402 ff; Lenaerts/Van Ypersele, above n. 155; and A.G. Toth, "Is Subsidiarity Justiciable?" (1994) 19 *ELR* 268–85.

[169] See also sect. 4.2.

[170] See Kapteyn, above n. 155, 48–9; P. VerLoren van Themaat, "De rol van beginselen bij de integratie van geografische economische, sociale en politieke systemen en bij de integratie van vakgebieden", in K. Hellingman (ed.), *Europa in de steigers: van Gemeenschap tot Unie* (Deventer, 1993), 133. In this sense also R. Dehousse, "Centralisation and Decentralisation in the European Community" in K. Hailbronner (ed.), *Europa der Zukunft—Zentrale und decentrale Lösungsansätze* (Köln, 1994), 33–44.

[171] Case C–233/94, [1997] ECR I–240.

[172] See Emiliou, above n. 152, at 405.

the principle of proportionality. In addition, even where no reference is made to the discretionary powers of the Community under Article 100a or 235, it is important to recall that the Court has confirmed that Community action in adopting measures in emergency situations relating to dangerous products is appropriate and not excessive in relation to the underlying objectives of health and safety protection and the proper functioning of the internal market.[173]

4.2. The Proportionality Principle

Much of what has been said about the subsidiarity principle may also be true for the proportionality principle, elevated to general Community law by the third paragraph of Article 3b. Yet, the proportionality principle is mainly restricted to a problem of means and ends, and does not necessitate complex efficiency tests for its application.[174] In accordance with this provision, the Community may not take action that goes beyond what is necessary to achieve the objectives of the Treaty. This principle is also enunciated in the second paragraph of Article 3b on subsidiarity which requires that the Community may take action only to the degree that the objectives of the proposed action cannot sufficiently be achieved by the Member States.[175] The proportionality principle was already a part of Community law, being introduced and developed by the Court in its jurisprudence.[176] In Case 15/83, *Denkavit*, the Court defined the principle as meaning that a Community measure must not exceed what is appropriate and necessary to attain the objective pursued.[177] In applying the principle, the Court generally examines whether the means applied by a Community measure correspond to "the importance of the aim, and . . . whether they are necessary for its achievement".[178] However, where Community institutions possess wide discretionary powers, the Court consistently applies a somewhat deferential proportionality test, and solely examines whether the relevant Community measure is vitiated by manifest error, misuse of powers, or a clear case of *ultra*

---

[173]   Case C–359/92, above n. 3, at I–3713–15.

[174]   Dehousse, above n. 151, 114–15.

[175]   Lenaerts considers the two appearances of the proportionality principle as due to an error in the drafting process: Lenaerts, above n. 155, at 25. Albeit some differences in emphasis in the two provisions exist, the European Council of Edinburgh has given a single interpretation to this principle meaning that any burden resting upon the Community, national (local) authorities, economic operators and citizens should be minimised and proportionate to the objective to be achieved; Community measures should leave room for national decisions as much as possible, whilst such measures should provide Member States with alternative ways to achieve the objectives of the measure: Conclusions of the Presidency, Bull. EC, 12–1992, Annex I to part A, at 20.

[176]   See, in general, N. Emiliou, *The Principle of Proportionality in European Law: A Comparative Study* (The Hague, 1996) and G. De Búrca, "The Principle of Proportionality and its Application in EC Law" (1993) 13 *YEL* 105–50.

[177]   [1984] ECR 2171, at 2175. See also Case C–174/89, *Hoche* [1990] ECR I–2681, para. 19, and Case C–359/92, above n. 3, para. 44.

[178]   See, for instance, Case C–118/89, *Lingenfelser* [1990] ECR I–2637; Case C–155/89, *Philipp Brothers* [1990] ECR I–330.

vires.[179] As argued above, this test will be generally applied to health and safety issues.

5. THE INSTITUTIONAL BALANCE OF POWERS

5.1. The Principle of the Institutional Balance of Powers

Any deepening of Community action in health and safety matters must also respect the institutional balance of powers laid down in the Treaty.[180] This principle dates back to the early days of the Community. It was introduced for the first time by the Court in the *Meroni* cases of 1958.[181] In these cases, the Court held that Article 3 of the ECSC Treaty (which is analogous to Article 4 EC) lays down "a balance of powers which is characteristic of the institutional structure of the Community". According to the Court, this balance of powers was a fundamental guarantee for the subjects of the Community, in particular, undertakings and associations of undertakings.[182] Subsequently, the Court also applied this principle to the E(E)C context, particularly in relation to Article 4, which requires that the five Community institutions carry out the tasks entrusted to the Community, whilst each institution must act within the limits of the powers conferred upon it by the Treaty. At present, it has acquired a central place within the Community legal system.[183] In the Court's view:

"[t]he Treaties set up a system for distributing powers among the different institutions of the Community, assigning to each institution its own role in the institutional structure of the Community and the accomplishment of the tasks entrusted to the Community".[184]

The principle of the institutional balance thus dictates that:

"each institution must exercise its powers with due regard for the powers of the other institutions. It also requires that it should be possible to penalise any breach of that rule which may occur".[185]

---

[179] See, for instance, Case C–331/88, *The Queen v. The Minister for Agriculture, Fisheries and Food and the Secretary of State for Health, ex parte Fedesa and others (Fedesa)* [1990] ECR I–4023; Case C–405/92, *Etablissements Armand Mondiet SA v. Armement Islais SARL (Mondiet)* [1993] ECR I–6133; Case C–280/93, *Germany v. Council* [1994] ECR I–4973.

[180] See, in general on this principle, G. Guillermin, "Le principe de l'équilibre institutionnel dans la jurisprudence de la Cour de Justice des Communautés européennes" (1992) 119 *Journal du droit international* 319–46 and S. Prechal, "Institutioneel evenwicht: balanceren op een onzichtbaar koord" (1991) 40 *Ars Aequi* 934–43.

[181] Case 9/56, *Meroni & Co., Industrie Metallurgiche S.p.A. v. High Authority* [1957–8] ECR 133 and Case 10/56, *Meroni & Co., Industrie Metallurgiche S.p.A. v. High Authority* [1957–8] ECR 157.

[182] Case 9/56, above n. 181, at 152; Case 10/56, above n. 181, at 173.

[183] See, e.g., Case 25/70, *Köster*, above n. 118 and Case 30/70, *Scheer*, above n. 118; Case 294/83, *Parti écologiste "Les Verts" v. European Parliament* [1986] ECR 1339; Case 149/85, *Wybot v. Faure* [1986] ECR 2391; Case 34/86, *Council v. Parliament* [1986] ECR 2155.

[184] Case C–70/88, *Parliament v. Council (Chernobyl)* [1990] ECR I–2041, at I–2072 (para. 21).

[185] *Ibid.*, para. 22.

This means that for the implementation of its health and safety measures, particular importance is to be attached to the power of the Commission to implement the rules laid down by the Council (and Parliament) by virtue of Article 145, third indent.[186]

5.2. The Principle of the Institutional Balance—More than a Re-statement of Article 4?

Notwithstanding the use of the term "balance", the principle of the institutional balance does not require that a true equilibrium be maintained between the institutions. According to the Court, the principle of the institutional balance of powers refers to the balance of powers created by the Treaty.[187] The principle is not always easy to apply since it has evolved alongside the Community, and has thus varied over time as the Treaties have been amended.[188] This variability has led to the criticism that the principle of the institutional balance of powers was a mere "snapshot" (*"Momentaufnahme"*) of the current division of competences and functions, and rejected it as not being a useful normative criterion.[189] However, the flexibility of the principle of the institutional balance does not necessarily frustrate its potential usefulness. In contrast, it may even be advantageous since, in this manner, the factual exercise of powers by the institutions may be taken into account, which may lead to the adaptation of the balance of powers by means of the creation of new institutions and/or the reinforcement or weakening of existing ones. In the national (Dutch) context, for example, attempts have been made to counterbalance the increasingly top-heavy nature of administration through the enhancement of parliamentary control, the quality of legislation, and the judicial review of administrative decisions.[190] This might also be applied in the Community context.

In its more recent case law in relation to the role of the Parliament amongst the other institutions, the Court has tended to indicate that the institutional balance of powers principle (of which the Court itself is a part in its policing task[191]) is

---

[186] See sect. 6.1.

[187] See, for instance, Case 109/75R, *National Carboning Company* v. *Commission* [1975] ECR 1193; Case 138/79, *SA Roquettes Frères* v. *Council* (*Isoglucose*) [1980] ECR 3333; Case 139/79, *Maizena GmbH* v. *Council* (*Isoglucose*) [1980] ECR 3393. See also Guillermin, above n. 180 and Prechal, above n. 180.

[188] Guillermin, above n. 180, 332–3. See also Prechal, above n. 180, at 941.

[189] T. Läufer, *Die Organe der EG—Rechtsetzung und Haushaltsverfahren zwischen Kooperation und Konflikt* (Bonn, 1990), 219–22.

[190] See, in the national (Dutch) context, W.J. Witteveen, *Evenwicht van machten* (Zwolle, 1991), 71–2.

[191] In particular, Case C–70/88, above n. 184, at I–2073. Prechal argues that the recognition by the Court of a limited right of appeal to the Parliament in order to ensure the institutional balance in this case has tilted the balance to a small extent in favour of the Court itself. Prechal, above n. 180, at 941.

something more than a mere restatement of Article 4.[192] As early as 1979, the consultation of the Parliament was considered by the Court to be an essential factor within the institutional balance. It viewed that the existence of the Parliament confirmed the Community's commitment to the fundamental democratic principle that the people should play a part in the exercise of power through an intermediary representative assembly.[193] Furthermore, whilst Article 173 EEC made no provision for the review of parliamentary acts, this did not prevent the Court from considering an appeal against an act of the Parliament.[194] This (*contre legem*) recognition of the "passive legitimation" of the Parliament was justified by the Court since, in the absence of judicial review, the measures adopted by the Parliament might encroach on the powers of the Member States or the other institutions or even be *ultra vires*.[195] Subsequently, the further step of assigning an active right of appeal to the Parliament was easily taken. In *Chernobyl*, the Court ruled that, since the Treaty assigned it the task of ensuring that the interpretation and application of the Treaty be in accordance with the law, it likewise needed to ensure the institutional balance, and was thus entitled to review whether parliamentary prerogatives had been observed. In the Court's opinion, the absence of an explicit provision assigning the Parliament the right of appeal might very well create a procedural vacuum, but this could not be allowed to negate the fundamental interest that the institutional balance laid down in the Treaty be observed.[196] Today, this case law has been codified by Article 173.[197]

5.3. Functions of the Principle of Institutional Balance

It follows from the preceding sections that the principle of the institutional balance ensures that the Community institutions do not step outside the boundaries of the powers conferred upon them by the Treaty. It, therefore, may be said to find its legal expression in the legal basis requirement which likewise fulfils this guarantee function.[198] By demanding that the institutions respect each other's powers, the principle of institutional balance thus constitutes a guarantee for the rights and competences of the actors within the Community legal order. In addition, it may also be said to reinforce the Community Rule of

---

[192] See Rodrigues, who argues that with the judgment in Case C–70/88, above n. 184, the observance of the institutional balance has been attributed a high-ranking position: G.C. Rodrigues, "Der Gerichtshof der Europäischen Gemeinschaften als Verfassungsgericht" (1992) 27 *EuR* 3, 233.

[193] See the *Isoglucose* cases (Case 138/79, at 3360 and Case 139/79, at 3424), above n. 187 and, more recently, Case C–65/93, *Parliament v. Council* [1995] ECR I–643.

[194] *Les Verts*, above n. 183.

[195] *Ibid.*, at 1366.

[196] Case C–70/88, above n. 184, at I–2073. Shortly before this judgment, however, the Court had still rejected this right: see Case 302/87, *Parliament v. Council (Comitology)* [1988] ECR 5615.

[197] See, as regards the prerogatives of the Parliament, Case C–316/91, *Parliament v. Council* [1994] ECR I–625; Case C–156/93, *Parliament v. Commission* [1995] ECR I–2019; and Case C–303/94, *Parliament v. Council* [1996] ECR I–2943.

[198] See Chap. 1.

Law[199] in so far as the measures of both its Member States and its institutions cannot escape the judicial review of the Court.[200] It thus not only entails a horizontal guarantee that the institutions do not step outside the powers allocated to them by the Treaty, thus encroaching upon the powers of the other institutions, but also safeguards the status of Member States and their citizens, both being "subjects" of Community law,[201] ensuring that Community institutions never act *ultra vires*. Thus, the institutional balance principle also offers a guarantee that the rights of Community citizens will be protected.[202]

5.4. The Principle of the Institutional Balance and the *Trias Politica*

In this way, the institutional balance principle functions as a guarantee to the Member States and to the citizens of Member States, protecting them against any misuse of power by the Community institutions. It guarantees the system of "checks and balances" laid down in the Treaty. The principle of the institutional balance of powers, as developed by the Court, thus bears a strong resemblance to the *trias politica* doctrine when it is understood as a balance rather than a separation of powers.[203]

---

[199] See, for instance, *Les Verts*, above n. 183, in which the Court explicitly ruled that the European Community is a Community based on the rule of law in so far as both its Member States and its institutions cannot avoid judicial review of the measures adopted by them in conformity with the Treaty, which is the constitutional charter of the Community. The Court reiterated this view in *Opinion 1/91*, above n. 123.

[200] In this sense, Guillermin, above n. 180, 344–6. See also Rodrigues, above n. 192.

[201] See for instance Case 26/62, *Van Gend en Loos* [1963] ECR 1 and, more recently, *Opinion 1/91* (above n. 123) in which the Court held that "As the Court of Justice consistently has held, the Community treaties established a new legal order for the benefit of which States have limited their sovereign rights, in ever wider fields, and the subjects of which comprise not only the Member States but also their nationals".

[202] *Meroni* cases, above n. 181.

[203] In the national context alongside the separation of powers principle, other interpretations of the *trias politica* exist. These equally adhere to the basic idea of protecting the liberties of individuals against a concentration of powers in one single authority, but rather focus on relationships and interconnections between the branches. See, for the interpretation of the *trias politica* as a balance of powers, recently, Witteveen, above n. 190. See also P.L. Strauss, "The Place of Agencies in Government: Separation of Powers and the Fourth Branch" (1984) 84 *Columbia Law Review* 573–669. Such an interpretation of *trias politica* as requiring a balance of powers instead of a separation of powers was already advanced within the American context by Hamilton, Madison and Jay under the pseudonym "Publius" in 1787 (see also the ideas of Smith in his Lectures on jurisprudence of 1762–6). They proposed a political structure in which autonomous state organs control each other: a system of checks and balances. Their thoughts have been published in a series of newspapers, the Federalist Papers: see C. Rossiter (ed.), *The Federalists Papers* (1787) (New York, 1961). In contrast to separation of powers, the balance of powers or checks and balances idea does not suppose a radical division of government into three parts, with specific functions precisely divided among them. Rather, it seeks both an effective independence and interdependence between the various actors: Strauss, at 578. Such an interpretation is, as Witteveen convincingly argues, in accordance with Montesquieu's device of *"le pouvoir arrête le pouvoir"*. Wittenveen points out that even where Montesquieu discusses separation of powers in chap. 6 of Book XI, he already gives important exceptions to a strict separation of powers, which may be interpreted as visualising a balanced constitution. Such a reading is reinforced where Montesquieu observes that *"Ces trois puissances*

Upon closer analysis, however, salient differences do in fact emerge. The unique Community institutional structure was designed in the mid-twentieth century with the specific objective of allowing the Member States to achieve a common goal without necessarily abandoning their national interests.[204] The institutional structure of the Community and the division of tasks among the institutions, the Council, the Commission, the Parliament and the Court of Justice were primarily inspired by the concerns of the founding Member States that an autonomous organ, such as the Commission, should not become too powerful. Thus, the balance of powers enshrined within the Treaty seems to derive more from power interests than from a liberal political ideology.[205] However, though not designed to protect the liberties of individuals against a far too powerful state,[206] the Community's institutional structure was indeed created to avoid the concentration of powers within one single body, which is, in fact, the main element of the principle of the *trias politica*. In practice, the constitutional reality which exists within the Member States does indeed closely resemble that of the Community.[207] Therefore, despite its different origin, the institutional balance principle may be argued to function in the same manner as the principle of the *trias politica* does at national level.[208]

5.5. The Member States within the Institutional Balance of Powers

If the principle of the institutional balance is to capture the complexity of the Community structure fully, two further elements need to be taken into account: the other bodies created by the Treaty, in addition to the institutions, as well as the role played by the Member States within the Community setting. As regards the former point, it is generally recognised that, to a certain extent, the distinction between institutions and organs has been blurred, since various organs, with powers of their own, have been inserted into the Treaty.[209] Examples of

---

devraient former un repos ou une inaction. Mais comme, par le mouvement nécessaire des choses, elles sont contraintes d'aller, elles seront forcées d'aller de concert": Witteveen, above n. 190, 34 ff. Both Witteveen and Strauss therefore consider it more appropriate to adopt an interpretation of the *trias politica* as a balance of powers, in combination with a review of the functions to be carried out by the various actors.

[204]   Pescatore, above n. 113, at 406.

[205]   Dehousse, above n. 114, at 777.

[206]   See Pescatore, above n. 113.

[207]   De Witte, above n. 115, at 7. See also Everson, who compares the Community balance of powers with its American counterpart: above n. 113, at 197.

[208]   See, in this sense, albeit in comparison with the principle of separation of powers, Guillermin, above n. 180, at 344. As this principle constitutes a guarantee of rights and competences of the actors of the Community legal system, the author proposes to speak of *"le principe de la Communauté de droit"*. See equally Everson, above n. 113, at 197.

[209]   By distinguishing from *organs*, a terminology commonly used in public international law, the founders of the Rome Treaty wanted to express that the *institutions* possess discretionary powers, which may directly affect (bind) the citizens of the Community: see Kapteyn/VerLoren van Themaat *et al.*, above n. 117, at 190.

these are the European Investment Bank[210] and the future European Central Bank.[211] In its case law, the Court has already shown a degree of readiness to place such organs on a par with the institutions.[212]

As regards the Member States, the Court appears to interpret the institutional balance in a purely horizontal manner (a balance between the "institutions"), and does not include the Member States within it. However, the balance of powers between the Member States and the Community is of vital importance;[213] as argued earlier, the strict division of powers between the institutions may be argued to be a reflection of the Member States' concern that the integrity of their own powers be maintained and thus acts as a shield against too great an institutional concentration of powers, particularly within the hands of the Commission. Thus, a functional understanding of the institutional balance starts from questioning why specific powers have been distributed among which institutions and generally recognises that without Member State acceptance, it is impossible for the Community to develop or carry out regulatory policies. Therefore, the entire complexity of the Community structure may only be understood if the institutional balance of powers is widely defined. This definition must not only encompass the balance between the individual Community institutions, but must also include the balance between the Community and the Member States.

6. DIFFICULTIES FLOWING FROM THE INCREASING RELIANCE ON THE COMMISSION IN HEALTH AND SAFETY REGULATION

The deepening of Community involvement in health and safety regulation entails a fundamental shift from the national to the Community level. It leads to far greater Community activity, with a corresponding workload for the Community legislature. The delegation of greater power to the Commission originates from, and in a classical analysis is justified by,[214] the dual need for greater efficiency and a reduction in the work load of the Council/Parliament. Furthermore, the specific nature of risk regulation necessitates an intricate process of risk assessment and management, and a degree of flexibility, which is perhaps best supplied during the implementing phase; an institution such as the Commission is better adapted to these tasks than the Council, which must

---

[210] See Arts. 4b and 198d–e.

[211] See Arts. 4a and 105 ff.

[212] In Case C–370/89, *SGEEM* v. *European Investment Bank* [1992] ECR I–6211, for instance, the Court held that the term "institutions" in Art. 215 also covered Community organs such as the European Investment Bank. Such a readiness can also be read in the Court's judgment in *Les Verts*, above n. 183.

[213] See also Everson, above n. 113, 196–8.

[214] See in general on the issue of delegation of powers, for instance, Vereniging voor wetgeving en wetgevingsbeleid, *Delegatie van bevoegdheden* (Alphen aan de Rijn, 1992); including two preliminary reports of R.G. Mazel, "Delegatie van wetgevende bevoegdheid; de inhoud van het wetsbegrip", 9–45 and W.J. Witteveen, "Delegeren is communiceren", 46–98.

observe a cumbersome (co-decision) decision-making process (with the Parliament).

Yet, the greater reliance on the Commission is not without difficulties. As argued above, the delegation of powers to the Commission needs to respect the institutional balance of powers. In this context, the exact wording of Article 145, third indent, must be examined so as to establish the Commission's prerogatives relating to the implementation of Community policies. In addition, delegation of ever more discretionary powers to this institution results in an increasing move away from the legitimacy of the Community legislature which was obtained through the attribution of powers to the Community. Therefore, the increasing role of the Commission inevitably raises the concurrent problem of how to enhance legitimacy. Furthermore, the growing reliance on the Commission likewise places a greater burden upon it and reveals its limits in relation to the capacity and the supply of expertise and information. Whilst the following chapters will analyse the specific structures of health and safety regulation which the Community has established in an attempt to overcome these and other problems, this chapter will examine its more general features and requirements.

6.1. Delegation of Implementing Powers to the Commission

6.1.1. *The Concept of Delegation*

For the purpose of our analysis, the concept of delegation within the Community context[215] must first be defined. In the Treaty itself, no mention is made of delegation as such. However, the possibility that powers may be delegated is implicitly alluded to in Article 145, third indent, and Article 155, fourth indent.[216] These Articles stipulate that the Commission exercises the powers conferred on it by the Council for the implementation of the rules laid down by the latter. In its early case law, the Court was faced with this delegation issue. By virtue of its judgments in the famous *Meroni* cases of 1958, it seems that the Court distinguishes between a "true" delegation of the powers conferred upon the delegating authority, and a situation where the authority grants the powers to a delegate, the performance of which remains subject to oversight by the authority, which assumes full responsibility for the decisions of the delegate.[217] According to the Court, in the latter situation no "true" delegation takes place.

---

[215] See Schindler, who points out that a common notion of delegation in the Member States does not exist: P. Schindler, *Delegation von Zuständigkeiten in der Europäischen Gemeinschaft* (Baden-Baden, 1972), 54–68.

[216] See H.H Maas, "Delegatie van bevoegdheden in de Europese Gemeenschappen" (1967) 15 *SEW* 3. See also J.V. Louis, "Delegatie van bevoegdheden in de Europese Gemeenschappen" (1978) 26 *SEW* 12, 802–14. See, in this context, in particular Case 16/88, *Commission* v. *Council*, above n. 129.

[217] *Meroni* cases, above n. 181, at 147–9 and at 169–71.

Delegation of powers may accordingly be defined as the transfer of powers from one organ to another, which the latter exercises under its own responsibility. Delegation must be distinguished from *attribution*. This concept arises where the Treaty confers a particular power upon an institution; a power which the institution exercises under its own responsibility. As argued in Chapter 1, the principle of attributed powers thus refers to the powers conferred upon each institution by the Treaty. Legally speaking, the field of health and safety regulation entails both such situations: attribution and delegation of powers: further powers—in particular the powers to implement Community law—are shifted from the Member State to the Community level, where the Community legislature decides which powers are to be delegated to the Commission. In practice, however, this means that health and safety regulation and its implementation are shifted from the Member States to the Commission.

6.1.2. The Introduction of Article 145, Third Indent, by the Single European Act

The Paris Summit of 1974 highlighted the importance that full use be made of the Treaty which allowed the implementing powers to be delegated to the Commission. Subsequent to the failure of the "traditional approach", the need for more efficient and faster decision-making prompted the reconsideration of Article 155, fourth indent. In 1978, in its Communication to the Council entitled "The transitional period and the institutional implications of the enlargement" (Fresco I), the Commission suggested for the first time that its executing tasks might be enlarged.[218] It suggested amending Article 155 into a general competence to exercise administrative and executive competences, though leaving the Council with sufficient room to oversee such activity. The Council would, therefore, retain the possibility, in politically sensitive cases, of deciding for itself. Alternatively, the Council would provide for oversight of Commission activities by means of supervisory committees, in accordance with already established procedures.[219] Although not directly responding to the proposals made by the Commission, the Report on the European Institutions by the Committee of Three (Biesheuvel, Dell and Marjolin)[220] subsequently suggested the "rationalisation" of Council work and proposed the drawing up of standard formulae covering each distinct category of committee; formulae which might be inserted into new decisions involving the delegation of powers.

In its "Fresco II" Communication, the Commission combined the ideas contained in Fresco I with the Report of the Three Wise Men, and proposed the amendment of Article 155 to lay down an implementing power for the

---

[218] Suppl. Bull. EC 2/78, at 16.
[219] These procedures will be discussed in Chap. 3. The Spinelli project proposed to confer a very large executive competence to the Commission. See R. Bieber/J.P. Jacqué/J.H.H. Weiler, *L'Europe de demain*, coll. "Perspectives européennes" (Luxembourg, 1985), at 31.
[220] 13th General Report on the activities of the European Communities (1979), at 27.

Commission, subject to the assent of the Council, and also put forward four formulae which the Council might use to subject the exercise of implementing powers by the Commission to conditions.[221] During the IGC on the SEA, the Commission presented a proposal for the amendment of Article 155, similar to that made in its Fresco II Communication. The IGC recognised the need to confer more powers upon the Commission and, at the same time, underlined the need to rationalise the work of the Council through the stipulation of the conditions which the Commission was obliged to respect. It nevertheless decided to opt for a more cautious approach and inserted a construction into Article 145 which explicitly obliged the Council to confer each implementation power upon the Commission, instead of granting the Commission a general, autonomous, power of implementation.[222] This compromise text, as eventually inserted by the SEA, stipulates that the Council shall:

> "confer on the Commission, in the acts which the Council adopts, powers for the implementation of the rules which the Council lays down. The Council may impose certain requirements in respect of the exercise of these powers. The Council may also reserve the right, in specific cases, to exercise directly implementing powers itself. The procedures referred to above must be consonant with principles and rules to be laid down in advance by the Council, acting unanimously on a proposal from the Commission and after obtaining the Opinion of the European Parliament".

Both the Maastricht and the Amsterdam Treaties left this provision untouched.

6.1.3. The Scope of Delegation

The extent to which the Council may delegate powers to the Commission has long been disputed. It was unclear whether the Council was obliged to lay down, in the main regulation, the exact content and extent of the rule-making powers to be delegated to the Commission,[223] or whether it only needed to lay down general rules. Enlightenment in this matter was supplied by the Court. In its well-known *Rey Soda* judgment, the Court rejected the notion that the power of the Commission might be restricted to an executive competence, allowing it to execute only pre-determined rules.[224] The Court emphasised that where the Council had conferred broad powers upon the Commission, the limits of these powers were primarily to be determined according to the general objectives of the organisation of the market, and not through too great regard for the literal meaning of the authorisation.[225] As explained above, the Court yet again

---

[221] C.-D. Ehlermann, "Compétences d'exécution conférées à la Commission—la nouvelle décision-cadre du Conseil" (1988) 316 *RMC* 233. See, equally, W. Nicoll, "Qu'est-ce que la comitologie?" (1987) 306 *RMC* 168.

[222] Ehlermann, above n. 221, at 234.

[223] Maas, above n. 216, at 3.

[224] Case 23/75, *Rey Soda* v. *Cassa Conguaglio Zucchero*, above n. 120.

[225] *Ibid.*, at 1301.

determined that the concept of implementation used in Article 155 be given a broad interpretation;[226] an interpretation confirmed, in particular, in the *Fisheries* case.[227]

In *Köster*, the Court had already decided that the interpretation of the powers conferred on the Commission had to take into account the system and the objectives of the authorisation and the regulation as such.[228] In this case, the Court drew from the distinction between measures based on the Treaty and measures deriving from it which were intended to ensure its implementation, the conclusion that the Council could not be required to draw up all details of all regulations in accordance with the procedures laid down by the Treaty. According to the Court, the Council would need only to adopt the fundamental elements of the matter concerned, while the Commission might determine detailed implementation rules.[229] This ruling has been confirmed in recent case law.[230] This means that the Commission can be delegated broad powers.

6.1.4. Delegation of Implementing Powers to the Commission and the Institutional Balance of Powers

The need to respect the institutional balance raises the question of the exact nature of the delegation. Must the exercise of the implementing powers by the Commission be considered to be the Commission's prerogative? In other words, does Article 145 oblige the Council to delegate powers to the Commission? The wording of Article 145 third indent, "the Council shall confer on the Commission", indicates that it entails more than a mere authorisation to delegate, and instead places an obligation upon the Council to delegate "powers for the implementation of the rules which it lays down".[231] This obligation, however, is tempered by the discretion given to the Council to determine in which cases it will exercise the implementing powers itself, and whether it will impose certain requirements upon the Commission.

The possibility of the Community legislature reserving implementing powers for itself is limited to specific cases. Grounds for reserving implementing powers may include the highly political sensitivity of decisions, uncertainty at the

---

[226] See sect. 3.2.

[227] Case 16/88, above n. 129.

[228] Case 25/70, *Köster,* above n. 118.

[229] See, *inter alia,* Case 25/70, *Köster,* above n. 118, para. 6.

[230] See Case C–240/90, *Germany* v. *Commission,* above n. 124; Case C–417/93, *Parliament* v. *Council* [1995] ECR I–1185; Case C–156/93, *Parliament* v. *Commission,* above n. 197; and Case C–303/94, *Parliament* v. *Council,* above n. 197.

[231] See C. Blumann, "Le pouvoir exécutif de la Commission à la lumière de l'Acte unique européen" (1988) 24 *RTDE* 1, 30; K.St.C. Bradley, "Comitology and the Law: Through a Glass, Darkly" (1992) 29 *CMLRev.* 703; H.J. Glaesner, "Die Einheitliche Europäische Akte" (1986) 21 *EuR* 2, 146; O. Harnier, "Artikel 145", in H. Von der Groeben/J. Thiesing/C.-D. Ehlermann, *Kommentar zum EWG-Vertrag* (Baden-Baden, 1991), 4247, no. 17; J.P. Jacqué, "L'Acte unique européen" (1986) 22 *RTDE* 595. See also the answer given by the Commission on WQ no. 1058/88 [1989] OJ C121/21.

moment of adoption as to the scope of the powers, and the risk of resistance from the Member States.[232] As mentioned above, decisions involving health and safety issues are politically sensitive so that the retention of decisional powers in these matters may be considered to be a "specific case". When making use of this exception, however, the Council must state in detail the grounds for its decision.[233]

The possibility of imposing certain conditions on the delegation of powers to the Commission refers to the long-standing practice of the conditional delegation of powers, which requires the Commission to consult certain committees composed of national representatives before adopting an implementing decision. The procedures to consult these committees have subsequently been laid down in Decision 87/373/EEC of 13 July 1987.[234] So, while there is an obligation to delegate, the Council may nonetheless decide how much power will be delegated to the Commission.[235] Moreover, the Council's obligation to delegate to the Commission does not affect its powers to leave implementation to the Member States. However, when it decides to exercise implementing powers at Community level, it must respect the Commission's competence relating to the implementation of Community legislation. The ever-growing workload of the Community in health and safety generally and the increasing reliance on the Commission, however, leads in turn to the trend of leaving specific tasks to bodies other than the institutions.[236]

6.2. The Concept of Legitimacy

The deepening of Community activities in the field of health and safety regulation, accompanied by the increasing role of the Commission through the means of a greater delegation of powers, inevitably raises legitimacy problems. Legitimacy is however an equivocal concept and raises various conceptual difficulties.[237] For the purpose of this book, some of its more general features may be highlighted.

---

[232] Harnier, above n. 231, point 24; Blumann, above n. 231, at 41.

[233] As required by the Court in Case 16/88, above n. 129, para. 10. See, also, J. Forman, "Case 16/88 *Commission* v. *Council*" (1990) 27 *CMLRev*. 872–82. In this vein, it may be questioned whether these requirements have been fulfilled in, for instance, Dir. 89/107/EEC on food additives, which retains some major decision-making powers in the Council, where it merely states in its preamble that "the drawing-up of lists of categories of food additives to be covered by a directive is a matter to be decided by the Council acting under the procedure laid down in Article 100a of the Treaty".

[234] Council Dec. 87/373/EEC laying down the procedures for the exercise of implementing powers conferred on the Commission [1987] OJ L197/33. See, in more detail, Chap. 3.

[235] See R. Dehousse, "Completing the Internal Market: Institutional Constraints and Challenges", in R. Bieber/R. Dehousse/J. Pinder/J.H.H. Weiler (eds.), *1992: One European Market? A Critical Analysis of the Commission's Internal Market Strategy* (Baden-Baden, 1988), 322, albeit not viewing delegation to be an actual obligation.

[236] On how far the institutional balance of powers allows this will be examined in the next chaps.

[237] See, for instance, A. Hyde, "The Concept of Legitimation in the Sociology of Law" (1983) 54 *Wisconsin Law Review* 379–426, who pleads for the abandonment of the concept of legitimation.

6.2.1. Legitimacy

"Legitimus" means "following a law", or, interpreted more generally, "following a rule or principle".[238] These rules must find a degree of social acceptance among the citizenry. In this context, Max Weber associated legitimacy with three sources: legality, tradition and charisma.[239] Acceptance, however, can also stem from other factors such as: indifference, fear of sanctions, expedience, convenience or profit, or from the conviction that the rules are "just" and that the institutions which promulgated them were legally authorised to do so. For all these reasons, political institutions and rules promulgated by them may be accepted, notwithstanding the possible disagreement of citizens with their substance. In legal science, acceptance is generally limited to the latter, normative ground: legitimacy in the sense of acceptance of rules because they are just, whilst the promulgating institutions are legally authorised to make them. Hence, not only factual acceptance is considered here, but also a normative element of "justice".

In most national concepts of the Rule of Law, citizens can only be bound by laws. These laws derive their legitimacy from the representative character of a legislature, which is directly elected. Rules issued by government or administration obtain indirect legitimacy as the latter are deemed to act solely on the basis of laws adopted by the legislature.[240] Yet, the requirements of the modern welfare state have inexorably led to a general withdrawal of the legislature in favour of the administration and to non-governmental actors. Many "discretionary" powers are at present generally delegated to the administration. This wide degree of discretion may accordingly be argued to have weakened the administration's claim to be acting solely on the basis of the legislature's duly enacted laws and, thus, to have undermined administrative legitimacy. The move away from this "transmission belt" model of administrative law,[241] therefore, underlines the importance of additional means to enhance administrative legitimacy.[242] Here administrative law is increasingly concerned with the provision of a surrogate political process to ensure the fair representation of a wide range of affected interests in the process of administrative decision.[243] Such additional measures include, therefore, greater democratic and judicial control, increased transparency, greater expertise and stronger participation of citizens

---

[238] See G. Winter, "Drei Arten gemeinschaftlicher Rechtssetzung und ihre Legitimation", in G. Brüggemeier (ed.), *Verfassungen für ein ziviles Europa* (Baden-Baden, 1994), 48.

[239] M. Weber, *Economy and Society: An Outline of Interpretive Sociology,* edited by G. Roth/C. Wittich (Berkeley/Los Angeles/London, 1978), i, 215.

[240] See, in the Dutch context, for instance, inspired by the writings of Weber, M. Oosting, *Beginselen van bestuur* (Alphen an den Rijn, 1980), 9.

[241] See R. Stewart, "The Reformation of American Administrative Law" (1975) 88 *Harvard Law Review*, 1669–70. This applies also to the European Community.

[242] See in this context, M. Everson, "Administering Europe?" (1998) 36 *JCMS* 195–216.

[243] Stewart, above n. 241, at 1670. See also Everson, above n. 242.

in the decision-making process, by means of representative interest groups, open hearings and public debate.[244]

However, these additional measures for their part raise various problems. The inclusion of diffuse interests in decision-making, for example, gives rise to problems concerning the articulation, representation and organisation of the interests: every consumer wants his/her health and safety to be protected, but has different hierarchies of values and preferences. Hence, the "diffuseness" of the interests makes their recognition as public or general interests difficult.[245] The same may apply to the reliance on greater expertise. This, in turn, necessitates the development of procedural rules as additional legitimising mechanisms.

6.2.2. Legitimacy in the Community Context

However, legitimacy concerns as they appear in national contexts cannot simply be transposed to the Community level. Not a state, but a system of multi-level governance, the Community is beset by additional difficulties inherent in the need to respect the regulatory concerns of the Member States and the differing linguistic and cultural systems and the "representativity" of socio-economic interests. The due process of Community decision-making becomes particular important where, in view of differing habits and traditions, the Community is required to promote solutions based on criteria acceptable throughout Europe and is, thus, likely to resort to regulatory schemes which seek to gain acceptance through their reliance on culturally neutral scientific standards.[246] Sight must, nevertheless, not be lost of the fact that health and safety regulation, which requires the assessment and management of risks, cannot and should not be understood as a task solely to be performed by experts, whose work is isolated from broader social developments, cultural traditions and values.[247] Rather, health and safety regulation should be recognised as a process permeated by policy considerations[248] and thus also leave room for the participation of political actors together with socio-economic interests, originating from the entire Community.[249]

---

[244] See De Haan/Drupsteen/Fernhout, above n. 112.

[245] N. Reich, *Internal Market and Diffuse Interests* (Louvain-la-Neuve, 1990), 15–16.

[246] See Ch. Joerges, "Social Regulation by the Community: The Case of Foodstuffs", in F. Snyder (ed.), *A Regulatory Framework for Foodstuffs in the Internal Market*, EUI Working Paper LAW 94/4 (Florence, 1994), 52.

[247] See also Dehousse/Joerges/Majone/Snyder/Everson, above n. 4, 52.

[248] See also C.F. Cranor, *Regulating Toxic Substances. A Philosophy of Science and the Law* (New York/Oxford, 1993), 131; S. Jasanoff, *The Fifth Branch. Science Advisers as Policymakers* (Cambridge, Mass./London, 1990), 249; K.S. Shrader-Frechette, *Risk and Rationality: Philosophical Foundations* (Berkeley/Los Angeles, 1991), 190 and 218.

[249] See below, sects. 6.3. and 6.4.

6.3. Participation of Member States in the Exercise by the Commission of Implementing Powers on Health and Safety

Increasing implementation of health and safety regulation inevitably touches upon the question of what role is left for the Member States. The non-majoritarian approach to market integration, defended by Majone, holds that the integrated market can be managed by "insulation" from political concerns by non-majoritarian technical experts.[250] I take the view, however, that for risk regulation to be legitimate, it cannot be left to technocrats/experts alone, but needs to be decided by political and socio-economic actors.[251] Clearly, participation of Member States' democratically elected representatives cannot be placed on the same footing as the participation of socio-economic interest groups. The plea for the participation of Member States in the implementation of risk regulation by the Community is founded on several normative and pragmatic arguments, which are advanced below.

6.3.1. Explaining the Participation of the Member States from the Institutional Balance of Powers

Whether a "Member State-oriented" understanding of the principle of the institutional balance developed above will ever have legal value will largely depend upon the Court. It may, nonetheless, be useful to explain the institutional frameworks of Community health and safety regulation and why Member States and their national institutions not only want to retain a voice in the legislative process, but also desire to have a degree of influence on the process of the implementation and application of Community law. Where powers are exercised by an intergovernmental institution such as the Council—in co-decision with the Parliament—this control is ensured. Yet, where—retaining implementing powers at Community level—the Council and the Parliament delegate such powers to the Commission, national influence is no longer guaranteed. From this perspective, the altering of the balance of powers in favour of the Community and, ultimately, of the Commission may explain the Member States' insistence on an ongoing role in such "Community" activity.[252] In this way, the principle of the institutional balance accommodates the recognition of transnational governance structures between the Community and the Member States.

---

[250] See G. Majone, *Regulating Europe* (London, 1996).
[251] See the Introduction to this book.
[252] Such an understanding of the principle of the institutional balance would, for instance, explain the view of J.P. Jacqué, Director of the Legal Service of the Council, that the question of comitology belongs to the affairs of the Member States. This view was expressed during the EUI Conference on Comitology held in Florence in Dec. 1996.

6.3.2. The Sui Generis *Character of the Community*

First, as argued in the introduction to this book, the Community is not a state. Instead, it can be identified as a system of multi-level or transnational governance. Governance in such a system, with a non-hierarchical structure, can only be accomplished through co-operation between power holders, which are both the Member States and the Community institutions.[253] The multi-level approach sees to decision-making by different levels of government and shifting fields of competence[254] and appears to be compatible with the conservation of national administrative powers and the assumption of national powers by the Community. It accommodates a concept of shared competences for risk regulation, as developed in the previous chapter.

6.3.3. National Constitutions

Furthermore, the continuing interest of the Member States in such regulation is understandable in view of the fact that many countries are required by their national constitutions to provide for the health and safety of their citizens.[255] The view that the nation-state is obliged to protect the health and safety of its citizens has been developed, in particular, in the German literature. In this context, reference has been made to the philosophies of Hobbes, Locke and Rousseau, all of whom are concerned with the justification of the nation-state: human beings being prepared to give up their sovereignty in favour of a higher institution, ensuring peace, safety and freedom.[256] Although these philosophies can be questioned and would no longer serve to justify the nation-state, one only needs to point to the German Basic Law which can be interpreted as laying down an obligation on the German State to protect human health and safety.[257]

6.3.4. Community Law: Article 36 and Secondary Law

The responsibility of Member States for human health and safety is recognised in the Treaty itself: Article 36 explicitly stipulates that Member States may adopt measures constituting trade barriers provided that they are justified for

---

[253] See, e.g., Ch. Joerges/J. Neyer, "From Intergovernmental Bargaining to Deliberative Political Processes: The Constitutionalisation of Comitology" (1997) 3 *ELJ* 273–99.

[254] G. Marks/L. Hooghe/K. Blank, "European Integration Since the 1980s: State-centric versus Multi-level Governance" (1996) 34 *JCMS* 343; D. Curtin, "'Civil Society' and the European Union: Opening Spaces for Deliberative Democracy?", in *Collected Courses of the Academy of European Law* (Florence, 1996, forthcoming 1998).

[255] See H.-W. Micklitz, "Consumer Rights", in A. Cassese *et al.* (eds.), *Human Rights in the European Community: The Substantive Law* (Baden-Baden, 1991), 53–109, and Micklitz/Roethe/Weatherill, above n. 167.

[256] W. Köck, "Risikovorsorge als Staatsaufgabe" (1996) 121 *Archiv für öffentliches Recht* 13.

[257] Art. 1 I, in combination with Arts. 2 II and 14 of the Basic Law. See Köck, above n. 256, and Micklitz, above n. 255. Importantly, the recognition of the precautionary principle as a legal principle in several acts also points in this direction.

reasons of, *inter alia*, the protection of health and life of humans. This responsibility is further recognised in many Community acts on health and safety issues and is expressed in the development of a concept of shared competence on health and safety.

6.3.5. *The Specific Nature of Risk Regulation*

National administrations have historically been very active in regulating risks: on the one hand, overseeing the delicate matter of the weighing of normative values often deeply rooted in national traditions and cultures, and, on the other, seeking to fulfil their constitutional obligation to provide for the health and safety of their citizens, as argued above. The normative, ethical, cultural and political dimensions of risk regulation make themselves equally or even more strongly felt at Community level: not only do they speak against the delegation of risk assessments entirely and exclusively to expert bodies but they also render it highly unlikely that one single body (the Commission) will be able to come up with uniform decisions which are in any way socially acceptable throughout the whole internal market. Member States may accordingly be argued to have a very strong interest in health and safety matters. Seen in this light, it would thus seem expedient to ensure that the increased transfer of implementing powers to the Community level, be accompanied by the evolution of mechanisms (committees and agencies) which allow the Member States to retain a degree of influence over the exercise of such powers.

6.3.6. *Addressing Subsidiarity*

The need to include the Member States in Community risk regulation may also be viewed as a means of addressing subsidiarity. The political character of subsidiarity cast doubts whether the Court is the appropriate institution to judge on the implementation of the subsidiarity principle.[258] For example, the House of Lords Select Committee on the European Communities retained that:

> "subsidiarity is a political principle which should permeate all stages of the Community legislative process, but the responsibility for its application should lie with the legislators and not with the judges".[259]

Sharing this opinion, I argue that the decision on the level at which specific tasks can best be achieved should be left to the political process.[260] This does not, however, mean that the principle of subsidiarity is completely irrelevant. The subsidiarity principle furnishes the clear message that Member States should not be excluded from the process of creating a European Union based upon the rule of law, democratic principles and solidarity (regardless of the constitutional form which it may ultimately take). In this context, Dehousse has

---

[258] See Dehousse, above n. 151, 112 ff.
[259] Above n. 167, point 165 (see also points 23 and 24).
[260] Of this opinion, also Dehousse, above n. 151, at 119.

pointed to other means to implement the philosophy of subsidiarity.[261] Subsidiarity might thus be given a procedural dimension, not only focusing attention upon the question of *who* acts, but also upon that of *how* and *in what way* decisions are drafted.[262] In other words, subsidiarity as a management tool: procedural subsidiarity, as opposed to a substantive subsidiarity, which relates more to questions of political content.[263]

In order to address the Member States' concerns as regards unnecessary Community interference, mechanisms which provide for co-operation between all the levels concerned might be designed.[264] As regards health and safety regulation, the existing committee mechanisms might, for example, ensure that the Member States are able to exercise on-going control over the decision-making process whilst, at the same time, securing constant co-operation between all the authorities concerned. Likewise, agencies could also serve this purpose. In this way, the subsidiarity philosophy would largely be met. This issue will be addressed in the following chapters.

6.3.7. Compliance

Finally, from a more pragmatic viewpoint too, Member States' participation in Community health and safety regulation may be argued to be necessary; the production of regulatory provisions is of little use where these rules are not complied with by Member States. As argued above, non-compliance is amongst the factors which push the Community in its third phase of integration towards ever-increasing activity in this field. It has indeed become clear that one of the general problems facing Community integration at the present moment is that "non-compliance" is no longer a phenomenon restricted to the confines of recalcitrant states.[265] Non-compliance may partly be attributed to gaps in policy formation,[266] or to the fact that Member States can no longer block Community legislation in areas which were previously constrained by the unanimity voting requirement but which are now subject to qualified majority voting (such as in the area of social regulation). In addition, compliance problems may be argued to occur due to administrative difficulties in the application and implementation of Community law at national level, often stemming from mutual distrust.[267]

---

[261] See Dehousse, above n. 151, 124–5.

[262] *Ibid.*

[263] Z. Bankowski, "Subsidiarity, Sovereignty and the Self", in K.W. Nörr/T. Oppermann (eds.), *Subsidarität: Idee und Wirklichkeit. Zur Reichweite eines Prinzips in Deutschland und Europa* (Tübingen, 1997), 23–39.

[264] Dehousse, above n. 151, 124–5.

[265] M. Mendriou, "Non-compliance and the European Commission's Role in Integration" (1996) 3 *JEPP* 1, 4.

[266] For instance, during the transgovernmental and transnational negotiations which take place at various levels between Community institutions, national administrations and interest groups: see Mendriou, above n. 265, 6–7.

[267] See Ch. Joerges/E. Vos, "Structures of Transnational Governance and Their Legitimacy", in J. Vervaele (ed.), *Compliance and Enforcement of EC Law* (Kluwer Law International, forthcoming).

The need for co-operation and deliberation with the Member States is only accentuated by the large extent of mutual distrust between national administrations. Therefore, by allowing Member States to participate in the implementing phase too (by means of committees or agencies) these problems may be overcome.

6.4. Means to Enhance Legitimacy

As argued above, the delegation of discretionary powers to the Commission moves away from its legitimacy claim to act on a legislative mandate, thus enhancing the importance of searching for additional means of legitimacy for the Commission's actions: expertise, interest representation, transparency, due process requirements which ensure respect for the individuals and fairness of the procedures and accountability.[268] The analysis of the legitimacy of the structures by which the Community regulates health and safety issues will accordingly focus on these requirements as additional means of legitimacy. This section addresses general aspects of these requirements, and deduces some principles from the Court's case law and the Treaty of Amsterdam.

6.4.1. Scientific Expertise

It can be said that the greater the expertise involved, in general leading to "better" informed decision-making, the greater the degree of acceptance shown by the citizens of the Community.[269] The participation of various qualified scientific experts in Community decision-making, therefore, potentially enhances the quality of decisions and thus their legitimacy.[270]

The conferral on the Commission by the Amsterdam Treaty in Article 100a(3) of an obligation to take account of "any new development based on scientific facts" when proposing harmonisation measures recalls the Court's case law reviewing the proportionality of national legislative measures causing trade barriers. In these cases, the Court has consistently obliged Member States which invoked Article 36 or safeguard clauses to base their views on scientific research,[271] in particular, requiring them to take account of the findings of international scientific research.[272] The amendment by the Amsterdam Treaty thus mirrors the Court's jurisprudence: the Commission is also obliged to take account of the newest scientific evidence.

---

[268]   See, in general, R. Baldwin, Rules and Government (Oxford, 1995), 41–6.

[269]   See R. Baldwin/C. McCrudden, *Regulation and Public Law* (London, 1987), 49.

[270]   See Winter, above n. 238, at 48.

[271]   See Ch. Joerges, "Scientific Expertise in Social Regulation and the European Court of Justice: Legal Frameworks for Denationalised Governance Structures", in Ch. Joerges/K.H. Ladeur/E. Vos (eds.), *Integrating Scientific Expertise into Regulatory Decision-Making. National Traditions and European Innovations* (Baden-Baden, 1997), 302 ff.

[272]   See, e.g., Case 178/84, *Commission v. Germany (Reinheitsgebot)* [1987] ECR 1227.

However, the obligation to take account of scientific facts is, according to the wording of the amendment, conferred on the *Commission* and not on the Community legislature: the Parliament and the Council. This does not however mean that the Community legislature is not obliged to base its legislative acts on scientific expertise. At first sight, the wording calls readily to mind the Court's case law in which it demonstrated great reluctance to question "the wisdom of any measures approved by the Council",[273] merely examining whether the relevant measure was vitiated by a manifest error, misuse of powers or whether the authority in question had manifestly exceeded the limits of its discretion.[274] In the *Hormones* case,[275] the Court had to consider the correct legal basis of Council Directive 85/649/EEC prohibiting the use of hormones in livestock farming.[276] The United Kingdom argued that, in view of its health protection objectives, Article 100 was the correct legal basis while the Council defended its choice for Article 43.[277] After having determined Article 43 to be the correct legal basis of this Directive, the Court was asked to judge whether the Council had a duty to consider a scientific report, to which it would have to refer in its statement of reasons. Without going into scientific details, the Court, however, formalistically ruled that since the main directive in question[278] imposed such an obligation solely on the Commission, the Council was not obliged to refer to such aspects.[279] Advocate General Lenz had correctly observed that the scientific report highlighted only one aspect of the problem, the health of consumers, whilst account was also to be taken of the prejudices of consumers towards hormones in meat.[280] Yet, he superficially continued that once it was established that the Hormones Directive served the agricultural policy objective, there was:

> "really no reason to examine the health problem in particular . . . and so the fact that in the preamble to the contested directive the Council did not go into the partial findings of the scientific group, which the Commission did make available to the Council, certainly cannot be regarded as a failure to state reasons".[281]

Clearly, in the case at issue scientific evidence had considered the substances in question to be harmless to human health; the reasoning of both the Court and the Advocate General would never have been followed in the opposite situation. Such superficial reasoning must, nevertheless, be rejected in any case and should not be followed when interpreting the Amsterdam amendment. It is true that in

---

[273] Joerges, above n. 271, at 316.

[274] Case C–331/88, *Fedesa*, above n. 179. See also Case C–405/92, above n. 179.

[275] Case 68/86, *United Kingdom* v. *Council* [1988] ECR 855.

[276] Council Dir. 85/649/EEC [1985] OJ L382/28.

[277] See, in particular, Joerges, above n. 271.

[278] Council Dir. 81/602/EEC on the prohibition of certain substances having a hormonal action and of any substances having a thyrostatic action [1981] OJ L222/32, to which Dir. 85/649/EEC, above n. 276, was complementary.

[279] *Hormones* case, above n. 275, at 899–900.

[280] Reflecting, in particular, the negative attitude of consumers towards meat treated with such hormones.

[281] *Hormones* case, above n. 275, at 882.

view of scientific uncertainty, adequate solutions cannot and should not be furnished by science and scientists alone.[282] The wording of Article 100a(3) indeed does not (and cannot) oblige the Commission to adhere to scientific "facts", but to "take account" of them, thus keeping a potential resort to the precautionary principle[283] on the part of the Community legislature in this field open.[284] The recent judgment of the Court on the emergency measures taken by the Commission in the BSE case seems to confirm this, where the Court expressly rules that:

> "[w]here there is uncertainty as to the existence or extent of risks to human health, the institutions may take protective measures without having to wait until the reality and seriousness of those risks become fully apparent".[285]

At the same time, this obligation ensures that scientific evidence may not be disregarded, implicitly extending the obligation to base measures on scientific facts to the Community legislature as well. This is underlined by the fact that scientific advice becomes increasingly the basis on which the Community must justify its safety measures in international fora such as the World Trade Organisation (WTO); for example, where the Community needs to defend its ban on hormones in beef on the basis of sound scientific expertise.[286]

6.4.2. Public Interest and Interest Participation

The transfer of powers which affect the "public good" to the Community level touches also upon the question whether and how various interests should participate in the decision-making process. The task of bringing the viewpoints of various socio-economic interests into Community decision-making is generally performed by the Economic and Social Committee in accordance with the Treaty provisions.[287] The need to include a more direct form of participation of the social partners on specific topics of Community decision-making[288] in order

---

[282] See also the Court in Case C–331/88, *Fedesa*, above n. 179, at 4062. See, in this sense, also Case C–84/94, *United Kingdom* v. *Council* [1996] ECR I–5755.

[283] See, for a discussion of the precautionary principle, e.g., O. Godard, "Social Decision-Making under Conditions of Scientific Controversy, Expertise and the Precautionary Principle", in Ch. Joerges/K.H. Ladeur/E. Vos (eds.), *Integrating Scientific Expertise into Regulatory Decision-Making. National Traditions and European Innovations* (Baden-Baden, 1997), 39–73.

[284] Of a different opinion: R. Barents, "Het Verdrag van Amsterdam en het Europees Gemeenschapsrecht. De materieelrechtelijke en institutionele veranderingen" (1997) 45 *SEW* 10, 353.

[285] Case C–157/96, *The Queen* v. *Ministry of Agriculture, Fisheries and Food, ex parte National Farmers' Union et al.* [1998] ECR I–2211, para. 63 and Case C–180/96, *United Kingdom* v. *Commission*, above n. 92, para. 99.

[286] For Art. XX of GATT 1994 explicitly stipulates that the contracting parties may still adopt measures "necessary to protect human, animal or plant life or health", provided that such measures do not constitute arbitrary or unjustifiable discrimination between countries or a disguised restriction on international trade. See, for instance, B. Eggers, "Die Entscheidung des WTO Appelate Body im Hormonfall" (1998) 9 *EuZW* 5–6, 147–51.

[287] See, in general, Art. 4.

[288] See, for instance, C. Harlow, "A Community of Interests? Making the Most of European Law" (1992) 55 *MLR* 331–50.

to enhance its legitimacy was, however, recognised as early as the Paris Summit of 1972.[289] However, "no really specific thinking has taken place at EU level on the way in which interest representation should be introduced into decision-making".[290] The next chapters will therefore examine in what way interests are represented in Community health and safety regulation. Particular attention will be paid to the traditionally "under-represented" interest in this field: consumer representation.[291] Such groups have insisted on being included in the regulatory process, pointing out various factors which seem to suggest that industrial interests are favoured in Community decision-making. For example, the Commission's Directorate-General III, concerned with foodstuffs, pharmaceuticals and standardisation, is often closely identified by consumer organisations with industry's interests.[292] Hence, our search for a more democratic and procedural account of rationality in Community risk regulation should take particular account of the "human dimensions" of risk assessment and management. Subjective concerns stemming from normative questions of social perceptions and demands which are deeply rooted in the different cultures and traditions are not easily approached in a purely "objective" manner. Therefore, a public debate on such issues at Community level is of great significance.

6.4.3. *Transparency and Access to Documents*

Risk assessment is difficult to separate from societal and political values and this is underlined by the fact that, in situations where scientific activities attract great attention from the public, scientists are likely to be subject to powerful political pressure. This was, for example, openly admitted by scientists working within various scientific committees on the BSE case.[293] This makes the need for enhanced transparency in risk evaluation even more important. The need for greater transparency was underlined by the Intergovernmental Conference on the Maastricht Treaty affirming that:

> "the transparency of the decision-making process strengthens the democratic nature of the institutions and the public's confidence in the administration".[294]

Accordingly, the Commission and the Council have undertaken various initiatives on public access to their documents, resulting in the adoption of a

---

[289] See Sixth General Report of the European Communities, 11 ff.

[290] Curtin, above n. 254.

[291] See recently, Commission Communication on Promoting the Role of Voluntary Organisations and Foundations in Europe, COM(97)241 final.

[292] These critiques were expressed in relation to the Community's regulatory policy on pharmaceuticals: see L. Hancher, *Regulating for Competition. Government, Law, and the Pharmaceutical Industry in the United Kingdom and France* (Oxford, 1990), 107 ff. See, in more detail, Chap. 4. In the context of competition policy, Everson makes mention of the reservations expressed as regards the independence of DGIV of the Commission in this field: Everson, above n. 113, at 196.

[293] See Chap. 3.

[294] Declaration no. 17 on the right to access to information annexed to the Maastricht Treaty. The necessity to make the Community more open had further been repeated by the European Council in Birmingham in Oct. 1992.

common Code of Conduct.[295] This Code, subsequently included in both a Commission Decision[296] and a Council Decision on this issue,[297] lays down as a general principle that citizens should have access to Commission and Council documents. Two categories of exceptions are provided for: the first relates to the protection of third parties in the general public interest (mandatory) whilst the second category sees to the protection of internal deliberations of the institution (discretionary). Where an institution invokes one of these exceptions, it must explain in detailed its reasons for it.[298] Subsequently, the Parliament,[299] the Economic and Social Committee[300] and other bodies[301] have also adopted their own rules on access to documents.

Following the Treaty of Amsterdam, the Community's commitment to transparency will be officially laid down in the Treaty (Article A(2) TEU), whilst Union citizens are explicitly granted the right of access to the documents of the Parliament, the Council and the Commission (Article 191a).

6.4.4. Due Process Requirements

(a) Duty to Examine all Relevant Aspects of the Individual Case Carefully and Impartially: Consultation of Scientific Experts

The Commission is, however, not completely free in consulting scientific experts. It follows from the *Angelopharm* case that when the Commission has itself set up a scientific committee with the purpose of providing the Commission with the most recent scientific and technical research, it is obliged

---

[295] See the Commission's Communication to the Council, the Parliament and the Economic and Social Committee on public access to the institutions' documents (COM(93)191 final) and its Communications on openness in the Community (COM(93)258 final) and increased transparency in the work of the Commission (SEC(92)2274 final), leading to the adoption of a Code of Conduct concerning public access to Council and Commission documents (93/730/EC) [1993] OJ L340/41.

[296] Commission Dec. 94/90/ECSC, EC, Euratom [1994] OJ L46/58, as amended by Commission Decision 96/567/Euratom, ECSC, EC [1996] OJ L47/45. See, also, the Commission's Citizen's Guide (http://europa.eu.int/comm/sg/citguide/en/citgu.htm).

[297] Council Dec. 93/731/EC on public access to Council documents [1993] OJ L340/43, as amended by Council Dec. 96/705/EC, ECSC, Euratom [1996] OJ L325/19. See on the unsuccessful attempt at the annulment of this Dec., Case C–58/94, *Netherlands* v. *Council* [1996] ECR I–2169.

[298] See Case T-105/95 *WWF (UK)* v. *Commission* [1997] ECR II-313; Case T-124/96, *Interporc Im- und Export GmbH* v. *Commission* [1998] ECR II-231; Case T-83/96 *Van der Wal* v. *Commission* [1998] ECR II–545.

[299] European Parliament Dec. 97/632/EC, ECSC, Euratom on public access to European Parliament documents [1997] OJ L263/27.

[300] Economic and Social Committee Dec. on public access to ESC documents [1997] OJ L339/18.

[301] See Dec. on public access to European Environment Agency documents [1997] OJ C282/5; Rules on public access to documents adopted by the Bank's management Committee [1997] OJ C243/13; Dec. of the Governing Board on Public Access to European Training Foundation Documents [1997] OJ C369/10; Dec. of the Committee of the Regions concerning public access to documents of the Committee of the Regions [1997] OJ L351/70; Rules for access to Translation Centre documents [1998] OJ C46/5; Dec. 9/97 concerning public access to administrative documents of the European Monetary Institute [1998] OJ L90/43. See, also, the Special Report from the European Ombudsman to the European Parliament following its own-initiative inquiry into public access to documents [1998] OJ C44/9.

to consult it.[302] In addition, some requirements have been set about which scientific experts need to be consulted by the Commission. In *Technische Universität München*,[303] the Court considered the duty-free importation of scientific apparatus under Council Regulation 2784/79.[304] Under this Regulation, the Commission was required, before adopting any decision, to consult the Member States or, if necessary, a group of experts gathered together in the Committee on Duty-Free Arrangements.[305] The Court first determined that the equal need to guarantee individual rights under the Community legal order, especially individual rights in procedural matters, determined that the Commission be likewise obliged carefully and impartially to examine all relevant aspects of the individual case. This obligation extended to a further obligation that where the Commission resorts to such a group of experts (most often being its only source of information, as was admitted by the Commission) it must also ensure that the persons in this group possess the necessary *technical* knowledge or, alternatively, that they seek advice from experts in the specific field under consideration.[306]

(b) Right to a Hearing

In addition to underlining the existence of the individual right to have an adequately reasoned opinion and placing a duty upon the competent institution to examine carefully and impartially all the relevant aspects of the individual case, the Court ruled in *Technische Universität München* that the person concerned also had the right to make his or her views known so that the Court might verify whether decisions adopted in accordance with discretionary powers satisfied all factual and legal requirements.[307] These requirements may be argued to apply *mutatis mutandis* to health and safety regulation.

6.4.5. Judicial Control and the Duty to State Reasons

Where it is not known what the institutions do or the reasons for it, it is impossible to exert control. Therefore, the duty to state reasons under Article 190 constitutes an important instrument for judicial control. It is not surprising that when asked to judge upon Community measures involving intricate scientific evaluations, the Court has been very cautious and has attached much value to procedural matters, particularly to the duty to state reasons. In *Technische Universität München*,[308] the Court held that since procedural rights granted to

---

[302] Case C–212/91, *Angelopharm v. Freie und Hansestadt Hamburg* [1994] ECR I–171. See, in more detail, Chap. 3.
[303] Case C–269/90, *Hauptzollamt München-Mitte v. Technische Universität München* [1991] ECR I–5469.
[304] [1979] OJ L318/32.
[305] Art. 7(3)–(5) of this Reg.
[306] Case C–269/90, above n. 303, at I–5500/–1. See also Case C–185/91, *Bundesanstalt für den Güterfernverkehr v. Gebrüder Reiff* [1993] ECR I–5801.
[307] Case C–269/90 above n. 303, I–5499.
[308] *Ibid.*

individuals by the Community legal order were deemed to be vitally important, there was need for a clear and unequivocal statement of the reasons for the decision which would enable the persons concerned (and the Court) to appraise the reasons for the measure and to defend their rights, where necessary.[309] This duty was of even greater importance in complex and technical administrative procedures where the Commission necessarily has power of appraisal. The emphasis on the duty to state reasons under Article 190 was reiterated more recently in, for instance, *Pentaclorophenol*, where the Court was called upon to judge on the validity of a Commission decision under Article 100a(4).[310] Here, the Court ruled that where the Commission wished to authorise a derogation under Article 100a(4) based on the protection of health, it could not merely refer to the fact that the national rules in question were aimed at health protection, but had to produce the relevant scientific and legal arguments itself.[311]

6.4.6. *Accountability of Community Health and Safety Regulation*

Greater Community activity in health and safety regulation leads to parallel demands for greater accountability and control. Democratic legitimacy of Community health and safety regulation is strongly linked to the Parliament's right to participate in and control the decision-making process. The Parliament considers its power to scrutinise and monitor implementing Commission decisions to be of crucial importance to democratic accountability.[312] The power to supervise the Commission's activities is laid down, in particular, in Article 144, which empowers the Parliament to issue a motion of censure against the Commission as a whole (although not the individual Commissioners).[313] Further control is expressed in various Treaty Articles, which enable the Parliament to criticise the Commission (for example, Article 143). However, where Community health and safety regulation relies on other bodies for implementation, problems of accountability and the ultimate control over these bodies in turn arise.[314]

7. CONCLUSION

In this chapter, three phases of integration in relation to health and safety regulation were identified. The first period ran up to the SEA. During this period, the Community gave preference to the detailed harmonisation of each national act. Yet, the original Community work programme for harmonisation—the

---

[309] Case 205/85, *Nicolet Instrument* v. *Hauptzollamt am Main-Flughafen* [1986] ECR 2049.

[310] Case C–41/93, *France* v. *Commission* [1994] ECR I–2509.

[311] See, in detail, Chap. 1.

[312] See F. Jacobs/R. Corbett/M. Shackleton, *The European Parliament* (London, 1992), 233.

[313] See, in general, P.J.G Kapteyn/P. VerLoren van Themaat, edited by L. Gormley, *Introduction to the Law of the European Communities* (Deventer, 1990), 138–40.

[314] See Chaps. 3–5.

detailed harmonisation of each piece of national legislation—was to fail early due to the increasing Community workload, and the cumbersome nature of the decision-making procedures. The disappointing results persuaded the Community institutions to reform their harmonisation strategy. In the second period, between the SEA and the Maastricht Treaty, the Community sought to speed up its decision-making through the adoption of innovative regulatory techniques and through the use of the minimum harmonisation method. The application of the mutual recognition principle to health and safety regulation, however, raised the spectre that a "race to the bottom", and a deterioration of health and safety regulation, would ensue. In practice, however, this has not occurred. Instead, the Community has promoted the protection of human health and safety and has increasingly intervened in health and safety regulation.

"Post-Maastricht", we are witnessing a third phase of integration which involves the deepening of Community involvement, and a greater degree of implementation of Community rules at Community level. Divergent national safety concepts, the unwillingness of Member States to accept different concepts, mainly due to mutual distrust in national administrative practices, in no small part necessitate this deepening and encourage the Community to further "genuine" product safety issues in addition to "purely" internal market objectives.

Several arguments plead for the Community competence to execute its own legislation. First, the distinction between legislation and execution has itself been blurred. Further, the Treaty does not itself distinguish between legislation and execution; a distinction generally based on the principle of the separation of powers. Instead, Treaty provisions speak of "measures" in general or "measures for the implementation of the rules". This concept of implementation is a broad concept and comprises both the drawing up of rules and the application of such rules to specific cases. The Community's competence to adopt implementing measures concerning health and safety issues may, in general, be based on Article 100a, 129a or 235. Although Article 100a limits Community action to the *harmonisation* of national provisions, the Court has confirmed the broad interpretation of the latter concept, determining that harmonisation includes both measures relating to a specific product or class of products and individual measures concerning these products. Contrary to what may have been argued, the instrument of harmonisation has demonstrated itself to be quite broad and flexible, and is thus still relevant in the matter of health and safety regulation.

The deepening of the Community's activities in health and safety regulation will not be subject to challenge from the principles of subsidiarity and proportionality. Given the inextricable link between health and safety protection and the internal market objective, the Community institutions will have no difficulty in proving that further Community action in health and safety regulation is necessary. Where the Community deepens its involvement in health and safety regulation, it must likewise observe the principle of the institutional balance.

This principle refers to the balance of powers between the institutions as laid down in the Treaty, and has been developed mainly by the Court. Under this principle, each institution must exercise its powers with due regard for the powers of the other institutions. Similarly, it guarantees that the Community institutions exercise their powers within the limits laid down by the Treaty, and so reinforces the rule of law on which the Community is based. However, although the Court views the principle of the institutional balance as being something more than a simple restatement of Article 4, it has not developed its vertical aspects and has thus disregarded the vital role played by the Member States within the institutional balance. Only the inclusion of the Member States within the principle of the institutional balance would allow a full understanding of the Community's institutional structure and would therefore do full justice to its complexity.

The delegation of greater powers on health and safety issues to the Commission stems from the need for greater efficiency and a reduction in the Council's workload—a need felt even by the infant Community—as well as the obligation to respect the institutional balance. Moreover, it results from the specific nature of health and safety regulation which requires a high degree of flexibility. However, the intensification of Community activity in this area, particularly Commission activity, gives rise to problems relating to its legitimacy. Although not an unequivocal concept, legitimacy can generally be understood in the sense of acceptance of rules because they are just, and, consequently, the promulgating institutions are legally authorised to make them. In national contexts, the increasing role of administration—moving further away from their "legitimate" basis of acting on the legislatures' acts—emphasises the search for additional means of administrative legitimacy, such as greater expertise, increased transparency, stronger citizen participation and democratic and judicial control. In contrast to the national level, the multi-level governance structure of the Community is troubled with further problems relating to the need to include the Member States in the implementation phase, in particular, differing linguistic and cultural habits, and the "representativity" of interests.

The need to include Member States in health and safety regulation by the Commission can be explained from the functional "Member State-oriented" interpretation of the principle of the institutional balance of powers and stems from a procedural interpretation of the subsidiarity principle. The development of mechanisms, such as committees and agencies, is exactly to ensure the participation and co-operation of all levels. Normative arguments which plead for a right of Member States to participate in risk regulation include the *sui generis* character of the Community, the constitutional obligations of Member States on health protection, a responsibility which is recognised in both Article 36 and various secondary legislative acts, the specific nature of risk regulation, and, of a more pragmatic nature, compliance. Requirements of legitimacy of health and safety regulation by the Commission further focus on scientific evidence, interest representation, increased transparency and accountability as a basis of decision-making, whilst particular attention should be paid to the requirements laid down by the Court obliging the Commission to examine carefully and impartially all the relevant aspects of each single case, together with the duty to state reasons and to provide for the right to be heard.

In this legal setting, the growing reliance on the Commission places a greater burden upon it and reveals its limits in relation to the capacity and the supply of expertise and information. The fact that Community involvement in health and safety regulation may be considered to be an accidental consequence of the market integration objective may, in turn, explain why the Community has not been well-equipped to face these and other difficulties, and has instead sought institutional responses through committees, agencies and private bodies. The deepening of Community health and safety regulation therefore results in an increasing Community reliance on these structures and necessitates their evaluation.

3

Health and Safety Regulation through Committees—the Case of Foodstuffs

1. INTRODUCTION

The first regulatory model by means of which the Community regulates health and safety issues consists of committees. The intensification of Community activities in health and safety regulation is undoubtedly accompanied by a "creeping" importance of committees in the Community decision-making process. In an attempt to overcome its general lack of scientific expertise, the Commission has created committees composed of highly qualified scientific experts who provide scientific data and evaluations. Other committees, composed of representatives of interest groups, have been established to inform the Commission of their point of view. Such committees are broadly comparable to the various advisory organs found in the Member States in every regulatory field,[1] the consultation of which serves to enhance the legitimacy, rationality and effectiveness of decision-making.[2] Yet, the situation at Community level is more complex. Here, committees have also been established to provide Member States with a means of ensuring their continuing influence over Community decision-making should implementing powers on health and safety issues be delegated to the Commission. Since these issues are strongly intertwined with national traditions and cultural habits, it is not surprising that Member States have from the outset been very unwilling to surrender their influence over such decisions. Where the increasing workload of the Community and its search for efficient decision-making as well as the specific nature of health and safety regulation nonetheless result in a greater delegation of more powers to the Commission, committees become of ever-increasing importance.

This chapter examines how the Community regulates health and safety issues through committees and highlights the problems to which this gives rise. The resort to committees by the Community institutions is a general phenomenon which has recently attracted great academic attention.[3] This plethora of com-

---

[1] These bodies have particular expertise in a specific area and advise decision-makers on possible regulatory difficulties and solutions. See, however, the debate in the Netherlands on whether or not to abolish most of the existing advisory organs, discussed *inter alia* by P. De Haan, "Herstructurering van adviesraden" (1993) 21 *NJB* 778–83 and I.C. Van der Vlies, "Adviesorganen moeten blijven" (1993) 13 *NJB* 450.

[2] See H.R.B.M. Kummeling, *Advisering in het publiekrecht* (Den Haag, 1988), 19 ff.

[3] See, for instance, K.St.C. Bradley, "Comitology and the Law: Through a Glass, Darkly" (1992) 29 *CMLRev.* 693–721; G.J. Buitendijk/M.P.C.M. Van Schendelen, "Brussels Advisory Committees:

mittees which exists within the Community's institutional setting is often referred to as "comitology". A typical example of Brussels jargon,[4] this term is also used in a stricter sense, encompassing only those committees composed of national representatives who assist the Commission in the exercise of its implementing powers. These latter committees, in particular, have been controversial.

The complexity of the committee model requires a separate discussion. Therefore, before examining the operation of committees in health and safety regulation, this chapter first gives a general overview of the origins of the committees, their typology and number, and then analyses the main legal problems which have arisen due to the unforeseen rise of committees within the Community's institutional structure. The early days of the Community saw legal debate concentrate upon the question whether Community institutions possessed the competence to create such committees. More important and still topical today is the debate on the legality of committees composed of national representatives which must be consulted by the Commission in the exercise of its implementing powers. Delegation of implementing powers to the Commission, which is subject to review and oversight by these committees, has been argued to upset the institutional balance of powers, interfering particularly with the Commission's right of decision and the Parliament's power of control.[5] Since the Maastricht Treaty, which granted the Parliament co-legislative powers in many areas, among which are measures based upon Article 100a, such committees have once again become the focus of debate as the Parliament reiterated its right to be involved in the implementing phase of the decision-making process. This "authentic jungle"[6] of committees has also been controversial in terms of their lack of efficiency and effectiveness.

A Channel for Influence?" (1995) 20 ELR 37–56; G. Della Cananea, "Cooperazione e integrazione nel sistema amministrativo delle comunità europee: la questione della comitologia" (1990) 40 Riv. Trimestrale di diritto pubblico 655–702; J. Falke/G. Winter, "Management and Regulatory Committees in Executive Rule-making", in G. Winter (ed.), Sources and Categories of European Union Law. A Comparative and Reform Perspective (Baden-Baden, 1996), 541–82; Ch. Joerges, Die Beurteilung der Sicherheit technischer Konsumgüter und der Gesundheitsrisiken von Lebensmitteln in der Praxis des europäischen Ausschußwesens ("Komitologie"), ZERP–Diskussionspapier 95/1 (Bremen, 1995); Ch. Joerges/J. Neyer, "Transforming Strategic Interaction into Deliberative Problem-solving: European Comitology in the Foodstuffs Sector" (1997) 4 JEPP 609–25; J. Neyer, "Administrative Supranationalität in der Verwaltung des Binnenmarktes: Zur Legitimität der Komitologie" (1997) Integration 24–37; W. Sauter/E. Vos, "Harmonisation under Community Law: the Comitology Issue", in P. Craig/C. Harlow, Law-making in the European Union (London, The Hague, Boston, 1998), 169–86; R.H. Pedler/G.F. Schaefer (eds.), Shaping European Law and Policy: The Role of Committees and Comitology in the Political Process (Maastricht, 1996); D. Sidjanski, "Communauté européen 1992: gouvernement de comités?" (1989) 48 Pouvoirs 71–80. See also the European Law Journal's special issue on Comitology, 3/3 of 1997. See also Ch. Joerges and E. Vos (eds.), EU Committees: Social Regulation, Law and Politics (Hart Publishing Oxford, forthcoming).

   [4] To the horror of some writers. See Nicoll who states: "Un mot affreux, qui appartient au Volupuk européen, s'est glissé dans le vocabulaire de tous le jours: «Comitologie»". W. Nicoll, "Qu'est-ce que la comitologie?" (1987) 306 RMC 185.
   [5] This is asserted in particularly by the Parliament. See, e.g., Bradley, above n. 3.
   [6] See S. Cassese, "La Costituzione Europea" [1991] Quaderni costitutionali 487–508.

As Jacques Delors said in 1994:

"Elle implique par ailleurs de supprimer la comitologie qui constitue une entrave lourde et invalidante aux différentes étapes de l'élaboration des décisions et de leur application".[7]

The examination of these questions of a more general nature is followed by scrutiny of the specific role of committees in Community health and safety regulation. Analysis is focused upon one particular field of health and safety regulation: the food sector. This field, which is among the Community's first priorities for harmonisation, is an excellent example of the difficulties the Community has faced over the years in the regulation of health and safety issues. It demonstrates how the Community endeavours to overcome problems by means of committees and the impact that the BSE crisis had on the manner of dealing with these problems. The food sector is characterised by the existence of mainly three committees: the Scientific Committee on Food, the Advisory Committee on Foodstuffs and the Standing Committee on Foodstuffs. The increasing activities of the Community in the food sector, accompanied by greater delegation of implementing powers to the Commission, inevitably results in a greater resort by the Community institutions to these committees. However, their interaction with the Community institutions and the Member States in the regulatory process is far from clear and causes problems of transparency. Analysis of the role of these committees is therefore of great importance. Furthermore, Community decision-making through these committees is examined with regard to its legitimacy. The increasing reliance on the committees has been criticised as posing a danger to the overall legitimacy of Community decision-making. From the point of view of democratic principles, for instance, the fact that decisions taken by the Council, following an unsuccessful Commission attempt, would largely escape parliamentary control may be objectionable. In this context, the committee procedures are particularly criticised since it is feared that the threat of renewed referral to the Council/ Parliament might make the Commission more likely to follow the opinion of the committees consulted so as to avoid complication and delay.[8] In this manner, committees would conceivably blur national and Community responsibilities thus frustrating democratic scrutiny and public accountability, since neither an individual civil servant, in his/her role as a committee member, nor the Commission would carry full responsibility for the decisions adopted.[9] On the other hand, seemingly paradoxically, comitology-based decision-making in the food sector has recently been argued to enhance legitimacy and constitute "deliberative supranationalism". This committee model, primarily advocated by Christian Joerges, is based upon the idea that market integration and risk

[7] J. Delors, before the French National Assembly, Commission of Foreign Affairs, *compte rendu*, n. 26 of 3 Nov. 1994 under the Presidency of M. Giscard d'Estaing, 5.

[8] P.J.G. Kapteyn/P. VerLoren van Themaat, edited by L. Gormley, *Introduction to the Law of the European Communities* (Deventer, 1990), 244.

[9] F. Jacobs/R. Corbett/M. Shackleton, *The European Parliament* (London, 1992), 233.

regulation cannot be left to scientific and market actors alone but require political guidance. According to this view, Member States, and not single citizens, are the bearers of legitimacy which balance normative values. It does not consider the supranational law of the EU as a set of rules which has precedence over and pre-empts national systems. Rather, it gives great importance to the manner in which the actual law is produced. Law, in this view, derives its validity and legitimacy from the deliberative quality of its production.[10]

This chapter, therefore, analyses the committee system in the food sector in the light of its legitimacy and concentrates on the search for the additional means of legitimacy identified in the previous chapter: accountability, transparency, interest participation, expertise and due process requirements.

2. THE RISE OF COMMITTEES WITHIN THE COMMUNITY'S INSTITUTIONAL STRUCTURE

2.1. Origins of Committees

Generally speaking, committees[11] have sprung up within the Community's institutional structure in response to the dual need to carry out the ever-increasing Community activities effectively and to ensure the continuing presence of the Member States within the Community decision-making process. Committees composed of national representatives have been participants in the Community decision-making process ever since the Council decided to delegate implementing powers to the Commission. It was not by accident that, in the early 1960s, committees arose in the agricultural sector.[12] Clearly needing to reduce its ever-increasing workload, the Council chose to delegate to the Commission certain discretionary powers implementing the Community's agricultural policy. The strong national resistance to an unconditional delegation of powers to the Commission together with the need for close co-operation between the Community institutions and the Member States, however, forced the Council to improvise and to oblige the Commission to consult a committee made up of national representatives prior to adopting any decision. The Commission was free to adopt the measure where this committee, by qualified

---

[10] Ch. Joerges/J. Neyer, "From Intergovernmental Bargaining to Deliberative Political Processes: The Constitutionalisation of Comitology" (1997) 3 *ELJ* 273–99.

[11] The committees which find their basis directly in the Treaty itself fall beyond the scope of our research. These include, for example: the Transport Committee (Art. 83), the Social Fund Committee (Art. 124), the Committee of Permanent Representatives (habitually known under the French abbreviation COREPER, Art. 151 (1)), the Economic and Social Committee (Art. 193) and the Committee of the Regions (Art. 198a).

[12] See C. Bertram, "Decision-making in the E.E.C.: The Management Committee Procedure" (1967–8) 5 *CMLRev.* 246–65; P. Schindler, "The Problems of Decision-making by Way of the Management Committee Procedure in the European Economic Community" (1971) 8 *CMLRev.* 184–205; H. Schmitt von Sydow, *Die Verwaltungs- und regelungsausschussverfahren der Europäischen Wirtschaftsgemeinschaften* (Brussels, 1973). See also R.H. Lauwaars, "Art. 235 EEG als grondslag voor de schepping van een Europees merkenrecht" (1981) 29 *SEW* 9, 533–48.

majority voting, agreed upon the Commission measure or failed to reach a decision. However, when this committee rejected the draft decision, the Commission had to refer the matter back to the Council. By means of this so-called "management committee procedure", the Council thus retained its oversight powers, being able to reject or to adopt Commission measures on the basis of a qualified majority.[13] Another committee procedure was introduced in 1968. Termed the "regulatory committee procedure", it placed more restrictions on the Commission's exercise of implementing powers.[14]

In the following years, more of these committees, together with less powerful "advisory committees" were created by the Council in a variety of areas. In addition, encouraged by the Paris Summit of 1972,[15] the Commission, too, established committees composed of interest representatives in specific fields in an attempt to provide for the increased participation of various categories of economic and social interests in the Community policy-making process.[16] Moreover, the Commission again created still more committees in an effort to satisfy its voracious demand for technical and scientific information. In time, the number of committees participating in the preparation and implementation of Community policies has burgeoned alongside the expansion of Community activities.

2.2. Typology of Committees

Committees can be categorised according to three criteria. A first criterion is based upon the *bindingness of the consultation*. Committees can accordingly be divided into committees whose consultation is compulsory in the procedure for drafting Community legislation, and committees whose consultation is not compulsory.[17] Depending on the weight of their opinion, the first category of committees can be further subdivided into *advisory*, *management* and *regulatory* committees.[18] This twofold distinction, however, is not rigid: committees may be transferred to the first category should either the Community legislature or the Court decide that their consultation needs to be made obligatory.[19] For

---

[13] See Reg. 19 on the progressive establishment of a common market organization in cereals (1962) OJ No. 30/933.

[14] In particular in the field of customs law, see, for instance, Council Reg. 802/68 [1968] JO L165 and Council Reg. 803/68 [1968] JO L170.

[15] Sixth General Report of the EC of 1972, 11.

[16] See, as an example in the agricultural sector, the advisory committee on cereals, on pigmeat, on poultrymeat, on eggs, on sugar, on feedingstuffs, on raw tobacco, on wine, on hops, on milk and milk products [1987] OJ L45/1.

[17] Such a division is adhered to by the Community in the Community budget.

[18] In view of the various procedures by which the committees operate, a distinction was made as early as 1968 by the Legal Affairs Committee of the European Parliament, between advisory committees, the consultation of which is compulsory but whose opinion is not binding, and management and regulatory committees. EP Doc 115/1968–69 (Jozeua-Marigné report). See Bradley, above n. 3, at 695.

[19] See Case C–212/91, *Angelopharm* v. *Freie und Hansestadt Hamburg* [1994] ECR I–171.

example, the Scientific Committee on Food was considered so important as to make consultation indispensable.[20]

Another classification may be made according to the *legal basis* by which committees have been created. Committees may thus be divided into committees set up by a Council act, and committees set up by a Commission act. The first are established by a separate act of the Council, or are included in a Council (and Parliament) act regulating a specific subject-matter. The latter are, in general, created by a specific Commission act. In general, committees set up by Council act, in order to assist the Commission in implementation, need to be consulted in the procedure for drafting Community legislation, whilst other committees, commonly set up by the Commission, do not require compulsory consultation.

A third classification may be made on the basis of committee *functions*. Roughly speaking, three types of committees can be distinguished: *scientific* committees, *interest* committees and *policy-making/implementation* committees, each of which correspond to the different aspects of regulatory decision-making.[21] Similarly, committee composition varies in accordance with their function. *Scientific* committees are composed of independent scientific experts. *Interest* committees consist of the representatives of the various interest groups, whilst *policy-making/implementation* committees are composed of the representatives of the Member States. Committees composed of scientific experts have been created by the Commission in response to the need for expertise and form the basis of any decision. These committees thus operate both in the preparatory and the implementing phase. Committees composed of representatives of socio-economic interests groups have been set up where the Commission thought it necessary to canvas a wider body of opinion.[22] Committees composed of national representatives operate mainly in the implementing phase of the decision-making process, where the Council has delegated powers to the Commission. Obligatory consultation of such committees by the Commission follows a specific procedure.[23]

2.3. Committees in Figures

Uncertainty exists as regards the exact number of committees which operate within the ambit of the Community structure. In the literature, different

[20] See, for instance, Art. 6 of Council Dir. 89/107/EEC on food additives authorised for use in foodstuffs intended for human consumption [1989] OJ L40/27. This compulsory obligation is now expressed in the Community budget.

[21] See also R. Dehousse/Ch. Joerges/G. Majone/F. Snyder (with M. Everson), *Europe After 1992. New Regulatory Strategies*, EUI Working Paper LAW 92/31 (Florence, 1992), 21.

[22] See, for a subdivision of the latter group, Economic and Social Committee of the European Communities, *Community Advisory Committees for the Representation of Socio-Economic Interests* (Aldershot, 1980).

[23] See also the attempt to classify the committees made in 1975 by M. Ayral, "Essai de classification des groupes et comités" (1975) 187 *RMC* 330–42.

estimates are found, each based on different calculations. Streeck and Schmitter, following Grote,[24] arrive at a total of 1,336 consultative bodies for 1988.[25] Wessels, in turn, reports the existence of 537 expert committees and 218 management committees in 1985,[26] while for that same year the Commission itself lists somewhat more than 300 committees.[27] A recent study by Buitendijk and Van Schendelen, calculated there to be approximately 1,000 committees.[28] An explanation for these considerable differences in the numbers of committees may be the inclusion by some authors of the various working-groups and subcommittees of the different committees.[29] In this book, however, such working-groups will not be taken into account and the calculation of the number of existing committees relies on the annual overview of committees listed on the Community budget.[30] The calculation of the number of committees thus listed gives a more modest result, although it is noted that the Community budget gives an overview of committees which are expected to meet and therefore does not include "dormant" committees.[31] The latter committees are set up by Community acts, but may remain inoperational for a certain period of time.[32] In more than twenty years of Community activity, the number of committees has multiplied by five: from 93 in 1975 to 477 in 1998.[33]

A glance at Figure 1 reveals that whereas the number of committees in the 1980s remained relatively stable, rising from approximately 220 to 230, the most explosive growth in committee numbers has come in the 1990s, growing from

---

[24] J. Grote, *Guidance and Control in Transnational Committee Networks: The Associational Basis of Policy Cycles at the EC Level* (1989), unpublished manuscript.

[25] W. Streeck/P.C. Schmitter, "From National Corporatism to Transnational Pluralism: Organized Interests in the Single European Market" (1991) 19 *Politics and Society* 137. See also V. Eichener, *Social Dumping or Innovative Regulation? Process and Outcomes of European Decision-Making in the Sector of Health and Safety at Work Harmonization*, EUI Working Paper SPS 92/28 (Florence 1992), 48. Hilf mentions a number of 1,355 groups and committees listed in an internal document of the Commission as early as 1975: M. Hilf, *Die Organisationsstruktur der Europäischen Gemeinschaften* (Berlin/Heidelberg/New York, 1982), 111, n. 5.

[26] W. Wessels, "Administrative Interaction", in W. Wallace (ed.), *Dynamics of European Integration* (London, 1990), 229–41.

[27] See Commission of the European Communities, *Committees* (Luxembourg, 1985). See for 1980, Bull EC, 2/80.

[28] Buitendijk/Van Schendelen, above n. 3, at 40. This calculation is made on the basis of a Commission document of 1990. See, very confusingly, SEC(90)2025 final, which mentions 994 committees for 1990. In a report on the budget appropriations of 1989, the Commission mentions 1,000 committees, SEC(89)1728 final. Here it must be noted that the Commission also includes groups of experts. The number of committees listed in the final budget for 1990 amounted, however, to 272 (see Fig. 1).

[29] Hilf speaks, in fact, of groups and committees: above n. 25, at 111.

[30] See also J. Falke, "Comitology and Other Committees: A Preliminary Empirical Assessment", in R.H. Pedler/G.F. Schaefer (eds.), *Shaping European Law and Policy: The Role of Committees and Comitology in the Political Process* (Maastricht, 1996), 117–65.

[31] See SEC(89)1728 final, 5.

[32] For instance, the Community budget for 1993 mentions the Standing Committee on Medical Devices, appropriating an amount of 4,800 ECU to the meetings of this committee; no account is made for this committee on the budgets for 1994 and 1995.

[33] The very few working groups or sub-committees occasionally mentioned in the Budget have not been included in this calculation.

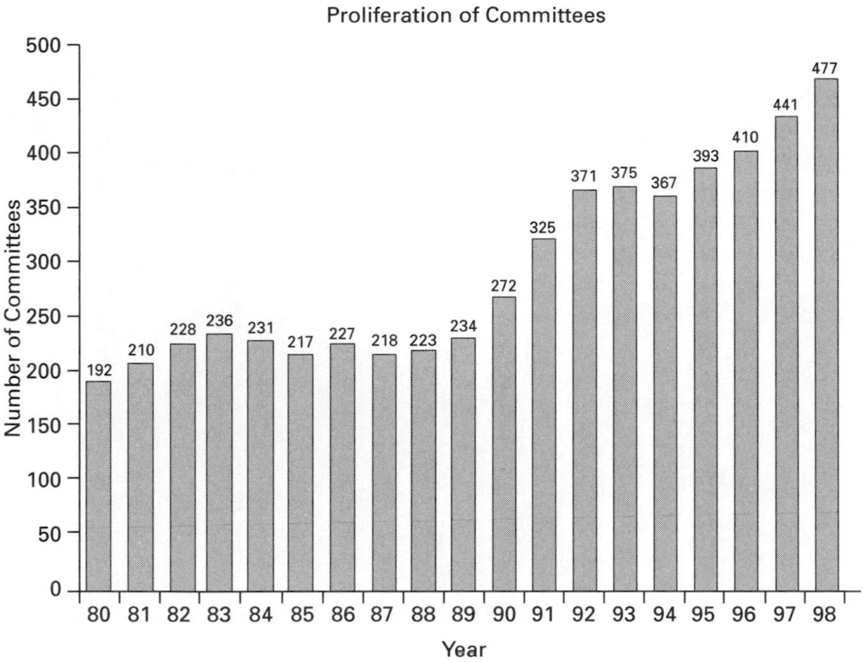

Proliferation of Committees

Figure 1. Proliferation of committees set up by secondary Community legislation since 1980.

Source: Community budgets.

272 to 477. In part, this may be explained by the growing awareness of the need for co-ordination subsequent to the New Approach and the SEA—a function which committees may perform.[34] The substantive increase in the importance of committees within the Community decision-making process is perhaps best highlighted by budgetary figures. Figure 2 shows that whilst annual Community expenditure on committees increased from approximately 3.8 million to 8 million ECU in the years 1980 to 1989, in the 1990s committee expenditure has dramatically increased to 19.5 million ECU for 1998.[35]

3. THE COMPETENCE OF THE COMMUNITY TO CREATE COMMITTEES

The growing importance of committees touches upon a rather old debate on the competence of the Community institutions to create such bodies. As argued

[34] See, in this context, e.g., the creation of the Advisory Committee for the Co-ordination in the Internal Market Field by Commission Decision 93/72/EEC [1993] OJ L26/18.

[35] It must be noted, however, that the accession of the three new Member States in 1995 has automatically added members of the new Member States to all committees, thus increasing Community expenditure on the meetings of these committees. See, on this problem, the Commission in SEC(95)248 final.

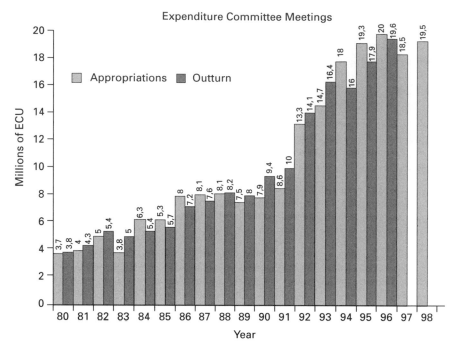

Figure 2. Appropriations and expenditure of committee meetings 1980–98.
Source: Community budgets.

above, the absence of a specific Treaty provision on the setting up of new auxiliary organs has never prevented the Community institutions from setting up many such organs.[36] A few indications that committees may be created are found in the Treaty itself. For example, in the context of judicial review by the Court, Article 177(c) grants jurisdiction to the Court to give preliminary rulings concerning the interpretation of the statutes of bodies established by an act of the Council.[37] Another indication is found in Article 130n which allows the Community to set up joint undertakings, or any other structure, necessary for the efficient execution of Community research, technological development and demonstration. In addition, Article 188c requires the Court of Auditors to examine all Community revenue and expenditure. When executing this task, it must also examine "the accounts of all revenue and expenditure of all bodies set

---

[36] See H. Schmitt von Sydow, *Organe der erweiterten Europäischen Gemeinschaften—Die Kommission* (Baden-Baden, 1980), 173.

[37] I.E. Schwartz, "Artikel 235. Allgemeine Ermächtigungsklausel", in H. Von der Groeben/ J. Thiesing/C.-D. Ehlermann, *Kommentar zum EWG-Vertrag* (Baden-Baden, 1991), 5826, points 180–1; J. Pipkorn, "Bericht Europäische Gemeinschaften", in C. Starck (ed.), *Erledigung von Verwaltungsaufgaben durch Personalkörperschaften und Anstalten des öffentlichen Rechts* (Baden-Baden, 1992), 113; F. Merz, "Bedarf die errichtung eines Europäischen Kartellamtes der Änderung des EWG-Vertrages?" (1990) 1 *EuZW* 13, 407.

up by the Community in so far as the relevant constituent instrument does not preclude such examination". Moreover, Article 214 imposes an obligation, not only on members of Community institutions, officials and other servants of the Community, but also on the *members of committees* not to disclose any information relating to the duty of professional secrecy.[38] Yet, these Articles merely create a *presumption* that the institutions may set up committees, and it is not clear on which basis the institutions may do so.[39] This question will be addressed below.

3.1. The Power of the Council to Create Committees

Committees established by a Council act generally serve to assist and supervise the Commission or to provide for a general framework in which opinions can be exchanged between the Commission and the Member States.[40] The competence of the Council to set up such committees through the delegation of powers to the Commission is laid down in Article 145 as amended by the SEA.[41] In its third indent, this Article stipulates that the Council may impose certain requirements in respect of the exercise of these powers. In view of the fourth phrase of this indent and the Declaration of the ICG on the implementing powers of the Commission, this Article must be interpreted as allowing for the inclusion of a requirement to follow committee procedures where the Council delegates powers to the Commission.[42]

3.2. The Power of the Commission to Create Committees

The power of the Commission to set up committees is imputed, particularly by French literature, to its self-organisational power.[43] This power is invested in the Commission by Article 16 of the Merger Treaty.[44] Yet, this power relates solely to the internal organisation of the Commission, its services and its offi-

---

[38] In contrast to Art. 153, this Art. is not restricted to committees provided for by the Treaty.

[39] Schmitt von Sydow, above n. 36, at 173.

[40] See for instance the Pharmaceutical Committee, set up by Council Dec. 75/320/EEC [1975] OJ L147/23, the consultation of which is not obligatory.

[41] Prior to the SEA, in 1970, the Commission also considered that the Decs. setting up the Standing Veterinary Committee and the Standing Committee on Foodstuffs were validly created by the Council on the basis of Art. 145: Written Question, no. 3/70 [1970] OJ C56/13. Schmitt von Sydow denied that these Arts. would form the correct basis: above n. 36, 172–3. Hilf considered in that period the legal basis to be found in Art. 155(4): above n. 25, 120–4. The same opinion was expressed by the Court in the well-known *Köster* case, Case 25/70, [1971] ECR 1161. See also C. Blumann, "La Commission, agent d'exécution du droit communautaire. La comitologie", in J.-V. Louis/D. Waelbroeck (eds.), *La Commission au coeur du système institutionnel des Communautés européennes* (Bruxelles, 1989), 58.

[42] See also Chap. 2.

[43] Blumann, above n. 41, at 57.

[44] See *inter alia* Case 54/75, *De Dapper* v. *Parliament* [1976] ECR 1381.

cials.[45] Although the Commission controls these committees to some extent and forms the secretariat, it does not exercise hierarchical control or power over personnel.[46] Although committee members (national experts or interest group representatives) are officially nominated by the Commission, this is no more than a mere formal confirmation of Member State and interest group proposals. Moreover, such committee members act on *"titre personnel"*, or represent the opinion of the interest group to which they belong. Therefore, these committees do not form part of the Commission's internal structure which determines that the power to create such committees cannot be derived from its self-organisational power. More plausible is a thesis, mainly followed in German literature,[47] which states that the power to create such committees is implied in existing legislative and implementing powers (implied powers).[48] The power to adopt decisions or proposals conferred by the Treaty on the Community institutions would, in this way, include the power to set up the committees necessary for the preparation of such decisions.[49]

4. COMMITTEES AND THE INSTITUTIONAL BALANCE OF POWERS

The Community's increased reliance on committees has not been devoid of legal problems. The main legal problems to which committees give rise relate to the delegation of powers to the Commission and the institutional balance of powers. Generally, only committees whose consultation is compulsory by the Commission in the implementation of rules laid down by the Council have been controversial. The establishment of advisory committees has no legal consequence, apart from the creation of the obligation to consult. In contrast, divergence of opinion with management and regulatory committees compels the Commission to refer the draft measures it plans to adopt back to the Council. The latter committees have, therefore, been the subject of much controversy. In particular, the Commission and the Parliament have accused them of taking away their rights of decision and control, thus distorting the Community's insti-

[45] Nor do the Commission's rules of procedure devote a specific Art. to the setting up and working of committees.

[46] Hilf, above n. 25, at 115. This can also be derived from the fact that in the Community budget these committees are put under the heading of expenditure on formal and other meetings [1993] OJ L31.

[47] Schmitt von Sydow, above n. 12, 125–6 and Schmitt von Sydow, above n. 36, 174; Hilf, above n. 25, 237 and 300–2; G. Nicolaysen, "Zur Theorie von den implied powers in den EG" (1966) 1 *EuR* 135 ff.

[48] As early as 1956, the theory of implied powers was defined by the Court in the interpretation of the ECSC Treaty, as "a rule of interpretation . . . according to which the rules laid down by an international treaty or law presuppose the rules without which that treaty or law would have no meaning or could not reasonable and usefully be applied": Case 8/55, *Fédération Charbonière de Belgique* v. *High Authority* (judgment of 29 Nov. 1956) [1954–6] ECR 292, at 299. See also Chap. 1, n. 81. See, in general, on the theory of implied powers, Kapteyn/VerLoren van Themaat, above n. 8, 117–19.

[49] Schmitt von Sydow, above n. 12, at 126.

tutional balance. From the Commission's viewpoint, the regulatory committee procedure entails a considerable restriction of the Commission's freedom of action.[50] The Parliament's ardent opposition to management and regulatory committee procedures, and its incessant support of the Commission's implementation rights, can be explained by its desire to be considered as a co-legislature, and its right of political supervision which only applies to Commission and not to Council activities.[51] Interestingly, such problems were to give rise to open institutional conflict only when the Community, prompted by a desire to achieve the goals of the internal market more efficiently, finally sought to streamline and formalise the presence of committees within the Community's institutional structure.

4.1. The Search for More Efficient Decision-making

The Commission's White Paper of 1985 was designed to accelerate the decision-making procedure and make it more efficient.[52] Fast and efficient decision-making was to be accomplished through a more "rational" and disciplined process of delegating implementing powers to the Commission.[53] Consequently, the plethora of committees which the Commission was obliged to consult before adopting any decision, was to be re-appraised drastically, as these committees would not only delay the decision-making procedures considerably, but also entail considerable cost.[54] However, in the preparatory negotiations on the SEA, which was to introduce the institutional corollary of the New Approach, Article 100a, it soon became clear that national political distrust determined that a further delegation of powers to the Commission would only be possible if existing committee procedures were confirmed and formalised, thus allowing the continuing control of Commission activities by the Council.

Therefore, the Council's obligation to delegate implementing powers to the Commission, which was inserted by the SEA as a third indent to Article 145, was attenuated by certain exceptions; in specific cases, the Council would have the discretion to exercise such powers itself or to impose "certain requirements". Stipulating that "the procedures referred to above" must be in accordance with the principles and rules laid down by the Council, the wording of Article 145,

---

[50] See, in particular, the report from the Commission to the European Parliament on delegation of executive powers to the Commission, SEC(89)1591 final.

[51] See Art. 144. Other instruments are *inter alia* the oral and written questions to the Commission and the obligation of the Commission to submit annually a general report to the Parliament (Art. 143). See also Art. 158(2).

[52] COM(85)310 final. See, in more detail, Chaps. 2 and 5.

[53] C.-D. Ehlermann, in evidence to the House of Lords Select Committee on the European Communities, *Report on the Delegation of Powers to the Commission*, Session 1986–7, 3rd report (London, 1987), 17.

[54] See the Resolution of the European Parliament on the cost to the EC budget and effectiveness of committees of a management, advisory and consultative nature [1983] OJ C277/194.

third indent, itself implies that these "certain requirements" refer to committee procedures.

Confirmation that committee procedures were to be formalised nonetheless prompted a fast and furious debate between the Community institutions. On the one hand, the Commission proposed a simplified structure, with the number of committee procedures reduced to three: an advisory, a management and a regulatory procedure.[55] On the other hand, however, the Parliament reiterated its long-held position, arguing that continued reliance on the regulatory committee procedure would not only distort the Community's institutional balance, undermining the Commission's independent implementing task and thus the Parliament's right of supervision, but would also cause delays in, or even block, the Community's decision-making process. Urging that this procedure be eliminated, the Parliament likewise demanded that it be given the opportunity to express its opinion whenever a proposal was referred back to the Council.[56] The Council nevertheless continued to insist upon the formal confirmation of the regulatory committee procedure. Following months of quarrelling, the Council finally adopted Decision 87/373/EEC, commonly termed the Comitology Decision,[57] and thereby definitively laid down the committee procedures to be applied where implementing powers are delegated to the Commission.

4.2. The Comitology Decision

The Comitology Decision consolidates the three classical procedures which had grown out of established Community practice. Implementing powers delegated by the Council to the Commission are thus subject to review by advisory, management and regulatory committees, with the management and regulatory committee procedures being further subdivided into a *filet* and *contre-filet* variant. In addition, the Comitology Decision also provides for a safeguard committee procedure. Despite the procedural consultation obligation, the substantive opinion of the advisory committee has no legal standing. In contrast, negative opinion from management or regulatory committees results in a compulsory reference of the draft decision to the Council.

Procedure I: The Advisory Committee Procedure

The advisory committee procedure requires the Commission to consult a committee for an opinion. This committee consists of representatives of the Member

---

[55] [1986] OJ C70/6. This proposal was originally based on Art. 235, but this was merely a technical device to present it as early as Mar. 1986. Once the SEA came into force, the proposal was based on Art. 145, see, Ehlermann, above n. 53.

[56] Debates of the European Parliament (1986) OJ C227/55. See Parliamentary amendments (1986) OJ C297/95. See also C.-D. Ehlermann, "Compétences d'exécution conférées à la Commission—la nouvelle décision-cadre du Conseil" (1988) 316 *RMC* 234–235.

[57] (1987) OJ L197/33.

States and is chaired by a Commission representative. The latter submits the draft measures to the committee which delivers its opinion within a time limit laid down by the chair according to the urgency of the matter. If necessary, the committee adopts its opinion through a vote. The opinion is recorded in the minutes of the committee and each Member State may have its position registered in these minutes. When adopting its final decision, the Commission must take the "utmost" account of the committee's opinion and further inform the committee of the manner in which its opinion has been taken into account.

Procedure II: The Management Committee Procedure

The management committee procedure largely reproduces the traditional formula established in the agricultural area. Under this procedure, the Commission is required to consult a committee composed of representatives of the Member States and chaired by a representative of the Commission. The Commission representative submits a draft of the measures it wants to adopt to the committee which, in turn, delivers its opinion within a time limit laid down by the chair according to the urgency of the matter. The opinion of the committee is adopted by a qualified majority in accordance with Article 148(2), whilst the chair does not have a vote. Subsequently, the Commission adopts the measures, which have immediate effect. However, if these measures are not in accordance with the opinion of the committee, the Commission is obliged to communicate them to the Council forthwith. In such cases, there are two possible procedures:

- *Variant (a) (filet):* the Commission may defer the application of the measures which it has decided upon, for a period not longer than one month from the date of communication to the Council. Within this period, the Council may take a different decision by qualified majority.
- *Variant (b) (contre-filet):* in variant (b) the Commission is obliged to defer application of the measures for a period to be laid down in each Council act of up to a maximum of three months from the date of communication to the Council. Within this period the Council may adopt a different decision by qualified majority.

Procedure III: The Regulatory Committee Procedure

The regulatory committee procedure varies from the management committee procedure in that, if the Commission wishes to adopt measures which are not in accordance with the committee's opinion, or in the absence of an opinion, it must without delay submit to the Council a proposal of the measures to be adopted. The Council then acts by qualified majority. In this case too, two variants exist:

- *Variant (a) (filet):* if, on the expiry of the time limit laid down in each Council act (a maximum of three months from the date of referral to the

Council) the Council has not acted, the Commission adopts the proposed measures.

• *Variant (b) (contre-filet)*: if, on the expiry of the time limit laid down in each Council act (up to a period of three months from the date of referral to the Council) the Council has not acted, the proposed measures are adopted by the Commission, save where the Council has decided against the said measures by simple majority.

Safeguard Procedure

This procedure may be applied where the Council confers on the Commission the power to decide on safeguard measures. In accordance with the procedure, the Commission notifies the Council and the Member States of any decision regarding safeguard measures. In its enabling act, the Council may stipulate that, before adopting this decision, the Commission must consult the Member States in accordance with procedures to be determined in each case. Any Member State may refer the Commission's decision to the Council within a certain time limit to be determined in the act in question. This procedure, too, has two variants:

• *Variant (a)*: in accordance with variant (a) the Council may take a different decision if it acts by qualified majority within a certain time limit determined in the main act.
• *Variant (b)*: under variant (b) the Council may, by qualified majority, confirm, amend or revoke the decision of the Commission within a certain time limit. If, within this period, the Council has not acted, the Commission decision is deemed to be revoked.

4.3. Inter-institutional Controversies

4.3.1. Shortcomings of the Comitology Decision

Given that the main objective of the Comitology Decision was an increase in the efficiency of the decision-making process, it is open to a degree of criticism.[58] First, the Decision contains no measures to counteract the dangers of delay or blocking of decisions inherent in the regulatory committee procedure.[59] In addition, the Decision is only *ex post* applicable to committees,[60] while those exist-

[58] See, generally, C. Blumann, "Le pouvoir exécutif de la Commission à la lumière de l'Acte unique européen" (1988) 24 *RTDE* 23–59.
[59] W. Meng, "Die Neuregelung der EG-Verwaltungsauschüsse. Streit um die «Comitologie»",(1988) 49 *ZaöRV* 222. See also, K. De Gucht, *Besluitvorming in de Europese Unie* (Antwerp/Apeldoorn, 1994), 82–4.
[60] See the Parliament's critique in its Institutional Affairs Committee Report on the executive powers of the Commission (Comitology) and the role of the Commission in the Community's external relations (Rapporteur: Roumeliotis), 19 Nov. 1990, Doc. A 3–0310/90, PE 141.457/fin, 11.

ing at the time of its adoption remain unaffected. Although the Council may bring existing committees into line with the procedures prescribed by the Comitology Decision,[61] more than seven procedures continue to exist in practice. In addition, the efficiency of the decision-making processes is called into question where the Comitology Decision does not take into account the risk of delays in the decision-making process as the regulatory committee procedure allows only for a best-case postponement of decision-making until the next Council session and a worst-case postponement *ad calendas graecas*.[62] The principles governing the selection of committee procedures are not determined, either.

More importantly, however, the Decision did little to avert the brewing controversy between the Community institutions, but instead brought the issue to a head. The regulatory committee procedure (especially in its *contre-filet* variant) remained a thorn in the flesh of both the Commission and the Parliament. The explicit obligation to delegate implementing powers to the Commission rekindled hopes, in particular those of the Parliament, that a successful attack could be made on the validity of the Comitology Decision which confirmed the contested regulatory committee procedures. Having brought the case before the Court, however, the Parliament's argument that the Decision infringed upon the institutional balance of powers and Article 145, third indent, failed for lack of *locus standi*.[63]

4.3.2. The Plumb–Delors Agreement

After its unsuccessful attempt to attack the validity of the Comitology Decision, the Parliament proceeded with a more subtle approach to the comitology issue.[64] It decided systematically to convert regulatory committee procedures into advisory or management committee procedures.[65] In practice, this strategy was rather unsuccessful, as the Council appeared more likely to abandon delegation than to renounce the (*contre-filet*) regulatory committee procedure.[66] This was particularly the case in sectors touching upon very sensitive issues such as health and safety. Moreover, in cases relating to consumer and environment protection, some members of the Parliament even contested the autonomy of the Commission,[67] implicitly approving a stricter committee procedure.

---

[61] Art. 4 of the Comitology Dec., above n. 57.

[62] See Meng, above n. 59, at 222.

[63] Case 302/87, *Parliament v. Council (Comitology)* [1988] ECR 5615. See, in particular, J.H.H. Weiler, "Pride and Prejudice—Parliament v. Council" (1989) 14 *ELR* 334–46; Case C–70/88, *European Parliament v. Council* [1990] ECR I–2041, recognised the right of Parliament to bring legal proceedings before the Court. See comments of Bebr in (1991) 20 *CMLRev.*, 663–80.

[64] See, on the Parliament's crusade against committees, in particular K.St.C. Bradley, "The European Parliament and Comitology: On the Road to Nowhere?" (1997) 3 *ELJ* 230–54.

[65] See Jacobs *et al.*, above n. 9, at 232.

[66] Commission Report, SEC(89)1591 final, 5–6.

[67] Jacobs *et al.*, above n. 9, at 232.

At the same time, the Parliament officially asked the Commission to be informed of all proposals which the Commission submitted to advisory, management or regulatory committees. This proposition was formalised in an exchange of letters between the President of the Parliament, Plumb and the President of the Commission, Delors—the so-called Plumb–Delors Agreement.[68] In accordance with this agreement, the Commission was obliged to forward all draft measures, usually referred to committees of national representatives in the implementing phase, with the exception of routine management documents of a limited period of validity or of minor importance, and documents whose adoption was complicated by considerations of secrecy or urgency. In practice, the Commission forwarded relatively few documents[69] and often did not even indicate the time limit in which the committee concerned had to express its opinion. This made it difficult for the Parliament to react to proposals.

However, the Parliament, too, offered up a *mea culpa* by admitting that it had not provided for an adequate follow-up of this new procedure.[70] One occasion on which the agreement was successfully put into motion, however, concerned a proposal of the Commission on powdered milk for infants. Being of the opinion that the Commission's proposal was not sufficiently strict,[71] the Parliamentary Environment and Consumer Protection Committee raised a question in a plenary hearing which adopted a resolution on this issue in April 1991. As a result, the Commission modified its proposal significantly, thus answering the Parliament's concerns.[72]

4.3.3. *The* Modus Vivendi

The long-awaited chance for Parliament to impose its views on the comitology issue came after the adoption of the Maastricht Treaty, which conferred upon the Parliament co-legislative powers under the co-decision-making procedure (Article 189b), obligatory for Article 100a measures. Not surprisingly, having

---

[68] Jacobs *et al.*, above n. 9, at 234.

[69] European Parliament, Roumeliotis Report, above n. 60, at 5. See also the Parliament's complaint addressed to the Commission of not having implemented the Plumb-Delors agreement as regards its decision on organic production of agricultural products: Parliament Resolution B3–349/93 [1993] OJ C115/274. The procedure subsequently brought before the Court against the Commission Reg. in question (No. 207/93 [1993] OJ L25/5) was however rejected by the Court in Case C–156/93, *Parliament* v. *Commission* (*organic production*) [1995] ECR I–2019. During various interviews carried out by me, it even appeared that not all Commission officials were aware of the existence of this procedure.

[70] See in this context the Roumeliotis Report calling upon the parliamentary committees to be vigilant in applying the procedure: above n. 60, at 5.

[71] The Parliament was of the opinion that the Dir. in question should not allow manufacturers of infant formula milk to distribute free samples to young mothers without the provision of independent medical advice and should limit the advertising of such products to medical journals, this being in accordance with WHO principles.

[72] Jacobs *et al.*, above n. 9, at 234. See Commission Dir. 91/231/EEC on infant formulae and follow-on formulae [1991] OJ L175/35.

once been granted such powers, the Parliament seized the opportunity to voice its disapproval of the inclusion of existing committee procedures in the co-decision procedure.[73] The Parliament was quick to argue that the Council no longer possessed an exclusive power of delegation in cases which prescribed the co-decision procedure, and that the modes of delegation prescribed in Article 145, third indent, would, in any case, not apply to cases of co-decision. Clearly distinguishing between acts adopted by the Council and acts adopted by the Parliament and Council acting in concert, it argued that Articles 145 and 155 related solely to the delegation of powers by acts adopted by the Council acting alone.[74] As a result, within co-decision negotiations the Parliament consistently rejected all proposals including committee procedures.[75] Although the Parliament's reasoning could be argued to be erroneous in reference to the fact that Articles 145 and 155 had been implicitly modified by virtue of the requirement made in Article 191(1) that acts adopted in accordance with the co-decision procedure be signed by the Presidents of both the Parliament and the Council,[76] the strategy of the Parliament to block the decision-making procedure was ultimately to prove successful.

Following a failed attempt by the Commission to reach inter-institutional agreement on this issue,[77] a *modus vivendi* was adopted between the three institutions in December 1994.[78] This *modus vivendi* requires the Commission, when sending the draft measures to the policy-making/implementation committee in question, to send these documents (at the same time and under the same conditions) to the appropriate parliamentary committee as well. In this sense, the *modus vivendi* mirrors the *Plumb–Delors* agreement. In addition,

[73] See Bradley, above n. 3, at 696 and K.St.C. Bradley/A. Feeney, "Legal Developments in the European Parliament" (1993) 13 *YEL* 405.

[74] Resolution of the Parliament [1994] OJ C20/176. Hereto the wording of Art. 145, third indent (not amended by the Maastricht Treaty) was referred to, which states that the Council confers on the Commission, "in the acts which the Council adopts, powers for the implementation of the rules which the Council lays down". See the draft resolution and the explanatory memorandum by the rapporteur De Giovanni of the Committee on Institutional Affairs on questions of comitology relating to the entry into force of the Maastricht Treaty of 6 Dec. 1993, Doc. A3–417/93, PE 206.619/fin.

[75] See in particular the bargaining on mechanical coupling devices, recreational craft and the Open Network Provision (ONP) voice telephony discussed by D. Earnshaw/D. Judge, "Early Days: The European Parliament, Co-decision and the European Union Legislative Process post-Maastricht" (1995) 2 *JEPP* 634–6. See, also, Falke/Winter, above n. 3, 562–5.

[76] This interpretation is strengthened by the Court's recent judgment in Case C–259/95, *European Parliament* v. *Council* [1997] ECR I–5303, where the Court explicitly held that "[a]cts of the Council, without further qualification, are those adopted by that institution, either alone or together with the Parliament under the co-decision procedure. It is clear from the various provisions of the EC Treaty . . . that acts adopted jointly by the Council and the Parliament are regarded as acts of the Council" (para. 26).

[77] SEC(94)645 final. See J. Monar, "Interinstitutional Agreements: The Phenomenon and its New Dynamics after Maastricht" (1994) 31 *CMLRev.* 693–719 and F. Snyder, "Interinstitutional Agreements: Forms and Constitutional Limitations", in G. Winter (ed.), *Sources and Categories of European Union Law. A Comparative and Reform Perspective* (Baden-Baden, 1996), 453–66.

[78] *Modus vivendi* between the European Parliament, the Council and the Commission concerning the implementing measures for acts adopted in accordance with the procedure laid down in Art. 189b of the EC Treaty [1996] OJ C102/1.

where the policy-making/implementation committee fails to agree, or is not able to adopt an opinion, thus obliging the Commission to submit the matter to the Council, the Parliament must be given the possibility of issuing an opinion to which the Council must pay due attention. Although the very general formulation of this agreement gives room for various interpretations,[79] the *modus vivendi* has, in practice, achieved its aim of unblocking the decision-making procedure and developing (apparent) agreement amongst the institutions on comitology.

The *modus vivendi* is, however, of a temporary nature. Where, in addition to blocking co-decision-making, the Parliament can also obstruct the operation of committees by blocking their budget allocations,[80] the practical need to find a permanent solution to comitology is readily apparent. The comitology issue was therefore set by both the Parliament and the Commission on the 1996–7 IGC agenda for a revision of the Maastricht Treaty.[81] The Parliament once again emphasised its desire to be involved in the committee procedures and submitted a proposal for a single committee procedure. It argued that:

> "It would be wrong for the Parliament to get involved in unnecessary detail but if the Council considers that a Comitology 'detail' is so politically or commercially significant that it does not want to give 'carte blanche' to the Commission it should be recognised that the Parliament should also have a legitimate interest in such matters".[82]

The Commission,[83] however, supported the retention of the three existing committee procedures without the *contre-filet* variants.[84] Not being able to reach agreement on comitology, a majority of the Reflection Group for the IGC chaired by C. Westendorp recognised the necessity of a simplification of the present committee system.[85] The IGC nonetheless failed to consider comitology as a topic in need of Treaty amendment and restricted itself, in a Declaration attached to the Treaty of Amsterdam, to soliciting the Commission to submit a proposal to amend the Comitology Decision to the Council by the end of 1998.[86]

---

[79] Whilst the Parliament views the *modus vivendi* to be a concertation procedure leading to a compromise solution, one national government underlines that it does not compel the Council to adopt the Parliament's opinion: see Earnshaw/Judge, above n. 75, 635–6.

[80] See, for instance, the 1995 budget where the Parliament appropriated only 1.9 million ECU to committee meetings, and only provisionally appropriated the greater sum of 17 million ECU.

[81] See, in general, C. Blumann, "Le Parlement européen et la comitologie: une complication pour la Conférence intergouvernementale de 1996" (1996) 32 *RTDE* 1–24.

[82] See European Parliament Committee of Institutional Affairs, Report on the European Parliament's opinion for the IGC (Art. N of the TEU) and assessment of the work of the Reflection Group (rapporteurs Dury and Maij-Weggen), 5 Mar. 1996, A4–0068/96/Part B, 48.

[83] Commission Opinion for the IGC 1996, Reinforcing Political Union and Preparing for Enlargement, 1995, 13–14.

[84] See for an overview of the positions of the Member States and the institutions on this point, S. Griller (ed.), Regierungskonferenz 1996: Ausgangspositionen, IEF Working Paper Nr. 27 (Vienna 1996), 87 ff.

[85] Westendorp Report of 5 Dec. 1995, reprinted in J.A. Winter, *Reforming the Treaty on European Union—The Legal Debate* (The Hague, 1996), 481–518. See K.St.C. Bradley, "Institutional Aspects of Comitology: Scenes from the Cutting Room Floor", in Ch. Joerges/E. Vos (eds.), *EU Committees: Social Regulation, Law and Politics* (Hart Publishing, Oxford, forthcoming).

[86] Declaration no. 31. See also sect. 5.11.

4.4. The Court's Approval of Committee Procedures

Parliamentary disquiet notwithstanding, the Court has failed to find any legal objection to the participation of committees in the exercise of implementing powers by the Commission. The legality of the use of the management committee procedure was contested immediately following its introduction in 1962. In *Köster*, it was argued that this procedure was contrary to the EEC Treaty, not only since it interfered with the Commission's independent right of decision, but also since the use of a body not foreseen by the EC Treaty would distort the established institutional relationship between the Commission and the Council.[87] The Court, however, emphasised that a delegation of powers to the Commission under Article 155 EEC was entirely optional and held that Article 155 EEC did not preclude the Council from subjecting delegated powers to detailed rules for their exercise. Since the ultimate decision-making power did not rest with the Committee, but remained with either the Council or the Commission, the Court concluded that the improvised insertion of management committees into the Community's established institutional structure was not contrary to the Community's institutional balance under Article 4 EEC.[88]

The legality of this procedure was further confirmed by the Court in *Rey Soda*. The Court repeated that this procedure was a legally valid mechanism which entailed a great advantage, in that the Council might confer exceptionally wide powers of implementation upon the Commission, whilst reserving the right to intervene "where necessary".[89] This notwithstanding, in *Dulciora* the Court expressly underlined that only in cases where a management committee had actually adopted a negative opinion did draft measures have to be referred back to the Council by the Commission; in cases where such a committee failed to produce an opinion, the Commission could adopt its proposed measure without giving the Council the possibility of adopting a different opinion.[90] Where no committee procedures are included in the basic act, only the Commission has the power to implement the rules in question.[91] In the internal market context, however, this will rarely occur, as committee procedures have proved to be indispensable for delegating powers to the Commission.

In its subsequent case law, the Court has tackled various other instances of the overall objections raised about comitology, concluding in each case that

---

[87] Case 25/70, *Einfuhr- und Vorratstelle für Getreide und Futtermittel v. Köster, Berodt & Co.* [1970] ECR 1161.

[88] *Ibid.*, at 1171. See also Case 30/70, *Scheer v. Einfuhr- und Vorratstelle für Getreide und Futtermittel* [1970] ECR 1197, at 1208–9.

[89] Case 23/75, *Rey Soda v. Cassa Conguaglio Zucchero* [1975] ECR 1279, at 1301. See also Joined Cases 279, 280, 285 & 286/84, *Rau and others v. Commission (Christmas butter)* [1987] ECR 1069.

[90] Case 95/78, *Dulciora v. Amministrazione delle Finanze dello Stato* [1979] ECR 1547, at 1568.

[91] This may be deduced form Case 30/88, *Greece v. Commission* [1989] ECR 3711, concerning the financing of projects in the context of special aid to Turkey, at 3740.

they were unfounded.[92] In *Tedeschi*, the Court rejected fears that comitology might not accelerate but instead paralyse the Community decision-making process, and concluded that the *contre-filet* variant of the regulatory committee procedure would not necessarily lead to decisional impasse, since the Commission was always free to submit a new proposal.[93] In addition, comitology was held not to interfere with the Commission's independent powers conferred upon it by the Treaty. In a ruling from 1988,[94] the Court was called in to adjudicate in the long-standing conflict between the Commission (supported by the Parliament[95]) and the Council on the use of committee procedures within the Commission's own budgetary power under Article 205.[96] The subject-matter of litigation was the adoption of a regulation on fisheries research programmes by the Council which included a management committee procedure.[97] The Commission argued that its own decisional powers under Article 205 were unfairly restricted by the management committee procedure, since the powers delegated to it involved mere budget appropriations and did not fall under the concept of "implementation" within the meaning of Article 145, third indent. The Council, however, countered. It claimed there was a clear distinction between powers to adopt acts of general and individual application covered by Articles 145 and 155 and the budgetary powers under Articles 203 and 205. It asserted that the budget might not be implemented without a substantive decision on the legal basis of the expenditure. The Court, whilst establishing the limits to Article 205, nonetheless confirmed the Council's broad interpretation of the concept of "implementation" within Article 145, third indent,[98] and approved the Council's use of a management committee procedure.[99]

In *Parliament* v. *Council* the Court further considered Parliament's interest in committee procedures, investigating the question whether the Council might alter a Commission proposal for a management committee into a regulatory

---

[92] However, where no committee procedures are included in the basic act, only the Commission has the power to implement the rules in question. This may be deduced from Case 30/88, *Greece* v. *Commission*, concerning the financing of projects in the context of special aid to Turkey in which no committee procedure was included in the basic act, and where the Court considered that only the Commission had the power to lay down the detailed rules for the use of the aid in question and for the approval of specific projects [1989] ECR 3711, at 3740.

[93] Case 5/77, *Tedeschi* v. *Denkavit Commerciale Srl.* [1977] ECR 1555, at 1580.

[94] Case 16/88, *Commission* v. *Council (Fisheries)* [1989] ECR 3457. See the comments by Blumann, in [1900] *RTDE* 173–90, and J. Forman, "Case 16/88, *Commission* v. *Council*" (1990) 27 *CMLRev.* 872–82.

[95] See EP session documents 3/78 (paras. 33–4) and 400/78 (paras. 66–9) of 1978.

[96] See C.-D. Ehlermann/M. Minch, "Conflicts between the Community Institutions within the Budgetary Procedure: Article 205 of the EEC Treaty" (1981) 16 *EuR* 23–42.

[97] Council Reg. (EEC) 3252/87 on the co-ordination and promotion of research in the fisheries sector [1987] OJ L314/17.

[98] Case 16/88, above n. 94, at 3485.

[99] Following this judgment, two analogous Cases (250/88 and 308/88) on food aid were withdrawn. Nevertheless, in the Interinstitutional Agreement on budgetary discipline and improvement of the budgetary procedure, the Commission reiterates its preferences for the advisory committee procedure [1993] OJ C331/1.

committee procedure (*filet*) without re-consulting Parliament.[100] Importantly, the Court did recognise that the choice between the various types of committees could have a substantive effect upon the decision-making process, although *in casu* this choice had not decisively affected the overall balance of the powers allocated to the Commission and the Council.[101]

5. HEALTH AND SAFETY REGULATION THROUGH COMMITTEES: THE CASE OF FOODSTUFFS

It follows from the preceding sections that, formally speaking, committees do not give rise to particular problems in relation to the institutional balance of powers, as interpreted and confirmed by the Court. However, it is difficult to deny the great impact which committees have on Community decision-making and the important functions they fulfil within the institutional setting: scientific committee opinions generally form the basis of Community acts, whilst other committees possess important means to influence the outcome of the decision-making procedure. This raises questions of the control, legitimacy and transparency of committee activities within the Community decision-making process. In this context, the fact that decisions referred to the Council by the Commission largely escape oversight by the Parliament has been argued to be, from the viewpoint of democratic legitimacy, unacceptable.[102] The Parliament does not, however, constitute the only legitimising element in the Community structure. As argued in the previous Chapter, with the increasing transfer of decision-making powers to the Commission, additional legitimising sources, such as the quality of expertise, the representation of diffuse interests and the transparency of the decision-making process have gained in importance. More generally, the shift of health and safety regulation to the Community level raises concerns about the formulation of public opinion on the issues under discussion.

This section analyses, therefore, how committees assist the Community institutions in regulating health and safety issues, in particular, in the food sector. The field of processed foodstuffs[103] is of exemplary importance as it

---

[100] Case C–417/93, *Parliament v. Council (TACIS)* [1995] ECR I–1185. See also Case C–156/93, above n. 69. An earlier attempt by the Parliament to annul the regulatory committee procedure in a Council reg. by means of its intervention in a case between the Commission and the Council was rejected as the Parliament, in the role of an intervening party, was not allowed to raise a subject-matter not addressed by one of the main parties: Case C–155/91, *Commission v. Council* [1993] ECR I–939, at I–969.

[101] Case C–417/93, above n. 100, paras. 25 and 26.

[102] See Kapteyn/VerLoren van Themaat, above n. 8, at 244.

[103] For the purpose of this book I shall only consider processed foodstuffs, the regulation of which at national level generally constitutes trade barriers; thus leaving unprocessed foodstuffs, which are generally considered agricultural products which fall under the Community's Common Agricultural Policy regulation, outside the scope of our study. It is admitted though, that in some cases (as the BSE crisis demonstrates) the distinction is difficult to draw.

demonstrates the difficulties which the Community encounters in regulating health and safety issues, whilst likewise displaying all three of the committee models which the Community deploys to tackle such problems: a scientific committee, an interest committee and a policy-making/implementation committee. The increasing involvement of the Community in this sector, accompanied by a growing delegation of implementing powers to the Commission has led to a concurrent increase in the importance of the committees operating in this sector. Close examination of the food sector serves to determine the impact of the committees on the Community's decision-making and to explore the interaction between the Community institutions and the Member States, subjecting this field to analysis of whether and how the search for these additional means of legitimacy is implemented.

5.1. The Peculiarities of Foodstuffs

Food is the key to the good health and well-being of persons since it supplies essential nutrients, "feeding" the individual's needs. Food is, by its very nature, a means of survival for human beings and the ensuring of its safety and quality is therefore of the utmost importance to consumers, producers and public authorities. At the same time, the imperatives of fair trading need to be respected. This immediately explains the difficulties which are encountered in the regulation of food issues.

Food law has a long-rooted tradition at national level, where regulators combat food adulteration, fraud and dangerous food.[104] Foodstuffs were thus among the Community's first priorities for harmonisation to eliminate trade barriers arising from national provisions. Annually, numerous new food products enter the market, increasing the range of products and processes the Community needs to regulate. The Community must take account of both traditional products, generally, locally produced according to customary methods, and fabricated products, often produced by big industries using modern technology. Food regulation by the Community must accommodate health and consumer protection,[105] fair competition, new technologies, requirements relating to the Community's poorer regions, etc. These difficulties are enhanced by continuously changing public attitudes to food and by the enormous economic consequences of the Community's harmonisation activities in the food industry, which is one of its largest industries.[106] For example, for 1997 European food

[104] The United Kingdom, for instance, adopted its first regulatory statute on food in 1860, which was elaborated by the statute of 1875. Germany adopted its first act in 1879, France in 1885 and Belgium in 1890: see Ch. Lister, *Regulation of Food Products by the European Community* (London/Dublin/Edinburgh/Brussels, 1992), 16. Lister mentions as examples of the practices in the early nineteenth century of adulterated and often dangerous food production, the darkening of green coffee-beans by lead and the brightening of confectioneries by a variety of toxic substances.

[105] See, e.g., M. Chambolle, "Food Policy and the Consumer" (1988) 11 *JCP* 441.

[106] Lister, above n. 104, 2–3.

consumption (including drink and tobacco) was estimated to exceed 550,000 million ECU.[107]

5.2. The Community's Regulatory Approaches to Foodstuffs

5.2.1. The "Traditional" Approach to Foodstuffs

As early as 1962, the Community proceeded to the harmonisation of food laws as the different national provisions on food constituted obstacles to trade. Among the very first directives ever adopted by the Community was the Council Directive on the use of colourings in foodstuffs.[108] This directive was the beginning of a sequence of Community directives on foodstuffs.[109] In accordance with the "traditional" approach to harmonisation,[110] aiming at a total harmonisation of national food laws, approximately 50 "vertical" directives relating to one single foodstuff were to be adopted under a strict timetable. The first directive adopted under this approach was the directive on cocoa and chocolate.[111] Difficulties, however, were encountered *inter alia* where the efforts to harmonise all existing food laws, defining detailed requirements on the composition ("recipes") of specific foodstuffs, touched upon sensitive questions of culinary cultures and traditions.[112] Not surprisingly, therefore, negotiations on the harmonisation of one particular foodstuff under Article 100 EEC, requiring unanimous voting, took much time and often were not completed within the time-limits laid down. The Directive on fruit jams, jellies, marmalades and chestnut puree,[113] for instance, was adopted after 14 years of negotiation.[114]

5.2.2. The New Approach to Foodstuffs of 1985

The slow and cumbersome decision-making procedures[115] in food regulation finally led the Commission to declare the "New Approach to Technical Harmonisation and Standards"[116] also applicable to foodstuffs.[117] Recognising

---

[107] European Commission, DGIII, *Panorama of EU Industry 1997*, Vol. 1, 3–3.

[108] [1962] OJ L115/2645. This Dir. does not have an EEC number as, at the time of adoption, no formal numbering system had been worked out. See P. Gray, "Food Law and the Internal Market. Taking Stock" [1990] *Food Policy* 111.

[109] See, in general, N. Nentwick, *Das Lebensmittelrecht der Europäischen Union* (Vienna, 1994); Lister, above n. 104; P. Deboyser, *Le droit communautaire rélatif aux denrées alimentaires* (Louvain-la-Neuve, 1989); A. Gérard, *Food Law in the Europe of Today* (Brussels, 1987).

[110] As adopted by the Council in its Resolution [1969] OJ C76/1. See, in detail, Chap. 2.

[111] Council Dir. 73/241/EEC [1973] OJ L228/23.

[112] Gray, above n. 108, at 112.

[113] Council Dir. 79/693/EEC [1979] OJ L205/5.

[114] See D. Welch, "From 'Euro Beer' to 'Newcastle Brown', A Review of European Community Action to Dismantle Divergent 'Food' Laws" (1983–4) 22 *JCMS* 57.

[115] In 1985, dirs. had been adopted in only 14 of the 50 sectors identified by the general harmonisation programme, COM(85)603 final, 3.

[116] Council Resolution on a New Approach to Technical Harmonisation and Standards [1985] OJ C136/1. See Chaps. 2 and 5.

[117] Communication from the Commission to the Council and the European Parliament on the completion of the internal market: Community legislation on foodstuffs, COM(85)603 final.

the specific nature of food as a regulatory problem, the Commission took the view that Community legislation on food should be limited to provisions justified by the need to protect the health of persons, the need to provide consumers with information and protection on matters other than health and the need to ensure fair trading and provide for the necessary public controls. Referring to *Cassis de Dijon*, the Commission revealed that it would abandon the detailed regulation of compositional rules, as labelling would suffice. It recognised, however, that such an approach would require a comprehensive system of labelling. As regards the health protection aspects of food, the Commission announced that it would follow a horizontal approach concentrating on the regulation of the substances processed into food. At the same time, the Commission demanded that it should be delegated greater power together with the Standing Committee on Foodstuffs. Whilst the Council would always adopt the basic rules of Community food law, there would be delegated to the Commission, for reasons of efficiency and flexibility, the task of implementing these rules under the conditions laid down by the Council. This New Approach has subsequently formed the main device for the regulation of food issues by the Community.[118]

5.2.3. *Various Regulatory Patterns of Food Regulation*

On the basis of the New Approach for foodstuffs, a wide-ranging set of horizontal directives has been adopted, relating to additives,[119] extraction solvents,[120] flavouring agents,[121] colours,[122] sweeteners,[123] food additives other than colours and sweeteners,[124] materials and articles in contact with foodstuffs[125] and official control.[126] Under this approach, directives establish horizontal requirements, applicable to a broad range of diverse products independent of whether they belong to the same product categories. Many such directives are framework directives which are supplemented by implementing measures by the Commission, in accordance with a regulatory committee procedure.

The vertical approach nevertheless still forms a part of the practice. Hence, the updating and replacing of the directives concerning specific food categories

---

[118] See, equally, Communication from the Commission on the free movement of foodstuffs within the Community [1989] OJ C271/3.

[119] Council Dir. 89/107/EEC [1989] OJ L40/27, as lastly amended by European Parliament and Council Dir. 94/34/EC [1994] OJ L237/1.

[120] Council Dir. 88/344/EEC [1988] OJ L157/28, as lastly amended by European Parliament and Council Dir. 97/60/EC [1997] OJ L331/7.

[121] Council Dir. 88/388/EEC [1988] OJ L184/61, as amended by Commission Dir. 91/71/EEC [1991] OJ L42/25.

[122] European Parliament and Council Dir. 94/36/EC [1994] OJ L237/13.

[123] European Parliament and Council Dir. 94/35/EC [1994] OJ L237/3.

[124] European Parliament and Council Dir. 95/2/EC [1995] OJ L61/1, as amended by European Parliament and Council Dir. 96/85/EC [1997] OJ L86/4.

[125] Council Dir. 89/109/EEC [1989] OJ L40/38.

[126] Council Dir. 89/397/EEC [1989] OJ L186/23.

adopted in the 1970s, such as cocoa and chocolate,[127] certain sugars,[128] honey,[129] fruit juices,[130] dehydrated milk,[131] jams and jellies,[132] caseins and caseinates[133] and mineral water[134] still remains a Community activity.

In addition, a third approach, which lies between the horizontal and vertical approach, can be identified. In practice, this approach stipulates horizontal requirements for what are similar product categories.[135] An example of this approach is the directive on quick-frozen food[136] which regulates the processing of foodstuffs by rapid freezing but does not address all regulatory issues regarding the categories of food which may be frozen. Another example is the directive on foodstuffs intended for particular nutritional use,[137] which combines a horizontal framework directive with the possibility of adopting vertical directives on specific foodstuffs. The latter directives are generally adopted by the Commission in accordance with a regulatory committee procedure.[138] At present, these approaches are used concurrently by the Community in its effort to find practical solutions for issues which have arisen.

5.2.4. Towards a Third Phase of Integration: The Deepening of Community Food Regulation

The distinction made by the New Approach to foodstuffs between health issues regulated by the Community and issues other than health issues which might be tackled through a comprehensive labelling mechanism has been heavily criticised. The abandonment of compositional rules has been argued to lead to a decline in the quality of foodstuffs.[139] The general dissatisfaction with this situation, though not directly related to the ensuring of health protection (although in some cases quality may be strongly interrelated with safety), has therefore led the Community to regulate the quality of food in a similar way.[140]

---

[127] Council Dir. 73/241/EEC [1973] OJ L228/23, as amended by Council Dir. 89/344/EEC [1989] OJ L142/19.

[128] Council Dir. 73/437/EEC [1973] OJ L356/71.

[129] Council Dir. 74/409/EEC [1974] OJ L221/10.

[130] Council Dir. 75/726/EEC [1975] OJ L311/40, as consolidated by Council Dir. 93/77/EEC [1993] OJ L244/23.

[131] Council Dir. 76/118/EEC [1976] OJ L24/49.

[132] Above, n. 113.

[133] Council Dir. 83/417/EEC [1983] OJ L237/25.

[134] Council Dir. 80/778/EEC [1980] OJ L229/11. See the Commission's amended proposal COM(97)228 final.

[135] See Lister, above n. 104, 32–7.

[136] Council Dir. 89/108/EEC [1989] OJ L40/34.

[137] Council Dir. 89/398/EEC [1989] OJ L186/27, as amended by European Parliament and Council Dir. 96/84/EC [1997] OJ L48/20.

[138] See, for instance, Commission Dir. 91/321/EEC on infant formulae: above n. 72.

[139] See O. Brouwer, "Free Movement of Foodstuffs and Quality Requirements: Has the Commission Got it Wrong?" [1988] 25 *CMLRev.* 237–62.

[140] See Council Reg. (EEC) 2081/92 on the protection of geographical indications and designations of origin for agricultural and foodstuffs [1992] OJ L208/1, as amended by Council Reg. 535/97 (1997) OJ L83/3 (see also Commission Reg. 2037/93 [1993] OJ L185/5, as amended by Commission

In health matters, the Community has undoubtedly made important progress through the New Approach. Yet, the free movement of foodstuffs within an internal market, together with the specific nature of risk regulation, has nonetheless required the Community to deepen its involvement in the regulation of foodstuffs; a deepening which entails an increasing delegation of implementing powers to the Commission in this area. Several more specific factors may explain this tendency:

Mutual Distrust: Control and Inspection Systems

Existing national food laws provoke many complaints that they constitute trade barriers. For the year 1995, for instance, the Commission recorded 66 complaints concerning trade barriers in the food sector. This sector was listed second on the record of sectors being complained against, just after the car sector, for which 71 complaints were registered.[141] The main obstacles to the trade in food are currently identified as being those national procedures which require prior authorisation for foodstuffs, so that the composition of the food may be controlled and the presence, in particular, of food supplements and/or additives may be detected.[142] The carrying out of such inspection procedures by the Member States may be explained by the lack of mutual confidence in each other's products.[143] As set out in Chapter 2, the Court has consistently approved such inspection procedures, provided that they are justified to protect human health under Article 36 and do not constitute arbitrary discrimination or a disguised restriction on imported goods.[144] Thus, Community directives need to regulate all aspects of health protection (leading to full harmonisation) and also establish Community procedures to monitor compliance, so that Article 36 may no longer be validly invoked by the Member States.[145] This explains the neces-

Reg. 1428/97 [1997] OJ L196/39) and Council Reg. (EEC) 2082/92 on certificates of a specific character for agricultural products and foodstuffs [1992] OJ L208/9. This was already pointed out in the Commission's Communication of 1989, above n. 118. See O. Brouwer, "Community Protection of Geographical Indications and Specific Character as a Means of Enhancing Foodstuffs Quality" (1991) 28 *CMLRev.* 615–46. See, for an overview of the critiques, Lister, above n. 104, at 102.

[141] In total, 258 complaints were recorded, of which 15 related to chemicals, 10 to pharmaceuticals, 9 to telecommunications, 6 to construction and 81 to other categories, including language problems in the use of labelling. See the Report from the Commission to the Council and the European Parliament—The Single Market in 1995, COM(96)51 final, 24.

[142] *Ibid.*, at 25.

[143] See R. Streinz, "Economic Aspects of Technical Regulations", in F. Snyder (ed.), *A Regulatory Framework for Foodstuffs in the Internal Market*, EUI Working Paper LAW 94/4 (Florence, 1994), 84 and 101 ff. See, on the problem of mutual trust in general, G. Majone, *Mutual Trust, Credible Commitment and the Evolution of Rules for a Single European Market*, EUI Working Paper RSC 95/1 (Florence, 1995).

[144] See, for instance, Case 132/80, *United Foods and Van den Abeele* v. *Belgium* [1981] ECR 995, at 1023.

[145] See, in particular, Case 247/84, *Motte* [1985] ECR 3887 and Case 304/84, *Muller* [1986] ECR 1511. See also Chap. 2. However, in accordance with the proportionality principle, a double check in the exporting country and in the importing country may, as the Court has consistently held (depending on the circumstances) be more than Art. 36 allows in cases where other possibilities exist which are an equally effective to protect human health: see, *inter alia*, Case 132/80, *United Foods*, above n. 144, at 1025.

sity for the Community to establish uniform control and inspection procedures for foodstuffs.[146] In 1989, therefore, the Council issued a directive on the official control of foodstuffs,[147] the need for which had already been recognised by the New Approach for foodstuffs. With this directive the Community has above all sought to co-ordinate national inspection activities, by requiring the Member States to stipulate their inspection programmes exactly in accordance with the appropriate criteria.

From 1993 onwards, the Commission has drawn up, in annual agreement with the Standing Committee for Foodstuffs, co-ordinated programmes with recommendations relating to the sampling of specific food products;[148] a move designed to contribute to the establishment of mutual confidence between the competent national authorities.[149] Yet, the mere co-ordination of national control procedures has appeared to be insufficient, *inter alia* due to the lack of common quality control standards and the different interpretations of basic statistical concepts.[150] This has led the Council to adopt additional measures on the official control of foodstuffs, requiring the Member States to comply with the general criteria for the operation of testing laboratories laid down in a European Standard.[151]

In addition, a Community inspection service,[152] now brought under the umbrella of the Community's Food and Veterinary Office, has been set up by this Directive in order to foster co-operation with the national authorities and evaluate the equivalence and effectiveness of official food control systems.[153] This inspectorate undertook its first control missions in 1995.[154] An important aspect of the control of foodstuffs is the control of food hygiene. In order to increase confidence in the standard of food hygiene and generally to improve the level of food hygiene, it was necessary to supplement these rules with a directive laying down general rules on food hygiene and the procedures for the

---

[146] See the Commission of the European Communities, *Second Symposium on Control of Foodstuffs* (Luxembourg, 1992).

[147] Council Dir. 89/397/EEC [1989] OJ L186/23.

[148] See the Commission Recommendations for 1993 [1992] OJ L350/85; for 1994 [1994] OJ L80/25; for 1995 [1995] OJ L65/27; for 1996 [1996] OJ L109/24; for 1997 [1997] OJ L22/27; and for 1998 [1998] OJ L36/10.

[149] COM(94)567 final, 6.

[150] See the Report from the Commission to the Council and the European Parliament on the application of Art. 13 of Council Dir. 89/397/EEC on the official control of foodstuffs, COM(94)567 final.

[151] Council Dir. 93/99/EEC on the subject of additional measures concerning the official control of foodstuffs [1993] OJ L290/14.

[152] In its report of 1994 the Commission proposed to start with 6 Commission officials (4 A, 1 B and 1 C grade), with 2 A officials being recruited annually during 1995–6. See COM(94)567 final.

[153] Art. 5 of Dir. 93/99/EEC, above n. 151.

[154] COM(96)51 final, 28. According to the financial sheet attached to the Commission report on the application of Dir. 89/397, above n. 150, in 1995 the costs of this inspectorate, including travel expenses, staff and publication of mission reports, were estimated at 421,000 ECU. For 1996 the cost estimate was 298,500 ECU.

verification of compliance with such rules.[155] The next step was the establishment of Community procedures to combat contaminants in food.[156]

The Increasing Public Concern about Food Issues and Mutual Distrust: Creation of New National Provisions on Food

The food sector has been identified as one of the sectors in which various new national provisions continue to be proposed.[157] In part, the creation of new national provisions on food may again be explained by mutual distrust. However, the tightening up of national systems for food regulation may also be explained by the increasing public awareness of food and nutrition issues and a growing number of illnesses derived from the consumption of food products,[158] a concern reflected in governmental regulation.

Free Movement of Dangerous Foodstuffs in the Community Market and Worldwide Accidents

Where foodstuffs may freely circulate throughout the Community, hazardous products affect not only the national market but potentially the whole Community market. The Commission established, therefore, as early as the 1980s, an informal alert system on dangers arising from foodstuffs.[159] This system was formalised on an experimental basis for four years by Decision 84/133/EEC[160] covering both food and non-food products and was prolonged by Decision 89/45/EEC.[161] This system has been activated with regard to a large number of issues,[162] including the toxic oil syndrome[163] and the Chernobyl accident.[164] The directives on official control and contaminants must, therefore, be

[155] Council Dir. 93/43/EEC on the hygiene in foodstuffs [1993] OJ L175/1.

[156] Council Reg. (EEC) 315/93 laying down Community procedures for contaminants in food [1993] OJ L37/1.

[157] See, recently, the Commission's Green Paper on Food Law, COM(97)176 final, 19. Earlier, see COM(96) 51 final, 3, and COM(93)632 final, 7. Member States are obliged to notify their draft regs. on the basis of the notification procedures under Council Dir. 83/189/EEC laying down a procedure for the provision of information in the field of technical standards and regulations ([1983] OJ L109/8, amended by European Parliament and Council Dir. 94/10/EC [1994] OJ L100/30), and since 1988 also applicable to food and pharmaceuticals: see Council Dir. 88/182/EEC amending Council Dir. 83/189/EEC [1988] OJ L81/75.

[158] For example, a study carried out in the UK reported twice as many cases of food poisoning in 1984 as in 1968. See Lister, above n. 104, at 263.

[159] This system consisted of the creation of a network of contacts points in the Member States and the installation of a "red" telephone—a direct line at the Food Unit of DGIII, as well as a telex link—on which information could be received from the national contact points. See Deboyser, above n. 109, 223–30.

[160] Council Dec. 84/133/EEC introducing a Community system for the rapid exchange of information on dangers arising from the use of consumer products [1984] OJ L70/16.

[161] [1989] OJ L17/51, as amended by Council Dec. 90/352/EEC [1990] OJ L173/49.

[162] See the Report from the Commission on the system for the rapid exchange of information on dangers arising from the use of consumer products in accordance with Art. 8 (2) of Council Dec. 84/133/EEC, COM(88)121 final.

[163] See I. De Uriarte y de Bofarull, *Consumer Legislation in Spain* (Louvain-la-Neuve, 1987), 132, and Deboyser, above n. 109, 417–18.

[164] Although it had not been foreseen that this system would be used for cases of radio-activity following nuclear accidents, COM(88)121 final, 7. See Deboyser, above n. 109, 230–4.

viewed in the light of such contamination accidents as well. Although under this system, the role of the Commission is confined solely to the transmission of information, the General Product Safety Directive, which places the alert system on a permanent footing,[165] has granted the Commission decision-making powers in emergency situations.[166]

The need for the Community to intervene (indissolubly linked to the Community's agricultural policy) may be illustrated by the BSE scandal. In this case, the circulation of meat derived from cows affected by this disease throughout the Community market potentially endangered the health of Community citizens and thus necessitated Community action.[167] Likewise, the above-mentioned Chernobyl accident, which had Community-wide effects, also forced the Community to impose monitoring and control provisions relating to the radioactive contamination of food products and animal feedstuffs.[168]

Use of New Technologies

The use of new technologies in the production of food likewise pushes the Community towards more intervention. Innovative means of increasing meat production have resulted in perilous cattle diseases, such as BSE. In addition, new technologies have made it possible to retrieve food ingredients artificially from chemical compounds, or to give new properties to such ingredients. These "novel" food ingredients and biotechnology processes have caused considerable public concern, which relates both to a decline in food quality and a reduction in safety,[169] and are included within the regulatory activities of national legislatures. Since differences between these laws may hinder the free movement of these products and create conditions of unfair competition, the Community has stepped into this new field, too.[170]

---

[165] Art. 7 ff. of Dir. 92/59/EC [1992] OJ L228/24.

[166] Art. 9 of Dir. 92/59/EC, above n. 165. See the unsuccessful recourse against this provision by Germany: Case C–359/92, [1994] ECR I–3681. See, in more detail, Chap. 2.

[167] Commission Dec. 96/239/EC on emergency matters to protect against BSE [1996] OJ L78/47. See sect. 5.3.1.2.

[168] See, for instance, Council Dec. 87/600/Euratom on Community arrangements for the early exchange of information in the event of a radiological emergency [1987] OJ L371/76, and Council Reg. (EEC) 2219/89 on the special conditions for exporting foodstuffs and feedingstuffs following a nuclear accident or any other case of radiological emergency [1989] OJ L211/4; Commission Reg. (Euratom) 944/89 laying down maximum permitted levels of radioactive contamination in minor foodstuffs following a nuclear accident or any other case of radiological emergency [1989] OJ L101/17.

[169] See Lister, above n. 104, at 121.

[170] European Parliament and Council Reg. 258/97 on novel foods and novel food ingredients [1997] OJ L43/1. See the special issue on the Novel Foods Regulation of the *Zeitschrift für das gesamte Lebensmittelrecht* 1/98, in particular, R. Streinz, "Anwendbarkeit der Novel Food-Verordnung" (1998) ZLR 19–37. See also R. Streinz (ed.), *Novel Food* (Bayreuth, 1993).

5.3. Main Committees Set Up in the Food Sector: Description

Regulation of food is characterised by the existence of all of the main committee models identified according to a functional criterion: a scientific committee: the Scientific Committee on Food, an interest committee: the Advisory Committee on Foodstuffs, and a policy-making/implementation committee: the Standing Committee on Foodstuffs. The Scientific Committee on Food and the Advisory Committee are consulted by the Commission in both the preparatory stage and the implementing stage of the regulatory process. The Standing Committee operates mainly in the implementing phase, where the Commission, in the exercise of its delegated powers, is obliged to consult it. In addition, the Consumer Committee (CC), an interest committee, is sometimes consulted. This book will concentrate primarily on the examination of these committees, which are all involved in the regulation of health and safety issues raised by processed foodstuffs.[171] Other scientific committees, such as the Scientific Committee for Plants, the Scientific Veterinary Committee[172] and various advisory committees in the agricultural area, which also play a role in the decision-making on foodstuffs, but which are primarily concerned with unprocessed food, fall outside the scope of this book.

5.3.1. *Scientific Committee: The Scientific Committee on Food*

Since its establishment, the Scientific Committee for Food (SCF) has been the main source of scientific expertise for Community food regulation. Over the years, the SCF has gained an outstanding reputation due to its serious and independent working methods.[173] Confidence in the work of the SCF was expressed by the Court in several cases, when it ruled that when Member States consider for approval or refusal the circulation of a product on their markets, they should take account of the findings of international scientific research and, in particular, the work of *inter alia* the SCF.[174] The same confidence has led the Community legislature in many directives to make the consultation of the SCF by the Commission compulsory where questions of human health protection have been involved. Therefore, the functioning of this Committee and the rules developed by the Commission attracted neither significant political nor academic attention.

Yet the outbreak of the BSE crisis demonstrated that where highly political matters are involved, the pragmatic approach of the Commission to the consul-

---

[171] Excluding the committees set up for other food issues such as labelling.

[172] See Commission Dec. 97/579/EC setting up Scientific Committees in the field of consumer health and safety [1997] OJ L237/18.

[173] See K. Van der Heijden, "The Scientific Committee for Food: Procedures and Program for European Food Safety" [1992] Food Technology, 102–6.

[174] See, for instance, Case 178/84, *Commission* v. *Germany* [1987] ECR 1227; Case 247/84, above n. 145; and Case 304/84, above n. 145.

tation, composition and independence of scientific committees, as well as their qualitative output and supervision, is not sufficient to guarantee effective health and safety protection of consumers. For a better understanding of the consequences which the BSE crisis had on the Commission's approach to food safety, this section gives a brief overview of the activities of the SCF prior to the BSE crisis, followed by an account of the BSE crisis and, in particular, the findings of the Temporary Committee of Inquiry into BSE of the Parliament on the role the Commission played in the BSE case. Subsequently, the Commission's new approach to scientific committees and, in particular, the SCF is discussed.

5.3.1.1. The Scientific Committee for Food prior to the BSE Crisis

Very soon after the promulgation of the first Community directives in the food sector,[175] the need for a body to advise the Commission on food safety and to give "objective" evaluations became readily apparent.[176] Thus, the Commission created the Scientific Committee for Food in 1974.[177] The rules on the operation of this Committee were generally laid down by the instituting Commission Decision:

- the SCF could be consulted by the Commission on any problem relating to the protection of the health and safety of persons, whilst it could also draw the attention of the Commission to any such problem independently;[178]
- the number of SFC members could not exceed 18;[179]
- the members were nominated by the Commission from highly qualified scientific persons, having competence on the consumption of food (in particular, on the composition of food), processes modifying food, food additives and other processing aids and contaminants;[180]
- SCF members were appointed for a period of three years;[181]
- the SCF appointed its president and two vice-presidents from amongst its members;[182]
- the SCF could form working groups from among its members;[183]
- the Commission provided the secretariat of the SCF and its working groups.[184]

---

[175] In the absence of a European body, the safety evaluations for the 1962 Dir. on food colours, for instance, had still been made on a national basis or extracted from international evaluations: see Gray, above n. 108, at 111.

[176] See Gray, above n. 108. See, in general, Van der Heijden, above n. 173, 102–6 and E. Poulsen, "Consultation at the Commission Level. Scientific Advice: the Scientific Committee for Food", in A. Gérard (ed.), *Food Law in the Europe of Today* (Brussels, 1987), 129–36.

[177] Commission Dec. 74/234/EEC [1974] OJ L136/1.

[178] Art. 3 of Commission Dec. 74/234/EEC, as amended by Decision 86/241/EEC (1986) OJ L163/40.

[179] Art. 2 of Commission Dec. 74/234/EEC, above n. 177.

[180] Ibid., Art. 4.

[181] Ibid., Art. 6.

[182] Ibid., Art. 5.

[183] Ibid., Art. 7.

[184] Ibid., Art. 8.

Other rules were developed in practice. For example, where formal procedural rules on the appointment of members were lacking, the Commission *ad
hoc* invented a system by which it appointed the members following proposals
from national governments,[185] and operated a fixed quota system: one member
per Member State with two members from the larger Member States.[186] Thus it
could happen that members of the SCF were at the same time members of the
other scientific committees such as the Scientific Committee on Cosmetology.[187]
Furthermore, in practice, the SCF not only gave opinions on Commission draft
proposals, for either Council directives or for implementing acts, but also acted
as "arbiter" (in an advisory status) in conflicts between Member States as
regards the free movement of certain foodstuffs and provided scientific assessments of the requests for approval for any compound or preparation of food by
a manufacturer, which were submitted to the Commission.[188]

In addition, practice demonstrated that it was difficult, if not impossible, to
find highly qualified scientists who were not involved in industry-paid research.
In order to ensure some degree of independence from industrial and commercial
interests, rules were subsequently developed to detect and eliminate potential
conflicts of interests.[189] These rules required the members, when taking up their
positions, to fill in a declaration of commercial consultancies and interests (existence of a pecuniary relationship between the member and a commercial firm).
The Commission maintained a confidential register of the declarations received.
Any interest acquired after the initial declaration needed similarly to be declared
to the Commission. When a matter was to be considered at a SCF meeting in
which a member had an interest, s/he had to declare that interest at the outset.
This requirement was explicitly laid down in a new Commission Decision of
1995.[190] This Decision further stated that the SCF was to be consulted whenever
a legal act required it,[191] while it generally defined the areas of consultation of
the SCF and competence of its members as relating to the consumption of food,
in particular, nutrition, hygiene and toxicology.[192] This Decision also made a
long-standing practice of the Commission compulsory, namely that the SCF
opinions were to be published in reports by the Commission and made available
to the general public.[193]

---

[185] Interview with a SCF member.
[186] See the Composition of the Scientific Committee for Food [1995] OJ C218/3.
[187] Interview with a SCF member.
[188] See Van der Heijden, above n. 173, at 104.
[189] See R. Hankin, "The Role of Scientific Advice in the Elaboration and Implementation of the
Community's Foodstuffs Legislation", in Ch. Joerges/K.H. Ladeur/E. Vos (eds.), *Integrating
Scientific Expertise into Regulatory Decision-Making. National Traditions and European
Innovations* (Baden-Baden, 1997), 158.
[190] Art. 11 of Commission Dec. 95/273/EC [1995] OJ L167/22.
[191] Art. 2 of Commission Dec. 95/273/EC, above n. 190.
[192] Arts. 2 and 4 of Commission Dec. 95/273/EC, above n. 190.
[193] Art. 9 of Commission Dec. 95/273/EC, above n. 190. See the series published by the European
Commission, food science and techniques, reports of the Scientific Committee for Foods,
Luxembourg, which include general reports on issues such as flavourings and opinions on the safety
aspects of specific substances.

The Commission's DGIII formed the SCF's secretariat. Where necessary, the Commission organised, on an *ad hoc* basis, meetings between the SCF and interested industry parties and consumers. In general, SCF opinions were reached through consensus.[194] Where a draft opinion was ambiguous or was not acceptable to all members, the text was sent back to the working groups. If consensus still could not be reached, the different positions taken in the course of the deliberations were set out in a report drawn up under the supervision of the Commission. Plenary sessions of the SCF were held approximately four to five times per year.[195] SCF working groups assembled on a more frequent basis according to need. In 1995, for instance, 30 meetings of the various working groups were scheduled.

5.3.1.2. The Outbreak of the BSE Crisis and the Findings of the Temporary Committee of Inquiry into BSE

The official announcement by the British Government on 20 March 1996 that a link between BSE and Creutzfeldt-Jacob Disease (CJD) in human beings could not be ruled out provoked an unprecedented crisis among the EU institutions, the European public and the European beef industry.[196] Although the Commission immediately reacted with an export ban on British beef,[197] it must be said that it had not acted so promptly in the years before the outbreak of this crisis. A Temporary Committee of Inquiry into BSE (hereafter: Inquiry Committee) was set up by the Parliament in July 1996 to investigate, in particular, the Commission's (non-)policy on this topic in the years before 1996.[198] Following the Report of this Committee of 7 February 1997,[199] the main evidence of mismanagement of the BSE crisis can be traced back to the 1990–4 period when the disease had reached crisis levels.

The events subsequently discovered by the Inquiry Committee resemble science fiction. The Committee detected several elements which indicated that during this period the Commission had followed a policy of "disinformation".[200]

---

[194] Interview with a Commission official of DGIII.

[195] Commission of the European Communities, Directorate-General for Industry, *The Scientific Committee for Food* (Brussels, 1995), 5.

[196] See M. Westlake, "'Mad Cows and Englishmen'—The Institutional Consequences of the BSE Crisis", in N. Nugent (ed.), *The European Union 1996: Annual Review of Activities* (1997) 35 *JCMS Annual Review* 11–36.

[197] Commission Dec. 96/239/EC on emergency matters to protect against BSE [1996] OJ L78/47. The UK's attempt to attack this Dec. before the Court was unsuccessful: see Case C–180/96, *United Kingdom* v. *Commission*, [1998] ECR I–2265 (see on the request for interim measures [1996] ECR I–3903). See, also, Case C–157/96, *The Queen* v. *Ministry of Agriculture, Fisheries and Food, ex parte National Farmers' Union et al.* [1998] ECR I–2211.

[198] [1996] OJ C261/132. See also European Parliament Resolution on the Commission's information policy on BSE since 1988 and the measures it has taken to ensure compliance with the export ban and eradicate the disease [1996] OJ C261/75.

[199] Report on the alleged contraventions or maladministration in the implementation of Community law in relation to BSE, without prejudice to the jurisdiction of the Community and the national courts of 7 Feb. 1997, A4–0020/97/A, PE 220.544/fin/A.

[200] Although the Commission denied having followed such a policy.

The Committee concluded that this policy had not been confined to misleading public opinion, but had played a major role in relations between the Community institutions. Legislative activity by the Community on BSE was suspended and the Council held no debates on BSE. Furthermore, in 1990 scientific evidence had been already found that the disease could be transmitted to cats and pigs. Whereas such information should have prompted the acceleration of scientific research, from 1990 onwards, hardly any scientific result on this topic was produced in the UK.[201] In addition, the Committee found that when, in 1990, both France and Germany had considered restricting the import of British beef, the then Commissioner on Agriculture, MacSharry, had prevented them from doing so by threatening them with Court proceedings.

The greater part of the evidence found by the Committee indicated that the UK held the major responsibility for the crisis. It had *inter alia* put pressure on the Commission not to include BSE in its general inspections of slaughterhouses in the UK. The UK insisted that it could handle the problem without interference from outside. Happy to let a British problem be dealt with by the British, the Commission and the other Member States were eager to believe this. The influence of "British thinking" on the Commission was increased by the presence of many persons of British nationality on the two committees operating in this field: the Scientific Veterinary Committee (a scientific committee) and the Standing Veterinary Committee (a policy-making/implementation committee). The operation of the Standing Veterinary Committee during this period had been put under political pressure and it was only partly aware of the information which had been diffused by the Scientific Veterinary Committee. The latter information, however, had also not been free from political influence.[202]

The Inquiry Committee discovered that the Scientific Committee's Sub-Group on BSE, in particular, had been overwhelmed by the presence of British experts and officials from the British Ministry of Agriculture. Although this dominance could initially be explained by the fact that the UK had the most experience with BSE, it was no coincidence that the BSE Sub-Group had practically always been chaired by a British official, whilst its minutes were drawn up by a temporary Commission official of British nationality. In addition, committee members from other Member States had apparently been discouraged from attending the Sub-Group's meetings by the Commission's non or low reimbursement practices. From this, the Inquiry Committee concluded that the Scientific Veterinary Committee tended to reflect the position of the British Ministry of Agriculture, since:

"the UK was able to control [the Scientific Veterinary Committee] through the convening of the meetings, the agendas and attendance, and the drafting of minutes".[203]

---

[201] Inquiry Committee Report, above n. 199, 5–6.
[202] *Ibid.*, at 10.
[203] *Ibid.*, at 16.

Taken together, these elements led the Inquiry Committee to call for greater transparency regarding the action to combat BSE, particularly in relation to the conditions of the functioning and work of the scientists on the scientific committees. It *inter alia* urged greater transparency and reform of the rules governing the work of the scientific committees to ensure independence and appropriate funding of the scientists and the publication of debates and dissenting opinions.[204]

5.3.1.3. The Commission's New Approach to Food Safety in the Aftermath of BSE

As is the case with many tragedies, the BSE crisis has been an important lesson for the Community institutions regarding how to deal with risk regulation, particularly in the area of foodstuffs. It was clear that the activities of both the Commission and the committees had been put under strong political pressure whilst transparency in decision-making had been notably lacking. As a result, the President of the Commission, Jacques Santer, responding to the accusations of a lack of transparency and of manipulation by the Parliament,[205] hastened to announce to Parliament shortly after the publication of the Inquiry Committee's Report that the Commission had developed a new approach to food safety and that it would radically reform the Directorates dealing with human health.[206]

Thus, in its rapidly designed New Approach to Consumer Health and Food Safety, the Commission moves away from an approach emphasising food security, concerned with the provision of food in the context of agricultural policy as laid down in Article 39(1), towards an approach emphasising food safety, linked to the protection of consumers.[207] It finally endeavours to base its approach to food regulation on three principles: separation of the responsibility for legislation and scientific advice, separation of the responsibility for legislation and inspection, and greater transparency and information throughout the decision-making process and inspection. In order to avoid future intermingling between economic (industrial or agricultural policy) interests and health protection, the Commission further decides to place all the relevant scientific committees under the authority of DGXXIV, renamed the Directorate-General on Consumer Policy and Consumer Health Protection,[208] and to issue a new decision regulating the activities of the scientific committees.

Hence, the Commission proclaims three instruments as being essential for an

---

[204] *Ibid.*, 38–40.
[205] Parliament Resolution on the results of the Temporary Committee of Inquiry into BSE [1997] OJ C85/61.
[206] Speech of 18 Feb. 1997, Bull. EU 1/2 1997.
[207] J.-L. Valverde/A.J. Piqueras García/M.D. Cabezas López, "La «nouvelle approche» en matière de santé des consommateurs et sécurité alimentaire: la nécessité d'une agence européenne de sécurité des aliments" [1997] *RMUE* 4, 33.
[208] Communication from the Commission on consumer health and food safety, COM(97)183 final. See http://europa.eu.int/comm/dg24/ (homepage).

effective consumer health policy: scientific advice, risk analysis and control. It stresses that *scientific advice* is and will be the basis for all the regulatory activities of the Community and is mainly obtained from the scientific committees. The functioning of these committees will be based on the *excellence* of their members (risk evaluation is undertaken by eminent scientists), their *independence* (to ensure that the scientists are free from conflicting interests) and the *transparency* of their activities (easy access to information on the activities of the committees and their advice).

The Commission recognises risk analysis as falling within its remit. It defines it as a systematic procedure including risk assessment, risk management and risk communication. Risk assessment, defined by the Commission as scientific evaluation of hazards and the probability of their emergence in a given context, forms the foundation of scientific advice offering the Commission a sound basis for proposals and measures on health and safety. Risk management is viewed by the Commission as the assessment of all measures making it possible to achieve an appropriate level of protection, which will include the evaluation of policy alternatives which result from scientific assessment and the desired level of protection. Risk communication, the exchange of information with all parties concerned, should be as transparent as possible.

Lastly, the Commission announces a new approach to control and inspection. It emphasises the need for risk assessment procedures in order to identify control priorities, the reorganisation of control activities to ensure that the whole production chain is covered and the introduction of formal audit procedures to allow assessments by national authorities. This approach will be implemented through its Food and Veterinary Office, which will be responsible for monitoring the observance of food hygiene, and veterinary and plant health regulation.

Together, these principles form part of six basic goals identified by the Commission in its Green Paper on the General Principles of Food Law in the EU, which it presented in addition to its New Approach:

— to ensure a high level of protection of public health, safety and the consumer;

— to ensure the free movement of goods within the internal market;

— to ensure that the legislation is primarily based on scientific evidence and risk assessment;

— to ensure competitiveness of European industry and enhance its export prospects;

— to place the primary responsibility for safe food on industry, producers and suppliers, using hazard analysis and critical control point (HACCP) type systems, which must be backed by effective official control and enforcement.[209]

---

[209] Commission Green Paper on the general principles of food law in the European Union, COM(97)176 final.

5.3.1.4. The New Scientific Committee on Food

In July 1997, the Commission formally adopted a new decision on the eight scientific committees operating in the institutional structure of the Community.[210] It laid down general requirements which are applicable to all of these committees. This Decision aims to put into practice the principles of excellence, independence and transparency. The relevant changes for the SCF, now officially named the Scientific Committee *on* Food, are the following. The Decision reduces the number of members on the Committee from 20 to 17, confirming seven former SCF members and selecting 10 new members.[211] Whilst before the BSE crisis it was possible for SCF members to be members of other scientific committees at the same time, this is now explicitly prohibited.[212] Importantly, the Commission agrees to remunerate the committee members in addition to the reimbursement of travel and subsistence allowances;[213] in the past, the lack of funds had made it difficult to attract scientific experts of a high reputation. Under its new statute, the SCF held its 109th plenary meeting in November 1997.

The task of the SCF and the other committees is generally formulated as providing scientific advice on matters of consumer health and food safety. According to Article 2(3) of Decision 97/579/EC, it shall in particular:

- critically examine risk assessments made by scientists belonging to Member States" organisations;
- develop new risk assessment procedures in areas such as food-borne diseases and the transmissibility of animal diseases to man;
- draft scientific opinions designed to enable the Commission to evaluate the scientific basis of the recommendations, standards and guidelines prepared in international fora;
- evaluate the scientific principles on which Community health standards are based, taking into account the risk assessment techniques developed by the international organisations concerned.

The Committee remains competent to draw the Commission's attention to any specific problem on foodstuffs on its own initiative.[214] For the carrying out of its tasks, the SCF obtains scientific assistance and co-operation from the Member States.[215] Since the BSE case had illustrated the lack of co-ordination between the scientific committees and the conflict as to which committee was competent in matters which touched upon different policy areas, it is now explicitly regulated that when a question is common to several scientific committees, the SCF together with the other relevant scientific committees may,

---

[210] Commission Dec. 97/579/EC, above n. 172.
[211] See the alphabetical list of committee members published in [1997] OJ C342/8.
[212] Art. 3(3) of Commission Dec. 97/579/EC, above n. 172.
[213] *Ibid.*, Art. 5(3).
[214] *Ibid.*, Art. 2(5).
[215] See sect. 5.5.5.

after the approval of the Scientific Steering Committee, set up a common working group.[216]

SCF members are still appointed for three years, but may not remain in office for more than two consecutive terms.[217] The SCF appoints its president and two vice-presidents from among its members.[218] Importantly, although it is not provided in the Decision, the Commission's DGXXIV forms the SCF's secretariat. In order to carry out some in-depth analyses, at present, eight working groups have been set up by the SCF and are composed of one or more Committee members and specialised external experts.[219] They work on additives, contaminants, materials in contact with food, nutrition and dietetic foods, intake and exposure, food hygiene and microbiology, novel foods and processes and flavourings. For these working groups, too, the secretariat is provided by DGXXIV. The SCF needs to adopt harmonised rules of procedure in collaboration with the Scientific Steering Committee.[220] These rules must ensure that the SCF performs its tasks in the "best possible way", in accordance with the principles of excellence, independence and transparency. In particular, they must lay down procedures with a view to:

— appointing rapporteurs to assemble information packages and documents and prepare draft opinions for the SCF;
— verifying that rapporteurs are in a position to perform their assignments as independently as possible, free from outside influence;
— delivering an opinion as quickly as possible, and, in any event, within the period required by the Commission.

Opinions are adopted by majority voting.[221] More transparency on the activities of the SCF is ensured through publication of its membership, agendas, minutes and opinions (including minority opinions) whilst respecting the need for commercial confidentiality.[222] These principles will be examined in more detail in section 5.5.

5.3.2. *Interest Committees: The Advisory Committee on Foodstuffs and the Consumer Committee*

5.3.2.1. The Advisory Committee on Foodstuffs

Led by self-legitimising objectives, the Commission decided in 1975 to set up an Advisory Committee on Foodstuffs.[223] The Advisory Committee consists of 10 permanent members and 20 experts. These persons are drawn equally from five

---

[216] Art. 2(2) of Commission Dec. 97/579/EC, above n. 172.
[217] *Ibid.*, Art. 5(1).
[218] *Ibid.*, Art. 4.
[219] *Ibid.*, Art. 7.
[220] *Ibid.*, Art. 8.
[221] *Ibid.*
[222] *Ibid.*, Art. 10.
[223] Commission Decision 75/420/EEC, setting up an Advisory Committee on Foodstuffs [1975] OJ L182/35, amended by Commission Dec. 78/758/EEC [1978] OJ L251/18. See, in general,

economic groups representing industry, consumers, agriculture, commerce and workers.[224] One observer from each group may attend the Committee meetings. The representative organisations in these five fields[225] each propose to the Commission four member-candidates of different nationalities and appoint the experts who will assist them. The Commission appoints the members from among these candidates. In addition, four observers from the economic groups, have been appointed to provide administrative liaison with the secretariat of the Committee. The permanent members elect the Committee chairperson and the two vice-chairpersons. The Committee can create working parties in order to examine technical subjects relating to the drafting of regulatory measures on foodstuffs. The Commission provides the Committee and the working parties with a secretariat, which draws up the agenda for meetings, invites members whose attendance is required and supplies the necessary documentation.

The Advisory Committee may be consulted by the Commission on all problems arising from the harmonisation of legislation on foodstuffs. In general, the Committee is not able to engage in detailed discussion of all draft Community legislation (both Council and Commission acts) which the Commission submits to it. Rather, the Committee deals with fundamental questions of foodstuffs legislation, as well as specific issues concerning specific foodstuffs or substances. In addition, the Advisory Committee has also had occasion to discuss self-regulatory agreements. Advisory Committee discussions have thus included a draft agreement on a code of conduct for competition between breast milk substitutes in the Community; an agreement submitted to it by the Association of Dietetic Food Industries. Although, from a formal point of view, questions could be raised regarding the conformity of such practice with the Commission Decision setting up the Committee, these discussions have been considered by the Committee itself to be quite satisfactory. The former chairman of the Committee even suggested that such associations should formulate their own proposals more often and submit these to the Committee for discussion.[226]

In practice, discussion on Commission proposals is very informal and, in general, no voting takes place.[227] In view of the diverse interests represented in this

B. Peinemann, "Consultation at the Commission Level. Socio-professional Advice: Advisory Committee on Foodstuffs", in A. Gérard (ed.), *Food Law in the Europe of Today* (Brussels, 1987), 137–44.

[224] Commission Dec. 80/1073/EEC, establishing a new statute of the Advisory Committee on Foodstuffs [1980] OJ L318/28. The experience gained in the operation of the Committee from 1974 had shown the need for the establishment of a new statute (preamble).

[225] As listed in the annex to Commission Dec. 80/1073/EEC (above n. 224), namely, for agriculture: the Committee of Agricultural Organisations of the EEC (COPA), jointly with the General Committee for Agricultural Co-operation in the EEC Countries (COGECA), for commerce: the most representative organisations are, for consumers: the Consumer Consultative Committee (now the Consumer Committee), for industry: the Union of Industries of the European Communities (UNICE), for workers: the European Trade Union Confederation (ETUC).

[226] Peinemann, above n. 223, at 139.

[227] *Ibid.*, at 138. The informal character of the Committee meetings was confirmed in an interview with a Commission official of DGIII, who described these meetings as a "*discussion café du commerce*".

single committee, it is difficult to reach a single opinion. The result is often rather controversial. However, discussions in the Committee present the Commission with an opportunity to learn more about the particular viewpoints of the various interests concerned and the problems which its draft measures may entail for them. The Commission, in its role of secretariat, draws up a draft summary record of the discussions and submits this to the members for approval. If no requests for modifications are made by participants within a determined time limit, the record is considered to have been approved. The records may report the adoption of an opinion (although in such cases no strict counting takes place), the mere registration of the different opinions or the reaching of a common posi-tion.[228] The records of the discussions are communicated upon request to the Council and the Standing Committee on Foodstuffs.[229]

However, the Commission is not obliged to consult the Committee. The chairperson of the Committee may nevertheless indicate to the Commission that the Committee feels it should be consulted on any matter falling within its com-petence on which no opinion has been sought. Although the Commission seem-ingly had imposed upon itself a general obligation to consult this Advisory Committee at each decision-making stage,[230] the Committee appears at present not to be active and has no visible function in the implementation process.[231] On a parliamentary question in 1990 asking why the Advisory Committee had not been convened for the last 18 months, the Commission replied that during that time several directives had been prepared for adoption by the Council, which had not been given cause to involve the Committee.[232] At present, much to the frustration of Committee members, the Commission appears to be taking no steps to remedy this situation.[233] Hence in practice, although its scheduled expenditure on the Community budget mysteriously increases (from 63.000 ECU in 1996 to 89.000 ECU in 1997 and 1998—see Table 1), this Committee seems to have become "dormant".

5.3.2.2. The Consumer Committee

In 1973, recognising the need to hear the voice of consumers on proposals of spe-cific interest to consumers and to provide some balance against more powerful interests, the Commission officially established a committee solely representing consumer interests, the Consumers' Consultative Committee. This Committee would enable the Commission to maintain close and continuous contact with consumer organisations at Community level.[234] The workings of this

---

[228] Interview with a Commission official of DGIII.
[229] Peinemann, above n. 223, at 138.
[230] Interview with a Commission official of DGIII.
[231] See Joerges/Neyer, above n. 10.
[232] See WQ no. 1154/89 by Mr Ford [1990] OJ C303/11.
[233] See Joerges/Neyer, above n. 10.
[234] Commission Dec. 73/306/EEC [1973] OJ L283/18, as last amended by Dec. 80/1087/EEC [1980] OJ L320/33. This Committee replaced the Contact Committee for Consumer Questions, established in 1962.

Committee were, however, criticised by certain consumer groups, since the Commission consulted it on major proposals only after these proposals had been agreed upon in the Commission, and similarly failed to provide adequate funding.[235] The amount of the work done by this Committee was considered to be quite unsatisfactory.[236] This and the growing impact of Community policies on consumer issues, together with the introduction of Article 100a(3) by the SEA, which required the Commission to take account of a high level of consumer protection in its internal market proposals, led to the 1989 Commission Decision to replace the Consumers' Consultative Committee with the Consumers' Consultative Council (CCC).[237] The CCC was composed of 48 representatives of European, national and regional consumer organisations and institutions.[238] Its seats were apportioned amongst the latter organisations and institutions according to nationality. The Consumer Council was to advise the Commission on all problems relating to consumer interests. In order to examine the specific subjects more thoroughly, six working groups ("sections") were set up on foodstuffs, health and safety, economic and financial questions, justice and transactions, information and education, and standardisation.

Shortly after the inauguration of this new body, however, two problems came to the surface. First, some interest groups, which had no representatives on the CCC, displayed their desire to become members of the CCC. This was, for instance, the case with tenants' organisations and automobile clubs. Secondly, an old conflict between some members of the CCC escalated at a crucial moment. The European consumer organisation BEUC,[239] representing many national consumer organisations, although certainly not all of them, refused to recognise the European Trade Unions Council (ETUC) and the European Federation of Consumer Co-operatives (EUROCOOP) as "true" consumer organisations. Initiatives were soon taken for yet another reform of the CCC. The former Commissioner in charge of consumer affairs, Mrs Christiane Scrivener, warned however that it was not the Commission's task to resolve the internal problems of consumer organisations and that any reform would require

---

[235] See Memorandum by the Consumer in the European Community Group (UK), submitted to the House of Lords Select Committee on the European Communities, *Report on the Delegation of Powers to the Commission*, Session 1986–7, 3rd report (London, 1987), 39. See also the memorandum of the Consumers' Association in the same report, 32 ff. In general, M. Goyens, "Development of EC Consumer Protection", in T. Askham/A. Stoneham, *EC Consumer Safety* (London/Dublin/Edinburgh, 1994), 31.

[236] Krämer mentions as the main reasons for this: the insufficient status of the Committee; the inactive attitude of the four member organisations to defend the opinions of the Committee and the fact that Committee opinions were not published by the Commission. L. Krämer, *EEC Consumer Law* (Louvain-la-Neuve, 1985), 51. From 1973 to 1985 the Consumers' Consultative Committee issued 97 opinions.

[237] Commission Dec. 90/55/EEC [1990] OJ L38/40, as last amended by Commission Dec. 95/13/EC (1995) OJ L21/17.

[238] See, for the nomination of members of the Consumers' Consultative Council, before accession of the three new Member States [1994] OJ C189/3.

[239] Bureau Européen des Unions des Consommateurs, based in Brussels.

reciprocal recognition as such by all parties.[240] Tired of these internal problems,[241] the Commission decided in June 1995 to replace the Consumers' Consultative Council with the Consumer Committee,[242] as the former did not "adequately meet the Commission's need as regards effectiveness and speed of consultation".[243]

The number of members on this new Committee has been reduced to 20: one member per Member State together with five members from the five European consumer organisations (one member per organisation).[244] The members are appointed by the Commission for a period of two years. The Commission provides the secretariat for the Committee and organises its work, whilst a Commission representative also chairs Committee meetings. Recently, however, problems have arisen with regard to the appointment of the members of this new Committee, as the Commission has refused to appoint persons who had already been members of the old CCC. Only the future will demonstrate whether this Committee is able to overcome its internal difficulties and whether it can be of true significance in the Community decision-making process.[245]

5.3.3. Policy-making/implementation Committee: The Standing Committee on Foodstuffs

Not surprisingly, the delegation of implementing powers to the Commission in this politically sensitive field is generally accompanied by the obligation on the Commission to consult the Standing Committee on Foodstuffs. This Committee was created in 1969 by a separate Council Decision[246] in order to ensure close co-operation between the Member States and the Commission.[247]

The Standing Committee is composed of representatives from the Member States and is chaired by a Commission representative. Each Member State is represented by not more than five officials, who are together considered to be a single member of the Committee.[248] The composition of this Committee may be subject to change, dependent on the subject-matter dealt with. It is for the

[240] L. Maier, "Institutional Consumer Representation in the European Community", in N. Reich/G. Woodroffe (eds.), *European Consumer Policy after Maastricht* (Deventer, 1994), 89–90.

[241] The new Commissioner, Mrs Emma Bonino, explicitly stated that the Commission was not going to pay for consumers' organisations to come and litigate in Brussels.

[242] Commission Dec. 95/260/EC [1995] OJ L162/37.

[243] *Ibid.*, third recital.

[244] Previously, the larger Member States were represented by 2 people, while the 5 organisations had 22 members.

[245] See http://europa.eu.int/comm/dg24/policy/committee/index_en.html.

[246] Council Dec. 69/414/EEC [1969] OJ L291/9. Originally this Committee was named the Standing Committee for Foodstuffs. As recent Community legislation, however, speaks of the Standing Committee on Foodstuffs, I shall adhere to the latter terminology.

[247] First recital of the preamble to Council Dec. 69/414/EEC, above n. 246.

[248] Art. 6 of the Rules of Procedure of the Standing Committee on Foodstuffs, adopted in accordance with Art. 3 of Council Dec. 69/414/EEC, published in European Commission, *Foodstuffs. Co-ordinated instruments* (Luxembourg, 1994), 25–7.

Member States to decide who is to represent them on this Committee. Membership is not made public, in stark contrast to other committees, such as the SCF. According to a general study on committee practices, compositional changes occur relatively infrequently.[249] Often, Member State representatives on this Committee have already participated in the preparation of directives under the umbrella of the COREPER. If necessary, the representative of one Member State may represent another Member State. The Committee may set up working parties to consider specific issues, whilst experts on specific issues may also be heard upon the request of a member or upon the initiative of the chairperson. Such experts generally come from professional organisations.[250] The latter, however, do not take part in the decisions of the Committee.[251]

The secretariat is provided by the Commission. The Committee adopts its opinions, in the framework of the regulatory committee procedure, by qualified majority in accordance with Article 148(2). If necessary, the opinion of the Committee may be reached through a written procedure. Under such a procedure, Member States will be deemed to agree with the draft measures if they fail to communicate either their opposition to a measure, or their intention to abstain from taking a position, within a certain time limit. If, however, a Member State requests the draft measures to be reconsidered during a Committee meeting, the written procedure ceases.[252] The Commission representative draws up a summary record of each meeting held, which is sent to the Committee members, who can then make comments. Disagreement may result in a proposed amendment being discussed at the next meeting.[253] The Committee's meetings take place behind closed doors, and its opinions are not made public.

The Standing Committee on Foodstuffs is consulted in all food matters which have been delegated to the Commission. It may, moreover, consider any other question in relation to foodstuffs legislation referred to it by its chairperson on his or her own initiative or at the request of a Member State.[254] Thus, for instance, the Committee may also be consulted in the preparatory phase of Community decision-making or in relation to strategy orientation or problems in application.[255]

---

[249] Institut für Europäische Politik, *Study on Comitology. Characteristics, Performance and Options*, Preliminary Final Report (Bonn, 1989).

[250] Interview with a Commission official of DGIII.

[251] Art. 7 of the Rules of Procedure, above n. 248.

[252] *Ibid.*, Art. 8.

[253] *Ibid.*, Art. 10.

[254] Art. 2 of Council Dec. 69/414/EEC, above n. 246; Art. 2 of the Rules of Procedure, above n. 248.

[255] Interview with a Commission official of DGIII.

Table 1. Scheduled expenditure of the relevant committees in the food sector (in thousands of ECU).

Committees	1993	1994	1995	1996	1997	1998
Scientific Committee on Food	214	345	345	345	345	144
Advisory Committee on Foodstuffs	42	63	63	63	89	89
Standing Committee on Foodstuffs	32	89	89	89	89	89
Consumer Committee	400	400	540	112	112	112
Committee on Product Safety Emergencies	—	22.5	40	40	40	40

Source: Community budgets.

5.4. The Interrelation between the Member States and the Community Institutions through the Standing Committee on Foodstuffs

The increasing workload of the Community on food issues and the specific nature of food regulation determine that increased powers are delegated to the Commission to implement the general rules established by the Council/ Parliament, in accordance with the 1985 New Approach. Although, in general, such powers have been very broad, in the field of additives in particular, the Council has reserved some major decision-making powers for itself, whilst it has subjected the exercise of the implementing powers to the consultation of the Standing Committee on Foodstuffs. In addition, Member States retain powers to adopt measures where the health and safety of persons are endangered.

The powers thus conferred on the Commission vary from strict powers merely to adopt monitoring and sampling procedures (quick-frozen food-stuffs[256]) together with purity criteria (extraction solvents and food additives[257]), to broader powers of management (scientific co-ordination[258] and

---

[256] See Commission Dir. 92/1/EEC on the monitoring of temperatures in the means of transport, warehousing and storage of quick-frozen foodstuffs intended for human consumption [1992] OJ L34/28; Commission Dir. 92/2/EEC laying down the sampling procedures and the Community method of analysis for the official control of the temperatures of quick-frozen foodstuffs intended for human consumption [1992] OJ L34/30.

[257] See, for instance, Commission Dir. 95/45/EC laying down specific purity criteria concerning colours for the use in foodstuffs [1995] OJ L226/1.

[258] See, *inter alia*, Commission Dec. 94/652/EC establishing the inventory and distribution of tasks to be undertaken within the framework of co-operation by Member States in the scientific co-operation of questions relating to food [1994] OJ L253/29, amended by Commission Dec. 95/142/EC [1995] OJ L92/26.

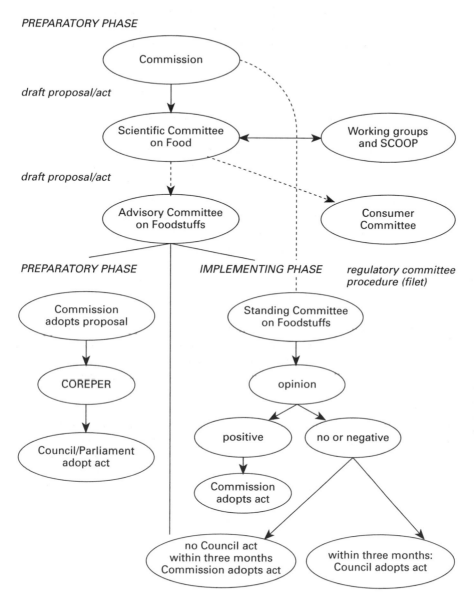

Figure 3. Simplified scheme of consultation and decision-making procedure in the food sector.

------- = the Commission practice of, at times, consulting the Standing Committee before drafting Community acts also in the preparatory phase.

------▶ = consultation not always takes place.

official control[259]), powers to adopt specific directives on groups of products (materials and articles in contact with foodstuffs[260] and particular dietetic foods[261]) and powers to adopt specific (emergency) measures where human health is endangered (hygiene).

5.4.1. Bridging between the Member States and the Commission

The role which the Standing Committee on Foodstuffs plays in the regulation of food issues is without doubt very important. The delicate process of risk assessment and the management of foodstuffs, during which all relevant interests must be weighed, may explain why Member States wish to remain involved where food regulation is increasingly transferred to the Community and, in particular, to the Commission. This then explains why committees are composed of solely Member State representatives and not of Parliament representatives as well under co-decision. As previously argued,[262] the development of committee-based implementation might be argued to be an attempt to restore the institutional balance between the Member States and the Community, compensating for the shift in favour of the Commission. Recent actions brought before the Court by Member States which have contested the validity of Commission decisions upon the grounds that they were not properly consulted within the framework of the other policy-making/implementation committees,[263] demonstrate that these committees, in practice, play a vital role within the internal market; Member States are not only well aware that such committees guarantee them a continuing role in an increasingly centralised decision-making processes, but are also prepared to defend this role.

Thus, it comes as no surprise that consultation of the Standing Committee generally follows the regulatory committee procedure which gives the Member States greater weight in decision-making. As a regulatory committee, the Standing Committee is able to influence the decision-making of the Commission to a great extent.[264] Although the Commission continues to propose that the consultation of this Committee should follow the advisory procedure,[265] the Council has systematically replaced this procedure with a regulatory (*filet*) committee procedure (see Table 2). The Commission has, however, generally

---

[259] Annually the Commission adopts co-ordinated programmes for the official control of foodstuffs; for 1995 [1995] OJ L65/27; for 1996 [1996] OJ L109/24; for 1997 [1997] OJ L22/27; for 1998 [1998] OJ L36/10.

[260] See, for instance, Commission Dir. 90/128/EEC relating to plastic materials and articles intended to come into contact with foodstuffs [1990] OJ L75/19; Commission Dir. 93/10/EEC relating to materials and articles made of regenerated cellulose film intended to come into contact with foodstuffs [1993] OJ L93/27.

[261] See, for instance, Commission Dir. 91/321/EEC on infant formulae, above n. 72, as amended by Commission Dir. 96/4/EC [1996] OJ L49/12 and Commission Dir. 96/5/EC on processed cereal-based foods and baby foods for infants and young children [1996] OJ L49/17.

[262] See Chap. 2.

[263] See below, sect. 5.9.

[264] Interview with a Commission official of DGIII.

[265] See, e.g., its proposal for a Council Reg. on novel foods [1992] OJ C190/3.

Table 2. The inclusion of committee procedures in Community food legislation involving health and safety issues (StCF = Standing Committee on Foodstuffs).

Council/Parliament Directive	StCF: Procedure	Variant	Safeguard Clause
88/344/EEC on extraction solvents [1988] OJ L157/28	Regulatory committee (Art. 6)	a) *filet*	Regulatory committee procedure (Art. 5)
88/388/EEC on flavourings [1988] OJ L184/61	Regulatory committee (Art. 10)	a) *filet*	Regulatory committee procedure (Art. 8)
89/107/EEC on food additives [1989] OJ l40/27	Regulatory committee (Art. 11)	a) *filet*	Regulatory committee procedure (Art. 4)
89/108/EEC on quick-frozen foodstuffs [1989] OJ L40/34	Regulatory committee	a) *filet*	Not included
89/109/EEC on materials intended to come in contact with foodstuffs [1989] OJ L40/38	Regulatory committee (Art. 9)	a) *filet*	Regulatory committee procedure (Art. 5)
89/397/EEC on official control [1989] OJ L186/23	Not included	Not included	Not included
89/398/EEC on foodstuffs for particular nutritional uses [1989] OJ L186/27	Regulatory committee (Art. 13)	a) *filet*	Regulatory committee procedure (Arts. 11 and 12)
93/5/EEC on scientific co-operation [1993] OJ L52/18	Regulatory committee (Art. 5)	b) *contre-filet*	Not included
Regulation 315/93 on a Community procedure for contaminants of food [1993] OJ L37/1	Regulatory committee (Art. 8)	b) *contre-filet*	Regulatory committee procedure (Art. 4)
93/43/EEC on hygiene [1993] OJ L175/1	Regulatory committee (Art. 14)	b) *contre-filet*	Special Procedure and Regulatory committee procedure (Art. 11)
93/99/EEC on official control (additional measures) [1993] OJ L290/14	Regulatory committee (Art. 8)	a) *filet*	Not included
94/35/EC on sweeteners [1994] OJ L237/3	Regulatory committee	a) *filet*	Not included
94/36/EC on colours [1994] OJ L237/13	Regulatory committee (Art. 5)	a) *filet*	Not included
95/2/EC on food additives other than sweeteners and colours [1995] OJ L61/1	Regulatory committee (Art. 6)	a) *filet*	Not included
Regulation 2232/96 on a Community procedure for flavouring substances [1996] OJ L299/1	Regulatory committee (Arts. 7 and 8)	a) *filet* and b) *contre-filet*	Regulatory committee procedure (Art. 3(3))
Regulation 258/97 on novel foods and novel food ingredients [1997] OJ L43/1	Regulatory committee (Art. 13)	a) *filet*	Regulatory committee procedure (Art. 12)

accepted the inclusion of the latter committee procedure in relation to important health issues.[266] Even the Parliament, being the most fervent defender of the
advisory committee procedure, tends, in this field, to accept the *filet* variant of
the regulatory committee procedure.[267] The Commission has also accepted the
contre-filet variant of this procedure in some important cases where it was likely
that the Council would otherwise simply abandon its delegation of powers.[268]

Practice has demonstrated that the Commission's draft decisions are rarely
sent back to the Council.[269] Two factors would seem to offer explanations for
this state of affairs: first, the Commission rarely disregards the Committee opinion; second, the Committee is hesitant to either adopt a negative opinion or fail
to issue one.

The Commission's stance would seem to be motivated by its interest in the
correct implementation of the measures adopted; it will therefore rarely try to
enforce measures against the will of the Member States.[270] Additionally, the
Commission is aware that a negative committee opinion on its draft measures
under the regulatory committee procedure is unlikely to be overturned by the
Council: the Member States which voted against a measure in the committee are
highly unlikely to vote for it in the Council. This may be explained by the fact
that the representatives on policy-making/implementation committees often
also participate in the COREPER working groups.[271] Thus, the importance of
the fact that the Standing Committee is a regulatory committee should not be
underestimated. Whilst some of the national representatives on the Standing
Committee seem not to be aware of the type of committee they sit on,[272] the
Commission is certainly well aware of the potential power of Committee members and is, therefore, bound to take the positions of the Member States seri-

---

[266] COM(89)1591 final, 11.

[267] This may be concluded from a case study on the decision-making process leading to the adoption of the Sweeteners Dir. The authors merely note that in the common position of the Council, the
advisory committee procedure, as proposed by the Commission, was changed into a regulatory one.
Yet the most important element of the Council's common position was the insertion of a footnote
applying to alcohol-free and low-alcohol beers. It was the latter footnote and not the inclusion of
the regulatory committee procedure (although in a second reading the Parliament reinstated
the advisory committee procedure) which led to the outbreak of an institutional conflict. See
D. Earnshaw/D. Judge, "The European Parliament and the Sweeteners Directive: From Footnote to
Inter-Institutional Conflict" (1993) 31 *JCMS* 103–16. In contrast, in the field of telecommunications,
for instance, the comitology issue led to the blocking of the proposal on the Open Network
Provision, as was reported by the same authors. See Earnshaw/Judge, above n. 75.

[268] See COM(90)2589 final, 10.

[269] *Ibid.* This was confirmed during an interview with a Commission official of DGIII. In the field
of technical products, too, the Commission hardly ever deviates from the opinion of the Committee
on Technical Standards and Regulation set up by Dir. 83/189/EEC (above n. 157); interview with a
Commission official of DGIII involved with the latter Committee.

[270] S. Pag, "Interdependence between the Commission and National Bureaucracies", in
S. Cassese (ed.), *The European Administration* (Brussels, 1988), 463.

[271] This is confirmed by the interviews carried out by me with Commission officials in the field
of technical goods, in relation to the New Approach dirs. referring to technical standards (such as
the Machinery Dir.). See also Pag, above n. 270, at 470.

[272] See Joerges/Neyer, above n. 10.

ously. In this sense, the Standing Committee is not a mere advisory organ but is actually quite influential.[273]

Yet this does not mean that the Commission is without any influence: its power to steer and guide these committees by means of its position as chair must by no means be undervalued. Of particular importance is the power to set the time-limit within which committees must deliver their opinion. This task is granted to the chairperson, a Commission official. In setting the time-limit, which must pay due regard to the urgency of the matter to be decided, the chairperson has discretionary power. A decision on such a time-limit can, according to the Court, only be revoked in cases of obvious error or misuse of powers.[274] On the whole, the Commission possesses considerable power and appears to be a dominant actor.[275] In this sense, the Commission seems fully aware of its responsibility for decisions adopted in accordance with committee procedures. If committee members are hostile towards its proposal, the Commission will evaluate the situation and decide whether or not it will accept a compromise solution. In this, the abovementioned elements are of great importance.

The Committee's hesitancy in this context[276] would seem to be attributable to the fact that this Committee is generally used as a *forum* for discussion between the Commission and the national administrators.[277] Within the framework of the Standing Committee, the Commission officials together with the national civil servants seek a compromise solution. Here, the Commission will often seek consensus amongst the members. The Standing Committee has many important achievements behind it in terms of co-operation and co-ordination. The fact that members on the Committee are familiar with one another, having sat together for many years, may certainly contribute to the creation of a "good spirit" of co-operation.[278]

5.4.2. The Paradox of Denationalisation and the Growing Importance of National Interests

Members on the Standing Committee are both bureaucrats and national representatives. On the one hand, the participation of Committee members as national *bureaucrats* may be considered as one element in the general process of the denationalisation of Community decision-making, towards a more transnational decisional approach, characterised by the relative lack of importance of

---

[273] See in general Buitendijk/Van Schendelen, above n. 3, 46–7; J. Dondelinger, "Relations avec les administrations nationales", in J. Jamar/W. Wessels, *Community Bureaucracy at the Crossroads* (Bruges, 1985), 94. See also Della Cananea, above n. 3, at 677.

[274] Case 278/84, *Germany v. Commission* [1987] ECR 1, at 41 (para. 13).

[275] See, also, Joerges/Neyer, above n. 10, and, in general, Pag, above n. 270, at 464.

[276] Interview with a Commission official of DGIII.

[277] See, in general, Pag, above n. 270, at 461.

[278] Interview with a Commission official of DGIII. In the field of technical products a similar situation may also be observed: members of the 83/189 Committee on Technical Standards and Regulation (above n. 157) have been on this Committee for an undetermined period. It has actually happened that a member was on this Committee for more than 12 years: interview with a former member of this Committee. See Chap. 5.

the national element in decision-making, with technical expertise, economic and social interests and administration replacing national interests.[279] However, on the other hand, the fact that members on the Standing Committee are the *representatives* of the Member States may be considered as an element detrimental to supranational decision-making.[280]

Hence, on the one hand, we can observe a trend towards a centralisation of decision-making by the Community in which national interests are diminishing, while, on the other, we note an opposing tendency: the growing importance of national interests. The Standing Committee in this way forms a bridge between the horizontal and vertical distribution of powers between Community and national level, thus developing multi-level policy-making.[281] Balancing and bridging these two levels, the Standing Committee and other similar committees may, therefore, be an important means of addressing the issue of subsidiarity:[282] first, since they reassure the Member States that they continue to have influence over the exercise of powers by the Community institutions during all phases of the decision-making process; and secondly, since they provide for constant co-operation between national and Community authorities.

Thus, the Standing Committee is a forum in which both Member States and the Commission exchange views and discuss the possible problems which have arisen in relation to the matter under decision. In this regard, it is important to underline that the Standing Committee is composed of national *officials*. For good and effective decision-making, it is essential that discussions are held with the national bureaucrats who are dealing with the same issues at national level and that they reach agreement. This, at the same time, also enhances the quality of decision-making. Collaboration between national officials and the Commission[283] is of particular importance in a field where there is a degree of mutual distrust amongst the Member States as regards each others' administration. In this respect, the Standing Committee also constitutes an indispensable forum for interaction and co-operation between the national administrations and the Commission.[284] This has been termed "bureaucratic interpenetration".[285] Through the Committee the building up of co-ordination and the establishment of (administrative) partnership through committees is increas-

---

[279] See J.H.H. Weiler/ U.R. Haltern/ F.C. Mayer, "European Democracy and Its Critique" (1995) 18 *West European Politics* 3, 24–5.

[280] See J.H.H Weiler, "The Community System. The Dual Character of Supranationalism" (1981) 1 *YEL* 290.

[281] See Sauter/Vos, above n. 3 and, in general, F.W. Scharpf, "Community and Autonomy: Multi-level Policy-making in the European Union" (1994) 1 *JEPP* 2, 219–42.

[282] See Chap. 2 and also Buitendijk/Van Schendelen, above n. 3, at 55.

[283] Wessels speaks in this context of the possible creation of a "megabureaucracy": see W. Wessels, "Verwaltung im EG-Mehrebenensystem: Auf dem Weg zur Megabürokratie?", in M. Jachtenfuchs/B. Kohler-Koch (eds.), *Europäische Integration* (Opladen, 1996), 165–92.

[284] See S. Cassese, *Le basi del diritto amministrativo* (Turin, 1989), 303–4. See also Della Cananea, above n. 3, at 694.

[285] Pag, above n. 270, at 447, quoting the definition of Scheinmann: "[i]n its most simple form, bureaucratic interpenetration is the intermingling of national and international bureaucrats in various working groups and committees in the policy-making context of the EEC".

ingly striven for.[286] In this vein, the Standing Committee may foster effective and good decision-making in the area of health and safety regulation where mutual distrust and incorrect implementation have to date hindered the achievement of the internal market. The committee system has therefore been argued to be an institutional option which may be capable of bridging the gaps between political sensitivities and the rationality of expertise and between European and national administrative bodies, between governmental and non-governmental actors.[287]

5.4.3. Safeguard clauses

Most directives include safeguard clauses in accordance with Article 100a(5) which reserves to the Member States the power to protect health and safety. These clauses allow Member States to adopt temporary measures, which are, however, subject to approval by the Community institutions (see Table 2). In principle, the power to decide upon such measures is conferred upon the Commission. Here, too, the Standing Committee on Foodstuffs plays a special role. Although the Comitology Decision provides for a special procedure which may be applied for safeguard measures, virtually no use is made of this procedure in the food sector.[288] Instead, resort is made to the regulatory committee procedure.[289]

In general, the procedure to be followed is as follows. For reasons of health protection, Member States may, under certain conditions, temporarily suspend or restrict trade in a product on their territory, even though it complies with the directives. They must immediately inform the Commission and the other Member States and give reasons for their decisions. As soon as possible, the Commission must examine the evidence and consult the Standing Committee. While in cases in which a Commission proposal for an implementing measure is discussed, the Committee may not (in accordance with Article 5) question the subject-matter on which agreement within the Council has been reached, in these situations members on the Committee may nonetheless again express their national position.

Subsequently, the Commission delivers its opinion and takes the appropriate measures. Where the Commission is of the opinion that amendments to the directive concerned are necessary, it must consult the Standing Committee following the same procedure applied in relation to implementing measures (see Table 2). In Directive 89/398/EEC on foodstuffs intended for a particular nutritional use, this procedure is also prescribed where Member States are allowed to

---

[286] See Joerges/Neyer, above n. 3.

[287] See Joerges/Neyer, above n. 10.

[288] With the exception of the Hygiene Dir. which includes in Art. 10 a procedure in accordance with Art. 3 of the Comitology Decision in addition to the procedure on safeguard measures, for situations in which a hygiene problem is likely to pose a serious risk to human health or spreads into the territory of a non-member country: above n. 155.

[289] The same applies to the field of technical consumer products. See Chap. 5.

suspend or prohibit products, not listed in this Directive, but which do not comply with the provisions spelled out in the Directive or which endanger human health. More recently, Council Regulation 315/93 on contaminants and Council Directive 93/43/EEC on hygiene provide that the Commission must in all cases take measures in accordance with the *contre-filet* regulatory committee procedure as prescribed for other implementing measures.

5.4.4. *The Use of the Regulatory Committee Procedure in Food Regulation*

Although the IGC, which approved the SEA,[290] expressly advocated the use of the advisory committee procedure, the Council has, in practice, often rejected Commission proposals for an advisory committee, and instead favoured more restrictive management and regulatory committees.[291] This tendency has been strongest in relation to politically sensitive regulatory issues. In the food sector, the Council has proved itself willing to delegate implementing powers to the Commission only if delegation is overseen by a regulatory committee procedure; and it has sometimes even insisted on the use of the *contre-filet* variant of this procedure (see Table 2). Hence, from the beginning, the Standing Committee has operated in accordance with a regulatory procedure which was laid down by the Council in a separate Resolution in 1969.[292] Recent directives have generally adapted the procedures to the Comitology Decision.

At present, most directives concerning foodstuffs require the Commission to consult the Committee under the *filet* (*a*) variant of the regulatory procedure. In a few cases, i.e. scientific co-operation, contaminants, hygiene and flavouring substances,[293] the much-criticised *contre-filet* (*b*) variant of the regulatory committee procedure is prescribed. This variant of the regulatory committee procedure is also imposed in emergency situations where a serious and immediate risk to the health and safety of consumers exists, now formalised under the General Product Safety Directive which requires the consultation of the Committee on Product Safety Emergencies. In other fields touching upon health and safety issues and the environment, the Council has preferred to include this variant as well. While generally opposed to the regulatory committee procedure, the Commission has admitted[294] that the use of its *filet* variant might be justified in sensitive areas of social regulation, which involve politically controversial issues of great concern to the Member States. Moreover, the Parliament itself is inter-

---

[290] See the Declaration on the implementing powers of the Commission attached to the SEA.

[291] See Commission Communication to the Council on the conferment of implementing powers on the Commission, SEC(90)2589 final, 7. See also SEC(89)1591 final, 5–6.

[292] Council Resolution [1969] OJ C148/1.

[293] Here both the *filet* and *contre-filet* variant are used: the *filet* variant is prescribed for the establishment of a register on flavouring substances, whilst the *contre-filet* variant is prescribed for the adoption of a positive list on flavourings: Arts. 7 and 8 of European Parliament and Council Reg. 2232/96 on a Community procedure for flavouring substances [1996] OJ L299/1. In addition to this peculiarity, this procedure is also special in that it allows matters to be referred to the Committee by a Member State representative.

[294] See the Commission in SEC(89)1591 final, 11.

nally divided upon the issue of whether the Commission should be fully autonomous in cases relating to consumer and environment protection, and has implicitly approved the more stringent committee procedures.[295]

5.4.5. Objections to the Use of the Contre-filet Variant of the Regulatory Committee Procedure in Emergency Cases and Administrative Procedures

The use of the *contre-filet* variant (b) of the regulatory committee procedure in food regulation and health and safety regulation in general regulation must, however, be regretted. Particularly in health and safety regulation, it is conceivable that the Council rejects a Commission proposal by a simple majority, but is not able to reach its own decision on the basis of qualified majority.[296] The risk arises that notwithstanding the recognised need for a decision, no decision will be taken at all,[297] thus endangering the health and safety of persons. The formal reasoning of the Court in *Tedeschi* which generally approved the validity of this variant of the regulatory committee procedure should therefore be rejected.[298] The use of the *contre-filet* variant (b) procedure should particularly be rejected in the following situations:

"Emergency Situations"

This variant of the regulatory committee procedure has been included in various acts concerning health and safety issues, with a few cases in food legislation. For instance, one of the most important acts for consumer health and safety, the General Product Safety Directive,[299] obliges the Commission to follow the *contre-filet* variant of the regulatory committee procedure in situations which require an immediate decision in order to ensure the safety of European citizens.[300] In view of the high political sensitivity of such cases, it is not unlikely that in the event of a negative committee opinion, or in the absence of such an opinion, the Council may not be able to reach the qualified majority necessary for the adoption of a decision, but may nonetheless choose by a simple majority to block the measures proposed by the Commission. This could have serious consequences for the health and safety of persons.

"Administrative Matters"

Another example of the serious problems which may arise due to the application of the *contre-filet* procedure, is the use of this procedure in administrative matters where the rights of individuals are directly involved. As explained in

---

[295] Jacobs *et al.*, above n. 9, 232.
[296] See H.H. Maas, "Wetgevingskroniek EG 1977 en 1978" (1979) 27 *SEW* 10/11, 695. See, also, the critiques of Bradley, above n. 3, 710–11.
[297] See WQ 760/74 (Jahn) [1975] OJ C108/26.
[298] Case 5/77, above n. 93. See sect. 4.4.
[299] Above, n. 165.
[300] Art. 11 of Dir. 92/59/EEC, above n. 165.

previous chapters, such administrative matters are increasingly being transferred to Community level. In the third phase of integration the need for greater Community involvement in health and safety regulation results in a centralisation of decision-making on health and safety issues. This entails more implementation by the Community institutions, and thus the adoption of decisions of direct interest to individuals. This is, for example, the case of applicants for authorisation of new flavouring substances under the new Community procedure for flavourings.[301]

This can be most clearly demonstrated by an example from a related field regarding applications for authorisations of pharmaceutical products. Under the new Community authorisation system of medicinal products,[302] the Commission has been empowered to decide upon applications by individuals for the authorisation of medicines under a centralised or decentralised procedure.[303] After the adoption of a draft decision,[304] the Commission is required to consult the Standing Committee on Medicinal Products for Human Use according to the procedure. Although doubts may be raised about the appropriateness of the consultation of this Committee in these cases,[305] the consultation of the committee under this procedure may give rise to particular problems (see Figure 4). The least troublesome problem relates to those cases where the measures envisaged are in accordance with the opinion of the Standing Committee, and the Commission accordingly adopts the measures. However, if the proposed measures are not in accordance with the opinion of the Committee or in the absence of a Committee opinion, the Commission must submit the draft proposal to the Council. In this case, four possible scenarios may be envisaged:

(1) the Council adopts a decision by qualified majority, confirming the Commission's proposed measures;
(2) the Council adopts a decision by unanimity, amending the Commission's proposed measures (practice of the institutions);
(3) the Council does not act within three months[306] and consequently on its expiry the Commission adopts its proposal;
(4) the Council does not reach a decision with qualified majority within three months, but decides against the Commission proposal by simple majority.

---

[301] European Parliament and Council Reg. 2232/96, above n. 293.

[302] Council Reg. (EEC) 2309/93 laying down Community procedures for the authorisation and supervision of medicinal products for human and veterinary use and establishing a European Agency for the Evaluation of Medicinal Products [1993] OJ L214/1 and Council Dir. 93/39/EEC amending Dirs. 65/65/EEC, 75/318/EEC and 75/319/EEC in respect of medicinal products [1993] OJ L214/22.

[303] For a detailed description of these procedures, see Chap. 4.

[304] This draft decision is, in principle, in accordance with the opinion of the Agency for the Evaluation of Medicinal Products; see Art. 10(3) of Council Reg. 2309/93, above n. 302.

[305] See Chap. 5.

[306] The time limit set by Art. 73 of Council Reg. 2309/93, above n. 302.

Scenarios (2) and (4) are the most problematic. Scenario (2) relates to both the *filet* and the *contre-filet* variant of the regulatory committee procedure. Although the text of the Comitology Decision is unclear on this point, in practice the Community institutions apparently follow the general rule laid down in Article 189a(1) that a Commission proposal can be amended only by a unanimity decision of the Council.[307] This rule was, for example, adopted in the case of genetically modified maize. In this case,[308] the Commission had proposed to approve the marketing of genetically modified maize, but could not obtain the necessary support in the relevant standing committee under the *filet* procedure. The proposal was sent back to the Council. Although most Member States were against the Commission's proposal, the Council could not reach unanimity. The Commission could therefore freely adopt its approval of the marketing of transgenic maize, notwithstanding the disapproval of most Member States.[309] However, whilst, in view of its different character, it is doubtful that this unanimity rule applies to the committee-based implementing procedure, Article 189a(1), as inserted by the Maastricht Treaty, would currently not apply to the co-decision procedure,[310] which is the procedure generally applicable to the adoption of health and safety regulation (Article 100a). Application of this rule to the implementing phase should in any event be rejected since it risks reviving the traditional harmonisation approach "through the backdoor".

Scenario (4) is typical of the *contre-filet* and is full of uncertainties. In theory, should the Committee give a negative opinion but the Commission wish to approve an authorisation, the Council may reject the Commission approval by a simple majority. Equally, the Commission may not wish to issue an authorisation where the Committee is in favour. In this case, too, in view of the politically sensitive character of the authorisation of medicinal products, the Council may fail to act by a qualified majority, but nonetheless vote by a simple majority to block the proposed authorisation. Here, a political struggle between the Commission and the Council could greatly impinge upon the legal rights of the applicant for the authorisation of a medicinal product. The new authorisation system for medicinal products has sought to establish a rapid authorisation procedure,[311] and accordingly includes specific time limits within which decisions or opinions must be taken and given. Its inclusion of the *contre-filet* variant of the regulatory procedure, however, may lead to unacceptable delays and the undesirable result of the applicant not receiving a decision upon his or her

---

[307] See Opinion 4264/91 of the Legal Service of the Council of 22 Jan. 1991 (although in relation to the former Art. 149(1) EEC); Bradley, above n. 85; H.C.H. Hoffmann/A.E. Toeller, "Zur Reform der Komitologie: Grundsätze und Regeln" [1998] *Staatswissenschaft und Staatspraxis* 2 (forthcoming).

[308] Decided under the former Art. 149(1) EEC.

[309] K.St.C. Bradley, "Alien Corn, or the Transgenic Procedural Maze", in M.P.C.M. Van Schendelen (ed.), *EU Committees as Influential Policy-makers* (forthcoming).

[310] See J. Schoo, "Artikel 189a", in H. Von der Groeben/H. Thiesing/C.-D. Ehlermannn (eds.), *Kommentar zum EU/EG Vertrag* (Baden-Baden, 1997), 4/1064–1072.

[311] 7th recital of the preamble of Council Reg. (EEC) 2309/93, above n. 302.

request for authorisation.[312] Similarly, even where the Council's "no"[313] might be considered to be a decision,[314] implicitly refusing authorisation of the medicinal product in question, this seems to be contrary to the obligation to state reasons by virtue of Article 190 and, in particular, to the right of individuals in administrative procedures to receive an adequately reasoned decision.[315] The use of this procedure should therefore be abolished.

5.5. Integrating Scientific Expertise in Community Food Regulation through the Scientific Committee on Food

5.5.1. *The Resort to the Scientific Committee on Food as a Source of Scientific Advice*

In its 1985 New Approach on Foodstuffs, the Commission underlined the necessity of obtaining the opinion of the SCF prior to adopting any decision involving health issues.[316] In subsequent directives, the Council actually made the consultation of the SCF compulsory on any question affecting human health protection. Currently, therefore, the Commission is obliged to obtain the advice of a body which it had originally intended to be of a purely advisory nature.

The obligation to consult a scientific committee was the subject of litigation in *Angelopharm*.[317] In this case, the Court was asked for a preliminary ruling on the validity of a German prohibition of a hair restoration product which was based on a Commission Directive[318] implementing the general Council Directive 76/768/EEC on cosmetics.[319] Without going into scientific details, the

---

[312] This person may, in such cases, demand a decision under Art. 175(3).

[313] The text stipulates literally: "save where the Council has decided against the said measures by a simple majority". Compare the French, Italian and Dutch text in which a more neutral terminology is used namely when the Council *"s'est prononcé à la majorité simple contre lesdites mesures"*, *"si sia pronunciato a maggioranza semplice contro tali misure"*, *"zich met gewone meerderheid van stemmen tegen genoemde maatregelen heeft uitgesproken"*.

[314] In this context, it is established case law of the Court that "any measure the legal effects of which are binding on, and capable of affecting the interests of, the applicant by bringing about a distinct change in his legal position is an act or decision which may be the subject of an action under Article 173 for a declaration that it is void": Case 60/81, *IBM v. Commission* [1981] ECR 2639, recently reiterated by the Court of First Instance in Case T–3/93, *Air France v. Commission* [1994] ECR II–121. See also Case 22/70, *Commission v. Council (ERTA)* [1971] ECR 263; Case C–325/91, *France v. Commission* [1993] ECR I–3283; Joined Cases C–181/91 & C–248/91, *Parliament v. Council and Commission (Bangladesh)* [1993] ECR I–3685; and Case C–325/91, *France v. Commission* [1993] ECR I–3283. See, e.g., R. Greaves, "The Nature and Binding Effect of Decisions under Article 189 EC" (1996) 21 *ELR* 3–16.

[315] As the Court expressly held in Case C–269/90, *Hauptzollamt München-Mitte v. Technische Universität München* [1991] ECR I–5469, at I–5499. Similar objections may be expressed to the inclusion of this procedure, for instance, in the new Community system on the Community trade mark, see Art. 141 of Council Reg. (EEC) 40/94 on the Community trade mark [1994] OJ L11/1.

[316] COM(85)603 final, 16–19.

[317] Case C–212/91, above n. 19.

[318] Twelfth Commission Dir. 90/121/EEC [1990] OJ L71/40.

[319] [1976] OJ L262/169.

Regulatory committee procedure (*contre-filet*)

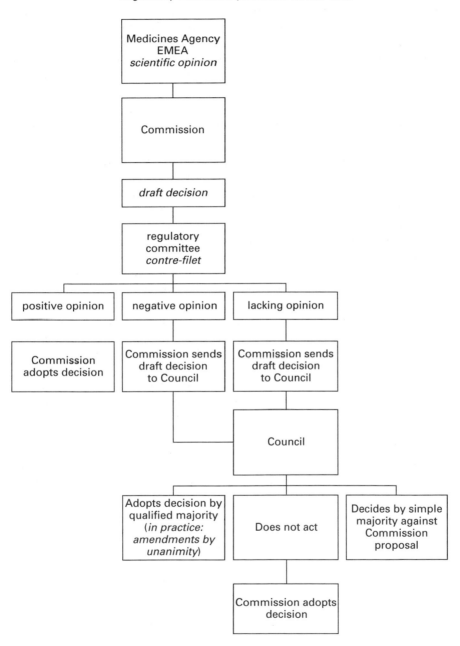

Figure 4. The *contre-filet* variant of the regulatory committee procedure used in the authorisation of medicinal products.

Court concentrated on the procedural requirements relating to the adoption of the Commission Directive, which underlay the German prohibition. The question arose whether the Commission was generally obliged to consult the Scientific Committee for Cosmetology before adopting its decisions, or whether consultation of this Committee was necessary only when the Commission or a Member State so requested. The relevant Article stipulated on this point that:

> "The amendments necessary for adapting annexes II to VII to technical progress shall be adopted in accordance with the same procedure, after consultation of the Scientific Committee for Cosmetology at the initiative of the Commission or of a Member State".[320]

The Court considered that the purpose of the Scientific Committee on Cosmetology, consisting of highly qualified persons in the relevant disciplines, was to provide the Commission with the assistance and information necessary to examine the complex scientific and technical problems which the drafting and adaptation of Community rules entailed. As the Commission in this case itself accepted, the consultation of this Committee made it possible to ensure that the measures to be taken had a scientific basis, taking into account the most recent scientific and technical research, and that only prohibitions necessary on grounds of health protection were imposed. Therefore, even if the text of the relevant directive was ambiguous on this point, the Court held that the consultation of this Committee must be mandatory in all cases. The Court argued that neither the Commission (as it had itself admitted) nor the Standing Committee on Cosmetic Products, composed of national representatives, was in the position to carry out scientific assessments, as the latter would require assistance by scientific and technical experts delegated by the Member States.[321] Although perhaps not laying down a "meta-positive principle",[322] the Court clearly indicated its preference for the development of scientific expertise in the Community context, rather than in the national setting.

From this ruling it might be deduced that where the Commission has set up a scientific committee to ensure that its measures have a scientific basis and take account of the most recent scientific and technical research, and that only measures are adopted which are necessary to protect human health, the Commission is obliged to consult this committee.[323] Is this conclusion still valid in the BSE aftermath? Here, particular notice must be taken of Commission Decision 97/579/EC on scientific committees, which explicitly stipulates that the scientific committees must be consulted in the cases laid down by Community legislation.[324] From this, it could be concluded that in other cases consultation would

---

[320] Art. 8(2) of Commission Dir. 90/121/EEC, above n. 318.

[321] Case C–212/91, above n. 19, at I–211.

[322] See Ch. Joerges, "Scientific Expertise in Social Regulation and the European Court of Justice: Legal Frameworks for Denationalised Governance Structures", in Ch. Joerges/K.H. Ladeur/E. Vos (eds.), *Integrating Scientific Expertise into Regulatory Decision-Making. National Traditions and European Innovations* (Baden-Baden, 1997), at 314.

[323] E. Vos, "The Rise of Committees" (1997) 3 *ELJ* 3, 210–29.

[324] Art. 2(1), above n. 172.

not be obligatory. However, even where Community legislation is silent on this point, consultation of scientific committees for issues which affect consumer health and safety should be preferred. First, it would ensure that the scientific advice resorted to is based on principles such as excellence, independence and transparency, and is not dependent on an *ad hoc* approach of the Commission. Secondly, this would enable the Commission to fulfil its obligation under the new text of Article 100a(3) inserted by the Amsterdam Treaty to take account of "any new development based on scientific facts".[325]

5.5.2. *Principles of Excellence and Independence of Scientific Expertise*

In the BSE aftermath, the Commission intends to follow a more coherent approach to risk regulation. To this end, the principles of *excellence* of the members of the scientific committees, their *independence* and the *transparency* of their activities[326] currently guide the Commission when dealing with scientific advice and the scientific committees.

In accordance with the principle of excellence, the Commission has itself set selection criteria for the appointment of the committee members. Consequently, a selection jury composed of members of the Scientific Steering Committee (which co-ordinates the scientific committees)[327] will give "preference"[328] to candidates who possess the criteria laid down in the "Call for expressions of interest for the post of member of one of the Scientific Committees", designed by the Commission:

- professional experience in the field of consumer health and more specific-ally in the areas covered by the field of competence of the committee con-cerned;
- experience in risk assessment;
- experience in delivering scientific opinion at national or international level;
- professional experience in a multidisciplinary and international environ-ment;
- attested scientific excellence;
- experience in scientific management.

As regards the principle of independence, Commission Decision 97/579/EC determines that the members of the SCF act "independently of all external influ-ence".[329] To this end, SCF members must annually inform the Commission of any interests which might be considered prejudicial to their independence, and they (as well as external experts) have to declare at each meeting any specific interest potentially conflicting with their independence. Of further importance

---

[325] See Chaps. 1 and 2.

[326] See, for a discussion of the latter principle, sect. 5.7.

[327] Commission Dec. 97/404/EC setting up a Scientific Steering Committee [1997] OJ L169/85.

[328] See call for expressions of interests for the post of Member of one of the Scientific Committees, as published on Internet: http://europa.eu.int/comm/dg24/health/sc/call_en.html.

[329] Art. 6(1), above n. 172.

for the independence of committees is that their agenda is drawn up by the Committee itself and not by the Commission. Although provisions on this point are lacking, this has already occurred in practice.[330]

5.5.3. Diversification of Expertise on the SCF

When setting up scientific committees, the Commission must pay adequate attention to the need that the composition of such bodies represent all disciplines relevant to the matter under discussion. This duty may be readily deduced from the Court's judgment in *Technische Universität München*,[331] discussed in the previous chapter. According to the Court, the Commission's obligation to examine all relevant aspects of the individual case carefully and impartially extended to a further obligation that where it need resort to a committee composed of expert representatives of the Member States (which is most often the Commission's only source of information) it must also ensure that the persons on this committee possess the necessary *technical* knowledge or, alternatively, that they seek advice from experts in the specific field under consideration.[332]

In accordance with the principle of "excellence", the relevant fields of expertise for SCF members have been identified as toxicology, pathology, human and veterinary medicines, food allergies, public health, epidemiology, molecular/ genetic biology, genetics, science and food technology, microbiology and food hygiene, human food, food composition and consumption, analytical chemistry and biotechnology.[333] The new composition of the SCF reflects these disciplines.[334]

5.5.4. Towards the Building Up of European and International Scientific Expertise through the SCF

Although the SCF members do not represent their Member States, they represent the different schools of thought inherent in their own national cultures and education systems. Notwithstanding the fact that, in accordance with the principle of excellence, members are selected on their expertise, some kind of geographical quota system (which the Commission previously operated) may be detected in the composition of the SCF, although experts from some small Member States (Portugal, Luxembourg and Finland) are lacking. Hence, at present, the Committee has two members from the bigger Member States: the United Kingdom, Italy, Germany and France, with the exception of two members from the Netherlands (probably because of its established experience in this

---

[330] Interview with a SCF member.
[331] Case C–269/90, above n. 315.
[332] *Ibid.*, at I–5500/5501. See, also, Case C–185/91, *Bundesanstalt für den Güterfernverkehr* v. *Gebrüder Reiff* [1993] ECR I–5801.
[333] See call for expressions of interest for the post of Member of one of the Scientific Committees, above n. 328; part of these fields is laid down in the Annex to Commission Dec. 97/579/EC, above n. 172.
[334] See [1997] OJ C342/8.

field) and one member from the smaller Member States: Greece, Austria, Ireland, Sweden, Spain, Denmark and Belgium.[335]

These national scientific experts must attempt to find a common denominator on specific topics, acceptable to all members on the Committee. Practice has demonstrated that divergent safety ideologies are not necessarily insurmountable hurdles to the Community's attempt to develop a true Community safety philosophy. In their search for the latest research, scientists, more than any other people, are already accustomed to co-operation within an international epistemic community. By means of the SCF, therefore, national scientific expertise is co-ordinated, enhancing the scientific consistency of Community legislation. At the same time co-ordination with international organisations such as the World Health Organisation, the Codex Alimentarius Commission and the American Food and Drug Administration is also ensured.

5.5.5. The Scientific Co-operation Model (SCOOP)

The Court's judgment in *Technische Universität München*[336] clearly underlines the vital need for the Commission itself to obtain scientific evidence. The growing involvement of the Community with the food sector and the increasing implementation tasks of the Commission are hence accompanied by a greater reliance on, and overburdening of, the SCF. Thus, some way of alleviating the increasing pressures on the SCF appeared necessary. Although initially the Commission seriously considered the creation of an agency in this field,[337] this idea was abandoned at the beginning of 1991.[338] Instead, the Council adopted a system of scientific assistance and co-operation in the scientific examination of food issues,[339] thus underlining the practical insufficiency of the co-operation obligation under Article 5. Under this system (in Brussels' jargon "SCOOP"[340]) Member States are required to co-operate with the Commission through their competent authorities and bodies, and to support the scientific examination of food questions, particularly in relation to human health. The goal is the co-ordination of existing national resources in support of Community activities in co-operative assessment.[341] The management of this co-operation is entrusted to the Commission together with the Member States in the framework of the Standing Committee on Foodstuffs, under the criticised *contre-filet* regulatory committee procedure.

---

[335] *Ibid.*

[336] Case C–269/90, above n. 315. See in this context also the *Pentachlorophenol* case where the Court ruled that the Commission cannot merely rely on the evidence provided by the Member States: Case C–41/93, *France* v. *Commission* [1994] ECR I–1829.

[337] See the discussions in F. Snyder (ed.), *A Regulatory Framework for Foodstuffs in the Internal Market*, EUI Working Paper LAW 94/4 (Florence, 1994).

[338] COM(91)16 final—SYN 332, 9.

[339] Council Dir. 93/5/EEC on assistance to the Commission and co-operation by the Member States in the scientific examination of questions relating to food [1993] OJ L52/18.

[340] Thus abbreviating the terms "scientific co-operation".

[341] Gray, above n. 108, at 116.

Scientific co-operation serves to strengthen the resources of the SCF.[342] In this way, national authorities collect and review the best available scientific information in the Member States, organise food intake surveys and investigate dietary products and prepare reports for the risk evaluation of certain substances.[343] The information thus gathered serves as a solid basis for the risk assessment carried out by the SCF. Whilst some confusion has arisen about the role of the SCF within this system—it was feared that scientific co-operation would bypass the SCF and deprive it of its tasks[344]—the Commission has ensured that the SCF will continue to be the main centre of scientific advice on the regulation of food issues by the Community.[345] In this context, the creation of a food agency remains topical. Following the BSE disaster, this option was once again seriously considered by the Commission in relation to veterinary and phytosanitary inspection,[346] but subsequently withdrawn again.[347] Transforming the SCF into an agency[348] could provide greater organisational independence and, in view of its ever-increasing workload, ensure increased administrative resources, its own independent secretariat and scientific support staff.[349] This is, to some extent, already provided for through the reorganisation of the Commission.

Whilst the scientific co-operation model will effectively function in certain areas and relieve the SCF's workload to some extent, the SCF nonetheless remains the body ultimately responsible for risk evaluation and must process all information transmitted by the national co-ordinatory bodies. It might nevertheless be doubted whether all Member State authorities can realistically participate in the carrying out of a wide range of tasks.[350] In this sense, scientific co-operation is likely to take into consideration the current division of scientific resources amongst the Member States, the southern States having considerably fewer scientific resources. When endeavouring to develop a true Community safety philosophy the Community must, therefore, recognise the imbalance of scientific expertise and develop a mechanism for the redistribution of scientific resources.[351] This also touches upon the problem of the economic implications of the setting of high safety standards and the development of highly sophisticated regulatory schemes which inevitably operate in favour of Member States

---

[342] See also Recommendation no. 17 of the Sutherland Report, *The Internal Market After 1992. Meeting the Challenge* of 26 Oct. 1992.

[343] See European Commission, DGIII/E/1, Scientific co-operation on questions relating to food. Tasks in the inventory established in Commission Dec. 95/492/EC, internal report of Nov. 1995.

[344] Interview with a SCF member.

[345] See Hankin, above n. 189, 162–4.

[346] See the Commission's proposal for a Council Reg. establishing a European Agency for Veterinary and Phytosanitary Inspection [1996] OJ C239/9.

[347] Commission Communication to the European Parliament and the Council on Food, Veterinary and Plant Health Control and Inspection, COM(98)32 final.

[348] See Commissioner Van Miert in [1991] *Eurofood* 2.

[349] See, also, Lister, above n. 104, at 300.

[350] *Ibid.* 299.

[351] This problem was recognised during an interview with a Commission official of DGIII.

with technically highly-developed industries. Action through the Structural Funds (Article 130 ff.) may be one means of addressing these distributional concerns.[352]

5.6. Interest Participation by Means of Committees?

5.6.1. *The Need for Plural Decision-making on Food Issues*

Community food regulation draws a distinction between risk assessment and risk management: it leaves the risk assessment of foodstuffs to the SCF, whilst management is carried out by the Commission in close collaboration with the Standing Committee. Where food issues are politically sensitive—likely to provoke disagreement amongst the Member States—it is not surprising that the Commission tends to follow the opinion of the SFC closely. This functional decentralisation[353] may contribute to the Commission's and the general Community's legitimacy, enhancing the quality of Community food regulation. On the other hand, the normative nature of risk assessment presupposes that SFC members are likely to enter into normative assessments as well. A more normative assessment is likely to be introduced, for example, where the Commission has apparently requested the SFC to take into account, in addition to "purely scientific considerations" the needs of industry and the alleged impossibility of reaching specific standards.[354] The normative character of risk regulation together with the potential of technocratisation of Community food regulation makes the participation of other "non-scientific" interested parties in food regulation increasingly important.

5.6.2. *The Role of the Economic and Social Committee*

The task of bringing the viewpoints of various social and economic interests into Community decision-making is generally performed by the Economic and Social Committee (hereafter ESC) in accordance with the Treaty provisions. In the 1970s, the Commission's efforts to increase socio-economic interest participation in its own decision-making through the creation of other, new interest committees for specific fields was, consequently, received very critically by the ESC.[355] The ESC feared that the existence of these committees would weaken its pre-eminent position as the consultative body for socio-economic interests and lead to an overall dilution of consultation in the Community, undermining its

---

[352] See Joerges/Neyer, above n. 10, 278–9.

[353] See, recently, L.F.M. Besselink/H.J.S Albers/W.T. Eijsbouts, "Subsidiarity in Non-federal Contexts: the Netherlands and the European Union" (1994) 42 *SEW* 5, 293.

[354] Interview with a SCF member.

[355] See the ESC opinion on the place and the role of the Economic and Social Committee in the institutional machinery of the Community in the context of a possible evolution thereof [1974] OJ C115/40.

general responsibility for social and economic matters as conferred upon it by the Treaty. These fears notwithstanding, it admitted that for technical matters of minor importance consultation by means of highly specialised committees composed of officials, management committees or committees for individual products, could nonetheless be justified.[356] Although for a limited time the Commission reduced its recourse to such committees, it has nonetheless continued to establish and resort to these committees for advice. In addition, the Commission has recently created a new kind of committee in the field of environment: a general consultative forum, composed of both socio-economic interests and representatives from regional and local authorities.[357]

In view of the fact that the ESC is never consulted during the implementing phase, the significance of the consultation of interest committees with regard to health and safety regulation would appear to have been amplified if the recent trend towards the deepening of Community involvement in this area is considered. Interest committees, being *"little ESCs"*, which specialise in health and safety matters such as food, may then serve particularly well to open up public debate on health and safety matters and may even be the corner-stone of a genuinely European process of public-opinion formation.[358] By means of such committees, potentially pluralistic decision-making is fostered as is the quality and thus the legitimacy of Community decision-making in general.

5.6.3. *Participation of Various Interests through Committees*

Standing Committee on Foodstuffs

Not only the Parliament, but also the ministers within the Council, may contribute to democratic legitimacy. The ministers taking part in the decision-making procedure in the Council are accountable to their national parliaments for their actions and thus to their national electorates.[359] From this perspective, it may even be argued that the Standing Committee and other policy-making/implementation committees, acting as *"little Councils"*[360] and comparable with the COREPER,[361] may enhance democratic legitimacy as the

---

[356] See the ESC opinion on the place and the role of the Economic and Social Committee in the institutional machinery of the Community in the context of a possible evolution thereof [1974] OJ C115/40. In relation to the food sector, for instance, a report of 1972 of the ESC revealed the desirability of the creation of an advisory committee composed of representatives of the various economic and social interests concerned—similar to those existing in the context of organisation of agriculture markets. See the second recital of the preamble to Commission Dec. 75/420/EEC setting up an Advisory Committee on Foodstuffs [1975] OJ L182/35.

[357] Commission Dec. 93/701/EC [1993] OJ L328/53.

[358] See, in this context, F.W. Scharpf, "Europäisches Demokratiedefizit und deutscher Föderalismus" [1992] *Staatswissenschaften und Staatspraxis* 3, 293–306.

[359] See the House of Lords Select Committee on the European Communities, above n. 53, 12–13.

[360] See V. Eichener, *Social Dumping or Innovative Regulation? Process and Outcomes of European Decision-Making in the Sector of Health and Safety at Work Harmonization*, EUI Working Paper SPS 92/28 (Florence 1992), 48.

[361] Weiler, above n. 280, at 288.

members of these committees *represent* the Member States and act on behalf of their indirectly elected governments.

At present, the Standing Committee provides for a forum in which problems are addressed through "deliberation" between the various actors with different interests. In this vein Committee-based decision-making fits perfectly into the multi-level structure of the Community and addresses tensions between the dual supranational and intergovernmentalist structure of the Community and its problem-solving tasks. In this light, committees have been argued to contribute to the legitimacy of Community decision-making, based upon a model of "deliberative supranationalism".[362] However, although this system seems to work satisfactorily, the fact is that deliberation among the participants of comitology does not include the participation of socio-economic interests. Therefore, consideration should be given to the case for inviting interested parties to (certain) meetings of the Standing Committee (which deliberates at closed doors), hereby taking account of the need for a certain amount of "secrecy" so as not to obstruct deliberation.[363]

Advisory Committee on Foodstuffs

To a certain extent, the "deliberation" which takes place through the committees resembles the regulatory practices of both the American Food and Drug Agency and the Environmental Protection Agency which support a negotiation model of hazard assessment and management, as advocated by some social studies of science.[364] This model, however, is specific in so far as it refers to the need for negotiation with citizens. In a search for a more democratic and procedural account of rationality so as to reflect the human dimensions of risk assessment and management, the model recognises that the process of risk assessment is highly value laden and needs the explicit consent of those who are most vulnerable to risks, i.e. the users of products.[365] In this context, negotiation, rather than mere expert decision-making, is argued to be of vital importance for ensuring free, informed consent in situations of controversial risks.[366] However, as argued earlier, in the Community context, "deliberation" through committees in the food sector at present includes solely the negotiation process between scientists, national representatives and the Commission.[367]

Although the views of the various interests involved may conflict, the discussion of a specific subject-matter between the representatives of industry, consumers and the other interests involved within the framework of the Advisory

---

[362] Joerges/Neyer, above n. 10.

[363] See the ESC Opinion on the Commission's Green Paper on Food and its New Approach to Food Safety [1998] OJ C19/61.

[364] See S. Jasanoff, *The Fifth Branch. Science Advisers as Policymakers* (Cambridge, Mass./London, 1990), 234 ff. and K.S. Shrader-Frechette, *Risk and Rationality: Philosophical Foundations* (Berkeley/Los Angeles, 1991), 206 ff.

[365] Shrader-Frechette, in the context of environmental protection, above n. 364, 169–218.

[366] *Ibid.*, at 206.

[367] Joerges/Neyer, above n. 10.

Committee might very well contribute to the deliberative formulation of sensible and appropriate, and thus more legitimate, food law by the Community.[368] At present, however, this Committee is not operative. This is due to the fact that consultation of the Advisory Committee depends entirely upon the Commission, which currently does not convene this Committee. The non-consultation of the Committee by the Commission is confirmed by recent empirical research and may be explained by the fact that the Commission is no longer in need of information about the different viewpoints through this Committee, as it is now approached directly by the interested parties concerned.[369] Clearly, those who will lose most from this development are the consumers, who, in comparison with industry, are already greatly under-represented. Further examination is, therefore, needed to examine whether it is feasible and worthwhile to increase the consultation of this Committee, for example, by giving the Committee the right to request the Commission to be consulted[370] and/or make its consultation obligatory.[371] This will largely depend on which model of citizen participation should be operated for Community health and safety regulation.

Account must here be taken of another problem posed by the Advisory Committee which derives from the fact that it is composed only of interest groups selected by the Commission. Here, the general problem arises, touched upon in Chapter 2, of how to select "the" representatives of certain interests; a problem which may be exemplified by the difficulties which have arisen around the Consumer Committee. As regards the Advisory Committee, this Committee does not include representatives of environmental organisations. This may be explained by the fact that this Committee was set up in the early 1970s, when not much attention was paid to environmental issues. At present, however, in view of the environmental impact of the substances used in foodstuffs, it would seem to be essential that the representatives of environmental groups be included in this Committee.

Consultation of the Advisory Committee as a sole interest-group representative body would thus inevitably risk excluding other interested parties. These difficulties underline the need for further means of enabling wider consultation of all parties concerned, irrespective of the question whether or not to make the consultation of the Advisory Committee compulsory. Examples of such mechanisms might be a more systematic use of green papers and a kind of public notice

---

[368] See Peinemann, above n. 223, at 139.

[369] See Joerges/Neyer, above n. 10, at 279. Whatever its reason, looking at the problem from the other side, namely what will interested parties do if the Committee is no longer convened, it is likely that they will intensify lobbying. This would, in turn, necessitate the regulation of lobbying by interested parties, as already identified by the Commission. See Commission Communication on an open and structured dialogue between the Commission and special interest groups [1993] OJ C63/2.

[370] This has been granted to the advisory committees in the agricultural sector by Art. 1(3) of Commission Dec. 98/235/EC on the advisory committees dealing with matters covered by the common agricultural policy [1998] OJ L88/59.

[371] See the ESC Opinion on the Commission's Green Paper, above n. 363.

and comment procedure, such as the one set forth in the US Administrative Procedures Act,[372] publishing decisional intentions in the Official Journal or on the Internet and inviting all interested parties to make their observations or comments known. The need for a greater use of green papers was recognised by the Sutherland report and the Commission's follow-up to this report[373] and has been partly put into practice by the Commission, which plans to publish green papers on various topics relevant to consumers.[374] At present, the Commission is already making intensive use of the Internet to make information available to the citizens. For foodstuffs, the Commission has presented its Green Paper on the General Principles on Food Law in the European Union, which was intended to launch a public debate on food regulation.[375] This and the introduction of a kind of public notice and comment procedure could ensure a wider participation of all interested parties in Community food regulation.

5.7. Transparency and Access to Documents

At present, the activities of committees are generally shrouded in secrecy. In general, it is unclear how committees operate: often rules of procedures do not exist or are not made public, whilst information on membership, meeting dates and committee agendas is similarly not available. This is particularly true for the policy-making/implementation committees. Although the Standing Committee on Foodstuffs is an exception to this in that it has adopted and published its rules of procedures, it also does not publish information to its members, its meetings and agendas. Only through empirical research and personal contacts may a layer of this secrecy be peeled away.[376] In addition, no data are available on the opinions issued by these committees. Recently, upon the insistence of the Parliament, which had threatened not to adopt the Community budget,[377] the Commission finally disclosed certain details and published an overview of the committee opinions.[378] Although impressive in volume,[379] this document merely lists the subjects which have been discussed by the committees, and does not divulge the content of the opinions of the committees. The same obscurity surrounds the Advisory Committee on Foodstuffs.

[372] 5 USC Sec. 553(c). See S. Breyer/R. Stewart, *Administrative Law and Regulatory Policy* (3rd edn., Boston, Mass., 1992) and R. Baldwin, *Rules and Government* (Oxford, 1995), 75 ff.
[373] Communication from the Commission to the Council and the European Parliament on the operation of the Community's internal market after 1992. Follow-up to the Sutherland report, SEC(92)2277 final, 5–6.
[374] Communication from the European Commission to the Council on the Priorities for Consumer Policy, 1996–8, COM(95)519 fin.
[375] Green Paper, above n. 157.
[376] See, in particular, sects. 5.3.3. and 5.4.
[377] Resolution of the Parliament [1995] OJ C308/134.
[378] Budget 1995. "Comitology, volume I, XIX/A7/0067/95, Decisions taken in 1994 by the committees listed in Annex I to Part A (Administrative appropriations) of Section III (Commission) of the general budget for the European Union for 1994" [1994] OJ L34.
[379] It comes to more than 1,000 pages.

The situation is different for the Scientific Committee on Food. Here, the BSE crisis served to open up the activities of all scientific committees, and particular use is now made of the Internet to publicise agendas, minutes and membership of these committees.[380] It was already common Commission practice to publish in the Official Journal the membership of the SCF and its opinions in a series on food science and techniques (albeit with considerable delay).[381] In the BSE aftermath, efforts are being made to guarantee greater transparency of the activities of the SCF particularly, through the use of the Internet: membership, agendas, minutes of meetings and opinions of the SCF are all published on the Internet.[382]

For an effective use of the principle of transparency in this field, however, it does not suffice just to have a SCF homepage on the Internet. The Commission should also be committed to updating regularly the information provided and putting new information on it, which seems, at present, not always to occur. It equally requires access to the documents not only of the scientific committees, but also of the other committees. In this context, the Code of Conduct on access to documents adopted both by the Council and the Commission[383] should also apply to the committee documents.[384] For documents regarding the policy-making/implementation committees, however, the Commission can in principle refuse access by referring to the protection of the confidentiality of the Commission's internal deliberations (in addition to the protection of commercial and industrial secrecy[385]), which is a formal exemption to the right of access to its documents.[386] In such situations, the Commission will nonetheless be required to balance explicitly the interests of citizens in gaining access to its documents against any interest of its own in maintaining the confidentiality of its deliberations.[387]

---

[380] See http://europa.eu.int/comm/dg24/health/sc/index_en.html (homepage for the scientific committees).

[381] Previously, general SCF reports on issues such as flavourings and SCF opinions on the safety aspects of specific substances were already published by the Commission, in its series: food science and techniques, reports of the Scientific Committee for Foods, Luxembourg.

[382] See http://europa.eu.int/comm/dg24/health/sc/ncomm1/index_en.html (homepage SCF).

[383] Code of Conduct concerning public access to Council and Commission documents (93/730/EC) [1993] OJ L340/41 and Council Dec. 93/731/EC on public access to Council documents [1993] OJ L340/43, as amended by Council Dec. 96/705/EC, ECSC, Euratom [1996] OJ L325/19 and Commission Dec. 94/90/EC, ECSC, Euratom [1994] OJ L46/58 as amended by Commission Dec. 96/567/EC, ECSC, Euratom [1996] OJ L47/45.

[384] See Annex II to COM(93)258 final, para. 9.

[385] The other exemptions are: protection of the public interest (public security, international relations, monetary stability, legal proceedings, inspections and enquiries); protection of the individual and of privacy; protection of the financial interests of the Community and protection of confidentiality if it has been requested by a supplier of information or, if the supplier is a Member State, because that country's legislation requires it.

[386] See its Communication on increased transparency in the work of the Commission, SEC(92)2274 final.

[387] Analogy may be sought in *Carvel and Guardian Newspapers* v. *Council*. In this case, the applicants had sought access to a number of documents, including preparatory COREPER reports, the minutes, voting records and decisions of certain Council sessions under Council Dec. 93/731/EC. The CFI annulled the Council's decision refusing the applicants access to the documents because of its failure to balance the various interests: Case T–194/94, [1995] ECR II–2767.

5.8. Accountability of Community Food Regulation

Although the Commission is formally accountable for the implementing decisions it adopts, the Standing Committee on Foodstuffs and other standing committees have an important impact on the outcome. If the Parliament takes its power to scrutinise and monitor implementing decisions seriously, its involvement by means of an information procedure such as the *modus vivendi* (in contrast to a formal consultation obligation[388]) may well contribute to the democratic legitimacy of the Community decision-making process, serving a public debate function and bringing about greater openness as regards the operation of the Standing Committee. This can only be achieved if the Parliament itself determines which information may be of interest to it, without prior filtering by the Commission.[389] It is therefore essential, as experience with the Plumb-Delors agreement demonstrated, that the Commission's forwarding of all information be matched by an adequate parliamentary follow-up. In this regard, the Parliament must first address its own internal problems, in particular, the cultural division concerning the need to be involved in executive decisions.[390] The question which emerges here is thus one of whether the Parliament's apparent desire to be involved in the implementation of Council/Parliament rules is similarly underpinned by a convincing concept of parliamentary control of Community food regulation.[391]

5.9. Towards Indirect Judicial Review of Committee Activities

Although committee opinions cannot be formally reviewed by the Court, in practice, committee activities seem no longer to escape judicial review. Recently, both private parties and Member States have discovered the importance of committee activities in the Community's decision-making as a means of initiating court proceedings for procedural infringements of Commission decisions. This has led the Court to take a close look at the internal rules of procedure of several committees. Thus, several recent judgments open up the ways in which to have committee activities reviewed before the Court and shine some

---

[388] See the House of Lords Select Committee on the European Communities, above n. 53, at 13.

[389] See, however, Falke/Winter, above n. 3, at 579, who take the view that the Parliament should not be involved in the initial stage in which proposals are sent to the committees as the Parliament would be flooded with politically uninteresting information. In their opinion, only in very rare and carefully selected cases should the early involvement of Parliament be made possible. Such a view, however, raises the question as to who must carefully select the relevant cases. The Commission, being the interested party in question, seems not to be suitable.

[390] Some members, in particular from countries where the traditional view has been that detailed regulatory matters should be left to the government, believe that the Parliament should focus on major political debates and primary legislation, whilst other members, originating from a strong tradition of MPs being involved in detailed implementation, consider the consultation procedures to be important: see Jacobs *et al.*, above n. 9, at 235.

[391] See Joerges, above n. 322.

light on the arcane world of comitology.[392] In *Accrington Beef* the applicants *inter alia* argued that the Commission had failed to consult the Beef Management Committee properly,

> "because consultation of the Management Committee was arranged as late as possible so that the committee members were not given the opportunity to reflect on the matter or to consult traders in the beef sector".[393]

The Court, however, refused to go into procedural details and superficially replied:

> "It is sufficient to note in that regard that the Management Committee was consulted on the Commission's proposal for a regulation and gave a favourable opinion".[394]

More recently, however, the Court was more willing to have a closer look at the procedural rules of committees. In *Moskof,* the Court examined in detail various drafts of the regulation and the minutes of the Tobacco Management Committee on the applicants' complaint that the Commission should have resubmitted a draft regulation to the Committee, as the text of this regulation would have been changed after approval of this Committee. The Court, however, concluded that the Management Committee procedure had been observed.[395] In *Azienda Agricola "Le Canne" Srl* v. *Commission*, the applicant challenged the validity of a Commission decision reducing financial aid relating to the development of aquaculture and the establishment of protected marine areas *inter alia* on the grounds of failure to consult the Standing Committee on the Fishing Industry. The Court, however, rejected the applicant's claim here, too, and held that no consultation of the Standing Committee was required, since the decision in question did not constitute a reduction but an observation that part of the applicant's expenditure fell outside the scope of its originally approved project.[396]

Member States have also used irregularities in the procedure before the standing committees to seek annulment of Commission decisions. In the *Construction Products* case,[397] Germany clearly indicated its desire to be taken seriously in its participation in the Commission's decision-making through the Standing Committee on Construction Products[398] by attacking a Commission Decision[399] which implemented the Construction Products Directive.[400] It

---

[392] Bradley, above n. 85.

[393] Case C–241/95, *The Queen* v. *Intervention Board for Agricultural Produce, ex parte Accrington Beef Co. Ltd and Other* [1996] ECR I–6699, para. 43.

[394] *Ibid.*, para. 44.

[395] Case C–244/95, *Moskof AE* v. *Ethinikos Organismos Kapnou* [1997] ECR I–6441, para. 46.

[396] Case T–218/95, *Azienda Agricola "Le Canne" Srl* v. *Commission* [1997] ECR II–2055, para. 56.

[397] Case C–263/95, *Germany* v. *Commission* (*Construction Products*) [1998] ECR I–441.

[398] Also other Member States have insisted upon participation through committees. See, for example, Case C–147/96, *Netherlands* v. *Commission* (relating to Standing Veterinary Committee), pending before the Court. See [1996] OJ C197/9.

[399] [1989] OJ L40/12.

[400] [1995] OJ L129/23.

accused the Commission of not having sent the German version of the draft Commission Decision within the prescribed time-limit of 20 days. In addition, the Commission had completely disregarded its express request to postpone voting at the meeting of the Standing Committee, a possibility allowed for in the rules of procedure in case of delay. The Commission, however, replied that Germany had received an English version of the draft decision and that it was unreasonable to ask for a postponement one day before the meeting.

Faced with this clear disregard of procedural rules, the Court decided this time to teach the Commission a lesson. It first confirmed that the sending of an English version of the document in question was contrary to Article 3 of Council Regulation 1 on the languages to be used by the Community,[401] according to which documents which are sent by a Community institution to a Member State need to be drafted in the language of that State.[402] The Court continued by examining the requirements stipulated in the Rules of Procedure of the Standing Committee, in particular, the requirement to send the document to the offices of the Permanent Representatives of the Member States and to their representatives on the Committee, together with the requirement that there was no possibility of shortening the period of notice of 20 days. It held that these requirements indicated the intention to ensure that Member States had enough time to study the documents, which could be particularly complex and require time for discussion between the different administrative authorities or consultation of external experts.[403] From these requirements, together with the fact that the vote had not been postponed despite Germany's explicit request, it concluded that there had been an infringement of essential procedural requirements and annulled the Commission's Decision.

5.10. Right of Hearing

Individuals are increasingly required to apply to the Commission directly for an authorisation under Community legislation of a substance to be used in food. For example, this is the case for additives, where the specific substance must be added to the positive list. At present, however, no provisions which guarantee a right of hearing for the individual applicant submitting his/her request exist, the importance of which was underlined in *Technische Universität München*.[404] Therefore, rules need to be developed to include such a right in the relevant procedures.

[401] [1952–8] OJ Spec. Ed. 59.
[402] Case C–263/95, above n. 398, para. 27.
[403] *Ibid.*, para. 31.
[404] Case C–269/90, above n. 315.

5.11. Reform of the Comitology Decision

It is clear from the foregoing analysis that for comitology to be a legitimate model for Community food regulation, the committee system needs to be improved. The revision of the Comitology Decision scheduled for the end of 1998, called for by the IGC, is therefore a great opportunity to submit comitology to the more general principles of legitimacy, as discerned in this book. In view of the Member State-oriented understanding of the institutional balance, the participation of the Member States within the implementing phase should be generally recognised. The degree of Member State participation could be linked with the committee procedure to be followed, for example, through the identification of potentially politically sensitive topics, such as health and safety regulation.

Proposing one single committee procedure as the Parliament did[405] would probably mean renouncing the advisory committee procedure, a procedure which in some fields may be very acceptable. Therefore, without abandoning the possibility of resorting to the advisory committee and in view of the Council's readiness to block delegation, the three committee types should be retained.[406] Importantly, these procedures should be clarified, simplified and made more open. Committees should further be obliged to draw up rules of procedure which would, for example, also include rules on the language in which the Commission needs to send its draft decisions.

First, the *contre-filet* variant should be abolished. As indicated above, this variant could under certain circumstances endanger the health and safety, or have a negative impact on the rights, of EU citizens. Furthermore, it must be clear that the overall logic behind committee procedures would seem to indicate that where the Commission and the relevant management or regulatory committee cannot agree, the matter must again be referred to the Community legislature, i.e. in cases of co-decision (Article 100a) to both the Council and the Parliament.[407] The establishment of some kind of hierarchy of Community rules would seem to be indispensable here.[408] In these cases, the nature of the measure (implementing measure of general rules—"fundamental elements"[409]—already considered by the legislature) and efficiency recommend the adoption of a strongly simplified form of co-decision within strict time-limits. In other cases,

[405] See sect. 4.3.3.

[406] See, however, Demmke and Haibach, who want to abolish the regulatory *filet* (IIIa) procedure: C. Demmke/G. Haibach, "Die Rolle der Komitologieausschüsse bei der Durchführung des Gemeinschaftsrechts und in der Rechtsprechung des EuGH" [1997] *Die Öffentliche Verwaltung* 718.

[407] See, also, Falke/Winter, above n. 3, 578–80. See, in this context, the practice in some Member States of the parliament retaining some form of involvement in executive rule-making: Jacobs *et al.*, above n. 9, at 235 and K.-H. Ladeur, "Sources and Categories of Legal Acts—Germany", in G. Winter (ed.), *Sources and Categories of European Union Law. A Comparative and Reform Perspective* (Baden-Baden, 1996), 257.

[408] See, in general, *ibid.*

[409] See Chap. 2, sect. 6.1.3.

the same reasons demand that the Council should be able to decide by qualified majority in the case of amendments, too. Here, the practice of the institutions applying Article 189a(1) to measures referred back to the Council (and Parliament), demanding unanimity for amendments by the Council, should be abolished. Moreover, the Comitology Decision must also take account of the urgency of the matter in question: where human health and safety are endangered, the Commission should be able to set strict deadlines for the Council and/or Parliament to decide depending on the emergency, and it should be able to adopt temporary measures in such cases. This would make the special safeguard procedure, in practice rarely operated (see Table 2), redundant.

The Parliament should, however, not become active in the committees themselves, but rather strengthen its instrument of control of committee activities. It should obtain a right to be informed of what the committees and the Commission do and a right of "revocation".[410] The latter right would enable the Parliament to require the Commission to interrupt its decision-making procedure and to refer the matter back to the Community legislature.

Clearly, the obscurity which currently governs the committee system should definitely be dispelled. Although the "success" of deliberation admittedly depends on a certain degree of confidentiality in the environment in which deliberation takes place,[411] this should not prevent committee activities from being brought into the daylight (such as the American "sunshine committees").[412] Greater transparency could be ensured by the publication of dates of the meetings and agenda, as well as the committee members, whilst open ("enlarged") meetings could be organised with interested parties.[413]

Very recently, the Commision submitted its proposal, which retains the basic structures, but cautiously reforms and simplifies their operational principles.[414] The proposal is to be welcomed for taking up some of the issues already discussed: it retains the three committee procedures, indeed abandons the *contre-filet* procedures, obliges committees to draw up rules of procedure and finally requires that all existing committee procedures are brought into line with the new procedures. The proposal is, however, disappointing in several other aspects: importantly, it fails to generate the more general principles as described above, such as the openness of committee activities. Similarly Parliamentary influence remains limited to being informed and there is a lack of clarity as to the position of the Parliament when it has severe objections against the committee opinions or the draft Commission proposal. Clearly, the extent to which this proposal will be acted upon by the other institutions remains to be seen.

---

[410] See J. Neyer, "The Comitology Challenge to Analytical Integration Theory", in Ch. Joerges/ E. Vos (eds.), *EU Committees: Social Regulation, Law and Politics* (Hart Publishing, Oxford, forthcoming).

[411] Joerges/Neyer, above n. 10.

[412] See Federal Advisory Committee Act, s. 10, 5 USCS Appx (1994).

[413] As currently happens with the Committee on Technical Standards and Regulations set up by Dir. 83/189/EEC (above n. 157); see Chap. 5.

[414] [1998] OJ C279/5.

6. CONCLUSION

The Community has set up various committees to provide for assistance in the regulation of health and safety issues. These committees are an *ad hoc* institutional evolution which meets the, at times unexpected, functional demands of an ever-expanding European Community for technical information and expertise. In addition, the committees also serve as a forum in which the views of interested parties may be aired. Although committees are broadly comparable with various advisory organs found in the Member States in every regulatory field, the consultation of which serves to enhance the legitimacy, rationality and effectiveness of decision-making, the situation at the Community level is more complex. Here, committees have also been established to provide the Member States with a means of ensuring their continuing influence over EC decision-making when implementing powers have been delegated to the Commission. Committees may be classified according to the bindingness of their consultation (committees whose consultation is obligatory and committees whose consultation is not compulsory) and according to the legal basis on which they have been created (Council act or Commission act). In addition, a functional typology distinguishes between policy-making/implementation committees, interest committees and scientific committees, each of which corresponds to the different aspects of regulatory decision-making.

While estimates of the overall number of committees operating within the Community's institutional structure differ widely, this book has relied on the number of committees listed on the Community budget, amounting to approximately 477 committees for 1998. The substantive increase in the importance of committees within the Community decision-making process is perhaps best highlighted by budgetary figures which show that, whilst annual Community expenditure on committees increased to 8 million ECU in 1989, for 1998 approximately 20 million ECU was set aside for this purpose.

The participation of this plethora of committees in the Community decision-making process, however, has raised various questions about their legality and legitimacy. In particular, the obligation of the Commission to consult policy-making/implementation committees in the implementation of Council/Parliament decisions has been contested in conformity with the Community's principle of the institutional balance of powers. In this chapter, however, I concluded that committees generally do not disturb the institutional balance as interpreted by the Court. This conclusion does nonetheless not deny the importance of committees in the implementation of Community policies. Rather than neglecting committees, as the Court seems to do, emphasis should be laid on the importance of controlling the committees within the Community's system of checks and balances, and monitoring their impact on the legitimacy of the Community decision-making process.

Analysis of the operation of the committee model in the food sector reveals how the Community addresses its need for greater expertise and need to guar-antee the on-going approval of the Member States through resorting to the three types of committees. This field, which has a long-rooted regulatory tradition at national level, finds itself moving towards a third phase of integration, in which the Community needs to regulate and control the implementation of its rules closely, mainly due to the mutual distrust between the Member States. Other factors explaining this trend are the increasing public concern about food issues resulting in new national legislative initiatives, the use of new technologies, the risk of free movement of dangerous foodstuffs and worldwide accidents.

The food sector exhibits all the three committee models (according to the functional typology): a scientific committee: the Scientific Committee on Food; an interest committee: the Advisory Committee on Foodstuffs; and a policy-making/implementation committee: the Standing Committee on Foodstuffs. All three committees each have a particular function: the Scientific Committee is designed to incorporate scientific advice into the decision-making process; the Advisory Committee exists to inform the Commission of the opinions of the various interests involved, and the Standing Committee on Foodstuffs is designed to ensure the political approval of the Member States in the imple-menting phase.

Community food regulation distinguishes between risk assessment and risk management, which is expressed in its institutional design; the Community leaves the risk assessment of foodstuffs to the SCF which, apparently, restricts itself to dealing with the scientific aspects of a specific subject-matter; the polit-ical decision is subsequently taken by the Commission together with the Standing Committee on Foodstuffs. Since foodstuffs issues are politically sensi-tive, it comes as no surprise that the Commission tends to follow closely the opinion of the SCF which has acquired an outstanding reputation. Although this Committee has largely been neglected in the (institutional) debate on comitol-ogy, analysis of the food sector reveals it to be one of the most important com-mittees, determining the scientific basis for every decision on food. The activities of the SCF have been regulated by rules laid down by the Commission in its deci-sion on scientific committees, and/or have been developed by the Commission on an *ad hoc* basis. The SCF is supported by the Member States in the frame-work of an obligatory scientific co-operation model set up by the Community. This model, however, is not an adequate regulatory tool and moreover fails to take into account the present imbalance in the distribution of scientific resources throughout the Community. Furthermore, in view of the increasing workload of the SCF, its resources should be strengthened by its having its own secretariat and appropriate scientific staff. From a long-term perspective, the formal trans-formation of the SCF into an agency would seem desirable.

The special position that Member States retain in decision-making on food issues through the Standing Committee may be explained by a Member-State-oriented understanding of the institutional balance of powers. Further, their participation in this phase of decision-making can be justified by the delicate nature of food law, in which traditionally determined interests are weighed. Both the obligatory consultation of the Standing Committee on Foodstuffs in its role as a regulatory committee and the inclusion of safeguard procedures reassure the Member States that their views will be taken into account. For good and effective decision-making, deliberative interaction with the Member States appears to be of the utmost importance. Here, on the one hand, the Standing Committee, composed of national bureaucrats, functions as a forum of interaction and co-operation between the Member States and the Commission, thus encouraging the centralisation of decision-making. In this way, the significance of purely national interest is diminished, contributing to the overall trend of greater transnational decision-making, in which national interests are replaced by technical expertise, socio-economic interests and administration. On the other hand, however, the Committee, composed of national representatives, enhances the importance of the national interests and contributes to the decline of supranational decision-making. The Standing Committee is consequently a means of bridging the horizontal and vertical division of powers and might be argued to have pragmatically secured subsidiarity and to have created a framework for co-operative and deliberative multi-level policy-making.

Committees in the food sector have generally functioned well and may be argued to promote greater effectiveness and legitimacy of Community decision-making. In this vein, committees have been argued to be a forum for the development of novel and mediating forms of interest formation and decision-making and thus to contribute to the legitimacy of Community decision-making, based upon a model of "deliberative supranationalism".

Until the outbreak of the BSE crisis, many of the Community's rules relating to committees had been created on an *ad hoc* basis and/or developed in the Court's jurisprudence. However, the BSE crisis has clearly demonstrated that where important political interests are at stake, the *ad hoc* approach followed by the Commission to food regulation is not sufficient to guarantee decision-making free from manipulation and capture. This is underlined by the fact that in such situations even the scientists are likely to be subject to powerful political pressure, as was openly admitted by scientists working on the BSE case within various scientific committees. This makes the need for enhanced legitimacy and greater transparency in risk evaluation even more imperative. It further highlights the need for the development of a rationality based on "objective" and refined scientific expertise.

In response to the BSE crisis, the Commission has, in fact, presented a more coherent approach to food safety based on true "principles", namely, excellence, independence and transparency of scientific advice delivered by the scientific committees. Although these criteria are certainly acceptable, the question nonetheless arises (precisely in view of the BSE disaster) whether the Commission should be allowed to draw up its own rules—some of which are not even laid down in a decision but in a publication of the Commission looking for candidates for committee members. Here, general principles which stipulate under what conditions and what principles the Commission should carry out its (implementing) tasks should be laid down by the Community legislature.

In addition, the Commission's new approach only sees to scientific advice given by the scientific committees and does not extend these principles to the rest of the process of risk regulation. It thus fails to take account of the role of Member State representatives within the Standing Committee or of interest-group representatives within the Advisory Committee or otherwise. Where, for example, the Standing Committee is often very secretive and neither its activities nor its members are made public, the need for greater transparency and for more information upon committee membership and activities becomes particularly clear.

Consequently, the incoherence which has resulted from the essentially pragmatic approach of the Community institutions to comitology now needs to be compensated for through general rules. Thus, a more general mechanism should be set up by the Community legislature to ensure more openness and legitimacy in regulatory decision-making on food as well as greater consistency and generality of application. The revision of the Comitology decision should, therefore, lay down principles such as Member State participation, parliamentary control, openness, access to documents and specific meetings, specific provisions on emergency matters, and abolish the *contre-filet* variants of the committee procedures. The drafting of these and other principles on scientific expertise may lead towards the establishment of a kind of European administrative procedures act.[415] Such an act could include, for example, the composition of committees, the appointment of the members, public meetings and access (such as the American "sunshine" committees), publications, transparency, quality of expertise, interest participation and hearing rights.

Importantly, the drafting of such an act would need to address the question of how interested citizens may participate in Community risk regulation to ensure its legitimacy. Here, the limits of science together with the normative character of risk assessment require foodstuffs not to be regulated solely by scientific experts and/or national and European bureaucrats in a closed and often secretive, albeit deliberative, circle. Greater use of green papers and a system of public notice and comment procedure, for example, through the Internet, should be considered. This may contribute to the opening up of a truly Community-wide public debate on risks inherent in food; a debate noticeable at present only for its absence. The organisation of a forum with all interested parties, as is now occasionally organised by the Commission, may be of great importance. In addition, it should be asked whether the consultation of the Advisory Committee on Foodstuffs should be made compulsory. Laying down these general principles, such an act will further legitimise Community policies on food and, more generally, Community health and safety regulation.

---

[415] See, in the US context, e.g. M. Shapiro, *Who Guards the Guardians Judicial Control of Administration* (Athens/London, 1988), 39 ff. See also 'The Administrative Procedure Act: A Fortieth Anniversary Symposium' (1986) 72 *Virginia Law Review* 215–492.

4

Health and Safety Regulation through Agencies—the Case of Pharmaceuticals

1. INTRODUCTION

The second regulatory model applied by the Community to regulate health and safety issues is that of agencies.[1] The Community has adopted this model in the field of pharmaceuticals. Recourse to an agency in this area is part of a recent general trend which favours the greater use of agencies within the Community's institutional structure. Although a few agencies were created in the 1970s, it was the 1990s which witnessed a "boom" in newly set up agencies. These agencies can be distinguished from committees in that they possess legal personality and, supported by their own administrative structures, have a degree of administrative independence.

The renewed resort to agencies in the 1990s can largely be explained by the increased requirement for information and co-ordination at the Community level as well as by the need to lighten the Commission's workload in various policy areas; a workload growing increasingly heavy as a result of general implementation problems and the need to deepen Community action in these areas.[2] The existing agencies support Community institutions and national authorities in identifying, preparing and evaluating specific policy measures and guidelines.[3] Thus, on the one hand, agencies are a response to growing and complex Community tasks and are an aid in its search for more efficient and effective decision-making. On the other hand, however, the agency structure also underlines the continuing responsibilities of the Member States.

This chapter examines first the general problems which the creation of agencies by the Community has given rise to; more specifically, the legal basis for these agencies and the difficulties attendant upon such delegation of powers

---

[1] For the purposes of this book, the term "agency" is used in its widest sense and also includes bodies entitled fund, foundation or office. Where such bodies have specific regulatory powers, mirroring US and national agencies, they are referred to as "regulatory agencies".

[2] See, for a general discussion, A. Kreher (ed.), *The New Agencies. Conference Report*, EUI Working Paper RSC 96/49 (Florence, 1996) and *id.*, *The EC Agencies between Community Institutions and Constituents: Autonomy, Control and Accountability, Conference Report*, EUI RSC Working Paper (Florence 1998).

[3] See, in general, M. Everson, "Independent Agencies: Hierarchy Beaters?" (1995) 1 *ELJ* 180–204.

(closely related to the issue of the institutional balance of powers). Subsequently, analysis is focused on the agency regulatory structure in the field of pharmaceuticals. Here the specific role of the agency set up in this area will be examined, with a view in particular to the assertion that agencies are the true functional alternative to decision-making in the framework of comitology.[4] As with foodstuffs, the regulation of pharmaceuticals has always had a high priority on the Community agenda. Yet the unique features of the pharmaceutical market, together with the even greater degree of political sensitivity on this issue, have led the Community to adopt a somewhat different approach. In this field, no source of scientific expertise existed, unlike in the food sector, where since the 1970s the internationally renowned Scientific Committee on Food furnished a basis for "European expertise". A committee had been created in this sector, too, to ensure the development of a common technical position amongst the Member States. This was, however, in large part a mere political organ, composed of national representatives. The Community, therefore, proceeded with the creation of an agency to assist the Commission in the authorisation of medicinal products, the European Agency for the Evaluation of Medicinal Products (EMEA). In addition to the need for European scientific expertise, Community involvement in this field has also necessitated post-market control of authorised medicines and the provision of information to third parties by the Community. These tasks have typically been entrusted to this Agency. This new regulatory pattern, however, has given rise not only to questions about its legal basis and delegation of powers, but also to questions about its legitimacy. Decision-making based upon greater expertise may arguably entail greater legitimacy, so that the EMEA entrusted with supplying expertise might, in principle, constitute a legitimising element within the decision-making process. Concerns might nonetheless be raised about the manner in which the EMEA drafts its scientific opinions (in particular about the selection of experts consulted and the "objectivity" of the scientific opinion), transparency, accountability and interest participation in Community decision-making. In conclusion, it needs to be asked whether the EMEA should not be transformed into a true "independent" regulatory agency, thus relieving the increasing workload of the Commission in this area.

2. THE RISE OF AGENCIES WITHIN THE COMMUNITY'S INSTITUTIONAL STRUCTURE

2.1. Origins of Agencies

The Community first created agencies in the early 1970s. The origins of the first agency, the European Monetary Co-operation Fund, may be traced back to the

---

[4] See R. Dehousse, "Regulation by Networks in the European Community: The Role of European Agencies" (1997) 4 *JEPP* 246–61.

The Hague Summit of 1969, where plans were developed to achieve an economic and monetary union.[5] The need for the co-ordination of economic and monetary policy was further emphasised by the Council[6] and reiterated by the Heads of State at the Paris Summit of 1972.[7] The European Monetary Co-operation Fund was accordingly established in 1973.[8] At the same Paris Summit of 1972, political agreement was reached on the need to design action programmes on social and environmental policy. The two action programmes subsequently drawn up[9] resulted in the creation in 1975 of both the European Centre for the Development of Vocational Training[10] and the European Foundation for the Improvement of Living and Working Conditions,[11] each charged with the task of providing information and co-ordination.

Although over the years the creation of bodies such as a European Cartel Office[12] and a European Trade Mark Office[13] was discussed,[14] no further agencies were set up until the 1990s. Between 1990 and 1994, no fewer than seven new agencies saw the light of the day:[15] the European Environment Agency,[16] the European Training Foundation,[17] the European Monitoring Centre of Drugs and Drug Addiction,[18] the European Agency for the Evaluation of

---

[5] See R.H. Lauwaars, "Auxiliary Organs and Agencies in the EEC" (1979) 16 *CMLRev.* 365–87.

[6] Resolution of the Council and the Representatives of the Governments of the Member States on the attainment by stages of economic and monetary union in the Community [1971] OJ C28/1.

[7] Bull. EC 1972, no. 10, 17.

[8] Council Reg. 907/73 [1973] OJ L89/2. See C.-D. Ehlermann, "Die Errichtung des Europäische Fonds für Währungspolitische Zusammenarbeit" (1973) 8 *EuR* 3, 193–208.

[9] See Council Resolution concerning a social action programme [1974] OJ C13/1 and Council Resolution on the programme of action of the European Community on the environment [1973] OJ C112/1.

[10] Council Reg. 337/75 [1975] OJ L39/1.

[11] Council Reg. 1365/75 [1975] OJ L139/1.

[12] See the discussions in the (mainly German) literature, e.g., K. Holderbaum, "Chancen für eine Europäische Kartellbehörde?" (1967) 2 *EuR* 116–33; U. Everling, "Zur Errichtung nachgeordneter Behörden der Kommission der Europäische Wirtschaftsgemeinschaft", in W. Hallstein/H.-J. Schlochauer (eds.), *Festschrift für Ophüls, Zur Integration Europas* (Karlsruhe, 1965), 33–49. At present, the discussion on the need for such an office is still very much alive, see F. Merz, "Bedarf die Errichtung eines Europäischen Kartellamtes der Änderung des EWG-Vertrages?" (1990) 1 *EuZW* 13, 405–8 and C.-D. Ehlermann, "Reflections on a European Cartel Office" (1995) 32 *CMLRev.* 471–86. See also K. Van Miert, "The Proposal for a European Competition Agency" (1996) 2 *EC Competition Policy Newsletter* 2. See, for a discussion on the need to create a European Telecommunications Agency, W. Sauter, "The ONP Framework: Towards a European Telecommunications Agency. The Growing Demand for a European Regulator" (1994) 5 *Utilities Law Review*, 140–6 and *id.*, *Competition Law and Industrial Policy in the EU* (Oxford, 1997), 207 ff.

[13] See the Commission's proposal [1980] OJ C351/5, amended by its proposal of 1984 [1984] OJ C230/1. See R.H. Lauwaars, "Art. 235 EEG als grondslag voor de schepping van een Europees merkenrecht" (1981) 29 *SEW* 9, 533–48.

[14] See, in general, M. Hilf, *Die Organisationsstruktur der Europäischen Gemeinschaften* (Berlin/Heidelberg/New York, 1982), 147 ff.

[15] See the brochure by the European Commission, *The Agencies of the European Union* (Luxembourg, 1996) and http://europa.eu.int/en/agencies.html (homepage of the European agencies).

[16] Council Reg. (EEC) 1210/90 [1990] OJ L120/1.

[17] Council Reg. (EEC) 1360/90 [1990] OJ L131/1, amended by Council Reg. (EC) 2063/94 (1994) OJ L216/9.

[18] Council Reg. (EEC) 302/93 [1993] OJ L36/1.

Medicinal Products,[19] the Office for Harmonisation in the Internal Market (Trade Marks, Designs and Models),[20] the European Agency for Safety and Health at Work[21] and the Community Plant Variety Office.[22] In order to meet the translation needs of these newly set up bodies a specific "agency", the Translation Centre, was created.[23] In 1997, another agency was set up, the European Monitoring Centre on Racism and Xenophobia.[24]

The location of these bodies became the subject of a heated political discussion. The struggle for the siting of the Environment Agency, for example, determined that, for more than three years, this agency existed only on paper. The creation of other agencies was obstructed for the same reasons. In October 1993, this situation was finally resolved following the adoption of a common agreement of the Representatives of the Governments of the Member States on the location of the agencies.[25] In accordance with this agreement, agencies are currently sited all over the Community.[26] The increasing importance of these agencies within the Community's institutional structure may be illustrated by a glance at agency expenditure (see **Figure 5**).[27]

2.2. Classification of Agencies

Following a functional approach, agencies can broadly be classified into three categories:[28]

— agencies which have as their main function providing information and are generally charged with the co-ordination and supervision of this information and the creation of networks;

— agencies which need to provide specific services and specific measures to implement Community regimes;

— agencies which provide specific information, expertise and services, and are the compulsory basis for decision-making but do not have decision-making powers of their own.

[19] Council Reg. (EEC) 2309/93 [1993] OJ L214/1.

[20] Council Reg. (EC) 40/94 [1994] OJ L11/1.

[21] Council Reg. (EC) 2062/94 [1994] OJ L216/1.

[22] Council Reg. (EC) 2100/94 [1994] OJ L227/1.

[23] Council Reg. (EC) 2965/94 [1994] OJ L314/1, as amended by Council Reg. (EC) 2610/95 [1995] OJ L268/1.

[24] Council Reg. (EC) 1035/97 [1997] OJ L151/1.

[25] [1993] OJ C323/1.

[26] The seats of the agencies mentioned are as follows: the Environmental Agency (Copenhagen), the Training Foundation (Turin), the Monitoring Centre for Drugs and Drug Addiction (Lisbon), the EMEA (London), the Agency for Health and Safety at Work (Bilbao), Trade Mark Office (Alicante), the Plant Variety Office (Angers, temporarily located in Brussels) and the European Centre on Racism and Xenophobia (Vienna).

[27] The agencies are mainly funded by the Community. Exceptions hereto are both the Trade Mark Office and the EMEA which for approximately 50% of their income rely on revenue acquired from the registration fees paid by companies.

[28] See A. Kreher, "Agencies in the European Community—a Step towards Administrative Integration in Europe" (1997) 4 *JEPP* 236–8.

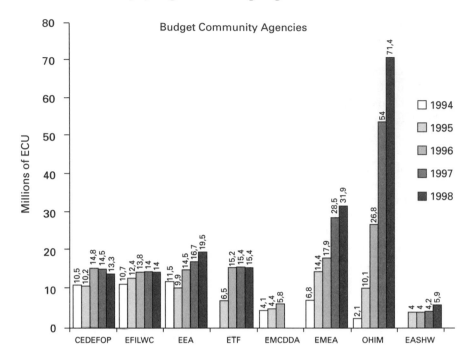

Figure 5. Budget of the Community Agencies 1994–8.

Abbreviations: CEDEFOP: the European Centre for the Development of Vocational Training; EFILWC: the European Foundation for the Improvement of Living and Working Conditions; EEA: the European Environment Agency; ETF: the European Training Foundation; EMCDDA: the European Monitoring Centre of Drugs and Drug Addiction; EMEA: the European Agency for the Evaluation of Medicinal Products; OHIM: the Office for Harmonisation in the Internal Market and EASHW: the European Agency for Safety and Health and Work.

Source: Community budget and Agency budgets.

The first category of agencies can be subdivided into two sub-categories. The first sub-category needs to collect, analyse and disseminate information relating to its specific policy areas. This group comprises the European Centre for the Development of Vocational Training and the European Foundation for the Improvement of Living and Working Conditions (the two "older" agencies) and the European Training Foundation. The second sub-category of agencies is those agencies which, in addition to the general information function, need to create and co-ordinate networks of experts. These networks comprise the appointment of national focus points which need to co-operate with the agencies and co-ordinate at national level the activities in relation to the agencies" work programmes. They offer Member States greater influence than they would have otherwise had under an alternative approach of centralised information and planning within the Commission.[29] The agencies charged with these tasks are the European Environment Agency, the European Agency for Safety and Health at Work and the European Monitoring Centre for Drugs and Drug Addiction. The significance of the information produced by all these agencies is evident where it forms the basis of regulatory decision-making within the Community. Hence, the provision of information and evidence by such agencies has been argued to constitute "regulation by information". In this context, the agency model has been conceptualised as being based upon non-majoritarian thinking and preferring administrative market integration to be carried out by fully independent agencies. In this view, the Community's activities should be restricted to the correction of market failures and be isolated from any redistributive social concerns.[30] As argued in the previous chapters, however, this view neglects the normative nature of risk regulation.

The second category of agencies includes the Office for Harmonisation and the Community Plant Variety Office. These agencies see to the provision of services and the implementation of the newly created Community regimes on trade marks and plant variety rights through specific registration procedures and are empowered to take decisions on the registration of applications for a Community trade mark or plant variety right.

The third category is a mixture between the first and the second categories and comprises the European Agency for the Evaluation of Medicinal Products. Although formally providing solely information and specific expertise, this Agency bears a strong resemblance to the second category in that it has been allotted a specific role in the new Community authorisation system of pharmaceuticals but does not have formal decision-making powers.

3. THE COMPETENCE TO ESTABLISH AGENCIES UNDER THE TREATY PROVISIONS

The emergence of agencies within the organisational structure of the Community raises questions regarding the Community's competence to establish such bodies and which powers may be delegated to them. As argued in the previous chapter, although several Treaty provisions do raise presumptions that further organs may be created in addition to the named Treaty institutions, there is no specific provision to allow this. This requires examination of the precise legal basis upon which agencies can be founded and the powers which may be conferred upon them.

---

[29] See K.-H. Ladeur, *The European Environment Agency and Prospects for a European Network of Environmental Considerations*, EUI Working Paper RSC 96/50 (Florence, 1996).

[30] G. Majone, *Independence vs. Accountability? Non-Majoritarian Institutions and Democratic Government in Europe*, EUI Working Paper SPS 94/3 (Florence, 1993) and *id.*, "The New European Agencies: Regulation by Information" (1997) 4 *JEPP* 262–75.

3.1. The Legal Basis for Agencies

Virtually all the agencies listed above were based on the general Treaty provision of Article 235. The only exception is the Environment Agency, which was founded on Article 130s. In addition, Article 100a has been regularly discussed as a valid legal basis for the creation of agencies. This Article was, for example, proposed as the legal basis for the European Agency for the Evaluation of Medicinal Products by the Commission, although rejected by the Council. This section therefore discusses these three Articles as potential legal bases for Community agencies.

3.1.1. Article 235

Arguments for the creation of agencies by virtue of Article 235 may first be found in an analogous interpretation of the Court's *Opinion 1/76*.[31] Here, the Court was asked by the Commission for an opinion on the compatibility with the Treaty of the draft agreement establishing a European Laying-up Fund for Inland Waterway Vessels. In reply, the Court explicitly confirmed the Community's competence to set up additional bodies and held that, as expressly provided by Article 75(1)(c) EEC, the Council was empowered to lay down "any other appropriate provisions" for achieving the common transport policy. In the Court's view, this provision not only entitled the Council to enter into contractual relations with a non-member country, but also empowered it to establish "appropriate" bodies such as the proposed public international institution, the European Laying-up Fund for Inland Waterway Vessels.[32]

The text of Article 235 is similar to that of Article 75, in that it allows the Council to take "the appropriate measures". Applying the reasoning of the Court analogously, this, in principle, would also include the setting up of agencies with legal personality.[33] These bodies must, however, be "necessary to attain one of the Community objectives". Article 235 is, therefore, generally a valid legal basis for agencies if such bodies are created in order to overcome difficulties hindering the pursuit of the internal market and the Community objectives laid down in Articles 2 and 3. For example, where requirements of the free circulation of medicines and health protection give rise to a need for an agency to ensure a single scientific evaluation of the quality, safety and efficacy of medicines, Article 235 may be called upon. The same applies to the establish-

---

[31] *Opinion 1/76* [1977] ECR 741.

[32] *Ibid.*, at 755. See P.J.G. Kapteyn, "Het advies 1/76 van het Europese Hof van Justitie, de externe bevoegdheid van de Gemeenschap en haar deelneming aan een Europees oplegfonds voor de binnenscheepvaart" (1978) 26 *SEW* 4, 276–88 and (1978) 26 *SEW* 5/6, 360–9.

[33] See I.E. Schwartz, "Artikel 235. Allgemeine Ermächtigungsklausel", in H. Von der Groeben/J. Thiesing/C.-D. Ehlermann, *Kommentar zum EWG-Vertrag* (Baden-Baden, 1991), 5829, points 188–9 and 191–2; Lauwaars, above n. 5, 371 ff; P.J.G. Kapteyn/P. VerLoren van Themaat, edited by L. Gormley, *Introduction to the Law of the European Communities* (Deventer, 1990), 115.

ment of the Safety and Health at Work Agency. In addition, the Office for Harmonisation in the Internal Market (trade mark and designs) may be based on Article 235 since it assists in the administration of Community trade marks and enables undertakings to spread their activities over the whole of the internal market.[34] In contrast to Article 100a, Article 235 does not require a direct link with the operation of the common market. This allows for the creation of agencies, such as the European Drugs Centre, whose link with the common market is less evident, but which might nonetheless be argued to contribute to Community objectives, such as the raising of living standards and the quality of life, public health protection or the harmonious development of economic activities within the Community.

The two limits to the scope of Article 235, identified in Chapter 1, must nonetheless be emphasised: first, Article 235 cannot be used to change the institutional structure of the Community and alter its balance of powers; and secondly, Article 235 may not be applied if other Treaty provisions are available. The former limit is of particular importance in relation to the powers to be conferred upon agencies. It determines that agency powers must not encroach upon those of the Treaty institutions. This means that agencies may not be endowed with regulatory powers, at the expense of the powers of the Community institutions and, in particular, the Commission's implementing powers. Therefore, under current Community law the creation of "independent" regulatory agencies in the American style would seem to be precluded.[35] For this, a revision of the Treaty under Article N(1) TEU in the framework of an intergovernmental conference would be necessary. The second limit refers to the generally residual character of Article 235 and necessitates scrutiny of both Article 130s, upon which the Environment Agency is based, and Article 100a, which was originally proposed as the legal basis for the EMEA.

However, the use of Article 235 as the legal basis for setting up agencies has met with diverse criticism, mostly related to the limited role of the Parliament in the decision-making procedure involved (mere consultation). As a representative of the Parliament asserted in this context:

> "I do think that the question of a new act based on Article 235 was the argument of the conspiracy of the initiators. Art. 235 was a way to move the Community forward at a time when the general public was sleeping. It was the theory of the implicit powers, that a Council behind closed doors, together with the Commission, could work in a system to do all kind of things which the founding fathers had never imagined. But I believe Art. 235 is dead after the next negotiations. In order not to go back to a structure in which the bureaucrats run the European Union, but to achieve a structure where democracy and control will lead to a new Europe which is indeed more democratic and transparent, we need to have accountability structures".[36]

---

[34] See the preamble to Council Reg. 40/94, above n. 20.

[35] See, in more detail, sects. 3.2 and 4.10.

[36] L.J. Brinkhorst, "The Future of European Agencies: A Budgetary Perspective from the European Parliament", in A. Kreher (ed.), *The New Agencies. Conference Report*, EUI Working Paper RSC 96/49 (Florence, 1996), 81.

Therefore, the Article 100a procedure based on co-decision has been preferred to the use of Article 235. In addition, although the procedure of Article N(1) again eschews co-decision and merely requires that Parliament be consulted, it nonetheless demands the approval of national governments[37] and would, for reasons of democratic legitimacy, be preferable for such fundamental issues, at least until Article 235 allows for parliamentary co-decision.

3.1.2. Article 130s

Article 130s enables the Council to decide which action is to be taken by the Community in relation to the environment. At the time of the agreement on the European Environment Agency (EEA), prior to the Maastricht Treaty, this Article determined that:

> "1. The Council, acting unanimously on a proposal from the Commission and after consulting the Parliament, and the Economic and Social Committee, shall decide what action is to be taken by the Community.
> 2. The Council shall under the conditions laid down in the preceding subparagraph, define those matters on which decisions are to be taken by a qualified majority".

In line with the Court's reasoning in *Opinion 1/76*, Community action may include the establishment of an agency, where this is necessary to attain the objectives laid down in Article 130r, in particular those stipulated in paragraph 3. The latter paragraph states that the Community must pay regard to all available scientific and technical data, when drawing up environmental policy. The Environment Agency, mainly collecting, processing and analysing environmental data, is therefore validly founded on Article 130s. Although the amendment of Article 130s by the Maastricht Treaty currently allows Community action to be adopted under the Article 189c procedure, the co-operation procedure, this will not affect the rationale which allows agencies to be created on the basis of this Article.

3.1.3. Article 100a

Although various committees have been created under Article 100a,[38] this Article has never been used for the establishment of agencies. However, for the

---

[37] See P.J.G. Kapteyn/P. VerLoren van Themaat *et al.*, *Inleiding tot het recht van de Europese Gemeenschappen: na Maastricht* (Deventer, 1995), 151.

[38] There are abundant examples of advisory committees created by harmonisation measures based upon Art. 100 or 100a. A few examples in the pharmaceutical sector are: Council Dir. 75/319/EEC on the approximation of provisions laid down by law, regulation or administrative action relating to proprietary medicinal products ([1975] OJ L147/13), based on Art. 100, created a "Committee for Proprietary Medicinal Products"; Council Dir. 78/25/EEC on the approximation of the laws of the Member States relating to the colouring matters which may be added to medicinal products ([1978] OJ L11/18), based on Art. 100, set up a "committee for the adaptation to technical progress of the Directives on the elimination of technical barriers to trade in the sector of colouring matters which may be added to medicinal products"; Council Dir. 89/105/EEC relating to the

reasons of parliamentary participation mentioned above, it is nonetheless of interest to examine whether this Article may offer a valid legal basis for agencies' creation. In contrast to the general formulation of Articles 75, 130s and 235, Article 100a requires that measures are adopted for the "approximation" of national provisions. Therefore, measures other than harmonisation measures may not be based on Article 100a, notwithstanding their close connection to the achievement and functioning of the internal market.[39] Hence, Article 100a is a valid legal basis only where it can be shown that the creation of a Community system or agency might be considered to be a harmonisation measure, necessary for the completion of the internal market.[40] Harmonisation requires the changing and supplementing of national legislation. This means that Community measures of a mere institutional character do not constitute harmonisation measures in the sense of Article 100a. The creation of an agency by virtue of Article 100a therefore seems to be ruled out. However, where this is secondary to the main purpose of a specific measure, i.e. harmonisation, Article 100a may still offer a valid legal basis for an agency. The question whether an agency might be based on Article 100a must therefore be examined in the light of the "centre of gravity" of the proposed measure:[41] does it seek to eliminate existing or future differences between national legislative provisions, and is the agency dependent upon such harmonisation measures?[42]

The importance of the harmonisation requirement in determining the validity of Article 100a as a legal basis for agencies can be exemplified by the discussions surrounding the Commission's proposal for a new Community authorisation procedure for medicines including the creation of the European Agency for the Evaluation of Medicinal Products (EMEA).[43] Although political agreement had been reached within the Council on the substance of the proposed system, the Commission's resort to Article 100a as its legal basis and its use for the establishment of the EMEA was ardently debated. The Legal Service of the Council contested the Commission's broad use of the concept of harmonisation to justify the adoption of the proposed authorisation system under Article 100a. It maintained that the vital criterion for harmonisation, namely, that the Member States should retain the ability to formulate their own rules on

---

transparency of measures regulating the pricing of medicinal products for human use and their inclusion in the scope of national health insurance systems ([1989] OJ L40/8), based on Art. 100a, instituted a "Consultative Committee for the implementation of Directive 89/105/EEC relating to the transparency of measures regulating the pricing of medicinal products for human use and their inclusion in the scope of national health insurance systems": see, further, chap. 3.

[39] J. Pipkorn, "Artikel 100A, Angleichung von Vorschriften mit Bezug auf den Binnenmarkt", in H. Von der Groeben/J. Thiesing/C.-D. Ehlermann, *Kommentar zum EWG-Vertrag*, Band 2 (Baden-Baden, 1991), 2844, point 36.

[40] J. Pipkorn, "Bericht Europäische Gemeinschaften", in C. Starck (ed.), *Erledigung von Verwaltungsaufgaben durch Personalkörperschaften und Anstalten des öffentlichen Rechts* (Baden-Baden, 1992), 114.

[41] See Chap. 1.

[42] Pipkorn, above n. 39, at 2847, point 41.

[43] COM(90)283 final—SYN 309 to 312.

this subject-matter in implementing procedures, had not been met. Eventually, the centralised authorisation procedure and the establishment of the EMEA were achieved under Article 235.[44]

Like the Legal Service of the Council in relation to the EMEA, some academics argue that the notion of "harmonisation" within the terms of Article 100a is only present where Community measures must be implemented by national rules and allow for action at Member State level. In this view, the creation of a parallel Community system independent from the national system is not compatible with the concept of harmonisation.[45] Measures such as the regulation on the Community trade mark or the proposed regulation on a European limited liability company *("Aktiengesellschaft")*,[46] which exist independently of national provisions, would therefore need to be based on Article 235. However, I take the view that the criterion that action at the level of the Member States should continue to be possible should not be considered decisive to determine whether harmonisation takes place. It fails to take account of the fact that a harmonisation measure is generally accepted even when it only partly replaces national provisions. For example, a harmonisation measure may affect only actions with cross-border aspects, whilst leaving the rest of the national legal order unaffected,[47] as is the case with optional harmonisation.[48] Furthermore, in contrast to the concept of harmonisation under Article 100, the notion of harmonisation under Article 100a does not specify the type of act the Community institutions may adopt. Hence, both directives and regulations may be adopted, of which the latter are directly applicable in the Member States and do not require national legislative action. Harmonisation of national provisions can thus take place through a regulation which replaces any conflicting national legislation. The use of the latter instrument is particularly well suited to situations which require the complete uniformity of the legal requirements which allow for the circulation of certain products (total harmonisation).[49]

Seen in this light, arrangements such as the Community authorisation system for medicinal products might be argued to be no more than the consolidation of national uniform rules on the same subject-matter. This system could be considered to be necessary to ensure the free movement of goods and to be based on, rather than replace, the existing national authorisation procedures and the pooling of national resources.[50] In this sense, the establishment of such a system

---

[44] See, however, the suspicions of Brinkhorst, above n. 36.

[45] See I.E. Schwartz, "30 Jahre EG-Rechtsangleichung", in E.J. Mestmäcker/H. Möller/H.P. Schwarz, *Eine Ordnungspolitik für Europa* (Baden-Baden, 1987), 365, and P.-Ch. Müller-Graff, "Die Rechtsangleichung zur Verwirklichung des Binnenmarktes" (1989) 24 *EuR* 129. This opinion is shared by A. Dashwood, "The Limits of European Community Powers" (1996) 21 *ELR* 120.

[46] [1989] OJ C263/41, amended by COM(91)174 final.

[47] E.g., national provisions dealing with purely internal issues.

[48] See Pipkorn, above n. 39, 2844–9.

[49] See Pipkorn, above n. 39, at 2845 and the discussion by D. Calleja/D. Vignes/R. Wägenbaur, *Commentaire Megret. Dispositions fiscales, rapprochement des legislations* (Brussels, 1993), 351.

[50] See the Commission in its Explanatory Memorandum to COM(90)283 final—SYN 309 to 312.

would be compatible with the concept of harmonisation.[51] The definition of harmonisation recently given by the Court, including both general rules and the application of rules to specific cases,[52] leads in this direction. The broad concept of harmonisation is further confirmed by the practice of the Community institutions, which have taken Article 100a as a basis for action programmes relating to matters such as vocational training for customs officials[53] and the exchange of national officials engaged in the implementation of Community legislation on the internal market.[54]

Having established that such a system is one of harmonisation, the focus of analysis then turns to the determination of whether the creation of the agency is an end in itself or whether it specifically facilitates and is secondary to the harmonisation system. Only in the latter case can the agency be established under Article 100a. In the case of the EMEA, the centralised system on medicinal products had as its main objective the market integration of medicines and could itself be based on Article 100a.[55] The Agency clearly has a supplementary character in relation to the harmonisation goal of the common authorisation system of medicines: it provides the indispensable scientific basis for Community decisions.[56] Moreover, as the closer co-operation and the building of mutual confidence between national administrations at which the agency is aimed, is needed to ensure such uniform application, the supplementary character of the agency is confirmed. Hence, Article 100a could provide a valid legal basis for an agency such as the EMEA.[57] However, an agency would no longer possess the supplementary character if proper decision-making powers were delegated to it and these powers were exercised without Commission supervision. The delegation of these powers to an agency would be of such institutional importance that it would not fall within the concept of harmonisation. The same would apply to cases in which a *de facto* delegation of decision-making powers to agencies occurs. Such cases would then necessitate recourse to Article 235 or Article N.1, depending on whether the institutional balance of powers is affected or not. Hence, although the creation of new agencies is generally not troublesome,[58] the

[51] Pipkorn, above n. 39, at 2847 and at 2849.

[52] Case C–259/92, *Germany* v. *Council* (*general product safety*) [1994] ECR I–3681. See, in detail, Chap. 2.

[53] Council Dec. 91/341/EEC on the adoption of a programme of Community action on the subject of vocational training of customs officials (Mattheus programme) [1991] OJ L187/41.

[54] Council Dec. on the adoption of an action plan for the exchange between Member States administrations of national officials who are engaged in the implementation of Community legislation required to achieve the internal market [1992] OJ L286/65.

[55] See, for a description of this system, sect. 4.2.2.

[56] See Pipkorn, above n. 39, at 2849, point 45. The same may be argued to apply to the provisions on pharmacovigilance. However, in his analysis of the European Monetary Co-operation Fund, the European Centre for the Development of Vocational Training and the European Foundation for the Improvement of Living and Working Conditions, Lauwaars argues that "just because the new organ, possessing legal personality, may lead its own life, I further believe that such legal personality may only be granted by virtue of Article 235": Lauwaars, above n. 5, at 376.

[57] Doubts are expressed by Calleja/Vignes/Wägenbaur, above n. 47, at 351.

[58] See Lauwaars, above n. 5, at 371.

choice of the legal basis for these agencies, particularly between Articles 235 and 100a, depends, in the final analysis, upon the powers to be delegated to these bodies.

3.2. Delegation of Powers to Agencies

3.2.1. The Meroni *Principles*

When dealing with delegation of powers to bodies possessing legal personality, other than the institutions referred to in Article 4, one is inevitably confronted with the early case law of the Court in the ECSC context.[59] In the *Meroni* cases of 1958,[60] the Court was called upon to decide upon the validity of a delegation of powers under Article 53 ECSC by the High Authority to two scrap equalisation bodies established under Belgian private law.[61] Although the ECSC Treaty made no explicit provision for such delegation, the Court ruled that:

> "the possibility of entrusting to bodies established under private law, having a distinct legal personality and possessing powers of their own, the task of putting into effect certain 'financial arrangements common to several undertakings', as mentioned in subparagraph (a) of Article 53 ECSC, cannot be excluded".[62]

The Court considered that the power of the High Authority to authorise or to undertake personally any financial arrangements, as provided for in Article 53 ECSC, entitled it to entrust certain powers to such bodies, subject to conditions determined by it and subject to its continuing oversight. The Court considered, however, that the exercise of such delegated powers could not be exempted from the conditions to which they would have been subject if they had been directly exercised by the High Authority (*"nemo plus iuris transferre potest quam ipse habet"*), referring, in particular, to the obligation to state reasons and the need for judicial control of decisions. In the Court's view, the delegation of powers, which implied a wide margin of discretion to allow for the practical execution of economic policy, could not be accepted:

> "since it replaces the choices of the delegator by the choices of the delegate and brings about an actual transfer of responsibility".[63]

The Court concluded that only "clearly defined executive powers" may be delegated, the use of which must always remain subject to the supervision of the

---

[59] See *inter alia* H.H. Maas, "Delegatie van bevoegdheden in de Europese Gemeenschappen" (1967) 15 *SEW* 2–18; J.-V. Louis, "Delegatie van bevoegdheden in de Europese Gemeenschappen" (1978) 26 *SEW* 802–14; Lauwaars, above n. 5, and, in particular, K. Lenaerts, "Regulating the Regulatory Process: "Delegation of Powers" in the European Community" (1993) 18 *ELR* 23–49.

[60] Case 9/56, *Meroni & Co. Industrie Metallurgiche S.p.A.* v. *High Authority* [1958] ECR 133; Case 10/56, *Meroni & Co. Industrie Metallurgiche S.p.A.* v. *High Authority* [1958] ECR 157.

[61] Namely the Imported Ferrous Scrap Equalisation Fund and the Joint Bureau of Ferrous Scrap Consumers.

[62] Case 9/56, at 151, Case 10/56, at 172, both above n. 60.

[63] Case 9/56, above n. 60, at 152.

High Authority. The Court justified its reasoning by referring to the balance of powers, "which is characteristic of the institutional structure of the Community", and which would be distorted if discretionary powers were delegated to bodies other than those established by the Treaty.[64]

In accordance with this case law, the following conditions would apply for the admissibility of the transfer of sovereign powers to subordinate authorities outside the EC institutions:

— the Commission cannot delegate broader powers than it enjoys itself;
— only strictly executive powers may be delegated;
— no discretionary powers may be delegated;
— the exercise of delegated powers cannot be exempted from the conditions to which they would have been subject if they had been directly exercised by the Commission, in particular, the obligation to state reasons and judicial control of decisions;
— the delegated powers remain subject to conditions determined by the Commission and subject to its continuing oversight;
— the institutional balance between the EC institutions may not be distorted.

3.2.2. The Influence of the Meroni Principles on Community Practice

Although the *Meroni* judgments related to the ECSC Treaty, their validity for the EC Treaty is generally accepted.[65] In accordance with this jurisprudence, the "older" agencies were set up with mere executive powers.[66] When designing the new agencies, however, the Community institutions have been clearly guided by these *Meroni* principles, too. As, for example, the Commission explained in its proposal concerning the EMEA:

"In accordance with the principles underlying the Community treaties, the tasks of the new Agency are purely advisory, and it is neither possible or appropriate to delegate to the Agency the power to take decisions on the authorisation of new medicinal products which would be binding on the Community and the Member States. Such decisions can only be taken by the existing Community institutions".[67]

Similar arguments were advanced by the Commission in relation to the creation of the European Environment Agency, and in answer to Parliament's

---

[64] *Ibid.*

[65] Maas, above n. 59, 13–14; Louis, above n. 59, 806–9; Lauwaars, above n. 5, 371 ff; Lenaerts, above n. 59, 41.

[66] One exception hereto is the European Monetary Co-operation Fund, which possessed discretionary powers. In the legal literature, this situation has been justified by the special nature of the tasks to be carried out and the position of the Central Banks in the Member States: see Louis and Ehlermann, referred to by Lauwaars, who underlined the provisional nature of such measures and the need for a revision of the Treaty in such a case. Lauwaars, above n. 5, 373–4. See also R.H. Lauwaars, "Art. 235 EEG als grondslag voor de schepping van een Europees merkenrecht" (1981) 29 *SEW* 533–48.

[67] Explanatory memorandum, above n. 50, at 21.

demands for a regulatory agency.[68] The Council has followed this reasoning to its extreme in the final adoption of the new Community authorisation system on medicines: the EMEA was not granted any decision-making powers, not even to draft the application form for authorisation. By contrast, the Council has been less strict as regards the Trade Mark Office and the Community Plant Variety Office to which it delegated decision-making powers on the granting of Community trade marks and Community plant variety rights. However, the granting of decision-making powers to these agencies seems to contrast with the Court's judgment in *Romano* (this time in relation to the EEC context), where the Court invalidated a delegation of power (even though it was only "executive") to adopt acts having the force of law to the Administrative Commission on Social Security for Migrant Workers.[69] This seemingly contradictory situation underlines the importance of analysing the possibility of delegating decision-making powers to agencies.

3.2.3. *The Relevance of* Meroni *for the Creation of Agencies: The Institutional Balance of Powers*

Doubts may be expressed whether the *Meroni* principles prohibiting the delegation of discretionary powers to third bodies in the ECSC context should be strictly applied in relation to the EC Treaty.[70] A few differences should be noted. First, the ECSC Treaty and the EC Treaty differ in nature: the ECSC Treaty has been drafted as a *traité-loi*, whilst the EC Treaty has been designed as a *traité-cadre*. The limited scope for a possible delegation of powers could still be justified in the case of the ECSC Treaty, since it explicitly assigns specific powers to the Commission. In this case, the delegation of such powers would be more difficult to accept since it would boil down to a *"carte blanche"* delegation. However, the *traité-cadre* nature of the EC Treaty implies that the powers conferred on the institutions, in particular those conferred on the Council, are often broadly formulated. Here it would seem more appropriate to lay down clear and precise principles to establish which powers might usefully be delegated and to design appropriate means of control, herewith restricting free decision-making powers, instead of prohibiting all freedom to delegate. Another difference is that the *Meroni* cases related to the delegation of powers to private bodies external to the Community's institutional structure. In addition, the distinction between "discretionary" powers and "strictly executive" powers made by the Court in the *Meroni* cases has largely been blurred in the Court's subsequent case law. For example, in its *Opinion 1/76* on the Draft Agreement establishing a European

[68] See D.A. Westbrook, "Environmental Policy in the European Community: Observations on the European Environment Agency" [1991] *Harvard Environment Law Review* 262.

[69] Case 98/80, *Romano* v. *Inami* [1981] ECR 1241, at 1256, para. 20. See, in this sense, H.H. Maas, "The Administrative Commission for the Social Security of Migrant Workers. An Institutional Curiosity" (1966–7) 3 *CMLRev.* 51–63.

[70] See Kapteyn/Verloren van Themaat, above n. 33, at 121. See also Ladeur, above n. 29, and Everson, above n. 3, 196–7.

Laying-up Fund for Inland Waterway Vessels, the Court did not see any reason to examine the possibility of delegation of discretionary powers to the Fund, since the Statute of the Fund defined and limited the delegated powers "so clearly and precisely that in this case they are only executive powers".[71] However, the powers which the Court pointed out included the powers of the Fund to establish the contributions to be levied on all vessels using the inland waterways, the conditions of payment and the basic rate for contributions for the first year, as well as the power to amend the rate of contributions (both the basic rate and the adjustment coefficients). Hence, the broad interpretation of "executive powers" used by the Court in this case[72] together with its broad interpretation of the concept of implementation[73] clearly approach "discretionary" powers.

Thus, the significance of the *Meroni* doctrine for the delegation of powers to agencies does not lie in the distinction between a delegation of "mere executive" and a delegation of "discretionary" powers, the latter at any rate being prohibited. Rather, attention should be focused on the principle of the institutional balance of powers from which the Court derived this case law. The requirements relating to judicial review and the duty to state reasons can also be traced back to the principle of the institutional balance of powers. The emphasis on the institutional balance of powers in these cases is in line with the Court's overall case law. In the abovementioned *Romano* case,[74] for instance, the Court prohibited the Administrative Commission on Social Security for Migrant Workers from being given the power to adopt acts on the implicit grounds that the institutional balance of powers had not been properly observed.

Hence, it follows that at present the *Meroni* principles are only relevant for the delegation of powers to agencies in so far as they relate to the principle of the institutional balance of powers. At present, the existing agencies tend to ameliorate the implementation of Community law at national level[75] and mainly produce information, monitor information, co-ordinate national implementation mechanisms and carry out studies. "Delegation" of such powers to agencies cannot but improve the quality of Community law-making and its legitimacy. Such "delegation", therefore, does not distort the institutional balance of powers.[76]

4. HEALTH AND SAFETY REGULATION THROUGH AGENCIES:
THE CASE OF PHARMACEUTICALS

The particular agency-based framework of Community health and safety regulation will be examined in one important, heavily regulated field: pharmaceuticals.

---

[71] Opinion 1/76, above n. 31, at 759–60.
[72] See Kapteyn, above n. 32, at 365.
[73] See Case 16/88, *Commission v. Council (Fisheries)* [1989] ECR 3457, discussed in Chap. 2.
[74] Case 98/80, *Romano v. Inami*, above n. 69.
[75] See Lenaerts, above n. 59, at 43.
[76] See further sect. 4.10.1.

Like foodstuffs, medicinal products have been subject to Community regulation since the very early days of the Community. Different national approaches to the regulation of medicines on product safety and market authorisation of pharmaceuticals, price differences and reimbursement controls and property rights have resulted in barriers to trade.[77] Therefore, the Community has been active in the field since the 1960s. In this book, analysis is concentrated on product safety and market access of medicinal products for human use.[78]

In order to achieve a single market for medicinal products, the Community introduced in 1993 a new system on market authorisation for pharmaceuticals. Within this system, the European Agency for the Evaluation of Medicinal Products (EMEA) plays an important role. This agency frees the Community institutions from some of the new responsibilities which have arisen due to the introduction of new Community authorisation procedures for medicinal products and the corresponding need to monitor the medicinal products now freely circulating on the Community market.[79] It thus provides for scientific analysis, co-ordination of supervision, transmission of assessment reports, recording of the status of marketing authorisations and provision of technical assistance for the maintenance of a database on medicinal products, etc. The introduction of the agency-based decision-making process of the Community on the authorisation of medicinal products raises, however, general questions of its legitimacy. Here, the importance of the quality of the scientific expertise used, the participation of interest representatives and the transparency of the decision-making process again all come into play.

4.1. The Peculiarities of Pharmaceuticals

Although pharmaceuticals are designed to cure persons, they are, at the same time, general hazards to human health. The degree of hazard may vary according to the degree of knowledge, but it is never completely eliminated. These, by their very nature, toxic and potentially harmful products are, therefore, subject to a very high degree of regulation. Regulatory activities in this field can further be explained by the particular nature of the pharmaceutical market. This market is characterised on the supply side by highly professional and scientifically sophisticated producers and on the demand side by a peculiar interplay between three parties: the consumer intermediary (doctor), the party which reimburses (social security system) and the actual consumer, alias the patient.[80] The latter

---

[77] See A. Geddes, "Free Movement of Pharmaceuticals within the Community: The Remaining Barriers" (1991) 16 *ELR* 295–306.

[78] See, for a discussion of the various activities of the Community on medicines, R. Thompson, *The Single Market for Pharmaceuticals* (London, 1994). Medicinal products for veterinary use are excluded from the scope of this book.

[79] See Explanatory Memorandum, above n. 50, at 34.

[80] D. Hart/N. Reich, *Integration und Recht des Arzneimittelmarktes in der EG* (Baden-Baden, 1990), 9.

is not generally able to form an opinion on the safety or efficacy of the various medicinal products, either because of a lack of information or a lack of competence, nor is he or she in a position to choose the correct medicine. In general, this choice depends largely on the doctor and on whether the product in question will be reimbursed in accordance with the national health scheme.

Confronted with a market to which the "normal rules" of supply and demand do not apply, all Member States have adopted a "paternalistic" approach towards the regulation of pharmaceuticals, based on the protection of patients against harmful adverse effects.[81] At present, therefore, modern societies are founded on a preventive approach to drug safety and require authorisation of medicines prior to their being placed on the market (formally based on the criteria of safety, quality and efficacy) and include regulatory frameworks for the post-market control of medicines (pharmacovigilance). In contrast to foodstuffs, the authorisation of medicines is based on a product-related approach.

Official controls of the quality or purity of medicinal products can be traced back to the seventeenth century when quasi-official pharmacopoeias were published as guides to the formulation and quality of pharmaceuticals and were designed to prevent the adulteration of products. By the nineteenth century, rudimentary legislation had emerged on the training of pharmacists, the establishment of pharmacies and the legal role of the pharmaceutical profession in guaranteeing the quality of the medicinal products they had prepared.[82] The pharmacopoeias did not address the safety and the efficacy of medicines since there was little necessity to do so as long as most medicines were distilled from herbs, the effects of which were supposedly commonly well-known.

Safety and efficacy assessments were included in the regulation on medicines in the mid-nineteenth century. This coincided not only with the rise of large-scale manufacturing and of techniques of chemical synthesis, but also with an increasing awareness of the potential harmfulness of medicines.[83] The Thalidomide tragedy, in particular, led most Member States to tighten up their laws on medicines.[84] Prescribed to pregnant women for treatment of morning

[81] See D. Hart, "Drug Safety as a Means of Consumer Protection: The Approximation of Laws in the EC Medicinal Products Market and Its Limitations" (1989) 12 *JCP* 344–5 and N. Reich, "Integration und Regulierung des Arzneimittelmarktes innerhalb der EG" (1984) 148 *ZHR* 358.

[82] In the UK, the Food and Drugs Acts 1909–49 regulated the quality and fraudulent claims of medicines, merely stipulating that medicinal products were not to be injurious to health. In France, the Act of 11 September 1941 *"fixant le statut général de la pharmacie"* was principally concerned with quality control. See L. Hancher, *Regulating for Competition. Government, Law, and the Pharmaceutical Industry in the United Kingdom and France* (Oxford, 1990), 107 ff.

[83] See Hancher, above n. 82, 107 ff.

[84] The French Act on the General Statute of Pharmacies of 1941 introduced an obligation of market authorisation for medicines, although it was mainly concerned with quality control and not particularly rigorous scientifically. See, N. Reich, *Arzneimittelregulierung in Frankreich*, ZERP-MAT 11 (Bremen, 1987) and Hancher, above n. 82, at 107. In the Netherlands, the Supply of Medicines Act of 1958 likewise introduced a medicines registration procedure: see M.-H.B.B. Schutjens, *Drug Regulation in the Netherlands*, ZERP-MAT 13 (Bremen, 1987). In the UK, the Medicines Act of 1968 was a direct reaction to the Thalidomide scandal: see L.J. Smith, *Legal Regulation of the British Pharmaceutical Market* (Baden-Baden, 1991), 8.

sickness, Thalidomide had disastrous adverse effects causing infant deformities in cases in which the foetus had been exposed to it.[85] This and other catastrophic events forced Member States to develop more stringent controls on the safety of medicinal products through the establishment of marketing authorisation procedures and pharmacovigilance systems.[86] At the same time, tragedies of this sort brought about a general acceptance of a high level of regulation of medicines in the Member States by both the industry and the general public.

4.2. The Community's Regulatory Approach to Pharmaceuticals

The market authorisation procedures established in the 1960s mirrored different ethical, clinical and historical considerations which influenced medical traditions in the Member States.[87] Existing divergencies between medical and regulatory cultures led to a wide variety of approaches to medicines and their safety.[88] These differences continued hindering the marketing, research and production of medicinal products throughout the Community. The consequent trade barriers and the European-wide impact of the Thalidomide tragedy[89] determined that the Community needed to become involved in the complexities of medicines regulation. Thus, as early as 1965, the Community adopted its first directive on the authorisation of medicines,[90] which had the dual objective of protecting human health and eliminating obstacles to trade.[91] This directive was the beginning of a long and thorny process towards the creation of an internal market for pharmaceuticals.

4.2.1. *Partial Harmonisation Combined with Mutual Recognition: The Former Authorisation Procedures*

Faced with substantial disagreement between the Member States on the choice to be made between harmonisation of decentralised controls based on the co-

---

[85] See W.W. Lowrance, *Of Acceptable Risk. Science and the Determination of Safety* (Los Altos, 1976), at 19. See also H. Sjöström, *Thalidomide and the Power of the Drug Companies* (Harmondsworth, 1972) and H. Teff/C. Munro, *Thalidomide: The Legal Aftermath* (Farnborough, 1976). Where recently discoveries point to the curative effect of Thalidomide in the battle against, for example, HIV, AIDS and cancer, the difficulties for regulators in dealing with such issues are evident. See, e.g., C. Blaney, "Second Thoughts About Thalidomide", National Center for Research Resources Reporter, Nov./Dec. 1995.

[86] L. Hancher, "The European Pharmaceutical Market: Problems of Partial Harmonisation" (1990) 15 *ELR* 11–12.

[87] See Geddes, above n. 77, 296, and J. Gardner, "The Still More Difficult Task: The European Agency for the Evaluation of Medicines and European regulation of Pharmaceuticals" (1996) 2 *ELJ* 52.

[88] See Hancher, above n. 86, at 12, and E. Kaufer, *The Regulation of Drug Development, In Search of a Common European Approach*, EUI Working Paper 89/411 (Florence, 1989).

[89] See Hart, above n. 81, 345.

[90] Council Dir. 65/65/EEC on the approximation of provisions laid down by law, regulation or administrative action relating to proprietary medicinal products [1965] OJ 22/369.

[91] Both objectives have been confirmed in the case law of the Court: see *inter alia* Case 227/82, *Van Bennekom* [1983] ECR 3900 and Case 301/82, *Clin-Midy* [1984] ECR 259.

ordinated mutual recognition of national authorisation or a centralised Community authorisation procedure,[92] the Community adopted, in Directive 65/65/EEC, a compromise solution on a gradual approach towards the mutual recognition of national market authorisation. This meant that market entry conditions for medicines (both procedural and scientific criteria) were harmonised in detail and would thus create the pre-requisites for the "automatic" mutual recognition of national licensing decisions.[93] Thus, Directive 65/65/EEC established that no medicinal product should be placed on the market without prior authorisation, whilst authorisation would only be granted if the application was accompanied by specific documentation guaranteeing safety, quality and therapeutic efficacy.[94]

These requirements were further refined by Directive 75/318/EEC, which harmonised the accompanying documentation, and Directive 75/319/EEC which set out procedural rules and established the Committee on Proprietary Medicinal Products (CPMP). This Committee, which has become of pivotal importance in the new Community authorisation system,[95] was composed of national representatives and had, as its main task, to advise national authorities whether a specific medicinal product should be licensed.[96] In order to promote progress towards mutual recognition, another committee was established, the Pharmaceutical Committee. This Committee was composed of national representatives who were also senior experts in public health matters, and advised the Commission on questions of general policy as opposed to purely scientific matters relating to medicinal products.[97]

4.2.1.1. The Multi-state Procedure

Notwithstanding these requirements, harmonisation proceeded at slow pace. The so-called *"multi-state"* procedure was founded on the principle that a medicinal product, manufactured and marketed in one of the Member States according to Community rules should be allowed into other Member States, which were required to pay due regard to the initial authorisation. Only in exceptional cases, in which national authorities persisted in their objections to the authorisation, would the case be referred to the CPMP for an advisory opinion. This Committee would then examine the case and issue a legally non-binding

---

[92] At that time, a centralised approach was strongly opposed by several Member States (including Germany) and by the industry. See Hancher, above n. 86, at 12.

[93] See L. Hancher, "Creating the Internal Market for Pharmaceutical Medicines—an Echternach Jumping Procession?" (1991) 28 *CMLRev*. 821–3.

[94] Arts. 3 and 4 of Dir. 65/65/EEC, above n. 90.

[95] See sect. 4.3. ff.

[96] Council Dir. 75/318/EEC on the approximation of the laws of the Member States relating to analytical, pharmacotoxicological and clinical standards and protocols in respect of the testing of proprietary medicinal products [1975] OJ L147/1 and Council Dir. 75/319/EEC on the approximation of provisions laid down by law, regulation or administrative action relating to proprietary medicinal products [1975] OJ L147/13.

[97] Council Dec. 75/320/EEC [1975] OJ L147/23.

opinion to the Member States concerned and to the applicant.[98] Taking this opinion into account, the Member States were then to decide whether or not to issue a market authorisation. However, this procedure was rarely used by the pharmaceutical industry, which was blocked, in particular, by the requirement to apply for contemporaneous marketing authorisation in five or more Member States after having obtained a first authorisation in one of the Member States.[99] In addition, the long delays in decision-making and the diversity of the decisions finally adopted, rendered the latter requirement highly costly.[100]

This led the Commission once again to consider the option of a centralised Community authorisation procedure. However, experiences with the Benelux Registration Office for medicinal products[101] reinforced the industry's resistance to a centralised procedure, which in the Benelux context had been felt to be unduly severe and inflexible. Commercial opposition was supported by "exporting" Member States that continued to lobby for the introduction of decentralised procedures for the mutual recognition of market authorisations. On the other hand, however, various "importing" Member States, encouraged by a number of consumer organisations, argued that the mutual recognition strategy would enable pharmaceutical companies to conform to the lowest national safety provisions, thus allowing for a dilution in safety standards and a regulatory "race to the bottom".[102] The Community institutions finally decided to strengthen and improve the existing multi-state procedure and to postpone mutual recognition until 1990.[103] Council Directive 83/570/EEC thus reduced the minimum threshold of Member States from five to two. Further innovations included the introduction of a right to a hearing, and the obligation to provide for a summary of product characteristics.[104] Although this procedure appeared far more attractive to the pharmaceutical industry,[105] it proved in-

---

[98] See C.A. Teijgeler, "The Role of the CPMP in the EEC", in S.R. Walker (ed.), *International Medicines Regulations: A Look Forward to 1992* (Dordrecht/Boston, 1989), 207–18.

[99] See the Commission's Report on the activities of the Committee for Proprietary Medicinal Products of 1988, COM(88)143 final, 10.

[100] See E. Kaufer, "The Regulation of New Product Development in the Drug Industry", in G. Majone (ed.), *Deregulation or Re-regulation? Regulatory Reform in Europe and the US* (London/New York, 1990), 161.

[101] This Office was instituted in 1972. However, partly because of the increasing importance of the Community legislation, and partly because of organisational/financial problems relating to this Office, it was abolished in 1982. See, for more details, R.H. Lauwaars/J.M. Maarleveld, *Harmonisatie van wetgeving in Europese organisaties* (Deventer, 1987), 319–24.

[102] See Hancher, above n. 82, 154–5.

[103] Council Dir. 83/570/EEC amending Dirs. 65/65/EEC, 75/318/EEC and 75/319/EEC on the approximation of provisions laid down by law, regulation or administrative action relating to medicinal products [1983] OJ L332/1.

[104] *Ibid.*

[105] From 1987 to the end of 1990, 142 applications were counted against 41 applications in the period 1978–86. One curiosity is worth mentioning: it appeared from the figures registered by the Commission that the benefit in reducing the threshold of Member States might have been psychological rather than actual since the average multi-state procedure concerned a little more than five recipient countries. See the Report on the activities of the Committee for Proprietary Medicinal Products of 1991, COM(91)39 final, 14–15.

efficient in operation. The idea behind the multi-state procedure, namely that Member States should mutually recognise market authorisation and only make exceptional use of the non-binding arbitration efforts of the CPMP, appeared to be elusive. In practice, virtually every application was opposed by the receiving Member State and the matter was systematically referred to the CPMP, even though initial authorisations had been issued by authorities noted for their scientific competence.[106]

Table 3. Frequency of systematic objections against the first market authorisation of a medicinal product raised by the Member States as a percentage.

Objecting States	B	DK	D	GR	E	F	IRL	I	LUX	NL	UK
Number of objections	88	83	85	48	67	74	55	93	0	92	86

Source: COM(91)39 final, 17.

4.2.1.2. The Concertation Procedure

In 1986, another authorisation procedure was introduced for medicinal products developed by means of new biotechnological processes and other highly-technological medicinal products.[107] At the same time, medicinal products were introduced within the scope of the so-called *standstill* regime, which required Member States to communicate to the Commission any draft of a technical regulation relating to the production and marketing of these products.[108] The new authorisation procedure, the so-called "concertation" procedure, was compulsory for most biotechnological medicines and optional for highly technological medicines. It aimed to resolve questions relating to the safety, quality and efficacy of these medicines at Community level within the CPMP, prior to the adoption by national authorities of any decision on market authorisation. It thus required that the application for authorisation was filed both with the national authorisations and with the CPMP. The final decision remained, however, with the Member States. This procedure functioned fairly satisfactorily.[109] This may be explained by the fact that production of these "high-tech" products is a recent development and no deeply-rooted traditions exist in the Member States as regards such products.

---

[106] See the 1991 Report on the activities of the CPMP, above n. 105, at 22.

[107] Council Dir. 87/22/EEC on the approximation of national measures relating to the placing on the market of high-technological medicinal products, particularly those derived from biotechnology [1987] OJ L15/38.

[108] Art. 5 of Council Dir. 87/22/EEC, above n. 107, in accordance with Arts. 8 and 9 of Dir. 83/189/EEC on information procedures [1983] OJ L109/8.

[109] Above n. 106.

4.2.2. The Deepening of Community Action on Medicinal Products

4.2.2.1. The Limits of the Voluntary Application of the Mutual Recognition Principle

In its White Paper of 1985 on the completion of the internal market the Commission had further committed itself to the achievement of an internal market for the pharmaceutical sector by 1992. Yet, its detailed agenda for eliminating trade barriers by this date appeared extremely difficult to carry out on the basis of the procedures described above.[110] In particular, the application of the principle of "automatic" mutual recognition to market authorisations as designed by the Commission was problematic. In practice, this principle has never worked in this field, as the Commission itself recognised.[111] Although over the years, a large number of Directives extending the scope of Directive 65/65/EEC,[112] and covering virtually every aspect of the risk assessment process and the authorisation procedure, had made the concept more attractive to the industry, the Member States continued to reject systematically the authorisation of medicinal products which had been approved in other Member States. This occurred notwithstanding the fact that applications had been prepared in accordance with the standardised Community format. The variation in the treatment of such applications, approved by the Court's case law,[113] can be explained by several factors,[114] such as different national traditions and ethics, different attitudes towards risk assessment procedures, differences in national clinical education, and distrust towards the authorisation methods of the other Member States.[115] Faced with this practice, the pharmaceutical industry appeared now ready to accept a centralised Community authorisation procedure.

[110] This agenda did not only include harmonisation of market authorisation (product safety) rules, but also national price and reimbursement controls (transparency) and advertising and retail distribution. See COM(85)310 final, annexes 17 and 18.

[111] See the the 1991 Report on the activities of the CPMP, above n. 105, at 22 and Commission, Completing the Internal Market: an area without internal frontiers, COM(90) 552 final, points 30–5. See also the Commission's programme for 1990, Address by J. Delors, President of the Commission, to the European Parliament and his reply to the debate: Bull. EC, Supp. 1/90, 19.

[112] See *inter alia* Dir. 89/341/EEC amending Dirs. 65/65/EEC, 75/318/EEC and 75/319/EEC on the approximation of provisions laid down by law, regulation or administrative action relating to proprietary medicinal products ([1989] OJ L142/11) removing the initial limitation set in Dir. 65/65/EEC on proprietary medicinal products to *all* medicinal products; Dir. 89/342/EEC extending the scope of Dirs. 65/65/EEC and 75/319/EEC and laying down additional provisions for immunological medicinal products consisting of vaccines, toxins or serums and allergens ([1989] OJ L142/14); Dir. 89/343/EEC extending the scope of Dirs. 65/65/EEC and 75/319/EEC and laying down additional provisions for radiopharmaceuticals ([1989] OJ L142/16); Dir. 89/381/EEC relating to products derived from human blood or plasma ([1989] OJ L181/44).

[113] The Court sanctioned Member State recourse to Art. 36 in cases of incomplete harmonisation, and within the limits of the proportionality principle, thus allowing for national licensing procedures. See Chap. 2.

[114] Commission, Completing the Internal Market: an area without internal frontiers, COM(90)552 final, points 30–5. See also R. Hankin, in evidence to the House of Lords Select Committee on the European Communities, *Report on the European Medicines Agency and Future Marketing Authorisation Procedures*, Session 1991–2, 3rd report (London, 1992), 57–8.

[115] See Kaufer, above n. 100, at 163. See also R. Dehousse/Ch. Joerges/G. Majone/F. Snyder (with

4.2.2.2. The New System for the Free Movement of Medicinal Products

The failure of the Member States to apply the mutual recognition principle voluntarily and the pressures from the pharmaceutical industry to have a European-wide licensing system forced the Commission to reconsider its approach towards the authorisation of pharmaceuticals.[116] In 1990, the Commission formally presented its new strategy, entitled the "future system for the free movement of medicinal products in the European Community".[117] After some dispute on the legal basis of the Commission proposal[118] and the political struggle for the location of the agency, the Council adopted this system with some modifications in July 1993 by virtue of Article 235.[119] This system is largely based on the experiences gained in relation to the multi-state and concertation procedures and introduces two new authorisation procedures, a centralised and a decentralised procedure, as well as an institutional novelty in this field: the EMEA.[120]

An important element of the new system is the introduction of legally binding Community decisions which are adopted following: an application for a Community market authorisation; arbitration where mutual recognition has not been accepted; failed arbitration by the CPMP where Member States have adopted divergent decisions on the authorisation of a medicinal product; identification of cases of Community interest and variations of Community authorisations. Clearly, the opening up of the national markets by the Community procedures has important economic advantages for the pharmaceutical industry, which has been identified as a substantial asset for the European economy,[121] being among the Community's best performing high-technology sectors with the highest output growth of 7 per cent per year.[122] Hence, the great interest of this industry in these procedures (and the EMEA) is evident.

M. Everson), *Europe After 1992. New Regulatory Strategies*, EUI Working Paper LAW 92/31 (Florence, 1992), 41, and G. Majone, *Mutual Recognition In Federal Type Systems*, EUI Working Paper SPS 93/1 (Florence, 1993), 17.

[116] See Kaufer, above n. 100, at 163.

[117] Above n. 43.

[118] See sect. 3.1.3.

[119] Council Reg. (EEC) 2309/93 laying down Community procedures for the authorisation and supervision of medicinal products for human and veterinary use and establishing a European Agency for the Evaluation of Medicinal Products [1993] OJ L214/1; Council Dir. 93/39/EEC amending Dirs. 65/65/EEC, 75/318/EEC and 75/319/EEC in respect of medicinal products [1993] OJ L214/22; Council Dir. 93/40/EEC amending Dirs. 81/851/EEC and 81/852/EEC on the approximation of the laws relating to veterinary medicinal products [1993] OJ L214/31. See, for the implementation and transitional measures of this system, the Commission's Communication on the implementation of the new marketing authorisation procedures for medicinal products for human and veterinary use in accordance with Council Reg. 2309/93 and Council Dirs. 93/39/EEC, 93/40/EEC and 93/41/EEC [1994] OJ C82/4.

[120] See Thompson, above n. 78, 91–140; Gardner, above n. 87, 55–63; and P. Deboyser, "Les nouvelles procédures communautaires pour l'authorisation et la surveillance des médicaments" (1995) *RMUE* 4, 31–78.

[121] Commission Communication on the outlines of an industrial policy for the pharmaceutical sector in the European Community COM(93)718 final, 4.

[122] European Commission, DGIII, *Panorama of EU Industry 1997*, 9–16. The study of the industrial policy pursued in relation to pharmaceuticals falls beyond the scope of this research.

4.2.2.3. The Centralised Market Authorisation Procedure

The centralised procedure laid down in Council Regulation (EEC) 2309/93 locates the competence to authorise innovative medicines at Community level. The procedure is compulsory for biotechnological medicines (as defined in part A of the annex), and optional for certain highly-technological medicines (defined in part B of the annex). In this manner, the dichotomy established by Directive 87/22/EEC is expressly preserved. The centralised procedure builds on the relatively successful concertation procedure under which the Member States had already been obliged to refer matters to the former CPMP before adopting any decision. The EMEA lies at the core of this system. Applications for marketing authorisations must be submitted directly to the EMEA. The Agency subsequently forwards the applications to the new CPMP, which forms an integral part of the EMEA.[123] This Committee examines the medicines for quality, safety and efficacy and formulates the agency's opinion. The Agency ensures that the opinion of the CPMP is delivered within 210 days of the receipt of a valid application.[124]

In the preparation of an opinion, the Committee may ask a state laboratory, or a laboratory designated for that purpose, to test the medicinal product for which market authorisation is sought.[125] Where the Committee intends to adopt a negative opinion or is of the opinion that the authorisation should be made subject to certain conditions, the applicant has the right of "appeal" against this opinion to the Agency. The CPMP will then reconsider the case.[126] The final opinion of the CPMP is forwarded by the EMEA as the agency's opinion to the Commission, the Member States and the applicant. Within 30 days, the Commission subsequently prepares a draft decision. This draft decision is generally in accordance with the Agency's opinion. If not, the Commission must supply a detailed explanation for its position.[127]

Before reaching a final decision, however, the Commission must consult a policy-making/implementation committee, the Standing Committee on Medicinal Products for Human Use[128] in the framework of the *contre-filet* variant of the regulatory committee procedure. The undesirable consequences

---

[123] It is noted that, notwithstanding the aim of Dir. 89/381/EEC (above n. 112) to extend the scope of Dirs. 65/65/EEC, 75/318/EEC and 75/319/EEC to all medicinal products, the deletion of the word "proprietary" was, by apparent oversight, not extended to Dir. 75/319/EEC. This oversight has led to inconsistency in the Dirs. and keeps the name of the "Committee for *Proprietary* Medicinal Products" intact.

[124] Art. 6 (4) of Council Reg. 2309/93, above n. 119.

[125] *Ibid.*, Art. 7(b).

[126] *Ibid.*, Art. 9.

[127] *Ibid.*, Art. 10.

[128] Set up by Dir. 87/19/EEC amending Dir. 75/318/EEC on the approximation of the laws of the Member States relating to analytical, pharmacotoxicological and clinical standards and protocols in respect of the testing of proprietary medicinal products [1987] OJ L15/31. This Committee, originally named "Committee on the Adaptation to Technical Progress of the Directives on the Removal of Technical Barriers to Trade in the Proprietary Medicinal Products Sector" was renamed by Art. 2 of Dir. 93/39/EEC, above n. 119.

which result from the use of this variant in authorisation procedures have already been explained in Chapter 3 (see further below).[129] The procedure to be followed is nonetheless special in that generally the opinion of the Standing Committee is obtained through a written procedure.[130] In the written procedure, the Commission representative, chairing the Committee, sends the Commission's draft decision on which an opinion is requested by mail or e-mail to the Committee members.[131] Within 30 days,[132] the Member States have to communicate to the chairperson their decision to accept or to refuse the draft, or to abstain. In their decision, Member States may include written comments. When a Member State does not take a position within the 30–day period, it is deemed to have agreed to the draft. Where a Member State however sends a duly written request to examine the draft decision during a meeting of the Standing Committee, the written procedure shall be terminated and the chairperson convenes the Committee as soon as possible. Where the Commission considers that written comments put forward by the Member States raise important new questions of a scientific or technical nature which have not yet been addressed, the procedure is suspended and the matter is referred back to the EMEA.[133] A new procedure is initiated in the 30 days following the receipt of the agency's reply by the Commission. The decision finally adopted by the Commission is binding on all Member States. The written procedure does nonetheless not apply in the "exceptional" cases in which the Commission's draft opinion is not in accordance with the Agency's opinion.

An authorised medicinal product is valid throughout the Community[134] for a period of five years.[135] Authorised medicines are entered in the Community Register of Medicinal Products.[136] The refusal of a Community market authorisation constitutes a prohibition on placing the product in question on the Community market.[137] Once authorised, a medicinal product may be suspended or withdrawn only by a decision of the Commission, advised by the CPMP. Where, however, urgent action is required to protect human or animal health or the environment, Member States may temporarily suspend the use of an authorised medicine. The Commission will consider the validity of the suspension and prepare a decision in accordance with the above-mentioned procedure.[138]

---

[129] See sect. 5.4.5. and Fig. 4 of Chap. 3.

[130] Commission Reg. (EC) 1662/95 laying down detailed arrangements for implementing the Community decision-making procedures in respect of marketing authorisations for (medicinal) products for human or veterinary use [1995] OJ L158/4.

[131] Art. 3 of Commission Reg. 1662/95, above n. 130.

[132] In emergency procedures, this period is reduced to 15 days: Art. 5 of Commission Reg. 1662/95, above n. 130.

[133] Art. 4 of Commission Reg. 1662/95, above n. 130.

[134] Art. 12 (1) of Council Reg. 2309/93, above n. 119.

[135] *Ibid.*, Art. 13.

[136] *Ibid.*, Art. 12(1). See http://dg3.eudra.org/register/index.htm.

[137] *Ibid.*, Art. 12(2).

[138] *Ibid.*, Art. 18(4).

4.2.2.4. The Decentralised Market Authorisation Procedure

For all other medicinal products, a decentralised procedure must be followed. This procedure updates and renders the former multi-state procedure more efficient. It thus starts from the mutual recognition principle and is also called the "mutual recognition" procedure. The procedure generally applies in situations where the company has already obtained a market authorisation for a medicinal product in one Member State and wants this product to be authorised in one or more other Member States.

The holder of an authorisation applies for recognition of the initial authorisation to the competent authorities of the Member States concerned, forwarding them the necessary documents. The application must be identical to the initial authorisation, otherwise the additions or amendments must be identified. Before submitting an application, the market authorisation holder informs the Member State which issued the initial authorisation (reference Member State)[139] that such an application has been made. For applications after 1 January 1998, the relevant Member States must themselves ask the reference Member State for an assessment report. Where a Member State discovers that an application for authorisation is still under active examination in another Member State, it may suspend the detailed examination and wait for the assessment report to be prepared by the other Member State.

When submitting the application, the applicant must also inform the CPMP and state which Member States are involved as well as submit a copy of the first authorisation. The Member State which issued the initial authorisation (reference Member State) acts as rapporteur, prepares an assessment report on the medicinal product concerned and forwards this to the relevant Member States. The Member States concerned are bound to recognise the marketing authorisation granted by the reference Member State within 90 days of receipt of the application,[140] unless there are grounds for supposing that the authorisation of the medicinal product in question presents a risk to public health (in terms of quality, safety and efficacy).[141] In the latter case, the opposing Member State formulates its objections and forwards its own assessment report to the applicant, the reference Member State, the other Member States concerned and the CPMP.

Subsequently, all Member States involved will "use their best endeavours to reach agreement on the action to be taken in respect of the application".[142] To this end, the Member States will clarify and discuss their concerns and deficiencies. They can meet within the Mutual Recognition Facilitation Group. This Group is composed of national representatives and, as its name suggests, aims to facilitate the mutual recognition of pharmaceuticals between the Member

---

[139] If more than one Member State has authorised the product, the Member States concerned will select the reference Member State from amongst them.

[140] Art. 9(4) of Dir. 75/319/EEC, as amended by Art. 3 of Dir. 93/39/EEC, above n. 119.

[141] *Ibid.*, Art. 10(1).

[142] *Ibid.*, Art. 10(2).

States. If no acceptable solution can be found within 90 days, the matter is referred to the CPMP for arbitration. The CPMP considers the matter and issues an opinion. To this end, it may appoint a rapporteur from amongst its members and appoint individual experts for advice on specific issues.[143] In this procedure, too, there is the possibility of "appeal" against an unfavourable opinion of the CPMP, whereupon this Committee itself will reconsider the matter. The final decision is taken by the Commission in accordance with the same regulatory committee *contre-filet* procedure which applies to the centralised procedure.[144] In contrast to the decision taken under the centralised procedure, however, the decision taken in the decentralised procedure is addressed solely to the applicant and the Member States involved and, in the Commission's opinion, would not prevent the other Member States from subsequently raising additional objections to the medicinal product in question.[145]

The CPMP procedure for arbitration may also be activated by a Member State, the Commission or the persons responsible for the authorisation of the pharmaceutical product in cases where the Member States have adopted divergent decisions on the authorisation of this product.[146] In addition, reference to the CPMP may be made by Member States, the Commission or the applicant for or holder of a market authorisation before reaching a decision on a request for a market authorisation (or its suspension or its withdrawal) "in specific cases where the interests of the Community are involved".[147] In these cases, the Member States, the Commission or the person invoking the procedure must clearly phrase the question which is referred to the CPMP.

Where a Member State finds that the variation of the terms of an existing authorisation or its suspension or withdrawal is necessary for reasons of health protection, it refers the matter to the CPMP, which will issue an opinion to be approved by the Commission. Where health protection requires urgent action, the Member State may temporarily suspend the marketing and use of the medicine on its territory, until the Commission takes a definitive decision.[148]

4.2.2.5. Supervision and Reinforced Pharmacovigilance

The Community's activities in the market authorisation of medicinal products similarly require it to be involved in the post-market surveillance of medicinal products on the Community market. Under the centralised procedure, the Community requires the person responsible for placing the medicine on the market to take account of technical and scientific progress and make any amendments necessary to enable the medicinal product to be manufactured and checked by means of generally accepted scientific methods. Amendments must

[143] *Ibid.*, Art. 13.
[144] *Ibid.*, Art. 14(2).
[145] Commission in its Explanatory Memorandum, above n. 50, at 17. This will ultimately be for the Court to consider.
[146] Art. 11 of Dir. 75/319/EEC, as amended by Art. 3 of Dir. 93/39/EEC, above n. 119.
[147] *Ibid.*, Art. 12.
[148] *Ibid.*, Art. 15a.

be approved according to the centralised authorisation procedure. At the same time, Council Regulation 2309/93 requires the national competent authorities to verify on behalf of the Community that the legal requirements governing medicinal products are complied with.[149] These authorities, therefore, carry out repeated inspections. The same applies to supervision under the decentralised procedure, although here the national authorities are not required to carry out the inspections "on behalf of the Community".[150]

The new systems aim to reinforce the former systems, under which the CPMP had already exchanged information on matters of pharmacovigilance.[151] Member States are now required to set up pharmacovigilance systems which collect the information necessary for the surveillance of medicines and, in particular, for the gathering of information relating to adverse reactions in humans. Equally, national systems provide the scientific evaluation of such information. These systems collate data on the consumption of medicinal products and information on frequently observed misuse and serious abuse of medicinal products. The Member States must report all suspected serious adverse reactions to medicines on their territory to the EMEA and to the person responsible for placing the product on the market. The latter person is required to have permanently at his or her disposal a person responsible for pharmacovigilance. This person must maintain records of all suspected adverse reactions, which, in turn, must be sent to the EMEA and to the Member States. In addition, Member States must encourage doctors and other health care professionals to report suspected adverse reactions. The Agency is responsible for the setting up of a database network for the rapid transmission of data between the Community authorities in cases of an alert relating to a faulty product, serious adverse reactions and other relevant information.

Where, as a result of inspections or the evaluation of adverse reaction reports, the national authorities consider withdrawing or suspending a medicinal product, the Commission will, in consultation with the EMEA, examine the reasons advanced by the Member States and request an opinion from the CPMP. Subsequently, the Commission adopts a decision in accordance with the procedure mentioned above.

4.3. The Agency for the Evaluation of Medicinal Products: Description

The new authorisation system clearly entails an increase in the workload of the Commission. It increases its need for scientific expertise and creates the need to register the authorised products, to follow-up and monitor these products and to provide information to third parties. The Commission's administrative capacity and, in particular, its scientific expertise have nonetheless their obvious

---

[149] Arts. 15–17 of Council Reg. 2309/93, above n. 119.
[150] Arts. 29a–29f of Dir. 75/319/EEC, as amended by Art. 3 of Dir. 93/39/EEC, above n. 119.
[151] *Ibid.*, Arts. 30–3.

limits. In this field, too, the Commission initially aimed to reinforce the existing committees: the CPMP and the CVMP. However, the specific characteristics of the field together with the different nature of these committees which, in contrast to the Scientific Committee on Food, were composed of national representatives, led the Commission to create an agency to deal with scientific expertise. In the Commission's view, in order for the CPMP and CVMP to function effectively (with proper co-ordination) logistical support and resources were necessary. Hence, the establishment of a new European Agency for pharmaceuticals was, in the words of the Commission:

> "essential in order to enable the Community institutions to discharge the major new responsibilities imposed upon them as a result of the introduction of the new Community authorisation procedures and the additional responsibilities in the field of pharmacovigilance and the supervision of manufacturers".[152]

4.3.1. *The Structure of the EMEA*

The EMEA, which came into operation in 1995, is composed of the former Committee for Proprietary Medicinal Products (CPMP), the Committee for Veterinary Medicinal Products (CVMP), a Secretariat, an Executive Director and a Management Board (see Figure 6).

The Committee for Proprietary Medicinal Products (CPMP) and the Committee for Veterinary Medicinal Products (CVMP)

Without doubt, the most important organs are the CPMP and the CVMP,[153] which are entrusted with the responsibility of formulating the scientific opinion of the EMEA. Through the establishment of this agency, an attempt is made to strengthen the scientific role and independence of these two committees,[154] which were formerly composed of the representatives of the Member States and the Commission. Today, the CPMP is composed of two members nominated by each Member State for a period of three years.[155] They are chosen for their role and experience in the evaluation of medicinal products for human use and represent their competent authorities.[156] The membership is made public.[157] In contrast to the former CPMP, the Commission is not represented on this Committee. Commission representatives are nonetheless entitled to attend the meetings of the CPMP.[158] The CPMP may establish working groups and expert groups.[159] Currently, permanent Working Parties deal with Efficacy, Safety, Pharmacovigilance and Biotechnology, while there is also a joint CPMP/CVMP

---

[152] Above n. 43, at 34.
[153] Discussion of this Committee falls beyond the scope of this research.
[154] Recitals 9–14 to Reg. 2309/93, above n. 119.
[155] *Ibid.*, Art. 52(1).
[156] *Ibid.*, Art. 52.
[157] *Ibid.*, Art. 54. See the list published in Annex 2 to the EMEA Activity Report of 1997.
[158] Art. 52(1) of Council Reg. 2309/93, above n. 119.
[159] *Ibid.*, Art. 50(2).

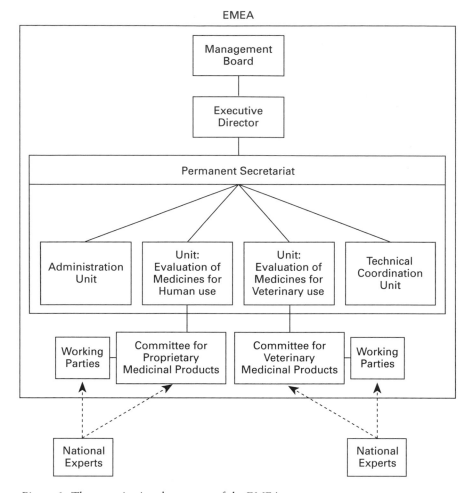

Figure 6. The organisational structure of the EMEA.

Quality Working Party.[160] In addition, *ad hoc* working parties may be set up, where necessary. Today *ad hoc* expert groups work on transmissible spongiform encephalopathies (TSE), third-generation oral contraceptives and cardiovascular risks, influenza vaccine, anti-retrovirals, herbal medicinal products and the summary of product characteristics.

To support its activities, the CPMP can count on a group of 2,112 experts (1,659 experts for human medicines and 453 for veterinary medicinal products), put at its disposal by the Member States.[161] These experts not only participate

---

[160] See the EMEA Activity Report of 1997, sect. 3.4. These groups already existed under the former system, see the 1991 Report on the activities of the CPMP, above n. 105, 8–11.

[161] In accordance with Art. 53(2) of Council Reg. 2309/93, above n. 119. See the EMEA Activity Report of 1997, sect. 1.3.

in the evaluation teams which support the work of the (co-)rapporteurs, but also participate in the CPMP's working parties and the activities of the International Conference on Harmonisation (ICH) at the international level. In general, the CPMP meets monthly. On average, these meetings last four days and ensure the intense involvement of the CPMP members. Participation in the activities of the CPMP and its Working parties thus entails a considerable workload for the national competent authorities for which no compensation is made. In addition to the obligation to issue objective scientific opinions, the members of the Committee are required to ensure co-ordination between the tasks of the EMEA and the work of the competent national authorities. When the CPMP is asked to evaluate a medicinal product, it appoints one of its members as rapporteur. In their work, both Committee members and experts rely heavily on the scientific assessments and resources available to the national marketing authorisation bodies. Each Member State must monitor the scientific quality of the evaluation carried out, and supervise the activities of the members and experts nominated, although they must refrain from giving the members any instruction which is incompatible with the tasks incumbent upon them.[162]

The Secretariat and Executive Director

The Secretariat of the Agency provides technical and administrative support for the Committees and ensures co-ordination between them.[163] Specific responsibilities are assigned to the Executive Director, who is the legal representative of the EMEA.[164] The Director is appointed by the Management Board following a proposal from the Commission. The current Director is Mr Fernand Sauer, former head of unit of DGIII and former deputy chairman of the CPMP. The Director is responsible for: the day-to-day administration of the Agency, the provision of technical support for the Committees, ensuring that the time limits laid down in Community legislation are respected, co-ordination between the two Committees, preparation of the revenue and expenditure statement and execution of the budget of the Agency and all staff matters. The Director prepares the report on the activities of the Agency and the working-programme, together with the budget and the annual accounts. In addition, the Director must approve all of the Agency's financial expenditure.

The Management Board

The Management Board is the EMEA's governing body and is responsible for budgetary matters, the appointment of the Executive Director and the monitoring of the Agency's performance. It consists of two representatives from each Member State, two representatives from the Commission and two representatives appointed by the European Parliament, one representative having specific responsibilities for medicinal products for human use and one for medicinal

---

[162] Art. 52(3) of Council Reg. 2309/93, above n. 119.
[163] *Ibid.*, Art. 50(1).
[164] *Ibid.*, Art. 55.

products for veterinary use.[165] The Executive Director provides the secretariat of the Board.

In 1997, the Management Board met four times. During these meetings various topics were discussed, among which were the regulatory challenges for the EMEA for the millennium for pharmaceuticals, the role of the EMEA in international activities, the identification and management of regulatory costs, information technology and quality standards.[166] The Board adopts the annual activity report, the working programme and the budget prepared by the Director. Decisions of the Board are adopted by a majority of two-thirds of its members. Furthermore, the Board develops the appropriate contacts between the EMEA and representatives of the industry, consumers, patients and health professions.[167]

4.3.2. *The Tasks of the EMEA*

The overall objective of the EMEA is to provide the Member States and the Community institutions with the best possible scientific advice on any question relating to the evaluation of the quality, the safety and the efficacy of medicinal products.[168] To this end, it will undertake the following tasks, some of which were already performed by the former CPMP:

- the co-ordination of the scientific evaluation of the quality, safety and efficacy of medicinal products, subject to marketing authorisations;
- the transmission of assessment reports, summaries of product characteristics, labels and package leaflets;
- the co-ordination of supervision of authorised medicinal products, giving advice on the measures necessary to ensure the safe and effective use of medicines and the creation of a database on adverse reactions (pharmacovigilance);
- advising on the maximum limits for residues of veterinary medicinal products which may be accepted in foodstuffs of animal origin;
- co-ordinating the verification of compliance with the principles of good manufacturing practice, good laboratory practice and good clinical practice;
- upon request, providing technical and scientific support for steps to improve the co-ordination between the Community, the Member States, international organisations and third countries on scientific and technical issues relating to the evaluation of medicinal products;
- recording the status of marketing authorisations for medicines obtained in accordance with the Community procedures;

---

[165] See the list of members published in the EMEA Directory of 1 Dec. 1997.
[166] The EMEA Activity Report of 1997, sec. 1.2.
[167] Art. 65 of Council Reg. 2309/93, above n. 119.
[168] *Ibid.*, Art. 51.

- providing technical assistance for the maintenance of a database on medicinal products, available for public use;
- assisting the Community and the Member States in the provision of information to health care professionals and the general public about medicinal products which have been evaluated within the Agency;
- where necessary, advising companies on the conduct of the various tests and trials necessary to demonstrate the quality, the safety and the efficacy of medicines.

Thus, although there is undoubtedly a degree of formal centralisation of powers on medicinal products at Community level, the activities entrusted to the EMEA at the same time ensure a measure of functional decentralisation.

4.3.3. The Operation of the EMEA and the Community Authorisation Procedures

After the new system came into force in January 1995, 18 applications pending under the concertation procedure were transferred to the new centralised procedure. Following a positive opinion from the CPMP, the very first Community authorisation was issued by the Commission in October 1995.[169] In its three years of operation, the EMEA has received 131 applications for human medicinal products for the centralised procedures. Of these applications, 49 concerned pharmaceuticals listed in part A (obligatory), whilst 82 applications related to medicinal products listed in part B of the Annex, for which the centralised procedure is voluntarily. The relatively high number of voluntary applications readily demonstrates the success of this procedure. This emphasises the great desire and interest of the pharmaceutical industry to obtain a European-wide authorisation of their products, instead of going through each and every national licensing procedure.

The decentralised or mutual recognition procedure, too, appears to function well. Between 1995 and 1997, a total of 659 procedures were completed, of which 240 related to new applications and 419 related to applications for variations to authorisations. Only five referrals for arbitration were made.[170] The Mutual Recognition Facilitation Group, which regularly meets to discuss the problems relating to the authorisation of a specific product, is likely to have contributed significantly to the proper-functioning of this procedure.

The growing importance of the EMEA in licensing is further confirmed by the fact that both the pharmaceutical industry and the Member States increasingly ask for scientific advice or opinions from the CPMP before applying for or deciding on authorisation. From 1995 to 1997, the CPMP gave 50 advisory

---

[169] Approving the product Gonal-F: see [1996] OJ C22/11.
[170] See the Report from the meeting of the Mutual Recognition Facilitation Group of Jan. 1998, published in annex to CPMP Press Release of January 1998 CPMP/069/98 (http://www.eudra.org/emea.html).

opinions to pharmaceutical companies,[171] whilst Member States demonstrated a growing interest in obtaining a CPMP opinion before adopting a decision on authorisation under the mutual recognition procedure.[172] The rapidly growing significance of the EMEA in the Community's pharmaceutical licensing is further illustrated by its budget, which has doubled over the last three years,[173] resulting in an expenditure of 28.5 million ECU for 1997 (see Figure 7). For that year, revenues were obtained from both EU subsidy (approximately 50 per cent) and evaluation fees paid by industry (approximately 50 per cent).[174]

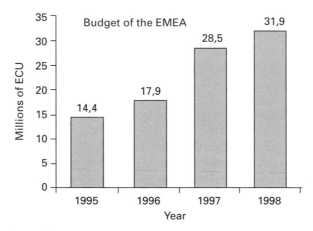

Figure 7. Budget of the EMEA 1995–8.
Source: The EMEA Activity Report of 1997 (Annex 6) and the Community Budget [1998] OJ L57.

4.4. The Interrelation between the Member States and the Community Institutions through the EMEA and Committees

Although Member States did agree upon the necessity of creating a new authorisation system, several conditions had to be met. First, the process of centralising authorisation powers at Community level created notable tension between Community internal market policy and national policies on the pricing of pharmaceuticals and reimbursement under national public health or security systems, which the Member States did not intend to surrender to the

---

[171] See Annex 1 to CPMP Press Release of Dec. 1997, CPMP/1138/97 (http://www.eudra.org/emea.html).

[172] In accordance with Art. 12 of Dir. 75/319/EEC, as amended by Art. 3 of Dir. 93/39/EEC, above n. 119.

[173] In 1994, the EMEA spent 6.8 million ECU on administrative costs relating to the creation of the Agency.

[174] In accordance with Art. 57(1) of Council Reg. 2309/93 and Council Reg. 297/95 on fees payable to the European Agency for the Evaluation of Medicinal Products [1995] OJ L35/1.

Community.[175] Consequently, the new system expressly excluded the powers of the Member States in this field from its scope.[176] In addition, the concerns of some Member States (in particular Ireland) that the obligation to admit medicinal products might conflict with national policies on birth control[177] were addressed through the introduction of a provision stating that authorisation by the Community does not affect the application of national legislation prohibiting or restricting the sale, supply or use of medicinal products as contraceptives or abortifacients.[178]

Furthermore, decision-making powers were not transferred to the Community level without a guarantee that the Member States would continue to have a voice in this politically sensitive matter. As argued in Chapter 2, this may be explained in terms of subsidiarity and a "Member State-oriented" understanding of the institutional balance of powers, of which the alteration in favour of the Community is compensated for by some new form of Member State control. Accordingly, the new institutional framework is carefully designed with particular attention to the need for close co-operation with the Member States. Member States have thus been granted influence upon the decision-making process through their close involvement and participation within the EMEA, whilst committees continue to exist in this field, too. Co-operation between Member States and the Community (Commission) is guaranteed not only by means of the EMEA, but also through the Standing Committee on Medicinal Products for Human Use, the Pharmaceutical Committee and the Mutual Recognition Facilitating Group.

4.4.1. The EMEA

The new authorisation system is therefore wholly dependent upon co-operation between the EMEA and the competent national authorities. The EMEA plays an important co-ordinating role between the Community and the Member States. It is generally responsible for the co-ordination of the scientific sources placed at its disposal by the competent authorities of the Member States. Being composed of representatives of the Member States, the Commission and Parliament, the EMEA contributes to improve co-operation and implementation at the national level. Allowing the Member States ample opportunity to participate actively in the decision-making process within the Agency goes some way towards overcoming the obstinate distrust between national authorities, which has been one of the main problems faced by the Community over the years. Community decision-making thus based on co-ordination and co-operation of

---

[175] See Gardner, above n. 87, at 50.

[176] Art. 65 of Council Reg. 2309/93 and Art. 3 of Council Dir. 65/65/EEC as amended by Council Dir. 93/39/EEC, above n. 119. This provision was not included in the Commission proposals.

[177] See the Commission in its Explanatory Memorandum, above n. 50, at 24.

[178] Art. 12(1) of Council Reg. 2309/93 and Art. 6 of Dir. 65/65/EEC, as amended by Art. 1 of Dir. 93/39/EEC, above n. 119.

the national authorities contributes to increased effectiveness and at the same time addresses the subsidiarity issue.

First, the EMEA's Management Board potentially contributes to greater co-ordination between the Community institutions and the Member States, simply by virtue of its composition. More specifically, it adopted in December 1996 a general "Statement of Principles governing the Partnership between the National Authorities and the EMEA".[179] This document summarises and reinforces several principles already set out in Council Regulation 2309/93. It thus stipulates that national competent authorities transmit to the EMEA a list of scientific experts in all relevant fields who are available to serve in the working parties or expert groups of the CPMP (and CVMP). To this end, the Member States must allow CPMP (CVMP) members and experts to rely on the scientific assessments and resources available to the national competent authorities, whilst they monitor the scientific level of the evaluation carried out and supervise Committee activities. However, it is again repeated that Member States must refrain from giving Committee members and/or experts any instruction which is incompatible with their tasks.

Furthermore, the CPMP has an important co-ordinating function within the EMEA too. In addition to giving scientific opinions, its members need to ensure that there is appropriate co-ordination between the EMEA and each national authority.[180] Where an exchange between the participants in this network is likely to improve the information or the scientific evaluation on which decisions are based, this results in enhanced Community decision-making[181] and thus greater legitimacy. In addition, the statement stipulates that the EMEA compensates the national competent authorities for the services of the rapporteurs, co-rapporteurs and experts in addition to the reimbursement of travel and accommodation expenses.[182] The activities thus undertaken by these experts on behalf of the EMEA are subjected to a contract between the EMEA and the national competent authority. In this contract, the national competent authority agrees to produce within a certain time limit an assessment report by the appointed rapporteur and experts in accordance with the mandate given by the CPMP. In the same contract the national authority undertakes once again to put all scientific resources at the disposal of the rapporteur, whilst guaranteeing respect for the scientific independence of rapporteurs and experts. The EMEA, for its part, undertakes the obligation to pay a fee to the national competent authority for the work done. Where, however, the CPMP views that the assessment report does not meet the expected quality requirements, the EMEA may withhold payment until an acceptable report is produced. In exceptional circumstances, the EMEA may break the contract.[183]

[179] EMEA/MB/030/95–final–Rev.1, published in annex to the Press Release of the 12th meeting of the Management Board of 4 Dec. 1996.
[180] In accordance with Art. 52(2) of Council Reg. 2309/93, above n. 119.
[181] See, also, Lenaerts, above n. 59, at 43.
[182] Art. 9 of the Statement, above n. 179.
[183] See the Standard Contract between the national competent authority and the EMEA, Annex II to the Statement, above n. 179.

4.4.2. The Standing Committee on Medicinal Products for Human Use, the CPMP and the Management Board

Like the Standing Committee on Foodstuffs analysed in the previous chapter, the Standing Committee on Medicinal Products for Human Use may potentially ensure the exchange of information and opinions between the Member States and the Commission and provide for a degree of co-ordination. Although deliberation between all regulatory actors involved is particularly important in this field (characterised by mutual distrust), some critical remarks may be made regarding the inclusion of the Standing Committee in the authorisation procedure and its relationship with the CPMP and the Management Board.

First, whilst the introduction of a standing committee in addition to a "true" scientific committee might be "justified" in order to ease the Member States' anxiety that they might lose their influence (as is the case in the food sector), it may be wondered whether the inclusion of the Standing Committee on Medicinal Products for Human Use, in addition to the CPMP/EMEA, is actually necessary and/or desirable in the authorisation of medicinal products. In this regard, it is helpful to recall that the Standing Committee was created within the framework of Directive 75/318/EEC on the harmonisation of analytical, pharmaco-toxicological and clinical standards and is composed of the representatives of the Member States.[184] It was not involved in the authorisation of medicines as such. This was the task of the CPMP, which was originally also composed of the representatives of the Member States.

Although under the new system, the CPMP members have been made more independent from their Member States, being selected for their role and experience in the evaluation of medicinal products, they continue to "represent their competent [national] authorities". However, as already set forth above, Member States are required to "refrain from giving any instruction" which is incompatible with the tasks of the Committee. These requirements are the outcome of lengthy debates on the composition of the CPMP, during which the Commission argued that a scientific committee which mirrored the structure adopted for foodstuffs should be created,[185] whilst the Member States demanded that they retain political involvement in view of the close link with questions of national health and medical practices.[186] This two-tiered manner of formulating a scientific opinion, however, means that national experts, representing their competent authorities, adopt an opinion only after consultation with a pool of national scientific experts. Within the framework of the CPMP, therefore, it is not highly-qualified scientists, but persons closely involved with the authorisation of medicines at the national level, who formulate the scientific opinion of the agency. Examination of the membership of the CPMP reveals

---

[184] It was set up by Dir. 87/19/EEC, above n. 128.
[185] See Arts. 10 and 50 of the Commission's proposal, above n. 43.
[186] See Hankin, above n. 114.

that the members of this Committee, of whom many were national representatives within the former CPMP,[187] belong to the national medicines agencies or health departments.[188] Furthermore, in practice some CPMP members also sit on the Standing Committee. In addition, it should not be forgotten that CPMP members are nominated by the Member States, which means that members who no longer support the position of their national authorities run the risk of not being renominated.

These elements seem to confirm that the forum function of the Standing Committee identified in Chapter 3, which, through "deliberative interaction", may contribute to effective and good decision-making and bring in the more political aspects, in practice is already undertaken within the framework of the CPMP. This interpretation seems to be strengthened by the fact that, as a general rule, the Standing Committee on Medicinal Products for Human Use is consulted by means of a written procedure during which Member States[189] can express their approval, disapproval or intention to abstain. This view is strengthened where the EMEA reports that:

> "The consistent and high scientific quality of the CPMP opinions prevented further scientific discussions during the Standing Committee phase. This facilitated the issuing of Commission Decisions granting Community marketing authorisations".[190]

Opinions adopted by the CPMP are thus likely to include not only purely scientific, but also normative (nationally-flavoured) elements (see below). However, further empirical research is needed to investigate this in more detail. Such research should also examine the intricate relationship between the Standing Committee and EMEA's Management Board, both composed of national representatives. It is current practice, for example, for a great number of members on the Standing Committee to sit on the Management Board, as well as on the Pharmaceutical Committee. The success of empirical research, however, will be fully dependent upon the Standing Committee creating greater transparency; at present, details on its composition and procedure are not publicly available.

In addition to the doubts about its usefulness or necessity, the consultation of the Standing Committee within the framework of the *contre-filet* variant of the regulatory committee procedure is in any case to be heavily criticised, since this variant potentially results in unacceptable delays or in the blocking of a Commission proposal by a simple majority vote in the Council.[191]

---

[187] See the 1991 Report on the activities of the CPMP, above n. 105.

[188] See, e.g., the list of the membership of the CPMP published in the EMEA Directory of 1 Dec. 1997.

[189] The switch in terminology between the committee members and the *Member States* in Art. 3 of Commission Reg. 1662/95 (above n. 130) seems, in this respect, to be significant.

[190] The EMEA Activity Report of 1997, sect. 3.2.

[191] See Chap. 3.

4.4.3. The Pharmaceutical Committee

The Pharmaceutical Committee was set up in 1975 as a counterpart to the CPMP.[192] Whilst the CPMP was designed to deal with scientific questions relating to the free movement of medicines, this Committee was created to foster mutual recognition by examining general questions relating to the application of the directives on proprietary medicinal products, or indeed any questions relating to such products. The Committee could be argued to be a policy-making/implementation committee, although no specific procedure is laid down for its consultation, and it was created to provide advice on only very general questions. In addition, there are particular requirements relating to the quality of the national representatives in that they must be senior experts in health matters.

Although the Community annually sets aside 45,000 ECU for this Committee,[193] and the consultation of this Committee by the Commission is compulsory for proposals on medicinal products, in particular for amendments to Directive 65/65/EEC,[194] most of the activities of this Committee have for too long remained cloaked in obscurity. For instance, the exact role played by the Committee during negotiations on the new authorisation system was far from clear, although in a Special Report on the Community's Committee Budget, the Commission did actually mentioned its involvement.[195] Recently, however, more light has been shed on this Committee and both its composition and the outcomes of its meetings are put on the Internet.[196] Nonetheless, in view of the tasks undertaken by the EMEA (in particular those of co-ordination) and for the sake of clarity, it seems that discussions on general questions relating to the authorisation of medicinal products brought up by the Commission or the Member States would best be carried out within the Agency itself. In this context, it is noteworthy that almost half of the members (and deputies) of the Pharmaceutical Committee are at the same time also members (and alternates) of the Management Board of the EMEA.[197]

---

[192] Council Dec. 75/320/EEC, above n. 97.

[193] This Committee is actually mentioned twice on the same budget in relation to committees whose consultation is compulsory, once under the sector industry and once under the internal market.

[194] Art. 2 of Council Dec. 75/320/EEC, above n. 97.

[195] See Budget 1995. Comitology, vol. I, XIX/A7/0067/95; Decisions taken in 1994 by the committees listed in Annex I to Part A (Administrative appropriations) of Section III (Commission) of the general budget for the European Union for 1994 [1994] OJ L34/20.

[196] See http://dg3.eudra.org/commit/index.htm#pharmacom for the composition of the Pharmaceutical Committee and http://dg3.eudra.org/dgiiie3/news.htm for the information on the outcomes of its meetings.

[197] Prior to the new system, the majority of the members of the Pharmaceutical Committee were CPMP members: Commission of the EC, Pharmaceutical Committee, Draft summary record of the meeting on 13 Mar. 1991, III/3176/91.

4.4.4. The Mutual Recognition Facilitating Group

Under the decentralised procedure, Member States must recognise a medicinal product authorised in another Member State, unless there are grounds for believing that it presents a risk to health. In order to facilitate the application of mutual recognition in this procedure, the Mutual Recognition Facilitating Group, composed of national representatives, was created.[198] The establishment of this Group is due to the experiences gained in relation to the CPMP within the former regime on medicinal products.[199] Although the Group was originally intended to be of a temporary nature,[200] it currently appears to have a more permanent structure and it continues to meet at the EMEA in parallel with the meetings of the CPMP. The EMEA hereby provides administrative support, in terms of meeting rooms and secretariat. Hence, through this group, a forum is created which serves to increase the mutual confidence between the national competent authorities.

Where for years the free movement of pharmaceuticals was plagued by the mutual distrust between national authorities, this strategy of encouraging a continuous and regular debate among the competent authorities while keeping in the background the "threat" of a binding Community decision finally appears to be bearing fruit: out of the 659 procedures completed between 1995 and 1997 only five were referred to the CPMP for arbitration. Yet, although minutes of the group's meetings are made available on the Internet,[201] it is unclear who precisely is involved in this debate, as well as the group's relationship with the other bodies involved. For example, the EMEA Third Activity Report of 1997 reveals on this point that Dr David Jefferys is its current chairman and appears to be also a member of the CPMP.[202] This fact would only confirm once again the two-tiered system of integrating scientific expertise into pharmaceutical regulation.

4.5. Integrating Scientific Expertise into Community Regulation on Pharmaceuticals through the EMEA

4.5.1. Models for the Authorisation of Medicinal Products

At the national level, different models for the authorisation of medicinal products have been adopted. Having examined the authorisation systems in the Member States, Hart and Reich identify the following models:

---

[198] See the EMEA Activity Report of 1995, 26.

[199] See the Commission Report on the activities of the CPMP, SEC(93)771, 11–12.

[200] The EMEA Activity Report of 1995 spoke still of the *"Ad Hoc"* Mutual Facilitating Group, 26.

[201] In an annex to the CPMP's monthly press releases.

[202] The EMEA Activity Report of 1997, sect. 3.5.

model (1) a situation in which the decision on authorisation is adopted by civil servants/employees who are experts (internal expertise);

model (2) a situation in which the decision on authorisation is adopted by civil servants/employees who are experts, after the consultation of an associated, external "independent" staff of scientists (internal and associated external expertise);

model (3) a situation in which the decision on authorisation is adopted by an associated external "independent" staff of scientists (external expertise).[203]

Most Member States generally rely on expertise provided by "independent" external scientists (models 2 and 3).[204] The Community approach to the authorisation of medicines comes close to model 2, albeit with some differences as regards the "independent" staff of scientists consulted.[205]

4.5.2. The Community's "Two-tiered" Model of Integrating Scientific Expertise

In the "two-tiered" model of integrating scientific expertise,[206] the work of the CPMP depends mainly on the national authorities. The CPMP members and the experts responsible for evaluating medicinal products must rely on national assessments and the resources made available to them by the national authorisation authorities.[207] The scientific evaluation of medicinal products thus remains in the hands of the Member States, who are required to monitor the scientific quality of the evaluation carried out and supervise activities, although they are similarly required to abide by a rather vague prohibition on interfering with the work of the CPMP. In this field, the extreme sensitivity of the Member States has prevented the use of the procedure applied to the food sector, where the Community has separated the scientific decision (to be taken by scientists within a European committee framework) from the political decision (to be taken by the Community institutions and Member State representatives). This confirms that risk assessment of medicinal products is difficult to separate from issues of risk management.[208] It is noteworthy that the Commission had originally proposed the creation of a Scientific Council. This body, composed of five to nine people of outstanding and international reputation and nominated by the Council, would review the activities of the CPMP and advise it on important questions of a general or ethical nature.[209] Not surprisingly, political sensitivity

[203] Hart/Reich, above n. 80, 51–6.
[204] Model 2 can be found in most Member States, while model 3 legally exists only in the Netherlands. *De facto*, however, the latter model can also be found in France and the UK, although in these countries model 2 is opted for legally. Model 1 combined with model 2 approaches the Danish situation: see Hart/Reich, above n. 80, 51–6.
[205] See sects. 4.5.2. and 4.5.3.
[206] See above, sect. 4.4.2.
[207] Art. 52(3) of Council Reg. 2309/93, above n. 119.
[208] See C.F. Cranor, *Regulating Toxic Substances. A Philosophy of Science and the Law* (New York/Oxford, 1993), 132.
[209] See Art. 65 of the Commission's proposal for a Council Reg., above n. 43.

has also impeded this kind of independent peer review.[210] Instead, Council Regulation 2309/93 merely contains vague hints that the CPMP "may seek guidance" on such questions.[211]

As argued above, opinions adopted by the CPMP are likely to include not only purely "scientific", but also normative elements. Therefore, once the CPMP has reached a consensus on the authorisation of a specific medicinal product (including all relevant considerations), it is probable that the Commission will follow this opinion, although this may be different should no consensus be reached and the CPMP adopt an opinion by a majority vote. This is confirmed by Council Regulation 2309/93 which presupposes that, in general, the draft decision of the Commission will be in accordance with the Committee opinion.[212] This finding is important in order to establish where interest representation might fit into this regulatory scheme, and at the same time where it may constitute a further argument in favour of a regulatory agency.[213] Nonetheless, it remains possible that with time the CPMP will grow more independent and less susceptible to Member States' influence, and thus emerge as a "true" scientific or epistemic community. It has been suggested that raising the EMEA's credibility (even at the expense of the national authorities) may serve the interests of the CPMP members, and raise their prestige to the level accorded to bodies such as the American Food and Drug Administration. In this vein, members would be more concerned to create a reputation on the basis of their scientific opinions, rather than seek to reflect the views of their Member States.[214] However, such an attitude of Committee members is difficult to imagine where the whole system is based on co-operation between the EMEA and the national competent authorities. Moreover, acting in this way, the members risk being denied re-appointment by the Member States, and could potentially suffer a loss of their own personal prestige. Evidently, in this matter further (empirical) research on the activities of the CPMP is necessary.

4.5.3. Principles of Objectivity and Independence

The Council has set two principles which the Community's new licensing system must follow: the principle of objectivity and the principle of independence. As regards "objectivity", the Council states in the preamble to Regulation 2309/93 that by means of the agency, the Community institutions aim "in the

---

[210] See, in general, S. Jasanoff, *The Fifth Branch. Science Advisers as Policymakers* (Cambridge, Mass./London, 1990), 61–79.

[211] Art. 50(3) of Council Reg. 2309/93, above n. 119. The House of Lords Select Committee on the European Community had already expressed its doubts about the purpose and status of such a body in its *Report on the European Medicines Agency and Future Marketing Authorisation Procedures*, Session 1991–2, 3rd report (London, 1992), 18. It believed it would be difficult to find eminent scientists to serve on this Council.

[212] Art. 10(1) of Council Reg. 2309/93, above n. 119.

[213] See sect. 4.10.

[214] See Gardner, above n. 87, 64–5.

interest of public health"[215] to meet the need to base licensing decisions "on the objective scientific criteria of the quality, the safety and the efficacy of the medicinal product concerned to the exclusion of economic or other considerations".[216] The EMEA accordingly needs to provide the Community institutions and the Member States with "the best possible scientific advice"[217] relating to the evaluation of medicines.

To this end, the CPMP provides "objective scientific opinions".[218] The principle of "objectivity" relates, in the Council's view, to the severance of health protection considerations from economic and other considerations. As argued earlier, however, the model adopted here in practice involves the indirect consultation of scientific experts: the CPMP is composed of national experts in the evaluation of medicines (many of whom were members of the former CPMP) who represent their competent national authorities and must, in turn, consult national scientific experts. The latter mechanism seems, to a certain extent, comparable with the "SCOOP" system in the food sector.

In a highly technical area such as medicines only a very limited number of persons are qualified to undertake highly technical research and analysis; research which is often commissioned by the pharmaceutical industry. It is therefore difficult to find experts in this field who are not in some way already working for the industry. In order to guarantee the "independence" of the EMEA's and the CPMP's work, Article 54 of Council Regulation 2309/93 prohibits members of the CPMP, of the Management Board, as well as rapporteurs and experts, from having any financial or other interest in the pharmaceutical industry which could affect their impartiality.[219] This principle is reinforced by the Statement of Principles governing the Partnership between the EMEA and the National Competent Authorities. This Statement stipulates first that Committee members will undersign a public declaration of interests. All these interests are entered in a register held by the EMEA which the public may consult. Although there is obviously a wide area for interpretation of the interest concerned and more precise rules will be necessary, this provision is a minimum step, providing at least more transparency in the decision-making process.[220] The statement further underlines the independence of Committee members and experts from their national competent authorities: Committee members and experts act for and on behalf of the agency, while the national authorities must respect and guarantee their scientific independence.[221]

In contrast to the food sector, where in the BSE aftermath the Commission explicitly adheres to the principle of *excellence* in relation to the composition of

---

[215] Third recital of the preamble to Council Reg. 2309/93, above n. 119.

[216] *Ibid.*

[217] Art. 51 of Council Reg. 2309/93, above n. 119.

[218] *Ibid.*, Art. 52(2).

[219] *Ibid.*, Art. 54(2).

[220] See Thompson, above n. 78, at 115.

[221] Art. 7 of the Statement in conjunction with Art. 3 of the Standard Contract, annex II to the Statement, above n. 179.

the scientific committees, underlining that risk evaluation should be undertaken by eminent scientists, such a principle is not applied in the pharmaceutical sector. Council Regulation 2309/93 does not require CPMP members to be "scientific experts". Instead members are:

> "chosen by reason of their role and experience in the evaluation of medicinal products for human and veterinary use as appropriate and shall represent their national authorities".[222]

A high level of scientific expertise is nonetheless striven for through the pool of experts made available by the Member States.[223] These experts must have proven experience in the assessment of medicinal products and indicate their qualifications and specific areas of expertise.[224] Again, this seems to confirm the two-tiered system of integrating scientific expertise into pharmaceutical regulation.

4.5.4. Requirements concerning the Plurality of Scientific Expertise

As with foodstuffs, national scientific expertise is co-ordinated within the working parties of the CPMP. Scientific data are evaluated by the various working parties of the CPMP. At the Agency's disposal are 1,659 experts from the Member States who may collaborate and assess the safety of specific medicinal products. In exceptional circumstances, the CPMP may appoint experts whose names are not on the list of experts held by the EMEA.[225] This system is attractive for its flexibility, the lack of which is one of the main difficulties which faces the American Food and Drug Administration (FDA), as it can attract scientifically qualified persons without overburdening them with administrative duties.[226]

Furthermore, in this manner, the Community attempts to encourage the creation of a common safety philosophy on medicinal products, satisfactory to the different scientific schools of thought to which such experts belong. The national experts, consulted in turn by this Committee, participate in international scientific networks and thus form part of an international epistemic community. In this way, co-ordination with new scientific and technical developments at both the national and the international level is guaranteed. The results furnished by the national experts are discussed within the general framework of the CPMP. Of particular importance is the participation of the CPMP and its Working Parties in the International Conferences on Harmonisation of Technical Requirements for Registration of Pharmaceuticals for Human Use

---

[222] Art. 52(1) of Council Reg. 2309/93, above n. 119.

[223] See the Commission in its Communication on the implementation of the new marketing authorisation procedures, above n. 119, point C.

[224] Art. 53(2) of Council Reg. 2309/93, above n. 119.

[225] These people, too, must first declare their interests. See Art. 5 of the Statement on Principles, above n. 179.

[226] Kaufer, above n. 100, at 163.

(ICH).[227] The latter is a joint regulatory/industry project to improve, through harmonisation, the efficiency of the process for developing and registering new medicinal products in Europe, Japan and the United States.[228]

Notwithstanding the great influence of the CPMP, it is nonetheless the Commission which must formally adopt a decision on the authorisation of a specific medicinal product. In so doing, it must ascertain that the experts consulted possess the necessary scientific knowledge for the authorisation of specific medicinal products. This is part of the obligation, placed on the Commission by the Court in *Technische Universität München*, to examine carefully and impartially all the relevant aspects of the case under consideration.[229] As argued in the previous chapters, this requirement also has an impact on the legitimacy of Community decision-making; a legitimacy which may be enhanced by the plurality of scientific expertise.

However, in contrast to the Commission proposal which required that the composition of the CPMP reflected the various scientific disciplines necessary for the evaluation of medicinal products,[230] Council Regulation 2309/93 contains no such requirement. The absence of such a requirement may be explained by the fact that the CPMP is still composed of representatives of the national authorities. The Court's case law seems nonetheless to indicate that the Commission may indeed need to demonstrate on a case-by-case basis that advice has been sought from experts possessing the necessary knowledge in the relevant fields. Hereby, the Commission will be able to point to the qualifications and the specific fields of expertise of the pool of experts listed by the EMEA.

4.5.5. The Scientific Committee on Medicinal Products and Medical Devices in the BSE Aftermath

The BSE crisis has also had consequences for the Community pharmaceutical regulation. Within the framework of the general reorganisation of the scientific committees, the Commission created a new scientific committee in the pharmaceutical area, too.[231] Accordingly, the Scientific Committee on Medicinal Products and Medical Devices advises the Commission on scientific and technical questions relating to Community legislation on pharmaceuticals. Like the Scientific Committee on Food, the Scientific Committee on Medicinal Products and Medical Devices must be consulted by the Commission where this is prescribed by Community legislation and may be consulted on other questions of particular relevance to consumer health.

---

[227] See its Internet site: http://www.ifpma.org/ich1.html.
[228] See, e.g., C. Hodgkin, "International Harmonisation—the Need for Transparency" (1996) 9 *International Journal of Risk & Safety in Medicine* 195–9.
[229] Case C–269/90, [1991] ECR I–5469. See Chaps. 2 and 3.
[230] Art. 50(1) of the Commission's proposal for a Council Reg., above n. 43.
[231] Commission Dec. 97/579/EC setting up Scientific Committees in the field of consumer health and food safety [1997] OJ L237/18.

The Committee is active "without prejudice to the specific competences given to the CPMP and the CVMP".[232] With this phrasing the Commission appears to draw a clear distinction between authorisation procedures of medicinal products and other regulatory activities on pharmaceuticals, such as (implantable) medical devices. This notwithstanding, the exact relationship between the Scientific Committee and the CPMP and the other bodies operating at present in this area is by no means clear.[233] Moreover, in practice at least one member is also a member of the Pharmaceutical Committee and the EMEA's Management Board as well as the Standing Committee. This not only appears to be in contrast to the spirit of Commission Decision 97/579/EC which explicitly prohibits members of one scientific committee from being members of one of the other scientific committees,[234] it is also raises questions regarding the difficulty of representing a Member State and at the same time "act[ing] independently of all external influence" as required by Commission Decision 97/579/EC.[235]

4.6. Participation of Interested Parties

Allowing the various interested parties to participate in the decision-making procedure in principle encourages plurality and the institutionalisation of informed discourse on the safety of medicinal products which, until recently, was largely lacking.[236] For example, prior to the new system, consumer interest groups, in particular, had complained about not being consulted. The European Consumers' Organisation, BEUC, for example, had expressed its discontent about its lack of official status in the former consultation procedures, which afforded the industry ample opportunity to collaborate with the CPMP. In the same vein, consumers had criticised the secrecy which surrounded decisions on regulatory medicinal policy, as well as the close links of the competent Directorate General (DGIII) of the Commission with the industry's interests.[237] This form of criticism could only grow stronger following the 1995 transfer of competence for pharmaceuticals from the internal market section of DGIII of the Commission (now DGXV) to the reorganised DGIII which has but one task: industrial policy. Moreover, it was argued that the system placed too great an emphasis on facilitating the marketing of medicinal products at the expense of

---

[232] Annex to Commission Dec. 97/579/EEC, above n. 231.

[233] In the summary report of its second meeting, this Committee announces its plans to review CPMP and CVMP guidelines (see http://europa.eu.int/comm/dg24/health/sc/ncomm7/out02_en.html).

[234] Art. 3(3) of Commission Dec. 97/579/EC (above n. 231) explicitly prohibits members of one scientific committee from being members of one of the other scientific committees, although it does not stipulate anything on the membership of other (non-scientific) committees.

[235] Art. 5(3) of Commission Dec. 97/579/EC, above n. 231.

[236] See Hart, above n. 81, at 353. See also D. Hart, "Harmonisierung des Marktüberwachungsrechts für Arzneimittel in der EG" (1990) 52 *Pharm.Ind.* 1075 and Hart/Reich, above n. 80, 45–6.

[237] See Hancher, above n. 82, at 158.

monitoring and other forms of post-market control.[238] In the debate on the Commission proposal on the new authorisation system, the former Consumer Consultative Council (CCC) had consequently suggested that both the CCC and the Parliament should be allowed to appoint experts to the Agency's Management Board and the CPMP.[239] Such a pluralistic structure is, for example, adopted in the case of the Administrative Board of the European Agency for Safety and Health at Work, which is composed of representatives of the Member States, trade union organisations, employers' organisations and the Commission.[240] This proposal was, however, not adopted, although representatives of the Parliament were admitted to the Management Board of the EMEA. Whilst, from the viewpoint of legitimacy, the inclusion of parliamentary representatives within the Management Board is to be applauded, there seems to be little or no feedback between the experts appointed by the Parliament (generally university professors) and the Parliament itself.[241]

Within the new system, consultation of interested parties is generally only prescribed when the Commission draws up detailed guidance on the form in which applications for authorisations are to be presented.[242] In addition, before determining the fee to be paid by the pharmaceutical companies for the authorisation, the Commission has to consult the representatives of the pharmaceutical industry.[243] For all other cases, Council Regulation 2309/93 prescribes that the Management Board, in agreement with the Commission, must develop "appropriate" contacts between the EMEA and the representatives of the industry, the consumers and the patients and the health professions.[244]

Clearly, the pharmaceutical industry has a great interest in the activities of the EMEA and seeks regular contacts with this body. The EMEA, for its part, seeks to encourage a dialogue between the agency and the pharmaceutical companies as future applicants. To this end, the EMEA held in 1997 several "Info-Days" which were attended by 100–200 representatives from the industry.[245] In addition, it expects greater dialogue with the future applicants through the giving of scientific advice (in accordance with Article 51(j) of Council Regulation 2309/93) to companies during the course of research and development programmes, sometimes many years before an application is submitted. Hearings with applicant companies are also organised. Furthermore, the EMEA is carrying out a joint project with the European Federation of Pharmaceutical

---

[238] *Ibid.*

[239] And the CVMP, see Resolution of the Consumer Consultative Council adopted on 12 Mar. 1991, point 3, printed in the 3rd report of the House of Lords Select Committee on the European Communities on the EMEA, above n. 211, at 66.

[240] See Art. 8 of Council Reg. 2062/94, above n. 21.

[241] This precarious situation was revealed by the Executive Director of the EMEA, Mr Sauer, during the Conference on the New Agencies, organised by the Robert Schuman Centre of the European University Institute, Florence, 1–2 Mar. 1996.

[242] Art. 6(5) of Council Reg. 2309/93, above n. 119.

[243] *Ibid.*, Art. 58.

[244] *Ibid.*, Art. 65.

[245] The EMEA Activity Report of 1997, sect. 2.3.

Industries' Association (EFPIA) to learn more about the performance of the new registration procedures by means of a questionnaire.[246] Moreover, joint EMEA/EFPIA workshops are held on project management issues in order to reach a common understanding on key issues of the management of centralised procedures with the industry.[247]

The wish on the part of the EMEA to build up a good relationship with the pharmaceutical companies is, however, brought to the extreme where it also organises a football match, EMEA *v.* Pharmaceutical Industry (EFPIA), to celebrate 9 May (Europe Day).[248] Since such situations risk transgressing the boundaries of a mere "good relationship" between the regulators and the regulated and could lead to "capture", they should, in my opinion, be avoided.

In order to avoid the EMEA being "captured", not only the transparency of the whole process but also the possibility of other interested parties participating in and being informed about the authorisation procedures and the activities of the EMEA and the CPMP gains in importance. Some initiatives in this direction are already taken today by the EMEA, which organises meetings with representatives from consumers, patients, health care professionals and the industry. Since decisions on authorisation or pharmacovigilance are most likely to be taken at the CPMP level, interested parties have demonstrated their desire to establish working relationships with the CPMP. Right from the beginning, both the EMEA and the Commission were approached by several European and international organisations with a request for a observer status on the CPMP and the CVMP. Following a proposal from the Commission, the Management Board decided to invite the European Pharmacopoeia to certain working groups.[249] Without granting them an official observer status, the EMEA has invited several other interested parties to CPMP meetings, immediately after a scheduled CPMP meeting. In 1997, for example, the EMEA invited various interested parties to such CPMP "debriefing" meetings, which the EMEA intends to hold on a quarterly basis, among which were both consumer representatives (the European Consumers' Organisation, BEUC) and the industry representatives (the European Federation of Pharmaceutical Industries' Association, EFPIA).[250] No information is, however, available about the form and content of such meetings.

---

[246] See, e.g., the CPMP's Press Release of 24 Oct. 1997 (CPMP/921/97).

[247] See the EMEA Newsletter Human Medicines Unit, no. 3, Nov. 1997, at 5.

[248] Annex IV to the CPMP's Press Release of 16 May 1997 (CPMP/389/97) thus reports: "To celebrate Europe Day, the European Medicines Evaluation Agency (EMEA) played football against the European Federation of Pharmaceutical Industries' Associations (EFPIA) on 12 May at Mile End (London). The EMEA team comprised representatives from the Committee for Proprietary Medicinal Products (CPMP) and the EMEA Secretariat. The composition of a very strong and able industry team was arranged by EFPIA, with the participation of AESGP. A collection took place in support of the Cancer Research Campaign. The score was as follows: Industry: 5—EMEA: 1. Congratulations to the winning team!."

[249] The EMEA Activity Report of 1995, 14.

[250] Other invitees were: the Association Européenne des Specialités Pharmaceutique Grand Public (AESGP), the European Generic Manufacturers Association (EGA), the Standing Committee

For interested parties, it is important to have discussions at Management Board level, too, since it is the Management Board which addresses general policy questions, such as the development of indicators and goals to be applied to the agency and examines how the agency can best contribute to the improvement of human and animal health.[251] Recognising this, the EMEA has organised workshops with the participants from the national authorities, European interest groups representing patients, consumers and the pharmaceutical industry and representatives of specialised media, to discuss, for example, transparency of and access to EMEA documents.[252] Although this initiative is certainly to be judged positively, the *ad hoc* and voluntary character of such arrangements seems insufficient to guarantee that interested parties participate or are informed.[253] The definition of "appropriate" contacts and the manner in which contacts are established ultimately depend on the goodwill of the Management Board and the Commission; they determine *who* may participate, *where* and *when*. In this field one should therefore give thought to a proper model of interest participation too.

As a model of interest participation in this field, the pluralistic approach adopted in the French authorisation scheme might be considered. In this case, two representatives of the pharmaceutical industry, one representative of health insurance funds and one representative of consumer associations may participate in the deliberations of the Commission d'Authorisation de Mise sur le Marché des Medicaments which advises on the authorisation of medicinal products and which is composed of pharmacological and medical experts.[254] These representatives have observer status and are also obliged to observe a rule of absolute secrecy.[255] Since, however, problems of "representativity" are bound to arise here, too, it seems desirable to have further means of enabling the wider participation of all parties concerned. One could again consider using a kind of public notice and comment procedure, publish decisional intentions in the Official Journal or on the Internet, and invite all interested parties to make their observations or comments known. The wide use the EMEA currently makes of the Internet to make information available to the public, together with its policy on access to its documents, goes in this direction.

---

of European Doctors and the Groupement des Pharmaciens de l'Union Européenne (GPUE). Other groups invited to the EMEA meetings were: the Drug Information Association (DIA) the European Association of Genetic Support Groups (EAGS), Health Action International (HAI), the International Federation of Associations of Pharmaceutical Physicians (IFAPP), the International Society of Drug Bulletins (ISDB) and the Pan-European Federation of Regulatory Affairs Societies (PEFRAS): the EMEA Activity Report of 1997, sect. 2.3.

[251] To this end, the Board in 1995 set up two Working Groups on Performance Indicators and Public Health, the EMEA Activity Report of 1995, 14.

[252] The EMEA Press Release of 31 Oct. 1997.

[253] See also sect. 4.7.

[254] In accordance with Act no. 84–309 of 26 Apr. 1984, JO of 28 April 1984. See Hancher, above n. 82, at 124 ff. and Reich, above n. 84, at 24.

[255] See also Hart, who suggests the adjudication of participatory rights to consumers which can appoint competent experts to take part as observers in the CPMP: Hart, above n. 81 at 353.

4.7. Transparency and Access to Documents

The very fact that a clearly identifiable agency with clearly defined tasks has been created, instead of an obscure Commission division or an equally opaque committee, should, in principle, create greater transparency. The EMEA's intentions of following an open and transparent policy have been made clear from the beginning.[256] Membership of both the Management Board and the CPMP is advertised and the assessment reports of the agency and the reasons for its favourable opinion are, on request, also made public to interested persons.[257] In this context, the Internet already plays an important and impressive role in providing information about the EMEA and details on the pharmaceutical sector in general. The so-called EudraNet (European Union Drug Regulatory Authorities Network),[258] for example, provides information on the EMEA in general, including its annual activity reports, its Management Board (press releases), the CPMP and CVMP (calendar of meetings, press releases, standard operational procedures, guidelines and European public assessment reports) and the addresses of the national authorities competent in the authorisation of medicines. This site also provides a link to the Commission's DGIII. The wide use of the Internet is, therefore, certainly an important step towards more open and public drug regulation.

Encouraged by the Code of Conduct on Access to Documents adopted by the Council and the Commission and the recommendation of the European Ombudsman that agencies, too, should adopt rules on access to documents,[259] the EMEA formally adopted in December 1997 a decision on access to its documents.[260] The Decision is based on the premise that the public should have the widest possible access to documents produced by the EMEA. Exceptions to this rule are made for confidential documents or preparatory documents as well as documents from third parties held by the EMEA.

4.8. Accountability of Community Pharmaceutical Regulation

Transparency is equally significant for the accountability of the Agency. An important instrument of control is the activity report, which the EMEA makes available to the public annually.[261] Further control of the EMEA is exercised by the Member States, the Commission and the Parliament, through their representatives on the Management Board. In addition to this instrument of control, the Parliament has significant power as regards the budget of the Agency. The impor-

---

[256] See the EMEA Activity Report of 1995, 6.
[257] Art. 12 of Council Reg. 2309/93, above n. 119.
[258] See http://www.eudra.org (homepage).
[259] See Chap. 2.
[260] Published within the framework of the EudraNet.
[261] *Ibid.*

tance of this instrument cannot be underestimated as, whilst it has financial resources of its own, the Agency depends for half of its revenues on the subsidies of the Community. The readiness of the Parliament to invoke this power to ensure control and transparency was underlined during a conference held in Florence on the "New Agencies",[262] where the representative of the Parliament stated that:

"It took until 1995, however, before the Parliament actually woke up and said: we will not grant any financial powers to these agencies, we will not inscribe them into the budget unless we have more clarity about a number of specific points. That is where the whole question of 'reserve' came in. The agencies here know that, in budgetary terms, they fall under the so-called non-compulsory expenditure. This non-compulsory expenditure part, which is about fifty per cent of the overall budget, is finally determined by the Parliament. The Parliament can, therefore, use its powers over non-compulsory expenditure, in a certain sense, to re-orient the budget".[263]

The Court of Auditors, which examines all the revenue, can further exercise control and expenditure of bodies established by the Community.[264]

4.9. The Right to a Hearing and Appeal Procedures

In many national authorisation procedures, the applicant is assigned the right to be heard and/or the right of appeal to a body other than the one issuing the opinion.[265] The possibility of forwarding written and oral explanations was introduced under the former multi-state procedure[266] and was also included within the pharmacovigilance procedure.[267] Under the Community system, however, the applicant may "appeal" should the CPMP plan to issue a negative opinion. Since this procedure consists of an "appeal" to the same body, composed of the same members, it is possibly best termed as a second reading rather than a proper appeal procedure. Consequently, doubts may be expressed about the authenticity and effectiveness of such a procedure. The industry has thus expressed its concern about the lack of a suitable system of hearings and appeals.[268] Since the right to a hearing has been recognised by the Court in

---

[262] Conference on "The New European Agencies", organised by the Robert Schuman Centre of the European University Institute, Florence, 1–2 Mar. 1996. See for the conference report, Kreher, above n. 2. The agencies are very much aware of the power of the Parliament, as was demonstrated by the lively discussion between the heads of the new agencies and the representative of the Parliament, L.J. Brinkhorst, rapporteur of the 1997 Community Budget, during this conference.

[263] See Brinkhorst, above n. 36, at 77.

[264] See, e.g., its Report on the financial statements of the European Agency for the Evaluation of Medicinal Products (EMEA, London) (Financial Year 1996), together with the agency's replies [1997] OJ C393/18.

[265] This is, for instance, the case in the Netherlands (Art. 3(3), Wet op de Geneesmiddelenvoorziening: see Schutjens, above n. 84, at 20, and in the United Kingdom, see Smith, above n. 84.

[266] Art. 14 of Dir. 75/319, as amended by Dir. 83/570/EEC, above n. 103.

[267] See the 1991 Report on the activities of the CPMP, above n. 105 and SEC(93)771.

[268] See the Memorandum by the Association of the British Pharmaceutical Industry, in written evidence to the House of Lords Select Committee on the European Communities, above n. 211, 67–8.

various cases,[269] its absence in the authorisation procedure should be considered to be an infringement of the general principles governing the Community. In order to repair this situation, one could think of an appeal system in which appeals are heard by a different panel within the CPMP and which enables representatives from the companies to appear in person.[270]

4.10.   The EMEA as an "Independent" Regulatory Agency?

In its current form, the EMEA is not an alternative to the former committee structure but it is actually *based on* the "scientific" committees, CPMP and CVMP. In particular, it provides an administrative framework in which these committees operate. Decision-making on licensing is, moreover, subjected to the regulatory committee procedure. Although the Commission had initially proposed that the EMEA should be given a few autonomous decision-making powers,[271] the extreme caution of the Council to remain within the limits allegedly set by the *Meroni* cases determined that even such powers were removed.[272] Instead, these powers were delegated to the Commission.[273]

As argued in section 4.4.2., however, it is highly likely that the EMEA *de facto* adopts the decisions on the authorisation or monitoring of medicines. Whether *de facto* delegation takes place will, in practice, depend on whether the Commission's final decision merely rubberstamps the CPMP opinion or whether it adopts it as its own. This question necessitates further empirical research, in which the particular role of the Standing Committee also needs to be scrutinised. It is nevertheless clear that to a certain extent the EMEA currently exhibits certain advantageous characteristics traditionally associated with "independent" regulatory agencies:[274] it provides scientific expertise and contributes to greater transparency and accountability. In terms of reducing the Commission's workload—another traditional rationale for regulatory agencies and the main reason for the creation of the EMEA—there would nonetheless be

[269] See, for instance, Case C–269/90, above n. 229. See also Chap. 2 and the case law referred to there.

[270] See Hankin, above n. 114 , at 65.

[271] See, for instance, Arts. 6(5) and 15(4) of the amended Commission proposal [1991] OJ C310/7.

[272] E.g., the Commission had proposed that the EMEA should have the power to adopt appropriate arrangements for the examination of variations to the terms of a marketing authorisation (Art. 15(4) of the Commission proposal) and to draw up guidance on the collection, verification and presentation of adverse reaction reports (Art. 24 of the Commission proposal). See above n. 43.

[273] Together with the removal of these few autonomous powers allotted to the agency by the Commission in its proposal, also the possibility for Member States, members of the Management Board and third parties directly involved, to refer any act of the agency to the Commission to be examined as regards its legality (Art. 59 of its proposal for a Council Reg., above n. 43) was deleted by the Reg.

[274] See, for instance, R. Baldwin/C. McCrudden, *Regulation and Public Law* (London, 1987), 4–7, and J.L. Boxum, "Zelfstandige bestuursorganen en de greep van ministers op de bestuurlijke organisaties", in J.W.M. Engels *et al.* (eds.), *De Rechtsstaat herdacht* (Zwolle, 1989), 255–65.

good reason to delegate the decision-making powers on the authorisation of medicines to the EMEA as well. Further, a more "independent" regulatory agency may address the concerns of consumer organisations (but not only these) that the Commission favours industrial interests far too much, although, in turn, it simultaneously raises fears for capture.

These elements, together with the assumption that the EMEA already takes *de facto* decisions on the authorisation or monitoring of medicines, may give credence to the argument that the Agency should be made formally independent, a model which has, for example, been adopted in the Netherlands.[275] This raises the question whether the current Treaty allows for the establishment of an independent regulatory agency in addition to the institutions.

4.10.1. *The Possibility of Delegating Decision-making Powers to the EMEA under Current Law*

On the basis of the arguments advanced in section 3.2. it could be argued that even under current law the EMEA can be delegated decision-making powers provided that the Community's institutional balance, its system of "check and balances", is respected. It stems from a "Member State-oriented" understanding of the principle of the balance of powers that the powers of both the institutions and the Member States need to be respected. Hereby, however, instead of prohibiting the delegation of free decision-making powers, the actual means of controlling the autonomy of the Agency should be focused upon.[276] The importance

---

[275] Here, the Medicines Evaluation Board (*College ter Beoordeling van Geneesmiddelen*) has officially been empowered to register medicinal products. See, for instance, Schutjens, above n. 84. Within the Community long traditions of such agencies exist. For instance, in France, the term *"autorité administrative indépendente"* was used for the first time by the legislature in 1978 to define the newly established *"Commission nationale de l'information et des libertés"*, created by the Act of 6 Jan. 1978. Whilst, before that date, independent administrative bodies had been instituted on a irregular basis (the first body being created in 1941), from that moment onwards various such bodies were created. See C. Teitgen-Colly, "Les autorités administratives indépendentes: histoire d'une institution", in C.A. Colliard/G. Timsitv (eds.), *Les autorités administratives indépendentes* (Paris, 1988), 21–6, and M.J. Guédon, *Les autorités administratives indépendentes* (Paris, 1991). In the UK, numerous Boards and Commissions dealing with matters of central and local administration were set up in the 18th century. See Constitutional Reform Centre, Regulatory Agencies in the United Kingdom, in: Parliamentary Affairs, 1991, 505–20. After a period of decline, agencies began to proliferate again with the growth of the welfare state. The creation of the Independent Television Authority in 1954, which was the first body having at its disposal a combination of powers (adjudicating issues between parties, developing general policies and enjoying relative independence), was followed by a host of regulatory agencies in the 1960s: see Baldwin/McCrudden, above n. 274, 13 ff. See also G. Majone, "The European Community: An 'Independent Fourth Branch of Government'?", in G. Brüggemeier (ed.), *Verfassungen für ein ziviles Europa* (Baden-Baden, 1994), 13 ff. See also R.A.W. Rhodes, *The New European Agencies. Agencies in British Government: Revolution or Evolution?*, EUI Working Paper RSC 96/51 (Florence, 1996). The American experience of regulatory bodies, which goes back to 1887 with the creation of the Interstate Commerce Commission (in relation to interstate railroad traffic) is well-known. See, in general, M. Shapiro, *Who Guards the Guardians Judicial Control of Administration* (Athens/London, 1988) and D.R. Whitnah (ed.), *Government Agencies* (Westport, Conn., 1983).

[276] See Chap. 2.

of controlling mechanisms, instead of prohibition of delegation of decision-making powers to bodies other than the institutions, has been emphasised by the Court in *Reiff*, concerning competition law.[277] In this case, the Court accepted the delegation of certain tasks to a German private (self-regulatory) commission of experts from the transport sector by the German Ministry of Transport. However, at the same time, it underlined the necessity for the public authorities to be able to substitute the decisions taken by that commission with their own decisions, and thus remain responsible.[278]

Thus, the EMEA as an "independent" regulatory agency should remain under "control".[279] In this way, the EMEA should be subject to the political oversight of the Parliament.[280] The control and influence by the Parliament could be guaranteed through its representatives on the Management Board as well as its appropriate budgetary powers, as currently occurs. Further, Member States' influence could be ensured through their participation in the EMEA, thus setting a transnational governance structure between the Community and the Member States. However, the conferring of powers to grant or refuse authorisation of medicinal products on the EMEA[281] might be particularly problematic in terms of how to ensure the Commission's supervision and the Court's controlling powers. These issues will be analysed separately.

4.10.1.1. The Commission's Powers: Supervision of the Agency

As regards the Commission's powers, the balance of powers remains intact even where acts having the force of law are delegated to the EMEA on the condition that the delegated powers are supervised by the Commission. In this way, the latter retains political responsibility for acts adopted by the EMEA. The practical supervision of the agency by the Commission might occur in several ways:

(a) Appeal to the Commission

One possibility is to make the agency's decisions subject to appeal to the Commission.[282] This solution is, for example, taken up by the Regulation on the Health and Safety at Work Agency:

> "Member States, members of the Administrative Board and third parties directly and personally involved may refer to the Commission any act of the Agency, whether express or implied, for the Commission to examine the legality of that act.

---

[277] Case C–185/91, *Bundesanstalt für den Güterfernverkehr* v. *Gebrüder Reiff* [1993] ECR I–5801.

[278] See also Ch. Joerges, "Scientific Expertise in Social Regulation and the European Court of Justice: Legal Frameworks for Denationalised Governance Structures", in Ch. Joerges/K.H. Ladeur/E. Vos (eds.), *Integrating Scientific Expertise into Regulatory Decision-Making. National Traditions and European Innovations* (Baden-Baden, 1997), 318.

[279] See M. Shapiro, "The Problems of Independent Agencies in the United States and the European Union" (1997) 4 *JEPP* 276–91.

[280] In the American context, agencies are, for instance, definitively under the control of Congress: see Shapiro, above n. 279.

[281] The same, e.g., applies to leaving questions of trade marks and plant variety rights to be decided by the Trade Mark Office (above n. 20) and the Plant Variety Office (above n. 22).

[282] Merz, above n. 12, at 408.

Referral shall be made to the Commission within fifteen days of the day on which the party concerned became aware of the act in question.

The Commission shall take a decision within one month. If no decision has been taken within this period, the case shall be deemed to have been dismissed".[283]

Such a construction equally ensures control by the Parliament and the Court.

(b) Control by Means of the Agency Budget

Commission supervision may also be secured through the control of the EMEA's budget. A right to supervise the budget of the EMEA and of other agencies constitutes an important instrument of control. At present, the EMEA is still 50 per cent financed by the Community, whilst Council Regulation 2309/93 requires it to submit to the Commission and the Court of Auditors detailed accounts of all its revenue and expenditure. Likewise, the Parliament has important powers of control over the agency and other agencies as it has a right of approval over the general Community budget. This is not only of great importance from the viewpoint of the principle of the institutional balance of powers, but certainly also from the point of view of accountability.

(c) The Definition of the Conditions under which the EMEA Should Operate by the Community Institutions

Another possible control method is that of the specification of the conditions which products have to meet by Community institutions, in order to prevent giving full discretion to the agency.[284] The task of the EMEA would then be simply to check whether these conditions had been fulfilled or not; a purely factual task. The latter option has been applied in the case of the registration of Community trade marks and Community plant variety rights, which in the main regulation obliges the Council to lay down the requirements for the registration of a Community mark or right. Council Regulation 40/94 on the Community trade mark, for example, requires the Trade Mark Office to examine applications for the Community mark, and possibly to refuse registration. The Commission's task is likewise more limited, being restricted to the specification of technical conditions, such as filing conditions and fees, in the implementation regulation.[285]

---

[283] Art. 22 of Council Reg. 2062/94, above n. 21. Both Art. 18 of Council Reg. 337/75 establishing the European Centre for the Development of Vocational Training (above n. 10) and Art. 22 of Reg. 1365/75 establishing the European Foundation for the Improvement of Living and Working Conditions (above n. 11) include an identical provision. The same provision was also included in the Commission proposal on the EMEA (Art. 59) (above n. 43) but was removed in the final version of the Reg. adopted by the Council.

[284] One could also imagine the situation in which the Commission gave a mandate to an agency to adopt a decision under its responsibility. However, the Treaty provisions and the Rules of Procedure of the Commission seemingly only allow for a situation in which the Commission empowers one or more of its members to take, on its behalf and under its responsibility, clearly defined management or administrative measures, provided that the principle of collective responsibility is respected. See Art. 11, Rules of Procedure of the Commission [1993] OJ L230/15, confirmed by the Court in, e.g., Case 5/85, *AKZO Chemie BV et al.* v. *Commission* [1986] ECR 2585.

[285] Art. 140 of Reg. 40/94, above n. 20. See Commission Reg. 2868/95 implementing Council Reg. 40/94 on the Community trade mark [1995] OJ L303/1.

The method applied in the Community Trade Mark System seems to mirror the Weberian belief in the superiority of rule-based governance.[286] In other words, the Council lays down very detailed rules on whether or not a trade mark may be registered as a Community trade mark, rules which also guide the Commission on how to determine more technical rules. The Trade Mark Office is merely required to check whether the conditions laid down in the Regulation have been met. Council Regulation 40/94 determines that where an application for a trade mark meets the requirements of the Regulation,[287] the trade mark shall be registered as a Community trade mark.

(d) Combination of the Various Options

The options discussed above, however, may give rise to several difficulties. Option (a) entails only *ex post* control and may be criticised as it continues to allow a body not foreseen by the Treaty to adopt measures which have an impact on the rights of citizens and the powers of the Member States. Thus, objections would arise particularly in relation to politically sensitive health and safety issues, since very technical fields, such as pharmaceuticals, must be regulated with an eye to normative values. The same may be true with regard to option (b) which does not even provide for the possibility that the Commission might make the final decision. Option (c) is likewise troublesome since it fails to answer the question whether individual decisions are subject to judicial review by the Court, and raises issues of legal uncertainty since individuals cannot be sure of judicial protection for their rights. The latter option may be equally difficult to apply to the specific case of health and safety regulation.

Therefore, a combination of these options seems most likely to ensure the balance of powers. An example of this combination is found in Article 53 Euratom in relation to the Supply Agency, which requires that:

> "1. The Agency shall be under the supervision of the Commission which shall issue directives to it, possess a right of veto over its decisions and appoint its Director-General and Deputy Director-General.
>
> 2. Any act, whether implied or expressed, performed by the Agency in the exercise of its right of option or of its exclusive right to conclude supply contracts, may be referred by the parties concerned to the Commission, which shall give a decision thereon within one month."

---

[286] M. Weber, *Economy and Society: An Outline of Interpretive Sociology*, edited by G. Roth/C. Wittich (Berkeley/Los Angeles/London, 1978), ii, 958–79. This belief was echoed by Lowi who called for a "juridical democracy": governance based on clear legislative standards for bureaucratic action or, failing that, on clear rules formulated by the bureaucracies themselves. This "juridical democracy" should, according to Lowi, restore democratic accountability, which had been obfuscated by the exercise of administrative discretion in the modern American state which would have led to the domination of the state by interest groups, thereby weakening popular control and creating new structures of privilege: Th.J., Lowi, *The End of Liberalism* (New York, 1969), 85–93. See also J.Q. Wilson, *Bureaucracy. What Government Agencies Do and Why They Do It* (New York, 1989), 335.

[287] And where no notice of opposition has been given or where such a notice has been definitively rejected.

A similar provision for agencies set up in the EC context would give the Commission ample powers to control and to intervene, if necessary, in the EMEA's decision-making. This, together with the budgetary powers, seems to be an optimal way to delegate decision-making powers to the EMEA, whilst leaving the Community institutions sufficient means of control and likewise ensuring judicial review. Thus, without prejudice to the need to reduce its workload, the Commission might be guaranteed control over the agency through a right to issue directives to it, a veto right over the agency's decisions and a right to appoint its Director. For reasons of legal certainty and coherency, a legal basis for the creation of agencies and the delegation of authority should nonetheless be introduced.[288]

4.10.1.2. Judicial Review

The question remains whether, under the current Treaty provisions, the Court can exercise judicial review where the EMEA would be empowered to adopt acts which have legal force and which are not made subject to an appeal to the Commission. Article 173 solely provides for the review of acts adopted jointly by the Parliament and the Council, acts of the Council, acts of the Commission and acts of the European Central Bank and the Parliament which are intended to produce legal effects *vis-à-vis* third parties.[289] Currently, this question arises in relation to, for example, the Trade Mark Office.

Can agency decisions be subjected to judicial review by the Court? One solution would be to include a provision giving the Court jurisdiction under Articles 173, 175, 177(b) and 184 in the founding agency legislation. The Trade Mark Regulation, for instance, stipulates that an appeal be made against decisions taken by any section of the Office (the Examiners, the Opposition Divisions, the Administration of Trade Marks and Legal Division and the Cancellation Divisions). Initially, the appeal goes to the Boards of Appeal,[290] though a procedure similar to the Article 173 action determines that such decisions are then subject to review by the Court. Article 63 of this Regulation determines that:

"1. Actions may be brought before the Court of Justice against decisions of the Boards of Appeal on appeals.

2. The action may be brought on the grounds of lack of competence, infringement of an essential procedural requirement, infringement of the Treaty, of this Regulation or of any rule of law relating to their application or misuse of power.

3. The Court of Justice has jurisdiction to annul or to alter the contested decision.

4. The action shall be open to any party to proceedings before the Boards of Appeal adversely affected by its decision.

5. The action shall be brought before the Court of Justice within two months of the date of notification of the decision of the Boards of Appeal.

---

[288] Ehlermann suggested that this should be done during the 1996–7 IGC: see Ehlermann, above n. 8, 484–5. However, the ICG has failed to address this topic.

[289] See H. Kruck, "Artikel 173. Gerichtshof", in H. Von der Groeben/J. Thiesing/C.-D. Ehlermann, *Kommentar zum EWG-Vertrag* (Baden-Baden, 1991), 4536 ff.

[290] Art. 57 of Council Reg. 40/94, above n. 20.

6. The Office shall be required to take the necessary measures to comply with the judgment of the Court of Justice".[291]

Furthermore, virtually all agencies have appointed the Court as the competent organ in disputes relating to non-contractual liability. The extension of judicial review to bodies other than those laid down in the Community's constitutional charter—the Treaty[292]—by simple legislative act may, however, be argued to be unconstitutional. However, the Court might even be willing to accept jurisdiction to review the legality of agency decisions, should the founding statutes not make provision for judicial review.[293] A first indication of this may be found in the Treaty itself, since Article 177(c) stipulates that the Court has jurisdiction in the interpretation of the statutes of bodies set up by a Council act, where those statutes so provide. Other indications are found in the case law of the Court itself. In this vein, particular attention must be paid to the Court's judgment in *Les Verts*, which could be applied *mutatis mutandis* to agency decisions, even though agencies do not qualify as "institutions".[294] In this case, the Court ruled that excluding parliamentary acts from review under Article 173 would be contrary "both to the spirit of the Treaty as expressed in Article 164 and to its system".[295] As the Court further elucidated, the Community is based on the Rule of Law, permitting the Court to review the legality of all acts[296] adopted by the institutions.[297]

From this reasoning, it might be deduced that no decisional act, including those emanating from bodies other than institutions, might escape judicial review, any Community act whatsoever being subject to the Community Rule of Law.[298] In addition, in *Sevince*,[299] which was decided in the context of an international agreement concluded between the Community and Turkey, the Court ruled that since it was competent to give preliminary rulings on the agreement in question, being an act adopted by one of the Community institutions,[300] it also had jurisdiction to give rulings on "the interpretation of the decisions adopted by the authority established by the agreement and entrusted with

---

[291] A similar provision is included in Council Reg. 2100/94 on Community plant variety rights (Art. 73), above n. 18. In the Reg. on the Drugs Monitor Centre, it is simply stipulated that the Court has jurisdiction in actions brought against the Centre under the conditions provided for in Art. 173 (Art. 17 of Council Reg. 302/93, above n. 14).

[292] See, *inter alia*, Case 294/83, *Parti Ecologiste "Les Verts"* v. *European Parliament* [1986] ECR 1339, at 1365, and *Opinion 1/91* [1991] ECR I–6079, at I–6102.

[293] See Lenaerts, above n. 59, 45–6.

[294] *Ibid.*

[295] Case 294/83, above n. 292, at 1366.

[296] The Court has always broadly interpreted "measures" as comprising "all measures taken by the institutions, whatever their nature or form, designed to produce legal effects": see, for instance, Case 22/70, *Commission* v. *Council (ERTA)* [1971] ECR 263 and, more recently, Joined Cases C–181/91 & C–248/91, *Parliament* v. *Council and Commission (Bangladesh)* [1993] ECR I–3685 and Case C–325/91, *France* v. *Commission* [1993] ECR I–3283.

[297] Case 294/83, above n. 292, at 1365.

[298] See Lenaerts, above n. 59, at 46.

[299] Case C–192/89, *Sevince* v. *Staatssecretaris van Justitie* [1990] ECR I–3461.

[300] See Case 181/73, *Haegeman* v. *Belgian State* [1974] ECR 449.

responsibility for its implementation".[301] Furthermore, the Court's Article 215 jurisprudence seems to adopt a broad interpretation of the term "institutions". In Case C–370/89, *SGEEM* v. *European Investment Bank*[302] the Court held that the term "institutions" also covered Community organs such as the European Investment Bank. Although the latter was an organ created by the Treaty itself and not by secondary Community legislation, taken together these elements seem nonetheless to indicate that the Court may be prepared to consider the legality of agency decisions under Article 173. However, from the point of view of legal certainty the inclusion of an explicit provision in Article 173 itself and in the specific regulations creating the agencies will be necessary.[303]

4.10.2. *Capture*

Arguments pleading for greater decisional independence for the EMEA, however, are often countered by one of the most frequently heard critiques of regulatory agencies: namely, that they are easily influenced and subverted to the ends of those who they are supposed to regulate; a phenomenon generally referred to as "agency capture".[304] It is indeed true that, at present, the pharmaceutical industry's attention is increasingly focused on the EMEA and that there is a certain risk of the EMEA being captured. Yet, the problem of capture is a general problem for all regulators and there is little reason to assume that the Agency would be more vulnerable to capture than the Commission would be.[305] This is clearly illustrated by the BSE crisis.[306] The problem of capture should, therefore, be addressed by ensuring transparency, political supervision and deliberative interaction with interested parties[307] rather than by preventing the EMEA from becoming a more "independent" regulatory agency.

5. CONCLUSION

In this chapter, the agency model was examined in the field of pharmaceuticals as a second regulatory approach to Community health and safety regulation. Recourse to an agency in this field is part of the general trend which sees a greater centralisation of powers at Community level, but also a functional decentralisation of tasks to agencies set up within the Community's institutional

---

[301] Case C–192/89, above n. 299, at I–3501. See, in this sense, Lauwaars, above n. 5, 379–80.

[302] [1992] ECR I–6211.

[303] See Lenaerts, above n. 59, at 46.

[304] See, for instance, Baldwin/McCrudden, above n. 274, 9–10; Majone, above n. 275.

[305] See, for instance, the above-mentioned criticism of consumer organisations against the Commission's practice in drug regulation.

[306] See Chap. 3.

[307] See, for instance, the Commission's initiatives to regulate lobby activities, in its Communication on an open and structured dialogue between the Commission and special interest groups [1993] OJ C63/2. See also S. Mazey/J. Richardson, "The Commission and the Lobby", in G. Edwards/D. Spence, *The European Commission* (London, 1994), 169–201.

architecture. Generally speaking, these agencies meet the ever-growing need for more information on specific topics and are of growing importance. The creation of agencies is, however, problematic, in that no Treaty provision explicitly provides for the possibility of creating agencies and the delegation of powers to them gives rise to varying opinions, legal uncertainty and, consequently, inconsistent behaviour on the part of the Community institutions. Close examination of the current Treaty provisions and the Court's case law reveals, however, that the agencies currently set up within the institutional setting of the Community are in conformity with Community principles. The existing agencies may potentially even enhance the quality and legitimacy of Community decision-making. They produce more information, which potentially leads to more informed decision-making, and are more visible, which possibly facilitates the political oversight of their activities.

The creation of an agency in the field of pharmaceuticals was the last step on the Community's lengthy road towards the establishment of one internal market for pharmaceuticals. Existing and strict national legislative provisions for many years had hindered the entry of foreign, legally marketed, medicinal products into national markets. The intense degree of drug regulation was foremost a direct result of the Thalidomide tragedy and stems from the very nature of products which, albeit produced to cure illnesses, are inherently toxic and potentially very harmful. Whilst the Community initially sought to force the Member States mutually to recognise each others' medicinal products, this approach failed since the Member States appeared not to be prepared to accept pharmaceuticals produced and marketed on the basis of divergent traditions and cultures. This, together with industry's pressures to force open national markets, in turn forced the Commission to design a new system which would transfer the powers on the authorisation of medicinal products to the Community level and to establish the EMEA.

In the first instance, however, this new authorisation system met with resistance from the Member States because of its impact on other related Member States' powers which they were not keen to give up—the pricing of and reimbursement for medicines under public health systems as well as national birth control policies. This dilemma was therefore addressed by expressly excluding the latter powers from the new authorisation system. Involvement in complex risk assessment and the management of medicines have nonetheless posed various other problems for the Commission, such as the need for scientific expertise, the need to respect the Member States' political interests and the need to balance socio-economic interests. By resorting to the EMEA and the Standing Committee on Medicinal Products for Human Use, the Commission has attempted to overcome these difficulties. The political sensitivity of Member States towards medicine regulation, in particular, made the Commission design the new institutional framework on the free movement of medicinal products carefully.

Analysis of the role of the EMEA reveals its important role in this new system. Significantly, it provides the scientific opinion which forms the basis for marketing authorisation or refusal. Further, it co-ordinates pharmacovigilance and, on the request of pharmaceutical companies, it also provides scientific advice prior to an application for market authorisation. The EMEA, moreover, has an important co-ordinative role, easing contact between the Member States and the Community. Being composed of representatives of the Member States, the Commission and Parliament, it contributes to improved co-operation and implementation and attempts to enhance mutual trust between national administrations; one of the main problems which the Community faces especially in this sector. In accordance with a "Member State-oriented" institutional balance of powers and addressing subsidiarity, it thus included Member States within the organisational structure of the EMEA as well as the decisional process, thereby developing a multi-level governance structure in this area.

This strategy currently seems to work very well: industry is very eager to apply for the centralised Community licensing, even when not obliged (for "high-tech" medicinal products) to do so, while Member States, faced with the alternative of a binding Community decision in the decentralised procedure, are also prepared to recognise each others' authorisations. This is particularly eased by the creation of a continuous debate between the national competent authorities within the framework of a monthly meeting.

However, the agency model thus adopted by no means excludes resorting to committees. On the contrary, the agency is actually based on two existing committees, whilst the Commission's decision-making powers are subjected to the consultation of the Standing Committee on Medicinal Products for Human Use under the *contre-filet* variant of the regulatory procedure. In addition, other committees also play a role. Where today there is an overlap both in functions (at times even contradicting) and committee members, these bodies should be streamlined and possibly brought within the framework of the EMEA itself.

The Council has set two principles which govern this agency: "objectivity" of scientific advice and "independence" of EMEA's activities. The principle of "objectivity" relates to the severance of health protection considerations from economic and other considerations. However, the model adopted in practice involves the indirect consultation of scientific experts: the CPMP is composed of national experts in the evaluation of medicines (many of whom were members of the former CPMP) who represent their competent national authorities, and must, in turn, consult national scientific experts. Although this "two-tiered" model is advantageous for its flexibility in approaching such national experts, it is presumed that the CPMP does not consider solely "scientific", but also more normative, considerations. In order to guarantee the "independence" of EMEA's and the CPMP's work, members of both the CPMP and the Management Board, as well as rapporteurs and experts, are prohibited from having any financial or other interest in the pharmaceutical industry which could affect their impartiality. This principle is reinforced by a Statement of Principles governing the partnership between the EMEA and the National Competent Authorities.

The agency model raises the presumption (although empirical research still needs to be undertaken) that the potential forum function of the Standing Committee, as revealed in the previous chapter, is carried out within the EMEA itself, more specifically, within the CPMP. Hence, in contrast to the committee model adopted in the food sector, the Community regime on medicines seems to be unable to draw a clear distinction between risk assessment and risk management of medicinal products. Hence, the balancing of the socio-economic interests presumably takes place within the CPMP and not within the framework of the Standing Committee on Medicinal Products for Human Use. This observation is important in relation to the need to identify at which exact stage of the regulatory process interest participation should take place. Although the EMEA increasingly seeks contacts with interested parties (as required by Community legislation), the way in which contacts are made depends on the goodwill of the Management Board and the Commission; they determine *who* may participate, *where* and *when*. In this field, too, one should therefore reflect on a proper model of interest participation. Whilst here the pluralistic approach adopted in France, allowing both industry and consumer representatives to make observations in the deliberations of the relevant advisory scientific body, may be considered, the problem of "representativity" underlines the need for further means of enabling wider participation by all parties concerned. Thus in this field, too, one could consider the use of a kind of public notice and comment procedure, publishing decisional intentions in the Official Journal or on the Internet, and inviting all interested parties to make their observations or comments known. The wide use that the EMEA currently makes of the Internet to make information available to the public together with its policy on access to its documents goes into this direction. This would be a further step in the formulation of a public discourse on drug safety.

The need to define such principles clearly gains in importance where the pharmaceutical industry's attention increasingly focuses on the EMEA and there is a risk of capture. Where, admittedly, efficiency reasons require a good relationship between both the industry and the EMEA, the establishment of such relations is clearly a very sensitive and fragile matter. Definition of these principles together with a true right of hearing, or an effective appeal procedure, encourages plurality and the institutionalisation of informed discourse on the safety of medicinal products. Only against this background and with a definition of clear principles of supervision, can the allocation of regulatory powers to the EMEA be considered.

Health and Safety Regulation through Private Bodies—the Case of Technical Product Standards

1. INTRODUCTION

As the third regulatory model of Community health and safety regulation, the Community seeks the assistance of self-regulatory structures and resorts to private standardisation bodies to regulate the safety of technical consumer products.[1] Lack of expertise leads the Community to draw from extensive technical expertise available at private European standardisation bodies. This, however, carries with it the risk that product safety regulation becomes a privatised matter, favouring private, market-driven interests above public interests of health and safety protection. Thus, with regard to regulating technical product safety, the Community is confronted with the troublesome interrelationship of public and private interests.

As Chapter 2 demonstrated, the New Approach to Technical Harmonisation and Standards was launched by the Community first and foremost for efficiency reasons to accelerate decision-making. Consequently, the New Approach concentrates on the harmonisation of essential health and safety requirements, which may form justified obstacles to trade, and confers on the private European standardisation bodies the task of elaborating these requirements into technical standards. The significance of these bodies in Community regulation will increase even further where the Commission intends to expand the use of standardisation into other Community policies.[2] Their growing importance also stems from the general safety obligation placed on the producers by the Council Directive on general product safety. Although not using the reference to standards technique, this Directive will undoubtedly have an impact on the standards producers use in manufacturing their products, where it stipulates

---

[1] This is also referred to as product safety in the "narrow" sense. See Ch. Joerges, "Paradoxes of Deregulatory Strategies at Community level: The Example of Product Safety Policy", in G. Majone (ed.), *Deregulation or Re-regulation? A Regulatory Reform in Europe and the United States* (London, 1990), 181. Product safety regulation in the "broad" sense includes the regulation of other consumer products, such as foodstuffs and pharmaceuticals.

[2] The fields of foodstuffs and pharmaceuticals increasingly encroach upon standardisation, too. For instance, standardisation activities are undertaken for methods of analysis or sampling and good hygiene practices. See, e.g., Communication from the Commission to the Council and Parliament on the broader use of standardisation in Community policy, COM(95)412 final.

inter alia that, in the absence of specific national rules, the conformity of a product to the general safety requirement is assessed with regard to voluntary national standards which implement European standards or, if these do not exist, national standards.[3]

With the inclusion of the reference to standards technique, the New Approach links up with the common domestic division between legal provisions and technical norms. In most Member States this technique has commonly been resorted to. Technical rules, transferred from legislative provisions to the allegedly more flexible level of self-regulation, permit quicker adaptation to technical progress and permit representative co-operation by interested parties in industry and the civil society at large (such as the economy, science and technical monitoring groups as well as other interested and expert groups).[4] Yet, the use of the reference to standards technique and the involvement of private bodies in the regulatory process are not without controversy. The general application of the reference to standards technique in the New Approach raises concern about the privatisation of the regulatory process where the private standardisation organisations, principally performing private and commercial activities, need to carry out risk assessments. The assessment of risks in technical goods is not only a matter of technical expertise but also concerns the integration of normative values. Allowing the standardisation bodies to define in technical terms the safety objectives stipulated in the directives creates the danger that, in practice, it is the standardisation bodies which determine the level of safety, which is an issue of public interest. Although under the New Approach manufacturers of technical products are left free to decide how to reach the safety level required by the single directives, in practice, manufacturers will generally use the harmonised standards, as they will give their products the advantage of the refutable presumption of conformity and thus easier access to national markets.[5]

Hence, the Community is faced with a well-known dilemma. On the one hand, resorting to the technical knowledge of the standards bodies is necessary: neither the Commission, nor the Council, nor the Member States have the technical knowledge to carry out the work currently accomplished by thousands of qualified persons all over Europe and co-ordinated by the European standardisation bodies CEN and CENELEC, nor should they take on this work. On the other hand, however, it raises a public–private divide problem, since private

---

[3] See, in particular, Art. 4(2) of Council Dir. 92/59/EEC on general product safety [1992] OJ L228/24.

[4] See P. Marburger, *Die Regeln der Technik* (Köln/Berlin/Bonn/Munich, 1979), 117 ff. and Ch. Joerges/J. Falke/H.-W. Micklitz/G. Brüggemeier, *Die Sicherheit von Konsumgütern und die Entwicklung der Europäischen Gemeinschaften* (Baden-Baden, 1988), 136–7 (see also the English version: *European Product Safety, Internal Market Policy and the New Approach to Technical Harmonisation and Standards*, EUI Working Papers LAW 91/10–14 (Florence, 1991; http://www.iue.it/LAW/WP-Texts/Joerges91/).

[5] See, for instance, J. Pelkmans/M. Egan, *Fixing European Standards: Moving Beyond the Green Paper*, CEPS Working Document 65, Standards Programme, Paper 3 (Brussels, 1992), 14.

standard-setting risks becoming a mainly industry-driven and market-led matter, constrained by a cost-benefit analysis, which would not pay sufficient attention to "public" interests, such as health and safety protection. In this vein, the normative quality of this process may be endangered as it cannot be expected that industries contemplate "genuine" product safety considerations when they themselves are responsible for the production of standards.[6]

At the national level, the constitutional admissibility of the reference to standards technique continues to attract academic attention[7] and legal requirements have been formulated to encounter the constitutional objections advanced by several (German) authors.[8] However, such requirements—developed in different states under various constitutional realities—cannot just be transposed to the Community level. The peculiarities of the Community arena must be taken into account.

This chapter thus examines the difficulties which the Community encounters in regulating product safety and addresses the legal questions stemming from its use of standards adopted by private bodies in public regulatory decision-making.[9] To this end, it examines whether the use of the reference to standards technique in the New Approach constitutes an unlawful delegation of decision-making powers to the standardisation bodies and scrutinises questions of legitimacy. It is argued that in view of their public interest character, the setting of standards cannot be left to the commercial cost-benefit approach of private actors alone and needs to observe principles of transparency, participation of interests and control.

2. HEALTH AND SAFETY REGULATION THROUGH PRIVATE BODIES: THE CASE OF TECHNICAL PRODUCT STANDARDS

2.1. The Peculiarities of Technical Consumer Products and Standardisation

The market in technical products is characterised by its reliance on standardisation. It is not surprising that where standards set the technical specifications of products, thereby giving products access to the market, they are of critical importance to industry, and that consequently self-regulatory structures have been developed to produce standards. These standards:

---

[6] Joerges *et al.*, above n. 4, at 59 (EUI Working Paper Law 91/10, at 29).

[7] See, for instance, F. Gambelli, *Aspects juridiques de la normalisation et de la réglementation technique européen. Guide sur le droit technique et la normalisation* (Paris, 1994) and C. Stuurman, *Technische normen en het recht—beschouwingen over de interactie tussen het recht en technische normalisatie op het terrein van informatietechnologie en telecommunicatie* (Deventer, 1995).

[8] See, for an overview, Joerges *et al.*, above n. 4.

[9] See, for case studies on the use of private standards in public policy in the USA, for instance, R.E. Cheit, *Setting Safety Standards. Regulation in the Public and Private Sectors* (Berkeley/Los Angeles/Oxford, 1990).

"meet the requirements of manufacturers and the marketplace. The characterisation of materials and products, test methods to measure and assess performance and safety levels and other common data and definitions are indispensable to enhance the technological and economic efficiency of industries and services and facilitate the supplier/client relationship".[10]

Standardisation can be defined as the activity of establishing provisions for common and repeated use, aimed at the optimum degree of order in a given context.[11] The use of technical standards is by no means new, and dates back to ancient times. For example, in ancient Egypt the pyramids were built with standard measurements, and the Romans constructed their aqueducts according to standard measures, too. Over the centuries, a more systematic approach to technical standards evolved; resulting, for example, in the adoption of an international metric system in the 1870s.[12] The use of standards in commercial activities was further increased by the industrial revolution. Reliance on standardisation was a consequence of the development of industrial mass production which generated the need for the interchange and combination of production elements.[13]

Where the novel technical developments gave rise to new risks in the workplace, national regulators had traditionally focused on the prevention of both accidents at work and occupational diseases. Other accidents, such as home and leisure accidents, caused by the use of technical products have, however, only recently been recognised as an objective of regulatory concern since they initially appeared to give rise to less dramatic accidents.[14] This may explain the fact that in this field comprehensive self-regulatory structures developed, with which regulators, plagued by the rapid development of modern technology,[15] could easily associate.

---

[10] Jacques Repussard, Secretary General of CEN, *European Standards to build the Common Market—an Introduction*, CEN document (Brussels, 1995), 1.

[11] This definition is adhered to by the International Organisation for Standardisation (ISO). See CEN, *Standards for Access to the European Market*, edited by J. Abecassis (Brussels, 1995), 22.

[12] See W. Brinkmann, *Rechtliche Aspekte der Bedeutung von technischen Normen für den Verbraucherschutz*, DIN-Normungskunde, Band 20 (Berlin/Köln, 1984), 9; R.H. Roth, *Technische Normung im Recht. Wesen, Struktur, Kooperation zwischen Fachverbänden und Staat* (Zürich, 1983), 35 ff. Even earlier, the Venetians had developed standardised warships which enabled them to hold these ships next to each other in battle.

[13] Marburger, above n. 4, at 181; Ch. Joerges, "The New Approach to Technical Harmonisation and the Interests of Consumers: Reflections on the Requirements and Difficulties of a Europeanisation of Product Safety Policy", in R. Bieber/R. Dehousse/J. Pinder/J.H.H. Weiler (eds.), *1992: One European Market? A Critical Analysis of the Commission's Internal Market Strategy* (Baden-Baden, 1988), 189. See also Joerges *et al.*, above n. 4, at 55 (EUI Working Paper LAW 91/10, at 29).

[14] See, for instance, Joerges, above n. 1, and W.H.J. Rogmans, "Consumer Interest in Safety Related Standards for European Consumer Products" (1989) 12 *JCP* 193–205.

[15] See, for instance, for the use of vague and indefinite terms by means of which the (German) legislature attempts to tackle these problems, K.-H. Ladeur, "The Integration of Scientific and Technological Expertise into the Process of Standard-Setting According to German Law", in Ch. Joerges/K.H. Ladeur/E. Vos (eds.), *Integrating Scientific Expertise into Regulatory Decision-Making. National Traditions and European Innovations* (Baden-Baden, 1997), 77–100.

Therefore, although the forms of interaction between the state and the private standardisation bodies (and the way in which formal rights of participation of social groups is ensured) differ in the Member States, one principle has been generally accepted in this field: the elaboration of technical safety regulations should be performed by private standardisation organisations, thus drawing on and taking advantage of the technical expertise of industries.[16] This is not surprising, since "it is expensive to reinvent the wheel".[17] Technical product safety regulation is therefore characterised by this interplay between regulators and private standardisers, based on principles of flexibility and co-operation.[18] It aims, on the one hand, to prevent damage from technical products to the health and safety of persons, to the environment and other goods; and on the other hand, to ensure the performance of commercial activities.[19]

2.2. Standard-setting by the European Standardisation Bodies CEN and CENELEC: Description

In order to comprehend fully the problems flowing from the reliance on the European standardisation bodies, it is important to understand how these bodies are structured and how they operate. Therefore, first an overview of both the European standardisation bodies and the standard-setting process will be given.

2.2.1. The Creation of CEN and CENELEC

The awareness that the different technical standards could thwart the free circulation of goods across borders led to the early creation of supranational, European standardisation organisations.[20] In 1961, the European Committee

---

[16] Joerges *et al.*, above n. 4, at 56 (EUI Working Paper Law 91/10, at 31). Some Member States, such as Spain, Portugal and Greece, have, however, only recently resorted to this system. See the comparative study on the legal status of standards in European legal systems, commissioned by the European Commission, which is presently being carried out at the Centre for European Law and Politics in Bremen. Results are forthcoming in J. Falke/H. Schepel (eds.), *The Legal Status of Technical Standards in the Member States of the EU and of EFTA* (Baden-Baden, forthcoming).

[17] R.W. Hamilton, "The Role of Non-governmental Standards in the Development of Mandatory Standards Affecting Safety or Health" (1976) 56 *Texas Law Review*, 1379 ff, cited in Joerges *et al.*, above n. 4, at 56 (EUI Working Paper Law 91/10, at 31).

[18] See, for instance, Marburger, above n. 4, at 111, and J. Falke, "Normungspolitik der Europäischen Gemeinschaften zum Schutz von Verbrauchern und Arbeitnehmern" [1989] *Jahrbuch zur Staats- und Verwaltungswissenschaft* 217–46.

[19] See Marburger, above n. 4.

[20] This phenomenon has not been restricted to the European market. See, for instance, the standardisation organisation COPANT (Comisión Panamericana de Normas Technicas), the African Organisation for Standardisation (ARSO), the Asian Standards Advisory Committee (ASAC), the Pacific Area Standards Congress (PASC) and the Caribbean Common Market Standards Council (CARICOM). See G. Breulmann, *Normung und Rechtsangleichung in der Europäischen Wirtschaftsgemeinschaft* (Berlin, 1993), 40 (n. 41).

for Standardisation, CEN,[21] was set up by the national standardisation organisations of the EC and EFTA countries.[22] CEN is currently made up of 19 members, consisting of the national standardisation bodies of the EC and EFTA countries and of the Czech Republic.[23] It is presently based in Brussels.[24] CEN is an international association governed by Belgian private law[25] and aims at implementing standardisation throughout Europe to facilitate the development of the exchange of goods and services, by the elimination of barriers set by provisions of a technical nature.[26] A similar objective is followed by the European Committee for Electrotechnical Standardisation, CENELEC, which is also based in Brussels. CENELEC was formed in 1973 through the amalgamation of two pre-existing groupings, CENEL[27] and CENELCOM.[28] CENELEC, too, has 19 members from the national electrotechnical committees of the EC and EFTA countries and the Czech Republic.[29] In correspondence with the international standards organisations, the International Electrotechnical Committee (IEC) and the International Organisation of Standardisation (ISO), CENELEC deals with the standardisation in the electrotechnical sector, whilst CEN oversees all other sectors, with the exception of telecommunications, for which another European Standardisation body was established in 1988, the European Telecommunications Standards Institute (ETSI).[30] Both CEN and CENELEC are mainly financed by their members organisations, the Community and the EFTA.

2.2.2. The Organisational Structure of CEN and CENELEC

Since the organisational structures of both CEN and CENELEC are almost identical, they will be discussed together and any differences will be mentioned.

The General Assembly

The General Assembly is the supreme body of both CEN and CENELEC. It is formed, on a permanent basis, by the national standardisation organisations of

---

[21] Art. 2 of the Statutes of CEN adopted by the General Assembly on 25 June 1992 officially declared CEN as the abbreviated name of this organisation, whilst its full name, in view of the three official languages of the organisation (French, English and German) may be indicated in French, *Comité Européen de Normalisation*, in English, European Committee for Standardisation, and in German, *Europäisches Komitee für Normung*. CEN Central Secretariat 1995–04–01.

[22] Initially, this organisation was called "*Comité Européen de Coordination des Normes*". See Breulmann, above n. 20, at 41.

[23] CEN—its mission, structure and activities, Apr. 1998. See http://www.cenorm.be (homepage).

[24] Art. 3 of CEN's Statutes. Until 1975, the organisation was domiciled in Paris.

[25] Art. 1 of CEN's Statutes.

[26] Art. 4 of CEN's Statutes.

[27] "*Comité Européen de Normalisation Electronique*".

[28] "*Comité Européen de Coordination des Normes Electrotechniques des Pays Membres de la Communauté Européenne*". See, for details on these organisations, Breulmann, above n. 20, 44–5.

[29] Statutes of CENELEC. See http://www.cenelec.be (homepage).

[30] For the purpose of this book, ETSI falls outside the scope of consideration. See, for details of this organisation, F. Nicolas/J. Repussard, *Common Standards for Enterprises* (Luxembourg, 1994), 34 ff. and http://www.etsi.fr.

the EC and EFTA countries (one member per country).[31] In response to the Commission's Green Paper and Follow-up Communication,[32] CEN now also allows European organisations that represent social and economic interests[33] to become "associates" and form part of the General Assembly, although they do not enjoy voting powers.[34] The General Assembly acts by simple majority, each national member having one vote whenever the quorums of presence or majority are not required by the statutes or by the rules of procedure. Acts of the General Assembly are binding for all national members even for those who were absent or voted against the acts.[35]

The President

CEN and CENELEC each have a President, who is appointed by the General Assembly for a period of two or three years, assisted by one or more vice-presidents. The President chairs the General Assembly and the Administrative Board, being a member by right of the latter organ. In CEN, the President (Mr Alain Perroy), in principle, has no voting right, although in cases where the voting requirements cannot be reached, he may intervene with a casting vote.[36] CENELEC's President (Mr Heinz Wanda) does not possess a voting right, unless he is at the same time the representative of a national delegation, in which case he may vote in his capacity of representative and not as President.

The Administrative Board

Both organisations are directed and managed by the Administrative Board. The composition of the Board, always including a Belgian member, is fixed by the internal rules.[37] The members are appointed for a period of two to three years by the General Assembly and act as a corporate body.[38] The Administrative Board acts as the representative of the General Assembly. It directs the work of the organisations and co-ordinates the action taken by all bodies. Except for matters which are expressly reserved to the General Assembly in the statutes, the Administrative Board has the broadest powers to administer and to handle all administrative matters and provisions relating to the objectives of the

---

[31] Art. 16 of CEN's Statutes and Art. 2 of CENELEC's Reg.

[32] See sect. 2.3.5.2.

[33] Art. 6.3 of CEN's Statutes. At present, CEN has the following associates: the European Association for the Co-ordination of Consumer Representation in Standardisation (ANEC), the European Chemical Industry Council (CEFIC), the European Computer Manufacturers Association (ECMA), the European Construction Industry Federation (FIEC), the European Office of Crafts, Trades and Small and Medium-sized Enterprises for Standardisation (NORMAPME) and the European Trade Union Technical Bureau for Health and Safety (TUTB). See CEN's Annual Report of 1996–7.

[34] See CEN document, Opening of CEN's management structures, 1992–7.

[35] Art. 16.2 of CEN's Statutes.

[36] *Ibid.*, Art. 21 read in conjunction with Arts. 24 and 30.

[37] *Ibid.*, Art. 25; Art. 12 of CENELEC's Statutes. CENELEC's Administrative Board is composed of eight members, including the President, three Vice-Presidents, a Treasurer, the former President, a Belgian member and the Secretary-General: CENELEC's Annual Report of 1996, 15.

[38] Arts. 25 and 26 of CEN's Statutes; Arts. 12–13 of CENELEC's Statutes.

standardisation organisations.[39] Each member of the Administrative Board is allowed one vote. Decisions are taken by a simple majority of votes expressed by the members present or represented. CEN's President has a casting vote when no majority can be reached.[40]

The Secretary General and the Central Secretariat

The Secretary General is appointed by the General Assembly upon proposal of the Administrative Board. This person is charged with the daily management of the organisations. The Secretary General ensures that the activities of the organs are carried out in accordance with the statutes, internal rules and adopted decisions, and he attends the meetings of the General Assembly and the Administrative Board in an advisory capacity.[41] The activities of the Secretary General are supported by the Central Secretariat which, in particular, performs preparatory and routine tasks. The Central Secretariat administers several bodies: the General Assembly, the Administrative Board, the Certification Board, CEN/ISSSS, the Technical Board and Sector Fora.

The Technical Board

The Technical Board (BT) steers and co-ordinates the standards programmes of CEN and CENELEC and promotes their rapid realisation by the central secretariat, Technical Committees and other bodies.[42] The functions of the Technical Board include, *inter alia*, advising on all matters relating to the organisation, co-ordination and planning of the standards work, monitoring the progress of the standards work, examining proposals for new projects, setting up and disbanding Technical Committees, imposing or releasing standstill obligations, organising technical liaison with intergovernmental organisations, deciding on questions of reference to national standards in European Standards (EN) and HD (Harmonised Documents), authorising the issue of reports if it is considered urgent or advisable to provide information to a CEN/CENELEC member, the Commission, the EFTA Secretariat or to other bodies, deciding on the European Standards and the Harmonised Documents, drafted by Technical Committees considering and ruling upon appeals on behalf a Technical Committee, another body or an officer of CEN/CENELEC and undertaking such tasks relating to standards work as requested by the General Assembly or the Administrative Board.[43]

The Technical Board consists of the President and/or the Vice-President(s) and one permanent delegate from each member organisation, who establishes

---

[39] Art. 28 of CEN's Statutes.

[40] *Ibid.*, Art. 30.

[41] *Ibid.*, Art. 33. The current Secretary General of CEN is Mr Georg Hongler and of CENELEC Mr Stephen Marriot. For CENELEC, the Secretary General is actually a member of the Administrative Board, see CENELEC's Annual Report of 1996.

[42] Art. 2.1.1. of the CEN/CENELEC Internal Regs., Part 2: *Common Rules for standards work*, 1996–6.

[43] *Ibid.*

the necessary contacts at the national level so as to represent the member organisation effectively. The Technical Board meetings are chaired by the President or a Vice-President.[44] Such meetings are convened by the Central Secretariat, which functions as the secretariat of the Board, on instructions of the chairperson or at the request of at least two members. Meetings of the Technical Board may be attended by representatives of the Commission and the EFTA Secretariat and, subject to contractual agreements, by other organisations as observers.[45] The Technical Board is required to report its activities to each meeting of the General Assembly or the Administrative Board, as appropriate.

Technical Sector Boards, Programming Committees and Sector Fora (CEN)

Until recently, the Technical Board could establish Technical Sector Boards (BTS) to ensure better co-operation in a specific sector between CEN's general administrative bodies and the business parties affected by the standardisation programmes.[46] To this end, the BTS were delegated powers *inter alia* to plan and co-ordinate the standards work, to co-operate with other BTS in CEN and with CENELEC to ensure consistency; to monitor fully and control the progress of standards work in its general field and of its relevant technical committees, to check the technical content of draft EC and EFTA mandates and to give advice to the BT on how to deal with them.[47] In addition to these Boards, the General Assembly, the Technical Board or the Joint Presidents Group could establish Programming Committees to provide coherent co-ordination, planning and programming of standardisation activities within a particular sector.[48] However, dissatisfied by the performance in particular of the BTS, CEN recently decided to review its organisational structure and to optimise its system by streamlining the technical work and reducing the CEN organs. It decided to drop the BTS level and thus reduced the technical work to three levels: policy setting (Technical Board/Administrative Board), programming (Technical Committee) and the drafting of standards (Working Groups). However, it will still be possible to carry out specific sector activities. To this end, "Sector Fora" can be established by the Technical Board. At present, three Sector Fora exist, dealing with: information technology, building and healthcare.[49]

[44] Art. 2.1.2. of the CEN/CENELEC Internal Regs., Part 2.

[45] Art. 2.1.3. of the CEN/CENELEC Internal Regs., Part 2.

[46] CEN's Revised rules for the Technical Sector Boards as approved by virtue of Resolution CA 34/1991.

[47] Art. 3 of CEN's Revised rules for the Technical Sector Boards.

[48] Art. 2.2. of the CEN/CENELEC Internal Regs., Part 2.

[49] See DIN-Mitt. 75 1996, Nr 1 and DIN-Mitt. 76. 1997, Nr. 1. See *Optimising CEN*, Communication following the decisions taken by CEN's Administrative Board on 28 June 1995 and on the planning for their implementation, Oct. 1995. See also the minutes of the 43rd Meeting of CEN/BT on 7–8 Apr. 1998, reported by the Swiss Standardisation Organisation SNV on the Internet: http://www.snv.ch/aktuell/bericht2_cen.htm.

Technical Committees

The Technical Committees (TCs) are the level at which the actual standards work is carried out. The TCs, created (and dissolved) by the Technical Board, have precise objectives, essentially to prepare CEN/CENELEC standards.[50] Joint CEN/CENELEC Technical Committees are set up by the Joint Presidents Group.[51] At present, CEN has 271 TCs, whilst CENELEC has 96 TCs. Technical Committees are principally required to take into account any ISO or IEC work. Each Committee ensures the approval of the Technical Board for its standards programme, which is supplied with precise title, scope and scheduled target dates for the critical stages of each project.[52] The members of the TCs are the CEN or CENELEC member organisations, hence the national standardisation bodies.[53] A Technical Committee meeting may not, however, be attended by more than three delegates of a member organisation at the same time. When forming and briefing its delegation to a Technical Committee, a member ensures that the delegation will convey a national position that takes account of all interests affected by the work. The chairperson of a Technical Committee is appointed by the Technical Board on nomination of the Technical Committee's secretariat for a period of a maximum of six years.[54] This person must be strictly impartial and must abstain from his/her national viewpoint and consequently, has no voting rights.

The chairperson attempts to obtain a unanimous decision of the Technical Committee.[55] Again, if no unanimity can be reached, the chairperson must seek consensus. The chairperson participates in the work of the *Comité de Lecture* and, on invitation, at meetings of the Programming Committees. When approved by the Technical Board, this person may represent CEN/CENELEC at meetings of other organisations in order to give technical advice on subjects within the scope of the Technical Committees.[56] Normally, the CEN/CENELEC member who holds the secretariat of the corresponding ISO/IEC Committee is in charge of the secretariat of the CEN/CENELEC Technical Committee. Otherwise, the allocation of the secretariat of a Technical Committee to a member is decided by the Technical Board.[57] In practice, it appears that often the Member States with a long-standing standardisation tradition and powerful standardisation bodies or the highly technically advanced Member States hold this important function of secretariat.[58] The secretary, appointed by the member

---

[50]   Art. 2.3.1. of the CEN/CENELEC Internal Regs., Part 2.

[51]   See, for details, *ibid.*, Art. 9.

[52]   Such target dates are reviewed at least once a year.

[53]   Art. 2.3.2. of the CEN/CENELEC Internal Regs., Part 2.

[54]   In exceptional cases, an extension of a maximum of three years is allowed for.

[55]   Literally Art. 2.3.3. of the CEN/CENELEC Internal Regs., Part 2, stipulates that "the chairman shall do everything possible to obtain a unanimous decision of the Technical Committee".

[56]   *Ibid.*, Art. 2.3.3.

[57]   *Ibid.*, Annex B. Guidelines for the allocation of technical secretariats.

[58]   See, for an overview of the national members who hold the secretariats of the TC's, Table 3 of J. Falke, "Achievements and Unresolved Problems of European Standardization: The Ingenuity of

holding the secretariat, is required to ensure, in consultation with the chairperson, that the Technical Committee functions efficiently and that agreed timetables are kept to. The secretary, obliged to maintain strict impartiality and divest him/herself of his/her national viewpoint, has no voting rights.

TC work is carried out mainly by correspondence. Meetings are held only when documentation is sufficiently well established to ensure satisfactory progress and with an agenda of sufficient substance, from the technical point of view, to justify the attendance of the delegates. Representatives of the Commission, the EFTA secretariat and other international and European organisations with a particular interest in the work, having been accorded formal liaison, may attend the TC meetings as observers without voting rights.[59] In general, each organisation is allowed to send only one observer to attend the meetings. The secretariat of a Technical Committee is required to submit a report on its work at least once a year.

A TC generally functions through Working Groups. It may, however, establish subcommittees which take on the responsibility for a large programme of work in which different expertise is needed for different parts of the work and/or when the range of separate activities needs co-ordination over long periods of time. The members on a subcommittee are CEN/CENELEC member organisations. The chairperson of a subcommittee is appointed by the parent TC for a maximum of six years. This period may be extended, in exceptional cases, by a maximum of three years. Working Groups are established in order to undertake a specific short term task by an agreed date and are usually dissolved when this task has been completed.[60] Working Groups are restricted to individual members appointed by the parent body or by CEN and CENELEC members, who act in a personal capacity. Experts from organisations which have observer status may also be included.

Comité de Lecture

The *Comité de Lecture* is a consultative body which assists the editing committees of Technical Committees and other bodies drafting CEN/CENELEC standards, by providing expert advice on editorial matters and on the presentation of European standards or harmonised documents. As a general rule, this Committee operates by correspondence. The *Comité de Lecture* is composed of an AFNOR[61]/UTE[62] representative (for the French language), a BSI[63] representative (for the English language), a DIN[64]/DKE[65] representative (for the German

Practice and the Queries of Lawyers", in Ch. Joerges/K.H. Ladeur/E. Vos, *Integrating Scientific Expertise into Regulatory Decision-Making. National Traditions and European Innovations* (Baden-Baden, 1997), 187–224.

[59] Art. 2.3.5. of the CEN/CENELEC Internal Regs., Part 2.
[60] *Ibid.*, Art. 2.5.1.
[61] *Association franÁaise de normalisation.*
[62] *Union Technique de l'Electricité.*
[63] British Standards Institute.
[64] *Deutsches Institut für Normung.*
[65] *Deutsche Elektrotechnische Kommission in DIN und VDE.*

language), the president and the secretary of the relevant Technical Committee and a representative of the Central Secretariat.[66]

Certification Bodies: CEN Certification Board and ELSECOM

CEN and CENELEC operate a system of voluntary testing and certification of product conformity to European standards, which is co-ordinated by the CEN Certification Board[67] and ELSECOM[68] (for CENELEC). Together, both standardisation bodies have developed a common set of certification rules for a CEN/CENELEC European Key Mark. This mark certifies that products comply with CEN/CENELEC standards.[69]

CEN's Information Society Standardisation System (CEN/ISSS)

In order to combine all the relevant European Information Society standardisation activities under one single umbrella CEN has recently set up the Information Society Standardisation System (CEN/ISSS).[70]

Liaison between the Organisations: The Joint Presidents Group (JPG)

A special co-ordination group has been established in order to ensure effective co-operation and to manage common boundaries between CEN, CENELEC and ETSI. This structure is made up of the Joint Presidents Group (JPG), which comprises up to seven senior representatives of the three standardisation organisations (including the Secretaries General of CEN and CENELEC and the Director of ETSI).[71] As a co-ordination group, it acts as a forum for discussion of matters of common policy. It prepares agreements on common matters. Its task is to assist CEN, CENELEC and ETSI in the development of common rules in order to ensure consistency and coherence of technical work, and to prevent the duplication of activities. Furthermore, the JPG promotes accessibility, for example through a common information system, and seeks to advance the evolution of European standardisation. It is assisted by two subordinate bodies: the Information Technology Steering Committee and the Joint Co-ordination Group.[72]

2.2.3. The Standard-setting Process

2.2.3.1. European Standards

European standardisation includes European Standards (EN), Harmonised Documents (HD), standards in the sense of the Information Directive, and

---

[66] Art. 4.8.2. read in conjunction with Art. 2.3.3. and 2.3.4. of the CEN/CENELEC Internal Regs., Part 2.

[67] *Ibid.*, Part 4: *Certification*, 1995–5.

[68] The European Electrotechnical Sectoral Committee for Testing and Certification.

[69] Art. 2 of the CEN/CENELEC Internal Regs., Part 4.

[70] See http://www.cenorm.be/isss/default.htm.

[71] See Art. 3.4.2. of the CEN/CENELEC Internal Regs., Part 2.

[72] *Ibid.*, Art. 3.4.3.

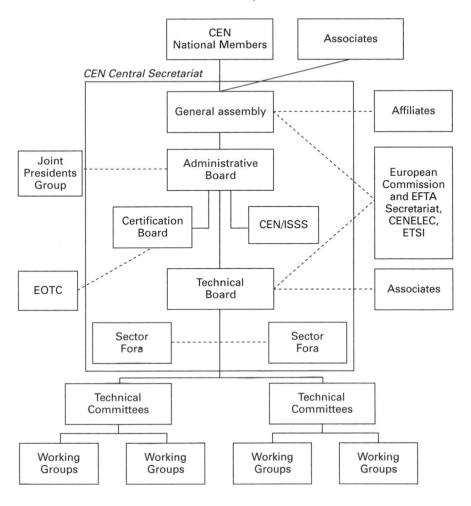

Figure 8. The organisational structure of CEN.
Source: CEN Central Secretariat 1998.

European Prestandards (ENV), the sum of which is, confusingly, referred to as "European standards". Community directives, however, speak of "harmonised standards". The term "harmonised standards" has created confusion amongst the European standardisation bodies, in particular. The Commission has consequently attempted to bring some clarity to the matter. In its *Guide on the Implementation of the New Approach Directives*, the Commission states that harmonised standards used in the New Approach Directives mean:

"the technical specifications adopted by a European standards organisation on the basis of the General orientations signed between the European standards organisations and the Commission on 13 November 1984, following a mandate by the Commission issued pursuant Directive 83/189/EEC".[73]

The Commission emphasises that harmonised standards used in the New Approach Directives do not refer to a specific category of standards adopted by the European standardisation bodies. According to the Commission, the terminology used in the Directives is a "legal qualification of documents existing in their own right in the framework of European standardisation".[74]

The difference between a European Standard (EN) and a Harmonised Document (HD) mainly lies in the degree to which they are binding for the national standardisation organisations. A European Standard (EN)[75] is a regionally valid standard which is drafted according to a uniform system of form and figuring, in the three official languages.[76] The adoption of a draft standard by CEN or CENELEC as a European Standard requires all member organisations to transpose this standard literally (identical on both technical content and presentation), in the time set by CEN/CENELEC, into its own national standardisation work.[77] This standard thus acquires the status of a national standard,[78] obliging the member organisations to withdraw all conflicting national standards.

A Harmonised Document (HD), following its adoption by CEN/CENELEC, creates the obligation of transposition by the member organisations in their national standards work. This is done by a public announcement of the HD number and title, whilst member organisations are required to withdraw any conflicting national standards. In contrast to the ENs, the HDs do not require a literal transposition of the text into national standards. Member organisations are free to maintain or issue a national standard dealing with a subject falling within the scope of the HD, provided that such a standard is equivalent in technical content.[79] However, in exceptional cases, national standards may deviate from the content of HD.[80]

At the outset of European harmonisation, the creation of HDs seemed to be the best possibility of bringing the national standards work closer together, without disturbing the traditional structures built up in the course of time in the Member States. In addition, recourse to these documents was favoured, since they allowed for autonomous standards work within the framework of CEN

---

[73] European Commission, *Guide to the Implementation of Community Harmonisation Directives Based on the New Approach and the Global Approach* (first version) (Brussels, 1994), 35. See, in this sense, for instance, Art. 4 of Council Dir. 89/106/EEC [1989] OJ L40/12.

[74] *Implementation Guide*, above n. 73, at 38.

[75] Next to these standards, Eurocodes exist which are very technical standards for the Iron and Steel sector. See for more details, Breulmann, above n. 20, 59–60.

[76] See Breulmann, above n. 20, at 54.

[77] Art. 5.2.2. of the CEN/CENELEC Internal Regs., Part 2.

[78] This is done either by publication of an identical text or by endorsement: see Arts. 5.2.2.2. and 5.2.2.3. of the CEN/CENELEC Internal Regs., Part 2.

[79] *Ibid.*, Art. 5.2.3. In this sense, the difference between Harmonisation Documents and European Standards is similar to that between Community dirs. and regs.

and CENELEC as well as the reproduction of ISO/IEC standards. Over the years though, it became clear that HDs were not an appropriate means of achieving one uniform standardisation system in the internal market.[81] In particular, there was a lack of comparability in the harmonised national standards work, as the title and scope of the harmonised standards in the single national standards works differed, while it was difficult to check whether the content of HDs had been incorporated into the national standards as the national deviation possibilities differed. The need for identical national standards has been recognised by CEN and CENELEC, declaring in their internal rules that preference should be given to the preparation of an EN.[82]

A European Prestandard (ENV) may be established as a prospective standard for provisional application, particularly in technically innovative fields (for example, information technology) or when there is an urgent need for guidance, and most importantly where aspects of safety for persons and goods are not involved. This standard, however, falls beyond the scope of this research.

2.2.3.2. The Drafting Process of European Standards

In the discussion of the organisational structures of the standardisation bodies, the way in which standards are being prepared has already been briefly touched upon. The basic principle which guides national, European and international organisations in the setting of standards is that of *consensus*. As one author concisely put it:

"standardisation = consensus".[83]

In this context, consensus does not signify that everyone has to agree upon a project, but rather that there is broad support for the project. EN 45020 defines consensus as:

"general agreement, characterised by the absence of sustained opposition to substantial issues by any important part of the concerned interests and by a process that involves seeking to take into account the views of all parties concerned and to reconcile any conflicting arguments".[84]

Thus, consensus does not mean that each member of a committee has a power of veto, which could easily lead to obstruction of the standard-setting process, but may be defined as the lack of tenacious opposition to a specific

---

[80] See, in particular, *ibid.*, Arts. 4.4. and 3.1.9.

[81] Breulmann, above n. 20, at 57.

[82] Art. 4.1.9. of the CEN/CENELEC Internal Regs., Part 2.

[83] M. Linder, "Adoption of European Testing Standards by CEN/CENELEC", CEN/CENELEC & ETSI (eds.), *Conformance Testing and Certification in Information Technology and Telecommunications* (Amsterdam/Washington/Tokyo, 1991), 113.

[84] EN 45020 of 1993, para. 1.7. See Arts. 5.1.1. and 2.3.3(3) of the CEN/CENELEC Internal Regs., Part 2. See, also, the Commission in its Green Paper on Standardisation, COM(90)456 final. See also Mohr, DIN-Mitt. Bd. 67 (1988), 536 and V. Eichener, *Social Dumping or Innovative Regulation? Process and Outcomes of European Decision-Making in the Sector of Health and Safety at Work Harmonization*, EUI Working Paper SPS 92/28 (Florence 1992), 65.

proposal. The use of consensus in the standard-setting procedure, above all, takes into account the *voluntary* nature of standardisation. National standardisation bodies, therefore, do not dispose of enforcement powers, but depend on the voluntary compliance of the business concerned.[85] Furthermore, some writers have explained the consensus principle in terms of competition, since the majority of manufacturers, who are members of national standardisation organisations, could outvote competitors and adopt standards which would be discriminatory against the manufacturers in minority.[86] Standards would therefore need to reflect common interests[87] and should not lead to economic advantages for single participants.[88] In practice, the search for consensus appears to be the main reason for the long duration of the standard-setting process, which takes rarely less than three years and, in exceptions, can last up to 10 years.[89]

Various bodies may propose to develop European standards: the Commission (relating to the New Approach Directives), the EFTA secretariat, national standardisation institutes, CEN and CENELEC's technical bodies or European trade, professional, technical or scientific organisations.[90] The Technical Board will subsequently decide whether a project will be pursued. Once agreed, European standards are mainly developed through one of three routes: Technical Committee (TC); Questionnaire Procedure (PQ) or International Standardisation (ISO).[91] In the absence of a suitable ISO or IEC document, the Technical Board may decide to adopt any other appropriate document as a basis for the work leading towards an EN or a HD.

After the adoption of a standards project by the Technical Board, the latter may initiate a Questionnaire Procedure.[92] This procedure serves to find out whether there is sufficient interest for the harmonisation of the subject proposed, the existing degree of national harmonisation on that subject and whether such a national document would be acceptable as an EN or a HD. The questionnaire is sent by the Central Secretariat to the national members.[93] At

---

[85] See, e.g., for Germany, Joerges *et al.*, above n. 4, at 182 (EUI Working Paper LAW 91/12, at 63).

[86] See Eichener, above n. 84, 64–5.

[87] See, for instance, the internal regs. of the German standardisation organisation DIN, DIN 820, part 1, standardisation principles, no. 2.

[88] See, on the relationship with competition law, in particular M. Schießl, *EG-Kartellrechtliche Anforderungen an die europäischen Normungsinstitutionen CEN, CENELEC und ETSI* (Frankfurt a.M., 1994). See also J. Falke/Ch. Joerges, *Rechtliche Möglichkeiten bei der Verfolgung und Sicherung nationaler und EG-weiter Umschutzziele im Rahmen der europäischen Normung*, Gutachten erstellt im Auftrag des Büros für Technikfolgen-Abschätzung des Deutschen Bundestages (Bremen, 1995), 43 ff.

[89] Eichener, above n. 84, at 65.

[90] Art. 4.1.3. of the CEN/CENELEC Internal Regs., Part 2.

[91] See CEN, above n. 11, at 26.

[92] Art. 4.2. of the CEN/CENELEC Internal Regs., Part 2.

[93] Two types of questionnaire may be distinguished: a Primary Questionnaire, which is used for an entirely new reference document, and an Updating Questionnaire, used for a revised reference document of which the previous edition has already adopted as an EN or a HD: Art. 4.2.2. of the CEN/CENELEC Internal Regs., Part 2.

this point, there is a stand-still obligation for the members not to take action during the preparation of an EN or a HD. If, upon evaluation of the replies to the questionnaires, the Technical Board takes the view that harmonisation is required, it can propose the reference document for a formal adoption as an EN or a HD or where, as in most cases, further technical work is required, refer it to a TC.

The actual standardisation work is effected by the Technical Committees and their working groups or sub-committees, which are generally required to take into account any ISO or IEC work already undertaken. TC work is only undertaken when no international results can be accepted as they stand or, on special request, for instance, from the Commission.[94] In the course of reaching unanimous or at least substantial support, working drafts may be circulated for discussion at Technical Committee meetings, for comments by correspondence or for written vote. Before a standard is accepted, each argument needs to be discussed in detail, until agreement is reached.

When consensus has been reached, the text agreed upon is submitted to CEN/CENELEC (Public) Enquiry.[95] In this procedure, the text is submitted by the secretariat of the Technical Committee to the Central Secretariat for the allocation of a draft EN (prEN) or a draft HD (prHD) number and distribution to the CEN/CENELEC members for public comment. Under this procedure, the members are allowed to comment on the document over a period of six months. Where the results of this inquiry show sufficient agreement (preferably consensus) on the content of the draft, a final text will be prepared by the Technical Committee secretariat for approval. If there is insufficient agreement, the Technical Committee may decide to have a second inquiry which lasts a further two months (a maximum of four). When this period has elapsed, no further enquiries are allowed, even if insufficient agreement still exists. In these cases no EN will be adopted. Preparation of a HD may be considered if a draft text does not obtain sufficient agreement.

Approval of the final text of an EN is achieved by a formal vote of the members, which has to be effected within a period of two months. The voting procedures of CEN and CENELEC, unified in accordance with the "General Orientations" agreement between the Commission and CEN/CENELEC, are mainly patterned on Article 148 EC.[96] However, if more than three members vote against, a proposal for an EN is not adopted.[97] If the voting is successful and no appeal has been lodged, the Technical Board notes the approval of the standard.

---

[94] *Ibid.*, Art. 4.3.1.
[95] *Ibid.*, Art. 4.3.4.
[96] Weighting of votes in accordance with *ibid.*, Art. 5.1: France, Germany, Italy and United Kingdom, each 10 votes; Spain 8 votes; Belgium, Greece, the Netherlands, Portugal and Switzerland, each 5 votes; Austria and Sweden, each 4 votes, Denmark, Finland, Ireland and Norway, each 3 votes; Luxembourg 2 votes and Iceland 1 vote.
[97] First votes from all members are counted, and the proposal is adopted if 71% or more of the weighted votes cast (abstentions not counted) are in favour.

An appeal may be lodged by a member against any action or inaction of a TC, another body or a CEN/CENELEC officer if that member considers that such action is contrary to the Statutes or Internal Regulations and the aims of CEN/CENELEC, or that it is not in the best interests of creating a European economic space, or contrary to public concerns such as health and safety or the environment.[98] Appeals will be considered by the Technical Board. Where appeals are lodged against Technical Board and Administrative Board decisions, they are considered by the General Assembly.

2.3. The Community's Regulatory Approach to Technical Consumer Products and Standards

The launch of the New Approach to Technical Harmonisation and Standards in 1985[99] was particularly inspired by the establishment of the internal market based on accelerated and efficient decision-making. Although the reference to standards developed by the European standardisation bodies had already been experimented with in the Low Voltage Directive of 1973,[100] its inclusion as a general regulatory instrument in the New Approach was certainly innovative at the Community level.[101] Although the New Approach to Technical Harmonisation and Standards was officially adopted in 1985, some important steps paving the way for its adoption had already been taken earlier.

2.3.1. The Information Directive of 1983

An initial step towards the New Approach had already been taken in 1983 with the adoption of Council Directive 83/189/EEC (the Information Directive).[102] In laying down a procedure for the provision of information in the field of technical standards and regulations, the Directive seeks to prevent the emergence of

[98] See CEN/CENELEC Internal Regs., Part 2, Annex A: Appeal mechanism.

[99] Council Resolution of 7 May 1985 on a new approach to technical harmonisation and standards [1985] OJ C136/1, based on the Communication from the Commission to the Council on Technical harmonisation and standardisation, a new approach, COM(85)19 final and drawing on the already approved principles of the Council in its Conclusions on standardisation of 16 July 1984, published as annex I to this Resolution.

[100] Council Dir. 73/23/EEC on the harmonisation of the laws of the Member States relating to electrical equipment designed for use within certain voltage limits [1973] OJ L77/29.

[101] In a 1982 Communication to the Council and the Parliament on the application of the Low Voltage Directive, the Commission had already expressed its intention to apply this model to other sectors of industry [1982] OJ C59/2. Moreover, next to the methods of total harmonisation and optional harmonisation, the Commission had already pointed to this technique in its original proposal for a General Programme for the elimination of technical barriers to trade of 1969 (the traditional approach to harmonisation, as above stated) and had been recommended by both the Parliament and the ESC. See Parliament Resolution [1969] OJ C108/39 and the ESC Opinion [1968] OJ C132/1.

[102] Council Dir. 83/189/EEC laying down a procedure for the provisions of information in the field of technical standards and regulations [1983] OJ L109/8.

technical barriers to trade and thus replaces the inefficient Gentleman's Agreement of the traditional approach: both Member States and national standardisation bodies are obliged to inform the Commission immediately of any technical draft regulation and draft standards,[103] whilst a standstill period is introduced where European standards or European legislation is under preparation.[104] Following the amendment of 1988, the scope of the Directive was extended to cover all industrial and agricultural products, thus including foodstuffs and medicinal products.[105] A further amendment of this Directive in 1994 aims to ensure greater transparency, to define more clearly which kind of information needs to be notified by the national standardisation bodies and to make the procedure more flexible and less cumbersome.[106] The Directive has been quite successful in the prevention of new trade barriers.[107]

2.3.2. The "General Orientations for Co-operation" of 1984

A second step towards the New Approach was taken in 1984. In that year, the Council formally recognised the need for a greater use of standardisation at European level and thus provided the political "green light" to the Commission for the development of a new approach based on the reference to standards technique.[108] However, the experimental use of the reference to standards technique in the Low Voltage Directive of 1973 had provoked severe criticism,[109] touching on the problem of the insertion of private standards into public law-making. Thus, before formally presenting a new approach, the Commission sought to influence the process of standard-setting by setting minimal "constitutional" guarantees for the safeguarding of public interests and looked for modes of co-operation with the European standardisation bodies CEN and CENELEC. On

---

[103] Arts. 8 and 4 of Dir. 83/109/EEC, above n. 102.

[104] On the basis of this procedure, the Commission received 362 notifications of draft national technical regulations from the Member States in 1992, 385 in 1993 and 389 in 1994. See the Commission's report on the operation of Dir. 83/189/EEC in 1992, 1993 and 1994, COM(96)286 final.

[105] See Art. 9 of Dir. 83/189/EEC, as amended by Council Dir. 88/182/EEC [1988] OJ L81/75.

[106] European Parliament and Council Dir. 94/10/EC materially amending for the second time Dir. 83/189/EEC laying down a procedure for the provisions of information in the field of technical standards and regulations [1994] OJ L100/30. For the consolidated version, see European Parliament and Council Dir. 98/34/EC, [1998] OJ L204/37, as amended by European Parliament and Council Dir. 98/48/EC, [1998] OJ L217/18, extending the scope of the notification procedure to information society services.

[107] See, in particular, S. Weatherill, "Compulsory Notification of Draft Technical Regulations: the Contribution of Dir. 83/189 to the Management of the Internal Market" (1996) 16 *YEL* 129–204.

[108] Conclusions on Standardisation Approved by the Council on 16 July 1984, published as Annex I to Council Resolution [1985] OJ C136/2.

[109] For the debate on the use of this technique, see, *inter alia*, E. Röhling, *Übertriebliche technische Normen als nichttarifäre Handelshemnisse im Gemeinsamen Markt* (Köln/Berlin/Bonn/Munich, 1972), 114 ff; R. Winckler, "Rechtsvorschriften für Anlagen, Geräte und Stoffe—Bestandsaufnahme und kritische Würdigung. Materialen und Geräte under besonderer Berücksichtigung des Gerätesicherheitsgesetzes, der 2. DurchfuhrungsVO zum EnWG unter der Niederspannungsrichtlinie", in Recht und Technik, *Rechtliche Regelungen für Anlagen, Geräte und Stoffe im deutschen und im europäischen Recht*, Studienreihe des Bundesministers für Wirtschaft, nr. 53 (Bonn, 1985), 26 ff.

13 November 1984, the Commission and the European standardisation bodies thus concluded a "General Orientations for Co-operation".[110] The following principles were agreed upon:

— The Commission, for its part, undertook to entrust CEN and CENELEC with the elaboration of European standards through mandates which provide for a financial contribution. Reserving the right to organise technical activities for the preparation of a standard without recourse to CEN/ CENELEC, the Commission ensured that, when doing so, it would invite qualified experts appointed by CEN/CENELEC to participate in these activities. Moreover, the Commission agreed to foster the diffusion and the use of European standards by the publication of the standard programmes conferred upon CEN/CENELEC and of the titles of the standards adopted in the Official Journal.

— CEN and CENELEC, for their part, guaranteed that the European standards developed satisfied the essential requirements on the protection of the citizens (for example, health and safety), which had been determined by the directives and by the mandates based on such directives. Moreover, they ensured that interested circles, in particular, the public authorities, industry, users, consumers and trade unions could, if they so desired, effectively take part in the elaboration of the European standards. Furthermore, CEN/CENELEC assumed the obligation to invite the Commission to assist the Technical Committees' sessions, whilst a representative of the Commission would be invited to assist the Technical Board meetings.

2.3.3. *The New Approach's Dichotomy between Law and Technical Specifications*

2.3.3.1. The New Approach to Technical Harmonisation and Standards

Following these events, the Commission officially presented the New Approach in its White Paper of 1985.[111] Focusing on the reduction of the Council's workload and accelerated decision-making procedures, this approach restricts legislative harmonisation to stipulating essential health and safety requirements, whilst the specification of these requirements in technical standards is left to the European standardisation bodies (CEN and CENELEC).[112] In this way, it

---

[110] Commission, DGIII, internal paper, published in DIN-Mitt. 64 (1985), 78–9. This Agreement has been published under CEN/CENELEC Memorandum No 4 as Appendix 4, in Nicolas/Repussard, above n. 30, at 197.

[111] COM(85)310 final. See Chap. 2.

[112] See on the New Approach, for instance, Joerges *et al.*, above n. 4; J. Falke, "Technische Normung in Europa: Zieht sich der Staat wirklich zurück?", in G. Winter (ed.), *Die Europäischen Gemeinschaften und das Öffentliche*, ZERP-Diskussionspapier 7/91 (Bremen 1991), 79–125; S. Farr, *Harmonisation of Technical Standards in the EC* (London, 1992); Joerges, above n. 13, 175–225; J. Pelkmans, "The New Approach to Technical Harmonisation and Standardisation" (1987) 25 *JCMS* 249–69; K. Schreiber, "The New Approach to Technical Harmonisation and Standards", in

attempts to overcome the difficulties associated with the slow process of agreeing upon such details. The distinction between the essential safety requirements and technical specifications constitutes the main characteristic of the New Approach. The New Approach herewith absorbs the common national dichotomy between law and technical norms.

Under the New Approach, products which are manufactured according to the harmonised standards are presumed to meet the essential safety requirements, although the technical specifications maintain their status of voluntary standards. Thus, in this manner, national authorities are obliged to recognise that products manufactured following harmonised standards are presumed to conform to the essential requirements established by a specific directive and thus to allow these products on their markets. The quality of harmonised standards is ensured by standardisation mandates, which are issued by the Commission to the European standardisation bodies. At the same time, the New Approach prescribes the inclusion of safeguard procedures in directives, under the management of the Commission and a standing committee, which allow the competent national authorities to challenge the conformity of a product, the validity of a certificate or the quality of a standard.[113]

2.3.3.2. The Model Directive

The New Approach sets a Model for each subsequent directive adopted.[114] This "Model Directive"[115] emphasises the following principles:

— "Member States have the responsibility of ensuring safety on their territory of persons, domestic animals and goods, or the respect of other essential protection requirements in the general interest such as health, consumer or environmental protection etc., with regard to the hazards covered by the Directive itself;
— the national provisions ensuring such protection must be harmonised in order to ensure the free movement of goods, without lowering existing and justified levels of protection in the Member States;
— CEN and CENELEC (one or the other, or both according to the products covered by the Directive) are the competent bodies to adopt European harmonised standards within the scope of the Directive, in accordance with the guidelines which the Commission, after consultation of the Member States, has signed with these bodies".[116]

The Model Directive sets various requirements concerning the main elements which need to be included in the directives based on the New Approach. First,

L. Hurwitz/Ch. Lesquesne, *The State of the European Community. Policies, Institutions & Debates in the Transition Years* (Boulder, Colorado/Harlow, Essex, 1991), 99–112.

[113] Guidelines for a New Approach, published as Annex II to the New Approach Council Resolution, above n. 99.

[114] Outlines of the principles and main elements which should make the body of the dirs., published as Annex II to the New Approach Council Resolution, above n. 99, 3–8.

[115] See, in particular, R. Lauwaars, "The 'Model Directive' on Technical Harmonisation", in R. Bieber/R. Dehousse/J. Pinder/J.H.H. Weiler (eds.), *1992: One European Market? A Critical Analysis of the Commission's Internal Market Strategy* (Baden-Baden, 1988), 151–73.

[116] Model Dir., above n. 114, at 3.

directives must contain a definition of their scope and, as a general rule, will be based on the method of total harmonisation. Products covered by the Directive may be placed on the market only if they do not endanger the safety of persons, domestic animals or goods and respect other essential requirements such as the protection of health and the environment. At the same time, it requires a general clause to be included setting out the responsibilities of the Member States in relation to the placing of goods on the market. Further, the Model Directive requires the essential safety requirements to be worded precisely enough to create legally binding obligations which can be enforced, and should be so formulated as to enable the certification bodies to certify products as being in conformity immediately.

In addition, these directives must include a "free movement clause": products that have been declared to conform to these requirements must be accepted by the Member States. Moreover, Member States must presume products to be in conformity with the essential safety requirements if these products are accompanied by one of the means of attestation provided for, declaring that they are in conformity with the harmonised standards or as a transitional measure with national standards. Furthermore, there must be several means of attestation which raise a presumption of conformity at the disposal of the producer. The producer may obtain a declaration of conformity with European standards or, in the absence of such standards, a declaration of conformity with national standards issued by a third party. In addition, the producer him/herself may issue a declaration of conformity, declaring that s/he has manufactured the product in conformity with the harmonised standards. The Model Directive provides a safeguard procedure, which enables the Member States to take appropriate temporary measures where a product may endanger the health and safety of their citizens. In addition, it provides for the creation of a standing committee, entrusted with the implementation of the directives. Where Member States or the Commission consider that a harmonised standard does not satisfy the essential safety requirements, the directives must provide for the possibility of bringing the matter before this committee.

2.3.4. The Success and Shortcomings of the New Approach

The New Approach and its institutional counterpart, Article 100a, have considerably accelerated decision-making by the Community institutions and have successfully tackled some of the shortcomings of the "traditional" approach.[117] In the years following the New Approach, a wide range of directives has been adopted with an average preparation period of only 18 months.[118] In accordance with the New Approach philosophy,[119] directives have been adopted, for

[117] See Pelkmans, above n. 112, 257 ff.
[118] See Falke, above n. 58.
[119] See, in general, CEN/CENELEC, *The New Approach. Legislation and Standards on the Free Movement of Goods in Europe* (2nd edn., Brussels, 1997).

instance, on simple pressure vessels,[120] toys,[121] construction products,[122] electromagnetic compatibility,[123] machinery,[124] personal protective equipment,[125] non-automatic weighing instruments,[126] active implantable medical devices,[127] appliances burning gaseous fuels,[128] telecommunications terminal equipment,[129] medical devices,[130] recreational craft[131] and lifts.[132] The adoption of these directives means that, in terms of efficiency, the New Approach can be considered to be a great success.[133]

However, although the New Approach has provided a coherent regulatory framework to ease the removal of technical barriers on paper, in practice, several shortcomings have been experienced.[134] The operation of the conformity assessment procedure in the New Approach immediately appeared to create confusion and was not very effective and consequently further Community action was needed on this point. In addition, some terms in the directives raised questions about their exact meaning, which resulted in a need for the clarification of certain basic concepts. The Commission responded by publishing a *Guide to the Implementation of Community Harmonisation Directives Based on the New Approach and the Global Approach*.[135] Furthermore, the practical application of the reference to standards technique appeared extremely troublesome. Difficulties arose primarily because of the delay of the standardisation work. The slow-down in bringing the New Approach into effective operation was nonetheless not only due to the standardisation organisations, as the

[120] Council Dir. 87/404/EEC [1987] OJ L220/48, amended by Council Dir. 93/68/EEC [1993] OJ L220/1.

[121] Council Dir. 88/387/EEC [1988] OJ L187/1, amended by Council Dir. 93/68/EEC [1993] OJ L220/1.

[122] Council Dir. 89/106/EEC [1989] OJ L40/12, amended by Council Dir. 93/68/EEC [1993] OJ L220/1.

[123] Council Dir. 89/336/EEC [1989] OJ L139/19, amended by Council Dir. 93/68/EEC [1993] OJ L220/1.

[124] Council Dir. 89/392/EEC [1989] OJ L183/9, amended by Council Dir. 91/368/EEC [1991] OJ L198/16, by Council Dir. 93/44/EEC [1993] OJ L175/12 and by Council Dir. 93/68/EEC [1993] OJ L220/1, as consolidated by European Parliament and Council Dir. 98/37/EC [1998] OJ L207/1.

[125] Council Dir. 89/686/EEC [1989] OJ L399/18, amended by Council Dir. 93/68/EEC [1993] OJ L220/1.

[126] Council Dir. 90/384/EEC [1990] OJ L189/1, amended by Council Dir. 93/68/EEC [1993] OJ L220/1.

[127] Council Dir. 90/385/EEC [1990] OJ L189/17, amended by Council Dir. 93/68/EEC [1993] OJ L220/1.

[128] Council Dir. 90/396/EEC [1990] OJ L196/15, amended by Council Dir. 93/68/EEC [1993] OJ L220/1.

[129] Council Dir. 91/263/EEC [1991] OJ L128/1, amended by Council Dir. 93/68/EEC [1993] OJ L220/1, as consolidated by European Parliament and Council Dir. 98/13/EC [1998] OJ L74/1.

[130] Council Dir. 93/42/EEC [1993] OJ L169/1.

[131] European Parliament and Council Dir. 94/25/EC [1994] OJ L164/15.

[132] European Parliament and Council Dir. 95/16/EC [1995] OJ L213/1.

[133] Only the Dirs. which concern technical consumer products and include the reference to standards technique are mentioned here. See, in general, CEN/CENELEC, above n. 119.

[134] See Pelkmans/Egan, above n. 5, at 3.

[135] Above n. 73. In addition, the Commission prepares information sheets on the various dirs. in force, for example "Machinery—Useful facts in Relation to Dir. 89/392/EEC", "PPE—Useful facts in relation to Directive 89/686/EEC", DGIII, 1997.

Commission preferred to believe,[136] but also due to the Commission itself and the Member States.[137]

Workload of CEN/CENELEC

Only a part of all the standardisation work undertaken by CEN/CENELEC is mandated by the Commission for the realisation of the essential requirements determined in the New Approach directives adopted by the Council.[138] Nevertheless, the adoption of directives in accordance with the New Approach considerably increased the workload of CEN/CENELEC and it appeared difficult for CEN and CENELEC to keep up with the Community's demand for standards. Without doubt, the delay in the adoption of European standards created significant problems for the actual implementation of the directives. It was extremely difficult for the manufacturers to meet the essential safety requirements since they were formulated in general terms and required specific formulation through standards.[139] In part, the delays in the standardisation process consequently caused delays in the achievement of the internal market.

In 1990, the Commission expressed its concern about the low annual production of standards by CEN/CENELEC as compared to the requests through the Commission's mandates: 150 standards as opposed to the 800 standards that had been requested.[140] At the end of 1991, CEN reported that of the 1,095 standards mandated by the Commission to CEN, concerning the directives on pressure vessels, toys, machinery, personal protective equipment, medical devices and gas appliances, only 47 standards had been adopted, whilst 250 draft standards were at the final stage of the procedure.[141] In June 1994, a certain improvement had been detected: the number of standards adopted by CEN had amounted to 218 whilst 652 standards were under enquiry,[142] out of the 1,709 standards mandated by the Commission.[143] Further progress can be observed in 1997, even though more mandates have been given to the standard-setting bodies.[144] CEN thus reports that of the 2,296 standards mandated in June 1997,[145] 656 had been ratified, and 927 were still being prepared (see Table 4).[146]

---

[136] See the Commission's Green Paper on the Development of European Standardisation, COM(90)456 final.

[137] Pelkmans/Egan, above n. 5.

[138] In 1991, the number of standards developed on Commission mandates represented 20% of CEN's total work programme, CEN's Annual Report of 1991, 9.

[139] See Schreiber, above n. 112, 105–7 in relation to the Dirs. on Construction Products and Machinery.

[140] Green Paper, above n. 136, at 13, point 6.

[141] CEN's Annual Report of 1991, 9.

[142] See on this procedure, sect. 2.2.3.2.

[143] CEN's Annual Report of 1993–4, 36.

[144] For an overview of the number of standards under development, under approval, ratified by the standardisation bodies and standards notified in the Official Journal on Apr. 1995, see Table 4 set out in Falke, above n. 58.

[145] These mandate figures also include some more recent dirs., such as Recreational Craft and Packaging and Packaging Waste.

[146] CEN's Annual Report of 1996–7, 14.

Table 4. Overview of the progress made by CEN in the development of standards in the framework of Commission mandates relating to the relevant New Approach Directives (involving safety standards) in June 1994 and in June 1997.

Directives	Ratified Standards		Standards Under Enquiry		Total Mandated Standards	
Year	1994	1997	1994	1997	1994	1997
Simple Pressure Vessels	21	35	18	8	42	47
Toys	6	6	0	0	6	6
Construction Products	65	147	323	238	757*	overall programme under development
Machinery (incl. static, lifting and mobility aspects)	23	144	142	337	462	708
Personal Protective Equipment	79	145	80	42	226	241
Gas Appliance	13	35	38	43	76	90
Active Implantable Medical Devices	7	29	19	13	38	46
Medical Devices	3	50	30	61	98	144
Recreational Craft	9	14	17	11	33	49
Lifts	—	1	3	4	8	14

Source: CEN's Annual Report of 1993/1994 and CEN's Annual Report of 1996–7.
* Interpretation depending on whether or not all items fall under the Directive.

The Commission's Working Methods

According to the Commission, "the final success of the New Approach . . . depends largely on the European Standardisation bodies".[147] However, the Commission itself was not without blame: its own policies and practices contributed to the delays in the development of European Standards. The Commission gave the European standardisation organisations an enormous workload to produce the standards within a fixed period of time. In view of the fact that it takes approximately seven years to develop an international standard and four years to generate a national one, it was unrealistic to expect European

[147] Green Paper, above n. 136, at 9.

standards to be developed within the tight deadlines set by the Commission. For example, the tight deadline set by the Council in the Machinery Directive raised various problems: this Directive came into force at the end of 1992, even though CEN still had many standards to prepare. The Council responded to these problems by extending the transitional period of a number of New Approach directives until January 1997.[148]

In addition, the overlap of the scope of various directives has further contributed to the confusion surrounding certain product standards.[149] This problem exists, in particular, with respect to the Low Voltages Directive, the Machinery Directive and the Construction Products Directive. The lack of prioritisation by the Commission in its mandates gave also rise to great difficulties for the standardisation bodies.[150] Furthermore, in the case of the Construction Products Directive, the Commission failed to adopt in time the additional criteria, necessary for the elaboration of standards for particular products, in so-called Interpretative Documents. Consequently, this led to a delay in the preparation of standards by CEN. Although the Construction Directive came into force in June 1991, CEN reported that by the end of 1991 of the 753 standards mandated, only seven standards had actually been adopted and 127 draft standards were still being prepared.[151] In these circumstances, it was very difficult for producers of technical consumer products to satisfy the requirements of the Directive.

The Delay in Implementation by the Member States

The delay in the implementation of the Council directives by the Member States also formed one of the drawbacks of the New Approach. For example, when the Construction Products Directive came into force on 27 June 1991, only three Member States had implemented this Directive into their national law.[152] To some extent, this delay was part of the general problem of prompt implementation of Community directives. The delay was, however, also part of a particular "policy" followed by Member States which, faced with the delay in the standardisation process, decided to postpone the putting into force of a number of New Approach directives.[153] The latter problem was addressed by the aforementioned amendment of New Approach directives.[154]

---

[148] Council Dir. 93/68/EEC amending Dirs. 87/404/EEC (simple pressure vessels); 88/378/EEC (toys); 89/106/EEC (construction products); 89/336/EEC (electromagnetic compatibility); 89/392/EEC (machinery); 89/686/EEC (personal protective equipment); 90/384/EEC (non-automatic weighing instruments); 90/385/EEC (active implantable medical devices); 90/396/EEC (appliances burning gaseous fuels); 91/263/EEC (telecommunications terminal equipment); 92/42/EEC (new hot water boilers fired with liquid or gaseous fuels) and 73/23/EEC (electrical equipment designed for use within certain voltage limits) [1993] OJ L220/1.

[149] This opinion was expressed by CEN in its comments on the Green Paper, European Commission, *Detailed Review of the Comments on the Green Paper* (Brussels, 1991), internal paper, at 20.

[150] Follow-up to the Green Paper, COM(91)521 final, 11.

[151] CEN's Annual Report of 1991, 9.

[152] Recently, the Court condemned Belgium for failure to implement this Dir.; see Case C–263/96, *Commission v. Belgium* [1997] ECR I–7453.

[153] See Pelkmans/Egan, above n. 5, 5 and 27.

[154] Above n. 148.

2.3.5. The Need to Deepen the New Approach

2.3.5.1. The Global Approach to Certification and Testing

Certification was obviously of growing importance, since it forms the means of proof which the economic operators require in order to comply with the legislative obligations.[155] Confusion surrounding the conformity assessment forced the Community institutions to refine their requirements constantly. It took the Commission until 1989, however, to adopt a more general approach to the issues of testing and certification. On 15 June 1989, the Commission presented a "Global Approach to Certification and Testing",[156] which aims to lay down a basis for the development of transparent and homogenous structures for certification, testing and quality. This approach was confirmed by the Council in its Resolution of 21 December 1989.[157] In the Global Approach, eight modules were developed for the conformity assessment, which relate to the design and production phases of products. The Global Approach also emphasises the need for the affixing of a CE marking.

The modules for the various phases of conformity assessment procedures were adopted by Council Decision 90/683/EEC.[158] According to this Decision, the essential objective of a conformity assessment procedure is to enable the public authorities to ensure that products placed on the market conform to the essential requirements, such as the health and safety of users and consumers, which are expressed in the provisions of the directives.[159] It determines a variety of modules which may be used by the directives.[160] In setting a wide range of possible modules, the directives attempt to leave as wide a choice as is consistent with ensuring compliance with the requirements.[161] The modules cover internal product control (module A), EC type-examination (module B), conformity to type (module C), production quality assurance (module D), product quality assurance (module E), product verification (module F), unit verification (module G) and full quality assurance (module H).[162] However, this general strategy also appeared insufficient to clarify and rationalise these modules and ensure coherency as regards the affixing of the CE marking. Clarification on the

---

[155] See J. McMillan, "La «certification», la reconnaissance mutuelle et le marché unique" [1991] *RMUE* 2, 182. See also J. Ensthaler, *Zertifizierung, Akkreditierung und Normung für den Europäischen Binnenmarkt* (Berlin, 1995); P. Andreini/G. Caia/G. Elias/F.A. Roversi Monaco (eds.), *La normativa tecnica industriale. Amministrazione e privati nella normativa e nella certificazione dei prodotti industriale* (Bologna, 1995), and Farr, above n. 112, 51 ff.

[156] A Global Approach to certification and testing. Quality measures for industrial products, COM(89)209 final—SYN 208.

[157] Council Resolution on a Global Approach to conformity assessment [1990] OJ C10/1.

[158] Council Dec. 90/683/EEC concerning the modules for the various phases of the conformity assessment procedures which are intended to be used in the technical harmonisation dirs. [1990] OJ L380/13.

[159] Annex to Council Dec. 90/683/EEC, above n. 158, Point I (a).

[160] *Ibid.*, Point I(d).

[161] *Ibid.*, Point I(f).

[162] *Ibid.*, Point II.

modules and rules on the affixing and use of the CE marking was brought by Council Decision 93/465/EEC.[163] More recent directives, such as the Medical Devices Directive,[164] include a classification of the devices and a variety of conformity assessment procedures.

In the Global Approach, the Commission also identified the need for a European infrastructure for the certification and testing in non-regulated areas, which depend on mutual recognition. For mutual recognition to work, confidence in the operators in the field of conformity assessment is essential. Consequently, the Commission promoted the creation of a flexible and non-bureaucratic structure which could constitute a central point for all interested parties.[165] The Council officially approved the creation of such a structure in its Resolution of 21 December 1991.[166] On 25 April 1990, the Commission, the EFTA secretariat, CEN and CENELEC signed a Memorandum of Understanding setting up the European Organisation for Testing and Certification (EOTC) for those products which do not fall within the ambit of EC directives.[167] This body aims to encourage mutual recognition agreements on certification and testing between the national bodies, to provide assistance and technical support to European legislation concerning questions on conformity assessment, the exchange of information and experiences of all parties, and to supplement the European standardisation process in the sector of conformity assessment.

2.3.5.2. The Green Paper on the Development of European Standardisation and its Follow-Up

It was the backlog in the European standardisation process that really pushed the Commission in 1990 to submit a "Green Paper on the Development of European Standardisation: Action for Faster Technological Integration in Europe".[168] Although both the Member States and the Commission had played their part in the slow-down in bringing the New Approach into effective opera-

---

[163] Council Dec. 93/465/EEC concerning the modules for the various phases of the conformity assessment procedures and the rules for affixing and use of CE conformity marking, which are intended to be used in the technical harmonisation dirs. [1993] OJ L220/23; Council Dir. 93/68/EEC consolidated the procedures of affixing the CE marking for the already adopted New Approach dirs. [1993] OJ L22/1. See Commission proposal for a Council Reg. (EEC) concerning the affixing and use of the CE marking of conformity on industrial products, COM(91)145 final—SYN 336 and amendment to the proposal for a Council Reg. (EEC) concerning the affixing and use of the CE marking of conformity on industrial products, COM(92)239 final—SYN 336.

[164] Above n. 130.

[165] Global Approach, above n. 156, Point III. C, and the Annex, Commission Memorandum on a Global Approach to certification and testing, Chap. 4, sect. four.

[166] Above n. 157.

[167] See McMillan, above n. 155, 201–2; Falke, above n. 112, 114–15; P. Andreini, "La normative tecnica tra sfera pubblica e sfera privata", in P. Andreini/G. Caia/G. Elias/F.A. Roversi Monaco (eds.), *La normativa tecnica industriale. Amministrazione e privati nella normativa e nella certificazione dei prodotti industriale* (Bologna, 1995), 45–98; L. Alunni, *Norme tecniche e certificazione della qualità. Politiche comunitarie, istituzioni e procedure* (Perugia, 1992), 103–5.

[168] Above n. 136.

tion,[169] the Commission preferred to blame mainly the standardisation organisations for the delay. In the Green Paper, the Commission gave clear priority to the acceleration of the standardisation process, but addresses some institutional issues, too.

Since the delay in the production of standards was, in the Commission's opinion, mainly due to CEN and CENELEC, its proposals were particularly aimed at improving the working methods of these bodies. In order to accelerate the standard-setting processes, it suggested: new methods for establishing common working documents (using, for instance, drafting secretariats to draw up a summary of the technical issues in one document); greater use of associated standardisation bodies; use of new technology to accelerate discussion on working documents; majority voting in technical committees; shorter and more flexible public enquiries; more rapid handling of comments; direct application of adopted standards, and the creation of one category of European standards, recognisable under their European identification number. Many proposals, such as majority voting in the TCs and the reduction of public enquiry periods, covered existing procedural working methods, while some proposals attempted to introduce completely new methods. The new methods included the introduction of novel procedures for drafting common working documents and the greater use of associated standardisation bodies to develop technical documents. In addition, the Commission proposed the creation of a European Standardisation System which would enhance co-ordination, transparency and the legitimacy of European standardisation.[170]

However, given the drastic nature of some of the proposals, the Green Paper was not received with great enthusiasm. Not surprisingly, the institutional reform of European standardisation was not particularly favoured by most of the participants in the European standardisation process, since the new system would considerably diminish their dominant position in European standardisation.[171] Further criticisms were expressed about the Commission's neglect of international standardisation, its sole focus on EC mandated standards, the misrepresentation of industrial involvement and the misunderstanding of operating practices in standardisation.[172] The Commission's proposals to accelerate the standardisation process by focusing on qualified majority voting in technical committees would, according to this criticism, completely ignore the characteristic core principle of consensus for the standardisation process.[173]

Consequently, in its Follow-up Communication, the Commission dropped most of its proposals. Instead, it proposed a more modest institutional reform, setting up a European Standardisation Forum, and some procedural changes,

---

[169] See sect. 2.3.4.
[170] The Commission's proposals related to the institutional reform of standardisation are discussed into more detail in sect. 4.1.
[171] Follow-up Communication, above n. 150, at 4.
[172] See Pelkmans/Egan, above n. 5, 15–22.
[173] See, on the principle of consensus, in particular, sect. 2.2.3.2.

such as the introduction of so-called programming mandates (specifying a full programme for the standards work for a specific sector in which clear priorities are set) and the reduction of public enquiry periods where national standards are simply adopted as European Standards. However, these proposals, too, were rejected by the standardisation bodies[174] and consequently not adopted by the Council.[175]

2.3.5.3. Increased Community Activities on Product Safety

Since the New Approach resulted in increasing the circulation of technical consumer products on the Community market, it also increased the chances of accidents resulting from the use of such products. As a result, there has been a clear need for the Community to undertake post-market-entry surveillance of products, which at the same time confirms the Community's commitment to safety protection.[176] The Parliament and Council have, for example, expressly stated in the preamble to their Decision setting up the Community System of information on home and leisure accidents that:

> "the establishment of a Community system of information on home and leisure accidents forms a component part of a policy of consumer protection and the prevention of accidents; . . . its importance in this respect can be seen from the fact that the data collected pursuant to the demonstration project set up by Decision 86/138/EEC, are being put to specific uses by several Member States for the adoption of measures in the area of product safety".[177]

As argued in Chapter 1, for reasons both of free movement and consumer health and safety protection, the Community has been required to adopt a firective on general product safety.[178] This directive not only places a general obligation on manufacturers to produce safe products but includes a notification and information procedure on the dangers arising from products. Based on this directive, a specific Community system has been created for the exchange of information of certain products which may jeopardise consumer health or safety.[179]

3. DELEGATION OF POWERS TO THE EUROPEAN STANDARDISATION BODIES?

The New Approach's generalised use of the regulatory model of the Low Voltage Directive was however highly debated. First, the regulatory technique

---

[174] Pelkmans/Egan, above n. 5, at 14.

[175] Council Resolution on the role of European standardisation in the European Economy [1992] OJ C173/1.

[176] See Chap. 2.

[177] First recital of the preamble to European Parliament and Council Dec. 3092/94/EC [1994] OJ L331/1, which confirmed a ongoing pilot project (EHLASS) initiated in 1986 by Council Dec. 86/138/EEC [1986] OJ L109/23.

[178] Council Dir. 92/59/EEC, above n. 3.

[179] Council Dec. 93/580/EEC [1993] OJ L278/64.

of the Low Voltage Directive presupposed specific conditions in the electrical sector. Secondly, although the Commission had attempted to design the New Approach carefully so as to meet the legal critique on the Low Voltage Directive, legal problems arising out of this directive were by no means entirely solved. Hence, today, legal debate continues to doubt the legality of the use of the reference to standards technique in the New Approach. One of the most controversial questions in legal literature remains whether it constitutes an illegal delegation of public decision-making powers to the private standardisation bodies, with no possibility of challenging their acts by judicial review. Although two cases on the interpretation of the Low Voltage Directive had been brought before the Court, in neither case did the Court express its opinion on the validity of this technique.[180] Hence, the question whether this technique entails an invalid delegation of powers to the standardisation bodies still needs to be tackled.[181]

3.1. The Reference to Standards Technique

3.1.1. Methods of Referring to Standards

Although the use of the reference to standards technique in the New Approach as a general regulatory model was innovative at Community level, it was not a new phenomenon for most Member States. At national level, there are mainly two methods of referring to standards:[182] *rigid* (*strict*) reference to standards and *sliding* (*dynamic* or *general*) reference to standards.

In the case of a *rigid* or *strict* reference, the legislature refers to technical standards, which are indicated by number, date, editions and if appropriate, the modifications of the standards. In this manner, the legislature is able to verify the content of a technical standard before incorporating it into the legal provisions. This description already indicates the main objection to this technique: in order to modify the standard, one must go through the lengthy legislative process, whilst the difficulty of modifying a standard could consequently hinder its technical developments. Rigid reference may, therefore, be an appropriate method only where one or few standards can be referred to or where technical development has been more or less closed off and major innovations are unlikely.

Sliding, dynamic or general reference alludes to the technique where reference is made to technical standards in their most current form.[183] This type

---

[180] Case 123/76, *Commission* v. *Italy* [1977] ECR 1449 and Case 815/79, *Cremonini and Vrankovich* [1980] ECR 3583. See, in general on these cases, T. Hartley, "Consumer Safety and the Harmonisation of Technical Standards: The Low Voltage Directive" (1982) 7 *ELR* 55–62.

[181] Joerges *et al.*, above n. 4, at 382 and Breulmann, above n. 20, 175–6.

[182] See, in particular, Marburger, above n. 4, 379–407. Also H.H. Eberstein, *Technische Regeln und ihre rechtliche Bedeutung* (Baden-Baden, 1969).

[183] Breulmann, above n. 20, 126–41, Marburger, above n. 4, 379–407; Joerges *et al.*, above n. 4, 136–41 (EUI Working Paper LAW 91/12, 6–12).

of reference uses, for example, indefinite terms, such as "the state of the art" in the legal text, which need to be specified by private standardisation bodies.[184] It may also include the reference to a technical standard indicating number and sometimes title, without displaying date or editions.[185]

Although some objections to the rigid reference technique might be solved by, for instance, referring to the technical standard in an administrative act, instead of a parliamentary act,[186] the advantages of the use of the sliding reference are apparent. Besides relieving the legislature of a burden and keeping legal texts free from complex technical details, this reference also allows a flexible adaptation of the content of the law to technical development and the participation of expert circles in law-making.[187] It is not surprising that preference is given to the sliding reference technique, particularly by the standardisation bodies.[188]

3.1.2. *Admissibility of the Reference to Standards Technique in the National Context*

The interwoven relationship between legal provisions and technical norms introduced in various Member States has not been free of criticism. Particularly in the German context, legal writers have raised major constitutional objections to the reference to standards technique. The rigid reference technique is generally not challenged here, since a precise standard is actually incorporated in the legislative norm and thus guarantees public intervention. However, particularly problematic is the use of the sliding reference to standards technique, since it would constitute a disguised delegation of decision-making powers to private persons. This would mean that, in practice, private bodies were to decide on the common good. This technique would allegedly be contrary to the principles of democracy, of constitutionality, in particular that of legal certainty, of openness and of the separation of powers.[189] The same objections have been sustained against the allowance of the sliding reference, supplementing the legal norms, which would boil down to giving *carte blanche* to private standardisation bodies.

Although the use of the sliding reference technique has provoked several constitutional problems in the Member States, it has not been abandoned. Instead of rejecting it, the practical need for this technique has been faced and legal requirements have been developed to obviate the objections forwarded. Various

---

[184] Breulmann, above n. 20, 136–8; Joerges *et al.*, above n. 4, 140–1 (EUI Working Paper LAW 91/12, 11–12). See, also, Falke, above n. 58, 216 ff.

[185] See G.M.F. Snijders, *Produktveiligheid en aansprakelijkheid* (Deventer, 1987), 47–9.

[186] *Ibid.*

[187] P. Marburger, *Die gleitende Verweisung aus der Sicht der Wissenschaft, Verweisung auf technische Normen in Rechtsvorschriften*, DIN–Normungskunde, Bd. 17 (Berlin/Cp;pgme, 1982), 29–30.

[188] Snijders, above n. 185, at 53.

[189] See references made in Joerges *et al.*, above n. 4, at 139, n. 34 (EUI Working Paper LAW 91/12, at 10, n. 34).

authors have thus attempted to formulate legal requirements, compliance with which would justify the sliding reference to standards technique. In the German context, for instance, Marburger has formulated the following minimum procedural requirements to which the German standardisation processes should adhere: standardisation committees should comprehensively represent all relevant expertise; all interests concerned should be represented in a balanced way in the standardisation procedure; the public should be enabled to influence the content of a standard, when developed; technical standards should be subjected to regular revision and the standard-setting procedure should be laid down in a binding way.[190] The main difficulties in satisfying such requirements generally lie in ensuring a balanced representation of all interests involved.

3.1.3. *The Reference to Standards Technique under the New Approach*

Several elements indicate that the technique used in the New Approach involves a sliding reference technique, leaving open the question of which standard is the technical specification. First, the New Approach's distinction between the legal safety requirements to be drawn up by the Community legislature, and the technical specifications to be elaborated by CEN and CENELEC, does not make reference to a specific standard. According to the Council:

> "One of the main characteristics of the New Approach is to make it possible to settle at a stroke, with the adoption of a single Directive, all the problems concerning regulations for a very large number of products, without the need for frequent amendments or adaptations to that Directive".[191]

In addition, the Model Directive and the directives based on it do not refer to specific standards by indicating their number and date. In practice, this would be almost impossible, since standards need to implement the essential safety requirements and are only drafted following the adoption of a specific directive. The Model Directive further emphasises that essential safety requirements must be worded precisely enough to create legally binding obligations which can be enforced.[192] These requirements demonstrate that the standards need to implement the essential requirements and not to supplement them.

3.2. Delegation of Powers to CEN and CENELEC?

The adoption of the Low Voltage Directive had been followed by various legal critiques, especially in German literature. Röhling, for instance, took the view that this technique in substance came down to an inadmissible delegation of

---

[190] Marburger, above n. 4, 138–46; see Joerges *et al.*, above n. 4, at 183 (EUI Working Paper LAW 91/12, 64).
[191] Criteria for choosing the priority areas in which the New Approach could initially be applied, Annex II, point 2 (b), at 9.
[192] Model Directive, above n. 114, Point B. III. 1.

powers, and if the Community were to take such standards into account, the Community ought to guarantee, *inter alia*, the Commission's influence on the standardisation process. In particular, the use of general and vague terminology to describe the safety objectives in the Low Voltage Directive were criticised as they would only allow preliminary assessments and would become applicable only by the standards. It is particularly this consequence of the reference to standards technique that the Commission in its White Paper intended to avoid.[193] According to the preparatory document of 31 January 1985, the essential safety requirements must be worded precisely enough "in order to create, on transposition into national law, legally binding obligations which can be imposed".[194] Consequently, the Model Directive requires that the essential safety requirements must be:

> "so formulated as to enable the certification bodies immediately to certify products as being in conformity, having regard to those requirements in the absence of standards".[195]

Although this phrasing was criticised for endangering the whole New Approach philosophy,[196] it did not quieten lawyers' concerns of an illegal delegation of powers to the European standardisation organisations.[197] In this context, most legal writers refer to the Court's case law in *Meroni*[198] which would allow for some degree of delegation, but under restricted conditions.[199] Several authors conclude from this case law that the New Approach entails an illegal delegation of powers to the standardisation bodies. Lauwaars, for example, concludes that compliance with the harmonisation standards grants a right to free movement, which implies a delegation of powers by the Council to the private standardisation bodies. In his view, this delegation would not be in accor-

---

[193] See for instance, Joerges *et al.*, above n. 4, at 346 (EUI Working Paper 91/13, at 132); P. Schloesser, "Europäische Gemeinschaft und Europäische Normung", in DIN Normungskunde n. 8, *Europäische Normung in CEN und CENELEC* (Berlin/Cologne, 1976), 132; M. Seidel, "Regeln der Technik und Europäisches Gemeinschaftsrecht" (1981) 34 *NJW* 1120–5.

[194] COM(85)19 final, 11.

[195] The New Approach Council Resolution, above n. 99.

[196] See Pelkmans, above n. 112, 265 ff. The European Parliament's Committee on Economic and Monetary Affairs and Industrial Policy also called for the deletion of this phrasing, PE Doc. A 2–54/86, 16 June 1986, point 7. See however the Commission's answer to a question of a MEP on this issue [1987] OJ C19/5.

[197] This concern is particularly debated in German literature. A short selection of recent literature on this subject is: E. Denninger, *Verfassungsrechtliche Anforderungen an die Normsetzung im Umwelt- und Technikrecht* (Baden-Baden, 1990); Falke, above n. 58; Falke/Joerges, above n. 88 and the preliminary experts' reports of U. Di Fabio/A. Bleckmann/H. Kubicek/P. Seeger (eds.), *Perspektive Techniksteuerung. Interdisziplinäre Sichtweisen eines Schlüsselproblems entwickelter Industriegesellschaften* (Berlin, 1993); G. Lübbe-Wolff, "Verfassungsrechtliche Fragen der Normsetzung" [1991] *Zeitschrift für Gesetzgebung* 219–48; P. Marburger/R. Enders, "Technische Normen im europäischen Gemeinschaftsrecht" [1994] *Jahrbuch für Umwelt- und Technikrecht*, 333–68;. A. Roßnagel, "Europäische Techniknormen im Lichte des Gemeinschaftsrechts" (1996) 111 *Deutsches Verwaltungsblatt*, 1181–5.

[198] Case 9/56, *Meroni & Co. Industrie Metallurgiche S.p.A. v. High Authority* [1958] ECR 133; Case 10/56, *Meroni & Co. Industrie Metallurgiche S.p.A. v. High Authority* [1958] ECR 157.

[199] See, in detail, Chap. 4.

dance with the *Meroni* case law since it fails to fulfil the requirement of judicial control.[200] More recently, Breulmann, too, denies the legality of the New Approach and its use of the sliding reference to standards technique. Yet he does not apply the *Meroni* conditions to allow for some delegation but severely rejects delegation as the Treaty does not provide for a specific provision allowing such delegation.[201] He concludes that a *de facto* delegation of decision-making powers to the standardisation bodies takes place, since the standards have legal binding effect on the national (judicial) authorities. The decisive factor here would be that Member States do not have autonomous powers to refuse the circulation of products in conformity with the harmonised standards on their market.[202]

Others, however, have denied delegation of decision-making powers to the standardisation bodies since the standards elaborated by CEN and CENELEC do not have legally binding consequences for the manufacturers or for the national authorities and the reference to them constitutes a refutable presumption.[203] Instead they generally point to the problems of legitimacy originating from a model based on interaction with private actors.[204] Thus, analysis of whether delegation takes place must focus on the nature of the standards and the presumption of conformity.

3.2.1. Nature of the Standards and the Presumption of Conformity

At first sight, the New Approach reveals that the standards referred to are non-mandatory and retain their status of *voluntary* standards.[205] The voluntary nature of the standards signifies that a manufacturer is free to *choose* whether or not to produce the products in conformity with the European standards. What is important is that the products satisfy the essential safety requirements laid down in the directives. In that case, however, the producer must prove that the products conform to the essential safety requirements. In the Commission's view, the reference to the standards is optional, so that corresponding standards cannot be mandatory and are therefore no more than mere *presumptions*.[206]

However, whether such presumptions are *refutable* or constitute *legal obligations* depends on the effect they have on the national (judicial) authorities.[207] Products manufactured in conformity with the standards drawn up by the European standardisation bodies are presumed to conform to the essential

---

[200] Lauwaars, above n. 115, 165–6.
[201] Breulmann, above n. 20, 175 ff.
[202] *Ibid.*, at 161–2.
[203] E.g., Falke, above n. 58; Falke/Joerges, above n. 88; A. Bücker, *Von Gefahrenabwehr zu Risikovorsorge und Risikomanagement im Arbeitsschutz. Eine Untersuchung am Beispiel der rechtlichen Regulierung der Sicherheit von Maschinen under dem Einfluß der Europäischen Rechtsangleichung* (Berlin, 1997), 213.
[204] See sect. 4.
[205] As stated in the Guidelines for the New Approach, above n. 113, at 3.
[206] Case 815/79, *Cremonini and Vrankovich*, above n. 180, at 3592.
[207] Breulmann, above n. 20, at 151 ff.

safety requirements determined in the directives. This presumption, as a general rule, obliges the Member States to allow such products on their markets. The presumption of conformity depends on both the publication of the reference by the Commission in the Official Journal, followed by the publication by the Member States of the references of the national standards transposed and the transposition of the European standards into national standards.[208] Use of the standard before its publication in the Official Journal by the Commission or by the Member States or non-transposition will not give rise to a presumption of conformity. It follows that Member States which ignore the harmonised standards are acting contrary to the obligations stemming from the relevant directive.[209] In this vein, compliance with the standards would constitute almost a right to free movement.[210] Yet the Member States are not legally bound by the standards since they do have powers to refute the presumption of conformity and thus no delegation takes place.[211] The two means which Member States have at their disposal for refusing products manufactured in accordance with harmonised standards are, as the Model Directive terms, the management of the list of standards and the safeguard clause.[212]

(a) Management of the Standards List

All directives contain a provision that the Member States can refer harmonised standards, which they deem not to be in conformity with the essential safety requirements, to the Committee on Technical Standards and Regulations[213] set up by Directive 83/189/EEC.[214] Although the Commission takes the ultimate decision on the conformity of the harmonised standards in this procedure, through the 83/189 Committee, the Member States can actively participate in shaping the decision, and ultimately, they can bring an action before the Court against this decision.

---

[208] Guidelines for the New Approach, above n. 113, fourth indent, at 3. Art. 5 of the Active Implantable Medical Devices Dir. (above n. 127), e.g., requires that "Member States shall presume compliance with the essential requirements referred to in Art. 3 in respect of devices which are in conformity with the relevant national standards adopted pursuant to the harmonised standards the references of which have been published in the Official Journal of the European Communities". Similar formulations can be found in other directives, such as Art. 5 of the Medical Devices Dir. (above n. 130); Art. 5 of the Toys Dir. (above n. 121); Art. 4 of the Construction Products Dir. (above n. 122) and Art. 5 of the Personal Protective Equipment Dir. (above n. 125).

[209] Breulmann, above n. 20, at 196.

[210] Lauwaars, above n. 115, at 165.

[211] See for instance, Falke, above n. 58; Falke/Joerges, above n. 88 and Bücker, above n. 203, at 213. See, however, the Construction Products Dir., which does not include a safeguard procedure.

[212] See, also, sects. 2.3.3.2. and 4.6.2.

[213] In accordance with Point VI of the Model Dir. (above n. 114). These procedures can be found in Art. 6 of the Toys Dir. (above n. 121); Art. 6 of the Active Implantable Medical Devices Dir. (above n. 127); Art. 5(2) of the Medical Devices Dir. (above n. 130); Art. 6 of the Machinery Dir. (above n. 124); Art. 5 of the Construction Products Dir. (above n. 122); Art. 7 of the Personal Protective Equipment Dir. (above n. 125).

[214] In accordance with Art. 5 of this Dir., above n. 102.

(b) Safeguard Clause Procedure

In addition, through the safeguard clause procedure the Member States may still restrict or prohibit the free circulation of those products on their markets which, although bearing the CE mark, could compromise the safety of persons.[215] These safeguard clause procedures allow the Member States to adopt solely temporary measures and once again the final word is for the Commission, in accordance with a committee procedure in which Member States again participate. Ultimately, Member States here, too, have the possibility of legal proceedings before the Court. The existence of such a Community procedure does not seem to prevent national judicial authorities from examining the harmonised standard in an individual action against a Member State which refuses to allow the entry of a product for safety reasons inherent in shortcomings of harmonised standards, even when confirmed by the Commission.[216] Hence, the standards elaborated by CEN and CENELEC do not have legally binding consequences for manufacturers or for the national authorities and the reference to them constitutes a refutable presumption. Thus, there is no delegation of decision-making powers to the European standardisation bodies.[217]

3.2.2. Delegation of Powers to the Commission

The assertion that an unlawful delegation takes place has been substantiated by the argument that harmonised standards have binding legal effect on national (judicial) authorities in particular because Member States do not have autonomous powers to prohibit circulation of products in conformity with the harmonised standards on their market. The main defendant of this thesis is Breulmann, who substantiates this assertion by referring to the fact that although Member States may indeed refuse products manufactured in conformity with the harmonised standards, they may do so only in limited cases and not under their own decision-making powers but under the control of the Commission.[218] However, in his reasoning Breulmann seemingly seeks comparison with the German situation as regards the reference to standards technique, and fails to recognise the complexity of the Community situation. Here, the New Approach empowers the Council and the Parliament to define the essential requirements and leaves the technical specification to the standardisation bodies, whilst the Member States remain responsible for ensuring the safety of

---

[215] Or domestic animals or property. See Point VII of the Model Dir. (above n. 114) and, for instance, Art. 7 of the Toys Dir. (above n. 121); Art. 7 of the Active Implantable Medical Devices Dir. (above n. 127); Art. 8 of the Medical Devices Dir. (above n. 130); Art. 7 of the Machinery Dir. (above n. 124); Art. 21 of the Construction Products Dir. (above n. 122); Art. 7 of the Personal Protective Equipment Dir. (above n. 125);

[216] See Bücker, above n. 203, at 214, who points in this context to Art. 11 of the Machinery Dir. Contra: Breulmann, above n. 20.

[217] Falke, above n. 58; Falke/Joerges, above n. 88, Bücker, above n. 203, at 213. Contra: Breulmann, above n. 20, 151 ff.

[218] Breulmann, above n. 20, 161–2.

products circulating on their markets. At the same time, the supervision and ultimate decision of the standards and the safety of products are entrusted to the Commission together with committees.[219] Therefore, the lack of autonomous powers of the Member States does not depend on the harmonised standards or the presumption of conformity, but on the fact that these powers are delegated to the Commission. Consequently, this argument does not alter the previous finding that no delegation takes place, either.

4. LEGITIMACY OF DECISION-MAKING AND STANDARD-SETTING

Instead of pointing to problems of delegation of powers, therefore, one should accept the need for the Community to resort to the standardisation bodies and seek to find a delicate balance between the regulation of public interests and the independence of the private standards bodies. It is clear that although harmonised standards are of a voluntary, non-binding nature and no delegation of decision-making powers takes place, the standards and the European standards organisations play an important role in Community health and safety regulation. Without doubt, manufacturers of technical products are left free to decide how to reach the safety level required by the individual directives. It is, however, clear that manufacturers will generally use the harmonised standards as these standards give their products the advantage of the refutable presumption of conformity and thus easier access to national markets.[220] In this sense, notwithstanding their voluntary nature, standards also have an influence on a person's safety and have a public interest character.

Hence, the law's task should be to make sure that the integrity of the standard-setting process is observed: that adequate means of controlling this process are provided and that this process is legitimate.[221] Co-operation between both public authorities and private bodies is essential here to bridge the public–private divide. The focus on possibilities of controlling the standardisation bodies and the standard-setting process would also be in congruity with the Court's judgment in *Reiff*.[222] As already set out in the previous chapter, the Court accepted here that private actors carried out specific tasks but emphasised the importance of procedural safeguards to ensure that the public interest is respected.[223] This avenue has been followed by the Commission in its Green Paper and Follow-up Communication.[224]

---

[219] See sect. 4.2.

[220] See, also, for instance, Pelkmans/Egan, above n. 5, at 14.

[221] See, also, Falke, above n. 58; Falke/Joerges, above n. 88.

[222] Case C–185/91, *Bundesanstalt für den Güterfernverkehr* v. *Gebrüder Reiff* [1993] ECR I–5801.

[223] See Ch. Joerges, "Scientific Expertise in Social Regulation and the European Court of Justice: Legal Frameworks for Denationalised Governance Structures", in Ch. Joerges/K.H. Ladeur/E. Vos (eds.), *Integrating Scientific Expertise into Regulatory Decision-Making. National Traditions and European Innovations* (Baden-Baden, 1997), 318.

[224] See below.

Consequently, this section investigates the efforts of the Commission in regulating the self-regulatory standardisation process and the legitimacy requirements, which have been examined in the previous chapters: the manner in which the standards are drafted and the quality of expertise, interest participation, transparency and means of control and accountability of standard-setting and what means for co-operation exists between the Commission, the Member States and CEN/CENELEC.

4.1. The Commission's Attempts to Democratise the Standardisation Process

4.1.1. A European Standardisation System

With its proposal for creating a European Standardisation System in the 1990 Green Paper on Standardisation, the Commission attempted to address the long-standing critique of leaving public risk regulation to be carried out by private standard bodies, by calling for the increased involvement of interested parties. According to the Commission, such a system would clearly define the role of all the participants at national level and European level in terms of agreed objectives and allow for greater transparency and participation of all interested parties. This system would allow for both the diversity of organisation and the autonomy of management within spectrally-based standardisation and would also ensure the co-ordination, transparency and legitimacy of European standardisation by applying common rules to all standardisation bodies within this system. These rules would have to be developed by a European Standardisation Council. This body would provide the overall policy of European standardisation activities and be composed of representatives of industry, consumers, users, trade unions, the Commission and the EFTA secretariat. In addition to this body, a European Standardisation Board—the executive body of the Standardisation Council—would strengthen co-ordination between the standardisation bodies. It would be composed of the officers of the European standardisation bodies and the secretary of the Standardisation Council. The European standardisation bodies would enjoy complete autonomy in the programming, financing, preparation and adoption of European standards, which would be subject to compliance with the rules of the European Standardisation System.[225]

In the Commission's view, this system would have the benefit of increasing flexibility by providing additional sectoral organisations where industrial sectors feel the need for greater autonomy. Accordingly, the pace of production of standards would be increased, since European industry would participate as associated bodies and thus offer its services and expertise. The participation of European industry would likewise mean more financing, an issue which reappears in the final part of the Green Paper, where the Commission expresses its

---

[225] Green Paper, above n. 136, 23–30.

concern about the long-term financial stability of European standardisation, in view of the growing dependence of the standardisation bodies on public money.[226] The Commission thus proposed that members of the European standardisation bodies should be subject to long-term financial commitment; to change the present system of collecting revenue from sales and to institute member fees for those industries participating in European standardisation (as associated bodies).

4.1.2. A European Standardisation Forum

However, the proposal for creating a European Standardisation System was ill-received by most participants in the European standardisation process.[227] The standardisation bodies, in particular, opposed the creation of new bodies, composed of representatives of the Commission, the EFTA secretariat, industry, consumers, users and trade unions, which would supervise the activities of the standardisation bodies, since this would threaten their autonomous position in European standardisation. For the same reasons, the national standardisation bodies rejected the proposal to allow associated bodies to participate directly in European standardisation. Similar oppositions was expressed by CEN, CENELEC and ETSI to the proposal to create new sectoral standardisation organisations. Industry did not approve the Commission's reform since it would need to contribute money and expertise to the standard-setting procedure.

Faced with these negative reactions, the Commission could clearly only retreat from its proposals. Abandoning most of its proposals, the Commission insisted nonetheless in its Follow-up Communication on the activation of a "process of democratisation of standardisation, which now gets more competences".[228] This Follow-up was, in the Commission's words:

> "intended to assist and promote democratic self-management of standardisation by indicating the changing political context in which European standardisation takes place, the fundamental principles on which standardisation should be based and the organisational changes which may be needed to ensure that those principles are fully observed".[229]

Although the Commission dropped the idea of radical institutional reform, it did however persist in its idea of creating some kind of institutional structure. It insisted that a kind of discussion panel should be established and suggested the creation of a European Standardisation Forum, instead of the previously proposed European Standardisation Council, which would comprise all interested parties and would further discussions about European standards policies. Its design would be similar to that of the proposed Standardisation Council,

---

[226] Green Paper, above n. 136, 37 ff.

[227] Follow-up Communication, above n. 150, at 4.

[228] J. Farnell, "Der Standpunkt der Generaldirektion III" (1992) *TGB* at 104; quoted in Eichener, above n. 84, at 93.

[229] Follow-up Communication, above n. 150, at 7.

although with an increased membership. This body would be able to address any issue relevant to the "success" of European standardisation, such as the current activity of the European standardisation bodies, the application of basic principles such as openness, participation of interested parties by the standardisation bodies, and the relationship between public authorities and the standardisation bodies. Whereas the conclusions of the Forum could be presented in non-binding resolutions, they would in all likelihood carry considerable weight in view of the fact that the representatives of the interested parties would be on the Forum. In addition, as an alternative to its proposed European Standardisation Board, it suggested the strengthening of the Joint Presidents Group which had been set up in the meantime in order to ensure permanent co-ordination between CEN, CENELEC and ETSI. Moreover, the Commission called upon the Member States to support the non-manufacturing interests to facilitate their participation in standardisation.[230] Furthermore, the Commission encouraged the more sectorally based industrial organisations to contribute to the standardisation process and European industrial organisations to participate directly in the work of the European standardisation bodies. However, this second more modest attempt to institutionalise and supervise standardisation was rejected by the European standards bodies, too.[231] Although the Council generally endorsed the principles set out by the Commission in its Green Paper and Follow-up, the institutional reform of standardisation was not pursued.[232] Unwilling to give up, the Commission very recently emphasised, next to efficiency, the importance of letting both public authorities and interested parties participate in the standardisation process and in strategic discussions and the elaboration of policy.[233]

4.2. The Interrelation between the Member States, the Community Institutions and the European Standardisation Bodies through Committees: Bridging the Public and Private Divide

Committees active in this field provide a means of supervision of the standard-setting process for the Member States and the Commission and supply a platform for co-operation between national public authorities, the Member States and the Commission, and the private standardisation bodies, CEN and CENELEC. In this vein, they bridge the public–private divide. Particular instruments to this end are the management of lists of the standards and the safeguard clauses.[234] Not surprisingly, the existence of committees and safeguard clauses

---

[230] See, on this issue, sect. 4.4.
[231] Pelkmans/Egan, above n. 5, at 14.
[232] Council Resolution, above n. 175.
[233] Report from the Commission to the Council and the European Parliament on efficiency and accountability in European standardisation under the New Approach, SEC(98)291, 10–12.
[234] See sect. 3.2.1.

here, too, encounters the Member States' insistence on remaining involved in decision-making delegated to the Commission, which attitude can be explained by the altered balance of powers between the Member States and the Community. Hence, committees guarantee the participation of the Member States in the implementation of the directives, while they forestall potential subsidiarity concerns.

In general, the committees active in technical product safety may legally be classified as committees whose consultation is obligatory. On a functional approach these committees may be classified as policy-making/implementation committees notwithstanding the fact that their consultation does not always follow the procedures prescribed by the Comitology Decision.[235] The following committees exist:

The Committee on Technical Standards and Regulations (83/189 Committee)

The Committee on Technical Standards and Regulations, set up by Directive 83/189/EEC[236] (the 83/189 Committee), plays a prominent role in the New Approach. It is composed of the representatives of the Member States, who may call for the assistance of experts or advisers and it is chaired by a representative of the Commission. Although there are no explicit provisions concerning the number of members, in practice, each Member State has one permanent and one alternate representative. Most representatives come from the Ministries of Economic Affairs and Trade and Industry.[237] Although a list of the Committee members seemingly exists, it is not made public.[238] The secretariat of the Committee is provided by the Commission. The Committee meets regularly, in general twice every three months. Further specific meetings may be held.[239] The Committee maintains a special relationship with the standardisation bodies. CEN and CENELEC representatives are often invited to attend its meetings.[240] At least twice a year, in so-called "enlarged" meetings, the Committee meets representatives of the national and European standardisation bodies.[241] Although Article 5 of Directive 83/189/EEC requires it to draw up its own rules of procedure, in practice this is ignored.[242] The lack of such rules and general information and transparency about the activities of this Committee clearly need to be improved.

The tasks of the Committee include: the giving of an opinion on problems which arise under the notification procedure; contact with the standardisation bodies, in particular through mandates; the development of Community standardisation policy towards the management of directives where no specific com-

---

[235] See Chap. 3.
[236] Above n. 102.
[237] Interview with a Commission official of DGIII.
[238] Interviews with a Commission official of DGIII and a former 83/189 Committee member.
[239] Interview with a former Commission official of DGIII.
[240] Interview with Commission officials of DGIII and CEN/CENELEC officials.
[241] Art. 6(1) of Dir. 83/189/EEC, above n. 102.
[242] Interview with Commission officials of DGIII.

mittees have been set up. Whilst no particular procedure for consultation has been instituted, in some cases the consultation of this Committee is obligatory, whereas in others it is voluntary. The Committee must be consulted and express its opinion on communications and proposals aimed at eliminating existing or foreseeable barriers to trade which the Commission submits to it.[243] In this connection, the Committee may propose, in particular, that the Commission request the European standards institutions to draw up a European standard within a given time limit, ensure where necessary that initially the Member States concerned decide amongst themselves on appropriate measures, or take all appropriate measures in order to avoid the risk of barriers to trade occurring.[244] Moreover, mandatory consultation is prescribed: where the Commission intends to amend the lists of standardisation bodies annexed to Directive 83/189/EEC; when it wants to draw up rules for the codified presentation of information and the planning and criteria for standards programmes; when it decides on the actual system whereby the exchange of information provided for in the Directive is to be effected and on any change to it; and when it reviews the operation of the system set up by the Directive.[245] Furthermore, the Committee must be consulted by the Commission when drafting a (programming) mandate to the European standardisation bodies,[246] while it may be consulted on any preliminary draft technical regulation received by the Commission.[247] The consultation of the 83/189 Committee is, in general, also required when a Member State invokes the safeguard clause for a product that does not conform to the safety requirements because of shortcomings in the standards.

Theoretically, it is possible for the Commission to deviate from the opinion of this Committee, but in practice, this appears hardly to occur.[248] In general, this Committee, too, has a forum function,[249] which enables the national representatives to exchange views with the Commission and the other Member States. Normally, no voting takes place in the Committee. As regards the process which is followed when adopting a mandate procedure, the Commission seeks a consensus among the members. Sometimes, therefore, it may take more than one Committee meeting before the Commission decides to send the mandate to CEN or CENELEC as appropriate.

The Standing Committees

The special role committees play in the New Approach has already been demonstrated: the Model Directive prescribes that each directive implementing the New Approach will set up a committee which is concerned with the implementation of the directive. Such a committee would, in particular, be consulted

---

[243] Art. 6(3) read in conjunction with Art. 6(2) of Dir. 83/189/EEC, above n. 102.
[244] *Ibid.*, Art. 6(3).
[245] *Ibid.*, Art. 6(4).
[246] *Ibid.*, Art. 6(4)(e).
[247] *Ibid.*, Art. 6(5).
[248] Interviews with Commission officials.
[249] See Chap. 3.

when the Commission or a Member State considered that a standard did not satisfy the essential safety requirements (list of standards), or where a Member
State found that a product might compromise the safety of persons (safeguard
clause). In practice, not every directive adopted according to the New Approach
principles establishes a separate committee for the implementation of that directive, but refers instead to the 83/189 Committee—this was the case with the
directives relating to simple pressure vessels, gas appliances and electromagnetic
compatibility.[250] Most of the other directives, however, operate a curious system of dealing with two committees. The tasks are divided between the committees: for all matters dealing with standards, it is necessary to invoke the
opinion of the 83/189 Committee; for any matter relating to the implementation
and practical application of the directive, a standing committee is set up. The
directives relating to construction products,[251] machinery,[252] active implantable
medical devices,[253] telecommunications terminal equipment,[254] medical
devices,[255] and recreational craft[256] have created their own standing committees.[257] These committees can be classified as policy-making/implementation
committees.

It thus happens that where, in the opinion of the Commission or the Member
States, a harmonised standard does not entirely meet the essential safety requirements, the matter is brought before both the 83/189 Committee and the relevant
Standing Committee. For example, problems involving construction products
require the Commission to consult both the Standing Committee on
Construction Products, and in the event of shortcomings in harmonised standards, the 83/189 Committee.[258] In addition, the Construction Products
Directive requires that before the Commission issue mandates for construction
products in conformity with Directive 83/189/EEC, the Standing Committee on
Construction Products be asked for an opinion. This latter Committee plays a
role in drawing up, managing and revising a list of products (which have little
influence on health and safety) and must be consulted under a regulatory (*filet*)
procedure.[259] This is exceptional, since nearly all other committees active in this

---

[250] By contrast, although the Toys Dir. clearly refers only to the 83/189 Committee, the
Community budget of 1998 claims that there also exists a Committee for the Adaptation to
Technical Progress of Toys. This committee also appears on the Community budget for previous
years.

[251] Art. 19 of Dir. 89/106/EEC, above n. 122.

[252] Art. 6(2) of Dir. 89/392/EEC, above n. 124.

[253] Art. 6(2) of Dir. 90/385/EEC, above n. 127.

[254] Art. 13 of Dir. 91/263/EEC, above n. 129.

[255] Art. 7 of Dir. 93/42/EEC, above n. 130.

[256] Art. 6(3) of Dir. 94/25/EC, above n. 131.

[257] There is one exception: the Personal Protective Equipment Dir. which refers to the Standing
Committee on Machinery: Art. 6(2) of Dir. 89/686/EEC, above n. 125.

[258] In addition, the Dir. stipulates that the Commission instruct technical committees, in which
the Member States participate, to draw up interpretative documents. However, more details concerning the composition, operation, etc. of such committees are not available.

[259] Art. 4 of Dir. 89/106/EEC, above n. 122.

field[260] follow the advisory committee procedure.[261] In contrast to the food and the pharmaceutical sectors where the regulatory committee procedure prevails, the Member States have here generally agreed to be consulted within the framework of the less stringent advisory committee procedure.[262] This may be explained by the fact that the field of technical goods has been less regulated since technical products were thought to be less risky than foodstuffs and pharmaceuticals. In the latter fields, strict regulation has commonly been accepted, as these products are often harmful by their very nature, and health risks are caused by their ingestion.[263]

In practice, the Member States have themselves responded to this complex "dual" committee system by "administrative simplification"[264] in which they send the same representatives to different committees. Depending on the tasks they have to carry out on behalf of their governments, committee members, who have often already been involved in the drafting of the respective directives (within the working-groups of the COREPER),[265] are also members on other committees. Thus, it is possible that an individual is involved in many directives at the same time and this person must participate in every committee that relates to those directives.[266] It happens, for example, that a member of the 83/189 Committee may also be member of the Standing Committee for Machinery.[267] A member would therefore be invited to meetings of different committees on the same day, and the group of members would "switch label" after each meeting.[268] Although in practice there is general satisfaction about the functioning of these committees by those taking part in the committee system, it must be stressed that the system in this field is by no means transparent, which makes the need to shed more light on these committees and their activities particularly compelling.[269] In this context, the very need to set up a standing committee for

[260] Except for the Standing Committee on Medical Devices consultation of which also takes place under the regulatory committee (*filet*) procedure: above n. 130.

[261] See Chap. 3 for a description of these procedures.

[262] As argued, construction products are politically more sensitive. These products require the consultation of the Standing Committee on Construction Products in the framework of the regulatory committee. That Member States want definitively to be consulted in this Committee may be deduced from the action brought by Germany against the Commission for infringement of essential procedural requirements where the opinion of the Standing Committee was allegedly not properly obtained. See Case C–263/95, *Germany* v. *Commission* (*Construction Products*) [1998] ECR I–441, discussed in Chap. 3, sect. 5.9.

[263] See Chaps. 3 and 4. See also E. Previdi, "The Organization of Public and Private Responsibilities in European Risk Regulation: An Institutional Gap Between Them?", in Ch. Joerges/K.H. Ladeur/E. Vos (eds.), *Integrating Scientific Expertise into Regulatory Decision-Making. National Traditions and European Innovations* (Baden-Baden, 1997), 225–41.

[264] S. Pag, "Interdependence between the Commission and National Bureaucracies", in S. Cassese (ed.), *The European Administration* (Brussels, 1988), 470.

[265] Interviews with Commission officials and a former 83/189 Committee member.

[266] Interview with a former 83/189 Committee member.

[267] Interviews with a Commission official of DGIII and a former 83/189 Committee member.

[268] Interview with a former member of these committees. See also Pag, above n. 264, at 470.

[269] See Chap. 3, and also see the study on comitology carried out by the Institut für Europäische Politik, *Study on Comitology. Characteristics, Performance and Options*, Preliminary Final Report (Bonn, 1989), 11.

each directive may be questioned. Future empirical research should not focus so much on the (well)functioning of committees, but rather on their necessity or superfluousness. The possibility of having only one standing committee on standardisation might be worth considering. The 83/189 Committee seems to be a "logical" candidate for this.

Other Committees Regulating Technical Product Safety

In addition to those mentioned in the New Approach, other committees influence the safety of technical products. These committees need not be specifically related to standardisation and could instead be related to more general questions of product safety. They include: the Consumer Committee,[270] the Committee on Product Safety Emergencies, which needs to be consulted both when the Commission becomes aware, through notification given by the Member States or through information provided by them, of the existence of a serious and immediate risk from a product to the health and safety of consumers in various Member States and is involved in the implementation of the Community system of information on home and leisure accidents,[272] and the Committee on a Specific Research and Development Programme in the Field of Measurements and Testing which is required to assist the Commission in the implementation of this programme.[273]

4.3. Integrating Technical Expertise into Community Regulation through CEN and CENELEC

Under the New Approach, the risk assessment of technical products is left to the European standardisation bodies. In this vein, the standardisation bodies can be compared with the Scientific Committee for Food in the food sector and the EMEA in the area of pharmaceuticals. However, in contrast to the food and medicine sectors where the production of scientific knowledge remains largely a public matter, the risk assessment in this field is made by private standardisation bodies. Since this assessment is not binding, it is not followed by a decision of the Commission. This means that at the level of the standards organisations the various interest values are counterbalanced.

---

[270] Set up by Commission Dec. 90/55/EEC [1990] OJ L38/40, as amended by Commission Dec. 94/146/EC [1994] OJ L64/28 and Commission Dec. 95/13/EC [1995] OJ L21/17. See Chap. 3.

[271] Set up by Art. 10 of Council Dir. 92/59/EEC on general product safety, above n. 3.

[272] See Art. 7 of European Parliament and Council Dec. 3092/94/EC, above n. 177.

[273] Council Dec. 92/247/EEC, adopting a specific research and technological development programme in the field of measurements and testing (1990–4) [1992] OJ L126/12. Of particular interest for this study are the research activities undertaken in the framework of this programme aiming at: the improvement of methods of obtaining reliable and internationally acceptable results for the application of Dirs., in particular on food products, industrial products and health; also aiming at providing a contribution to the implementation of the Global Approach to Conformity Testing of industrial products through support to European standardisation bodies, laboratory accreditation and mutual recognition, and the development of new methods of measurements and analysis.

4.3.1. The Co-ordination of Technical Expertise at Community and International level

Standards are made by thousands of qualified technical experts from all over Europe (EFTA countries included).[274] Clearly, these technical experts do not work in isolation and form part of the international standardisation organisation. In standard-setting by the Technical Committees of CEN/CENELEC, particular account is taken of the standards work of the international standardisation organisation, ISO.[275] In this manner, national technical expertise is co-ordinated at both Community and international level.[276]

4.3.2. The Diversification of Expertise

In previous chapters, it was argued that according to the Court's case law, where the Commission has been delegated powers to adopt individual decisions, it is required to examine carefully and impartially all the relevant aspects of the case. The Commission must ensure that the members of a specific expert committee possess the necessary technical knowledge or that they consult experts.[277] This obligation seemingly applies also to the situation in which the Commission examines (at the request of the Member States or on its own initiative) a harmonised standard or where its decision is needed in the framework of the safeguard clause. Whether and to what extent it would be appropriate to apply such requirements to the standard-setting process should also be considered.[278]

4.3.3. Unbalanced National Expertise?

It appears that countries with a long-standing tradition in standardisation and powerful standardisation organisations are quantitatively and qualitatively dominant in the process of standardisation. These are in the main Germany, the United Kingdom and France. It is noteworthy that the nationality of the individual who holds the secretariat or the presidency of the Technical Committee (albeit officially independent) is in practice not without importance. Both chair

---

[274] At present, approximately 300 technical committees are concerned with 10,000 standards. See COM(95)238 final, 51. Within the whole Community 132,301 experts are participating in the standardisation work: see Falke, above n. 58, Table 3, at 202.

[275] In 1995, 40% of the European Standards of CEN were identical as to their substance to ISO standards, whilst 95% of CENELEC standards were in conformity with the standards of the International Electrotechnical Committee (IEC): see Falke, above n. 58, at 200.

[276] See the Vienna Agreement for CEN–ISO and the Dresden Agreement for CENELEC–IEC. These Agreements are published as appendix in Nicolas/Repussard, above n. 30, 239 ff.

[277] Case C–269/90, *Hauptzollamt München-Mitte* v. *Technische Universität München* [1991] ECR I–5469.

[278] Here, one could consider the elements which point to the existence of a Community responsibility—in particular Art. 100a(3) as generally the Directives are adopted by virtue of Art. 100a—and the general task of the Commission to supervise the standards work entrusted to it in the single directives. See Chaps. 2 and 3.

and secretariat are often in the hands of one country. Hence, it does not seem accidental that the German standardisation organisation (DIN) currently holds the secretariat of many Technical Committees, followed by the French standards body (AFNOR) and the British standards body (BSI). In 1995, for instance, of the 269 existing Technical Committees, DIN held the secretariat of 74 TCs, whilst both AFNOR and BSI held the secretariat of 57 TCs.[279] In view of the strength of German industry in the field of machinery, it does not come as a surprise that DIN holds both the secretariat and the chair of the Technical Committee on the safety of machinery within CEN.[280] This situation raises the question of its "fairness" towards the Member States with less technical resources and, in particular, its impact on the setting of a high level of standards which may be difficult for the smaller (small- and medium-sized) industries of the Community to reach. It should be recalled that standards would need to reflect common interests and should not lead to economic advantages for single participants.[281]

4.4. The Participation of Interested Parties

The increasing use of standards in the production of technical products utilised by consumers and workers and having an impact on the environment accentuates the importance of such interests participating in the standard-setting process. Whilst the need for the representation of these interests in the national standardisation process is commonly recognised, it is, in part, their limited resources which restrict their actual participation. Clearly, where the standardisation process is transferred to the European level, the difficulties of interested parties in participating in the standardisation process are enhanced; apart from the question whether they are allowed to participate, interested parties are confronted with increased travel costs and language barriers. Confronted with the threat of the drastic institutional reform announced by the Commission in its Green Paper and Follow-up Communication, the European standardisation bodies have hastened to open up their structures to European socio-economic interest groups, too. The questions arise of the extent to which this has been done and what difficulties have remained. This book will concentrate on participation of consumer interests in standardisation, the need for which is traditionally recognised.[282]

---

[279] See Falke, above n. 58, Table 3, at 202. Other committees were chaired by the Italian UNI (20), the Dutch NNI (15), the Belgian IBN/BIN (14), the Danish DS (11), the Swedish SIS (7), the Spanish AFNOR (4), the Swiss SNV (4), the Irish NSAI (2), the Greek ELOT (1), the Norwegian NSF (1) and the STRI from Iceland (1). Portugal, Luxembourg and Austria did not hold the secretariat of Technical Committees.

[280] Eichener, above n. 84, at 68.

[281] See sect. 2.2.3.2.

[282] See, on consumer representation in the national and regional context, the study prepared by G. Langmann for the Consumer Policy Committee of ISO Study Day in May 1997 on this topic:

4.4.1. Consumer Participation in Standardisation

4.4.1.1. The Troubled History

Over the years, the need for consumer participation in European standard-setting work, long insisted upon by the European Consumer Organisation BEUC, has increasingly been recognised by the Community institutions and CEN/CENELEC. As early as 1977, CEN and CENELEC published a document in which the participation of consumers in their work was encouraged.[283] The standardisation bodies responded to the call of the Community institutions in the first Programme on a Consumer Protection Policy to take account of consumers' concerns in decisions which affected their interests.[284] However, the practical realisation still appeared a long way off.

In its second Consumer Protection Programme, the Council called upon the Commission to encourage adequate representation of consumers within the European standardisation bodies.[285] This political pressure resulted in the admission of representatives of the former Consumer Consultative Committee (CCC)[286] to participate as observers within the technical committees of CEN/CENELEC from 1982–3 onwards. Yet, with only limited financial resources, it appeared difficult to find qualified experts who were willing to represent the CCC without remuneration.[287] Consequently, in an agreement concluded with BEUC in October 1983, the Commission agreed to finance the representation of consumers in standardisation, which led to the creation of a European Secretariat for the co-ordination of standardisation (SECO).[288] This body was to improve the participation of consumers in standardisation and to support the work of observers, under the control of the former CCC working group on standardisation.[289]

In the "General Orientations" of 1984, the European standardisation bodies formally accepted the obligation to ensure that interested parties, such as consumers, could take part effectively in the elaboration of standards work. Following the New Approach, the Council further recognised the need to

Consumer Representation in Standardisation. A Review of the National Arrangements for Co-ordinating Consumer Representation in ISO-COLPCO Member Countries, available from the ANEC Internet site: http://www.anec.org.

[283] B. Farquhar, "La participation des consommateurs à la normalisation" [1994] *Revue européenne de droit de la consommation* 1, 29; *id.*, "Consumer Representation in Standardisation" [1995] *Consumer Law Journal* 56–68.

[284] Council Resolution on a preliminary programme of the European Economic Community for a consumer protection and information policy [1975] OJ C92/1.

[285] Council Resolution on a second programme of the EEC for a consumer protection and information policy [1981] OJ C133/1.

[286] See Chap. 3.

[287] These persons would only be reimbursed for travel expenses. This is a general problem for consumer organisations. See L. Maier, "Institutional Consumer Representation in the European Community", in N. Reich/G. Woodroffe (eds.), *European Consumer Policy after Maastricht* (Dordrecht, 1994), at 85.

[288] This body had its seat at BEUC's office.

[289] Farquhar, above n. 283, at 30.

improve the involvement of consumers in the process of standardisation in a Resolution of 4 November 1988,[290] which was reiterated by the Commission in its Green Paper and repeated again by the Council in its Resolution of 1992.

4.4.1.2. The Creation of ANEC

The absence of a more solid basis for consumer participation in standard-setting and the failure to adopt a European Standardisation Council or Forum, as proposed by the Commission, nonetheless provoked reconsideration of the existing structures. However, CEN's proposal to create a Consumer Consultative Committee within CEN[291] (a common construction in the national standardisation organisations[292]) was rejected by SECO as it feared that such a committee would be subject to the stringent internal rules of CEN and would be excluded from the possibility of being consulted in Commission draft directive proposals and mandates.[293] As a result, another avenue was explored in order to guarantee a greater degree of independence. In 1994, a new association was set up, the European Association for the Co-ordination of Consumer Representation in Standardisation, known by its French abbreviation ANEC.[294] This body aims to ensure the representation of consumer interests in the work of the European standardisation bodies and in any other body involved in standard-setting of interest to consumers, to comment on general questions of European standardisation and on draft directives involving standardisation, to facilitate the participation of consumers in the European standardisation process in general and to contribute to environmental protection.[295] To this end, ANEC performs the following tasks:

— to examine the essential safety requirements which need specification by the standardisation bodies;
— to give advice to the 83/189 Committee on the mandates;
— to establish the priorities for standards which concern consumers;
— to control the standardisation work and take initiatives to enhance consumers' influence in projects which concern them;
— to collect and distribute information relating to standardisation;

---

[290] [1988] OJ C293/1. See also its Consumer Protection Programme of 1989 [1989] OJ C294/1 and the call of the Parliament for more involvement of consumers in the European standardisation process: Resolution on consumer safety as a part of a new approach by the EC to technical harmonisation and standards, Doc. A. 2–267/88 [1989] OJ C12/72.

[291] Proposal for a CEN Consumer Consultative Committee (C4), internal CEN document.

[292] See, for a description of the Consumer Council in DIN, Joerges *et al.*, above n. 4, 185–9 (EUI Working Paper LAW 91/12, 68–72).

[293] SECO, *Annual Report on Consumer Participation in the Standardisation Process*, Oct. 1990, 6.

[294] *"Association de Normalisation Européenne pour les Consommateurs"*, governed by Belgian law.

[295] See Priorities for ANEC involvement in environmental standardisation, ANEC97/ENV/26, available on ANEC's Internet site: http://www.anec.org/whystds.htm. See also ANEC's call on the standards bodies in Europe to help protect the environment, Press Release of 25 June 1997 ANEC97/PR2, also available on the Internet.

— to prepare an annual declaration for the future activities of standardisation in the interests of consumers.[296]

Its General Assembly[297] is composed of one representative of a consumer organisation from the EC and EFTA, four representatives of the Consumer Committee and two from the remaining EFTA countries, with a total of 24 members. Observers from the Commission and EFTA, the standards organisations (CEN/CENELEC, ETSI and ISO) and other consumer organisations (for example, the European Consumer Safety Association ECOSA) can be invited to attend these meetings. A Steering Committee, composed of ten members, is chosen from among the members of the General Assembly. Six working groups, composed of consumer representatives and experts in specific sectors have been formed on: child safety, environment, electrical appliances, gas appliances, machinery and traffic safety. The Co-ordination Group oversees the working of these groups and provides a forum for the discussion of issues common to all groups and co-operation on various issues that fall outside the remit of the working groups.[298] ANEC is financed by the Community and EFTA.[299]

In 1995, ANEC officially became an associate member of CEN, which is, as previously observed, without voting rights.[300] At present, ANEC is very active. In 1995, for example, it issued 63 comments on various standardisation issues. These vary from comments of a more general nature, such as the proliferation of safety documents in CEN and the CEN/CENELEC certification mark, to more detailed comments on draft prENs.[301] ANEC attempts to exert more influence through active lobbying. To this end, it sends written comments to the relevant TCs of CEN/CENELEC, to the national representatives of, for example, the Committee on Product Safety Emergencies and to Commission officials working on specific topics of interest. Through its Co-ordination Group, it sends letters to the members of the working groups asking them to lobby their national members on the relevant Technical Committee or Technical Board of CEN to accept ANEC's position on a specific issue.[302]

4.4.2. The Remaining Difficulties

The general problem for the representation of diffuse interests in standardisation is that, although the need for such representation has been repeatedly acknowledged by both the Community institutions and the standardisation

---

[296] Farquhar, above n. 283, 29–36. ANEC press release of 2 Feb. 1995.

[297] This body met for the first time in Feb. 1995.

[298] ANEC's Annual Report for 1995, available at http://www.anec.org/public/anrep95.htm, 17–18.

[299] For 1995, the Community allocated a subvention of 750,000 ECU to ANEC's activities: ANEC press release.

[300] See sect. 2.2.2.

[301] ANEC's Annual Report for 1995, above n. 298, 37–40.

[302] All these and other activities are documented on ANEC's Internet homepage: http://www.anec.org.

bodies, no action is taken to guarantee it in practice. Some interest representatives, such as consumers and trade unions, have been given access to standards work. Others, however, such as environmentalists, are still struggling to attain observer status within the standardisation bodies and consequently feel that they are not sufficiently represented in standardisation work.[303] It goes without saying that here, too, problems of "representativity" arise.

Before its institutionalisation as an associate member of CEN, the success of the functioning of ANEC, for example, depended a great deal on the collaboration of both the Commission and the European standardisation bodies. In the past, SECO had accused the Commission of submitting its proposals relating to standardisation[304] after such a delay that it was nearly impossible to comment upon them.[305] In addition, the possibility of actually participating in technical standards work depends on financial resources, which interest groups generally lack. In practice, this problem has been solved by the Commission offering financial support to several interest groups.[306] However, these bodies remain dependent on the benevolence of the Commission for the carrying out of specific projects.[307]

Furthermore, even when endowed with observer status, interest groups have not been satisfied, since this observer status allowed them little chance to influence actual standards work.[308] Consequently, in their comments on the Commission's Green Paper, consumer organisations asked for the formal assignment of voting rights.[309] However, apart from the fact that it is highly unlikely that the standards organisations will accept such rights, as this would strongly interfere with their autonomy, even if voting rights were introduced, this would probably lead the standards organisations to apply majority voting, with which they would not only meet the Commission's strong desires expressed in the Green Paper, but could also outvote such interest groups. Giving voting rights to consumer or other interest representatives therefore seems inappropriate.

---

[303] See Falke/Joerges, above n. 88, 113–17. See also, very recently, the Commission in its Report on the efficiency and accountability of standardisation, above n. 233, at 10.

[304] E.g., proposals for a Council/Parliament dir. based on the New Approach, draft interpretative documents or draft standard mandates to CEN/CENELEC.

[305] E.g., it has happened that the Commission has submitted a draft proposal to SECO one day before the deadline.

[306] In addition to supporting ANEC, the Commission has, e.g., also provided the European Confederation of Trade Unions (ETUC) with the financial means to create the European Trade Union Technical Bureau for Health and Safety (TUTB) to represent trade union interests in standardisation.

[307] See, e.g., ANEC's failure to obtain Commission funding for projects specifically aimed at providing research and testing results in support of consumer priorities at technical level: ANEC's Annual Report for 1995, above n. 298, at 37.

[308] See, in general, Maier, above n. 287, at 87.

[309] Detailed review of the comments to the Green Paper, above n. 149, at 37.

4.4.3. In Search of a Discussion and Policy Platform: A European Standardisation Forum or Enlarging the "Enlarged" 83/189 Committee

In view of the difficulties, it would be desirable to have some kind of structure composed of all interested parties, both public and private, to allow a more coherent approach to addressing the problems to which standardisation gives rise, thus democratising the standardisation process. To this end, one could think of reviving the idea of creating a kind of European Standardisation Forum, suggested by the Commission in its Follow-up Communication.[310] Discussion of standards-related problems within this Forum would focus public attention on specific issues and open up public debate. A Forum could create a greater degree of coherence between the various interest representatives and allow them to discuss and/or detect specific problems of common interest. Depending on the outcome, the Community institutions could accordingly take action. This Forum could address general policy questions of product safety and standardisation and could assist the Commission in priority setting of mandates and generally keep up the relations with CEN/CENELEC. Extending the public enquiry procedure[311] to include interest representatives,[312] but without losing their observer or associate member status within CEN/CENELEC, interest representatives could signal problems they discover to this body.

The creation of yet another body in this field, however, runs the risk of overlapping functions already carried out by other bodies. Alternatively, one could develop and re-structure an already existing body: the 83/189 Committee.[313] As demonstrated above, this Committee already plays a central role in all issues related to standardisation and maintains a special relationship with the European standardisation bodies, from within the Committee's "enlarged" meetings. In addition to reinforcing their rights within the process of standard-setting, the opening-up of these meetings to the socio-economic interest groups, too, could provide a forum in which representatives from the Commission, the Member States, the national standards bodies, CEN, CENELEC and ETSI, as well as the socio-economic interest groups could address all standards-related issues and policy questions. Current developments are moving in this direction, ANEC recently having been invited to report on the national arrangements for consumer representation in standardisation in Europe within the "enlarged" meeting of the 83/189 Committee.[314] Clearly, this suggestion presupposes an improvement in the whole committee system and greater transparency in the activities of this Committee, as well as a perception of some approaches to the participation of interested parties also in the decision-making of the Community institutions (in particular, the Commission).

[310] See sect. 4.1.
[311] See sect. 2.2.3.2.
[312] See Falke/Joerges, above n. 88, at 161.
[313] Previdi proposes setting up an agency: see Previdi, above n. 263, at 241.
[314] ANEC Newsletter, Issue 5, Mar. 1998, available on ANEC's Internet site.

4.5. Transparency and Access to Documents

The European standardisation process has not been the greatest example of either openness or accessibility. The need for more transparency in the standard-setting process was once again emphasised by the Commission in its Green Paper and its Follow-up. Again, the Commission's proposal for institutional reform was an important warning to the European standardisation bodies to disclose more information on their activities and the standardisation process quickly. Consequently, several provisions were adopted to make the organisation and activities of the European standardisation bodies more public[315] and a *Bulletin of the European Standards Organisations (CEN, CENELEC and ETSI)* was created. This Bulletin provides a monthly overview of the developments concerning: the adopted European Standards and other documents; the Draft European Standards submitted to public enquiry; the decisions adopted by the European standardisation bodies (all indicated with their subject, number and the competent Technical Committee); official citations in the Official Journal of the European Community; and the standardisation mandates. The publication of these activities may be welcomed, as this enables the interested parties to learn about the projects of CEN and CENELEC and may serve to open up a public debate. In addition, both CEN and CENELEC publish their annual reports.

In this vein, at present, significant steps have already been undertaken towards ensuring greater openness in the standard-setting process. Both CEN and CENELEC have finally started to provide information on the Internet.[316] In this context, the recent agreement between the Commission and CEN to set up an Internet Network for European Standardisation (INES) is of particular interest.[317] This project is particularly aimed at small and medium-sized enterprises, consumers, workers and private and public buyers and will be of help to Central and Eastern Europe with a view to their possible accession to the EU. INES intends to produce specifications for the implementation and use of the Internet for the CEN Central Secretariat and the CEN national members. In addition, it aims to pilot and test new services amongst the developers and users of standards.

However, although CEN/CENELEC seem ready to make their documents accessible to various parties,[318] there is an absence of general rules on this point, with the result that the provision of documents depends largely on the willingness of the standardisation bodies. Clear rules governing the right of access to

---

[315] In particular CEN has been quite active, see for instance CEN, above n. 11.

[316] See http://www.cenorm.be (CEN's homepage) and http://www.cenelec.be (CENELEC's homepage).

[317] See ANEC News, http://www.anec.org/public/news/content.htm#Internet.

[318] It is noted that both organisations (in particular, CEN's Information Officer, Mr Stewart Sanson) have been very helpful in providing me with the documents necessary to carry out this research.

documents should therefore be established. This becomes of great importance if problems of "representativity" are to be encountered. In addition, it is note-worthy that an important document such as the *General Orientations* guidelines has never been published in the Official Journal and that other documents, such as mandates, have equally not been made public. Although the Commission has recently been obliged to publish the work mandated on an annual basis in the Official Journal,[319] queries remain concerning the accessibility of Commission documents in substance. On this specific issue, the general rules on access to Commission documents are unclear and need greater specification.[320] Moreover, as argued earlier, transparency of Community product safety regu-lation is obscured by the committee system in this field.

4.6. Accountability of Community Product Safety Regulation

Control mechanisms for the standardisation bodies and the standard-setting process are provided in the New Approach directives and developed in practice. The Commission is generally entrusted with the supervision of the standardisa-tion process, *inter alia*, by issuing standardisation mandates and monitoring whether the standards meet essential safety requirements. Other means of con-trol have been developed by the Commission in practice. The standardisation bodies nevertheless remain entirely responsible for the standards they adopt.

4.6.1. Supervision of the Standard-setting Procedure

Supervision of the standard-setting process enables the Commission to check whether public interests are truly balanced against the more market-driven interests of standard-setters and users. Some directives have themselves devel-oped a few techniques in order to clarify the essential safety requirements, which enable the Commission to exercise a certain degree of control, by specifying the essential safety requirements in *interpretative documents* (Construction Products Directive[321]) or drafting a *commentary* on the essential requirements (Machinery Directive[322]).

Furthermore, *standardisation mandates* should "potentially" provide the Commission with a measure of control. Yet, in practice, they are no more than "simple contracts between two contracting parties": the Commission and the standardisation bodies.[323] These mandates merely indicate the essential safety requirements of the directives for which standards are required, the date by which

---

[319] See Art. 11 of Council Dir. 94/10/EC amending Dir. 83/189/EEC [1994] OJ L100/30.

[320] See Commission Dec. 94/90/ECSC, EC, Euratom [1994] OJ L46/58.

[321] See Communication of the Commission with regard to the interpretative documents of Council Dir. 89/106/EEC [1994] OJ C62/1. See Falke, above n. 58, at 194.

[322] See European Commission, *Community Legislation on Machinery. Comments on Directive 89/392/EEC and Directive 91/368/EEC*, by P. Massimi/J.-P. Van Gheluwe (Luxembourg, 1993).

[323] J. Repussard, in CEN, above n. 11, at 189.

such standards have to be adopted and the financial voucher.[324] With the mandate, the Commission establishes the responsibility for the standards to comply with the essential safety requirements with the standardisation bodies.[325]

Closely linked with the standardisation mandates is the ability of the Commission to verify whether the terms of the mandate are fulfilled—and thus whether the standards meet the essential safety requirements. In the 1984 "General Orientations" guidelines, the standardisation bodies had already promised that the Commission could be present at the meetings of the technical committees and technical boards. Not surprisingly, it often appeared difficult to do so in practice. Consequently, the Commission proposed in 1990 to appoint its own *expert consultants* who would have the task of following CEN's activities and verifying the compatibility of standards with the essential requirements in the stage of drafting.[326] Whilst this would have been an adequate way for the Commission to exercise "proper" control,[327] it was probably for this very same reason that CEN did not agree upon the appointment of consultants who would be responsible to both the Commission and CEN. Consequently, consultants are currently appointed in agreement with the Commission on the proposal of CEN and are responsible only to CEN, although they have the opportunity of directly to contact the relevant Commission services.[328] In general, these consultants have already been involved in the preparation of the relevant directives and are already familiar with the essential requirements.[329] At present, there are 17 of these experts.[330] Although resort to these consultants certainly helps the Commission, which in general is well informed about proceedings within CEN,[331] to obtain more information about the ongoing drafting of these specific standards, it is apparent that the proper functioning of these experts entirely depends on the approval and co-operation of CEN. Since the consultants are

[324] Interviews with Commission officials of DGIII and XXIV.

[325] *Implementation Guide*, above n. 73, at 42. See also Falke, above n. 58, at 197.

[326] Commission, DGIII, internal paper, printed in DIN–Mitt 70, 1991, 106 ff., cited in Falke, above n. 112, 94–5.

[327] According to CEN, such consultants would have difficulty in translating the often generally and vaguely formulated essential requirements into standards. See CEN's comments on the Green Paper, reproduced in the Commission's detailed review of the comments on the Green Paper, above n. 149, at 20.

[328] See also Falke, above n. 58, at 197.

[329] See the interviews with P. Makin, consultant to CEN for safety of machinery, Compliance with a dir. and complexity of standards for safety of machinery, and A. Illingworth, consultant to CEN for pressure equipment, compliance with the pressure equipment and the harmonisation of supporting standards, published in CEN, above n. 11, 113–21. Both Makin and Illingworth have been involved in the drafting of the Machinery and the proposed Pressure Equipment Directives. Makin is a chartered mechanical engineer and, as member of the UK Health and safety executive, he was involved in the negotiations of the Machinery Directive. Illingworth is a chartered mechanical engineer and was seconded in 1989 to the Commission to assist in the writing of the proposed pressure equipment Dir.

[330] SEC(98)291, 14.

[331] It is noteworthy that the Director of Directorate B, Legislation and Standardisation; Telematic Networks of the Commission's DGIII, Mr E. Vardakas, was a former Secretary General of CEN and is thus well informed about the general proceedings of CEN.

seconded to CEN's administrative hierarchy, it seems unlikely that they will themselves seriously criticise CEN's standard-setting procedures to the Commission. Therefore, for these consultants to be an effective instrument of control they should be more independent of CEN.

Lastly, as argued above, the regular meetings between with the standardisation bodies within the framework of the "enlarged" 83/189 Committee equally serve to learn more about the standardisation activities and, more importantly, to create a basis for co-operation between national authorities, the Commission and the standardisation bodies. To enhance accountability, however, socio-economic interest groups should also be allowed to these meetings.[332]

4.6.2. Post-market Control of Harmonised Standards

Two important instruments of post-market control of standards which have been approved and used in the manufacturing of products are provided for in the New Approach directives themselves: the management of a list of the standards by the Commission and the safeguard clauses.[333] These instruments allow the Member States together with the Commission within the 83/189 Committee to submit harmonised standards to extensive control with regard to their health and safety and have proved to be effective.

Management of the List of Standards

The references of the harmonised standards drafted by CEN/CENELEC are published by the Commission in the Official Journal without, however, submitting them to checks as to their substance. Both the Commission itself and the Member States can nevertheless require more substantive checks of harmonised standards within the framework of the 83/189 Committee if they consider that these standards do not entirely meet the essential requirements. The Commission can thereafter take a decision to withdraw a standard from the list. As a result, a product manufactured in conformity with the standard withdrawn from the list is not presumed to conform. One recent example of this instrument of control is France's notification that parts of the European standard on the safety of mechanical presses[334] did not satisfy the essential safety requirements laid down in the Machinery Directive.[335] The Commission acknowledged the defects and commissioned a standardisation mandate to CEN to amend the standard as soon as possible. Its way of modifying the standard was to withdraw the relevant parts from the list of published standards for which it no longer granted the presumption of conformity.[336]

---

[332] See sect. 4.4.3.
[333] See sects. 2.3.3.2. and 3.2.1.
[334] EN 692.
[335] See Art. 3 of Dir. 89/392/EEC, above n. 124.
[336] Commission Dec. 98/100/EC on the publication of the reference of EN 692 standard "Mechanical Presses—safety" in accordance with Council Dir. 89/392/EEC (text with EEA relevance) [1998] OJ L23/34.

Safeguard Clauses

In addition, the safeguard clauses (without which the Member States would probably never have agreed upon the adoption of the New Approach) allow the Member States, together with the Commission within the framework of the 83/189 Committee, a "post-market control" of products which have been manufactured in conformity with the European standards and submit the standards to control.[337] A final decision is taken by the Commission. An investigation into the operation of the safeguard clause procedure in the Toys Directive reveals that the Member States readily invoke it: between 1990 and 1994, this procedure was initiated in 100 cases, of which 97 were considered to be justified by the Commission.[338]

5. CONCLUSION

The reliance on private bodies in the New Approach of the Community through the reference to standards technique has enabled the Community considerably to accelerate its harmonisation activities. Although the New Approach was successful, since it allowed several directives to be adopted within an average of 18 months, the shortcomings of this Approach readily became apparent. The unclear provisions on certification compelled the Community to develop a new system. Furthermore, the Community's policy aimed at the free circulation of technical products on the entire Community market required it to extend its activities also to the monitoring of product safety. The enormous delay in the elaboration of standards presented both the Community institutions and the Member States with further problems. Taken together, these elements required the Community to deepen its activities. The Community follows a "mixed" regulatory approach to technical consumer products: it regulates general safety requirements for the substance of certain product categories, without specifying the exact technical details. This is in contrast with both the food sector, where a "horizontal" regulatory approach which focuses on the risks of specific substances is adopted, and the pharmaceutical sector, which follows a "vertical" product approach and examines the risks of each and every medicinal product prior to its market entry.

The use of the reference to standards technique in the New Approach, however, incurs the risk that regulation of health and safety issues, a public interest, be carried out by private standardisation bodies. Hence, the Community is faced with the dilemma of, on the one hand, needing to resort to the technical

[337] Model Dir., above n. 114, point VII. See also Chap. 2.
[338] Communication from the Commission to the Council and the European Parliament on the Internal Market 1994, COM(95)238 final, 49. It is noteworthy that the bulk of the cases were started by the UK. See S. Weatherill, "Playing Safe: The United Kingdom's Implementation of the Toy Safety Directive", in T. Daintith (ed.), *Implementing EC Law in the United Kingdom—Structures for Indirect Rule* (Chichester, 1995), 241–69.

knowledge of the standards bodies, whilst, on the other hand, knowing that this will not guarantee that sufficient attention is given to "public" interests, such as health and safety protection.

The question whether the reference to standards technique entails an unlawful delegation of powers to the European standardisation organisations continues to be debated. According to some authors, the fact that harmonised standards would be legally binding on the national authorities signified that the reference to standards boiled down to a *de facto* delegation of decision-making powers to the European standardisation bodies. However, this argument must be rejected. First, standards are voluntary in their nature and producers are free to use other means of reaching the essential safety requirements prescribed in the New Approach directives. Secondly, the presumption of conformity is refutable, which means that the circulation of products manufactured in conformity with harmonised standards may be refused if they do not conform to the essential safety requirements. Member States may invoke a safeguard clause procedure, under which the final decision on the safety of products is delegated to the Commission together with various committees (in general, the 83/189 Committee).

This finding, however, does not belittle the importance of standards or the standards bodies in Community product safety regulation. Since products manufactured in accordance with the harmonised standards are presumed (albeit rebuttably) to meet the essential safety requirements, producers will be likely to use these standards because they facilitate access to foreign markets. These standards will, therefore, have an impact on the safety of people and have a public interest character. Thus, the setting of standards cannot be left solely to private actors, who, in addition to safety concerns, also need to balance other elements on a general market-driven cost-benefit analysis. When using the reference to standards technique, the Community must, therefore, be particularly vigilant concerning the legitimacy of standard-setting procedures. This need was already recognised in the 1984 "General Orientations" guidelines concluded between the Commission and the European standardisation bodies. The proposals by the Commission in its Green Paper for a radical institutional reform attempted to disclose and democratise the process of standard-setting. They nonetheless remained unsuccessful.

However, finding a balance between public interests and the independence of the private standards bodies is a delicate matter. The law's task in this matter should be to make sure that the integrity of the standard-setting process is observed: that adequate means to control this process are provided and that this process is legitimate. Instead of concentrating on the delegation issue, focus should concentrate on interaction and co-operation with the standardisation bodies and the legitimacy of the standard-setting process: the manner in which standards are drafted and the quality of expertise, interest participation and means of control, and the public accountability of the standard-setting procedures.

Committees ensure co-operation between the Member States, the Commission and CEN/CENELEC. Although the Model Directive of the New Approach in principle requires the creation of one standing committee, in practice, the 83/189 Committee is referred to. In some directives, a curious system of two committees is used, which provides, in addition to the 83/189 Committee, the consultation of a specific standing committee. For reasons of transparency and clarity, resort to one standing committee on standardisation should be considered.

In relation to technical expertise, the standardisation bodies themselves should counterbalance the various interests and adopt the standards. Risk management by the Commission in this field entails the supervision of the standard-setting procedure and ultimately (in addition to the Member States) the ensuring of the safety of products circulating on the Community market. Where the Commission is required to examine a harmonised standard or the safety of a product, the requirements set by the Court to examine all relevant aspects of the matter carefully and impartially seemingly apply. In practice, other problems relating to the distribution of expertise throughout the various Member States emerge. Where it appears that for the most part the technically more advanced Member States with strong standardisation traditions dominate the standardisation process, their impact on the level of standard-setting in relation to the smaller-sized industries in the Member States should be considered. In this vein, it should be recalled that standardisation needs to reflect common interests and should not lead to economic advantages for single participants.

Careful scrutiny of the modes of interest participation both in the regulation of technical products by the Community and in the process of standard-setting reveals several lacunae. An analysis of consumer representation, traditionally recognised as necessary for product safety, reveals its troubled history. Although, since the beginning of the Community, both the Community institutions and the standardisation bodies have called for consumer representation in standardisation process, it was not until recently that a more solid basis for consumer representation was established by means of the creation of a new body named ANEC. Although this body, financially supported by the Commission, has now become an associate member of CEN and has access to standards work, representatives of other interested parties, such as the environmentalists, are still struggling to attain observer status within the standardisation bodies or feel that they are not sufficiently represented in the standardisation work. Here one should reflect upon a more coherent approach to diffusing interest participation in Community (Commission) product safety regulation and establishing clear rules on this issue.

One could consider the creation of a European Standardisation Forum, similar to that suggested by the Commission, which would be composed of all interested parties. Such a Forum could create a greater degree of coherence between the various interest representatives and allow them to discuss and/or detect specific problems of common interest and open up public discourse on these issues.

Depending on the outcome, the Community institutions could accordingly take action. This Forum could address general policy questions of product safety and standardisation and could assist the Commission in the priority setting of mandates and generally maintain the relationship with CEN/CENELEC. By extending the public enquiry procedure to include interest representatives and without depriving them of their observer or associate member status, interest representatives could signal problems they discover to this body. Alternatively, avoiding the risk of overlapping functions with existing committees, the 83/189 Committee could be developed so as to extend its "enlarged" meetings also to socio-economic interested parties. It could provide a forum in which representatives from the Commission, the Member States, the national standards bodies, CEN, CENELEC and ETSI, as well as the socio-economic interest groups could co-operate and address standard-related issues and policy questions together. Improving and re-structuring the 83/189 Committee could strengthen co-operation between public authorities, private organisations and socio-economic interest representatives, thus enhancing "pre-market" control and accountability of standard-setting.

Clearly, this would require greater transparency in the operation of this and other committees active in product safety regulation and ensure access to documents to all interested parties. The latter is again important in order to confront possible representation problems relating to the selection of the parties who are allowed on to the enlarged 83/189 Committee. The same applies to the standard-setting organisations and procedures which admittedly make their activities increasingly public, but do not have precise rules concerning access to documents. Hence, for greater accountability and legitimacy of Community product safety regulation through private standard-setting bodies, principles of transparency, participation of socio-economic interest groups, and control and accountability which have to some extent already been developed by the Commission, should be reinforced and developed further. Such principles should not, however, be laid down in some hidden document such as the *General Orientations Guidelines* but require a decision by the Community legislature which will direct the Commission in its co-operation with the standardisation bodies and which could also be incorporated in a European administrative procedures act.

Conclusion

1. COMMUNITY HEALTH AND SAFETY REGULATION THROUGH COMMITTEES, AGENCIES AND PRIVATE BODIES

The involvement of the Community in health and safety regulation resulted from the spill-over effect of its pursuit of the internal market combined with a growing recognition of the importance of consumer health and safety protection. Although the competence of the Community in this field has been questioned, the Treaty provisions have proved flexible enough to cover Community action in this area. In general, Article 100a offers a valid legal basis for product regulation since it usually involves the internal market. Measures involving health and safety issues can generally be adopted under Article 100a, as the differences between national laws relating to such products hinder free movement. Where these national provisions aim to protect the health and safety of persons and thus form justified trade barriers, Community measures based on this Article reconcile both free movement and health and safety protection. Community competence in this field was strengthened by the Maastricht Treaty, which explicitly recognised the commitment of the Community to health protection (Article 3(o)) and consumer protection (Article 3(s)) and included a specific legal basis for health and consumer protection measures (Article 129a). The amendments to Articles 100a, 129 and 129a that will be introduced by the Amsterdam Treaty will further reinforce the Community's competence.

Although the competence of the Community in this area is not exclusive, the powers of the Member States on health and safety issues, recognised primarily in Article 36, can be pre-empted. In theory, this could lead to situations in which Member States can no longer legislate in this area, even in the absence of a specific Community act, as the Community has "occupied" this area. In practice, however, the Court has often allowed Member States to invoke Article 36 to justify their national acts protecting health and safety. Whilst legal debate has concentrated on formal issues of competence, Community practice has quietly carried on elaborating on the non-exclusive character of competence on health and safety issues laid down in the Treaty (Article 100a(4)) and, with regard to human health and safety, has developed a concept of shared competence between the Community and the Member States. On various occasions, the Commission has, for example, been prepared to allow Member States to "opt out" of harmonisation measures for reasons of health and safety protection, thus allowing for a more generous interpretation of pre-emption which favours national competence even after harmonisation. In addition, in its harmonisation measures on health and safety, the Community legislature has often not only recognised the competence of the Member States in this matter by introducing safeguard clauses in accordance with Article 100a(5), but has also expressly affirmed the powers of the Member States in this field. For example, analysis of the General Product Safety Directive discloses that Member State powers and Community powers on product safety are closely intertwined.

Although the New Approach to Technical Harmonisation and Standards, combined with the frequent resort to the new Article 100a (providing for qualified majority voting), proved a substantial aid to the completion of the internal market, the obstacles to trade within this market were by no means completely eliminated. Accordingly, in the "post-Maastricht" era, the Community, being increasingly confronted with the need to implement health and safety measures, has found itself involved in a third phase of integration. In this manner, the Community has been forced to confront health and safety regulation in all its complexity. Hence, instead of provoking a "race to the bottom", the New Approach has boiled down to a re-regulatory operation at the Community level. Several factors have prompted a deepening of Community activities in this area. Primarily, this need has resulted from the limits of mutual recognition as the sole regulatory instrument, as Member States have refused to accept each others' products because of different regulatory and cultural attitudes. At the same time, the mutual distrust between national administrations has led to the creation of new trade barriers, and the consequent blossoming in procedural rules. In addition, the use of vague terminology in directives and the wide degree of discretion left to Member States have given the Member States ample latitude for distinct or self-interested application, thus seriously threatening the achievement of one internal market. Moreover, the achievement of a single Community market, in which products may circulate freely, determines that potentially dangerous products are not restricted to one national market but may affect the entire Community market. Furthermore, there are some indications which suggest that the Community actually has a certain responsibility to protect the health and safety of persons.

However, this third phase of integration confronts the Community with several legal and practical problems. Legally speaking, the deepening of the Community's involvement in health and safety regulation has given rise to questions of competence, subsidiarity, proportionality, institutional balance, delegation of powers and legitimacy. Analysis of the Treaty Articles, however, has demonstrated that the relevant Treaty Articles do not distinguish between general legislative acts and implementing acts and are wide enough to cover delegation of broad implementing measures to the Commission. Furthermore, given the indissoluble link between health and safety protection and the internal market objective, the need to increase Community action in the area of health and safety is readily apparent: without regulating product safety, the internal market cannot be achieved. Thus, the principles of subsidiarity and proportionality are not likely to hinder more intense Community regulation of health and safety matters. In addition, the Community must ensure that the principle of the institutional balance is observed. This principle was developed by the Court and refers to the balance of powers between the institutions as laid down by the Treaty. It encompasses the notion that each institution must exercise its powers with due regard for the powers of the other institutions. It guarantees that the Community institutions do not exceed the limits of their powers as laid down in the Treaty, and thus reinforces the Community's rule of law and its system of "checks and balances". The strict division of powers between the institutions mainly reflects the concerns of the Member States about the continuing integrity of their own powers, and thus acts as a shield against a concentration of power in the hands of the Commission, in particular. Any functional understanding of the Community structure thus underlines the vital importance of giving the Member States and their national institutions a place not only in the legislative process, but also within the implementation and application of Community law, and further highlights their fundamental interest in effective judicial control. Such a "Member State-oriented" understanding of the notion of the institutional balance proves a useful tool in the interpretation of Community health and safety regulation and, in large part, explains the particular regulatory structures developed by the Community.

The delegation of greater powers on health and safety issues to the Commission stems from the requirement of greater efficiency and the necessity to reduce the Council's workload as well as from the obligation to respect the institutional balance. Moreover, it results from the specific nature of health and safety regulation, which requires a high degree of flexibility. The ever-growing involvement of the Community institutions, especially the Commission, in this area gives rise to various additional problems, relating in particular to legitimacy. In this book, legitimacy has generally been understood in the sense of acceptance of rules as just, and, consequently, the promulgating institutions are legally authorised to make them. In national contexts, the increasing trend towards leaving broad regulatory powers to the administration reduces the administration's claim that it is acting on the basis of the legislature's acts as the source of legitimation, and thus emphasises the need to look for additional means of administrative legitimacy. These means usually include increased transparency, greater expertise, stronger citizen participation, and democratic and judicial control. The Community's multi-level governance structure, however, cannot merely reproduce national models and is beset with further problems relating to the need to include the Member States in the implementation phase, the differing linguistic and cultural habits, and the "representativity" of interests.

Thus, this book has focused its analysis on the following requirements for the legitimacy of health and safety regulation by the Commission: Member State participation, scientific expertise, interest participation, transparency, due process requirements, judicial review and accountability as a basis of decision-making. The need to include Member States in Commission health and safety regulation can be explained by the functional "Member State-oriented" interpretation of the principle of the institutional balance of powers. The particular hesitancy of the Member States about simply accepting Community implementation of health and safety regulation may be explained by their potentially weakened position in the balance of powers; a balance which has shifted in favour of the Commission. In addition, the need for Member State participation in Community health and safety regulation also stems from a procedural interpretation of the subsidiarity principle, thus implementing the clear message that the Member States gave when elevating the notion of subsidiarity to a general principle of Community law; namely, that Member States should not be excluded from the process of building a European Union based on principles of the rule of law, democracy and solidarity. The development of mechanisms such as committees and agencies can be interpreted as a means of ensuring the participation and co-operation of all levels of decision-making. Normative arguments which plead for the right of Member States to participate in risk regulation include the *sui generis* character of the Community, the constitutional obligations of Member States on health protection (a responsibility recognised in both Article 36 and various secondary legislative acts), the specific nature of risk regulation, which requires a delicate weighing of normative values often deeply rooted in national traditions and cultures, and, more pragmatically, the need to ensure compliance.

Within this legal setting, the Community has also encountered certain practical difficulties. Greater Community intervention in health and safety regulation has increased the workload of the Community institutions, in particular the Commission. It must thus collect, produce and evaluate data, monitor activities at national level, and, last but not least, create emergency procedures to combat the circulation of dangerous products within the Community market (post-market control). This growing reliance on the Commission places a greater burden upon it and also reveals its limits in relation to its capacity to supply expertise and information.

The fact that Community involvement in health and safety regulation may be considered to be a spill-over of the market integration objective may, in turn, explain why the Community has not been well-equipped to face these and other difficulties. Despite the lack of general provisions allowing for the delegation of powers and the creation of bodies in addition to the institutions, the Community institutions have extended the Treaty provisions to design ingenious but complex regulatory patterns in order to address the tensions between market integration, product safety regulation and legitimate national regulatory concerns. General evaluation of the three regulatory structures confirms that risk regulation is increasingly carried out by and within bodies for which no provision was initially made in the Treaty. Although the subsidiary activities of such bodies alongside the institutions in the Community's institutional setting has met with various legal objections, I have argued in this book that such patterns are nonetheless in conformity with the overall Treaty provisions.

Committees

Analysis of the committee structure in the food sector has revealed the great impact which committees have on Community food regulation and the important functions they perform in food regulation. In this field, which has a deep-rooted regulatory tradition at national level, the Community finds itself moving towards a third phase of integration, in which it needs closely to regulate and control the implementation of its rules, mainly due to the mutual distrust between Member States. The committee structure in this area is characterised by the existence of the three main functional types of committees, namely: the Standing Committee on Foodstuffs (a policy-making/implementation committee), the Scientific Committee on Food (a scientific committee) and the Advisory Committee on Foodstuffs (an interest committee).

All three committees have a precise function: the Scientific Committee on Food is designed to incorporate scientific advice into the decision-making process; the Advisory Committee on Foodstuffs exists to inform the Commission of the opinions of the various interests involved; and the Standing Committee on Foodstuffs is designed to ensure the political approval of the Member States in the implementing phase. Herewith, the Community distinguishes between risk assessment (measuring the risk associated with specific substances) and risk management (deciding on what to do about the risks which the assessment reveals). Risk assessment is carried out by the SCF, which is designed to restrict itself to dealing with the scientific aspects of a specific subject-matter, while risk management is carried out by the Commission together with the Standing Committee on Foodstuffs. Although the Advisory Committee on Foodstuffs is intended to enhance the social acceptability of Community food regulation, it is currently not consulted by the Commission. Since foodstuffs issues are politically sensitive, it comes as no surprise that the Commission tends to follow closely the opinion of the SCF, which has acquired an outstanding reputation. Although this Committee has largely been neglected in the (institutional) debate on comitology, analysis of the food sector reveals it to be one of the most important committees, determining the scientific basis for every decision on food. Following the BSE crisis, the activities of the SCF have been regulated by the Commission through its Decision on scientific committees, and/or have been developed by the Commission on an *ad hoc* basis.

The political sensitivity of this field to the Member States may similarly explain the existence of the Standing Committee on Foodstuffs, which gives the Member States particular weight in the risk management of food by means of the regulatory committee procedure. In its role of regulatory committee, the Standing Committee on Foodstuffs is able to influence Commission decision-making to a very great extent, although the Commission nonetheless remains well aware of its own responsibility. In practice, the Standing Committee offers a forum for discussion and co-operation, and, in general, decisions are taken by the Commission in close co-operation with the Committee. Thus, it provides an institutional response to the legitimate concerns of the Member States to remain involved in the implementation of food regulation, and allows them to check the exercise of the powers by the Community institutions during any phase of the decision-making process. Consequently, the Standing Committee is a means of bridging the horizontal and vertical division of powers and might pragmatically be argued to have secured subsidiarity and to have created a framework for co-operative and deliberative multi-level policy-making.

Agencies

The agency structure adopted in the field of pharmaceuticals may be explained by the even greater political sensitivity of the Member States with regard to the regulation of these products, as well as the absence of an eminent source of scientific expertise similar to that of the Scientific Committee on Food. The EMEA responds, in particular, to the Commission's need for greater scientific expertise, but also functions to relieve it of some of its ever-increasing workload. Consequently, the EMEA is charged with the supplying of scientific data, the carrying out of risk assessments, the registration of medicines and the monitoring of drug safety.

However, the agency model thus adopted by no means rules out resorting to committees. First, it is noteworthy that the Agency is itself built on two existing committees: the Committee for Proprietary Medicinal Products (CPMP) and the Committee for Veterinary Medicinal Products (CVMP). In addition, the political sensitivity of these issues to the Member States again dictated that decision-making powers on the authorisation of medicines could not be transferred unconditionally to the Commission. Here a double "safety net" to ensure Member State control seems to have been built in; the authorisation procedure not only stipulates that the CPMP members continue to represent their competent national authorities, but also requires the Commission, prior to adopting any decision, to consult the Standing Committee on Medicines for Human Use through the framework of the troublesome *contre-filet* variant of the regulatory committee procedure. In addition, any Member State may suspend the use of authorised medicines within its territory for reasons of health protection. Decisions thus adopted by the Member States are, however, subject to Commission approval under the same decision-making procedure. The EMEA, moreover, has an important co-ordinating role in facilitating dialogue between the Member States and the Community. The EMEA's Management Board, composed of representatives of the Member States, the Commission and Parliament, also contributes to improved co-operation and implementation and attempts to enhance mutual trust between national administrations, which has been one of the main problems faced by the Community over the years, especially in this sector. In accordance with a "Member State-oriented" institutional balance of powers and in order to address subsidiarity, it has consequently included Member States within the organisational structure of the EMEA as well as in the decisional process, herewith developing a multi-level governance structure in this area.

Private Bodies

The field of technical consumer products has resorted to a self-regulatory structure based on private standardisation bodies. This construction has helped the Community to accelerate its harmonisation activities considerably. Thus, its New Approach to Technical Harmonisation and Standards of 1985 is based on the distinction between the harmonisation of essential safety requirements by the Community institutions and the resulting technical specifications by the European standardisation bodies. The latter bodies perform an important role, since they draft the actual standards which are presumed to implement the health and safety requirements set by the Community institutions. Hence, the standardisation bodies themselves counterbalance the various interests and adopt the standards. Risk management by the Commission in this field entails the supervision of the standard-setting procedure and ultimately (in addition to the Member States) ensuring the safety of products circulating on the Community market. This model, too, resorts to committees which ensure co-operation between the Member States, the Commission and CEN/CENELEC.

2. IN SEARCH OF LEGITIMATE COMMUNITY HEALTH AND SAFETY REGULATION

The growing involvement of the Community in risk regulation clearly indicates that it is moving away from its original conception as an "Economic Community" towards a European polity which is loosened from the nation-state, but nonetheless includes national interests and needs a constitutional framework. Integration theories such as neo-functionalism (despite being successful in explaining the "spill-over" of Community activities and corresponding competences into fields such as consumer protection), intergovernmentalism and supranationalism have their shortcomings as theoretical models of the Community. They all fail to recognise the complex and dynamic interplay of public and private actors at the several levels of the Community and focus too much on either state-centric or supranational views of Community decision-making. At present, the Community can be best conceptualised as a multi-level governance system, which is characterised by decision-making by different levels of government and shifting fields of competence. The multi-level approach respects both the conservation of national administrative powers and the assumption of national powers by the Community.

Examination of the three regulatory structures reveals that the apparent distinction between them tends to blur. I have observed that, in practice, the Community institutions have adopted a pragmatic approach in their design of the institutional structures so as to accommodate the complexities of science-based decision-making, rather than more theoretical conceptions. The models resemble each other in the apparent separation of risk assessment and risk management; bodies other than the formally competent institutions provide for the collection and assessment of scientific data, whilst risk management is carried out by the Commission in co-operation with national representatives on various committees. They nonetheless differ in the form of the bodies they have chosen to depend upon: a scientific committee (foodstuffs), an agency (pharmaceuticals) and private bodies (technical product standards). This situation may be explained by the differences between the fields concerned. The prevention of risks to human health which are derived from the use of potentially harmful substances has a long tradition of public regulation at the national level, with the significant strengthening of regulatory schemes following certain catastrophic events. The Community regulation of both foodstuffs and pharmaceuticals dates back to the early days of the Community, and has always included the use of committees. The protection of human safety in relation to the use of technical consumer products, however, has only relatively recently become a matter of regulatory concern and is commonly associated with the strong tradition of private standardisation, a technique which has been reproduced by the Community. In this field, the Community is faced with the dilemma of, on the one hand, needing to resort to the technical knowledge of private standards bodies, whilst, on the other hand, knowing that this will not guarantee that sufficient attention be given to "public" interests, such as health and safety protection. The reliance on private bodies is very much related to this specific field. However, although the strong national regulatory traditions in the food and pharmaceutical sectors indicate that "public" expert bodies are relied on for the production of scientific expertise, the Community, in particular the Commission, increasingly promotes the use of standards and thus advances the resorting to "private" expert bodies in these fields, too.

Despite these differences, close scrutiny of the institutional structures reveals that, in practice, all three patterns are ultimately based on committees to ensure Member State participation. Committees composed of Member State representatives, it has been argued in this book, form a flexible and appropriate way of including the interests of the Member States in risk management and of addressing subsidiarity concerns. Committees are flexible, fit easily within Commission decision-making and offer a platform for discursive and problem-oriented behaviour of the actors involved. At the same time, however, this flexibility creates obscurity about their precise activities. From the point of view of transparency, these committees leave much to be desired. In contrast, agencies are generally more visible and transparent by virtue of their own administrative structure. Scrutiny of the agency structure in the pharmaceutical sector, however, discloses that the EMEA, too, is built on two previously existing committees. Again in contrast, the Scientific Committee on Food, which resorts to a system of scientific co-operation with national administrative authorities, in practice resembles an agency, the only difference being that it lacks administrative resources of its own. Following the BSE crisis, the SCF, too, has become more visible and transparent, based on the principles of transparency, excellence and objectivity, which were rapidly designed for it by the Commission. In this respect, institutional frameworks do not seem to matter.

Another factor that the three structures have in common is that the Commission has not only sought to increase efficiency, flexibility and rationality through the inclusion of scientific expertise in the decision-making process, but has also been guided by its own pragmatic desire to balance efficiency and rationality in decision-making against the need to ensure acceptance for its decisions through the inclusion of socio-economic interest groups in decision-making procedures. As a result, there is no coherent approach to the inclusion of socio-economic representatives in Community risk regulation. At the same time, this book has revealed the difficulties relating to the participation of interested parties. The Commission has attempted either to institutionalise socio-economic groups within its own decision-making process (committees) or to finance such groups to participate in the standard-setting process by private bodies. Only within the EMEA structure is a trace of the explicit recognition of the need for "deliberation" with interested parties found in the legislative provisions of the Community's new authorisation system, which oblige the Agency to make contacts with such parties. Consequently, loose structures for *ad hoc* consultation of various interested parties have been created.

3. TOWARDS A THEORETICAL CONCEPTUALISATION OF COMMUNITY RISK REGULATION

Does all this mean that institutional frameworks do not matter? Certainly, ideological differences exist. The agency model, advocated primarily by Giandomenico Majone, is based upon non-majoritarian thinking, preferring administrative market integration to be carried out by fully independent agencies, and bringing together technical and economic expertise. In this view, the Community's activities should be restricted to the correction of market failures and be isolated from any redistributive social concerns. The committee model, maintained by Christian Joerges, is based upon the idea that market integration and risk regulation cannot be left to scientific and market actors alone but need political guidance. Member States, and not individual citizens, are the bearers of legitimacy to balance normative values. In this view, the constitutional basis of European risk regulation is formed by "deliberative supranationalism" as a mode of legal structuring of the political process. The supranational law of the EU is not seen as a set of rules which precedes and pre-empts national systems.

Rather, it gives great importance to the manner in which the actual law is produced. Law, in this view, derives its validity and legitimacy from the deliberative quality of its production. This model is not as distinct from the agency model as it claims: this model recognises a very limited redistributive concern only in relation to the apportioning of the costs of risks.[1]

Both models, however, have their weaknesses. The non-majoritarian governance model based on independent technocratic agencies fails to recognise the value-laden nature of risk regulation and does not take account of the tenacious desire of the Member States to participate in Community risk regulation and their consequent unwillingness to surrender their powers. Nor, significantly, does it include interest participation. The normative claim of deliberative supranationalism by means of committees is founded on a relatively small empirical study of two committees in the field of foodstuffs: the Scientific Committee on Foodstuffs and the Standing Committee on Foodstuffs. More importantly, however, it fails to recognise the importance of deliberation with interested parties.

Consequently, one should develop a theoretical concept of legitimate Community risk regulation which explicitly recognises that it is permeated by social and political considerations and is based on the main premise that the Community is a multi-level system of governance. At the same time, it is recognised that market integration based on risk regulation should not be left to scientific experts and/or national and European regulatory authorities alone: negotiation and deliberation with "civil society" should, in my view, be the basis of Community health and safety regulation. The need to let interested parties, in addition to Member States, participate in Community risk regulation stems from the fact that decisions affecting individuals are increasingly taken at Community level. Such interest participation offers diverse interest groups the opportunity to express their dissatisfaction or disagreement with specific national regulatory traditions and, in this way, helps them to overcome the obstacles posed by such traditions. Analysis of the manner in which interested parties may participate in Community health and safety regulation reveals the shortcomings of the Commission's current *ad hoc* approach. Clearly, this underlines the need to re-think the modes of interest participation in Community health and safety regulation. To this end, institutionalised interest participation through committees combined with the establishment of a public notice and comment procedure may be considered.

What can be observed is that the shortcomings of the current institutional arrangements stem from the lack of a comprehensive and coherent concept of risk regulation. The *ad hoc* approach of the Community can be explained by the fact the Community was not designed to deal with risk regulation. Not surprisingly, the BSE scandal, in which the Commission saw itself accused of having been heavily guided by market integration objectives instead of human health protection goals, has led to an increasing awareness of the role of scientific

---

[1] See M. Everson, "Administering Europe?" (1998) 36 *JCMS* 209.

expertise in regulatory Community decision-making by both Community regulators and the general public. Clearly, the institutional failures of the BSE crisis have, to a certain extent, been remedied by the principles of "excellence", "independence" and "transparency" which currently govern the production of scientific expertise by the Community's scientific committees. In relation to the EMEA, the Community legislature has also set some principles relating to the "objectivity" of scientific advice and the "independence" of the EMEA's activities. However, as demonstrated in this book, these principles are also not free from ambiguities.

Any conceptualisation of Community risk regulation should therefore take account of the increasing difficulties regarding the legal construction of scientifically controversial issues in Community law which result from the entanglement between law and science. It raises fundamental questions of the nature and purpose of risk assessment and management. For example, reliance on non-separatism of risk assessment from societal and political values calls for both greater scientific and methodological understanding, an understanding that allows for a critical scrutiny of uncertainties. Equally, this raises queries such as "how certain" is "certain enough", and entails the risk of creating a "scientific trap" in which the public could be encouraged to demand "certainty". Looking for political accountability for risk decisions could push regulators towards the establishment of a "scientifically correct" answer even when there is none, as has occurred, for example, in the USA.[2] Inevitably this leads to questions of the "frontiers of science" in litigation about decisions based on scientific evidence before the Court of Justice and risks resulting in endless litigation procedures.[3] Furthermore, scientific advice as a sound basis for decision-making not only gains increasing importance within the Community but increasingly becomes the basis on which the Community has to justify its safety measures in international fora, such as the World Trade Organisation, for example, where the Community needed to defend its ban on hormones in beef on the basis of sound scientific expertise. This signifies that emerging concepts of Community risk regulation need to be viewed in relation to the current trend towards the internationalisation of economic orders which is accompanied by the trend towards the internationalisation of scientific expertise and risk assessment procedures.

Certainly, these queries need further examination. What I do want to underline here is the need to develop general principles which, based on the premises mentioned above, will govern Community risk regulation, rather than declaring one specific institutional model exclusively to be the appropriate theoretical model for Community risk regulation. To this end, the principles set by the

[2] See S. Jasanoff, "Acceptable Evidence in a Pluralistic Society", in D.G. Mayo/R.D. Hollander (eds.), *Acceptable Evidence. Science and Values in Risk Management* (New York/Oxford, 1991), 29–47.
[3] See, in the American context, M. Shapiro, "The Frontiers of Science Doctrine: American Experiences with the Judicial Control of Science-Based Decision-Making", in Ch. Joerges/K.-H. Ladeur/E. Vos, *Integrating Scientific Expertise into Regulatory Decision-Making. National Traditions and European Innovations* (Baden-Baden, 1997), 325–42.

Commission (and/or Council and Parliament) and the Court should be reconsidered in a broader context. Both committees and agencies may still play an important role; both provide an expedient means of including Member States' concerns and scientific expertise, and take account of the peculiarities of the different product sectors. Principles of risk regulation could include rules (in part already developed by the Court and the Commission) on, for example, the appointment of committee/agency members, the composition of scientific committees or agencies, meetings in public, publications of activities, access to documents, transparency and the right of hearing. As regards the role of interested citizens, consideration should be given to a greater use of green papers and a form of public notice and comment procedure, for example through the Internet, which would contribute to the opening up of a truly Community-wide public debate on the risks inherent in consumer products. Sadly, this debate is only noticeable today by its absence. These rules could easily be included in a European administrative procedures act, and could actually prove a major step towards the development of a general theoretical conception of Community risk regulation.

Bibliography

ALUNNI, L., *Norme techniche e certificazione della qualità. Politiche comunitarie, istituzioni e procedure* (Perugia, 1992)

ANDREINI, P., "La normativa tecnica tra sfera pubblica e sfera privata", in P. Andreini/G. Caia/G. Elias/F.A. Roversi Monaco (eds.), *La normativa tecnica industriale. Amministrazione e privati nella normativa e nella certificazione dei prodotti industriale* (Bologna, 1995), 45–98

ARNULL, A., *The General Principles of EEC Law and the Individual* (London, 1990)

ASCH, P., *Consumer Safety Regulation, Putting a Price on Life and Limb* (New York/Oxford, 1988)

ASKHAM, T./STONEHAM, A., *EC Consumer Safety* (London, 1994)

AYRAL, M., "Essai de classification des groupes et comités" (1975) 187 *RMC* 330–42

BALDWIN, R., *Rules and Government* (Oxford, 1995)

—— McCrudden, C., *Regulation and Public Law* (London, 1987)

BANKOWSKI, Z., "Subsidiarity, Sovereignty and the Self", in K.W. Nörr/ T. Oppermann (eds.), *Subsidarität: Idee und Wirklichkeit. Zur Reichweite eines Prinzips in Deutschland und Europa* (Tübingen, 1997), 23–39

BARENTS, R., "New Developments in Measures Having Equivalent Effect" (1981) 18 *CMLRev.* 271–308

—— "Hormones and the Growth of Community Agricultural Law" [1988] 1 *LIEI* 1–19

—— "The Community and the Unity of the Common Market. Some Reflections on the Economic Constitution of the Community" (1990) 33 *German Yearbook of International Law* 9–36

—— "De wijzigingen van het materiële EEG-recht" (1992) 40 *SEW* 8/9, 684–701

—— "Milieu en interne markt" (1993) 41 *SEW* 1, 5–29

—— "The Internal Market Unlimited: Some Observations on the Legal Basis of Community Legislation" (1993) 30 *CMLRev.* 85–110

—— *The Agricultural Law of the EC* (Deventer, 1994)

—— "The Quality of Community Legislation" (1994) 1 *MJ* 101–14

—— "Het Verdrag van Amsterdam en het Europees Gemeenschapsrecht. De materieelrechtelijke en institutionele veranderingen" (1997) 45 *SEW* 10, 351–65

BEBR, G., "The balance of power in the European Communities" (1959) 5 *Annuaire européen* 53–75

BECHMANN, G. (ed.), *Risiko und Gesellschaft. Grundlagen und Ergebnisse interdisziplinärer Risikoforschung* (Opladen, 1993)

BECK, U., *Risikogesellschaft. Auf dem Weg in eine andere Moderne* (Frankfurt, 1986), translated by M. Ritter as *Risk Society: Towards a New Modernity* (London, 1991)

BECKER, U., "Von 'Dassonville' über 'Cassis' zu 'Keck'—Der Begriff der Maßnahmen gleicher Wirkung in Artikel 30 EGV" (1994) 29 *EuR* 2, 162–74

BERTRAM, C., "Decision-making in the E.E.C.: The Management Committee Procedure" (1967–8) 5 *CMLRev.* 246–65

BESSELINK, L.S.M./Albers, H.S.J./Eijsbouts, W.T., "Subsidiarity in Non-federal Contexts: Ghe Netherlands and the European Union" (1994) 42 *SEW* 5, 275–320

BIEBER, R./DEHOUSSE, R./PINDER, J./WEILER, J.H.H. (eds.), *1992: One European Market? A Critical Analysis of the Commission's Internal Market Strategy* (Baden-Baden, 1988)

BIEBER, R./JACQUÉ, J.P./WEILER, J., *L'Europe de demain*, coll. "Perspectives européennes" (Luxembourg, 1985)

BLANQUET, M., *L'article 5 du Traité C.E.E.—Recerche sur les obligations de fidélité des États membres de la Communauté* (Paris, 1993)

BLECKMANN, A., "Art. 5 EWG-Vertrag und die Gemeinschaftstreue" (1976) 91 *Deutsches Verwaltugsblatt*, 483–7

—— *Europarecht* (Köln/Berlin/Bonn/München, 1990)

BLUMANN, C., "Le pouvoir exécutif de la Commission à la lumière de l'Acte unique européen" (1988) 24 *RTDE* 1, 23–59

—— "La Commission, agent d'exécution du droit communautaire. La comitologie", in J.-V. Louis/D. Waelbroeck (eds.), *La Commission au coeur du système institutionnel des Communautés européennes* (Bruxelles, 1989), 49–69

—— "Le Parlement européen et la comitologie: une complication pour la Conférence intergouvernementale de 1996" (1996) 32 *RTDE* 1–24

BOHMAN, J./REHG, W. (eds.), *Deliberative Democracy* (Cambridge, Mass./London, 1997)

BOSCO, G., "Commentaire de l'acte unique européen des 17–18 fevrier 1987" (1987) 23 *CDE* 355–82

BOURGOIGNIE, TH. (ed.), *European Consumer Law* (Brussels, 1982)

—— "The Need to Reformulate Consumer Protection Policy" (1984) 7 *JCP* 307–21

—— *Eléments pour une théorie du droit de la consommation* (Louvain-la-Neuve, 1988)

—— "Consumer Law and the European Community: Issues and Prospects", in Th. Bourgoignie/D. Trubek, *Consumer Law, Common Market and Federalism in Europe and the United States* (Berlin/New York, 1987), 89–234

—— D. Trubek, *Consumer Law, Common Markets and Federalism in Europe and in the United States* (Berlin/New York, 1987)

BOXUM, J.L., "Zelfstandige bestuursorganen en de greep van ministers op de bestuurlijke organisaties", in J.W.M. Engels *et al.* (eds.), *De Rechtsstaat herdacht* (Zwolle, 1989), 255–65

BRADLEY, K.St.C., "The European Court and the Legal Basis of Community Legislation" (1989) 14 *ELR* 379–402

—— "Comitology and the Law: Through a Glass, Darkly" (1992) 29 *CMLRev.* 693–721

—— "The European Parliament and Comitology: On the Road to Nowhere?" (1997) 3 *ELJ* 3, 230–54

—— "Alien Corn, or the Transgenic Procedural Maze", in M.P.C.M. Van Schendelen (ed.), *EU Committees as Influential Policy-makers* (forthcoming)

—— "Institutional Aspects of Comitology: Scenes from the Cutting Room Floor", in Ch. Joerges and E. Vos (eds.), *EU Committees: Social Regulation, Law and Politics* (Hart Publishing, Oxford, forthcoming)

—— Feeney, A., "Legal Developments in the European Parliament" (1993) 13 *YEL* 383–425

BREKKE, O.A./ERIKSEN, E.O., *Technology Assessment and Democratic Governance*, Typescript, Norwegian Research Centre in Organisation and Management (Bergen, 1998)

BREUER, R., "Die internationale Orientierung von Umwelt-und Technikstandards im deutschen und europäischen Recht" [1989] *Jahrbuch des Umwelt- und Technikrechts* 43–116

BREULMANN, G., *Normung und Rechtsangleichung in der Europäischen Wirtschaftsgemeinschaft* (Berlin, 1993)

BREYER, S., *Breaking the Vicious Circle. Toward Effective Risk Regulation* (Cambridge, Mass., 1993)

—— Stewart, R., *Administrative Law and Regulatory Policy* (3rd ed., Boston, Mass., 1992)

BRINKHORST, L.J., "The Future of European Agencies: A Budgetary Perspective from the European Parliament", in A. Kreher (ed.), *The New Agencies. Conference Report*, EUI Working Paper RSC 96/49 (Florence, 1996), 75–81

BRINKMANN, W., *Rechtliche Aspekte der Bedeuting von technischen Normen für den Verbraucherschutz*, DIN-Normungskunde, Band 20 (Berlin/Cologne, 1984)

BROUWER, O., Free Movement of Foodstuffs and Quality Requirements: Has the Commission Got it Wrong? (1988) 25 *CMLRev.* 237–62

—— "Community Protection of Geographical Indications and Specific Character as a Means of Enhancing Foodstuffs Quality" (1991) 28 *CMLRev.* 615–46

BÜCKER, A., *Von Gefahrenabwehr zu Risikovorsorge und Risikomanagement im Arbeitsschutz. Eine Untersuchung am Beispiel der rechtlichen Regulierung der Sicherheit von Maschinen under dem Einfluß der Europäischen Rechtsangleichung* (Berlin, 1997)

BUITENDIJK, G.J./VAN SCHENDELEN, M.P.C.M., "Brussels Advisory Committees: A Channel for Influence?" (1995) 20 *ELR* 37–56

BYRNE, J.H., "Food law harmonization in the European Community" [1985] *Food Technology* 76–9

CALLEJA, D./VIGNES, D./WÄGENBAUR, R., *Commentaire Megret. Dispositions fiscales, rapprochement des legislations* (Brussels, 1993)

CARY, W.L., "Federalism and Corporate Law: Reflections Upon Delaware" (1974) 83 *The Yale Law Journal* 663–705

CASS, D.Z., "The Word that Saves Maastricht? The Principle of Subsidiarity and the Division of Powers within the European Community" (1992) 29 *CMLRev.* 1107–36

CASSESE, S., *Le basi del diritto amministrativo* (Turin, 1989)

—— "La Costituzione Europea" [1991] *Quaderni costitutionali* 487–508

CATH, I., "Freedom of Establishment of Companies: A New Step Towards Completion of the Internal Market" (1986) 6 *YEL* 247–61

CEN, *Standards for Access to the European Market*, edited by J. Abecassis (Brussels, 1995)

CEN/CENELEC, *The New Approach. Legislation and Standards on the Free Movement of Goods in Europe* (2nd ed., Brussels, 1997)

CHALMERS, D., "Repackiging the Internal Market—The Ramifications of the Keck Judgment" (1994) 19 *ELR* 385–403

CHAMBOLLE, M., "Food Policy and the Consumer" (1988) 11 *JCP* 435–48

CHAMBRAUD, A./FOUCHER, P./MORIN, A., "The Importance of Community Law for French Consumer Protection Legislation", in N. Reich/G. Woodroffe, *European Consumer Policy after Maastricht* (Deventer, 1994), 209–24

CHARNY, D., "Competition among Jurisdictions in Formulating Corporate Law Rules: An American Perspective on the 'Race to the Bottom' in the European Communities" (1991) 32 *Harvard International Law Journal* 423–57

CHEIT, R.E., *Setting Safety Standards. Regulation in the Public and Private Sectors* (Berkely/Los Angeles/Oxford, 1990)

CLOSE, G., "Harmonisation of Laws: Use or Abuse of Powers under the EEC Treaty?" (1978) 3 *ELR* 461–81

—— "The Legal Basis for the Consumer Protection Programme of the EEC and Priorities" (1983) 8 *ELR* 221–40

COHEN, J., Procedure and Substance in Deliberative Democracy", in S. Benhabib, *Democracy and Difference. Contesting the Boundaries of the Political* (Princeton, NJ, 1996), 95–119

—— "Deliberation and Democratic Democracy", in J. Bohman/W. Rehg (eds.), *Deliberative Democracy* (Cambridge, Mass./London, 1997), 67–91

—— Sabel, Ch., "Direct-Deliberative Polyarchy" (1997) 3 *ELJ* 313–42

COTTERLI, S./MARTINELLO, P./VERARDI, C.M, "Implementation of EEC Consumer Protection Directives in Italy", in N. Reich/G. Woodroffe, *European Consumer Policy after Maastricht* (Deventer, 1994), 249–68

CRANOR, C.F., *Regulating Toxic Substances. A Philosophy of Science and the Law* (New York/Oxford, 1993)

CRIJNS, F.C.L.M., *Het Europese perspectief van het Nederlandse staatsrecht* (Zwolle, 1989)

CROSBY, S., "The Single Market and the Rule of Law" (1991) 16 *ELR* 451–65

CROSS, E.D., "Pre-Emption of Member State Law in the European Economic Community: A Framework for Analysis" (1992) 29 *CMLRev.* 447–72

CURALL, J., "Some Aspects of the Relation between Articles 30–36 and Article 100 of the EEC Treaty with a Closer Look to Optional Harmonisation" (1984) 4 *YEL* 169–205

CURTIN, D., "The Constitutional Structure of the Union: A Europe of Bits and Pieces" (1993) 30 *CMLRev.* 17–69

—— " 'Civil Society' and the European Union: Opening Spaces for Deliberative Democracy?", in *Collected Courses of the Academy of European Law* (Florence, 1996, forthcoming 1998)

—— Heukels, T. (eds.), *Institutional Dynamics of European Integration. Essays in Honour of H.G. Schermers* (Dordrecht/Boston/London, 1994)

DAMM, R./HART, D. (eds.), *Rechtliche Regulierung von Gesundheitsrisiken* (Baden-Baden, 1993)

DASHWOOD, A., "The Limits of European Community Powers" (1996) 21 *ELR* 113–28

DE BURCA, G., "The Principle of Proportionality and its Application in EC Law" (1993) 13 *YEL* 105–50

DE GUCHT, K., *Besluitvorming in de Europese Unie* (Antwerp/Apeldoorn, 1994)

DE HAAN, P., "Herstructurering van adviesraden" (1993) 21 *NJB* 778–83

—— Drupsteen, T.G./Fernhout, R., *Bestuursrecht in de sociale rechtsstaat* (Deventer, 1986)

DE RUYT, J., *L'Acte unique européen: commentaire* (Brussels, 1989)

DE URIARTE Y DE BOFARULL, I., *Consumer Legislation in Spain* (Louvain-la-Neuve, 1987)

DE WITTE, B., "Community Law and National Constitutional Values" [1991] 2 *LIEI* 1–22

DEBOYSER, P., *Le droit communautaire rélatif aux denrées alimentaires* (Louvain-la-Neuve, 1989)

—— "Les nouvelles procédures communautaires pour l'authorisation et la surveillance des médicaments" [1995] *RMUE* 4, 31–78

DEHOUSSE, R. "Completing the Internal Market: Institutional Constraints and Challenges", in R. Bieber/R. Dehousse/J. Pinder/J.H.H. Weiler (eds.), *1992: One European Market? A Critical Analysis of the Commission's Internal Market Strategy* (Baden-Baden, 1988), 311–36

—— "1992 and Beyond: The Institutional Dimension of the Internal Market Programme" [1989] 1 *LIEI* 109–36

—— *Integration v. Regulation? Social Regulation in the European Community*, EUI Working Paper LAW 92/23 (Florence, 1992)

—— *Does subsidiarity really matter?*, EUI Working Paper LAW 92/32 (Florence, 1993)

—— "La Communauté européenne après Maastricht: vers un nouvel equilibre institutionnel?" [1993] *Rivista italiana di diritto pubblico comunitario* 1–21

DEHOUSSE, R. "Centralisation and Decentralisation in the European Community" in K. Hailbronner (ed.), *Europa der Zukunft—Zentrale und decentrale Lösungsansätze* (Cologne, 1994), 33–44

—— (ed.), *Europe after Maastricht. An Ever Closer Union?* (Munich, 1994)

—— "Community Competences: Are there Limits to Growth?", in R. Dehousse (ed.), *Europe after Maastricht. An Ever Closer Union?* (Munich, 1994), 103–25

—— "Comparing National Law and EC Law: The Problem of the Level of Analysis" (1994) 42 *The American Journal of Comparative Law* 761–81

—— "Some Reflections on the Crisis of the Harmonisation Model", in F. Snyder, *A Regulatory Framework for Foodstuffs in the Internal Market*, EUI Working Paper LAW 94/4 (Florence 1994), 43–9

—— "Regulation by Networks in the European Community: The Role of European Agencies" (1997) 4 *JEPP* 246–61.

—— Joerges, Ch./Majone, G./Snyder, F. (with M. Everson), *Europe After 1992. New Regulatory Strategies,* EUI Working Paper LAW 92/31(Florence, 1992)

DELLA CANANEA, G., "Cooperazione e integrazione nel sistema amministrativo delle comunità europee: la questione della comitologia" (1990) 40 *Riv. Trimestrale di diritto pubblico* 655–702

DEMMKE, C./HAIBACH, G., "Die Rolle der Komitologieausschüsse bei der Durchführung des Gemeinschaftsrechts und in der Rechtsprechung des EuGH" [1997] *Die Öffentliche Verwaltung* 710–18

DENNINGER, E., *Verfassungsrechtliche Anforderungen an die Normsetzung im Umwelt- und Technikrecht* (Baden-Baden, 1990)

DENYS, C., *Impliciete bevoegdheden in de Europese Economische Gemeenschap* (Antwerp, 1990)

DI FABIO, U./BLECKMANN, A./KUBICEK, H./SEEGER, P. (eds.), *Perspektive Techniksteuerung. Interdisziplinäre Sichtweisen eines Schlüsselproblems entwickelter Industriegesellschaften* (Berlin, 1993)

DI TROCCHIO, F., *Le bugie della scienza. Perché e come gli scienzati imbrogliano* (Milan, 1993)

DONDELINGER, J., "Relations avec les administrations nationales", in J. Jamar/W. Wessels, *Community Bureaucracy at the Crossroads* (Bruges, 1985), 89–98

DONNER, J.P.H., "De nationale wetgever en de Gemeenschap" (1992) 40 *SEW* 6, 464–74

DORN, D.-W., *Art. 235. EWGV—Prinzipien der Auslegung Die Generalermächtigung zur Rechtsetzung im Verfassungssystem der Gemeinschaften* (Kehl/Rhein, 1986)

DUE, O., "Artikel 5 van het EEG-Verdrag. Een bepaling met een federaal karakter?" (1992) 40 *SEW* 355–66

DUFF, A., "Ratification", in A. Duff/J. Pinder/R. Pryce, *Maastricht and Beyond. Building the European Union* (London, 1994), 53–68

—— (ed.), *The Treaty of Amsterdam* (London, 1997)

EARNSHAW, D./JUDGE, D., "Early Days: The European Parliament, Co-decision and the European Union Legislative Process post-Maastricht" (1995) 2 *JEPP* 624–49

EARNSHAW, D./JUDGE, D., "The European Parliament and the Sweeteners Directive: From Footnote to Inter-Institutional Conflict" (1993) 31 *JCMS* 103–16

EBERSTEIN, H.H., *Technische Regeln und ihre rechtliche Bedeutung* (Baden-Baden, 1969)

EGGERS, B., "Die Entscheidung des WTO Appelate Body im Hormonfall" (1998) 9 *EuZW* 5–6, 147–51

EHLERMANN, C.-D., "Die Errichtung des Europäische Fonds für Währungspolitische Zusammenarbeit" (1973) 8 *EuR* 3, 193–208

—— "The Internal Market following the Single European Act" (1987) 24 *CMLRev*. 361–404

—— "Compétences d'exécution conférées à la Commission—la nouvelle décision-cadre du Conseil" (1988) 316 *RMC* 232–9

—— "Ökonomische Aspekte des Subsidiaritätsprinzips: Harmonisierung versus Wettbewerb der Systeme" (1995) 18 *Integration* 1, 11–21

—— "Reflections on a European Cartel Office" (1995) 32 *CMLRev*. 471–86

—— Minch, M., "Conflicts between the Community Institutions within the Budgetary Procedure: Article 205 of the EEC Treaty" (1981) 16 *EuR* 23–42

EICHENER, V., *Social Dumping or Innovative Regulation? Process and Outcomes of European Decision-Making in the Sector of Health and Safety at Work Harmonization*, EUI Working Paper SPS 92/28 (Florence 1992)

—— *Entscheidungsprozesse in der regulativen Politik der Europäischen Union* (Habilitation, University of Bochum, 1997)

EMILIOU, N., "Subsidiarity: An Effective Barrier Against "the Enterprises of Ambition?" (1992) 17 *ELR* 383–407

—— "Opening Pandora's Box: The Legal Basis of Community's Measures before the Court of Justice" (1994) 19 *ELR* 488–507

—— *The principle of proportionality in European Law: A Comparative Study* (The Hague, 1996)

ENGEL, CH./BORRMANN, Ch., *Vom Konsensus zur Mehrheitsentscheidung. EG-Entscheidungsverfahren und nationale Interessenpolitik nach der Einheitlichen Europäischen Akte* (Bonn, 1991)

ENSTHALER, J., *Zertifizierung, Akkreditierung und Normung für den Europäischen Binnenmarkt* (Berlin, 1995)

EUROPEAN POLICY CENTRE, *Making Sense of the Amsterdam Treaty* (Brussels, 1997)

EVERLING, U., "Zur Errichtung nachgeordneter Behörden der Kommission der Europäische Wirtschaftsgemeinschaft", in W. Hallstein/H.-J. Schlochauer (eds.), *Festschrift für Ophüls, Zur Integration Europas* (Karlsruhe, 1965), 33–49

—— "Reflections on the Structure of the European Union" (1992) 29 *CMLRev*. 1053–77

EVERSON, M., "Independent Agencies: Hierarchy Beaters?" (1995) 1 *ELJ* 180–204

—— "Administering Europe?" (1998) 36 *JCMS* 195–216

FALKE, J., "Normungspolitik der Europäischen Gemeinschaften zum Schutz von Verbrauchern und Arbeitnehmern" (1989) *Jahrbuch zur Staats- und Verwaltungswissenschaft* 217–46

—— "Elements of a Horizontal Product Safety Policy for the European Community" (1989) 12 *JCP* 207–28

—— "Technische Normung in Europa: Zieht sich der Staat wirklich zurück?", in G. Winter (ed.), *Die Europäischen Gemeinschaften und das Öffentliche*, ZERP-Diskussionspapier 7/91 (Bremen 1991), 79–125

—— "Comitology and Other Committees: A Preliminary Empirical Assessment", in R.H. Pedler/G.F. Schaefer (eds.), *Shaping European Law and Policy: The Role of Committees and Comitology in the Political Process* (Maastricht, 1996), 117–65

—— "Achievements and Unresolved Problems of European Standardization: The Ingenuity of Practice and the Queries of Lawyers", in Ch. Joerges/K.-H. Ladeur/E. Vos, *Integrating Scientific Expertise into Regulatory Decision-Making. National Traditions and European Innovations* (Baden-Baden, 1997), 187–224

—— Joerges, Ch., *Rechtliche Möglichkeiten bei der Verfolgung und Sicherung nationaler und EG-weiter Umschutzziele im Rahmen der europäischen Normung*, Gutachten erstellt im Auftrag des Büros für Technikfolgen-Abschätzung des Deutschen Bundestages (Bremen, 1995)

—— Joerges, Ch., *"Traditional" Harmonisation Policy, European Consumer Protection Programmes and the New Approach*, EUI Working Paper Law 91/13 (Florence, 1991)

—— Winter, G., "Management and Regulatory Committees in Executive Rule-making", in G. Winter (ed.), *Sources and Categories of European Union Law. A Comparative and Reform Perspective* (Baden-Baden, 1996), 541–82

—— Schepel, H. (eds.), *The Legal Status of Technical Standards in the Member States of the EU and of EFTA* (Baden-Baden, forthcoming)

FALLON, M./MANIET, F. (eds.), *Sécurité des produits et mécanismes de contrôle dans la Communauté européenne* (Louvain-la-Neuve, 1990)

FARQUHAR, B., "La participation des consommateurs à la normalisation" [1994] *Revue européenne de droit de la consommation* 27–38

—— "Consumer Representation in Standardisation" (1995) 3 *Consumer Law Journal* 56–68

FARR, S., *Harmonisation of Technical Standards in the EC* (London, 1992)

FLYNN, J., "How Will Article 100A(4) Work? A Comparison With Article 93" (1987) 24 *CMLRev.* 689–707

FORMAN, J., "Case 16/88 Commission v. Council" (1990) 27 *CMLRev.* 872–82

FORWOOD, N./CLOUGH, M., "The Single European Act and Free Movement. Legal Implications of the Provisions for the Completion of the Internal Market" (1986) 11 *ELR* 383–408

FREESTONE, D., "European Community Environmental Policy and Law" [1991] *Journal of Law and Society* 135–54

FURRER, A., *Die Sperrwirkung des sekundären Gemeinschaftsrechts auf die nationalen Rechtsordnungen*. Dissertation Hochschule St. Gallen, no 1515 (Baden-Baden, 1994)

—— "The Principle of Pre-emption", in G. Winter (ed.), *Sources and Categories of European Union Law: A Comparative and Reform Perspective* (Baden-Baden, 1995), 521–40

FUSS, E.-W., *Die Europäischen Gemeinschaften und der Rechtsstaatgedanke* (Heule, 1963)

GAMBELLI, F., *Aspects juridiques de la normalisation et de la réglementation technique européen. Guide sur le droit technique et la normalisation* (Paris, 1994)

GARDNER, J., "The Still More Difficult Task: The European Agency for the Evaluation of Medicines and European Regulation of Pharmaceuticals" (1996) 2 *ELJ* 48–82

GEDDES, A., "Free Movement of Pharmaceuticals within the Community: The Remaining Barriers" (1991) 16 *ELR* 295–306

GEELHOED, L.A., *De interveniërende staat, aanzet tot een instrumentenleer* (The Hague, 1983)

—— "Het subsidiariteitsbeginsel: een communautair principe?" (1991) 39 *SEW* 7/8, 422–35

GEORGE, S., *Politics and Policy in the European Community* (New York, 1991)

GERADIN, D., "Trade and Environmental Protection: Community Harmonisation and National Environmental Standards" (1993) 13 *YEL* 151–99

GÉRARD, A., *Food Law in the Europe of Today* (Brussels, 1987)

GLAESNER, H.-J., "Die Einheitliche Europäische Akte" (1986) 21 *EuR* 119–52

GODARD, O, "Social Decision-Making under Conditions of Scientific Controversy, Expertise and the Precautionary Principle", in Ch. Joerges/K.-H. Ladeur/E. Vos (eds.), *Integrating Scientific Expertise into Regulatory Decision-Making. National Traditions and European Innovations* (Baden-Baden, 1997), 39–73

GOLDSCHMIDT, V. (ed.), Montesquieu, *"De l'esprit des lois"* (Paris, 1979)

GORMLEY, L.W., "Cassis de Dijon and the Communication from the Commission" (1981) 6 *ELR* 454–9

—— *Prohibiting Restrictions on Trade within the EEC* (Amsterdam/New York/Oxford, 1985)

—— "Two Years after Keck" (1996) 19 *Fordham International Law Journal* 866–86

GOYENS, M., "Consumer Protection in a Single European Market: What Challenge for the EC Agenda?" (1992) 29 *CMLRev.* 71–92

—— "Development of EC Consumer Protection", in T. Askham/A. Stoneham, *EC Consumer Safety* (London/Dublin/Edinburgh, 1994), 7–43

GOYENS, M., "Where There's a Will, There's a Way! A Practicioner's View", in N. Reich,/G. Woodroffe, *European Consumer Policy after Maastricht* (Deventer, 1994), 93–104

GRABITZ, E./SASSE, C., *Beiträge zur Umweltgestaltung* (Berlin, 1977)

GRAY, P., "Food Law and the Internal Market. Taking Stock" [1990] *Food Policy* 111–21

GREAVES, R., "The Nature and Binding Effect of Decisions under Article 189 EC" (1996) 21 *ELR* 3–16

GREEN, N./HARTLEY, T.C./USHER, J.A., *The Legal Foundations of the Single European Market* (Oxford, 1991)

GRILLER, S. (ed.), *Regierungskonferenz 1996: Ausgangspositionen*, IEF Working Paper Nr. 27 (Vienna, 1996)

GROTE, J., *Guidance and Control in Transnational Committee Networks: The Associational Basis of Policy Cycles at the EC Level* (1989), unpublished manuscript

GUÉDON, M.J., *Les autorités administratives indépendentes* (Paris, 1991)

GUILLERMIN, G., "Le principe de l'équilibre institutionnel dans la jurisprudence de la Cour de Justice des Communautés européennes" (1992) 119 *Journal du droit international* 319–46

GULMANN, C., "The Single European Act—Some Remarks from a Danish Perspective" (1987) 24 *CMLRev.* 31–40

HAAS, E.B., *The Uniting of Europe* (Stanford, 1958)

—— "International Integration: The European and Universal Process", in D. J. Hekius et al. (eds.), *International Security* (New York, 1964), 229–60

—— "Technocracy, Pluralism and the New Europe", in S.R. Graubard (ed.), *A New Europe?* (Boston, Mass., 1964), 62–88

—— Schmitter, P.C., "Economics and Differential Patterns of Political Integration: Projections about Unity in Latin America" (1964) 18 *International Organization* 705–37

HABERMAS, J., "Wie ist Legitimität durch Legalität moglich?" (1987) 20 *Kritische Justiz* 1–16

HAILBRONNER, K., "Der 'nationale Alleingang' im Gemeinschaftsrecht am Beispiel der Abgasstandards für Pkw" (1989) 16 *EuGRZ* 101–22

HANCHER, L., *Regulating for Competition. Government, Law, and the Pharmaceutical Industry in the United Kingdom and France* (Oxford, 1990)

—— "The European Pharmaceutical Market: Problems of Partial Harmonisation" (1990) 15 *ELR* 9–33

—— "Creating the Internal Market for Pharmaceutical Medicines—an Echternach Jumping Procession?" (1991) 28 *CMLRev.* 821–53

HANF, D., "Le jugement de la Cour constitutionnelle fédérale allemande sur la constitutionalité du Traité de Maastricht" (1994) 30 *RTD Eur* 3, 391–423

HANKIN, R, "The Role of Scientific Advice in the Elaboration and Implementation of the Community's Foodstuffs Legislation", in Ch. Joerges/K.-H. Ladeur/E. Vos (eds.), *Integrating Scientific Expertise into*

Regulatory Decision-Making. National Traditions and European Innovations (Baden-Baden, 1997), 141–67

HARLOW, C., "A Community of Interests? Making the Most of European Law" (1992) 55 *MLR* 331–50

HARNIER, O., "Artikel 145", in H. Von der Groeben/J. Thiesing/C.-D. Ehlermann, *Kommentar zum EWG-Vertrag* (Baden-Baden, 1991), 4239–53

HART, D., "Drug Safety as a Means of Consumer Protection: The Approximation of Laws in the EC Medicinal Products Market and Its Limitations" (1989) 12 *JCP* 343–55

—— "Harmonisierung des Marktüberwachungsrechts für Arzneimittel in der EG" (1990) 52 *Pharm.Ind.* 9, 1072–5

—— Reich, N., *Integration und Recht des Arzneimittelmarktes in der EG* (Baden-Baden, 1990)

HARTLEY, T., "Consumer Safety and the Harmonisation of Technical Standards: The Low Voltage Directive" (1982) 7 *ELR* 55–62

—— *The Foundations of European Community Law* (3rd ed., Oxford, 1994)

HAYDER, R., "Neue Wege der EG-Rechtsangleichung?" (1989) 53 *RabelsZ* 622–98

HERDEGEN, M., "Maastricht and the German Constitutional Court: Constitutional Restraints for an 'Ever Closer Union'" (1994) 31 *CMLRev.* 235–49

HÉRITIER, A./MINGERS S./KNILL C./BECKA M., *Die Veränderung von Staatlichkeit in Europa. Ein regulativer Wettbewerb: Deutschland, Großbritannien, Frankreich* (Opladen, 1994)

HESSEL, B./MORTELMANS, K., "Decentralised Government and Community Law: Conflicting Institutional Developments?" (1993) 30 *CMLRev.* 905–37

HILF, M., *Die Organisationsstruktur der Europäischen Gemeinschaften* (Berlin/Heidelberg/New York, 1982)

HODGKIN, C., "International Harmonisation—the Need for Transparency" (1996) 9 *International Journal of Risk & Safety in Medicine* 195–9

HOFFMANN, D., "Product Safety in the Internal Market: The Proposed Community Emergency Procedure", in M. Fallon/F. Maniet (eds.), *Sécurité des produits et mécanismes de contrôle dans la Communauté européenne* (Louvain-la-Neuve, 1990), 63–76

HOFFMANN, H.C.H./TOELLER, A.E., "Zur Reform der Komitologie: Grundsätze und Regeln" [1998] *Staatswissenschaft und Staatspraxis* 2 (forthcoming)

HOHM, K.-H., *Arzneimittelsicherheit und Nachmarktkontrolle* (Baden-Baden, 1990)

HOLDERBAUM, K., "Chancen für eine Europäische Kartellbehörde?" (1967) 2 *EuR* 116–33

HOUSE OF LORDS SELECT COMMITTEE ON THE EUROPEAN COMMUNITIES, *Approximation of legislation*, session 1977–8, 22nd Report and 35th Report, HL 131 and HL 199 (London, 1978)

HOUSE OF LORDS SELECT COMMITTEE ON THE EUROPEAN COMMUNITIES, *Report on the Delegation of Powers to the Commission*, Session 1986–7, 3rd Report (London, 1987)

HOUSE OF LORDS SELECT COMMITTEE ON THE EUROPEAN COMMUNITIES, *Report on Economic and Monetary and Political Union*, Session 1989–90, 27th Report (London, 1990)

HOUSE OF LORDS SELECT COMMITTEE ON THE EUROPEAN COMMUNITIES, *Report Political Union. Law-Making Powers and Procedures*, Session 1990–1, 17th Report (London, 1991)

HOUSE OF LORDS SELECT COMMITTEE ON THE EUROPEAN COMMUNITY, *Report on the European Medicines Agency and Future Marketing Authorisation Procedures*, Session 1991–2, 3rd Report (London, 1992)

HYDE, A., "The Concept of Legitimation in the Sociology of Law" (1983) 54 *Wisconsin Law Review* 379–426

INSTITUT FÜR EUROPÄISCHE POLITIK, *Study on Comitology. Characteristics, Performance and Options*, Preliminary Final Report (Bonn, 1989)

IPSEN, H.P., *Europäisches Gemeinschaftsrecht* (Tübingen, 1972)

ISAAC, G., *Droit communautaire général* (Paris, 1989)

JACHTENFUCHS, M., "Theoretical Perspectives on European Governance" (1995) 1 *ELJ* 115–33.

—— B. Kohler-Koch (eds.), *Europäische Integration* (Opladen, 1996)

—— and —— "Regieren im dynamischen Mehrebenensystem" in *id.* (eds.), *Europäische Integration* (Opladen, 1996), 15–44

JACOBS, F./CORBETT, R./SHACKLETON, M., *The European Parliament* (London, 1992)

JACQUÉ, J.-P., "L'Acte unique européen" (1986) 22 *RTDE* 575–612

JASANOFF, S., *The Fifth Branch. Science Advisers as Policymakers* (Cambridge, Mass./London, 1990)

—— "Acceptable Evidence in a Pluralistic Society", in D.G. Mayo/R.D. Hollander (eds.), *Acceptable Evidence. Science and Values in Risk Management* (New York/Oxford, 1991), 29–47

—— *Science at the Bar, Law, Science and Technology in America* (Cambridge, Mass./London, 1995)

—— Markle, G.E./Petersen, J.C./Pinch, T. (eds.), *Handbook of Science and Technology Studies* (Thousand Oaks/London/New Delhi, 1995)

JOERGES, CH., "Zielsetzungen und Instrumentarien der europäischen Verbraucherpolitik" (1979) 2 *JCP* 213–27

—— "The New Approach to Technical Harmonisation and the Interests of Consumers: Reflections on the Requirements and Difficulties of a Europeanisation of Product Safety Policy", in R. Bieber/R. Dehousse/J. Pinder/J.H.H. Weiler (eds.), *1992: One European Market? A Critical Analysis of the Commission's Internal Market Strategy* (Baden-Baden, 1988), 175–225

—— "Paradoxes of Deregulatory Strategies at Community Level: The Example of Product Safety Policy", in G. Majone (ed.), *Deregulation or Re-regulation?*

A Regulatory Reform in Europe and the United States (London, 1990), 176–97

—— "Product Safety Law, Internal Market Policy and the Proposal for a Directive on General Product Safety", in M. Fallon/F. Maniet (eds.), *Sécurité des produits et mécanismes de contrôle dans la Communauté européenne* (Louvain-la-Neuve, 1990), 177–213

—— "Market ohne Staat? Die Wirtschaftsverfassung der Gemeinschaft und die regulatieve Politik", in R. Wildemann (ed.), *Staatswerdung Europas? Optionen für eine politische Union* (Baden-Baden, 1991), 225–68

—— "Social Regulation and the Legal Structure of the EEC", in B. Stauder (ed.), *La securité des produits de consommation* (Zürich, 1992), 31–47

—— "European Economic Law, the Nation-State and the Maastricht Treaty", in R. Dehousse (ed.), *Europe After Maastricht. An Ever Closer Union?* (Munich, 1994), 29–62

—— "Legitimationsprobleme des Europäischen wirtschaftsrechts und der Vertrag von Maastricht", in G. Brüggemeier (ed.), *Verfassungen für ein ziviles Europa* (Baden-Baden, 1994), 91–130

—— "Social Regulation by the Community: the Case of Foodstuffs", in F. Snyder (ed.), *A Regulatory Framework for Foodstuffs in the Internal Market*, EUI Working Paper LAW 94/4 (Florence, 1994), 50–6

—— *Die Beurteilung der Sicherheit technischer Konsumgüter und der Gesundheitsrisiken von Lebensmitteln in der Praxis des europäischen Ausschußwesens ("Komitologie")*, ZERP-Diskussionspapier 95/1 (Bremen, 1995)

—— *States Without a Market? Comments on the German Constitutional Court's Maastricht Judgment and a Plea for Interdisciplinary Discourses*, NISER Working Paper (Utrecht, 1996)

—— "Scientific Expertise in Social Regulation and the European Court of Justice: Legal Frameworks for Denationalised Governance Structures", in Ch. Joerges/K.-H. Ladeur/E. Vos (eds.), *Integrating Scientific Expertise into Regulatory Decision-Making. National Traditions and European Innovations* (Baden-Baden, 1997), 295–323

—— "Challenging the Bureaucratic Challenge", in E.O. Eriksen/J.E. Fossum (eds.), *Integration through Deliberation? On the Prospects for European Democracy* (forthcoming)

—— Falke, J./Micklitz, H.-W./Brüggemeier, G., *Die Sicherheit von Konsumgütern und die Entwicklung der Europäischen Gemeinschaften* (Baden-Baden, 1988) (English version: *European Product Safety, Internal Market Policy and the New Approach to Technical Harmonisation and Standards*, EUI Working Papers LAW 91/10–14 (Florence, 1991; http://www.iue.it/LAW/WP-Texts/Joerges91/)

—— Ladeur, K.-H./Vos, E., *Integrating Scientific Expertise into Regulatory Decision-Making. National Traditions and European Innovations* (Baden-Baden, 1997)

JOERGES, CH. and Neyer, J., "From Intergovernmental Bargaining to Deliberative Political Processes: The Constitutionalisation of Comitology" (1997) 3 *ELJ* 273–99

—— and —— "Transforming Strategic Interaction into Deliberative Problem-solving: European Comitology in the Foodstuffs Sector" (1997) 4 *JEPP* 609–25

—— Vos, E., "Structures of Transnational Governance and Their Legitimacy", in J. Vervaele (ed.), *Compliance and Enforcement of EC Law* (Deventer, forthcoming)

—— and —— (eds.), *EU Committees: Social Regulation, Law and Politics* (Oxford, forthcoming)

KAISER, J.H., "Grenzen der EG-Zuständigkeit" (1980) 15 *EuR* 2, 97–118

KAPTEYN, P.J.G., "Het advies 1/76 van het Europese Hof van Justitie, de externe bevoegdheid van de Gemeenschap en haar deelneming aan een Europees oplegfonds voor de binnenscheepvaart" (1978) 26 *SEW* 4, 276–88 and (1978) 26 *SEW* 5/6, 360–9

—— "Community Law and the Principle of Subsidiarity" [1991] *Revue des Affaires européennes* 35–43

—— "Denemarken en het Verdrag van Maastricht" (1992) 25 *NJB* 781–3

—— "De complexe rechtsorde van het Unieverdrag: subsidiariteitsbeginsel en nieuwe bevoegdheden", in K. Hellingman (ed.), *Europa in de steigers: van Gemeenschap tot Unie* (Deventer, 1993), 41–52

—— VerLoren van Themaat, P. *et al.*, *Inleiding tot het recht van de Europese Gemeenschappen. Na Maastricht* (Deventer, 1995)

—— and —— edited by L. Gormley, *Introduction to the Law of the European Communities* (Deventer, 1990)

KAUFER, E., *The Regulation of Drug Development, In Search of a Common European Approach*, EUI Working Paper 89/411 (Florence, 1989)

—— "The Regulation of New Product Development in the Drug Industry", in G. Majone (ed.), *Deregulation or Re-regulation? Regulatory Reform in Europe and the US* (London/New York, 1990), 153–75

KELLERMAN, A.E., "The Quality of Community Legislation Drafting", in D. Curtin/T. Heukels (eds.), *Institutional Dynamics of European Integration, Essays in Honour of H.G. Schermers* (Dordrecht/Boston/London, 1994), 251–62

KEOHANE, R.O./HOFFMANN, S. (eds.), *Decisionmaking and Institutional Change* (Oxford, 1991)

KLÖSTERS, A., *Kompetenzen der EG-Kommission im innerstaatlichen Vollzug von Gemeinschaftsrecht* (Cologne/Berlin/Bonn/Munich, 1994)

KÖCK, W., "Risikovorsorge als Staatsaufgabe" (1996) 121 *Archiv für öffentliches Recht* 1–24

KOOPMANS, TH., "The Role of the Law in the Next Stage of European Integration" (1986) 35 *Int. and Com. Quarterly* 925–31

—— "Rechter, D-mark en democratie: het Bundesverfassungsgericht en de Europese Unie" (1994) 8 *NJB* 245–51

KORTMANN, C.A.J.M., "Post-Tchernobyl" (1991) 39 *SEW* 3, 163–72

KRÄMER, L., "EEC Action in Regard to Consumer Safety, Particularly in the Food Sector" (1984) 7 *JCP* 473–85

—— *EEC Consumer Law* (Louvain-la-Neuve, 1986)

—— "The Single European Act and Environmental Protection: Reflections on Several New Provisions in Community Law" (1987) 24 *CMLRev.* 659–88

—— "Environmental Protection and Article 30 EEC Treaty" (1993) 30 *CMLRev.* 111–43.

—— *EC Treaty and Environmental Protection* (London, 1995)

KREHER, A. (ed.), The New Agencies. *Conference Report,* EUI Working Paper RSC 96/49 (Florence, 1996)

—— *The EC Agencies between Community Institutions and Constituents: Autonomy, Control and Accountability, Conference Report,* EUI RSC Working Paper (Florence, 1998)

—— "Agencies in the European Community—a Step Towards Administrative Integration in Europe" (1997) 4 *JEPP* 225–45

KROMARECK, R., "Commentaire de l'Acte unique européen en matière d'environnement" [1988] *Revue juridique de l'environnement* 75–92

KRUCK, H., "Artikel 173. Gerichtshof", in H. Von der Groeben/J. Thiesing/ C.-D. Ehlermann, *Kommentar zum EWG-Vertrag* (Baden-Baden, 1991), 4536–71

KUHN, T., *The Structure of Scientific Revolutions* (Chicago, Ill., 1970)

KUMMELING, H.R.B.M., *Advisering in het publiekrecht* (The Hague, 1988)

LACHMANN, P., "Some Danish Reflections on the Use of Article 235 of the Rome Treaty" (1981) 18 *CMLRev.* 447–61

LADEUR, K.-H., "Sources and Categories of Legal Acts—Germany", in G. Winter (ed.), *Sources and Categories of European Union Law: A Comparative and Reform Perspective* (Baden-Baden, 1996), 235–72

—— *The European Environment Agency and Prospects for a European Network of Environmental Considerations,* EUI Working Paper RSC 96/50 (Florence, 1996)

—— "The Integration of Scientific and Technological Expertise into the Process of Standard-Setting According to German Law", in Ch. Joerges/K.-H. Ladeur/E. Vos (eds.), *Integrating Scientific Expertise into Regulatory Decision-Making. National Traditions and European Innovations* (Baden-Baden, 1997), 77–100

LANDFRIED, CH., "Beyond Technocratic Governance: The Case of Biotechnology" (1997) 3 *ELJ* 253–72

LANE, R., "New Community Competences Under the Maastricht Treaty" (1993) 30 *CMLRev.* 939–79

LANGEHEINE, B., "Rechtsangleichung unter Art 100a EWGV—Harmonisierung vs. nationale Schutzinteressen" (1988) 23 *EuR* 235–56

—— "Artikel 100A", in E. Grabitz, *Kommentar zum EWG-Vertrag* (Munich, 1990)

LANGMANN, G., *Consumer Representation in Standardisation. A Review of the National Arrangements for Co-ordinating Consumer Representation in ISO-COLPCO Member Countries*, Report prepared for ISO/COLPCO 1997 (http://www.anec.org)

LÄUFER, T., *Die Organe der EG—Rechtsetzung und Haushaltsverfahren zwischen Kooperation und Konflikt* (Bonn, 1990)

LAURSEN, F./VANHOONACKER, S. (eds.), *The Ratification of the Maastricht Treaty. Issues, Debates and Future Implications* (Maastricht, 1994)

LAUWAARS, R.H., *Lawfulness and Legal Force of Community Decisions* (Leiden, 1973)

—— "Auxiliary Organs and Agencies in the EEC" (1979) 16 *CMLRev.* 365–87

—— "Art. 235 EEG als grondslag voor de schepping van een Europees merkenrecht" (1981) 29 *SEW* 9, 533–48

—— "The 'Model Directive' on Technical Harmonisation", in R. Bieber/R. Dehousse/J. Pinder/J.H.H. Weiler (eds.), *1992: One European Market? A Critical Analysis of the Commission's Internal Market Strategy* (Baden-Baden, 1988), 151–73

—— Maarleveld, J.M., *Harmonisatie van wetgeving in Europese organisaties* (Deventer, 1987)

—— and —— "Het Britse Hogerhuis en de harmonisatie van wetgeving" (1979) 27 *SEW* 9–14

LAVE, L.B. (ed.), *Risk Assessment and Management* (New York/London, 1987)

LENAERTS, K., "Some Reflections on the Separation of Powers in the European Community" (1991) 28 *CMLRev.* 1–35

—— "Regulating the Regulatory Process: 'Delegation of Powers' in the European Community" (1993) 18 *ELR* 23–49

—— "Subsidiarity and Community Competence in the Field of Education" (1994/5) 1 *Columbia Journal of European Law* 1–28

—— Van Ypersele, P., "Le principe de subsidiarité et son contexte: étude de l'article 3B du Traité CE" (1994) 30 *CDE* 3–85

LINDER, M., "Adoption of European Testing Standards by CEN/CENELEC", in CEN/CENELEC & ETSI (eds.), *Conformance Testing and Certification in Information Technology and Telecommunications* (Amsterdam/Washington/Tokyo, 1991), 113–18

LISTER, Ch., *Regulation of Food Products by the European Community* (London/Dublin/Edinburgh/Brussels, 1992)

—— "The Naming of Foods: The European Community's Rules for Non-brand Product Names" (1993) 18 *ELR* 178–201

LOUIS, J.-V., "Delegatie van bevoegdheden in de Europese Gemeenschappen" (1978) 26 *SEW* 12, 802–14

LOWI, TH.J., *The End of Liberalism* (New York, 1969)

LOWRANCE, W.W., *Of Acceptable Risk. Science and the Determination of Safety* (Los Altos, 1976)

LÜBBE-WOLFF, G., "Verfassungsrechtliche Fragen der Normsetzung" (1991) 6 *Zeitschrift für Gesetzgebung* 219–48

LUHMANN, N., *Risk: A Sociological Theory* (Berlin/New York, 1993)

MAAS, H.H., "Delegatie van bevoegdheden in de Europese Gemeenschappen" (1967) 15 *SEW*, 2–18

—— "The Administrative Commission for the Social Security of Migrant Workers. An Institutional Curiosity" (1966–67) 3 *CMLRev.* 51–63

—— "Wetgevingskroniek EG 1977 en 1978" (1979) 27 *SEW* 10/11, 686–97

MADURO, M. POIARES, *We the Court. The European Court of Justice and the European Economic Constitution* (Oxford, 1998)

MAIER, L., "Institutional Consumer Representation in the European Community", in N.Reich,/Woodroffe, G. (eds.), *European Consumer Policy after Maastricht* (Deventer, 1994), 73–92

MAJONE, G. (ed.), *Deregulation or Re-regulation? A Regulatory Reform in Europe and the United States* (New York/London 1990)

—— *Controlling Regulatory Bureaucracies: Lessons from the American Experience*, EUI Working Paper SPS 93/3 (Florence, 1993)

—— *Deregulation or Re-Regulation? Policymaking in the European Community Since the Single Act*, EUI Working Paper SPS 93/2 (Florence, 1993)

—— *Mutual Recognition In Federal Type Systems*, EUI Working Paper SPS 93/1 (Florence, 1993)

—— "The European Community Between Social Policy and Social Regulation" [1993] *JCMS* 153–70

—— *Independence vs. Accountability? Non-Majoritarian Institutions and Democratic Government in Europe*, EUI Working Paper SPS 94/3 (Florence, 1994)

—— "The European Community: An 'Independent Fourth Branch of Government'?", in G. Brüggemeier (ed.), *Verfassungen für ein ziviles Europa* (Baden-Baden, 1994), 23–43

—— *Mutual Trust, Credible Commitment and the Evolution of Rules for a Single European Market*, EUI Working Paper RSC 95/1 (Florence, 1995)

—— *The Development of Social Regulation in the European Community: Policy Externalities, Transaction Costs, Motivational Factors*, EUI Working Paper SPS 95/2 (Florence, 1995)

—— *Regulating Europe* (London, 1996)

—— "The New European Agencies: Regulation by Information" (1997) 4 *JEPP* 262–75

—— Dehousse, R., "The Institutional Dynamics of European Integration: From the Single Act to the Maastricht Treaty", in S. Martin (ed.), *The Construction of Europe. Essays in Honour of Emile Noël* (Dordrecht/Boston/London, 1994), 91–112

MANCINI, G.F./KEELING, D.T., "Democracy and the European Court of Justice" (1994) 57 *MLR* 175–90

MARBURGER, P., *Die Regeln der Technik* (Cologne/Berlin/Bonn/Munich, 1979)

—— *Die gleitende Verweisung aus der Sicht der Wissenschaft, Verweisung auf technische Normen in Rechtsvorschriften*, DIN- Normungskunde, Bd. 17 (Berlin/Cologne, 1982)

—— Enders, R., "Technische Normen im europäischen Gemeinschaftsrecht" [1994] *Jahrbuch für Umwelt- und Technikrecht*, 333–68

MARKS, G./HOOGHE, L./BLANK, K., "European Integration since the 1980s: State-centric versus Multi-level Governance" (1996) 34 *JCMS* 343–78

MARTIN, B./RICHARDS, E., "Scientific Knowledge, Controversy and Public Decision Making", in S. Jasanoff/G.E. Markle/J.C. Petersen/T. Pinch (eds.) *Handbook of Science and Technology Studies* (Thousand Oaks/London/New Delhi, 1995), 506–26

MATTERA, A., *Le marché unique européen—ses règles, son fonctionnement* (Paris, 1988)

MAYNTZ, R., "Politische Steuerung: Aufstieg, Niedergang und Transformation einer Theorie", in K. Von Beyme/C. Offe (eds.), *Politische Theorien in der Ära der Transformation* (Opladen, 1996), 148–68

MAYO, D.G/HOLLANDER, R.D. (eds.), *Acceptable Evidence. Science and Values in Risk Management* (New York/Oxford, 1991)

MAZEY, S./RICHARDSON, J., "The Commission and the Lobby", in G. Edwards/D. Spence, *The European Commission* (London, 1994), 169–201

MCGEE, A/WEATHERILL, S., "The Evolution of the Single Market—Harmonisation or Liberation" (1990) 53 *MLR* 578–96

MCMILLAN, J., "La «certification», la reconnaissance mutuelle et le marché unique" [1991] *RMUE* 181–211

MENDRIOU, M., "Non-compliance and the European Commission's Role in Integration" (1996) 3 *JEPP* 1–22

MENG, W., "Die Neuregelung der EG-Verwaltungsauschüsse. Streit um die «Comitologie»" (1988) 49 *ZaöRV* 208–28

MERTENS DE WILMARS, J., "Het Hof van Justitie van de Europese Gemeenschappen na de Europese Akte" (1986) 34 *SEW* 9/10, 601–19

MERZ, F., "Bedarf die Errichtung eines Europäischen Kartellamtes der Änderung des EWG-Vertrages?" (1990) 1 *EuZW* 13, 405–8

MESTMÄCKER, E.-J., "On the Legitimacy of European Law" (1994) 58 *RabelsZ* 615–35

MICKLITZ, H.-W. (ed.), *Post Market Control of Consumer Goods* (Baden-Baden, 1990)

—— "Consumer Rights", in A. Cassese./A. Clapham/J.H.H. Weiler (eds.), *Human Rights in the European Community: The Substantive Law* (Baden-Baden, 1991), 53–109

—— "Die Richtlinie über allgemeine Produktsicherheit vom 29.6.1992" (1991) 5 *VuR* 261–7

—— Roethe, Th./Weatherill, S. (eds.), *Federalism and Responsibility. A Study on Product Safety Law and Practice in the European Community* (London/ Dordrecht/Boston, 1994)

—— Weatherill, S., "Consumer Policy in the European Community: Before and After Maastricht" (1993) 16 *JCP* 285–321

MONAR, J., "Interinstitutional Agreements: The Phenomenon and its New Dynamics after Maastricht" (1994) 31 *CMLRev.* 693–719

MOORE, S., "Revisiting the Limits of Article 30 EEC" (1994) 19 *ELR* 19, 195–201

MORTELMANS, K.J.M., "De interne markt en het facettenbeleid na het Keck-arrest: nationaal beleid, vrij verkeer of harmonisatie" (1994) 42 *SEW* 4, 236–50

MÜLLER-GRAFF, P.-Ch., "Die Rechtsangleichung zur Verwirklichung des Binnenmarktes" (1989) 24 *EuR* 107–51

MURPHY, F., "Towards a More Fairly Balanced and Better Quality of Life", in EEC Commission, *Thirty Years Community Law* (Brussels, 1983), 487–98

NENTWICK, N., *Das Lebensmittelrecht der Europäischen Union* (Vienna, 1994)

NEYER, J., "Administrative Supranationalität in der Verwaltung des Binnenmarktes: Zur Legitimität der Komitologie" [1997] *Integration* 24–37

—— "The Comitology Challenge to Analytical Integration Theory", in Ch. Joerges/E. Vos (eds.), *EU Committees: Social Regulation, Law and Politics* (Oxford, forthcoming)

NICOLAS, F./REPUSSARD, J., *Common Standards for Enterprises* (Luxembourg, 1994)

NICOLAYSEN, G., "Zur Theorie von den implied powers in den EG" (1966) 1 *EuR* 128–42

NICOLL, W., "Qu'est-ce que la comitologie?" (1987) 306 *RMC* 185–7

O'KEEFFE, D./TWOMEY, P.M. (eds.), *Legal Issues of the Maastricht Treaty* (London, 1994)

O'NEILL, M., "The Choice of Legal Basis: More than a Number" (1994) 1 *Irish Journal of European Law* 44–58

OECD, *Product Safety. Risk Management and Cost-Benefit Analysis* (Paris, 1983)

OLIVER, P., *Free Movement of Goods in the European Community Under Articles 30 to 36 of the Rome Treaty* (London, 1996)

OOSTING, M., *Beginselen van bestuur* (Alphen an der Rijn, 1980)

PAG, S., "Interdependence between the Commission and National Bureaucracies", in S. Cassese (ed.), *The European Administration* (Brussels, 1988), 445–80

PALACIO GONZALEZ, J., "The Principle of Subsidiarity (A Guide for Lawyers with a Particular Community Orientation)" (1995) 20 *ELR* 355–70

PEINEMANN, B., "Consultation at the Commission Level. Socio-professional Advice: Advisory Committee on Foodstuffs", in A. Gérard (ed.), *Food Law in the Europe of Today* (Brussels, 1987), 137–44

PELKMANS, J., *Opheffing van technische handelsbelemmeringen in de EG, Pilot Study in opdracht van het UNO* (The Hague, 1985)

PELKMANS, J., "The New Approach to Technical Harmonisation and Standardisation" (1987) 25 *JCMS* 249–69

—— Egan, M., *Fixing European Standards: Moving Beyond the Green Paper*, CEPS Working Document 65, Standards Programme, Paper 3 (Brussels, 1992)

—— Vollenbergh, A., "The Traditional Approach to Technical Harmonisation: Accomplishments and Deficiencies", in J. Pelkmans/ M. Vanheukelen (eds.), *Coming to Grips with the Internal Market*, Working document 85/05 (EIPA, Maastricht, 1986)

PEDLER, R. H./SCHAEFER, G.F. (eds.), *Shaping European Law and Policy: The Role of Committees and Comitology in the Political Process* (Maastricht, 1996)

PESCATORE, P., "L'exécutif communautaire: justification du quadripartisme institué par les traités de Paris et Rome" (1978) 14 *CDE* 387–406

—— "Die 'Einheitliche Europäische Akte'. Eine Ernste Gefahr für den Gemeinsamen Markt" (1986) 21 *EuR* 153–69

—— "Some Critical Remarks on the 'Single European Act'" (1987) 24 *CMLRev.* 9–18

PINDER, J., "Problems of European Integration", in G.R. Denton (ed.), *Economic Integration in Europe* (London, 1969), 143–70

PIPKORN, J., "Artikel 100A, Angleichung von Vorschriften mit Bezug auf den Binnenmarkt", in H. Von der Groeben/J. Thiesing/C.-D. Ehlermann, *Kommentar zum EWG-Vertrag*, Band 2 (Baden-Baden, 1991), 2822–95

—— "Bericht Europäische Gemeinschaften", in C. Starck (ed.), *Erledigung von Verwaltungsaufgaben durch Personalkörperschaften und Anstalten des öffentlichen Rechts* (Baden-Baden, 1992), 110–32

PITSCHAS, R., "Europäische Integration als Netzwerkkoordination komplexer Staatsaufgaben", in Th. Ellwein/D. Grimm/J.J. Hesse/G.F. Schuppert (eds.), *Jahrbuch zur Staats- und Verwaltungswissenschaft* (Baden-Baden, 1996), 379–416

POLLACK, M.A., "Creeping Competence: The Expanding Agenda of the European Community" (1994) 14 *Journal of Public Policy* 95–145

POULSEN, E., "Consultation at the Commission Level. Scientific Advice: The Scientific Committee for Food", in A. Gérard (ed.), *Food Law in the Europe of Today* (Brussels, 1987), 129–36

PRAKKE, L./KORTMANN, C.A.J.M., *Het bestuursrecht van de landen der Europese Gemeenschappen* (Deventer, 1986)

PRECHAL, S., "Institutioneel evenwicht: balanceren op een onzichtbaar koord" (1991) 40 *Ars Aequi* 934–43

PREVIDI, E., "The Organization of Public and Private Responsibilities in European Risk Regulation: An Institutional Gap Between Them?", in Ch. Joerges/K.-H. Ladeur/E. Vos (eds), *Integrating Scientific Expertise into Regulatory Decision-Making. National Traditions and European Innovations* (Baden-Baden, 1997), 225–241

PROSI, G., "The Harmonisation Issue in Europe: Prior Agreement or a Competitive Process?", in H. Siebert (ed.), *The Completion of the Internal Market* (Tübingen, 1990), 76–84

REAGAN, M.D., *Regulation. The Politics of Policy* (Boston/Toronto, 1987)

REICH, N., "Integration und Regulierung des Arzneimittelmarktes innerhalb der EG" (1984) 148 *ZHR* 356–66

—— *Arzneimittelregulierung in Frankreich*, ZERP-MAT 11 (Bremen, 1987)

—— *Internal Market and Diffuse Interests* (Louvain-la-Neuve, 1990)

—— "Binnenmarkt als Rechtsbegriff" (1991) 2 *EuZW* 7, 203–10

—— "Competition between Legal Orders: A New Paradigm of EC law?" (1992) 29 *CMLRev.* 861–96

—— "The 'November Revolution' of the European Court of Justice: *Keck, Meng* and *Audi* Revisited" (1994) 31 *CMLRev.* 459–92

—— Micklitz, H.W., *Consumer Legislation in the EC Countries—A Comparative Analysis* (London, 1980)

—— Woodroffe, G., *European Consumer Policy after Maastricht* (Deventer, 1994)

RENN, O., "Concepts of Risk: A Classification", in S. Krimsky/D. Golding (eds.), *Social Theories of Risk* (Westport, Conn./London, 1992), 53–79

RHODES, R.A.W., *The New European Agencies. Agencies in British Government: Revolution or Evolution?*, EUI Working Paper RSC 96/51 (Florence, 1996)

RODRIGUES, G.C., "Der Gerichtshof der Europäischen Gemeinschaften als Verfassungsgericht" (1992) 27 *EuR* 225–45

ROELANTS DU VIVIER, F./HANNEQUART, J.P., "Une nouvelle stratégie européenne pour l'environnement dans le cadre de l'Acte unique" (1988) 316 *RMC* 225–31

ROGMANS, W.H.J., "Consumer Interest in Safety Related Standards for European Consumer Products" (1989) 12 *JCP* 193–205

RÖHLING, E., *Übertriebliche technische Normen als nichttarifäre Handelshemmnisse im Gemeinsamen Markt* (Cologne/Berlin/Bonn/Munich, 1972)

ROSSITER, C. (ed.), *The Federalists Papers (1787)* (New York, 1961)

ROßNAGEL, A., "Europäische Techniknormen im Lichte des Gemeinschaftsrechts" (1996) 111 *Deutsches Verwaltungsblatt* 1181–5

ROTH, R.H., *Technische Normung im Recht. Wesen, Struktur, Kooperation zwischen Fachverbänden und Staat* (Zürich, 1983)

ROWE, W.D., "Risk Analysis", in M. Waterstone (ed.), *Risk and Society: The Interaction of Science, Technocracy and Public Policy* (Dordrecht/Boston/London, 1992), 17–31

SAGGIO, A., "Le basi giuridiche della politica ambientale nell'ordinamento comunitario dopo l'entrata in vigore dell'Atto unico" [1990] *Rivista di diritto europeo* 39–50

SAUTER, W., "The ONP Framework: Towards a European Telecommunications Agency. The Growing Demand for a European Regulator" (1994) 5 *Utilities Law Review*, 140–6

SAUTER, W., *Competition Law and Industrial Policy in the EU* (Oxford, 1997)

—— Vos, E., "Harmonisation under Community Law: The Comitology Issue", in P. Craig/C. Harlow, *Law-making in the European Union* (London, The Hague, Boston, 1998), 169–86

SCHARPF, F.W., "Europäisches Demokratiedefizit und deutscher Föderalismus" [1992] *Staatswissenschaften und Staatspraxis* 293–306

—— "Community and Autonomy: Multi-level Policy-making in the European Union" (1994) 1 *JEPP* 219–42

—— *Negative and Positive Integration in the Political Economy of European Welfare States*, Jean Monnet Chair Papers, EUI Working Paper RSC (Florence, 1995)

SCHIEßL, M., *EG-Kartellrechtliche Anforderungen an die europäischen Normungsinstitutionen CEN, CENELEC und ETSI* (Frankfurt a.M., 1994)

SCHINDLER, P., "The Problems of Decision-making by Way of the Management Committee Procedure in the European Economic Community" (1971) 8 *CMLRev.* 184–205

—— *Delegation von Zuständigkeiten in der Europäischen Gemeinschaft* (Baden-Baden, 1972)

SCHLOESSER, P., "Europäische Gemeinschaft und Europäische Normung" in DIN Normungskunde n. 8, *Europäische Normung in CEN und CENELEC* (Berlin/Cologne, 1976)

SCHMITT VON SYDOW, H., *Die Verwaltungs- und regelungsausschussverfahren der Europäischen Wirtschaftsgemeinschaften* (Brussels, 1973)

—— *Organe der erweiterten Europäischen Gemeinschaften—Die Kommission* (Baden-Baden, 1980)

—— "The Basic Strategies of the Commission's White Paper", in R. Bieber/ R. Dehousse/J. Pinder/J.H.H. Weiler (eds.), *1992: One European Market? A Critical Analysis of the Commission's Internal Market Strategy* (Baden-Baden, 1988), 79–106

SCHOO, J., "Artikel 189a", in H. Von der Groeben/H. Thiesing/ C.-D. Ehlermannn (ed.), *Kommentar zum EU/EG Vertrag* (Baden-Baden, 1997), 1064–72

SCHREIBER, K., "The New Approach to Technical Harmonisation and Standards", in L. Hurwitz/Ch. Lesquesne, *The State of the European Community. Policies, Institutions & Debates in the Transition Years* (Boulder, Colo./Harlow, 1991), 99–112

SCHUTJENS, M.-H.B.B., *Drug Regulation in the Netherlands*, ZERP-MAT 13 (Bremen, 1987)

SCHWARTZ, I.E., "30 Jahre EG-Rechtsangleichung", in E. J. Mestmäcker/ H. Möller/H.P. Schwarz, *Eine Ordnungspolitik für Europa* (Baden-Baden, 1987), 333–68

—— "Artikel 235. Allgemeine Ermächtigungsklausel", in H. Von der Groeben/J. Thiesing/C.-D. Ehlermann, *Kommentar zum EWG-Vertrag* (Baden-Baden, 1991), 5754–834

SCHWARZE, J., *Die Befügnis zur Abstraktion im europäischen Gemein-schaftsrecht* (Baden-Baden, 1976)

—— (ed.), *Der Gemeinsame Markt, Bestand und Zukunft in wirtschaft-srechtlicher Perspektive* (Baden-Baden, 1987)

—— (ed.), *Discretionary Powers of the Member States in the Field of Economic Policies and their Limits under the EEC Treaty* (Baden-Baden, 1988)

—— *Europäisches Verwaltungsrecht* (Baden-Baden, 1988)

—— *European Administrative Law* (London, 1992)

—— H.G. Schermers (eds.), *Structure and Dimensions of European Community Policy* (Baden-Baden, 1988)

SEDEMUND, J., " 'Cassis de Dijon' und das neue Harmonisierungs-konzept der Kommission" in J. Schwarze (ed.), *Der Gemeinsame Markt, Bestand und Zukunft in wirtschaftsrechtlicher Perspektive* (Baden-Baden, 1987), 37–54

SEIDEL, M., "Regeln der Technik und Europäisches Gemeinschaftsrecht" (1981) 34 *NJW* 1120–5

SEVENSTER, H.G., "Annotation to Case C-2/90, Commission v Belgium" (1994) 42 *SEW* 98–115

SHAPIRO, M., *Who Guards the Guardians Judicial Control of Administration* (Athens/London, 1988)

—— "Codification of Administrative Law: The US and the Union" (1996) 2 *ELJ* 26–47

—— "The Problems of Independent Agencies in the United States and the European Union" (1997) 4 *JEPP* 276–91

—— "The Frontiers of Science Doctrine: American Experiences with the Judicial Control of Science-Based Decision-Making", in Ch. Joerges/ K.-H. Ladeur/E. Vos, *Integrating Scientific Expertise into Regulatory Decision-Making. National Traditions and European Innovations* (Baden-Baden, 1997), 325–42

SHAW, J., *Law of the European Union* (2nd ed., Houndmills, 1996)

SHRADER-FRECHETTE, K.S., *Risk and Rationality: Philosophical Foundations* (Berkeley/Los Angeles, 1991)

SIDDHANTI, S.K., *Multiple Perspectives on Risk and regulation. The Case of Deliberate Release of Genetically Engineered Organisms into the Environment* (New York/London, 1991)

SIDJANSKI, D., "Communauté européen 1992: gouvernement de comités?" (1989) 48 *Pouvoirs* 71–80

SIEBERT, H., "The Harmonisation Issue in Europe: Prior Agreement or a Competitive Process?" in H. Siebert (ed.), *The Completion of the Internal Market* (Tübingen, 1990), 53–75

SJÖSTRÖM, H., *Thalidomide and the Power of the Drug Companies* (Harmondsworth, 1972)

SLOT, P.J., "Harmonisation" (1996) 21 *ELR* 378–97

SMITH, L.J., *Legal Regulation of the British Pharmaceutical Market* (Baden-Baden, 1991)

SNIJDER, G.M.F., *Produktveiligheid en aansprakelijkheid* (Deventer, 1987)

SNYDER, F., "Soft Law and Institutional Practice in the European Community", in S. Martin (ed.), *The Construction of Europe, Essays in Honour of Emile Noël* (Dordrecht/Boston/London, 1994), 197–225

—— "Interinstitutional Agreements: Forms and Constitutional Limitations", in G. Winter (ed.), *Sources and Categories of European Union Law. A Comparative and Reform Perspective* (Baden-Baden, 1996), 453–66

SOMSEN, H., "Comments to Case C-300/89, Commission v. Council (Titanium dioxide)" (1992) 29 *CMLRev.* 140–51

STEINDORFF, E., "Gemeinsamer Market als Binnenmarkt" (1986) 150 *ZHR* 687–704

—— *Grenzen der EG Kompetenzen* (Heidelberg, 1990)

—— "Unvolkommener Binnenmarkt" (1994) 158 *ZHR* 149–69

STEINER, J., "Drawing the Iine: Uses and Abuses of Article 30 EEC" (1992) 29 *CMLRev.* 749–74

STEWART, R., "The Reformation of American Administrative Law" (1975) 88 *Harvard Law Review*, 1669–813

—— "Madison's Nightmare" (1990) 57 *The University of Chicago Law Review* 335–56

STEYGER, E., *Medezeggenschap bij veiligheid en gezondheid* (Deventer, 1990)

STRAUSS, P.L., "The Place of Agencies in Government: Separation of Powers and the Fourth Branch" (1984) 84 *Columbia Law Review* 573–669

STREECK, W./SCHMITTER, P.C., "From National Corporatism to Transnational Pluralism: Organized Interests in the Single European Market" (1991) 19 *Politics and Society* 133–64

STREINZ, R., "Das Problem der 'umgekehrten Diskriminierung' im Bereich des Lebensmittelrechts" [1990] *ZLR* 487–517

—— (ed.), *Novel Food* (Bayreuth, 1993)

—— "Economic Aspects of Technical Regulations", in F. Snyder (ed.), *A Regulatory Framework for Foodstuffs in the Internal Market*, EUI Working Paper LAW 94/4 (Florence, 1994), 82–112

—— "Anwendbarkeit der Novel Food-Verordnung" [1998] *ZLR* 19–37

STUURMAN, C., *Technische normen en het recht—beschouwingen over de interactie tussen het recht en technische normalisatie op het terrein van informatietechnologie en telecommunicatie* (Deventer, 1995)

STUYCK, J., "Free Movement of Goods and Consumer Protection", in G. Woodroffe (ed.), *Consumer Law in the EEC* (London, 1984), 77–102

SUNSTEIN, C.R., "Protectionism, the American Supreme Court, and Integrated Markets", in R. Bieber/R. Dehousse/J. Pinder/J.H.H. Weiler (eds.), *1992: One European Market? A Critical Analysis of the Commission's Internal Market Strategy* (Baden-Baden, 1988), 127–47

—— *After the Rights Revolution. Reconceiving the Regulatory State* (Cambridge, Mass., 1990)

TASCHNER, H.C., "Artikel 100", in H. Von der Groeben/H. Thiesing/C.-D. Ehlermann (eds.), *Kommentar zum EWG-Vertrag* (Baden-Baden, 1991), 2791–822

TEFF, H./MUNRO, C., *Thalidomide: The Legal Aftermath* (Farnborough, 1976)

TEIJGELER, C.A., "The Role of the CPMP in the EEC", in S.R. Walker (ed.), *International Medicines Regulations: A Look Forward to 1992* (Dordrecht/Boston, 1989), 207–18

TEITGEN-COLLY, C., "Les autorités administratives indépendentes: histoire d'une institution", in C.A. Colliard/G. Timsitv (eds.), *Les autorités administratives indépendentes* (Paris, 1988), 21–73

TEMMINK, H.A.G., "Minimumnormen in EG-richtlijnen" (1995) 43 *SEW* 2, 79–105

TEMPLE LANG, J., "Article 5 of the EEC Treaty: The Emergence of Constitutional Principles in the Case Law of the Court of Justice" (1986–7) 10 *Fordham International Law Journal* 503–37

THOMPSON, R., *The Single Market for Pharmaceuticals* (London, 1994)

TINBERGEN, J., *International Economic Integration* (2nd ed., Amsterdam, 1965)

TIZZANO, A., "Lo sviluppo delle competenze materiali delle Comunità europee" [1981] *Rivista di diritto europeo* 139–210

TONNER, K., "The European Influence on German Consumer Law", in N. Reich/G. Woodroffe, *European Consumer Policy after Maastricht* (Deventer, 1994), 225–36

TOTH, A.G., "The Principle of Subsidiarity in the Maastricht Treaty" (1992) 29 *CMLRev.* 1079–105

—— "Is Subsidiarity Jusiticiable?" (1994) 19 *ELR* 268–85

—— "A Legal Analysis of Subsidiarity", in D. O'Keeffe/P. M. Twomey (eds.), *Legal Issues of the Maastricht Treaty* (London, 1994), 37–48

TRACHTMAN, J.P., "International Regulatory Competition, Externalisation and Jurisdiction" (1993) 34 *Harvard International Law Journal* 47–104

USHER, J.A., "The Gradual Widening of European Community Policy on the basis of Articles 100 and 235 of the EEC Treaty", in J. Schwarze/H.G. Schermers (eds.), *Structures and Dimensions of the European Community Policy* (Baden-Baden, 1988), 25–35

VALVERDE, J.-L./PIQUERAS GARCIA, A.J./CABEZAS LOPEZ, M.D., "La «nouvelle approche» en matière de santé des consommateurs et sécurité alimentaire: la nécessité d'une agence européenne de sécurité des aliments" [1997] *RMUE* 4, 31–58

VAN DER HEIJDEN, K., "The Scientific Committee for Food: Procedures and Program for European Food Safety" [1992] *Food Technology* 102–6

VAN DER MEULEN, B.J.M., *Rechterlijk toetsing van wetgeving in Europees perspectief, Bestuurrecht na 1992, preadviezen voor de Vereniging voor Administratief Recht* (Alphen an der Rijn, 1989)

VAN DER VLIES, I.C., "Adviesorganen moeten blijven" (1993) 13 *NJB* 450–2

VAN MALE, R.M., *Rechter en bestuurswetgeving* (Zwolle, 1988)

VAN MIERT, K., "The Proposal for a European Competition Agency" (1996) 2 *EC Competition Policy Newsletter* 2

VAUGHAN, D. (ed.), *The Law of the European Communities* (London, 1986)

VERENIGING VOOR WETGEVING EN WETGEVINGSBELEID, *Delegatie van bevoegdheden* (Alphen an der Rijn, 1992)

VERLOREN VAN THEMAAT, P., "De Europese Akte" (1986) 34 *SEW* 7/8, 464–83

—— "Some Comments of a Former Advocate-General at the Court of Justice of the European Communities", in M. Fallon/F. Maniet (eds.), *Sécurité des produits et mécanismes de contrôle dans la Communauté européenne* (Louvain-la-Neuve, 1990), 129–32

—— "Some Preliminary Observations on the Intergovernmental Conferences: The Relations between the Concepts of a Common Market, a Monetary Union, an Economic Union, a Political Union and Sovereignty" (1991) 28 *CMLRev.* 291–318

—— "De rol van beginselen bij de integratie van geografische economische, sociale en politieke systemen en bij de integratie van vakgebieden", in K. Hellingman (ed.), *Europa in de steigers: van Gemeenschap tot Unie* (Deventer, 1993), 121–40

VON DER GROEBEN, H./THIESING, J./EHLERMANN, C.-D., *Kommentar zum EWG-Vertrag* (Baden-Baden, 1991)

VON HEYDEBRAND U.D. LASA, H.-C., "Free Movement of Foodstuffs, Consumer Protection and Food Standards in the European Community: Has the Court of Justice Got It Wrong?" (1991) 16 *ELR* 319–415

VOS, E., "Market Building, Social Regulation and Scientific Expertise: An Introduction", in Ch. Joerges/K.-H Ladeur/E. Vos, *Integrating Scientific Expertise into Regulatory Decision-Making. National Traditions and European Innovations* (Baden-Baden, 1997), 127–39

—— "The Rise of Committees" (1997) 3 *ELJ* 210–29

WAELBROECK, M., "The Emergent Doctrine of Community Pre-emption— Consent and Re-delegation", in T. Sandalow/E. Stein (eds.), *Courts and Free Markets* (Oxford, 1982), ii, 548–80

WARD, A., "Effective Sanctions in EC Law: A Moving Boundary in the Division of Competence" (1995) 1 *ELJ* 205–17

WATERSTONE, M. (ed.), *Risk and Society: The Interaction of Science, Technocracy and Public Policy* (Dordrecht/Boston/London, 1992)

WEALE, A., "Environmental Protection, the Four Freedoms and Competition among Rules", in M. Faure/J. Vervaele/A. Weale (eds.), *Environmental Standards in the European Union in an Interdisciplinary Framework* (Antwerp/Apeldoorn, 1994), 73–89

WEATHERILL, S., "Regulating the Internal Market: Result Orientation in the House of Lords" (1992) 17 *ELR* 299–322

—— "Beyond Preemption? Shared Competence and Constitutional Change in the European Community", in D. O'Keeffe/P.M. Twomey, *Legal Issues of the Maastricht Treaty* (London, 1994), 13–33

—— *Law and Integration in the European Union* (Oxford, 1995)

—— "Playing Safe: The United Kingdom's Implementation of the Toy Safety Directive", in T. Daintith (ed.), *Implementing EC Law in the United Kingdom—Structures for Indirect Rule* (Chichester, 1995), 241–69

—— "Compulsory Notification of Draft Technical Regulations: The Contribution of Directive 83/189 to the Management of the Internal Market" (1996) 16 *YEL* 129–204

—— "After *Keck*: Some Thoughts on How to Clarify the Clarification" (1996) 33 *CMLRev.* 885–906

WEBER, M., *Economy and Society: An Outline of Interpretive Sociology*, edited by G. Roth/C. Wittich (Berkeley/Los Angeles, Cal./London, 1978)

WEILER, J.H.H, "The Community System. The Dual Character of Supra-nationalism" (1981) 1 *YEL* 257–306

—— "Community, Member States and European Integration: Is the Law Relevant?" (1982–3) 21 *JCMS* 39–56

—— *Il sistema comunitario europeo* (Bologna, 1985)

—— "The White Paper and the Application of Community Law", in R. Bieber/R. Dehousse/J. Pinder/J.H.H. Weiler (eds.), *1992: One European Market? A Critical Analysis of the Commission's Internal Market Strategy* (Baden-Baden, 1988), 337–58

—— "Pride and Prejudice—Parliament v. Council" (1989) 14 *ELR* 334–46

—— "Problems of Legitimacy in Post 1992 Europe" (1991) 46 *Aussenwirtschaft* 411–37

—— "The Transformation of Europe" (1991) 100 *The Yale Law Review* 2403–83

—— "Fin-de-Siècle Europe", in R. Dehousse (ed.), *Europe After Maastricht. An Ever Closer Union?* (Munich, 1994), 203–17

—— Haltern, U.R./Mayer, F.C., "European Democracy and Its Critique" (1995) 18 *West European Politics* 3, 4–39

WEINBERG, A.M, "Science and Trans-Science" (1972) 10 *Minerva* 209–22

WELCH, D., "From 'Euro Beer' to 'Newcastle Brown', A Review of European Community Action to Dismantle Divergent 'Food' Laws" (1983–4) 22 *JCMS* 47–70

WELLENS, K.C./BORCHARDT, G.M., "Soft Law in the European Community Law" (1989) 14 *ELR* 267–321

WESSELS, W., "Administrative Interaction", in W. Wallace (ed.), *Dynamics of European Integration* (London, 1990), 229–41

—— "Verwaltung im EG-Mehrebenensystem: Auf dem Weg zur Megabürokratie?" in M. Jachtenfuchs/B. Kohler-Koch (ed.), *Europäische Integration* (Opladen, 1996), 165–92

WESTBROOK, D.A., "Environmental Policy in the European Community: Observations on the European Environment Agency" (1991) 15 *Harvard Environment Law Review* 257–73

WESTLAKE, M.," 'Mad Cows and Englishmen'—The Institutional Consequences of the BSE Crisis", in N. Nugent (ed.), *The European Union 1996: Annual Review of Activities* (1997) 35 *JCMS, Annual Review* 11–36

WHITNAH, D.R. (ed.), *Government Agencies* (Westport, Conn., 1983)

WILLIAMS, S., "Sovereignty and Accountability in the European Community" (1990) 61 *Pol.Q.* 299–317

WILKE, M./WALLACE, H., *Subsidiarity: Approaches to Power-sharing in the European Community*, Discussion Paper 27 (Royal Institute of International Affairs, London, 1990)

WILSON, J.Q., *Bureaucracy. What Government Agencies Do and Why They Do It* (New York, 1989)

WILSON, R./CROUCH, E., *Risk/Benefit Analysis* (Cambridge, Mass., 1982)

WINCKLER, R., "Rechtsvorschriften für Anlagen, Geräte und Stoffe—Bestandsaufnahme und kritische Würdung. Materialen und Geräte under besonderer Berücksichtigung des Gerätesicherheitsgesetzes, der 2. DurchfuhrungsVO zum EnWG under der Niederspannungsrichtlinie", in Recht und Technik, *Rechtliche Regelungen für Anlagen, Geräte und Stoffe im deutschen und im europäischen Recht*, Studienreihe des Bundesministers für Wirtschaft, nr. 53 (Bonn, 1985)

WINTER, G., "Drei Arten gemeinschaftlicher Rechtssetzung und ihre Legitimation", in G. Brüggemeier (ed.), *Verfassungen für ein ziviles Europa* (Baden-Baden, 1994), 45–71

—— (ed.), *Sources and Categories of Europan Union Law: A Comparative and Reform Perspective* (Baden-Baden, 1995)

WINTER, J.A., *Reforming the Treaty on European Union* (The Hague, 1996)

WITTEVEEN, W.J., *Evenwicht van machten* (Zwolle, 1991)

WOODROFFE, G. (ed.), *Consumer Law in the EEC* (London, 1984)

WOOLCOCK, S., *The Single European Market. Centralisation or Competition among National Rules?*, Working Paper (The Royal Institute of International Affairs, London, 1994)

ZIEGLER, A.R., *The Common Market and the Environment: Striking a Balance*, Dissertation Hochschule St. Gallen nr. 1764 (Bamberg, 1995)

ZULEEG, M., "Die Kompetenzen der Europäischen Gemeinschaften gegenüber den Mitgliedstaaten" (1970) 20 *Jahrbuch des öffentlichen Rechts der Gegenwart* 1–66

Index

access to documents:
  CEN/CENELEC, 304–5, 310
  code of conduct, 103–4, 178, 238
  European Agency for the Evaluation of
    Medicinal Products, 238
  foodstuffs committees, 177–8
  legitimacy, 103–4
accountability:
  European Agency for the Evaluation of
    Medicinal Products, 238–41, 243
  foodstuff committees, 179
  legitimacy, 106
  product safety, 305–8
  standards, 305–9, 311
administrative law, 94–5
  "transmission belt" model, 94
Administrative Procedures Act, 177, 187, 311,
  323
Advisory Committee on Foodstuffs, 148–50,
  175–7, 184, 187
agencies:
  budget, 192
  capture, 147, 250
  classification, 191–3
  Commission, 188–203, 245
  committees, 188–9, 249, 317
  Community Plant Variety Office, 193, 202
  competence, 193–203
  co-ordination, 188
  decision-making, 193, 195, 199
  delegation of powers, 200–3, 248
  European Agency for the Evaluation of
    Medicinal Products, 189, 193–5, 197–9,
    202
  European Agency for Safety and Health at
    Work, 191–5
  European Environment Agency, 196, 201–2
  European Monetary Co-operation Fund, 190
  executive powers, 202–3
  harmonisation, 197–9
  functional decentralisation, 247–8
  implementation, 198–9
  independent, 195
  institutions, 189–94, 197–8
    balance of powers, 202–3
  judicial review, 245–7
  legal basis, 188–9, 194–200
  legal personality, 188, 194
  legitimacy, 196, 204, 248–50
  Meroni principles, 83, 200–3

origins, 189–91
Office for Harmonisation in the Internal
  Market (trade marks and designs),
  191–5, 202
pharmaceuticals, 189, 203–250, 317, 319–20
proliferation, 188, 190–5
regulation by information, 193
seats, 191
agriculture, 38, 40, 101, 144–5
Amsterdam Treaty *see* Treaty of Amsterdam
ANEC, 300–2, 310
approximation of laws *see* harmonisation
arbitration, 215, 228

barriers to trade, 14–18, 28–33, 55–8, 65–6,
  269, 293
Benelux Registration Office, 208
biotechnology, 68, 212
BSE crisis:
  Commission, 143–6, 186
  committees, 112, 145–8
  control, 146
  European Agency for the Evaluation of
    Medicinal Products, 231–4
  European Parliament, 145
  foodstuffs committees, 140–8, 178, 180, 186,
    320
  information, 146
  inspection, 146
  institutions, 143–4, 322
  New Approach to food safety, 145–6
  risk assessment and management, 146
  scientific expertise, 145, 186
  Temporary Committee of Inquiry, 143–5
  transparency, 145, 178, 186
  Treaty of Amsterdam, 36–8

CE marks, 277–8
CEN/CENELEC, 255–68
  access to documents, 304–5, 310
  Administrative Board, 257–8
  ANEC, 302
  bulletin, 204
  Central Secretariat, 258
  Comité de Lecture, 261–2
  Commission, 263–6, 284, 287–8, 293
  committees, 291–6
  creation, 255–6
  delegation, 280–9, 292, 309
  diversification of expertise, 297

CEN/CENELEC (*cont.*):
  EOTC, 278
  General Assembly, 256–7
  Information Society Standardisation System
      (ISSS), 262
  International Standardisation Organisation
      (ISO), 297
  Internet, 304
  mandates, 270, 305–6, 311
  Member States, 285–6
  membership, 256
  New Approach to Technical Harmonisation
      and Standards, 274–5, 283–4, 296
  organisational structure, 56–62
  President, 257
  risk assessment, 296
  seat, 256
  Sector Fora, 259
  Secretary-General, 258
  Technical Board, 258–9, 267–8
  technical committees, 260–1, 267, 297–8
  Technical Sector Boards, 259
  testing, 262
  voting, 257–8, 260, 265–7
  Working Groups, 261
  workload, 274–5
centre of gravity theory, 39–43, 51
certification, 262, 277–8
CJD *see* BSE crisis
Comitology Decision, 122–4, 182–3 *see also*
      committees
committees: *see also* foodstuffs, pharmaceuti-
      cals and standards
  advisory committee procedure, 122–3, 182–3
  agencies, distinction between, 188, 249, 317
  BSE crisis, 112, 140–8
  budget, 116, 118, 128, 130
  Comitology Decision, 122–4, 182–3
  Commission, 110–15, 119–21, 124–30, 184,
      316–17
  competence, 117–20
  Council, 113–15, 119, 121–31, 184
  European Parliament, 122, 125–8
  figures, in, 115–17, 184
  functions, 115
  institutions, 111, 113–18, 186–7, 319–20
    agreements between, 127
    balance of powers, 111, 120–31, 184
    controversies between, 124–8
  integration, 112–13, 316, 320
  interest committees, 115, 148–52,
  legitimacy, 182
  management committee procedure, 123, 182–3
  Member State participation, 182
  modus vivendi, 126–8, 182–3
  Plumb-Delors Agreement, 125–6
  policy-making/implementation committees,
      115, 152–4, 294

regulatory committee procedure, 123–4,
      182–3
    contre-filet variant, 157–8, 162–7, 182,
      225–6
  rise of, 113–17
  safeguard procedure, 124
  scientific committees, 115, 140–8
  scientific expertise, 110, 115, 166–73, 184,
      316
  subsidiarity, 98–9, 160
  transparency, 145, 177–8
  typology of, 114–15
Commission:
  Article 145, 89–91, 127–8
  balance of powers, 89
  BSE crisis, 143–6
  committees, 110–15, 119–21, 124–30, 184
  competence, 48–9
  delegation, 54–5, 88–93, 113, 287–8
  discretion, 54, 89
  harmonisation, 54–8
  implementation, 72–3, 89–93, 96
  legitimacy, 89, 93–5, 100–6
  mutual recognition, 60–4
  scientific expertise, 171, 186, 320
  workload, 89, 188, 315
competence:
  agencies, 193–203
  attributed powers, 21–2
  committees, 117–20
  concurrent powers, 43, 46–50
  consumer protection, 24–5, 34–5, 38–43
  environmental protection, 24–5, 38–43
  foodstuffs, 131–9
  harmonisation, 24–31, 46–50, 313
  implementation, 70, 75–7
  Kompetenz-Kompetenz, 27
  legal basis, 21–7, 75–7
  Member States, 16, 46–7, 74, 98
  mutual recognition, 60–5
  pharmaceuticals, 206–19
  product safety, 26, 49–50
  residual, 46–7
  safeguard clauses, 48–9
  shared, 46–51, 98, 312–13
  subsidiarity, 36
common market *see* internal market
compliance, 99–100
concurrent powers, 43–50
Consumer Committee, 150–4
consumer protection:
  action programmes, 20
  competence, 24–5
  demarcation, 39–44
  health and safety, 11
  integration, 19
  mutual recognition, 63
  product safety, 19

responsibility, 68
standards, 299–302
Treaty of Amsterdam, 38
Treaty on European Union, 34–5
Consumers' Consultative Committee, 150–1
Consumers' Consultative Council, 151–2
Council:
  agencies, 194, 198, 202
  balance of powers, 83–7
  Commission, 88–93
  committees, 113–15, 119, 121–31, 182–3
  delegation, 88–93
  foodstuffs, 134, 158, 162–6, 174–5
  workload, 88, 270, 314
Creutzfeldt-Jacob Disease *see* BSE crisis

dangerous products and free movement of
    goods, 67, 138–9, 313
delegation of powers:
  agencies, 200–3, 241–8
  Article 145, 89–91, 121–2, 126–8
  Article 155, 89
  attribution of powers, 90
  CEN/CENELEC, 283–9
  Commission, 54, 88, 89–93, 113, 287–8
  committees, 113, 115, 119, 121, 125, 127
  concept, 89–90
  Council, 90–3
  European Agency for the Evaluation of
    Medicinal Products, 241–7
  foodstuffs committees, 134
  illegality, 281
  implementation, 89–93
  institutional balance of powers, 92–3, 315
  Meroni principles, 83, 200–3
  scope, 91–3
  Single European Act, 90–1
  standards, 280–8, 292, 309
demarcation:
  agriculture, 38, 40
  Article 129a, 43
  Article 130s, 40–1, 43
  Article 235, 38–9
  barriers to trade, 39, 43
  centre of gravity theory, 39–43
  concurrent powers, 44
  consumer protection, 39–43
  environmental protection, 39–43
  free movement of goods, 43
  harmonisation, 38–43
  internal market, 43
  Titanium Dioxide case, 40–2
deliberation, 175, 178, 183, 225–6, 237, 247,
    250, 320–1
deliberative supranationalism, 112, 175, 320
denationalisation, 159–61
deregulation, 9, 60–5
derogation clauses, 31–3

distortion of competition, 29–30, 39–43
diversification of expertise, 170, 232–3, 297
duty to state reasons, 22, 105–6, 200

Economic and Social Committee (ESC), 173–4
  83/189 Committee, 292–4, 296, 303, 308,
    310–11
emergency procedures, 9, 163–6, 183
environmental protection:
  competence, 31–2
  demarcation, 39, 41, 43
  European Environment Agency, 190, 196,
    201–2
  mutual recognition, 63
  Pentachlorophenol case, 22, 33, 48
  opting out clause, 32–3
  working environment, 37
European Agency for the Evaluation of
    Medicinal Products:
  access to documents, 238
  accountability, 238–40, 243
  agency capture, 147, 236, 250
  appeals, 239–40, 242–3
  arbitration, 228
  authorisation, 216–17, 221–5, 228–30, 233,
    236, 240–2, 248, 317
  BSE crisis, 231–4, 247
  budget, 222, 238–9, 243
  centralised authorisation procedure, 212–3,
    221–2
  classification, 193
  Commission, 216–17, 227, 230, 233–6,
    238–47
  Committee for Proprietary Medicinal Products
    (CPMP), 217–19, 225–40, 249–50
  Committee for Veterinary Medicinal
    Products (CVMP), 217–19
  composition, 217–20
  concertation procedure, 221
  contraceptives or abortifacients, 223
  Council, 230–1, 249
  creation, 189, 191, 211
  decentralised authorisation procedure,
    214–15, 221–2
  delegation, 241–7
  European Federation of Pharmaceutical
    Products (EFPIA), 235–6
  European Parliament, 238–9
  Executive Director, 219
  experts, 218–19, 224, 227–9, 232–3
  free movement of goods, 228
  harmonisation, 219, 225, 232–3
  hearings, right to, 239–40
  independence, 230–2, 240–7, 249
  institutions,
    balance of powers, 241
    Member States and, interrelation
      between, 222–8

European Agency for the Evaluation of
    Medicinal Products (*cont.*:
  integration, 228–34
  Internet, 228, 237–8
  judicial review, 244–7
  legitimacy, 233
  Management Board, 219–20, 225–6, 234–8
  mutual recognition, 221–2, 228
  Mutual Recognition Facilitating Group, 228
  national authorities, 231, 233, 237, 249
  objectivity, 230–2, 249
  opinions, 222, 224–5, 230–1, 239
  participation of interested parties, 234–7,
    250
  Pharmaceutical Committee, 227
  risk assessment and management, 229, 232
  scientific advice, 220–1, 224, 228–34, 240,
    249
  Secretariat, 219, 220
  Standing Committee on Medicinal Products
    for Human Use, 225–6, 233–4, 248–50
    regulatory committee procedure (*contre-filet*), 226
  structure, 217–20
  subsidiarity, 224
  tasks, 220–1
  transparency, 236, 238–40
  working groups, 217–19
European Agency for Safety and Health at
    Work, 191–5
European Committee for Electrotechnical
    Standardisation *see* CEN/CENELEC
European Committee for Standardisation *see*
    CEN/CENELEC
European Environment Agency, 196, 201–2
European Federation of Pharmaceutical
    Products, 235–6
European Monetary Co-operation Fund, 190
European Parliament:
  balance of powers, 84–5
  BSE crisis, 145
  committees, 122, 125–8
  European Agency for the Evaluation of
    Medicinal Products, 219, 235
  foodstuffs committees, 158, 162–3
European Standardisation Council, 290–1
European Standardisation Forum, 290–1, 303,
    311
European Standardisation System, 289–90

foodstuffs:
  access to documents, 177–8
  accountability, 179
  administrative procedures, 163–6
  Advisory Committee on Foodstuffs, 148–50,
    175–7, 184, 187
  advisory committees, 148–50, 162, 175–7,
    316

barriers to trade, 132, 136
BSE crisis, 140–7, 178, 180, 186, 320
Commission, 132, 134, 136, 138–43, 147–87
committees, description, 140–54
Consumer Committee, 150–4
Consumers' Consultative Committee, 150–1
Consumers' Consultative Council, 151–2
control, 136–8
co-operation, 171–2
Council, 134, 158, 162–6, 174–5
dangerous, 138–9
denationalisation, 159–61
delegation, 134, 154–9
directives, 133–5, 161–2, 166, 168
diversification of expertise, 170
Economic and Social Committee (ESC),
    173–4
emergencies, 163–6
European Parliament, 158, 162–3
free movement of goods, 138–9
Green Paper on the General Principles of
    Food Law, 146
harmonisation, 132–3, 149, 165
hearings, right of, 181
horizontal approach, 134–5
implementation, 152–4, 156, 161–2, 174, 179,
    316
independence, 169–70
information, 172, 177–9
individuals right of hearing, 181
inspection, 136–8
institutions, 132
  balance of powers, 185
  Member States, interrelation between,
    154–66
integration, 135–9, 164, 166–73
interest committees, 148–52
interest groups, 176–7
judicial review of committee opinions,
    179–81
legitimacy, 110, 113, 173–5, 179, 182, 187
Member States, 154–66
monitoring, 154
New Approach to Food Safety, 133–4,
    136–7, 154
participation of interested parties, 150–1,
    173–7
peculiarities, 132–3
pharmaceuticals, 164–5
regulatory committee procedure (*contre-filet*), 157–8, 162–6, 171, 182
risk:
  assessment, 156, 172, 175, 185
  management, 173, 185
safeguard clauses, 161–2
Scientific Committee on Cosmetology, 168
Scientific Committee on Food, 140–3, 147–8,
    166–73, 178, 184–5, 320

Scientific Co-operation Model, 171–3
scientific expertise, 140–1, 166–73, 316
Scientific Steering Committee, 169
standards, 137, 173
Standing Committee on Foodstuffs, 152–66, 173–4 , 179–80, 185–6, 316
   subsidiarity, 160
   traditional approach, 133
   transparency, 146–8, 169, 177–8
   vertical approach, 134–5
free movement of goods, 13–14, 43, 138–9, 211, 228, 272, 280, 313
functional decentralisation, 173, 221, 247

harmonisation:
   agencies, 196–9
   Article 100a, 27, 29–32, 75–7
   barriers to trade, 32, 54–5, 57–8
   Cassis de Dijon case, 56–7
   CEN/CENELEC, 262–5, 284–5, 287
   competence, 24–5, 46–7, 313
   concurrent powers, 44–5
   definition, 30
   demarcation, 38–40
   derogation, 33
   exhaustive, 44, 47
   foodstuffs, 132–3, 140–54, 165
   implementation, 54–8, 75–7
   integration, 18–19
   minimum, 44
   mutual recognition, 57–8, 60–5
   New Approach to Technical Harmonisation and Standards, 56–8, 268–73
   optional, 44
   partial, 44, 47, 206–8
   pharmaceuticals, 206–8
   product safety, 27–42, 268–73
   qualified majority voting, 12–13, 27
   safeguard clauses, 31, 44, 47–8, 100
   Single European Act, 59–60
   standards, 44–5, 55–6, 251, 270–2, 288, 284, 307–11, 318
   total, 44, 47
   traditional approach, difficulties with, 54–8
   Treaty of Amsterdam, 37–8
   Treaty on European Union, 34

implementation:
   agencies, 199–200
   Commission, 72–3
   committees, 111, 115, 122, 128–30, 132, 184, 316
   competence, 70, 74
   concept, 72–4
   delegation, 89–93
   enforcement, 73
   foodstuffs committees, 184–5, 316
   General Product Safety case, 76

   harmonisation, 54–8, 75–7
   institutions, 71–5
   legal basis, 24–33, 75–7
   legislation, 53, 70–7
      blurring of legislation/execution distinction, 70–2
   Member States, 73–4, 315
   separation of powers, 70–1
   standards, 272, 276, 293–4
   subsidiarity, 80
inspections, 136–8, 146, 216
institutional balance of powers:
   agencies, 202–3, 240–7
   Article 4, 84–5
   comitology, 111, 120–31, 182–3, 186–7
   definition, 83–4
   delegation, 89–93, 131, 240–7
   functions, 85–6
   implementation, 71–5, 92–3
   legislation, 85
   Member States, 87–8, 96, 154–66, 222–8, 314
   rule of law, 85–6
   trias politica, 86–7
integration:
   harmonisation, 18–19
   internal market, 13
   mutual recognition, 9, 60–4
   negative, 13–19
   positive, 13, 18–20
interest committees, 115, 148–52
internal market, 11–13, 18–20, 27–33, 43, 52–69
International Conference on Harmonisation (ICH), 219, 232–3
International Standardisation Organisation (ISO), 256, 266, 297

judicial review, 179–81, 245–7

Kompetenz-Kompetenz, 27

legitimacy:
   access to documents, 103–4
   accountability, 106
   administrative law, 94–5
   BSE case, 103
   Commission, 58, 89, 93–5, 100–6
   committees, 110, 113, 182
   concept, 93–5
   Council, 101, 103–4
   decision-making, 95, 102–3, 131–2, 187, 204, 248, 288–9
   due process, 104–5
   duty to state reasons, 105
   European Agency for the Evaluation of Medicinal Products, 233
   foodstuffs committees, 173–8
   hearings, right to, 105

legitimacy (*cont.*):
  judicial control, 105–6
  Member States, 96–100, 320–2
  participation of interested parties, 102–3,
      173–8, 234–7, 298–304
  pharmaceuticals, 204, 229–40
  rule of law, 94
  scientific expertise, 100–2, 104–6
  standards, 285, 288–309, 311
  transparency, 103–4

Maastricht Treaty *see* Treaty on European
    Union
measures having equivalent effect, 14–15
medicinal products *see* pharmaceuticals
Member States:
  Article 36, 97–8
  competence, 16, 98
  concurrent powers, 43–50
  co-operation, 99–100
  implementation, 73–4, 96–100, 315
  institutions, 87–8, 314
    balance of powers, 96
    interrelation between, 154–66, 222–8
  participation, 96–100, 182
  subsidiarity, 98–9, 315
  sui generis nature of the Community, 97
  transfer of powers, 12
Meroni principles, 83, 200–3, 283–5
mutual recognition:
  compulsory, 64–5
  consumer protection, 63
  deregulation, 60
  environmental protection, 63
  harmonisation, 57–8, 65
  integration, 9
  pharmaceuticals, 210, 214, 221–2, 228
  race to the bottom, 60, 63
  regulatory competition, 60–5
  Single European Act, 63–4
  voluntary application, 210

national constitutions, 97
national laws, 16, 29–30, 32, 45, 48
New Approach to Food Safety, 133–4, 136–7,
    154
New Approach to Technical Harmonisation
    and Standards, 56–8, 251–3, 268,
    270–81, 283, 294, 296, 299–300, 305,
    309–10, 313, 318

obstacles to trade *see* barriers to trade
opting out clause, 31–2, 37

pharmaceuticals: *see also* European Agency for
    the Evaluation of Medicinal Products
  arbitration, 215
  Article 100a, 196–200

authorisation, 189, 197–8, 202, 204–16, 317
Benelux Registration Office, 208
biotechnology, 212
centralised authorisation procedure, 212–13,
    215–16
Commission, 208–13
committees, 189, 217–19, 225–8
concertation procedure, 209–10
decentralised authorisation procedure,
    206–8, 214–15
efficacy, 205
European Federation of Pharmaceutical
    Industries (EFPIA), 235–6
foodstuffs committees, 164–5
free movement of goods, 211
harmonisation, 206–9
information, 216
International Conference on Harmonisation
    (ICH), 219, 232–3
inspections, 216
internal market, 204, 210, 248
legitimacy, 224, 229, 235, 248–50
multi-state procedure, 207–9
mutual recognition, 206–10, 214–5
peculiarities, of, 204–6
pharmocovigilance, 215–16, 249
quality, 205
risk assessment and management, 210, 250
safety, 194, 205, 208
scientific expertise, 189
Standing Committee on Medicinal Products
    for Human Use, 213, 225–6, 317
subsidiarity, 80–1, 249, 317–18
Thalidomide tragedy, 205–6
transparency, 204
Plumb-Delors Agreement, 125–8
pre-emption, 45–6, 51, 312, 320–1
private bodies, 9, 251–311, 318
product safety, 19, 30–1, 49–50, 60–4, 251–4
    see also foodstuffs, pharmaceuticals,
    standards
proportionality, 17–18, 36, 77–9, 82–3, 100,
    313–14
protectionism, 18
public health, 34–5, 38

qualified majority voting, 11–12, 27–8, 63–4,
    279
quality of life, 19–20, 34
quantitative restrictions, 14

regulatory models, 9–10, 60–5
re-regulation, 64
risk:
  acceptable, 2–3
  assessment, 3–5, 8, 47, 156, 173, 175, 185,
      210, 229, 250, 252, 316, 319, 322
  competence, 5–6, 47

concept, 2–5, 320–3
decision-making, 6–9
definition, 2
EC law, under, 5–9
emergency procedures, 9
European Agency for the Evaluation of
    Medicinal Products, 229, 232, 250
foodstuffs committees, 156, 173, 175, 185
harmonisation, 8
institutions, 6–7, 9
integration, 6–7
management, 3, 5, 8, 185, 250, 318–19, 322
Member States, 98
monitoring, 2, 9
mutual recognition, 5
regulation, 2–5, 7–8, 98, 108, 320–3
"risk society", 3
scientific expertise, 8–9
standards, 252, 318
Treaty of Amsterdam, 9
Treaty on European Union, 5, 6
value-laden nature of, 4–5, 321
rule of law, 85–6, 94
rule of reason, 15–17

safeguard clauses, 31, 44, 161–2, 291–2, 287,
    297, 308–9
Scientific Committee on Cosmetology, 168
Scientific Committee on Food, 140–3, 147–8,
    166–73, 178, 184–5, 320
Scientific Co-operation Model (SCOOP),
    171–3
scientific expertise:
    agencies, 317
    BSE crisis, 145, 186
    Commission, 171, 186, 320
    committees, 110, 115, 132, 316
    diversification, 170
    European Agency for the Evaluation of
        Medicinal Products, 220–1, 224,
        228–34, 240, 249
    foodstuffs committees, 140–5, 166–73,
        184–5, 316
    independent, 229, 32
    legitimacy, 100–2, 104–6
    objectivity, 231, 322
    pharmaceuticals, 189
    plurality, 232–3
    risk, 9
    Treaty of Amsterdam, 37
Scientific Steering Committee, 169
self-regulation, 9, 252–3, 318
Single European Act, 11, 27–33, 30–1, 59–60,
    63–4
single market *see* internal market, Single
    European Act
standard of living, 19–20, 34
standards *see also* CEN/CENELEC

accountability, 305–9, 311
advisory committees, 295
ANEC, 300–2, 310
barriers to trade, 269, 293
CE marks, 277–8
certification, 277–8
Commission, 251, 269–70, 273, 275–80,
    288–942, 298–307, 310–11
Committee on Technical Standards and
    Regulations, *see* 83/189 Committee
control, 307–8
consensus, 260, 265–7
co-operation, 269–70, 307, 309
Council, 270, 278, 280, 299–300
directives, 272–3, 276–7, 294–5, 307, 309–10
delegation, 280–8
83/189 Committee, 292–4, 296, 303, 308,
    310–11
essential safety requirements, 285–6
European Parliament, 280
European Prestandards, 263–5
European Secretariat for the co-ordination
    of standardisation (SECO), 299
European Standards, 262–8
European Standardisation Council, 290–1
European Standardisation Forum, 290–1,
    303, 310
European Standardisation System, 289–90
foodstuffs committees, 137, 173
General Orientations for Co-operation,
    269–70, 299–300, 309
Harmonised Documents, 262–3
information, 278, 280, 293, 296, 304
    Information Directive 1983, 268–9
institutions, 279–80, 290, 298–303, 309
    Member States, interrelation with, 291–6
integration, 278–8
internal market, 268
International Standards Organisation (ISO),
    297
Internet, 304
legitimacy, 253, 288–309, 311
Low Voltage Directive, 280–1
management of list of, 286, 307
Model Directive, 271–2, 283, 310
monitoring, 305, 308
mutual recognition, 61, 278
national authorities, 271, 307, 309
New Approach to Technical Harmonisation
    and Standards, 56–8, 251–3, 268,
    270–81, 283, 294, 296, 299–300, 305,
    309–10, 313, 318
participation of interested parties, 255,
    289–90, 292, 298–302, 311
peculiarities, 253–5
pharmaceuticals, 208
presumption of conformity, 272–3, 277–8,
    307, 309

scientific expertise *(cont.)*:
  private bodies, 251–311, 318
  product safety, 252–4, 272, 280, 294, 296, 303, 305–9
  public-private divide, 252–3, 288, 291–6
  qualified majority voting, 279
  Questionnaire Procedure, 266–7
  reference to standards technique, 281–3
  rigid reference to, 281
  risk:
    assessment, 252
    management, 318
  safeguard clauses, 291–2, 308–9
  self-regulation, 252–3, 318
  sliding reference to, 281, 282–3
  standard-setting process, 262–8
  standing committees, 293–6, 310
  supervision, 305–7
  technology, 251–311, 317
  testing, 277–8
  transparency, 269, 289, 291, 304–5, 310–11

Standing Committee on Foodstuffs, 152–66, 173–4, 179–80, 184, 316
Standing Committee on Medicinal Products for Human Use, 225–6, 233–4, 248–50
subsidiarity, 78–82, 98–9, 315
supremacy, 45–6, 98–9

Thalidomide tragedy, 205–6
trade *see* barriers to trade
trade marks, 193, 195, 202, 243–6
transparency, 94, 103–4, 112, 131, 145–6, 177–8, 204, 236, 238–9, 269, 289, 291, 304–5, 310–11
Treaty of Amsterdam, 9, 21–2, 36–8, 100, 104, 128, 182–3 *see also* BSE crisis
Treaty of Rome, 11, 21, 24–7
Treaty on European Union, 5–6, 12–13, 21–2, 33–6, 58–60, 78–82, 107, 126–7
Trias Politica, 86–7

World Trade Organisation, 102, 322